Obituaries from Early Tennessee Newspapers 1794-1851

Edited By:
    The Rev. Silas Emmett Lucas, Jr.

SOUTHERN HISTORICAL PRESS
% The Rev.S. Emmett Lucas,Jr.
P.O. Box 738
Easley, South Carolina 29640

ISBN 0-89308-093-4

Introduction

These Obituaries from the earliest Tennessee Newspapers
previously had been available to the public in the card file of the
Tennessee State Library and Archives in Nashville, and hence were
unknown to many people working on families in Tennessee.

The Publisher wishes to thank Miss Kendall J.Cram,
Director of the State Library and Archives in Nashville for allowing
him to have these thousands of cards xeroxed for use in this book.

The reader will note that these notices cover the
entire state of Tennessee for the most part, beginning with the
earliest ones in 1794 in the Knoxville Gazette.

Abby, Margeret Elizabeth Infant daughter of Richard Abby. Died in
Davidson County on the 25th Feb.
National Banner & Nashville Whig. (Wednesday March 4, 1835.)

Abbey, Mary Ann S. Wife of Richard Abbey and the daughter of
William Compton of Davidson County. Died on the 28th ult. at
Commerce, Miss.
Nashville Whig. (Tuesday Feb. 1, 1842)

Abbott, Henry P. Harness Maker Died Sparta, Ga. A Native of Norfolk,
Virginia. Aged about 28 or 30 years.
National Banner & Nashville Whig. (Friday, Jan. 9, 1835.)

Abeel, Catherine Lately of Catskill in the State of New York. Died
At Westwood in the vicinity the residence of Mrs. Robert Woods on the
25th inst.
Nashville Whig. (Tuesday, February 28, 1843.)

Abel, Miss Susan daughter of Mr. James Abel. Died Northhampton, Eng.
National Banner & Nashville Whig. (Monday May 2, 1831)

Abernathy, Mrs. Ann Louise, Consort of Gilbert T. Abernathy. Died
In Nashville on the 18th inst. at the residence of Mr. Stephan D.
Watkins in the 27th year of her age she was the eldest daughter
Mr. Robert Baxter of Montgomery County.
The Christian Record. (Sat., Sept. 23, 1848)

Able, Mrs. Susan, aged 30 years. Died in Northhampton, England on the
23rd Jan.
Nashville Republican and State Gazette. (Thursday, May 19, 1831 No. 3
Vol. 7)

Achney, Mrs. Allen Consort of Mr. Jacob Achney. Died in Clarksville,
Tennessee of Cholera.
National Banner & Nashville Whig. (Wednesday July 8, 1835)

Acklen, James Camp Son of Col. John R. H. Acklen aged 3 years. Died
in Huntsville, Ala.
National Banner & Nashville Whig. (Friday, Feb. 6, 1835)

Acock, Miss Jane Died in Russellville, Ky.
National Banner & Nashville Daily. (Friday, April 12, 1833)

Adair, Esq. John Died in Knox County aged 95 years.
National Banner & Nashville Whig. (Sat., April 7, 1827)

Adair, Mrs. Martha W. Consort of Hon. William J. Adair aged 38 years.
Died in Triana, Ala.
National Banner & Nashville Whig. (Friday, March 6, 1835)

Adam, Hon. Thomas Boyleston Aged 59 years. Died in Quincy, Mass.
Only brother of Ex-President Adams.
Nashville Banner, Nashville Daily Advertiser. (Mon., April 2, 1832)

Adams, Mr. Andrew Merchant. Died in Philadelphia from injuries
received by upsetting a car on the rail road.
Nashville Whig. (Wednesday, July 10, 1839)

Adams, Mr. Benjamin of Davidson County. Died on 6th inst. he left
a wife and several children.
Impartial Review and Cumberland Repository. (Oct. 11, 1806)

Adams, Mr. C. Died in Danville, Ky. of Cholera.
National Banner & Nashville Daily Advertiser. (Mon., Aug. 5, 1833)

Adams, Mr. David At the Lafayett Iron Works. Died in Montogemry
County.
National Banner and Nashville Whig. (Vol. 19, No. 1280. Wednesday,
June 29, 1831)

1

Adams, Mrs. Elizabeth G. Wife of Alfred A. Adams Esqr. Died on Sunday night last. Aged 33 years and 9 months.
Nashville Whig (Thursday Nov. 2, 1843)

Adams, Mrs. Hannah Died in Scott County, Ky.
National Banner & Nashville Whig (Sat., Feb. 17, 1827)

Adams, Miss Hannah Died in Brookline, Massachusetts on the 16th ult.
National Banner & Nashville Daily Advertiser (Friday, Jan. 6, 1832)

Adams, Miss Hannah Died in Brooklin Mass. on the 16th ult.
Nashville Republican and State Gazette (Vol. 7 Tuesday, Jan. 10, 1832 No. 101)

Adams, John Robertson County. Died in the loss of Steam Boat Brandy-wine.
National Banner & Nashville Daily Advertiser (Monday, April 23, 1832)

Adams, The Hon. John Quincy Died in Washington on the night of the 23rd inst.
The Politician and Weekly Whig. (Friday, March 3, 1848)

Adams, Julia Consort of William Adams Esqr. Died in Dickerson County on the first of Aug.
Nashville Republican (Sat., Sept. 10, 1836)

Adams, Hon. Robert H. Senator in Congress from Mississippi died at Natchez.
National Banner & Nashville Whig (July 18, 1830)

Adams, Thomas P. Cashier of the branch of the Planters Bank. Died at Pulaski, Tennessee in the 43d year of his age.
Nashville Whig (April 14, 1841)

Adams, Mr. Tracy of Hamilton, Massachusetts. Died in New Orleans.
National Banner, Nashville Daily Advertiser (Fri., May 16, 1834)

Agun, Capt. D. of the revenue service. Died at sea off Key West.
National Banner & Nashville Daily Advertiser (Mon., May 26, 1834)

Agun, William Died at Versailles, Ky. 12 miles from Lexington of Cholera.
National Banner & Nashville Whig (Fri., Sept. 1835)

Aiken, William, Esq. Died in Charleston, S. C.
Nashville Republican and State Gazette (March 29, 1831)

Aimers, Thomas S. Aged 68 years. Died in Philadelphia a native Leicestershire England.
Nashville Whig (Monday, Nov. 19, 1838)

Akin, Mrs. Nancy, wife of Mr. Thomas Akin died at Knoxville
National Banner (Jan. 20, 1826)

Allcorn, James only son of the Col. John Allcorn. Died near Gallatin on the 22nd inst. in the 32d year of his age.
National Banner & Nashville Whig. (Wednesday, Oct. 1, 1834)

Alexander, Mrs. Frances Aged 45 years. Died in Pulaski on June 10 of Cholera.
National Banner, Nashville Daily Advertiser (Wed., June 19, 1833)

Alexander, Francis M. Who is said to have followed the Mercantile business in Mexico. Supposed he was murdered. See paper notice P. 3 Col. 3
National Banner and Nashville Daily Advertiser. (Vol. 20 Wednesday, June 20, 1832 No. 1518)

Alexander, Mr. James   Died in Nashville Tennessee
Nashville Republican and State Gazette (Tuesday, March 29, 1831
No. 110 Vol. 6)

Alexander, Mr. John Aged 30 years Died in New Orleans, La.
National Banner & Nashville Whig (Friday, Nov. 21, 1834)

Alexander, Mr. Levi Son of Daniel Alexander Esqr. Died in
Rutherford County on the 18th in the 25th year of his age.
National Banner & Nashville Whig (Thursday, Oct. 7, 1830)

Alexander, Mrs. Margeret A. W. Wife of Ebenzer Alexander Esqr.
and daughter of Hon. Hugh L. White. Died in Knox County on the 25th
ult.
National Banner & Nashville Whig (Wednesday, September 7, 1831)

Alexander, Mr. Peter of this town died on Tuesday the 9th inst.
Nashville Whig (April 16, 1816)

Alexander, Mr. Thomas Aged 55 years. Died in Courtland, Ala.
National Banner & Nashville Whig (Monday, March 21, 1831)

Alexander, Col. Walter B.
National Banner & Nashville Whig (Sat., July 29, 1826)

Alexander, Wm. Esq. Died at Murfreesborough on the 7th inst.
The Nashville Whig and Tennessee Advertiser (Aug. 15, 1818)

Alexander, Capt. William Died in Sumner County A soldier of the
Revolution. Aged 84 years.
National Banner & Nashville Whig (Thursday, Aug. 12, 1830)

Allan, Archibald Died at Louisville, Ky.
National Banner & Nashville Whig (Monday, March 21, 1831)

Allan, Mr. Archibald Died in Louisville, Ky.
Nashville Republican and State Gazette (March 19, 1831)

Allen, Mr. A. B., Merchant of Pensacola aged 32. Died in New Orleans.
National Banner & Nashville Daily Advertiser (Tuesday, June 24, 1834)

Allen, Miss Almira Ann Aged 15 daughter of Mr. Wm. B. Allen. Died
in Cahawba.
National Banner & Nashville Whig (Sept. 2, 1826)

Allen, Miss Caroline W. Died at Carthage aged 17 years.
National Banner & Nashville Whig (Sat., Jan. 19, 1827)

Allen, Mrs. Catherine K. Wife of Joseph Allen merchant of Carthage.
Died at Cartage Smith County on the 14th of April.
Daily Republican Banner (Wednesday, May 6, 1840)

Allen, Dixon of Nashville in the 27th year of his age. Died at Gallatin on the 26th.
National Banner & Nashville Whig (Monday, Sept. 29th, 1824)

Allen, Mrs. Elizabeth   Died in Sumner County, Wife of Capt. David
Allen.
National Banner & Nashville Whig (Sat. Feb. 23, 1828)

Allen, George W. Died in Hasville on Sunday Morning last.
National Banner & Nashville Whig (Tuesday, May 11, 1830)

Allen, Mr. Gideon R. Died at Paris, Tennessee.
National Banner & Nashville Whig (Sat., June 16, 1827)

Allen, Hiram A. In the 33rd year of his age. Died at the residence of
his brother Thomas Allen in Clinton County, Ky. on the 15th April.
The Politician and Weekly Nashville Whig (Fri., May 14, 1847)

Allen, Mr. James. Aged 72, died in Maury County.
National Banner (Sat., Nov. 7, 1829)

Allen, Mr. James. Died in New Orleans was the Editor of the Chilicothe
(Ohio) Times.
Nashville Republican and State Gazette (Thursday, March 31, 1831,
No. 111, Vol. 6)

Allen, Mrs. Letitia. Wife of Mr. John Allen and daughter of Mr. James
Saunders Esqr. Died in Sumner County.
National Banner & Nashville Daily Advertiser (Mon., Dec. 3, 1832)

Allen, Paul Esq. Died in Baltimore
National Banner & Nashville Whig (Sept. 9, 1826)

Allen, Mr. Robert. Died in Madison County, Ala.
National Banner & Nashville Whig (Sat., Nov. 18, 1826)

Allen, Col. Robert. Died at his residence Greenwood near Carthage
Smith County on the 19th inst. He was 66 years and two months old.
Nashville Whig (Sat., Aug. 24, 1844)

Allen, Mr. Taylor B. Late of Davidson County, Tenn. Died in New
Orleans on the 25th ult. Was the brother of Mr. J. W. Allen of
Nashville, Tennessee.
Nashville Union (Thursday, Jan. 18, 1838)

Allen, Theordore F. Son of S. W. Allen, died in Nashville the 18th inst.
of Scarlet Fever. Aged 3 years and 5 months.
The Politician and Weekly Nashville Whig (Fri., March 24, 1848)

Allen, Capt. Thomas J. Merchant of the House of Allen and Anderson,
formerly of the Steam Boat Ellen Kirkman. Died on Monday Night,
March 28th.
Nashville Whig (Sat., April 2, 1842)

Allen, Gen. Vine. Died in Craven County N.E.. Aged 50 years.
National Banner (Sat., Aug. 22, 1829)

Allen, Mr. William. In the 60th year of his age. Died in Sumner County.
National Banner and Nashville Daily Advertiser (Wed., Jan. 30, 1833)

Allen, William. Died in Todd County, Ky. on the 25th of August.
National Banner & Nashville Whig (Wednesday, Sept. 2, 1835)

Allen, Capt. William B. Company K. with First Regiment Tenn. Volunteers
Died - was killed in the Battle of Monterey, with the Mexicans, Sept.
21st.
Nashville Whig (Sat., Oct. 24, 1846)

Allen, William Hart. Infant son of Thomas J. and Jane D. Allen aged
7 months and 27 days. Died on the 15th inst.
Nashville Republican (Sat., Feb. 27, 1836)

Alley, Mrs. Lydia. Wife of Micajah Alley of Nashville. Died on
Wednesday last 8th inst. in the 43 year of her age the deceased was
a native of Mass.
National Banner & Nashville Whig (Wednesday, Oct. 15, 1834)

Alliback, James. Died at Cincinnati Ohio on 13th of Cholera.
National Banner & Nashville Daily Advertiser (Sat., Oct. 20, 1832)

Allison, Rev. Burgess. Died in Trenton, N. J.
National Banner & Nashville Whig (Sat., March 31, 1827)

Allison, Mrs. Eliza. Daughter of Mr. James Allison. Died in Logan
County, Ky.
National Banner & Nashville Whig (Sat., Jan. 20, 1827)

Allison, Mr. Franklin. Died in Logan County, Ky.
National Banner and Nashville Daily Advertiser (Jan. 2, 1832)

Allison, James H. Company J. First Regiment Tenn. Volunteers. Died
Was killed in the Battle of Monterey with the Mexicans on Sept. 21st,
1846.
Nashville Whig (Sat., Oct. 24, 1846)

Allison, Mrs. Jane. Wife of Capt. James Allison. Died in Logan County,
Ky.
National Banner & Nashville Daily Advertiser (Mon., Jan. 7, 1833)

Allison, Mrs. Mary. Died in Shelby County, Ky.
National Banner (March 17, 1826)

Allison, Mr. Robert Senr. A Native of Scotland. Aged 84 years, 8
months and 29 days. Died in Bedford County on the 2nd inst.
National Banner & Nashville Daily Advertiser (Wed., June 6, 1832)

Allison, Col. Uriah S. Died Roane County
National Banner (Sat., June 6, 1829)

Allmond, Col. Albert. Died in Norfolk, Virginia
Nashville Republican and State Gazette (Tuesday, May 10, 1831 No. 128.
Vol. 6.)

Alloway, Mrs. Irena. Consort of Mr. John Alloway. Died in Nashville
on Monday, Nov. 26th. Obituary Nov. 29th
National Banner & Nashville Daily Advertiser (Tues., Nov. 27, 1832)

Alsop, Miss Eliza. Died in Danville, Ky of Cholera.
Nashville Daily Advertiser & National Banner (Mon., Aug. 5th, 1833)

Alsop, Hon. Walker. Died in Louisville, Ky. A Member of the Legislature from that city.
National Banner & Nashville Whig (Friday, March 13, 1835)

Alston, Dr. Alexander S. J. Died in Tipton County, Tennessee formerly
of Hillsborough, Tennessee.
National Banner & Nashville Whig (Wednesday, Nov. 26, 1834)

Alston, Gen. John. Aged 56 years. Died in Holifax County, N. C.
National Banner & Nashville Whig (Wednesday, April 27, 1831)

Alston, Col. William. An eminent soldier of the Revolution. Died
at Charlston, S. C. on the 26th ult.
Nashville Whig (Wednesday, July 17, 1839)

Alston, Hon. Willis. Died on the 19th ult. for many years a member
of Congress from the Halifax District in N. C.
Nashville Republican (Sat., May 13, 1837)

Alsup, Mr. Thomas. Died at Florence, Ala.
National Banner (March 17, 1826)

Alvard, Hon. James C. Member of the Congress from Springfield, Mass.
Died at his residence 28th ult.
Nashville Whig (Wednesday, October 16, 1839)

Amelian, Dr. John. A native of Jamaica. Died in Mobile, Ala.
National Banner Nashville Daily Advertiser (Fri., May 16, 1834)

Ament, Anthony H. Son of Capt. William Ament in the 9th year of his
age. Died in Nashville on Monday the 18th inst.
National Banner & Nashville Whig. (Friday, May 22, 1835)

Ament, Helen M. Daughter of Capt. William Lament. Died on Monday the
18th inst.
National Banner & Nashville Whig (Friday, May 22, 1835)

Ament, Samuel R. Infant son of Samuel Ament. Died in Nashville on the 1st Inst.
National Banner & Nashville Whig (Friday, October 2, 1835)

Ament, Mr. William. Aged 36 years, formerly of Nashville. Died at the Cumberland Rolling Mill, Stewart County, Tenn. on July 29th.
National Banner & National Whig (Friday, August 5, 1836)

Ament, Mr. William B. Aged 36 years formerly of Nashville. Died on the 29th July at the Cumberland Rolling Mills, Stewart County, Tenn.
Nashville Republican (Thursday, Aug. 11, 1837)

Ames, Frances. Aged 74 years. Died at Lowell, Mass. Relict of Hon. Fisher Ames.
Daily Republican Banner (Tuesday, Aug. 29, 1837)

Amos, Miss. Daughter of Mr. Asbury Amos. Died in Logan Cty., Ky.
Nation Banner & Nashville Whig (Wednesday, Feb. 25, 1835)

Amour, Mr. Solomon H. Died in Paris, Henry County. A Highly Respectable Gentleman and Merchant.
National Banner & Nashville Daily Advertiser (Wed., Jan. 22, 1834)

Anderson, Mrs. Adeline. Wife of Capt. John Anderson. Died on the 29th July in Woodford County, Ky. formerly of Nashville.
Daily Republician Banner (Monday, Aug. 12, 1839)

Anderson, Mr. Asa. Of Madison County. Died the next day after he married by hanging himself Louisville Journal.
Nashville Republican (March 1, 1836)

Anderson, Carolina. Daughter of John H. Anderson. Died in Shelbyville, Tenn. of Cholera.
National Banner & Nashville Daily Advertiser (Thurs., July 11, 1833)

Anderson, Catherine Elizabeth. Infant daughter of Mr. William Anderson. Died on Thursday 14th in Nashville.
Nashville Whig (Sat., March 16, 1844)

Anderson, Catherine Mary Jane. Daughter of William E. Anderson, Esq. Died in Nashville on 24th inst.
National Banner and Nashville Advertiser (Vol. 20 Tuesday, Sept. 25th 1832 No. 1600)

Anderson, George Washington. Aged 23 years. Died in Jefferson County, Tenn. 7th son of the Hon. Joseph Anderson Comptroller of the U. S. Treasury.
National Banner & Nashville Whig (Friday, Jan. 9, 1835)

Anderson, Mr. Henry A. Died at Holly Springs formely of Florence, Ala.
Nashville Whig (Tuesday, April 21, 1846)

Anderson, Captain Henry H. Aged 27 years. Died in Bedford County, Tenn.
National Banner & Nashville Whig (Wednesday, Dec. 17, 1834)

Anderson, Mr. Jasper. Of the firm Crockett, Anderson and Co. Died in Nashville on the 24th.
National Banner & Nashville Daily Advertiser (Mon., Aug. 25th, 1834)

Anderson, John. Son of John H. Anderson. Died in Shelby, Tennessee of Cholera.
National Banner & Nashville Daily Advertiser (Thurs., July 11, 1833)

Anderson, Mr. John F. Aged 40. Died in Madison County, Ala.
National Banner & Nashville Whig (Monday, August 1, 1831)

Anderson, Mr. John F. Merchant of this County. Died in Nashville on

the evening of the 13th inst.
National Banner & Nashville Daily Advertiser (Tues., June 19, 1834)

Anderson, John W., Esq. Attorney at law of the firm of Anderson &
Lindsey. Aged about 28 years.
Dailey Republician Banner (Tuesday, Oct. 1st, 1839)

Anderson, Hon. Joseph. Late Comptroller of the Treasury of the United
States. Died in the City of Washington on Monday the 17th April.
National Banner & Nashville Whig (Wednesday, May 3, 1837)

Anderson, Joseph. Late Comptroller of the Treasury. Died in Washington
City.
Nashville Republican (Sat., April 29, 1837)

Anderson, Hon. Joseph. Late Comptroller of the Treasury and formely
a Senator in Congress from Tennessee. Died at Washington City.
The Union (Sat., May 6, 1837)

Anderson, Mr. K. Died in Shelbyville of Cholera.
National Banner & Nashville Daily Advertiser (Thurs., July 11, 1833)

Anderson, Mrs. Keziah. Died in Madison County T.
National Banner & Nashville Whig (Sat., Sept. 9, 1826)

Anderson, Louis Arthur. Only son of the late Hon. Richard E. Anderson.
Died in Louisville, Ky.
National Banner & Nashville Whig. (Mon., Aug. 15, 1831)

Anderson, Miss Mary. Second daughter of James Anderson Esqr. Died on
the 10th inst. in Kentucky near Winchester. Residing in Davidson
County near the Hermitage. (Obituary Oct. 7)
The Christian Record (Sat., Sept. 16, 1848)

Anderson, Mr. Mathias. Died in Sparta.
National Banner & Nashville Whig (Sat., July 22, 1826)

Anderson, Mr. Nathaniel S. Died on Friday morning last about 8
o'clock. Mr. Nathaniel S. Anderson merchant of the town. His death
was produced by a wound received in a duel the proceding day.
The Nashville Whig (May 28, 1816)

Anderson, Mrs. Pauline C. Consort of William C. Anderson in the 43rd
year of his age. Died in Nashville on the morning the 16th inst.
(Obituary)
The Christian Record (Sat., March 20, 1847)

Anderson, Mrs. Rachel. Wife of John Anderson. Died in Sullivan County.
National Banner & Nashville Whig (Wednesday, March 16, 1831)

Anderson, Mrs. Rachel. Died in Sullivan County, Tennessee
Nashville Republican and State Gazette (Tuesday, March 15, 1831
No. 101 Vol. 6)

Anderson, Richard C. Died in Jefferson County, Ky. Aide to General
Lafayette in the revolutionary war.
National Banner & Nashville Whig (Sat., Oct. 28, 1826)

Anderson, Robert. Aged 72 years. Died in this County this morning.
National Banner (May 13, 1826)

Anderson, Robert H. Son of P. H. Anderson, Canton, Ky. Died in
Amsterdam, Mi.
National Banner & Nashville Whig (Wednesday, Jan. 21, 1835)

Anderson, Susan. Died lately at the resident of John Anderson Esqr.
near Nashville at the age of 80th years.
The Nashville Whig & Tennessee Advertiser (May 2, 1818)

Anderson, Theophilus R. Died in Shelbyville, Tenn. of cholera.
National Banner & Nashville Daily Advertiser (July 11, 1833)

Anderson, William. Aged 71 years. Died in Knox County.
National Banner & Nashville Whig (Monday, Dec. 27, 1830)

Anderson, Capt. Wm. In the 79th year of his age. Died in Maury Co.,
Tennessee. A Soldier of the Revolution.
National Banner & Nashville Daily Advertiser (Wed., May 7, 1834)

Anderson, Capt. William. In the 79th year of his age. Died in
Davidson County, on the 5th inst. A Soldier of the Revolution.
National Banner & Nashville Daily Advertiser. (Friday, May 16, 1834)

Anderson, William E. Esqr. In the 29th year of his age. Died near
Franklin on the 1st inst. William E. Anderson Esqr. in the 29th
year of his age.
The Weekly Review, Franklin, Tennessee (Friday, Nov. 2, 1832)

Anderson, William E., Esqr. Aged 28 A young lawyer. Died at Franklin.
National Banner & Nashville Daily Advertiser (Monday, Nov. 5, 1832)

Anderson, Col. Wm. P. Died in Winchester, Tenn. Aged 56.
Nashville Republican and State Gazette (Tues., May 25, 1831 No. 5 Vol.7)

Anderson, William P. Died in Winchester in the 56th year of his age.
On Monday the 25th ult.
National Banner & Nashville Whig (Monday, May 23, 1831)

Anderson, William S. Died in Sommerville Fayette County.
National Banner & Nashville Whig (Sat., July 29, 1826)

Andres, The Rev. Felix de. Died on the 14th October last in St. Louis,
Missouri after a painful and lingering illness in the 43rd year of his
age, the Rev. Felix De Andres. Vicar General of Louisana and Superior
of the Congregation of the Mission.
The Clarion and Tennessee Gazette, Vol 1, No. 12, Whole No. 156.
(November 21, 1820)

Andrews, Ann. Eldest of the Daughters of John and Eliza Andrews.
Aged seven years. Died in the Vicinity on the 27th inst.
Nashville Whig (Friday Oct. 1, 1841)

Andrews, Mary Mrs. Aged 38. Died at Florence, Ala. Wife of Major
Patrick Andrews.
National Banner (Sat., Aug. 29, 1829)

Anthony, John D. Died in Knoxville, Tennessee with the Fever.
Daily Republican Banner (Sat., October 13, 1838)

Anthony, Capt. Thomax. Of Philadelphia. Died in St. Louis, Mo.
Formely of the Indian Department.
National Banner & Nashville Daily Advertiser (Tues., July 15, 1834)

Anthony, William B. The funeral of Wm B. Anthony who was killed in
battle of the 28th of December (1814) at New Orleans, will be preached
by the Rev. James Gwin on the 3rd Sabbath of this Month, June 18, 1815,
at this place where his family now lives in Sumner County.
Nashville Whig (June 6, 1815)

Archer, John. Aged 25 years. Died at Mobile, Ala.
National Banner (March 17, 1826)

Armour, John. Died in Hardeman County. Late of Baltimore in the 22d
year of his age.
Nashville Whig (October 4, 1824)

Armstrong, Mr. Alexander. Died in Huntington, Ohio.
National Banner & Nashville Whig. (Sat., Sept. 9, 1826)

Armstrong, Mr. Alexander. Aged 65 years. Died in Claiborne County, Mi.
National Banner & Daily Advertiser (Wednesday, Aug. 20, 1834)

Armstrong, Johnson. Died of Cholera. Copied from the Maysville Eagle
and Monitor Extra.
National Banner & Nashville Daily Advertiser (Thurs., June 6, 1833)

Armstrong, Mrs. Mareret. Wife of Benjamin D. Armstrong. Died at Athens.
National Banner & Nashville Whig (Monday, Jan. 31, 1831)

Armstrong, Mrs. Margeret. Aged 93 years. Died in Knox County, Tenn.
Nashville Republican (Tuesday, June 27, 1837)

Armstrong, Mrs. Margeret D. In the 37th year of her age. Died in
Nashville on the evening of the 29th consert of Col. Robert Armstrong
and daughter of the late Joshiah Nichols Esquires.
National Banner & Nashville Daily Advertiser (Monday, June 30, 1834)

Armstrong, Gen. Martin. Of this County. Died yesterday of a lingering
illness.
Impartial Review and Cumberland Repository (August 25, 1808)

Armstrong, Mrs. Nancy. Consort of Capt. William Armstrong. Died at
the Choctaw nation on the 28th Sept. Aged 32 years 11 months.
National Banner & Nashville Whig. (Monday, Oct. 24, 1836)
(Nashville Republican Tuesday, Oct. 25, 1836?)

Armstrong, Mrs. Nancy. Consort of Capt. William Armstrong. Died at
the Choctaw Agency on the 28th Sept.
Nashville Republican (Tuesday, Oct. 25, 1836)

Armstrong, Mr. Samuel M. Late of Knoxville. Died at Athens.
National Banner & Nashville Whig (Sat., Dec. 30, 1826)

Armstrong, Miss Susan Wells. Second daughter of the late Capt. William
Armstrong. Died in Nashville at the residence of Mrs. Irwin on Wed-
nesday last. (Obituary Sept. 9,)
The Christian Record (Sat., Sept. 2, 1848)

Armstrong, Mrs. Susannah W. Late of East Tennessee. Mother of Col.
Robert Armstrong. Postmaster and of Capt. William Armstrong, Mayor
of Nashville. Died of Cholera on the 29th May.
National Banner & Nashville Daily Advertiser (Thurs., May 30, 1833)

Armstrong, Mrs. Margeret. Wife of Mr. Benjamin Armstrong. Died at
Athens.
National Banner and Nashville Whig. Vol. 18 No. 1216 (Monday, Jan.
31, 1831)

Armstrong, Maj. William. In his 52 year of his age. Died on the 12th
inst. (Obituary)
The Christian Record. (Sat., July 17, 1847)

Arnett, Mr. John. Died in Rutherford County.
National Banner & Nashville Whig (Sat., Nov. 3, 1827)

Arnold, Mrs. Wife of Mr. Samuel Arnold. Died in Logan Co., Ky.
National Banner & Nashville Whig (Sat., Nov. 22, 1828)

Arnold, Mrs. Elizabeth. Wife of Samuel Arnold Esq. Died in Logan
County, Ky.
National Banner, Nashville Whig. (Sat., Dec. 20, 1828)

Arnold, Mr. John. Late of Lynchburg, Va. Died in Russellville, Ala.
National Banner & Nashville Whig (Friday, Feb. 12, 1830)

Arnold, Mr. John. Died in Henderson County on the 12th inst.
National Banner & Nashville Whig (Monday, August 30, 1830)

Arnold, Private Robert. With the 14th Regiment, infantry, Commanded
by Gen. Pillow. Died -- was killed in the battle before Mexico City.
The Politician and Weekly Nashville Whig (Fri., Oct. 29, 1847)

Arnold, Robert (Private). With the 14th Regiment part of the third
Division Commanded by Gen. Pillow. Died -- was killed in the last
Battle before the city of Mexico.
The Christian Record (Sat., Oct. 30, 1847)

Armstrong, Capt. W. Of the 6th U. S. Infantry. Died at Pensacola.
National Banner & Nashville Whig. (Sat., March 17, 1827)

Arnold, Mr. William. Died in Henderson County on the 15th Inst.
National Banner & Nashville Whig (Monday, Aug. 30, 1830)

Arnold, Gen. William of Tennessee. Died in Velasco, Texas.
National Banner & Nashville Daily Advertiser (Mon., July 29, 1833)

Arratt, Mr. David. Of the House of Lockhart & Arratt. Died at New
Orleans.
National Banner & Nashville Daily Advertiser (Mon., Aug. 25, 1834)

Asbridge, Rev. G. W. A native of Philadelphia. Died at Louisville, Ky.
National Banner & Nashville Daily Advertiser (Tuesday, May 20, 1834)

Ashby, William H. Son of Dr. M. C. Ashby. Died at Richmond, Ky.
National Banner & Nashville Whig. (Sat., Sept. 20, 1828)

Asher, Esq. John. An old and highly esteemed citizen. Died in
Florence, Ala.
Daily Republican Banner (Tuesday, March 13, 1838)

Ashley, Mr. Benjamin. A native of Virginia. Aged 51 years. Died
near New Albany, Indiana.
National Banner & Nashville Daily Advertiser (Thurs., June 19, 1834)

Ashley, William H. Died at Boonville, Mo. on the 26th.
Daily Republican Banner (Friday, April 6, 1838)

Ashton, Col. Henry. Marshall of the District of Columbia. Died in
Washington City.
National Banner & Nashville Daily Advertiser (Wed., March 19, 1834)

Ashton, Mr. Richard. Died in Lexington Ky. an old and highly
respected citizen.
National Banner & Nashville Daily Advertiser. (Mon., Aug. 19, 1833)

Ashum, Esq. John Hooker. Royall professor of law at Howard University.
Died suddenly on Monday morning.
National Banner & Nashville Daily Advertiser (Mon., April 22, 1833)

Askew, Mr. Abner L. Of Limestone County, Ala. Died in Bedford County.
National Banner & Nashville Whig. (Thurs., Nov. 11, 1830)

Atchison, Mr. John. Aged 47. Died in Warren County.
National Banner & Nashville Daily Advertiser (Mon., May 13, 1833)

Athy, Capt. Thomas. Died at Louisville, Ky. on the 19th inst.
National Banner (Sat., Aug. 29, 1829)

Atkeison, Elder John. In the 82d year of his age. Died in Williamson
County on the 2d inst of drapsy.
National Banner & Nashville Whig. (Wed., April 19, 1837)

Atkeisson, Mrs. Mary. Wife of Silman Atkeisson and daughter of Mr. Robert White. Died in Sumner County, Tenn.
National Banner & Nashville Daily Advertiser (Tues., July 5, 1834)

Atkins, Mrs. Elizabeth Y. Aged 28 years. Died in Bolivar.
National Banner & Nashville Whig (Mon., Aug. 16, 1830)

Atkins, Mrs. Harriet. Wife of Mr. Charles W. Atkins. Died at Knoxville
National Banner & Nashville Whig (Tuesday, April 20, 1830)

Atkins, James Esq. Age 64, after a illness of only 12 hours. Died in Washington County 27 ult.
National Banner & Nashville Advertiser, Vol. 20 No. 1561 (Friday, August 10, 1832)

Atkins, Rev. S. Late of Knoxville. Died at At____?, Va.
National Banner and Nashville Whig. (Sat., Sept. 15, 1827)

Atkinson, Mrs. Arobella C. Died on Sat., Nov. 25 at the residence of her father Robt. West in Dickson County, wife of O. C. Atkinson of Memphis, Tenn.
Daily Republican Banner (Dec 1st, 1837)

Atkinson, Brig. Gen. Henery. U. S. Army. Died at Jefferson Barracks near St. Louis on 14th inst.
Nashville Whig (Sat., June 25, 1842)

Atterbury, William. Of Hart County, Ky. Died in the loss of the Steam Boat Brandywine.
National Banner, Nashville Daily Advertiser (Mon., April 23, 1832)

Atwood, William Esq. Died in Huntsville, Ala. Late Post Master at that Place.
Nashville Republican (Sat., Sept. 24, 1836)

Auld, Mr. James. Died in Washington City.
National Banner & Nashville Daily Advertiser (Fri., Sept. 20, 1833)

Ault, Miss Dicy Patterson. Only daugther of Fredick Ault. Died in Knox County, Aged 20.
National Banner & Nashville Daily Advertiser (Mon., July 2, 1832)

Ault, Dicy Patterson. Age 20. Daughter of Frederick and Margeret Baker Ault. Death by suicide on Wednesday last.
National Banner and Nashville Daily Advertiser, Vol. 20, No. 1530 (Wednesday, July 4, 1832)

Ault, Mrs. Nancy. Died in Knox county.
National Banner & Nashville Whig (Sat., Dec. 2, 1826)

Ault, Mrs. Nancy. Died in Knox County, Mrs. Nancy Ault.
National Banner and Nashville Whig, Vol. 15, No. 46 Whole No. 774 (Dec. 2, 1826)

Austin, Capt. James. Formely a resident of Davidson County. Died in Giles County.
Daily Republican Banner (Tuesday, Oct. 27, 1840)

Austin, Mr. John. In the 42nd year of his age. Died last evening in Nashville.
Daily Republican Banner (Thurs., Feb. 13, 1840)

Austin, John. Died in Nashville on the 12th inst. of consumption.
Nashville Whig. (Friday, Feb. 14th, 1840)

Austin, Mrs. Millie. Wife of Edwin Austin. Died in Davidson County on the 20th inst. in the 25th year of his age.
Daily Republican Banner (Friday, Sept. 25th, 1840)

Austin, Mr. Milton. Of Nashville. Son of Mr. George Austin. Died
at Princeton, Ky.
National Banner & Nashville Whig (Monday, Sept. 27, 1830)

Austin, Stephen F. Died in Texas near Columbia on the 25th ult.
Nashville Republican (Thursday, Jan. 26, 1837)

Austin, Col. Stephen F. The founder of Austin Colony. Died at Velasco,
Texas on the 26th of Dec.
The Union (Saturday, Jan. 28, 1837)

Avery, Dr. Nathan. Aged 54. Died in Memphis on the 6th inst.
Nashville Whig (Thursday, March 19, 1846)

Ayer, Lieut. Lewis M. Died on the 15th inst. at the residence of
Capt. Kingsby, Lieut. Lewis M. Ayer, late of the United States Infantry.
Nashville Whig (Tuesday, Jan. 24, 1815, Page 3, col. 3)

Aykroyd, James. Son of Mr. & Mrs. James Aykroyd. Aged of 8 years.
Died in Nashville Yesterday.
National Banner & Nashville Daily Advertiser (Tues., Nov. 6, 1832)

Ayres, Mr. Benjamin. Died at St. Louis.
National Banner (Sat., Sept. 26, 1829)

Bachalor, Mrs. Mary Ann. Consort of Mr. Bachalor, L. Died in Frankfort
Ky. on the 3rd inst.
National Banner & Nashville Daily Advertiser (Sat., Aug. 10, 1833)

Backus, Mrs. Charlotte S. Wife of Geo. Backus Esq. Died in Louisville, Ky.
National Banner & Nashville Whig (Friday, April 22, 1831)

Backus, Mrs. Charlotte. Died in Louisville, Kentucky.
Nashville Republican and State Gazette (Sat., April 23, 1831)

Backus, Frances H. Aged 6 years daughter of Mr. George Backus. Died
at Louisville, Ky.
National Banner and Nashville Whig (Friday, Feb. 18, 1831)

Backus, George Mr. Formerly of Nashville. Died at New Orleans.
National Banner Nashville Whig (Wednesday, June 8, 1831)

Bacon, Elizabeth Mrs. Aged 21 years. Died in Frankfort, Ky. Wife
of Mr. Robert B. Bacon.
National Banner & Nashville Whig (Monday, March 30, 1835)

Bacus, Miss. Francis H. Age 16. Daughter of George Bacus. Died at
Louisville, Ky.
National Banner and Nashville Whig (Friday, Feb. 18, 1831)

Bacus, Mr. George. Formerly of Nashville. Died at New Orleans.
National Banner and Nashville Whig. (Wednesday, June 8, 1831)

Bacus, Mr. George. Formerly of this place. Died in New Orleans.
Nashville Republican and State Gazette (Thursday, June 9, 1831)

Bagby, Capt. Daniel. Died in Carroll County on the 20th in the 66 year
of his age.
National Banner and Nashville Whig (Sat., Sept. 6, 1828)

Bagless, Mr. Cullen. Died in Dover, Stewart County on Friday 1st
inst. a respectable citizen of that place.
Nashville Republican (Tuesday, Feb. 16, 1836)

Bagwell, Nicholas E. Esq. Died in Montgomery County, Tenn. on Wed.,
the 18th inst. in the 38th year of his age.
National Banner & Nashville Whig (Monday, April 6, 1835)

Bailey, Mr. Gabriel. Died in Logan County, Ky.
National Banner and Nashville Whig. (Sat., May 19, 1827)

Bailey, Mr. Henry L. Eldest son of Major Charles Bailey in the 30th
year of his age. Died on the 16th day in Clarksville, Tennessee.
The Christian Record (Sat., March 4, 1848)

Bailey, Mrs. Martha. Wife of George Bailey. Died in Logan County,
Ky.
National Banner (Sat., Aug. 15, 1829)

Bailey, Maj. Robert. Of Ky. Candidate for Congress next election.
Died in this County on Thursday last.
National Banner & Nashville Whig (Sat., July 14, 1827)

Bailey, Mr. Robert. Aged 83. Died in Shelby County, Ky.
National Banner & Nashville Whig. (Monday, March 7, 1831)

Bailey, Gen. Theodorus. Postmaster aged 70. Died in New York.
National Banner & Nashville Whig. (Sat., Sept. 27, 1828)

Baily, Mr. Henry. Of Nashville. Died on the 3d inst. at Eddyville
of the scalds he received on the Steamboat Sen. Robertson. Aged
28 years.
The Nashville Gazette. (Sat., May 12, 1821)

Baily, Mr. James. Died at Brazoria, (Texas)
National Banner and Nashville Daily Advertiser. (Thurs., Jan. 31, 1833)

Baily, Mrs. Martha. Wife of George Bailey. Died in Logan County, Ky.
National Banner. (Sat., Aug. 8, 1829)

Bainbridge, Commodore William. Of the United States Navy. Died
at Philadelphia on Sat. the 27th inst.
National Banner & Nashville Daily Advertiser (Wed., Aug. 7, 1833)

Baird, Mrs. Eleanor. Died in Rutherford County.
Nashville Whig. (Tuesday, July 21, 1846)

Baird, Gen. Thomas. Died in Shelby County, Ky.
National Banner & Nashville Whig. (Monday, March 7, 1831)

Baird, Mr. William Ferrill. Of Tennessee, A Member of the Medical
Class of Transylvania University. Died at Lexington, Ky. on the
1st inst.
National Banner and Nashville Daily Advertiser (Mon., Jan. 9, 1832)

Baker, Mrs. Fifth Street, West of Western Row. Died in Cincinnati
of Cholera on the 10th inst.
National Banner & Nashville Daily Advertiser. (Wed., Oct. 17, 1832)

Baker, Amelia. Daughter of William H. & Feleciana Baker. Age
11 months and 12 days. Died in Nashville on Monday 26th inst.
The Politician and Weekly Nashville Whig. (Fri., July 30, 1847)

Baker, Mr. Charles. Died in Todd County, Ky.
Nashville Republican and State Gazette. (Thursday, March 31, 1831,
No. 111. Vol. 6.

Baker, Mr. Charles M. Of Marshfield, Mass. Died in New Orleans,
La.
National Banner & Nashville Whig. (Friday, October 31, 1834)

Baker, Major Isaac L. Died at Attakapas, La.
National Banner & Nashville Whig. (Mon., Aug. 30, 1830)

Baker, Mr. James W. In the 52nd of his age. Died at his residence
in Sumner County, Tennessee of Consumption.
The Politician and Weekly Nashville Whig. (Fri., June 18, 1847)

Baker, Major John. Died at his residence in Montogemery County
on the 22nd inst.
National Banner and Nashville Whig. (Friday, Jan. 1st, 1830)

Baker, Rev. John. Of the Presbyterian Church. Died in Columbus,
Ga.
National Banner & Nashville Daily Advertiser. (Wed., July 9, 1834)

Baker, Col. Joshua. Age 54. Died on Monday last. A Revolutionary
Soldier.
Nashville Whig. (Vol. 4 Tuesday, March 18, 1816, No. 186)

Baker, Mrs. Mary A. Died in Montgomery County.
Nashville Republican and State Gazette. (Thursday, March 17,
1831, No. 102. Vol. 6)

Baker, Mrs. Mary L. Wife of Caleb H. Baker. Died in Knoxville.
Nashville Whig. (Tuesday, April 14, 1846)

Baker, Mrs. Nancy. Wife of James Baker. Died in Sumner County.
National Banner & Nashville Whig. (Thursday, Aug. 12, 1830)

Baker, Mrs. Robert. Died in Logan County.
National Banner & Nashville Whig. (Sat., Sept. 1, 1827)

Baker, Miss Sarah Ann. Wife of L. D. Baker. Died in Nashville on
Saturday last.
Daily Republican Banner. (Monday, July 20, 1840).

Baker, Mrs. Sarah Ann. Wife of L. D. Baker, Esq. Died in Nashville
on Saturday Last.
Nashville Whig. (Monday, July 20, 1840)

Baker, W. Of N. Y. Died in New Orleans of Yellow Fever.
Daily Republican Banner. (Wednesday, Sept. 27, 1837)

Baker, William Alexander. Aged six months. Died on Wednesday
Morning last, infant son of Eleazer and Elenora Baker.
The Nashville Gazette. (Sat., July 29, 1820)

Balch, Alfred Newnan. Aged 19 years. Died in Washington City on
the 19th only son of Judge Alfred Balch of Florida and formerly
of Nashville.
Daily Republican Banner. (Tuesday, June 30, 1840)

Balch, Mrs. Ann Newnan. Wife of Alfred Balch Esq. of Nashville.
Died in Nashville on Monday evening.
Nashville Union. (Wednesday, Oct. 24, 1838)

Balch, Mrs. Ann Newnan. Wife of Alfred Balch, Esq. of Nasvhille.
Died in Washington City on the 8th inst.
Nashville Whig. (Wednesday, Oct. 24, 1838)

Balch, Mrs. Elizabeth. Wife of Rev. Stephan B. Balch D. D.
Died at Georgetown D. C.
National Banner & Nashville Whig. (Sat., Dec. 20, 1828)

Balch, George Beall, Esq. Third son of Dr. S. B. Balch. Died at
Georgetown D. C.
National Banner & Nashville Whig. (Wednesday, Nov. 2, 1831)

Balch, Mrs. Mary. Consort of Alfred Balch Esq. formerly of Nashville.
Died in Washington County on the 8th inst.
Daily Republican Banner. (Tuesday, Oct. 23, 1838)

Baldwin, Mrs. E. Front St. near corp line. Died 18th at Cincinnati,
Ohio of Cholera.
National Banner & Nashville Daily Advertiser. (Fri., Oct. 26, 1832)

Baldwin, Benjamin J. Treasurer of the White Creek Springs Co.
Died at Vicksburg, Miss.
Nashville Whig. (Monday, Nov. 5, 1838)

Baldwin, Charles Esq. Counsellor at law. Died in New York
suddenly of Apoplexy.
National Banner & Nashville Daily Advertiser. (Mon., June 30, 1834)

Baldwin, Hon. Henry. One of the Associates Judges of the supreme
Court of the United States. Died at the Merchant Hotel in Phila-
delphia on Sunday night last.
Nashville Whig. (Thursday, May 2, 1844)

Baldwin, Judge Isaac. Died at New Orleans on the 27th inst.
National Banner & Nashville Daily Advertiser (Monday, May 13, 1833)

Baley, Mrs. Sarah W. Died at Hartsville Sumner County, Tenn.
National Banner & Nashville Whig. (Sat., Oct. 13, 1827)

Ball, Mr. Eliphalet Elemming. Aged 38 years 10 Months. Died
Nashville on the 8th inst. (Obituary)
Nashville Whig. (Sat., Sept. 12, 1846)

Ball, Fayette Esq. Died in Leesburg, Va.
National Banner & Nashville Daily Advertiser (Mon., May 26, 1834)

Ball, Mr. James. Died in Nashville on Monday 3rd inst.
National Banner & Nashville Whig. (Sat., March 22, 1828)

Ball, Mrs. Sarah. Aged 42 years. Died in Sommerville, Tenn. On
the 16th of Sept. Consort of Major John H. Ball.
National Banner & Nashville Whig. (Friday, Oct. 16, 1835)

Ballad, Miss Hope. Died in Mobile. Aged 16 years.
National Banner and Nashville Whig. (Sat., Oct. 7, 1826)

Ballenger, Capt. Henry F. Died at Lynchburg, Va.
National Banner and Nashville Daily Advertiser. (Wed., March 5, 1834)

Ballew, Miss Agnes. Aged 18 years. Died in New Orleans.
National Banner & Nashville Daily Advertiser. (Tues., June 24, 1834)

Balthrop, Mrs. Sally. Wife of Frances Balthrop of Davidson County.
Died on the 24th inst.
Daily Republican Banner. (Friday Oct. 27, 1837)

Bancraft, Charles H. of Con. Died in New Orleans of Yellow Fever.
Daily Republican Banner (Wed., Sept. 27, 1837).

Bang, Mrs. Catherine. Aged 51 years. Died in Nashville and formerly
of Baltimore.
Daily Republican Banner. (Sat., Sept. 30, 1837)

Bankhead, Eunice Waters. Daughter of James and Elizabeth Bankhead,
in the 6th year of her age. Died on Sunday evening.
The Politician & Weekly Nashville Whig. (Wed., Sept. 29, 1847)

Banks, Maj. C. Died at Mountsterling, Ky.
National Banner. (Jan. 27, 1826)

Banks, Capt. George. A Stranger supposed to be lately from
Baltimore. Died at Louisville, Ky.
National Banner & Nashville Whig. (Mon., Dec. 10, 1831)

Banks, George Esq. Died in Stafford County, Va. Aged 58 years.
National Banner & Nashville Whig. (Monday, July 31, 1837)

Banks, Mr. Israel. Of New Orleans. Died at sea on his passage to
New York.
National Banner & Nashville Whig. (Sat., Sept. 30, 1826)

Banks, Gen. James. Died near Memphis.
National Banner & Nashville Whig. (Friday, July 25, 1828)

Banks, Mrs. Sarah. Died at Gallatin.
National Banner & Nashville Daily Advertiser (Sat., Nov. 24, 1832)

Bannister, Maj. Thomas. Died at Huntsville, Ala. Aged 78 years.
National Banner. (Jan. 20, 1826)

Barbarin, Mr. Joseph. Eldest son of Mr. Louis Barbarin. Died in
New Orleans, La.
National Banner & Nashville Whig. (Friday, Nov. 21, 1834)

Barbaus, Philip Pendleton. Only child of Thomas Barbaus, M.D.
Professor of Chemistry in La Grange College. Died in La Grange, Ala.
on the 6th inst. of April. Ages 3 years 7 months 15 days.
National Banner and Nashville Whig. (Friday, April 21, 1837)

Barbee, Mr. H. L. Died at Natchez, Miss.
National Banner & Nashville Daily Advertiser. (Mon., Jan. 9, 1832)

Barber, Mr. John M. Died in Oldham County.
National Banner & Nashville Whig. (Sat., Sept. 30, 1826)

Barclay, Mrs. Elizabeth. Wife of Mr. Philander Barclay and daughter
of Richard Garrett Esq. of Glasgow. Died at Russellville, Ky.
National Banner & Nashville Daily Advertiser. (Sat., July 28, 1832)

Barclay, Mr. Hugh. In the 84th year of his age. Died near Bowling
Green, Ky.
National Banner & Nashville Whig. (Friday, Oct. 31, 1834)

Barfield, Mr. Daniel H. Died in Crittenden County, Ark.
National Banner & Nashville Daily Advertiser. (Wed., June 5, 1833)

Barkdale, Mrs. Nancy G. Consort of the late Nathaniel Barkdale of
Halifax County, Virginia. Died in Rutherford County, Tenn. of
Cholera on the 13th of July.
National Banner & Nashville Whig. (Wed., Aug. 19, 1835)

Barker, Mr. Charles. Died in Todd County, Ky.
National Banner & Nashville Whig. (Friday, April 1, 1831)

Barker, Hon. David. Died in New Hampshire.
National Banner & Nashville Daily Advertiser (Fri., May 16, 1834)

Barker, Edward S. Esq. Died on Thursday 25th of June at his
residence in Clarksville. (Obituary)
Nashville Whig. (Monday, July 13th, 1840)

Barker, John Major General. Aged 72 years. He was an officer in
the Revolutionary Army. Died on the 3rd inst. at Philadelphia.
The Nashville Whig & Tenn. Advertiser. (May 2, 1818)

Barker, Mrs. Mary Minor. Wife of Mr. John Barker. Died in Montgomery
County.
National Banner & Nashville Whig. (Wed., March 16, 1831)

Barkley, Capt. David. Died at Fulton T.
National Banner. (Sat., May 30, 1829)

Barkley, Mr. John. In the 78 year of his age. Died in Smith County.
National Banner & Nashville Whig. (Fri., Feb. 11, 1831)

Barkman, Mr. Jacob. Died at Huntsville, Ala.
National Banner & Nashville Whig. (Tues., Feb. 2, 1830)

Barlow, Mrs. Fanny M. G. Wife of Mr. Benjamin D. Barlow. Died in
Ruthford County.
National Banner & Nashville Daily Advertiser. (Sat., May 18, 1833)

Barlow, Mrs. Ruth. Widow of the late Joel Barlow. Died lately at
Kalorama.
The Nashville Whig and Tennessee Advertiser. (June 27, 1818)

Barnard, Gen. Isaac. Late Senator in Congress from Tenn. Died in
Westchester, Pa.
National Banner & Nashville Daily Advertiser. (Sat., March 15, 1834)

Barnard, John Bateman. Son of Joseph and Susan Barnard. Died in
Nashville.
Daily Republican Banner. (Wed., Jan. 30, 1839)

Barnes, Mr. Absolom. Died at Smithville.
National Banner & Nashville Whig. (Sat., July 22, 1826)

Barnes, Mrs. Rhoda. In the 81st year of her age. Died in Davidson
County on the 12th inst. at the residence of her son Bartley Barnes.
The Politician and the Weekly Nashville Whig. (Fri., March 17, 1848)

Barnes, Mrs. Rhoda. In the 81st years of her age. Died at the
residence of her son Bartley M. Barnes. Sheriff of Davidson County
on the 12th inst.
The Christian Record. (Sat., March 18, 1848)

Barnes, William. Died near Bolivar. Aged 106 years. He was one of
thos who fought at Braddock's Defeat in 1775 and subsequently at
Bunker's Hill, Brandywine and numerous other engagements in the
revolutionary wars, and volunteered his services in the late Indian
war, but was discharged because of his age and inability.
Nashville Banner and Nashville Whig. (Vol. 2 No. 84 July 28, 1827)

Barnett, Mrs. Margaret. Consort of William Barnett, Est. in the 67th
year of her age. Died in Waynesboro, Tenn. on the 14th of August.
National Banner & Nashville Daily Advertiser. (Fri., Sept. 20, 1833)

Barnett, Mr. Nathan M. Formerly of Madison County. Son of the late
Joseph Barnett. Died in Lincoln County, Ky.
National Banner & Nashville Daily Advertiser (Sat., Aug. 10, 1833)

Barnett, Mrs. Sally. Aged 67 years. Died in Antauga County. (Wantauga?)
National Banner & Nashville Whig. (Sat., Sept. 16, 1826)

Barnett, Rev. William. Died in Logan County, Ky.
National Banner & Nashville Whig. (Sat., Oct. 6, 1827)

Barr, Mr. Samuel H. Died in Florence, Ala.
National Banner & Nashville Whig. (Sat., Dec. 9, 1826)

Barrett, Mr. James. Died at his residence in Louisana.
The Politician and Weekly Nashville Whig. (Fri., July 23, 1847)

Barrett, Richard. Died on Tuesday last, Richard infant son of Mr.
James Barrett.
National Banner & Nashville Whig. (Sat., April 28, 1827)

Barrow, Mrs. Ann E. Died in Nashville on the Saturday last, Widow
of the late Willie Barrow Esq.
National Banner & Nashville Whig. (Monday, Aug. 15, 1831)

Barrow, David Esq. Late of Nashville. Died at Smithland on Friday
1st on his way from Louisana to Nashville to pay a visit to his friends.
National Banner & Nashville Whig. (Wed., July 6, 1831)

Barrow, Willie. Infant son of Washington Barrow Esq. Died in Nashville on Wednesday last.
National Banner & Nashville Whig. (Friday, Aug. 26, 1831)

Barry, Hugh L. W. Aged 7 years, son of the late R. H. Barry. Died on Thursday at the residence of Mrs. Judge Overton of Davidson County.
Daily Republican Banner. (Sat., Dec. 7, 1839)

Barry, Hugh Lawson White. Aged 7 years eldest son of the late Richard Henry Barry, formerly of Nashville. Died at the residence of his grandmother Mrs. Judge Overton.
Nashville Union. (Monday, Dec. 9, 1839)

Barry, Richard H. Died his funeral at the residence of Judge Overton at ten o'clock this morning.
Daily Republican Banner. (Monday, May 6, 1839)

Barry, Richard H. Died at his residence near Nashville yesterday.
Nashville Whig. (Monday, May 6, 1839)

Barry, Hon. W. T. Minister to Spain and late postmaster Gen. Died in England.
The Union. (Monday, Oct. 26, 1835)

Barstow, Joshua of the Army of Texas. Died at Orozimbo, Texas on the 24th Sept. a native of Massachusetts and late of Nashville.
Nashville Republican. (Nov. 17, 1836)

Barstow, Joshua of the Army of Texas. Died at Orozimbo, Texas on the 24th Sept. a native of Mass. and late of Tenn.
National Banner and Nashville Whig. (Nov. 18, 1836)

Barthe, Mr. Charles S. Aged 32. Died at Jackson.
National Banner & Nashville Whig. (Sat., July 15, 1826)

Bartholomew, Mr. Joseph. A Revolutionary soldier aged 66. Died at Knoxville.
National Banner & Nashville Whig. (Mon., May 23, 1831)

Bartlett, Mr. John. Died at Bayou Sarah, La.
National Banner & Nashville Whig. (Sat., Aug. 19, 1826)

Barton, Mr. Benjamin Died in Henry County.
National Banner & Nashville Whig. (Fri., Feb. 12, 1830)

Barton, David. Formerly a Senator from Missouri. Died in St. Louis.
Daily Republican Banner. (Sat., Oct. 14, 1837)

Barton, Rev. Isaac. Aged 85 years. Died in Jefferson County.
National Banner & Nashville Whig. (Mon., Nov. 28, 1831)

Barton, Mr. Lewis. Died in Caswell City, N. C.
Nashville Republican and State Gazette. (Thursday, October 16, 1831. No. 63 Vol. 7)

Barton, Mrs. Margaret. Died in Knox County. Aged 77 years.
National Banner (Feb. 10, 1826)

Barton, Wesley Esq. Died in Arkansas. A native of Tennessee.
National Banner and Nashville Whig. (Sat., Dec. 2, 1826)

Bascom, Mrs. Margaretta. Wife of Hiram D. Bascom. Died at St. Louis, Mo.
National Banner & Nashville Daily Advertiser. (Wed., July 9, 1834)

Basinger, Lieut. William E. 2nd Artillery. Died in the battle with the Seminole Indians in Florida.
The Union. (Saturday, Jan. 23, 1836)

Baskins, Mr. George St. John. Died in Fayetteville, Tenn.
National Banner & Nashville Daily Advertiser. (Tues., Feb. 11, 1834)

Bass, Mr. George M. Died at Jackson.
National Banner & Nashville Whig. (Wed., Dec. 14, 1831)

Bass, Mr. Hartwell. Died in Rutherford County.
National Banner & Nashville Whig. (Sat., Feb. 10, 1827)

Bass, Mr. James Sr. Died in Rutherford County.
National Banner, (March 3, 1826)

Bass. Malvina Grundy. Died on the 14th inst. at the residence of
Col. John McGavock near Franklin daughter of John M. and Malvina C.
Bass. (Obituary March 18)
The Christian Record (Sat., March 11, 1848)

Bass, Miss Mary A. Yesterday 11th of October. Died in Nashville.
See paper for Obituary.
National Banner and Nashville Advertiser. (Friday, Oct. 12, 1832
No. 1615, Vol. 20.)
Bass, Mr. Peter. Died at Smithland, Ky. On the 18th inst. in the
60th years of his age. was of the State of Missouri, and for many
years a native of this town.
National Banner. (Sat., May 30, 1829)

Bass, Doctor T. C. Formerly of Tennessee. Died near Natchez, Miss.
On the 28th of Sept.
National Banner & Nashville Whig. Wednesday, Oct. 21, 1835)

Bassett, F. B. Died in Huntsville, Ala.
National Banner & Nashville Whig. (Friday, Jan. 22, 1830)

Basye, Mr. Lewis M. Aged 53 years. Died in Davidson County on 26th
inst.
Daily Republican Banner, (Tursday, Oct. 29, 1840)

Bate, Virginia Augusta. 2nd daughter of Gov. Wm. B. Bate. Obituary.
Republican Banner and Nashville Whig. (No. 188, Tuesday, July 29, 1853)

Bateman, Mrs. Amelia. Consort of Mr. Evan Bateman. Died at her
residence at Davidson County on the 25th inst. in the 65th year of
her age. Obituary.
Nashville Union. (Friday, March 15, 1839)

Bateman, Dr. Ephraim. Late Senator in Congress. Died in New Jersey.
National Banner & Nashville Whig. (Sat., Feb. 21, 1829)

Bateman, Mr. Henry. Aged 69 years. Died yesterday at the residence
of his son-in-law W. H. Kindrich.
Nashville True Whig. & Weekly Commercial Register. (Fri., May 3, 1850)

Bateman, Mr. John D. Son of the Henry Bateman Esq. of this vicinity.
Died in Columbia, Texas on the 3rd Sept.
Daily Republican Banner. (Thursday, Oct. 29, 1840)

Bateman, Mr. Loama S. Died in Williamson County.
National Banner. (Sat., June 6, 1829)

Bates, Mrs. Elizabeth. Aged 75 years. Died in Haywood County.
National Banner & Nashville Whig. (Sat., March 17, 1827)

Bates, Fleming Esq. Died in Northumberland County, Virginia.
Nashville Republican and State Gazette. (Thursday, Feb. 24, 1831
No. 93, Vol. 6)

Bates, John P. Esq. Attorney at law of Anson County by the use of
laudanum, voluntarily put an end to his existence on the 5th inst.
National Banner & Nashville Daily Advertiser Mon. 1/2/1832 V.20 N1373

Bates, William Gray. Son of John Bates Esq. of the firm of Baring, Brothers & Co. Died in England on the 20th Dec. in the 20th year of his age.
National Banner & Nashville Whig. (Wed., March 4, 1835)

Batson, Esq. Thomas. Died in Montgomery County.
National Banner & Nashville Whig. (Thurs., Nov. 18, 1830)

Battelle, Jonathan Esq. Died at New York while on a journey for his health. Jonathan Battelle Esq. Editor of the Mobile Commercial Register.
Nashville Whig. (Nov. 15, 1824)

Battle, Mr. Henry. Aged 54 years. Died in Bedford County.
National Banner & Nashville Daily Advertiser. (Sat., Feb. 25, 1832)

Batts, George Washington. Died at Flemingsbourgh, Ky. Batts, George Washington. Age 50 years.
National Banner & Nashville Whig. (Sat., April 7, 1827)

Batts, Mr. John. Died in Shelbyville.
National Banner & Nashville Whig. (Sat., Sept. 13, 1828)

Bauchanan, George W. Esq. Late U. S. Attorney for the Western District of Pennsylvania. Died at Pittsburgh.
National Banner & Nashville Daily Advertiser. (Mon., Nov. 5, 1832)

Bauchanan, Dr. Joseph. Editor of the Focus. Died in Louisville, Ky.
National Banner. (Sat., Sept. 12, 1829)

Baugh, Mrs. Margaret. Died in Madison County, Ky.
National Banner. (March 24, 1826)

Bauguss, Mr. Richard. Formerly of Maury County. Died in Perry County.
National Banner & Nashville Whig. (Wed., Sept. 7, 1831)

Baulding, Dr. Amasa. Died in Franklin County.
National Banner & Nashville Whig. (Sat., Aug. 19, 1826)

Baum, Mr. Martin. Died in Franklin County.
National Banner & Nashville Whig. (Sat., Aug. 19, 1826)

Baum, Mr. Martin. Died at Cincinnati on the 11th inst.
National Banner & Nashville Whig. (Tues., Dec. 27, 1831)

Baum, Mr. Martin. Died at Cincinnati.
National Banner & Nashville Daily Advertiser. (Mon., Oct. 1, 1832)

Baxter, Mrs. Wife of Mr. D. Baxter. Died in Rutherford County.
National Banner & Nashville Whig. (Fri., May 20, 1831)

Baxter, Col. James. Died at Port Royal, Tenn. on Sunday the 7th instantly. A citizen of Clarksville and formerly of this place.
The Nashville Gazette. (Sat., Nov. 20, 1819)

Baxter, Mr. Jeremiah. Aged 55 years. Died in Maury County Aug. 20.
National Banner & Nashville Daily Advertiser. (Fri., Sept. 6, 1833)

Baxter, Mrs.Mary. Wife of Mr. Wm. Baxter. Died in Clark County, Ky.
National Banner. (May 16, 1829)

Baxter, Mr. Robert. Proprietor of the Tennessee Iron Works. Died on the 30th inst.
Nashville Tree Whig. Weekly Commercial Register. (Fri., May 17, 1850)

Baxter, Mrs. Ruth. Wife of Dr. John Baxter of New York. Died at New Harmony, Ind.
National Banner & Nashville Daily Advertiser. (Thurs., July 24, 1834)

Bayer, Mrs. Eliza Jane. Wife of Mr. Alfred J. Bayer. Died in Lexington, Ky.
National Banner & Nashville Daily Advertiser. (Wed., June 5, 1833)

Bayless, Abijah Wilson. Infant son of William B. and Ann M. Bayless of Nashville. Died Sunday Morning.
Nashville Whig. (Tues., May 21, 1844)

Bayless, Brittain Esq. Died in Stewart County, Tenn. On Thursday the 16th in the 77th year of his age.
National Banner & Nashville Whig. (Wed., Oct. 22, 1834)

Bayless, Mr. Cullen. Died in Dover, Stewart County on Friday 12th inst.
Nashville Republican. (Tuesday Feb. 16, 1836)

Bayless, Cullen. Died on Friday the 12th inst. in Dover, Stewart County, Tenn.
National Banner & Nashville Whig. (Friday, Feb. 26, 1836)

Boyless, Thos. Died near Jonesboro from being stabbed by one of his neighbors.
National Banner & Nashville Whig. (Wed., Aug. 9, 1837)

Bayless, Thos. Died near Jonesboro he was stabbed by one of his neighbors.
Nashville Republican. (Wed., Aug. 9, 1837)

Beach, Mrs. Catherine. Wife of Mr. James Beach. Died at Lexington, Ky.
National Banner & Nashville Whig. (Sat., April 14, 1827)

Beall, Mrs. Martha Y. Wife of Mr. James M. Beall. Died in Russelville Ky.
National Banner & Nashville Whig. (Sat., May 17, 1828)

Beall, Richard Esq. Of Alleghany County, Maryland. Died in Baltimore.
National Banner & Nashville Whig. (Wed., March 8, 1837)

Bean, Robert. Died lately, Robert Bean of Hawkins County. A distinquished soldier, a lover of peace and order and an esteemed citizen.
Knoxville Gazette. (Sat., June 1, 1793)

Bean, Mr. Russell. Died in Washington County on the 9th inst., the first man born in that county.
National Banner. (Jan. 27, 1826)

Bearden, Mrs. Eliza A. Wife of Mr. Marcus D. Bearden. Died in Knox County, Tennessee. Aged 32 years.
National Banner & Nashville Whig. (Friday, April 10, 1835)

Beatty, Mrs. Ann M. Died at Russellville, Ky.
National Banner. (Sat., Dec. 5, 1829)

Beauchamp, Thomas Esq. Aged 52 years. Died at Franklin, Ky. on the 29th ult.
National Banner & Nashville Whig. (Mon., Sept. 13, 1830)

Beavis, Mr. John L. Died at Frankford, Ky.
National Banner & Nashville Whig. (Sat., Nov. 3, 1827)

Beck, John E. Esq. U. S. Attorney for the district of West Tennessee. Died at his resident in this place on the 22nd inst.
The Nashville Whig and Tennessee Advertiser. (June 27, 1818)

Beck, Micajah Barrow. Infant son of Wm. C. and Delia D. Beck of
Gallatin. Died on Wednesday the 10th of Feb. aged 2 years and 2 mos.
Nashville Republican. (Tues., Feb. 18, 1836)

Beck, Mrs. Susannah. Consort of Mr. John Beck of Davidson County,
age 47. Died on the 19th Dec.
Impartial Review and Cumberland Repository. (Jan. 3, 1807)

Becker, Mrs. Fanny A. Died in Russellville, Ky.
National Banner & Nashville Whig. (Sat., Sept. 15, 1827)

Beckley, Mrs. M. Died at Lexington, Ky.
National Banner & Nashville Daily Advertiser (Thurs., July 25, 1833)

Beckwith, Miss Ann. Died near the place on Thursday last. The high
estimation in which this lady was held was manifested at her burial.
The Nashville Whig and the Tennessee Advertiser. (April 4, 1818)

Becton, Mr. George. Aged 94 years, a soldier of the Revolution.
Died in Davidson County.
National Banner & Nashville Daily Advertiser. (Mon., May 12, 1834)

Bedford, Mrs. Ann. Of Rutherford County, Tenn. in the 69 years of her
age. Died in this town in the residence of her son Mr. B. W. Bedford
National Banner and Nashville Whig. (Sat., Oct. 11, 1828)

Bedford, Dr. John R. Died in Limestone County, Ala.
National Banner & Nashville Whig. (Sat., April 7, 1827)

Bedford, Mr. John R. Died at Athens, Ala.
National Banner & Nashville Whig. (Sat., April 14, 1827)

Bee, Mr. Edwin B. Athens, Ohio. Died in the loss of the steam boat
Brandywine.
National Banner & Nashville Daily Advertiser. (Mon., April 23, 1832)

Beeler, Mrs. Wife of Joseph Beeler, Esq. Died in Grainger County.
National Banner. (Sat., Aug. 8, 1829)

Beirne, John Esq. Attorney at law aged 25 son of Col. Andrew Beirne
of Monroe County, Va. Died at Huntsville, Ala.
National Banner & Nashville Whig. (Thurs., July 29, 1830)

Belcher, Mary Francis. Daughter of Mr. N. & Mrs. E. Belcher. Died on
the 13th inst. age 15 months.
The Politician and Weekly Nashville Whig. (Fri., March 24, 1848)

Beldsnyder, Samuel B. Infant son of Mrs. Thomas Beldsynder. Died
in Nashville on the 2d inst.
National Banner & Nashville Daily Advertiser. (Tues., July 3, 1832)

Bell, Mr. Alexander. Died at Louisville Ky on the 20th inst.
National Banner & Nashville Whig. (Tuesday, Dec. 27, 1831)

Bell, Mr. George W. Died near Nashville a few days since.
The Western Weekly Review. (Friday, Dec. 23, 1831 Franklin, Tenn.)

Bell, Mr. George Washington. Died suddenly in Davidson County.
National Banner & Nashville Whig. (Mon., Dec. 19, 1831)

Bell, Mr. H. M. of Roane County. Died on board the Steamboat Atlantic
near Memphis.
National Banner & Nashville Daily Advertiser. (Wed., June 12, 1833)

Bell, Mr. Isaac T. Died in the vicinity of Helena, Ark.
National Banner & Nashville Whig. (Mon., Dec. 29, 1834)

Bell, Mr. James of Dumbarton, Scotland. Died in Nashville on the
20th inst. in the 34th year of his age.
Nashville Whig. (Sat., January 22, 1842)

Bell, Mr. John. Died in Todd County, Ky.
National Banner and Nashville Whig. (Sat., Sept. 16, 1826).

Bell, Capt. John M. of the U. S. Navy. Died in Westmoreland County,
Va.
National Banner and Nashville Daily Advertiser (Fri., Aug. 30, 1833)

Bell, Mrs. Mary M. H. Wife of Mr. James Bell of Nashville. Died
at Matanzas in the Island of Cuba.
National Banner and Nashville Whig. (Mon., May 18, 1835)

Bell, Mr. Nancy. Wife of Dr. Joseph E. Bell. Died in Greenville on
the 7th inst.
National Banner and Nashville Whig. (Monday, Sept. 26, 1831)

Bell, Nathaniel of Williamson County. Died Sept. 16th, 1848 a native
of Tennessee and about 58 years old.
The Christian Record. (Sat., Sept. 30, 1848)

Bell, Robert A. Esq. Died near Merridianville, Ala.
National Banner and Nashville Daily Advertiser. (Fri., Sept. 20, 1833)

Bell, Mrs. Sarah. Wife of Mr. Thomas Bell. Died in Hickman County
on the 20th inst. Daughter of Mr. Robin Johnson of Davidson County.
National Banner and Nashville Whig. (Wed., Jan. 26, 1831)

Bell, Mrs. Sarah L. Consort of Hon. John Bell. Died in Davidson
County. National Banner and Nashville Daily. (Fri., Sept. 29, 1832)

Bell, Zadock Esq. Attorney at law and formerly a student of this
place. Died in Montgomery Ala. on the 6th inst.
National Banner and Nashville Whig. (Sat., July 29, 1826)

Bellah, Mr. Samuel. Died in Rutherford County.
National Banner and Nashville Daily Advertiser. (Fri., Jan. 27, 1832)

Bellak, Mr. Samuel. Died in Rutherford County.
National Banner and Nashville Advertiser. (Friday, Jan. 27, 1832.
Vol. 20 No. 1395)

Bellknap, Morris B. Formerly of Pittsburg, Pa. Died at Smithland,
Ky.
Nashville Republican. Thursday, Aug. 3, 1837)

Bellsoover, Mrs. In the 46 years of her age. Died at the Cumberland
Iron Works on Sunday 14th inst.
National Banner & Nashville Whig. (Wed., June 24, 1835)

Beloat, Mr. Henry. Died at his residence in Sumner County on Thursday
evening the 29th in the 64th year of his age.
National Banner & Nashville Whig. (Sat., April 28, 1827)

Belsher, Mrs. Elizabeth Jane. Died in Montogomery, Ala.
National Banner & Nashville Whig. (Sat., Sept. 2, 1826)

Belt, Mr. W. Died in Frankfort, Ky.
National Banner & Nashville Daily Advertiser. (Sat., March 22, 1834)

Bender, Mr. Daniel. Aged 83 years. Died in Sumner County.
National Banner & Nashville Daily Advertiser. (Sat., Dec. 8, 1832)

Bender, Mrs. Feraba. In the 83rd year of her age. Died at the
residence of her son Berden Bender in Sumner County, Tenn.
The Politician Weekly & Nashville Whig. (Fri., Oct. 29, 1847)

Benham, Mrs. Isabella. Wife of Joseph S. Benham Esq. Died at Cincinnati.
National Banner & Nashville Whig. (Sat., Nov. 22, 1828)

Benie, Mr. Daniel Esq. Aged 45 years. Died in Davidson County, Tenn. on Friday, Nov. 11.
Nashville Republican. (Thursday, Nov. 17, 1836)

Bennett, Mr. Benjamin. Died in Columbia, Mo.
National Banner & Nashville Whig. (June 24, 1826)

Bennett, Hon. Caleb. Aged 78 years. Died in Wilmington, Delaware on May 7th. A soldier of the Republican Revolution.
National Banner and Nashville Whig. (Friday, May 27, 1836)

Bennet, Caleb P. Governor of Deleware. Died on the 9th instant. Aged 78 years. Died on the 9th inst.
The Union. (Tuesday, May 24, 1836)

Bennet, Mr. James. Aged about 60 years. Died near New Market, Tennessee.
National Banner & Nashville Daily Advertiser. (Fri., Aug. 16, 1833)

Benoit, Mr. Earnest. Died in Nashville.
National Banner & Nashville Whig. (Monday, Dec. 5, 1831)

Benoit, Mrs. Mary. Died on Saturday morning last. The Amiable consort of Mr. E. Benoit of this place.
The Nashville Whig. (Feb. 26, 1817)

Benson, Hon. Egbert. Aged 89 years. A member of the first Congress Convened. Died at Jamacia, Long Island. He was a soldier of the Revolutionary and lately a Judge of the Supreme Court of New York.
National Banner & Nashville Daily Advertiser. (Thurs., Sept. 12, 1833)

Benson, Mr. Joseph. Formerly of Philadelphia. Died on Sunday night the 23rd inst. brother of Sylvanus E. Benson of Nashville.
Nashville Whig. (Tues., Oct. 25, 1842)

Benson, Mr. William B. Died in Murfreesborough, Tenn.
National Banner & Nashville Whig. (Wed., Feb. 4, 1835)

Bentalow, Col. Paul. A Hero of the Revolution. Died at Baltimore.
National Banner & Nashville Whig. (Sat., Dec. 30, 1826)

Bentham, Jeremy. Died in Londan.
Nashville Republican and State Gazette. (Monday, July 30, 1832 Vol. 8, No. 34)

Benton, Charles F. Aged two years son of W. H. & E. Benton. Died on Sunday, August 2nd.
Daily Republican Banner. (Thursday, Aug. 6, 1840)

Berdwell, Mrs. Louise. Wife of Rev. Russell Berdwell. Died near New Market, Tenn.
National Banner & Nashville Daily Advertiser. (Friday, Sept. 20, 1833)

Berkley, Mr. C. H. D. of St. Louis. Died in the vicinity froze to death while out hunting.
Daily Republican Banner. (Thursday, Dec. 5, 1839)

Bernard, Mrs. Mildred. Died in Logan County, Ky.
National Banner & Nashville Daily Advertiser. (Mon., Sept. 9, 1833)

Bernard, Thomas H. Esq. Died at his residence in Bedford County on Saturday 31st of January after a short illness.
Nashville Whig. (Feb. 16, 1824)

Bernie, Edward Esq. A Native of Charleston, S. C. Died in New Orleans.
National Banner & Nashville Daily Advertiser. (Thurs., Aug. 8, 1833)

Berrien, Mrs. Rebecca. Wife of the Hon. John M. Berrien. Attorney
General of the United States. Died in Baltimore.
National Banner & Nashville Whig. (Thurs., Sept. 16, 1830)

Berry, Mr. A. F. Bookseller, brother of William T. Berry of Nashville.
Died at Memphis on the 4th inst.
Nashville Whig. (Tuesday, Sept. 10, 1844)

Berry, Charles Augustus. Only son of A. D. and Adeline Berry.
Died on the 2nd inst.
The Politican and Weekly Nashville Whig. (Dec. 10, 1847)

Berry, Charles Augustus. Only son of A. D. and Adeline Berry.
Died on the 2 inst. aged three years and four months.
The Christian Record. (Sat., Dec. 11, 1847)

Berry, Mrs. Elizabeth Virjane. Consort of Alfred Berry in the 17th
year of her age. Died in Robertson County, Tennessee March 14th
late of Nashville and the daughter of the late Isaac Herring.
Daily Republican Banner. (Wed., April 11, 1838)

Berry, Mrs. Elvina B. Consort of A. F. Berry. Died in Williamsport,
Maury County on the 20th ult.
Nashville Whig. (Mon., Aug. 6, 1838)

Berry, Horace Putnam. Infant son of A. D. Berry. Died on Tuesday
morning last aged ten months.
Nashville Whig. (Thurs., Oct. 22, 1846)

Berry, Mr. John S. Formerly of Knoxville, Tenn. Died in Tuscumbia,
Ala. on the 6th inst.
Nashville Whig. (Mon., Sept. 23, 1839)

Berry, Mrs. Mary C. On 23rd of Oct. late consort of Rev. M. Berry.
She died in the triumph of her faith and has left a family to mourn
the loss of a departed wife and mother.
Nashville Republican. (Tues., Jan. 19, 1836)

Berry, Mr. W. W. Died in Boliver, Tenn.
National Banner & Nashville Whig. (Monday Nov. 24, 1834)

Berry, Wilkins Tannehill. Infant son of William T. Berry, Bookseller
of Nashville. Died suddenly last evening.
Nashville Whig. (March 26, 1838)

Berryhill, Esq. William M. Died in Nashville.
Nashville Republican. (Sat., Oct. 15, 1836)

Berryhill, William M. Esq. Long favorably known as a merchant and
more recently as the Teller of the Union Bank. Died in Nashville
on the 13th inst.
The Union. (Sat., Oct. 15, 1836)

Berryhill, William M. Esq. Died in Nashville on Thursday 13th Oct.
National Banner & Nashville Whig. (Mon., Oct. 17, 1836)

Berson, Mrs. Lucinda. Consort of S. W. Berson and eldest daughter of
Henry Van Pelt, Editor of the Memphis Appeal. Died in Brownsville
on the 3rd inst.
Nashville Whig. (Thurs., March 12, 1846)

Berteau, Armistead. Printer aged about 20 years. Formerly from
Richmond and Baltimore. Died in New Orleans.
National Banner & Nashville Daily Advertiser. (Fri., Sept. 20, 1833)

Best, Dr. Robert. Died at Lexington, Ky.
National Banner & Nashville Whig. (Mon., Oct. 11, 1830)

Bethel, Gen. Wm. A citizen of Rockingham County, N. C. Died at Natchez, Mi.
National Banner & Nashville Daily Advertiser. (Thurs., Sept. 11, 1834)

Bethell, Miss Maria. Aged 19 years. Died in Jefferson County, Tenn.
National Banner & Nashville Daily Advertiser (Tues., Aug. 5, 1834)

Bibb, Charles S. Esq. Recently appointed United States Judge in the Territory of Arkansas. Died on the 15th near the Yellow Banks with Cholera.
National Banner & Nashville Daily Advertiser. (Mon., Oct. 22, 1832)

Bibb, Edward B. Esq. Late of Frankford, Ky. Died at Florence, Ala.
National Banner & Nashville Whig. (Sat., Feb. 10, 1827)

Bibb, Mrs. Elizabeth. Died In Logan County, Ky. Wife of Mr. Henry G. Bibb.
National Banner. (Feb. 10, 1826)

Bibb, Dr. George A. Died at Frankford, Ky. Aged 23 years.
Dec. 23, 1825

Bibb, Rev. James. Died in Madison County, Ala.
National Banner. (Feb. 24, 1826)

Bibb, Lieut. Lucien J. Of the United States Army, son of George M. Bibb Esq. of Frankford, Ky. Died at Bellona Arsenal on the Potomac.
National Banner & Nashville Whig. (Mon., Sept. 26, 1831)

Bibb, Mrs. Mary Ann. Wife of Rev. Richard Bibb. Died in Logan County, Ky.
National Banner & Nashville Whig. (Mon., March 28, 1831)

Bibb, Mrs. Mirian. Consort of Mr. James Bibb of Huntsville. Died in Madison County, Ala.
National Banner & Nashville Daily Advertiser (Mon., Sept. 9, 1833)

Bibb, Mrs. Sophia. Consort of Mr. Thos. Bibb and daughter of Col. W. Byrn in the 22nd year of her age. Died in Florence, Ala.
National Banner & Nashville Whig. (Wed., Nov. 16, 1831)

Bibb, William M. Governor of the State of Alabama. Died on the 9th of July last.
The Nashville Gazette. (Sat., Aug. 12, 1820)

Bibbs, William Sen. Esq. Aged 51 years. Died in Madison Co., Tenn.
National Banner and Nashville Daily Advertiser. (Thurs., June 19, 1834)

Bicknell, Robert T. Of Bicknell Reporter. Died in Philadelphia on the 9th inst. aged 33 years.
Daily Republican Banner. (Wed., May 22, 1839)

Bicknell, Mr. Wm. Of Belfast, aged 28. Died Pensacola.
National Banner & Nashville Whig. (Sat., March 31, 1827)

Bicknell, Mr. William F. Aged 19 years. Died in Tellico.
National Banner & Nashville Whig. (Fri., March 26, 1830)

Biddle, Chas. Esq. Died in Philadelphia on the 21st Dec.
National Banner & Nashville Whig. (Mon., Jan. 9, 1837)

Biddle, Charles Esq. In the 49th years of his age. Died in Philadelphia on the 21 ult.
Nashville Republican. (Tuesday, Jan. 10, 1837)

Biddle, Charles Esq. Died in Philadelphia on the 21st of Dec. in the 49th year of his age.
The Union. (Sat., Jan. 28, 1837)

Biddle, Mrs. Rebecca. Widow of the late Col. Clement Biddle. Died at Philadelphia.
National Banner & Nashville Whig. (Friday, Dec. 9, 1831)

Biddle, Richard Esq. High Sheriff. Died in Baurbon County, Ky.
National Banner, (May 10, 1826)

Biddle, Hon. Richard. Brother of Nicholas Biddle of Philadelphia and of Commodore Biddle of the Navy. Died at Philadelphia on the 6th inst.
The Politician and Weekly Nashville Whig. (Fri., July 16, 1847)

Bierne, Francis. Died in St. Stephans, Ala. Capt. Francis Bierne a Native of France.
National Banner & Nashville Whig. (Vol. 15, No. 21 Whole No. 750 September 2, 1826)

Biffle, Col. Jacob. Died in Wayne County on Wednesday morning the 29th Sept.
National Banner & Nashville Whig. (Thurs., Oct. 14, 1830)

Bigelow, Elijah Esq. Died at Jackson, Madison County on Saturday morning last aged 30 a native of Mass.
National Banner & Nashville Whig. (Thurs., Sept. 2, 1830)

Bigelow, Dr. Luther, aged 38 years. for many years an eminent and successful practioner of this state . Died in Nashville at the residence of Dr. Lawrence on the 6th inst.
National Banner & Nashville Daily Advertiser. (Oct. 8, 1832)

Biggs, Thomas. From Hawkins County. Died in the Tenn. State Prison of Cholera.
National Banner & Nashville Whig. (Friday, Aug. 14, 1835)

Bilbo, William Elias. Only son of William N. Bilbo of Nashville. Died at Columbus, Miss. on the 13th inst. Age one year and eleven months.
Nashville True Whig & Weekly Commerical Register. (Fri., April 26, 1850)

Billingsley, Mr. Barton. Died in Washington County, Ark.
National Banner & Nashville Daily Advertiser. (Fri., June 22, 1832)

Bills, Dr. Placebo M. Aged 65 years. Died in Maury County.
National Banner & Nashville Whig. (Sat., May 24, 1828)

Bills, Mrs. Prudence M. Wife of John H. Bills, Esq. Died in Bolivar, Hardeman County.
Nashville Whig. (Mon., Sept. 7, 1840)

Binkley, Captain Daniel. Of this County. A gentleman much respected by his acquaintance. Died on Monday last.
Nashville Whig. (Aug. 30, 1824)

Binney, Col. Amos. Aged 65 formerly Navy agent at this port. Died in Boston on the 10th ult.
National Banner & Nashville Daily Advertiser. (Mon., Feb. 4, 1833)

Bird, Owen D. One of the workmen in the branch mint. Died in New Orleans on the 15th inst. of Yellow Fever.
Daily Republican Banner. (Wed., Sept. 11, 1839)

Birth, Caroline Louise. Only daughter of James and Maria L. Birth. Died in the vicinity of Nashville on Tuesday morning.
The Politician & Weekly Nashville Whig. (Fri., March 17, 1848)

Birth, Caroline Louise. Only daughter of James and Maria L. Birth. Died in the Nashville Vicinity on the 14th inst.
The Christian Record. (Sat., March 18, 1848)

Biscoe, Samuel H. of Md. Died in New Orleans on the 15th of Yellow
Fever.
Daily Republican Banner. (Wed., Sept. 27, ____?)

Bishop, Wyat Esq. Died near his farm at Tuscumbia, Ala. In the 76
years of his age. A soldier of the Revolution.
National Banner & Nashville Whig. (Fri., Jan. 9, 1835)

Bissell, Gen. Daniel. Died Lately at St. Louis, Mo.
National Banner & Nashville Daily Advertiser. (Fri., Dec. 27, 1833)

Black, Ann. Daughter of John Black Esq. Died on the 18th inst. in
Nashville in the 15th year of her age.
Nashville Whig. (Thurs., Nov. 21, 1844)

Black, Rev. John. Pastor of the Fifth Presbyterian Church of
Pittsburgh. Died recently in Pittsburgh.
The Christian Record. (Sat., March 13, 1847)

Black, Dr. M. M. Aged 27 years and 6 months. Died in Maury County,
Tenn.
National Banner & Nashville Whig. (Wed., May 6, 1835)

Black, Mr. Peter. Died at Natchez.
National Banner. (Sat., July 11, 1829)

Black, Samuel P. Died in this vicinity on Thursday last.
Daily Republican Banner. (Tuesday, Sept. 5, 1837)

Black, Mrs. Sarah. Wife of Mr. John Black and daughter of Capt. Wm.
A. Sublett. Died in Rutherford County on the 31 ult.
National Banner & Nashville Whig. (Vol. 19, No. 1335. Friday,
Nov. 4, 1831)

Black, Col. William. Aged 57 years. Died in Madison County, Ky.
National Banner & Nashville Daily Advertiser. (Mon., March 26, 1832)

Blackburn, Mrs. Elizabeth Julia. Consort of Rev. George Blackburn.
Died in Woodford County, Ky. Jan. 28th. In the 40th year of her
age.
National Banner & Nashville Daily Advertiser. (Sat., Feb. 11, 1832)

Blackburn, Rev. Gideon. Died near Carlinsville, Illinois in August
last. Formerly of Nashville, Tenn.
Daily Republican Banner. (Mon., Oct. 8, 1838)

Blackburn, Rev. James. Died at Little Rock, Ark.
National Banner & Nashville Whig. (Sat., May 17, 1828)

Blackford, Mr. E. A respectable farmer and useful man. Died near
Bowling Green, Ky.
National Banner & Nashville Whig. (Friday, Feb. 6, 1835)

Blackman, Mr. Bennett. Aged 61 years. Died in Maury County.
National Banner & Nashville Daily Advertiser. (Wed., Sept. 25, 1833)

Blackman, Mrs. Elizabeth. Late consort of Hays Blackman and Eldest
daughter of William Compton. Died on the 3rd inst.
Daily Republican Banner. (Fri., Oct. 10, 1837)

Blackman, Mr. James. Late of Davidson County. Died near Boston,
Alabama on the 21st Aug.
National Banner & Nashville Whig. (Mon., Sept. 22, 1834)

Blackman, Mrs. James and two daughters Margarin and Adeline. Died
in the Boston Alabama about Oct. 1 formerly of Davidson County.
National Banner & Nashville Whig. (Wed., Nov. 12, 1834)

Blackman, John. In his 76 years. Died at his residence in Maury County on Sunday the 3rd inst.
Nashville Whig. (Thursday, Nov. 7, 1844)

Mrs. Evelina Blackmore. Wife of Dr. James A. Blackmore. Died in Gallatin.
National Banner & Nashville Daily Advertiser. (Sat., Jan. 19, 1833)

Major George D. Blackmore. In the 74th year of his age. Died in Sumner County, on the 27th Sept. a Revolutionary soldier.
National Banner & Nashville Daily Advertiser. (Sat., Oct. 5, 1833)

Mr. George D. Blackmore. Age 36 formerly of Sumner County, Tenn. Died in Chicot County, Ark.
National Banner & Nashville Daily Advertising. (Tues., Aug. 5, 1834)

Blackwell, Mrs. Melinda. Wife of Mr. Robert Blackwell. Died in Vandalia, Ill.
National Banner & Nashville Whig. (Sat., Dec. 20, 1828)

Blackwood, William, Esq. Died at Edinburg, Scotland, proprietor of Blackwood's Magazine.
National Banner & Nashville Whig. (Dec. 1, 1834)

Blain, Mrs. Jane Harriet. Died in Knoxville.
Nashville Whig. (Thursday, June 25, 1846)

Blair, Mr. James. Died in Roane County.
National Banner & Nashville Whig. (Sat., Dec. 2, 1826)

Blair, John Lieutenant Colonel. Died on the 14th ultimo, (May 14) Lieutenant Colonel John Blair of Hawkins County of a nervous fever. He was a brave, prudent, heroic officer, a valuable and highly esteemed citizen, an observer of the laws of his country, and always ready to fight and bleed in its defence.
Knoxville Gazette (Sat., June 1, 1793)

Blair, Mrs. Mary. Wife of Richard C. Blair, Esq. Formerly Sheriff of Grainger County aged 34 years 4 months and 22 days. Died in Henderson County on the 3rd ult.
National Banner & Nashville Whig. (Wed., March 23, 1831)

Blair, Mr. William. Clerk in the General Post Office. Died in Washington City.
National Banner & Nashville Whig. (Thurs., Nov. 4, 1830)

Blair, Lieut. Wm. P. Died at Frankfort, Ky.
National Banner. (Sat., July 4, 1829)

Blake, Martin Esq. Aged 47 years. Died in Louisville.
National Banner & Nashville Whig. (Sat., Sept. 30, 1826)

Blake, William. Of Boston Mass. Passenger. Died on the George Collier scalded to death on the 6th inst. about 80 miles below Natchez.
Daily Republican Banner. (Tuesday, May 14, 1839)

Blackemore, Mr. Fielding of Sumner County. Died on Sunday last 27th.
National Banner & Nashville Daily Advertiser. (Sat., Feb. 2, 1833)

Blackmore, William, (Gen.) Obituary.
Republican Banner and Nashville Whig. (No. 299, Mon., Dec. 12, 1853)

Blakenship, Mrs. Sarah W. Died at Murfreesborough.
National Banner. (Feb. 17, 1826)

Blanc, Mr. Yves Le. Died in New Orleans.
National Banner & Nashville Whig. (Sat., Sept. 9, 1826)

Blanchard, Mrs. Consort of Lieut. E. O. Blanchard of the U. S. Navy. Died in Louisville, Ky.
National Banner & Nashville Daily Advertiser. (Mon., June 9, 1834)

Blanchard, Mr. Edward Baily. Died in New Orleans, La.
National Banner & Nashville Whig. (Wed., Dec. 3, 1834)

Blanchard, Mrs. Mary H. Wife of Horace F. Esq. Died in Shelby Co.
National Banner. (Sat., Nov. 14, 1829)

Bland, Mrs. Consort of Mr. Thomas Bland. Died in Elizabethtown, Ky. Was Murdered by a Negro boy 15 years old.
National Banner & Nashville Whig. (Friday, Nov. 20, 1835)

Blanding, Col. A. President of the South Western Rail Road, Bank of South C. Died Copyed from Charleston Paper.
Daily Republican Banner. (Friday, Oct. 4, 1839)

Blanton, Mrs. Elizabeth. Consort of Harrison Blanton Esq. Died Frankfort, Ky.
National Banner & Nashville Whig. (Friday, March 13, 1835)

Blanton, Mr. John F. Died in Muffreesborough.
National Banner & Nashville Daily Advertiser. (Fri., June 14, 1833)

Blatchford, Alicia. Widow of the Rev. Samuel Blatchford, D. D. Died at Lansingburg, New York on the 2d ult. In the 80th year of her age.
The Christian Record. (Sat., June 2, 1847)

Mr. Allen Bledsoe. Aged 24. Died in Madison County, Ala.
National Banner & Nashville Whig. (Sat., Sept. 30, 1826)

Hon. Jesse Bledsoe. Died in Nacogdoches, Texas formerly a Senator in Congress from Kentucky.
National Banner & Nashville Whig. (Fri., Sept. 23, 1836)

Bledsoe, Judge Jesse. One time a Senator in Congress from Kentucky, the rival of Henry Clay died on 25th June last.
Nashville Republican. (Thursday, Sept. 22, 1836)

Judge Jesse Bledsoe. Died at Macodgoches, Texas on the 25th June last. He was at one time a Senator in Congress from Kentucky.
Nashville Republican. (Thursday, Sept. 22, 1836)

Mrs. George Ann Bledsoe. Daughter of the late Judge Humphreys. Died at the residence of Col. W. H. Humphreys in Nashville on the 22nd in the 31st year of her age.
The Christian Record. (Sat., May 27, 1848)

Blight, Mr. Isaac J. W. Died at Blount Springs, Ala.
National Banner & Nashville Whig. (Sat., July 22, 1826)

Block, Simon. Died 13th at Cincinnati, Ohio of Cholera.
National Banner & Nashville Daily Advertiser. (Tues., Oct. 23, 1823)

Blount, Capt. Charles. A soldier of the Revolution. Died in Campbell County, Va.
Nashville Republican and State Gazette. (Tuesday, April 12, 1831 No. 116, Vol. 6)

Blount, Jacob Tennessee. Died in October last, was the youngest son of the late William Blount.
Impartial Review and Cumberland Repository. (December 1, 1808)

Blount, Mrs. Mary. Died at Bakerdon on the 12th inst. in the 42d year of her age of a lingering illness which she bore with great fortitude. Wife of William Blount of Montgomery County and formerly Governor of this State. Nashville Whig. (May 24, 1824)

Blount, William G. Esq. Formerly Secretary of State. Died at Paris, Tenn.
National Banner & Nashville Whig. (Sat., June 16, 1827)

Blow, Mrs. Elizabeth. Died in St. Louis.
Nashville Republican and State Gazette. (Sat., Aug. 6, 1831 N. 37, Vol. 7)

Blow, Mr. Peter. Died at St. Louis.
National Banner & Nashville Daily Advertiser. (Sat., July 7, 1832)

Bloxton, Mrs. Mary. Of the Theatre. Aged 60 years. Died at Natchez.
National Banner & Nashville Whig. (Fri., June 17, 1828)

Bloxton, Mr. Thomas. A native of Virginia and lately a resident of Philadelphia. Died on Saturday last.
Nashville Whig. (Aug. 23, 1824)

Bludworth, Miss Emily. Died in Natchitoches.
National Banner & Nashville Whig. (Sat., Nov. 3, 1827)

Blythe, Mrs. Wife of Rev. James Blythe D. D. Died in South Hanover, Ind.
National Banner & Nashville Whig. (Wed., March 4, 1835)

Blythe, Mr. Richard. Died in Sunner County.
National Banner & Nashville Whig. (Fri., July 25, 1828)

Blythe, Samuel K. Esq. Formerly of Sumner County, Tenn. Died on Dec. 29th on Sulphur Rock of Red River in Texas.
Daily Republican Banner. (Mon., March 26, 1838)

Boardman, Daniel H., M.D. A native of New York, for some years past a resident of Tampico. Died in New Orleans, La.
National Banner & Nashville Whig. (Fri., Oct. 31, 1834)

Boatwright, Miss Martha. Daughter of Mr. Boatwright. Died in Russellville, Ky.
National Banner & Nashville Daily Advertiser. (Mon., Oct. 1, 1832)

Bobbs, Mr. Richard Henry. A native of North Carolina in the 22 year of his age. Died in Sumpton County, Ala.
National Banner & Nashville Whig. (Monday, Nov. 9, 1835)

Bobe, George. Died in Hillsborough Franklin County on the 17th ult. George, infant son of George Bobe.
Nashville Whig. (Oct. 4, 1824)

Boddie, Thomas H. Died in Madison County, Ala. Mr. Tho's H. Boddie aged 30
National Banner & Nashville Whig. (Sat., Sept. 30, 1826)

Bodley, Hugh S. Dr. Formerly of Lexington Ky. Died at Vicksburg, Miss. On Monday the 6th inst.
National Banner & Nashville Whig. (Mon., Aug. 3, 1835)

Bodwell, Dr. John A. Died in Methuen, Mass. For several years a resident of Nashville.
National Banner (March 3, 1826)

Boerstler, C. G. Died at New Orleans. Commission Merchant.
The Nashville Whig and Tennessee Advertiser. (Dec. 15, 1817)

Bogard, Mr. Abrah. Died in New Orleans on the 14th of July. One hundred and eighty four years ago.
National Banner & Nashville Daily Advertiser. (Thurs., Oct. 17, 1833)

Bogie, William. Died 15th at Cincinnati, Ohio of Cholera.
National Banner & Nashville Daily Advertiser. (Tues., Oct. 23, 1832)

Bogle, Samuel Junior and Miss Sarah Bogle. Children of Mr. Samuel
Bogle. Died in Blount County.
National Banner & Nashville Daily Advertiser. (Mon., June 17, 1833)

Bohanan, R. L. With the second Tenn. Regiment. Died was killed in
the battle of Sierra Garda with the Mexicans.
The Politician and Weekly Nashville Whig. (Fri., May 21, 1847)

Bohannon, Mrs. Wife of Dr. Richard Bohannon. Died in Versailles, Ky.
National Banner & Nashville Daily Advertiser. (Mon., June 18, 1832)

Bohannan, Mrs. Died in Frankfort, Ky. of cholera on Nov. 6th.
National Banner and Nashville Daily Advertiser. (Tues., Nov. 13, 1832)

Boles, John. Murdered on the 24th of May 1819. A Boat Passenger on
his way from Natchez thro the national was shot as is supposed by a
young Indian 3½ miles this side of the Chickasaw Agency.
Franklin Monitor. The Nashville Gazette. (June 5, 1819)

Bolles, J. Parks. Infant son of M. R. Bolles. Died in Rutherford
County, Tenn.
National Banner & Nashville Daily Advertiser. (Wed., May 7, 1834)

Bolles, William H. Son of Mr. Reuben Bolles, age 8 years. Died in
Murfreesboro, Tenn.
National Banner & Nashville Whig. (Mon., Oct. 20, 1834)

Bolls, Catherine Amonda. Infant daughter of Catherine and Reuben Bolls.
Died in Murfreesboro, Tenn.
National Banner & Nashville Daily Advertiser. (Mon., July 21, 1834)

Bond, John. From Perry County. Died at the Tennessee State Prison
of Cholera.
National Banner & Nashville Whig., (Fri., Aug. 14, 1835)

Bond, Mr. Wm. of Maryland. Died in this County on the 10th inst. after
a short illness.
National Banner & Nashville Whig. (Sat., Aug. 26, 1826)

Bondarant, Dr. Joseph. Died at Shelbyville, Ky. Dr. Bondurant, Dr.
Joseph.
National Banner and Nashville Whig. (Sat., Sept. 8, 1827)

Bondurant, Mrs. Sarah East. Wife of Maj. Benjamin Bondurant. Died in
Dresden, Weakley County, Tenn. On the 22nd day of August age 52 years
4 months and 18 days.
National Banner & Nashville Daily Advertiser. (Fri., Sept. 7, 1832)

Bondurant, Mrs. Unity Jolly. Consort of Maj. Hillary H. Bondurant.
Died in Nashville on the 26th Feb. in the 25th year of her age.
National Banner & Nashville Whig. (Fri., Feb. 27, 1835)

Bone, Catherine S. Died at Murfreesborough, Tenn.
National Banner. (Sat., May 9, 1829)

Bonie, Daniel Esq. Aged 45 years. Died in Davidson County, Tenn. on
Nov. 11th.
National Banner & Nashville Whig. (Wed., Nov. 16, 1836)

Bonnel, Mr. Aaron. He was a soldier of the revolution. Died
Wednesday Oct. 4th in the 79th year of his age.
Daily Republican Banner. (Fri., Oct. 20, 1837)

Bonner, Miss Sarah. Died in Wilson County.
Nashville Republican and State Gazette. (Thurs., June 23, 1831 No. 18,
Vol. 7)

Bonnevalle, Alexander. In the 55 year of his age. Died at New Orleans on the 18th of Aug.
National Banner & Nashville Daily Advertiser. (Wed., Sept. 3, 1834)

Booker, Dr. Frederick A. Died near Moulton, Ala.
National Banner & Nashville Whig. (Mon., April 11, 1831)

Booker, Richard L. Esq. Died on Sunday last at the residence of Dr. Ford of Sommerville, West Tenn. on his way to Nashville. He was of the House of N. & J. Dicks & Co. New Orleans.
Daily Republican Banner. (Sat., Aug. 3, 1839)

Booker, Mr. Richard M. Died in Maury County.
National Banner & Nashville Whig. (Thurs., Dec. 1, 1831)

Booker, Mrs. Susan M. Died in Maury County. Wife of Peter R. Booker, Esq.
National Banner. (Sat., June 27, 1829)

Boon, Mr. Richard. Departed this life on the 8th inst. In the town of Springfield after a lingering illness of about three weeks.
Nashville Whig. (January 15, 1823)

Boon, Mrs. Widow. Late of Johnson County, N. C. Died in Tipton County, Tenn.
National Banner & Nashville Daily Advertiser. (Monday, Sept. 9, 1833)

Boone, Daniel. Died on Tuesday 26th ult. At Charette Village, Missouri in the nintieth year of his age the celeberated Col. Daniel Boon., discovered the first settler in the state of Kentucky. His death was communicated to the Gen. Assembly on Thursday 28th inst. by Mr. Emmons, Senator from St. Charles County, and both branches of the Legislature through respect to his memory adjourned for the day, and passed a resolution to wear crepe on the arm for twenty days.
The Clarion and the Tennessee Gazette. (Vol 1, No. 8 Whole No. 152 October 24, 1820 [St. Louis. Eng.])

Booth, Mrs. Mary C. Wife of Zachariah Booth, Esq. Died at Knoxville
National Banner & Nashville Daily Advertiser. (Mon., Nov. 12, 1832)

Borland, Mr. James. Died in Roane County ages about 30 years.
National Banner & Nashville Whig. (Wed., Aug. 5, 1835)

Mr. Beal Bosley. 96 years of age. Died at his residence two miles west of Nashville, on the afternoon of the 7th inst. Funeral services by Rev. Mr. Bardwell.
The Nashville Daily Gazette. (Tues., May 8, 1860)

Bosley, Mr. Charles Jr. Died on the 21st Aug. at the residence of his father.
The Politician and Weekly Nashville Whig. (Wed., Sept. 1, 1847)

Bosley, Mrs. Martha Ann. Wife of Charles Bosley Esq. and daughter of A. D. Carden Esq. formerly a merchant of Nashville. Died Ma- 8th at the residence of Charles Bosley Esq. of Davidson County.
The Politician and Weekly Nashville Whig. (Friday, May 21, 1847)

Bosley, Miss Rachel. Died on Friday the 26th Dec. in Warren County, Ky. was the daughter of Mr. John Bosley of Davidson County.
Impartial Review and Cumberland Repository. (Jan. 3, 1807)

Bossen, Mrs. Susannah. Died at Cincinnati.
National Banner. (Feb. 24, 1826)

Bossuit, Joseph B. Of Boston, Mass. A passenger. Died on the Steamer George Collier about 80 miles below Natchez. Scalded to death.
Daily Republican Banner. (Tuesday, May 14, 1839)

Bostick, Mrs. Mary. Wife of Maj. John Bostick. Died in Williamson County.
National Banner & Nashville Daily Advertiser. (Tues., June 11, 1833)

Bostick, Miss Mary. Aged 17, daughter of Maj. J. G. Bostick. Died in Franklin County, Tenn.
National Banner & Nashville Daily Advertiser. (Fri., July 25, 1834)

Boswell, Charles. Son of Dr. John B. Boswell. Accidentally fell across the rails (Columbia Rail Road) instantly killed. Phil. Gaz.
National Banner & Nashville Daily Gazette. (Vol. 20, Friday, Nov. 9, 1832 No. 1639)

Boswell, Mr. George. Died in Lexington, Ky. From the Cholera.
National Banner & Nashville Daily Advertiser. (Mon., June 10, 1833)

Boswell, Col. Hartwell. Register of the land office. Died in Batesville, Ark. on the 13th Jan.
National Banner & Nashville Daily Advertiser. (Sat., Feb. 9, 1833)

Boswell, Mr. James M. Son of Gen. Wm. E. Boswell dec'd. Died in Harrison County, Ky.
National Banner & Nashville Daily Advertiser. (Thurs., Aug. 22, 1833)

Bosworth, Mrs. Died on Wednesday last. Consort of William Bosworth of this town.
The Nashville Whig. (Tues., Feb. 7, 1816)

Botsford, Mr. Russell. Died at Cincinnati.
National Banner (Sat., Sept. 19, 1829)

Bouie, Daniel Esq. In Davidson County, Tenn. on Friday Nov. 11. Aged 45 years, an old resident of this County.
Nashville Republican (Thurs., Nov. 17, 1836)

Bouin, Mr. Peter B. Died near Port Gibson, Miss.
National Banner & Nashville Whig. (June 24, 1826)

Bourne, Sarah Jane. Eldest daughter of Milton Bourne Esq. Aged 6 years and 2 weeks. Died in Robinson County on the 30th ult.
National Banner & Nashville Daily Advertiser. (Fri., Oct. 11, 1833)

Bowen, Mr. George T. Professor of Chemistry at the University of Nashville in the 28th year of age. Died in this town on Sat last.
National Banner & Nashville Whig. (Sat., Nov. 1, 1828)

Bowen, Mr. William. Died in Knox County.
National Banner & Nashville Daily Advertiser. (Tues., May 8, 1832)

Bowers, Samuel. Died 13th at Cincinnati, Ohio of cholera.
National Banner & Nashville Daily Advertiser. (Thursd., Oct. 25, 1832)

Bowman, Capt. Alexander. Aged 26 years. Died in Rutherford County.
National Banner & Nashville Whig. (Friday, May 20, 1831)

Bowman, Capt. Alexander. Died in Rutherford County, Tenn.
National Republican and State Gazette. (Sat., May 21, 1831. No. ? Vol. 7.)

Bowman, Mrs. Martha. Wife of Mr. Levi Bowman. Died in M'Minn. County.
National Banner & Nashville Daily Advertiser. (Wed., Jan. 23,1833)

Bowman, Rev. Matthew. Aged 62 years. Died in Amite County, Miss.
National Banner & Nashville Whig. (Sat., March 31, 1827)

Bowman, Mr. P. H. Aged 24 years. Died in Sumner County on the 13th inst.
National Banner & Nashville Whig. (Fri., April 22, 1831)

34

Bowman, Mr. P. H. Died in Sumner County.
Nashville Republican and State Gazette. (Sat. April 23, 1831 No. 121
Vol. 6)

Bowman, Mrs. Polly. Wife of George Bowman Esq. Aged 48 years. Died
in McMinn County.
National Banner & Nashville Whig., (Monday, March 14, 1831)

Bowman, Rev. Robert. Died at Woodville, Miss. the. Age. 77 years.
National Banner & Nashville Whig. (Sat., Dec. 23, 1826)

Bowman, Mr. Robert. Aged 87. Died in Woodford County, Ky.
National Banner & Nashville Whig. (Fri., June 27, 1828)

Bowman, Mr. Samuel of Davidson County. Died on Sunday Morning last
at the Nashville Inn.
Nashville Whig. (Tuesday, Feb. 28, 1843)

Boxley, Mr. John W. F. Aged 43. Died in Franklin, Tenn.
National Banner & Nashville Whig. (Friday, July 10, 1835)

Boyce, Mr. John. Died in Franklin, La.
National Banner & Nashville Daily Advertiser. (Sat., June 2, 1832)

Boyce, Rev. William A. Died in Arkansas by drowning off the traveling
connection of the Methodist Episcopal Church.
National Banner & Nashville Daily Advertiser. (Tuesday, Aug. 27, 1833)

Boyd, Mrs. Aged about 100 years. Died in Knox County.
National Banner & Nashville Daily Advertiser. (Mon., Jan. 9, 1832)

Boyd, George C. Esq. Attorney at Law. Died in Springfield at the
house of his father-in-law Mr. George C. Conrad.
The Politician and Weekly Nashville Whig. (Wed., Aug. 18, 1847)

Boyd, Mr. James. Died in the town on Tuesday.
National Banner & Nashville Whig. (Friday, July 25, 1828)

Boyd, Mr. James Kent. Died at New Orleans. On the Tuesday evening
3d inst. A native of New York and son of Samuel Boyd Esq. of that
City.
National Banner and Nashville Daily Advertiser. (Fri., Sept. 20, 1833)

Boyd, Captain John. An officer of the Revolution. Died in Northumberland, Penn. On the 13th of Feb. last. Aged 82 years.
National Banner & Nashville Daily Advertiser. (March 23, 1832)

Boyd, Maj. John. An old and highly respectable citizen. Died suddenly
in Nashville on Thursday last.
The Union. (Sat., Feb. 25, 1837)

Boyd, John. Died suddenly in Nashville on the 23rd Feb.
National Banner & Nashville Whig. (Monday, Feb. 27, 1837)

Boyd, Gen. John P. Naval Officer for the Port of Boston and Charlestown
Died in Boston.
National Banner and Nashville Whig. (Mon., Oct. 25, 1830)

Boyd, Julia Ellan. Daughter of Mr. Jeremiah Boyd aged 2 years. Died
in Washington County, Tenn.
National Banner and Nashville Whig. (Wed., April 8, 1835)

Boyd, Mrs. Lemira S. Consort of the late Maj. John Boyd. Died on
the 12th inst. near Nashville.
Nashville Union. (Wed., June 13, 1838)

Boyd, Mrs. Lemira L. Relict of the late Maj. Jno. Boyd. Died in this
vicinity yesterday.
Daily Republican Banner. (Thurs., June 14, 1838)

Boyd, Mrs. Martha. Wife of Dr. John C. Boyd. Died in Christian
County, Ky.
National Banner & Nashville Daily Advertiser. (Fri., Nov. 23, 1832)

Boyd, Miss Mary C. Daughter of Mr. Kenard Boyd. Died in Sommerville.
Nashville Whig. (Sat., April 11, 1846)

Boyd, Mrs. Rachel. Widow of the late Col. Richard Boyd. Died in
Nashville of Small Pox in the 45th years of her age.
National Banner and Nashville Whig. (Fri., Nov. 27, 1835)

Boyd, Major Whitmell H. Died in Davidson County on Monday 29th ult.
in the 24th year of his age.
National Banner & Nashville Whig. (Fri.,April 9, 1830)

Boyd, Maj. Whitnell H. Died in Davidson County.
National Banner & Nashville Whig. (Fri., April 2, 1830)

Boyd, Col. William. Of New Orleans. Died at sea.
National Banner & Nashville Whig. (Sat., Sept. 2, 1826)

Boyle, Hon. John. Died at his residence in Mercer County, Ky. Mourns
the lost of one of her abelest sons.
National Banner & Nashville Daily Advertiser. (Mon., Feb. 10, 1834)

Boyle, Dr. Jonathan H. Late of his town aged 27 years. Died in
Altrincham, England.
National Banner & Nashville Whig. (Sat., July 22, 1826)

Boyles, Mr. Barnabas. Aged 80. Formerly a resident of Davidson
County. Died in Lincoln County.
National Banner & Nashville Whig. (Fri., Sept. 23, 1831)

Boyles, Morris. Formerly of Tennessee. Died in Santa Fe, New Mexico
on the 13th of April last.
Nashville Whig. (Wed., Aug. 5, 1840)

Bradfoot, Thomas E. U. S. Attorney for the eastern District of
Virginia. Died lately at St. Augustine E. Florida.
National Banner & Nashville Daily Advertiser. (Fri., Dec. 27, 1833)

Bradford, Mr. A. B. Of Jefferson County, Miss. in the 44th year
of his age. Died near Tuscumbia on the 4th inst.
National Banner & Nashville Daily Advertiser. (Mon., July 15, 1833)

Bradford, Mrs. C. B. Wife of Major Thomas G. Bradford editor of the
Clarion in Nashville. Died on Monday morning last.
The Nashville Gazette. (Wed., March 15, 1820)

Bradford, Mrs. Eliza M. Consort of Mr. Simon Bradford. Died in
Nashville, Monday June 10.
National Banner & Nashville Daily Advertiser. (Tues., June 11, 1833)

Bradford, Miss Eliza Mills. Aged 14 years 8 months. Died on Wednes-
day the 9th inst. at Poplar Hill, the resident of Philip S Fall, near
Frankfort Ky. Youngest daughter of Capt. Simon Bradford, late of
Nashville.
The Politician and Weekly Nashville Whig. (Fri., Feb. 18, 1848)

Bradford, Mr. Fielding. Son of John Bradford Esq. Died in
Lawerceburg, Ind.
National Banner & Nashville Whig. (Mon., Aug. 2, 1830)

Bradford, Capt. John. In the 65 year of his age. Died in the County.
National Banner & Nashville Whig. (Sat., Feb. 3, 1827)

Bradford, Maj. Napoleon B. Aged 27 years 11 months & 27 days. Eldest
son of Gen. James Bradford. Died on Monday the 26th inst. Copies from

the Initial and New Market Telegraph.
National Banner & Nashville Daily Advertiser. (Fri., Sept. 6, 1833)

Bradford, Sarah Elizabeth. In the 4th year of her age. Died in Scott County, Ky. on the Thursday the 29th of Dec. Daughter of Col. Thos. Bradford.
National Banner & Nashville Daily Advertiser. (Thurs., Jan. 19, 1832)

Bradford, Mrs. Sophia wife of Mr. James M. Bradford. Died at St. Francisville.
National Banner & Nashville Whig. (Sat., Oct. 6, 1827)

Bradford, Susan Mary. Age 2. Died in Scott County, Ky. of the Scarlet fever on Monday 9, inst. daughter of Col. Tho. H. Bradford.
National Banner & Nashville Advertiser. (Vol. 20 Thursday, Jan. 19, 1832 No. 1388)

Bradford, Col. Theodorick F. Of Bradford County. Died in Bradford County on the 4th inst.
Daily Republican Banner. (Sat., April 11, 1840)

Bradford, Gen. Wm. Died at Cantonment Tawson, Ark. Aged 55 years.
National Banner & Nashville Whig. (Sat., Dec. 9, 1826)

Bradford, Capt. William. A soldier of the revolution. Died in Sumner County, Ten. on the 30th ult.
National Banner & Nashville Whig. (Wed., Aug. 3, 1831)

Bradford, Lieut. William. U. S. Dragoon. Died in Arkansas. Killed by the acccidental discharge of one of his own pistols.
National Banner & Nashville Daily Advertiser. (Mon., May 12, 1834)

Bradfute, Davidson Esq. Cashier of the Farmers Bank. Died at Lynchburg, Va.
National Banner & Nashville Whig. (Wed., Sept. 14, 1831)

Bradiord, John. Aged 83 years. Died in Lexington, Ky.
National Banner & Nashville Whig. (Fri., April 2, 1830)

Bradley, Miss. Daughter of Mr. Wm. Bradley. Died in Knox County.
National Banner & Nashville Whig. (Sat., Aug. 16, 1828)

Bradley, Abraham Esq. Died in this City on Monday night formerly Assistant Post Master General. (Nat. Intellenger)
Daily Republican Banner (Sat., May 18, 1838)

Bradley, Mrs. E. Died in Lexington, Ky. Of Cholera in the 1st ward.
National Banner & Nashville Daily Advertiser. (Tues., July 2, 1833)

Bradley, Mr. Edward. In the 32nd year of his age. Died in Smith County. On Sunday the19th ult.
National Banner & Nashville Whig. (Thurs., Oct. 7, 1830)

Bradley, James. Infant son of Maj. James Bradley of Huntsville. Died in Madison County, Ala.
National Banner & Nashville Daily Advertiser. (Mon., Sept. 9, 1833)

Bradley, Mrs. Lovey. Aged 39. Died in Wilson County, near Lebanon.
Nashville Republican and State Gazette. (Thursday, April 19, 1831 No. 119, Vol. 6)

Bradley, Mrs. Margaret. Wife of Thos. Bradley. Died in Williamson County.
National Banner & Nashville Whig. (Sat., June 14, 1828)

Bradley, Mrs. Oney. Mother of Mr. Robert Bradley. Died in Hopkinsville
National Banner & Nashville Advertiser. (Vol. 20 Thursday, Sept. 27, 1832 No. 1602

Bradley, Mr. Robert Junr. Died at Hopkinsville, Ky.
National Banner & Nashville Daily Advertiser. (Wed., Aug. 22, 1832)

Bradley, Mr. Robert. Aged 33 years. Died in Hopkinsville and the next day his mother Mrs. Oney Bradley.
National Banner and Nashville Advertiser. (Vol. 20 Thursday, Sept. 27, 1832 No. 1602)

Bradner, Mr. James J. From Cincinnita. Died in New Orleans.
National Banner & Nashville Daily Advertiser. (Thurs., Aug. 8, 1833)

Bradshaw, Mr. Eli. Died in Bedford County.
National Banner. (Sat., Aug. 29, 1829)

Bradshaw, Elias. Died in Maury County.
National Banner & Nashville Whig. (Fri., Oct. 20, 1826)

Bradshaw, Mrs. Elizabeth. Died in Maury County.
National Banner & Nashville Daily Advertiser. (Wed., Jan. 30, 1833)

Bradshaw, Mrs. Elizabeth. Relict of Wm. Bradshaw, dec'd. Died in Maury County on the 27th ult. after a lingering illness of several years.
National Banner & Nashville Daily Advertiser. (Mon., Feb. 4, 1833)

Brady, Col. Robert. Originally from Greenburg, Pennsylvania. Died at Cumberland Furnance Dickson County. on the 16th inst.
National Banner & Nashville Daily Whig. (Mon., Feb. 23, 1832)

Brady, Mrs. Sarah. Consort of Gen. H. Brady Aged 55 years. Died at Detroit Aug. 24.
National Banner & Nashville Daily Advertiser. (Mon., Sept. 9, 1833)

Brady, Gen. William. Died in Murfreesbarough, Tenn of Cholera.
National Banner & Nashville Whig. (Mon., July 27, 1835)

Brahan, Maj. Gen. John. Died in Florence, Ala.
National Banner & Nashville Daily Advertiser. (Mon., July 14, 1834)

Brahan, Mrs. Mary. Widow of the late General John Brahan and eldest daughter of Col. Robert Weakley of Tenn. Died on the 7th inst. Obituary from the Florence Ala. Gazette.
The Union. (Tuesday, Jan. 17, 1837)

Brahan, Mrs. Mary. Widow of the late Gen. John Brahan. Died in this vicinity on the 7th inst. She was the eldest daughter of Col. Robert Weakly of Tenn. Florence Al. Gaz.
National Banner and Nashville Whig. (Wed., Jan. 18, 1837)

Brahan, Mrs. Mary. Relic of the late Gen. John Brahan and daughter of Col. Robert Weakley. Died in the neighborhood of Florence, Ala.
Nashville Republican. (Thursday, Jan. 19, 1837)

Brain, Mr. Joseph N. Died in Madison County.
National Banner & Nashville Whig. (Sat., Aug. 19, 1826)

Branan, Thomas. A native of Maine. Died in New Orleans of the Yellow Fever.
Daily Republican Banner. (Friday, Sept. 29, 1837)

Brand, Andrew. Known as the Kentucky Fat boy. Died recently in Albany, N. Y. He was in the 16th year of his age and weighted 537 lbs.
The Nashville Tree Whig and Weekly Commerical Register. (Friday, October 4, 1850)

Brand, Samuel Brown. Son of John Brand Esq. Died in Lexington, Ky.
National Banner & Nashville Advertiser. (Tues., Sept. 4, 1832)

Brandon, John. From Lawerence County. Died at the State Prison at the Tenn. State Prison of Cholera.
National Banner & Nashville Whig. (Fri., Aug. 14, 1835)

Brandt, Mr. Edward. Died in Irvine, Ky.
National Banner & Nashville Whig. (Sat., July 8, 1826)

Branham, Mrs. Sarah. Died in Frankfort, Ky.
National Banner & Nashvilel Whig. (June 24, 1826)

Bransford, Samuel Wilson. Youngest son of the late Rev. John Bransford Died in Davidson County on the 16th of July aged 20 years 7 months and 24 days.
The Politician and Weekly Nashville Whig. (Fri., July 23, 1847)

Brant, Mrs. Elizabeth. Died at St. Louis.
National Banner & Nashville Whig. (Sat., Feb. 9, 1828)

Brantz, Lewis. President of the Baltimore and Port Deposit Rail Road Co. Died in Baltimore on the 20th inst. aged 80 years.
Nashville Whig. (Jan. 31, 1838)

Brashear, Miss Caroline. Daughter of Dr. Walter Brashear. Aged 18. Died at Attakapas, Louis.
National Banner & Nashville Whig. (Mon., Dec. 27, 1830)

Brashear, Mr. Walter. Aged about 23 years. Died on Thursday morning last in Frankfort, Ky.
National Banner & Nashville Whig. (Fri., Jan. 29, 1830)

Brawder, Mrs. Helen. Died in Logan County, Ky.
National Banner & Nashville Whig. (Sat., Aug. 18, 1827)

Brazelton, Mrs. Mary F. Wife of Col. Wm. Brazelton. Died at New Market, Jefferson County.
National Banner & Nashville Whig. (Sat., Dec. 30, 1826)

Breathett, Mrs. Elizabeth S. Died in Christan County, Ky. Wife of Jas. Breathett Esq.
National Banner & Nashville Whig. (Sat., April 7, 1827)

Breathitt, Dr. E. Died in Nashville on the Tuesday, Jan. 31st.
National Banner & Nashville Whig. (Wed., Feb. 1, 1837)

Breathitt, Dr. Edward. Died at his residence in Nashville this morning. One of our most highly and respectable citizens.
The Union. (Tuesday, Jan. 31, 1837)

Breathitt, Dr. Edward. Formerly of Franklin. Died in Nashville on Tuesday.
Nashville Republican. (Thurs., Feb. 2, 1837)

Breathitt, Mrs. Elizabeth. Mother of the late Gov. Breathitt. Died in Kentucky.
National Banner & Nashville Daily Advertiser. (Mon., April 7, 1834)

Breathitt, Mrs. Elizabeth S. Wife of James Breathitt, Esq. Died at Hopkinsville.
National Banner & Nashville Whig. (Sat., April 14, 1827)

Breathitt, Mr. George. Died at Hopkinsville, Ky. on the 23d inst.
National Banner & Nashville Daily Advertiser. (Tues., May 28, 1833)

Breathitt, Mr. James. Of Hopkinsville, Ky. Brother of the late Governor of Ky and of the late Dr. Breathitt of Nashville.
Daily Republican Banner. (Wed., Sept. 13, 1837)

Breathitt, His Excellency John. Govenor of Kentucky. Died at Frankfort, Ky.
National Banner & Nashville Daily Advertiser. (Fri., Feb. 28, 1834)

Breathitt, John Francis. Aged 13 son of the Govenor of Kentucky.
Died in Logan County, Ky.
National Banner & Nashville Daily Advertiser. (Tues., Jan. 22, 1833)

Breathitt, Lucy Ann. Daughter of Dr. E. Breathitt of Franklin in the
12th year of her age. Died in Franklin on Friday the 2d inst.
(Obituary)
The Western Weekly Review. (Friday, Dec. 9, 1831 Franklin, Tenn)

Breathitt, Lucy Ann. Daughter of Dr. E. Breathitt in the 12th year
of her age. Died in Franklin.
National Banner & Nashville Whig. (Mon., Dec. 10, 1831)

Breathitt, Lucy Ann. Daughter of Dr. E. Breathitt, aged 12.
National Banner and Nashville Whig. (Mon., Dec. 12, 1831 Vo. 19 No. 1359)

Breathitt, Mrs. Mary P. Relict of the late Dr. Edward Breathitt of
Nashville. Died on the 12th inst. at the Gayoso House in Memphis.
The Christian Record. (Sat., Feb. 20, 1847)

Breathitt, Mrs. Rebecca. Wife of Cardwell Breathitt Esq. Died at
Russellville, Ky.
National Banner & Nashville Whig. (Sat., June 16, 1827)

Breathitt, Mrs. Susan M. Wife of Hon. John Breathitt. Governor of
Kentucky. Died in Russellville, Ky.
National Banner & Nashville Daily Advertiser. (Mon., April 29, 1833)

Breazeale, John W. Esq. Died near Post Gibson, Miss.
National Banner & Nashville Daily Advertiser. (Wed., March 26, 1833)

Breckenridge, Gen. James. Died in Louisville, Ky.
National Banner & Nashville Daily Advertiser. (Fri., Sept. 20, 1833)

Breckenridge, Mrs. Margeret. Wife of Rev. John Breckenridge. and
daughter of Rev. Samuel Miller, D. D. Died at Princeton, New Jersey
on the 16th of June.
Nashville Whig. (Friday, June 29th, 1838)

Breeze, James. Died 17th at Cincinnita of Cholera.
National Banner & Nashville Daily Advertiser. (Thurs., Oct. 25, 1832)

Brennan, Mrs. Sarah. Died in Lexington, Ky.
National Banner & Nashville Whig. (Fri., July 18, 1828)

Brent, Mr. John L. Died in Bourbon County, Ky.
National Banner & Nashville Whig. (July 1, 1826)

Brent, Richard (Dec. 30, 1815) Died in Washington City at 4 o'clock
on the morning of the 30th of December, Richard Brent. A Senator of
the United States from the State of Virginia. His health, always
delicate, had been particularly so far sometime etc.
Nashville Whig. (January 24, 1815 Page 3, Col. 3)

Brevard, Miss D. Maria. Aged about 43 years. Died in Nashville Tuesday evening last. Formerly of Iredell County, N. Carolina.
Daily Republican Banner. (Sat., March 10, 1838)

Brevard, Mr. Joseph Eugene. Died in Fairfield District, S. C.
National Banner & Nashville Daily Advertiser. (Tues., Feb. 11, 1834)

Brewer, Mrs. A. A. Consort of Dr. Jas. Brewer. Died in Gibson County
on the 17th inst. in the 30th year of her life.
National Banner & Nashville Whig. (Mon., Oct. 31, 1831)

40

Brewer, Mrs. Ann. Wife of Dr. James Brewer formely of Nashville. Died in Gibson County on the 2nd July.
National Banner & Nashville Daily Advertiser. (Wed., July 30, 1834)

Brewer, Arthur A. Carpenter. Died was burned to death in St. Louis, Mo. on Sat., Aug. 31st.
Daily Republican Banner. (Mon., Sept. 9, 1839)

Brewer, Mr. Sterling. A Worthy and respectable citizen. Died in Nashville.
National Banner & Nashville Daily Advertiser. (Sat., July 7, 1832)

Brickell, Richard B. Esq. Editor of the Athenian. Died in Athens, Ala.
National Banner & Nashville Whig. (Wed., Jan. 21, 1835)

Bridgman, James. Died in Pikesville, Tenn. on the 20th inst. Aged 15 years.
Nashville Republican and State Gazette. (Sat., March 26, 1831 No. 109, Vol. 6)

Bridgus, Lycurgus. Only son of Thos. J. N. and Susan Bridgus, age 4 years and 5 months. Died at Coffeeville, Miss. on the 21st of May.
Nashville Republican. (Tues., May 30, 1837)

Briggs, Mrs. Hester. Wife of Mr. James T. Briggs. Died in Warren County, Ky.
National Banner & Nashville Whig. (Fri., March 18, 1831)

Briggs, John. Died in Shelbyville, Tenn. of Cholera.
National Banner & Nashville Daily Advertiser. (Thurs., July 11, 1833)

Bright, Lucius P. Youngest son of James Bright Esq. Died near Fayette-ville on Friday, May 8th.
Nashville Whig. (Wed., June 4, 1841)

Brin, Mr. William. Died in Franklin County, Ala. A citizen of Florence
National Banner. (Jan. 6, 1826)

Brinkley, Wesley H. Infant son of W. H. and Dorcas Brinkley. Died in Nashville on Monday the 8th inst.
Nashville Whig. (Tues., June 9, 1846)

Briscoe, Mr. Died at Forence, Ala.
National Banner & Nashville Daily Advertiser. (Wed., Aug. 7, 1833)

Brittian, Mrs. Died in Shelbyville, Tenn. of Cholera.
National Banner & Nashville Daily Advertiser. (Thurs., July 11, 1833)

Brittian, James. Died in Shelbyville, Tenn. of Cholera.
National Banner & Nashville Daily Advertiser. (Thurs., July 11, 1833)

Brittian, Joseph. Died in Shelbyville, Tenn. of Cholera.
National Banner & Nashville Daily Advertiser. (Thurs., July 11, 1833)

Broaddus, Mr. Thomas. Died in Madison County, Ky.
National Banner & Nashville Whig. (Sat., March 1, 1828)

Broadols, Mr. Edward. Died in Madison County, Ky.
National Banner & Nashville Whig. (Sat., Sept. 9, 1826)

Broadus, Mrs. Elizabeth. Died in Madison County.
National Banner & Nashville Whig. (Sat., Feb. 9, 1828)

Bronson, Enos. Esq. Editor of the United States Gazette. Died in Philadelphia.
Nashville Whig. (June 4, 1823)

Brooking, Samuel S. Esq. Died in Hart County, Ky.
National Banner & Nashville Whig. (Wed., Sept. 21, 1831)

Brooks, Mrs. Agnes. Died in Knox County.
National Banner & Nashville Whig. (Sat., Aug. 19, 1826)

Brooks, Mr. Benjamin. Of Nashville. Died at Smithland, Ky. of the
Cholera on the 8th of June last in the 27th year of his age.
National Banner & Nashville Daily Advertiser. (Sat., July 6, 1833)

Brooks, Mr. Benjamin H. Late of Nashville. Died in Smithland, Ky.
National Banner & Nashville Daily Advertiser. (Mon., June 17, 1833)

Brooks, Christopher C. Infant son of Mr. Christopher C. Brooks.
Aged 3 years. Died in Nashville.
National Banner & Nashville Whig. (Thurs., July 22, 1830)

Brooks, Eleanor. Daughter of P. Brooks. Died in Shelbyville, Tenn.
Of Cholera.
National Banner & Nashville Daily Advertiser. (Thurs., July 11, 1833)

Brooks, Dr. George C. Died at Cincinniti.
National Banner & Nashville Daily Advertiser. (Thurs., Jan. 19, 1832)

Brooks, George W. Aged 5 years son of Mr. Christopher Brooks. Died
in Nashville on Friday last.
National Banner & Nashville Whig. (Mon., July 5, 1830)

Brooks, Mrs. Harriet. Died in Tuscumbia, Alabama.
National Banner (Sat., June 27, 1829)

Brooks, Mrs. Harriett. Died in Tuscumbia, Ala
National Banner (Sat., Aug. 8, 1829)

Brooks, Mr. James. Died in Williamson County.
National Banner & Nashville Whig. (Sat., Jan. 13, 1827)

Brooks, Rev. James H. Pastor of the Presbyterian Church aged 45.
Died in Pulaski on June 7 of Cholera.
National Banner & Nashville Daily Advertiser. (Wed., June 19, 1833)

Brooks, Mrs. Melissa. Consort of Mr. M. D. L. H. Brooks and eldest
daughter of Robert B. McGowen of Maury County. Died yesterday in
Nashville.
Nashville Republican (Thurs., May 10, 1837)

Brooks, Mr. Moses. Aged 70 years. Died in Knoxville.
National Banner & Nashville Whig. (Fri., Feb. 12, 1830)

Brooks, Mrs. Sarah W. Aged 62 years. Died in Jackson, Tenn. on the
3rd Oct.
National Banner & Nashville Whig. (Mon., Oct. 17, 1836)

Brooks, Mr. Thomas. Aged 47 years. Died at Lexington, Tenn. on the
9th inst. A Native of Berry County, Ireland.
National Banner & Nashville Whig. (Mon., June 21, 1830)

Brookshire, Miss Mary. Died in McMinn County.
National Banner & Nashville Whig. (Wed., Sept. 7, 1831)

Broqua, Sheldon J. Of Poland, Ky. A Passenger. Died on the
steamboat George Collier, about 80 miles below Natchz. Scalded to
death.
Daily Republican Banner. (Tues., May 14, 1839)

Browder, Nicholas. Was from Washington County. Died at the Tenn.
State Prison of Cholera.
National Banner & Nashville Whig. (Fri., Aug. 14, 1835)

Brown, Mrs. A. Wife of R. W. Brown aged 44. Died at Wilmington, N. C.
National Banner and Nashville Daily Advertiser (Thurs., Jan. 2, 1834)

Brown, Alexander C. A member of Fire Company No. 1. Died in Nashville on Nov. 20th.
Daily Republican Banner. (Wed., Nov. 20, 1839)

Brown, Alexander C. Aged 22. Chief clerk in the office of Messss Foster & Fogg, Attornees. A native of Philadelphia. Died this morning at the county seat of Hon. E. H. Foster. Obituary
Nashville Whig. (Friday, Nov. 22, 1839)

Brown, Miss Ann. Died in Paris.
Nashville Banner and Nashville Whig. (July 28, 1827)

Brown, Mrs. Ann. Aged 63. Died in Frankford, Ky.
National Banner and Nashville Whig. (Sat., Aug. 12, 1826)

Brown, Mrs. Ann. Wife of James Brown Esq. late Minister of the United States in France. Died at Philadelphia.
National Banner and Nashville Whig. (Mon., Nov. 8, 1830)

Brown, Mrs. Ann B. Consort of Hon. W. T. Brown and daughter of Hon. Y. Gresham. Died in Memphis on 26th ult.
Daily Republican Banner. (Mon., June 4, 1838)

Brown, Mrs. Ann H. K. Died in Madison County.
National Banner and Nashville Daily Advertiser. (Wed., Oct. 3, 1832)

Brown, Hoh Anson. A representative in Congress from the District of Saratoga and Schenecady. Died last evening at his residence in Ballston, Spa.
Daily Republican Banner. (Wed., July 1, 1840)

Brown, Hon Anson G. Member of Congress from the Saratoba, New York District. Died at his home a few days ago.
Nashville Whig. (Fri., June 26, 1840)

Brown, Mr. Beverly. Died at Florence, Ala.
National Banner and Nashville Whig. (Sat., Feb. 23, 1828)

Brown, Mrs. Caroline M. Wife of George W. Brown. Died in Nicholasville, Ky.
National Banner and Nashville Daily Advertiser. (Wed., July 31, 1833)

Brown, Mrs. Carolina M. Consort of Geo. W. Brown, Esq. Died at Nicholasville, Ky.
National Banner and Nashville Daily Advertiser. (Sat., Aug. 10, 1833)

Brown, Mrs. Catharine. Wife of B. C. Brown, Esq. Died at Paris, Henry County.
National Banner and Nashville Daily Advertiser. (Tues., July 3, 1832)

Brown, Catherine age 2½. Died in Davidson County post humous daughter and only child of the late William L. Brown, Esq.
National Banner and Nashville Advertiser. (Sat., Nov. 24, 1832)

Brown, Catherine L. Aged 2½ years. Only child of the late William L. Brown, Esq. Died in Davidson County.
National Banner and Nashville Daily Advertiser. (Sat., Nov. 24, 1832)

Brown, Mr. Ch. L. Of the firm of Brown and Fisher. Died at Grand Gulf, Miss.
National Banner and Nashville Daily Advertiser. (Mon., May 26, 1834)

Brown, D. M. Died at Cincinnati, Ohio on 13th of Cholera.
National Banner and Nashville Daily Advertiser. (Sat., Oct. 20, 1832)

Brown, David and Jonathan. The former on Thursday afternoon the 30th and the latter on Saturday morning the 2nd May, were twin brothers 31 years of age. Died at South Orange, N. J.
National Banner. (Sat., June 13, 1829)

Brown, Mr. Dominic Jessop. Aged 19. Died in Estill County, Ky.
National Banner and Nashville Whig. (Sat., Aug. 26, 1826)

Brown, Mr. Duncan in the 68 year of his age. Died at his residence in Giles County, Tennessee on the 2nd of March. Obituary.
The Christian Record. (Sat., June 3, 1848)

Brown, Mrs. Elizabeth. Died in this county on Sunday last. Wife of William L. Brown, Esq.
National Banner and Nashville Whig. (Sat., March 1, 1828)

Brown, Mrs. Elizabeth. Died in this county on the 16th inst. Consort of Dr. Morgan Brown in the 64th year of her age.
National Banner. (Sat., April 25, 1829)

Brown, Mrs. Elizabeth wife of William Brown. Died on Monday, 17th instant in Lincoln County, Tennessee.
Nashville Whig. (Sat., Jan. 22, 1842)

Brown, Mrs. Elizabeth. Relict of the late Dr. Preston Brown of Frankfort, Ky. Died at the residence of her son J. P. W. Brown Esq. of Nashville.
Nashville Whig. (Sat., May 13, 1843)

Brown, Mrs. Frances. Aged 72. Died at Mobile.
National Banner. (Feb. 17, 1826)

Brown, Mr. George in the 71st year of his age. Died in Nashville on the 17th inst. at the residence of his son-in-law. (Nashville Inn)
The Christian Record. (Sat., May 20, 1848)

Mrs. H. Brown. Consort of W. M. Brown, Esq. Died in Paris, Tenn.
National Banner and Nashville Whig. (Fri., May 1, 1835)

Brown, Col. H. H. Of Perry County formerly a member of the Legislature of Tenn. Died in Nashville on Tuesday night last.
The Politican and Weekly Nashville Whig. (Fri., Oct. 22, 1847)

Brown, Hu Esq. Died in Knoxville of fever.
Nashville Whig. (Wed., Oct. 3, 1838)

Brown, Hugh. Died at the residence of Mr. F. S. Heeskell in Knoxville, Tenn.
Daily Republican Banner. (Sat., Oct. 6, 1838)

Brown, Huston. Died 17th at Cincinnati, Ohio of Cholera.
National Banner and Nashville Daily. (Thurs., Oct. 25, 1832)

Brown, Mr. Isaac C. Merchant. Died in Murfreesboro on the 7th inst.
Nashville Whig. (Mon., Jan. 14, 1839)

Brown, Mr. Isaac C. Died in Murfreeboro on the 7th inst. A merchant of that place.
Daily Republican Banner. (Wed., Jan. 16, 1839)

Brown, Mr. J. P. Died in Mobile on the 7th inst. he was proprietor and Manager of the Mobile Theatre, aged about 32 years.
National Banner and Nashville Daily Advertiser. (Thurs., June 19, 1834)

Brown, J. P. W. Esq. Died on Thursday evening at Mansfield the residence of Hon. E. H. Foster.
Nashville True Whig and Weekly Commercial Register. (Fri., May 10, 1850)

Brown, Mr. James P. Died in St. Louis.
National Banner and Nashville Whig. (Sat., July 22, 1826)

Brown, Mrs. Jane. Aged 91. Died in Maury County.
Nashville Republican and State Gazette. Thurs., June 9, 1831)

Brown, Jane. Born the 22nd of June 1740. Died in Maury County at
the residence of Col. Joseph Brown on the 3rd inst. in the 91 year of
her age.
National Banner and Nashville Whig. (Mon., June 13, 1831)

Brown, Jane B. Mrs. Consort of John L. Brown, formerly of Memphis.
Died on Tuesday, the 24th inst.
Nashville Whig. (Sat., Feb. 28, 1846)

Brown, Rev. Jefferson P. A native of Lebanon, Tenn. Died in
Nachitoches, La. on the 12th July aged 27 years.
National Banner and Nashville Whig. (Wed., Aug. 3, 1836)

Brown, Mr. Jeremiah. Died in Madison County.
National Banner and Nashville Whig. (Sat., Aug. 26, 1826)

Brown, Mrs. Joanna L. Wife of Mr. Edward L. Brown. Died at Knoxville.
National Banner and Nashville Whig. (Thursday, July 1, 1830)

Brown, Gen. John. Died in Stauton, Va.
National Banner and Nashville Whig. (Sat., Nov. 18, 1826)

Brown, John Esq. of Paris, Tenn. Died at New Orleans.
National Banner and Nashville Daily Advertiser. (Wed., Feb. 27, 1833)

Brown, Mr. John. Died in Nashville, on 24th Sept.
National Banner and Nashville Whig. (Mon., Sept. 28, 1835)

Brown, John. Of John Brown and Co. Boston. Died in the wreck of the
steam boat Lexington.
Daily Republican Banner. (Fri., Jan. 31, 1840)

Brown, Dr. John F. Aged 36 formerly of Wilson County. Died in Jackson.
National Banner and Nashville Whig. (Fri., May 7, 1830)

Brown, John P. Eldest son of Mr. W. W. Brown. Died in Davidson
County on the 29th Aug. in the year of his age.
National Banner and Nashville Whig. (Mon., Sept. 13, 1830)

Brown, John Preston. Infant son of Orlando Brown Esq. Died in
Frankfort, Ky.
National Banner and Nashville Whig. (Fri., March 13, 1835)

Brown, Mr. Jonathan. Aged 46. Died at Athens, Tenn.
National Banner. (Sat., May 9, 1829)

Brown, Mr. Joshua. Aged 68. Died in Madison County, Ky.
National Banner. (Feb. 10, 1826)

Brown, Mrs. Judith Ann. Died at Frankford, Ky.
National Banner and Nashville Whig. (Sat., Sept. 15, 1827)

Brown, Mrs. Julia May. Wife of J. S. Brown of Wheeling, Va. Died
at the residence of her brother Rev. J. T. Wheat of Nashville on 15th
inst.
Nashville Whig. (Tues., June 20, 1843)

Brown, Mr. Lawrence. Died in Philadelphia on the 22nd of Aug. Age
56.
National Banner and Nashville Daily (Sat., Sept. 6, 1834)

Brown, Mr. Leonard. Aged 93. Died in Sumner County.
National Banner and Nashville Daily Advertiser. (Tues., Nov. 19, 1833)

Brown, Mrs. Letitia. Wife of Capt. Edward M. Brown. Died in Giles
County.
National Banner and Nashville Daily Advertiser. (Fri., Dec. 21, 1832)

Brown, Mr. Lewis. Merchant aged about 30. Died in Mobile, Ala.
of Yellow Fever.
Daily Republican Banner. (Tuesday, Oct. 1, 1839)

Brown, Mrs. Mary. Consort of Maj. W. W. Brown in the 39th year of
her age. Died on Monday the 9th inst. at Hillsboro in the Davidson
County.
Daily Republican Banner. (Fri., March 13, 1840)

Brown, Mrs. Mary. Consort of Maj. W. W. Brown in the 37th year of
her age. Died near Hillsborough in Davidson County March 10th.
Nashville Whig. (Friday, March 13, 1840)

Brown, Mrs. Mary E. Consort of George Brown Esq. Died yesterday
morning the 2nd inst. of Davidson County.
Daily Republican Banner. (Friday, May 3, 1839)

Brown, Mrs. Mary Edwards. Wife of George Brown Esq. of Paradise
Hill Davidson County and mother-in-law of Joseph P. Brown. Died at
the Union Hall, Yesterday.
Nashville Whig. (Friday, May 3, 1839)

Brown, Mrs. Mary M. Died in Woodford County, Ky.
National Banner and Nashville Whig. (Sat., April 14, 1827)

Brown, Mrs. Mary W. Wife of Orlando Brown Esq. editor of the Frankfort Commonwealth. Died at the Blue Surphur Spring's in Virginia
on the 17th inst.
Nashville Whig. (Monday, Aug. 30, 1841)

Brown, Mrs. Matilda. Died in Nicholasville, Ky.
National Banner and Nashville Whig. (Sat., Oct. 6, 1827)

Brown, Dr. Morgan. Aged 83 years. Died on the 23rd near Nashville
father of the late Judge William L. Brown.
Daily Republican Banner. (Monday, March 9, 1840)

Brown, Morgan, Dr. Died on the 23d. ult. at his residence near this
city aged 83 years, father of the late Judge Wm. L. Brown and the
present Judge M. W. Brown. Native of Anson County, North Carolina
migrated into this stated in this year 1795.
Nashville Union. (Monday, March 9, 1840 Nashville, Tennessee)

Brown, Dr. Morgan. Father of the late Judge William L. Brown and the
present Judge M. W. Brown. Died on the 23rd ult. near Nashville the
deceased was a native of North Carolina.
Nashville Whig. (Monday, March 9, 1840)

Brown, Mrs. Nancy. Wife of Thomas Brown Esq. Died in Knox County.
National Banner and Nashville Whig. (Monday, Oct. 11, 1830)

Brown, Mrs. Nancy. Wife of Thomas Brown Esq. Died in Shelby County.
National Banner and Nashville Whig. (Thurs., Oct. 28, 1830)

Brown, Mr. Rayburn S. Aged 18. Died at Athens, M'Minn County.
National Banner and Nashville Whig. (Wed., Dec. 14, 1831)

Brown, Robert Breckenridge. Aged 14 months son of Robert Brown. Died
in Frankfort, Ky.
National Banner and Nashville Daily Advertiser. (Sat., Aug. 10, 1833)

Brown, Dr. Samuel. Died in Madison County, Ala. Formerly professor
of the theory and practice of physic in Transylvania University of
Lexington, Ky.
National Banner and Nashville Whig. (Tues., Jan. 26, 1830)

Brown, Samuel M. Post Office Agent of Lexington, Ky. Died killed
in the explosion of the Steamboat Lucy Walker just below New Albany.
Nashville Whig. (Tues., Oct. 29, 1844)

Brown, Mrs. Sarah. Aged 102 years. Died in Frankfort, Ky.
National Banner and Nashville Daily Advertiser. (Sat., Feb. 4, 1832)

Brown, Mrs. Sarah L. Wife of Rev. John R. Brown. Died in St. Louis.
National Banner and Nashville Whig. (Wed., June 8, 1831)

Brown, Sarah Virginia. In the fourth year of her age. Died in
Davidson County, on the 1st inst. second daughter of William W.
Brown.
National Banner Nashville Daily Advertiser. (Mon., Dec. 3, 1832)

Brown, Mrs. Sela. Wife of Mr. Henry W. Brown. Died in Hardeman County.
National Banner and Nashville Whig. (Mon., Aug. 30, 1830)

Brown, Dr. Silas. Treasurer of the State of Mississippi. Died in
the vicinity of Jackson, Miss. on a Monday last.
Daily Republican Banner. (Wed., June 12, 1839)

Brown, Mr. Thomas. Late Knox County. Died in Shelby County.
National Banner and Nashville Daily Advertiser. (Mon., June 17, 1833)

Brown, Thomas Esq. Died in Shelby County.
National Banner and Nashville Daily Advertiser. (Tues., July 2, 1833)

Brown, Mr. W. Died in Richmond, Ky.
National Banner and Nashville Whig. (Sat., Oct. 28, 1826)

Brown, W. F. With the second Tenn. Regiment. Died was killed in
the Battle of Sierra Gorda with the Mexicans.
The Politicans and Nashville Weekly Whig. (Fri., May 21, 1847)

Brown, Mr. William. Died in Dyer County.
National Banner and Nashville Whig. (Sat., Aug. 26, 1826)

Brown, Col. Wm. formerly of Cynthiana. Died in Jacksonville, Illinois
on the 20th inst.
National Banner and Nashville Daily Advertiser. (Sat., Nov. 23, 1833)

Bruce, Charles. Died at Versailles, Ky. 14 miles from Lexington,
Ky of Cholera.
National Banner and Nashville Whig. (Fri., Sept. 4, 1835)

Bruce, Joseph. Infant son of the Rev. Wm. Bruce aged 18 months.
Died in this town on Saturday morning 21st inst.
National Banner. (Jan. 27, 1826)

Bruce, Rev. Philip. Died in Giles County on the 11th inst. One
amongst the oldest and most useful preachers of the Methodist Church.
National Banner. (May 20, 1826)

Brun, M. Malte. Died in Paris, France. A celebrated author.
National Banner and Nashville Whig. (Sat., Feb. 24, 1827)

Bryan, Edmond. Died in Robertson County. A respectable Citizen.
The Nashville Whig and the Tenn. Advertiser. (Jan., 5, 1818)

Bryan, Harriet. Died on the 27th inst. at the resident [sic] of
Col. Henry H. Bryan Montgomery County, age about 10 years, she was
an amiable and interesting child.
Nashville Whig and Tenn. Advertiser. (Dec. 15, 1817)

Bryan, Col. Henry H. Died in Montgomery County. Formerly a representative from that District in Congress.
National Banner & Nashville Whig. (Fri., May 8, 1835)

Bryans, James. Late a citizen of Fayetteville, Tenn. Died at
Jackson, Mi. On the 28th ult. in the 60th year of his age.
National Banner & Nashville Daily Advertiser. (Wed., Aug. 14, 1833)

Bryan, James H. Esq. In the 75th year of his age. Died at his residence
in Robertson County. On the 23rd of March.
Nashville Whig. (Sat., April 27, 1844)

Bryan, Mrs. Margeret. Consort of James H. Bryan Esq. Died in
Robertson County on the Monday 27th inst. In the 50th year of her
age.
Nashville Whig. (Wed., Sept. 29, 1841)

Bryan, Mrs. Mary Macon. Wife of Col. William P. Bryan and daughter
of the late Newton Cannon. Died in Nashville on the Sunday the 20th
inst. aged 24 years one month and 24 days. (Obituary)
The Christian Record. (Sat., May 27, 1848)

Bryan, Mr. Thomas. Died in Frankfort, Ky.
National Banner & Nashville Daily Advertiser. (Fri., March 23, 1832)

Bryant, Dennis. Died 17th at Cincinnita, Ohio of Cholera.
National Banner & Nashville Daily Advertiser. (Thurs., Oct. 25, 1832)

Bryant, Mrs. Elizabeth. Died at Frankfort, Ky. Wife of Mr. Archibald
Bryant.
National Banner. (Sat., July 11, 1829)

Bryant, Tabitha Mrs. Consort of Mr. S. B. Bryant in the 25th year
of her age. Died in Murfreesborough, Tenn.
National Banner & Nashville Daily Advertiser. (Thurs., June 19, 1834)

Brysor, Mr. Peter. On the 1st inst. Died in Hardeman County.
Nashville Republican and State Gazette. (Vol. 7 Sat., Jan. 7, 1832
No. 102)

Buchanan, Mrs. Consort of Major John Buchanan. Died in Davidson
County, on Tuesday night 22, inst.
National Banner & Nashville Whig. (Wed., Nov. 23, 1831)

Buchanan, Mr. Alexander. Died during the last night in Davidson
County.
Nashville Republican (Sat., April 9, 1836)

Buchanan, Mr. David S. Late of Baltimore. Died at Louisville, Ky.
National Banner & Nashville Daily Advertiser. (Oct. 15, 1832)

Buchanan, George W. Esq. Late U. S. Attorney for the Western
District of Pennsylvania. Died in At Pittsburgh.
National Banner and Nashville Advertiser. (Mon., Nov. 5, 1832)

Buchanan, Maj. John. A Pioneer of the west one of the first settlers
in Tennessee and a veteran hero of the early war with the Indian.
Died in Davidson County.
National Banner & Nashville Advertiser. (Wed., Nov. 7, 1832)

Buchanan, Mr. Robert. Died in this town on Sat. last.
National Banner. (Sat., June 20, 1829)

Buchanan, Mrs. Sarah. Wife of Mr. George Buchanan. Died at Louisville,
Ky.
National Banner & Nashville Whig. (Mon., Feb. 14, 1831)

Buchanan, Mrs. Sarah L. Consort of John K. Buchanan. Died in Davidson County on the 23d of July.
National Banner & Nashville Daily Advertiser. (Mon., July 29, 1833)

Buckley, Joseph. Died at Cincinnita, Ohio on the 12th of Cholera.
National Banner & Nashville Daily Advertiser. (Sat., Oct. 20, 1832)

Bucknell, Mr. Robert Thaxter. The original proprietor and publisher
of this paper. Died on Thursday last, in the thirty third year of
his age.
Nashville Whig. (Wed., May 22, 1839)

Buckner, Mr. Arthur Presley Esq. Formerly of Kentucky. Died in Benton,
Miss.
National Banner & Nashville Daily Advertiser. (Sat., Aug. 24, 1833)

Buckner, Mrs. Lucy. Wife of Mr. James Buckner. Died in Hopkinsville,
Ky.
National Banner & Nashville Whig. (Mon., Sept. 12, 1831)

Buckner, Mrs. Mildred. Died in Christian County, Ky. Aged 17 years.
National Banner & Nashville Whig. (Sat., Aug. 12, 1826)

Buckner, Hon. Richard S., Sr. Died at his residence in Greensburg,
Green County, Ky. Aged about 64 years. Died on the 8th of last
month.
The Christian Record. (Sat., Jan. 8, 1848)

Buford, Mrs. Consort of Mr. John Buford. Died in Frankfort, Ky.
National Banner & Nashville Daily Advertiser. (Wed., July 9, 1834)

Buford, Mrs. Elizabeth. Died in Williamson County.
Nashville Republican and State Gazette. (Vol. 7 Tuesday, April 17,
1832 No. 144)

Buford, Philip T. A soldier of the Revolution. Died in Fayette County,
Western District, Tenn. and on the 15th of June.
National Banner & Nashville Daily Advertiser. (Sat., July 5, 1834)

Bugg, Miss Ann E. W. Daughter of the late Capt. Samuel Bugg. Died
on Saturday 2d near Gallatin.
Nashville Whig. (Vol. 4 Tues., Mar. 19, 1816 No. 186)

Bugg, Mrs. Francis. Aged 16 years. Died in Gallatin.
National Banner & Nashville Daily Advertiser. (Tues., June 11, 1833)

Buggs, Mr. Moore, Aged 90 years. Died in Cynthians, Ky.
National Banner. (March 17, 1826)

Bull, Amasa. Died 13th at Cincinnita, Ohio of Cholera.
National Banner & Nashville Daily Advertiser. (Tues., Oct. 23, 1832)

Bullitt, Hon. George. Died in the vicinity of Jackson, Mo.
Register of the Land Office at that place.
National Banner & Nashville Whig. (Mon., Dec. 29, 1834)

Bullock, Mrs. Wife of Walter Bullock, Esq. Died in Fayette County,
Ky.
National Banner & Nashville Whig. (Wed., Aug. 17, 1831)

Bullock, Col. David. Died at Richmond, Va.
National Banner & Nashville Daily Advertiser. (Thurs., Jan. 2, 1834)

Bullock, Mrs. Eliza A. Of Columbus, Ga. Died in Knox County.
National Banner & Nashville Whig. (Mon., Sept. 26, 1831)

Bullock, Col. Josias. A soldier of the revolution. Died in Wayne
County, Mi.
National Banner & Nashville Daily Advertiser. (Wed., March 5, 1834)

Bullus, Mr. M. Died at Gallatin on the 8th inst.
National Banner & Nashville Whig. (Sat., Nov. 18, 1826)

Bumpass, Capt. Robt. Near Statesville on 29th Jan. last an old and
respectable citizen died of inflammation of the lungs.
Nashville Republican. (Saturday, Feb. 27, 1836)

Burbridge, Mrs. Narcissa. Wife of Mr. Thomas H. Burbridge. Died in
Scott County, Ky.
National Banner & Nashville Whig. (Mon., July 12, 1830)

Burch, Captain Benjamin. Died in Washington on the 15th inst. Aged
seventy two years Door keeper of the House of Representatives of the
United States and a soldier of the Revolution.
National Banner Nashville Daily Advertiser. (Mon., May 21, 1832)

Burch, Mrs. Caroline. Consort of Mr. B. M. Burch 23 years. Died in
Puluski on June 8th of Cholera.
National Banner & Nashville Daily Advertiser. (Wed., June 19, 1833)

Burdine, Mr. Richard. Died near Whitesburgh, Ala. Aged 47 years.
National Banner. (March 3, 1826)

Burditt, Giles. Died in Shelbyville, Tenn. of Cholera.
National Banner & Nashville Daily Advertiser. (Thurs., July 11, 1833)

Burgess, Mr. Albert Bryan. Died in Nashville on Tuesda- 5th inst. in
the 28th year of his age.
Nashville Whig. (Fri., Feb. 8, 1839)

Burgess, Mr. Albert Bryan. Formerly of a Merchant and for several
years a resident of Nashville. Died in Nashville on Tuesday the
15th inst. in the 28th year of his age.
Nashville Union. (Mon., Feb. 11, 1839)

Burgess, Mr. Bryan. Died in Nashville on the 6th inst.
Daily Republican Banner. (Thurs., Feb. 7, 1839)

Burgess, Miss Jarncia. Died in Russellville, Ky.
National Banner & Nashville Whig. (Wed., Dec. 3, 1834)

Burgoyne, Lieutenant-General. Died in London on the 8th of August
1792. He went to bed in perfect health, after spending the day
cheerfully, and died at 4 in the morning.
Knoxville Gazette. (Sat., October 29, 1792)

Burin, Mrs. Nancy F. S. Died in Hawkins County.
National Banner & Nashville Whig. (Mon., Oct. 17, 1831)

Burke, Edmund. Infant son of Col. John B. Burke. Aged 2 years 5
months and 5 days. Died in Nashville on Sunday the 1st inst.
National Banner & Nashville Daily Advertiser. (Mon., Dec. 2, 1833)

Burkett, Private Charles B. Company K. with First Tenn. Regiment
Volunteer. Died was killed in the Battle of Monterey with the Mexicans
on Sept. 21st 1846)
Nashville Whig. (Sat., Oct. 24, 1846)

Burkhart, Col. Nicholas. Died in Howard Co. Mo.
National Banner & Nashville Daily Advertiser. (Wed., July 16, 1834)

Burnam, Mrs. Mary. Wife of Mr. John Burnam. Died in Warren County.
National Banner. (Sat., Sept. 5, 1829)

Burnet, Capt. George M. Died in Nashville on his way from Louisville
to Ala.
National Banner & Nashville Whig. (Mon., Sept. 27, 1830)

Burnett, Mr. William. Son of Col. William Burnett. Died in Bedford County, Tenn. Aged about 20 years.
National Banner & Nashville Whig. (Fri., March 27, 1835)

Burney, Mr. Dennis. Died in Montgomery County.
National Banner & Nashville Daily Advertiser. (Mon., Feb. 20, 1832)

Burns, Mr. R. J. (Printer) Died in Memphis, Tenn.
National Banner & Nashville Whig. (Wed., Jan. 14, 1835)

Burr, Colonel Aaron. Died at Staten Island on the 13th inst. formerly vice President of the United States Army in his 81st year.
National Banner Nashville Whig. (Wed., Sept. 28, 1836)

Burris, Susan. Aged 49. Died in Deerfield, Ohio.
National Banner & Nashville Whig. (Sat., July 29, 1826)

Burroughs, Stephen. The Counterfeiter, age about 80 years. Died at Three Rivers, Canada.
Daily Republican Banner. (Fri., Feb. 28, 1840)

Burrous, Ferdinand. Died 17th at Cincinnita, Ohio of Cholera.
National Banner & Nashville Daily Advertiser. (Thurs., Oct. 25, 1832)

Burton, Mrs. Agatha. Died in Granville City, N. Carolina.
Nashville Republican and State Gazette. (Thurs., March 3, 1831 No. 96 Vol. 6)

Burton, Mr. George H. Died in Nashville Tuesday coming last.
Nashville Whig. (Thurs., July 30, 1846)

Burton, Mr. Hutching G. Died in Iredel County, North Carolina. Formerly Governor of that State.
Nashville Republican. (Sat., May 7, 1836)

Burton, Mr. Jesse W. Died in Madison County, Ky.
National Banner & Nashville Whig. (Sat., Feb. 23, 1828)

Burton, Robert. Age 45 years. Died in Boonville, Ark. formerly of Tenn.
Nashville Whig. (Mon., Sept. 7, 1840)

Busby, Mrs. Matilda. Died in Versailles, Ky.
National Banner & Nashville Whig. (Sat., June 2, 1827)

Bush, Dr. John E. Died 15th at Cincinnita, Ohio of Cholera.
National Banner & Nashville Daily Advertiser. (Wed., Oct. 24, 1832)

Butcher, Thos. (Negro) From Washington County. Died at the Tenn. State Prison of Cholera.
National Banner & Nashville Whig. (Fri., Aug. 14, 1835)

Butler, Mr. Anthony. Nephew of General Andrew Jackson. Died on his passage from N. O. to New York on board the ship Virginia, Mr. Anthony N. Butler in the 23rd year of his age. The Deceased was the nephew of General Andrew Jackson.
Whig. (Nov. 8, 1824)

Butler, Mr. Edward Malister Butler. Son of Mr. Mann Butler of Louisville. Died at New Orleans.
National Banner & Nashville Whig. (Sat., June 7, 1828)

Butler, Emma Cora. Infant daughter of A. W. and Mary D. Butler. Died in Nashville on Tuesday the 20th inst.
Nashville Whig. (Fri., July 23, 1841)

Butler, Isaac Esq. Died in Rutherford County.
National Banner & Nashville Whig. (Tuesday, July 11, 1829)

Butler, Dr. Isaac. Died at Florence, Ala.
National Banner & Nashville Whig. (Tues., April 20, 1830)

Butler, Sarah Sylvia. Daughter of Rev. Zebulum and Mary Butler.
Aged 15 years. Died on the 17th August at the residence of her Uncle
Mr. John Murdock near Oakland College, Miss. (Obituary)
The Christian Record. (Sat., Oct. 14, 1848)

Butler, Mrs. Susan. Consort of Mr. E. C. Butler. Died on Nashville
on the 13th inst. Aged 27 years and 5 months and 15 days. (Obituary)
The Union. (Sat., Jan. 21, 1837)

Butler, Miss Theresa C. Died in Lincoln.
National Banner & Nashville Whig. (Sat., Sept. 1, 1827)

Butler, Capt. William. Died at Louisville, Ky.
National Banner & Nashville Whig. (Sat., Oct. 6, 1827)

Butts, Mr. Wiley. Died in Smith County.
National Banner & Nashville Daily Advertiser. (Sat., April 21, 1832)

Buxton, Mrs. Died in Sparta, Tenn. Consort of Rev. Stephens G.
Buxton.
Nashville Republican and State Gazette. (Sat., May 14, 1831 No. 1
Vol. 7)

Byles, Mr. John. Died in Gallatin.
National Banner & Nashville Advertiser. (Vol. 20 Mon., Dec. 3, 1832
No. 1659)

Bynum, Mrs. Maria. In Halifax, North Carolina on the 15th inst.
Mrs. Maria Bynum, consort of Hon Jesse A. Bynum Representatives in
Congress from that district.
Nashville Republican. (Tues., Oct. 11, 1836)

Bynum, Sergeant, H. L. With the Second Tenn. Regiment. Died was
killed in the Battle of Sierra Gorda with the Mexican.
The Politician and the Weekly Nashville Whig. (Fri., May 21, 1847)

Bynum, Mr. Madison. Of Mt. Pleasant, Tenn. Died at Camp Lane E.
Florida of measles.
National Banner & Nashville Whig. (Mon., Nov. 28, 1836)

Bynum, Mr. Madison. Of Mt. Pleasant, Tenn. Died at Camp Lane, E.
Florida of measles.
Nashville Republicans. (Mon., Nov. 28, 1836)

Bynum, Mrs. Maria. Consort of Hon. Jesse A. Bynum. Died in Halifax,
North Carolina on the 15th inst.
Nashville Republican. (Tues., Oct. 11, 1836)

Byrd. Mrs. Died in Princeton, Ky. of Cholera.
National Banner & Nashville Daily Advertiser. (Wed., July 9, 1834)

Byrd. Hon. Charles W. Died in Adam County, Ohio. Judge of the U. S.
Court for the District of Ohio.
National Banner & Nashville Whig. (Sat., Sept. 13, 1828)

Byrd, Mrs. Mary. Wife of Mr. Pleasant Byrd. Died in Limestone County,
Ala.
National Banner. (Sat., Oct. 10, 1829)

Byrn, Mrs. Frances. Wife of J. P. Byrn. Died in Dyer County, Tenn.
National Banner & Nashville Daily Advertiser. (Thurs., Sept. 11, 1834)

Byrn, Mrs. Frances. Consort of John P. Byrn Esq. Died in Dyer
County.
National Banner & Nashville Whig. (Wed., Oct. 1, 1834)

Byrn, Col. Jno. W. Formely of Sumner County and late sheriff of Lowndes County, Mi. Died on the 14th in Committing Suicide.
Daily Republican Banner. (Mon., Oct. 24, 1839)

Byrne, Miss Jane. Died in Lexington, Ky.
National Banner & Nashville Daily Advertiser. (Wed., July 31, 1833)

Byrne, Mr. John. Died in Russellville, Ky.
National Banner & Nashville Whig. (Sat., Aug. 9, 1828)

Byrne, Mrs. Martha. Died in Jackson County.
National Banner & Nashville Daily Advertiser. (Sat., April 21, 1832)

Byrnes, Patrick. Died at Cincinnita, Ohio of Cholera.
National Banner & Nashville Daily Advertiser. (Wed., Oct. 24, 1832)

Byrnes, Rev. Wm. Principal of St. Mary Semenary. Died on Wednesday evening at Bardstown, Ky. of Cholera.
National Banner & Nashville Daily Advertiser. (Sat., June 15, 1833)

Cabell, Dr. John C. Died at Lynchburg. An old and respectable citizen of that place.
National Banner & Nashville Daily Advertiser. (Sat., Sept. 6, 1834)

Cabet, Mrs. Age 65. Died in Mobile.
National Banner & Nashville Whig. (Sat., Sept. 16, 1826)

Cabler, Miss Margaret A. Daughter of Benjamin G. Cobler. Died in Nashville on the Friday the 8th inst. Aged 17 years and 3 months.
Nashville Whig. (Thurs., May 14, 1846)

Cadmus, Mr. Abraham Jr. Of Tuscumbia, Ala. Died in Lexington, Ky.
National Banner & Nashville Whig. (Sat., Sept. 6, 1828)

Cage, Mr. George W. A student of Medicine. Died at Cairo.
National Banner & Nashville Whig. (Sat., June 6, 1827)

Cage, Miss Jane. Died in Sumner County.
National Banner & Nashville Daily Advertiser. (Sat., June 1, 1833)

Cage, Mr. Jesse Jr. Died at 4 O'Clock P.M. on the 15th inst. at Cairo.
National Banner & Nashville Whig. (Sat., Sept. 23, 1823)

Cage, Capt. John. Died in Wilson County on the 9th inst.
National Banner & Nashville Whig. (Sat., May 26, 1827)

Cage, Mrs. Polly. Wife of Mr. Reuben Cage, aged 50. Died in Sumner County.
National Banner & Nashville Daily Advertiser. (Sat., Jan. 19, 1833)

Cage, Miss Sophia Ann. Died in Sumner County.
National Banner & Nashville Whig. (Wed., Aug. 17, 1831)

Cage, Mr. William. Formely of Sumner County, Tenn. Died near Lagrange, Tenn. On Friday 12th inst.
Nashville Republican (Tues., 23, 1836)

Cain, Mrs. Christiana Gregory. Aged 28 years. Died in Williamson County.
National Banner & Nashville Whig. (Sat., Aug. 5, 1826)

Cain, Geo. J. Died in Murfreesborough, Tenn. On the 17th of Cholera.
National Banner & Nashville Whig. (Fri., July 3, 1835)

Cain, Mr. James. Aged 44 formely of Petersburg, Va. Died at Tuscaloosa Ala.
National Banner & Nashville Whig. (Thurs., July 1, 1830)

Cain, Mrs. Martha M. Daughter of Capt. Benjamin Burch. Died at Washington City on the 21st Jan. late of Murfreesborough, Tenn.
National Banner & Nashville Whig. (Fri., Feb. 10, 1837)

Cain, Mrs. Mary. Consort of Mr. Robt. Cain and daughter of Dr. John Lawrence. Died in Nashville on the 9th of May.
National Banner & Nashville Whig. (Wed., May 11, 1836)

Cain, Mrs. Mary. Consort of Maj. R. B. Cain of McMinnville and daughter of Dr. W. P. Lawrence of Nashville. Died in Davidson County at the residence of Stockly Conelson Esq. on Monday the 9th inst.
The Union. (Thurs., May 12, 1836)

Caldwell, Mr. Daniel. Died in Ruthledge County. Aged 35 years.
National Banner. (April 14, 1826)

Caldwell, Dr. Daniel C. Aged about 50 years. Died in Russellville, Ky. on Tuesday the 11th.
Daily Republican Banner (Monday, Feb. 18, 1839)

Caldwell, Mr. David. Of Russellville, Ky. Died near Smithland.
National Banner & Nashville Daily Advertiser. (Mon., May 5, 1833)

Caldwell, Mrs. Drusilla. Wife of Mr. Charles Caldwell. Died in Gallatin.
National Banner & Nashville Daily Advertiser. (Sat., Jan. 19, 1833)

Caldwell, Mrs. Drusilla. Died in Gallatin, Tenn. on the 11th of January.
The Western Weekly Review. (Fri., Feb. 22, 1833 Franklin, Tenn.)

Caldwell, James Henry. Infant Son of D. P. Caldwell. Died at Christmasville Carroll County on the 13th inst. Aged about 20 months.
National Banner & Nashville Daily Advertiser. (Mon., Aug. 27, 1832)

Caldwell, Mr. John. Died at Hamilton, Ohio.
National Banner. (Feb. 17, 1826)

Caldwell, Mrs. Phebe. Died in Nashville on Yesterday morning. Age 71 years.
The Politician and the Weekly Nashville Whig. (Fri., March 24, 1848)

Caldwell, Mrs. Phebe. Relict of Mr. Thomas Caldwell. Died at her residence in Nashville on the 17th in the 71st year of her age.
The Christian Record. 6at., March 25, 1848)

Caldwell, Mr. Robert. In the 934d year of his age. Died at the residence of his son Thomas D. Caldwell in Campbell County, Va. on the 18th ult. A soldier of the Revolution.
Nashville Union. (Fri., March 22, 1839)

Caldwell, Mr. Samuel. Died in this town, suddenly.
National Banner. (April 28, 1826)

Caldwell, Dr. Silas M. Died in Haywood County.
Nashville Whig. (Tues., March 31, 1846)

Caldwell, William Esq. of Wadesborough. Died in Elkton.
National Banner & Nashville Whig. (Sat., Oct. 6, 1827)

Call, Mrs. Mary. Wife of Gen. Richard K. Call. Died in Tallahassee on the 28th Feb.
National Banner & Nashville Whig. (Mon., March 21, 1836)

Callahan, Francis Gregory. Infant son of Mr. Callahan. Died in Nashville.
National Banner & Nashville Daily Advertiser. (Wed., July 31, 1833)

Calloway, Mrs. Nancy. Wife of Joseph Calloway Esq. Died in Monroe County.
National Banner & Nashville Whig. (Mon., May 9, 1831)

Callender, Mrs. Mary. Wife of Mr. Thomas Callender. Died in Nashville on the 15th inst. in the 43r year of her age.
The Politician and the Weekly Nashville Whig. (Wed., Sept. 22, 1847)

Calloway, James S. Aged 24 years. Died at Grenada, Miss on the 24th.
Daily Republican Banner. (Tues., Feb. 6, 1838)

Calloway, Joseph Esq. Died in Monroe County.
National Banner & Nashville Daily Advertiser. (Mon., Nov. 12, 1832)

Calmes, Gen. Marquis. In the 80th year of his age. Died in Woodford County, Ky. On the 27th ult. He was a Captain in the Revolutionary Army.
National Banner & Nashville Daily Advertiser. (March 12, 1834)

Calvit, Mr. Tacitus G. Died at Alexandria, Lou.
National Banner (June 17, 1829)

Caman, Mr. John H. Died in Lawrence County, Ala.
National Banner & Nashville Whig. (Oct. 7, 1826)

Cameron, Robert Daniel. Aged 10 years and 10 months. Died in Nashville on the 10th inst. son of Daniel Cameron.
Nashville Union. (Wed., June 12, 1839)

Cameron, Mrs. Sarah A. Consort of John T. Cameron Esq. at Canton, Miss. Died on the 10th ult.
Nashville Whig. (Thurs., Aug. 3, 1843)

Cammack, Mrs. Wife of Mr. George Cammack. Died in Christian County, Ky.
National Banner & Nashville Whig. (Fri., Sept. 30, 1831)

Camp, Mrs. Eliza P. Died in Louisville, Ky.
National Banner & Nashville Daily Advertiser. (Mon., Nov. 19, 1832)

Camp, James. Died on Sunday morning between one and two O'clock Major James Camp merchant of the place. On Monday morning his remains were likewise buried with Masonic honors.
The Nashville Whig. (Tues. Feb 7, 1816)

Camp, Dr. John H. Formely a Speaker with the House of Representative of this State. Died on the 10th at Pulaski.
National Banner. (Sat., Nov. 21, 1829)

Campbell, Mrs. Consort of Mr. John Campbell of the firm of Msses Campbell and Peabody. Died on Sunday evening the 29th ult in Nashville.
The Union. (Thurs., Feb. 2, 1837)

Campbell, Rev. A. W. A Minister of the Presbyterian Church. Died at his residence in Paducah, Ky. on the 9th inst. Aged 45 years.
The Christian Record. (Sat., Feb. 5, 1848)

Campbell, Mr. Alexander. Son of Mr. Allen Campbell. Died at Russellville, Ky.
National Banner & Nashville Daily Advertiser. (Mon., Jan. 9, 1832)

Campbell, Mrs. Ann. Consort of Mr. James Campbell. In the 61st year of her age. Died in Knoxville, Tenn.
National Banner & Nashville Whig. (Mon., Oct. 20, 1834)

Campbell, Archibald Esq. Died in Richmond, Va. on the evening of the 27th aged about 65. Mr. Campbell was a brother of the Poet Campbell.
National Banner & Nashville Whig. (Fri., Dec. 31, 1830)

Campbell, Maj. Arthur L.   Died in Louisville, Ky. on the 19th inst.
Nashville Union. (Thurs., Jan. 25, 1838)

Campbell, Mrs. Catherine.   Died at Lexington, Ky.
National Banner. (Sat., April 18, 1829)

Campbell, Col. David.   Founder of Campbells Sta. in Knox County.
Died in Wilson County.
National Banner & Nashville Daily Advertiser. (Mon., Dec. 10, 1832)

Campbell, Duncan G. Esq.   Died in Wilkes County, Georgia.
National Banner & Nashville Whig. (Sat., Sept. 13, 1828)

Campbell, Mr. Edward.   Aged 30 years.   Died at Bellfront.
National Banner & Nashville Whig. (Fri., July 15, 1831)

Campbell, Edward.   Son of Capt. Robert Campbell in the 18th year of
his age.   Died in Maury County, Tenn.
National Banner & Nashville Whig. (Fri., Nov. 21, 1834)

Campbell, Mrs. Eliza.   Consort of James G. Campbell, Esq.   Died in
Fayette County, Va. on the 14th ult. formely of this County.
National Banner & Nashville Whig. (Fri., July 8, 1831)

Campbell, Mr. George.   Died near Columbia, T.
National Banner & Nashville Daily Advertiser. (Fri., Sept. 20, 1833)

Campbell, Dr. George W.   Of Columbia, Tenn.   Died at Paris in France
on the 20th of May last.
National Banner & Nashville Daily Advertiser. (Tues., July 29, 1834)

Campbell, Hon. George W.   Long a distinguished citizen of Tennessee.
Died in Nashville on Thursday last.   At a very advanced age.
The Politician and Weekly Nashville Whig. (Fri., Feb. 25, 1848)

Campbell, Hon. George Washington.   In the 80th year of his age.   Died
in Nashville on Thursday the 17th inst. (Obituary)
The Christian Record. (Sat., March 4, 1848)

Campbell, Private J. M. L.   Company K.   First Regiment Tenn. Volunteers.   Died was killed in the Battle of Montrey with the Mexicans
on Sept. 21st 1846.
Nashville Whig. (Sat., Oct. 24, 1846)

Campbell, James.   Infant son of James Campbell Esq.   Died in Nashville
on Tuesday last.
Nashville Whig. (Mon., Nov. 19, 1838)

Campbell, James G. Esq.   Died on the 4th inst. in Davidson County.
For the past 14 months a residence of Morgan County, Illinois.
Nashville Republican. (Sat., Feb. 18, 1837)

Campbell, James G. Esq.   Formely of Davidson County.   Died in Davidson
County on the 4th inst. for the last 14 months a citizen of Morgan
County.
National Banner & Nashville Whig. (Mon., Feb. 20, 1837)

Campbell, Gen. John.   Died at Charlestown Portage County, Ohio.
National Banner & Nashville Whig. (Sat., Sept. 8, 1827)

Campbell, Mr. John.   Son of Joseph and Rebecca Campbell in the 68th
year of his age.   Died in Rowen County, N. Carolina on the 26th of
May.
Daily Republican Banner (Mon., June 18, 1838)

Campbell, John Bell.   Son of James Campbell Esq.   Died in Nashville
Wednesday the 29th April.
Daily Republican Banner. (Fri., May 1, 1840)

Campbell, Mrs. Lucy A. Consort of Major William P. Campbell of Hillsboro. Died in Fayette County on the 17th June.
National Banner & Nashville Daily Advertiser. (Tues., July 2, 1833)

Campbell, Mrs. Margeret. Died in Brook County, Va. Wife of Rev. Alexander Campbell.
National Banner & Nashville Whig. (Sat., Nov. 17, 1827)

Campbell, Mrs. Maria W. Died on the 18th Nov.
Nashville Republican and State Gazette. (Vol. 7 Thursday, Dec. 1, 1831 No. 87)

Campbell, Mrs. Mary. At Bowling Green. Aged 70 years.
National Banner. (Sat., Aug. 15, 1829)

Campbell, Mary Caldwell. Infant daughter of William P. Campbell. Died on Wednesday night last.
The Western Weekly Review. (Fri., Feb. 1, 1833 Franklin, Tenn.)

Campbell, Matilda. Wife of Mr. James Campbell and daughter of Maj. James Peart. Died in Logan County, Ky.
National Banner & Nashville Daily Advertiser. (Tues., Feb. 14, 1832)

Campbell, Col. Michael. Died in Davidson County.
National Banner & Nashville Whig. (Fri., March 19, 1830)

Campbell, Mrs. Musadora. Consort of James Campbell Esq. Died in Nashville on the 1st inst.
The Union. (Sat., May 6, 1837)

Campbell, Philip. Sheriff of Davidson County. Died at his residence 4 miles south of Nashville.
Daily Republican Banner. (Thurs., June 28, 1838)

Campbell, Philip. Sheriff of Davidson County. Died at his residence eight miles south of Nashville.
Nashville Union. (Fri., June 29, 1838)

Cabaness, Mrs. Lucy. Died near Hazelgreen, Ala.
National Banner & Nashville Whig. (Sat., Jan. 12, 1828)

Campbell, Maj. Philip. Sheriff of Davidson County. Died at his residence in Nashville yesterday mroning and was buried with Masonic honors.
Nashville Whig. (Fri., June 29, 1838)

Campbell, Dr. Robert H. Of Nashville. Died lately on the Ohio River, a short distance from the Mouth of the Cumberland. He met death by drowning.
National Banner & Nashville Whig. (Fri., July 15, 1831)

Campbell, Mrs. Sarah. Consort of Mr. John Campbell. Died on Sunday the 29th inst. recently of Fayetteville, N. Carolina.
Nashville Republican. (Tues., Jan. 31, 1837)

Campbell, Mrs. Sarah. Consort of Mr. John Campbell. Recently of Fayetteville, N. C. Died in Nashville on Sunday 29th Jan.
National Banner & Nashville Whig. (Wed., Feb. 1, 1837)

Campbell, Mr. Thomas. Died in this town on the 21st inst in the 43rd year of his age.
National Banner & Nashville Whig. (Sat., Jan. 26, 1828)

Campbell, Thomas. Died at Louisville, Ky. On the 18th of Cholera.
National Banner & Nashville Daily Advertiser. (Mon., Oct. 22, 1832)

Campbell, Mr. Wiley. Died in Warren County, Ky.
National Banner & Nashville Whig. (Thurs., Aug. 5, 1830)

Campbell, Mr. William. Died in Knox County. Aged 43 years.
National Banner & Nashville Whig. (Sat., Feb. 23, 1828)

Campbell, Maj. William. Formely of Nashville. Died on the 11th
inst at the residence of his son J. W. Campbell of Jackson, Tenn.
Nashville Whig. (Tues., Jan. 25, 1842)

Campfield, Joseph S. Died in Augusta, Ga. of yellow fever.
Daily Republican Banner. (Fri., Oct. 4, 1839)

Cannon, Mrs. Elizabeth. Consort of Gen. Robert Cannon. Died in Shelbyville on the 15th inst.
Daily Republican Banner. (Sat., June 23, 1838)

Cannon, Mrs. Elizabeth. Consort of Gen. Robert Cannon. Died in
Shelbyville, Tenn. on Friday the 15th inst.
Nashville Whig. (Mon., June 25, 1838)

Cannon, Miss Jane. Died in Madison County.
Nashville Whig. (Tues., April 14, 1846)

Cannon, Mr. John M. Of Alandria, Lou. died in Bedford County.
National Banner and Nashville Advertiser. (Vol. 20 Wed., April 11, 1832
No. 1458)

Cannon, John M. Died at Shelbyville, Tenn. of Cholera.
National Banner & Nashville Daily Advertiser. (Thurs., July 11, 1833)

Cannon, Mr. John W. Died at Jackson, Tenn.
National Banner. (Sat., April 11, 1829)

Cannon, Mrs. Letitia. Consort of the late Minos Cannon deceased.
Died in Williamson County in the 79th year of her age.
National Banner & Nashville Daily Advertiser. (Fri., Jan. 27, 1832)

Cannon, Mrs. Lucy. In the 56th year of her age. Died on the 31st
ult. (Obituary)
The Western Weekly Review. (Fri., Feb. 10, 1832 Franklin, Tenn.)

Cannon, Mr. Minos Senior. Died in Williamson County on the 10th
inst. of May. He was a Native of Maryland.
National Banner. (Sat., Aug. 1, 1829)

Cannon, Narcissa W. Youngest daughter of Col. Newton Cannon.
National Banner & Nashville Whig. (Mon., Oct. 20, 1834)

Cannon, Theophilus A. Esq. In Rutherford County on the 10th inst.
In the 65th year of his age.
Nashville Republican. (Thurs., Jan. 14, 1836)

Cantrell, Mrs. Joyce. Wife of Mr. William Cantrell Esq. of Sumner
County. Died near Gallatin on the 23rd ult.
Nashville Whig. (Oct. 4, 1824)

Cantrell, Mrs. Juliet. Wife of Stephan Cantrell Esq. Died in Nashville on the evening of the 3rd inst.
Nashville Whig. (Fri., July 5, 1839)

Cantrell, Margaret Armstrong. Youngest daughter of Stephen Cantrell
Esq. in the 6th year of her age. Died in this vicinity on the 9th
inst.
National Banner & Nashville Daily Advertiser. (Wed., June 11, 1834)

Cantrell, Mrs. Mary. Died in Sumner County.
National Banner & Nashville Daily Advertiser. (Mon., March 3, 1834)

Cantrell, Mrs. Mary J. Wife of Mr. George C. Cantrell. Died in Sumner
County on the 21st inst. in the 27th year of her age.
Nashville Whig. (Tues., Jan. 27, 1846)

Cantrell, Mrs. Sally. Consort of Major Ota Cantrell of Rutherford County.
The Nashville Whig. (Sept. 17, 1816)

Cantrell, Mr. Stephen. A soldier of the Revolution. Died in Sumner County.
National Banner & Nashville Whig. (Sat., Feb. 10, 1827)

Cantrell, Mr. William M. Eldest son of William Cantrell Esq. of Sumner County. Died at the residence of Dr. John Cage on the 24th of Oct. age 22 years and one month. (Obituary)
Nashville Whig. (Thurs., Nov. 12, 1846)

Cantrell, Zebulon M. P. Son of Major Ota Cantrell. Died in Rutherford County.
National Banner & Nashville Whig. (Sat., Feb. 3, 1827)

Caperton, Mrs. Susannah. Wife of Mr. Thomas S. Caperton. Died in Salem, Franklin County, Tenn. on Sunday the 12th of Oct.
National Banner & Nashville Whig. (Sat., Nov. 1, 1828)

Carden, John Quincy. Son of Capt. A. L. Carden aged 14 months and 19 days. Died in Anderson County.
National Banner & Nashville Daily Advertiser. (Mon., Feb. 4, 1833)

Cardwell, Mrs. C. Wife of Henry H. Cardwell. Died in Knoxville, Tenn.
Daily Republican Banner. (Sat., Oct. 6, 1838)

Carey, Mrs. Wife of Mr. Thomas Cary. Died in Monroe County.
National Banner & Nashville Whig. (Sat., June 7, 1828)

Carey, Mr. Edward S. Died in Florence, Ala. Editor of the Register.
National Banner. (April 7, 1826)

Carey, Mr. Ludwell. Died in Fayette County.
National Banner & Nashville Whig. (Sat., Oct. 6, 1827)

Carey, Matthew. Died at Philadelphia a few days since of injuries received when thrown from his carriage.
Nashville Union. (Fri., Sept. 27, 1839)

Carle, Thomas. Died 13th at Cincinnita, Ohio of Cholera.
National Banner & Nashville Daily Advertiser. (Tues., Oct. 23, 1832)

Carlin, Mr. Of Wilson County. Died in Clarksville.
National Banner and Nashville Daily Advertiser. (Tues., June 11, 1833)

Carlisle, Mr. Robert. Died drown in the Kentucky River. Aged 33 years.
National Banner & Nashville Whig. (Sat., Aug. 19, 1826)

Carll, Mrs. Sarah. Died at Cincinnita.
National Banner. (May 13, 1826)

Carman, Robert. With the second Tennessee Regiment. Died was killed in the Battle of Sierra, Gorda. with the Mexicans.
The Politician and Weekly Whig. (Fri., May 21, 1847)

Carmichael, Mr. Aged 35 years. Died at Cincinnita, Ohio of the Cholera.
National Banner & Nashville Daily Advertiser. (Thurs., Oct. 18, 1832)

Carmicheal, Mr. Cah (Printer) Died at New Orleans on the 29th.
National Banner & Nashville Daily Advertiser. (Tues., Sept. 10, 1833)

Carmicheal, Col. Samuel W. Died in Monroe County at her residence.
Nashville Union. (Mon., Dec. 2, 1839)

Carelison, Mr. Thomas and Mrs. Elizabeth his wife. Died in Madison County, Ky.
National Banner & Nashville Whig. (Sat., Sept. 9, 1826)

Carnes, Mr. Alexander. A Soldier of the Revolution. Died in this town on Monday last.
National Banner & Nashville Whig. (Sat., March 8, 1828)

Carnes, Mrs. Susanna. In the 59th year of her age. Died at Vernon, Madison County, Monday Nov. 2nd.
National Banner & Nashville Whig. (Fri., Nov. 27, 1835)

Carpenter, Capt. Manning. Died at Huntsville, Ala.
National Banner & Nashville Daily Advertiser. (Wed., April 24, 1833)

Carpenter, Stephen Cullen. In the 78th year of his age. Died at Philadelphia on the 24th of July.
National Banner & Nashville Whig. (Mon., Aug. 23, 1830)

Carpenter, Mr. Walter. Died at Port Gibson, Miss.
National Banner & Nashville Whig. (Mon., Jan. 3, 1831)

Carpenter, Mr. William. Killed by the Accident discharge of a gun. Died at Port Gibson, Miss.
National Banner & Nashville Whig. (Mon., Feb. 21, 1831)

Carr, Mr. A. W. Formely of Lexington, Ky. Died in Lincoln County, Mo.
National Banner & Nashville Whig. (Wed., Sept. 28, 1831)

Carr, Mrs. Ann Marie. Aged 38 years. Died in St. Louis.
National Banner & Nashville Whig. (Sat., Sept. 2, 1826)

Carr, Dubney Overton. Formely of Albermarle County, Va. Aged 24. Died at Bogota on the 17th of Sept. last.
Republican and State Gazette. (Sat., Dec. 25, 1830 No. 69 Vol 6.

Carr, Miss Eliza. Died in Logan County, Ky.
National Banner & Nashville Daily Advertiser. (Tues., Nov. 27, 1832)

Carr, Mr. Henry. Died at Knoxville.
National Banner & Nashville Whig. (Sat., May 24, 1828)

Carr, Mr. James. Of Jackson. Died near Key Corney on the Forked Deer River, of the Cholera.
National Banner & Nashville Daily Advertiser. (Wed., June 5, 1833)

Carr, John Dabney. One of the Judges of the Court of Appeals. Died in Richmond, Virginia.
Nashville Republican. (Thurs., Jan. 26, 1837)

Carr, Overton. Principal Door-Keeper to the House of Representatives. Died at Washington on the 21st.
Daily Republican Banner. (Thurs., March 29, 1838)

Carr, Miss Sarah. Died near Memphis.
National Banner & Nashville Whig. (Sat., Feb. 9, 1828)

Carr, Thomas D. Died in Shelby County.
National Banner & Nashville Daily Advertiser. (Wed., Jan. 4, 1832)

Carr, Mr. William. Aged about 79 years. Died in Knoxville, Tenn. A soldier of the Revolution.
National Banner & Nashville Whig. (Fri., Jan. 23, 1835)

Carrick, Mrs. Consort of the Rev. Samuel Carrick of Knoxville Died lately.
Knoxville Gazette. (No. 25 of Vol. 2 Sat., Nov. 23, 1793 No. 51)

Carrick, Mr. Moses. Died near Sparta.
National Banner & Nashville Whig. (June 17, 1826)

Carrick, Samuel Mrs. Died since our last Mrs. Carrick the amiable
comfort of Rev. Samuel Carrick of this town Knoxville.
Knoxville Gazette. (Sat., Nov. 23, 1793)

Carrol, Mrs. Cecilia. Relict of the late Gov. Carrol. Died in
Nashville on the 12th inst. (Obituary Sept. 23)
The Christian Record. (Sat., Sept. 16, 1848)

Carrol, Charles. Of Carrollton. The late survioser of the signes
of the Declarationof the American Inpendence. Died at Carrollaton.
National Banner & Nashville Daily Advertiser. (Mon., Nov. 26, 1832)

Carroll, Mr. Elijah. Died in Logan County, Ky.
National Banner. (Feb. 17, 1826)

Carroll, Lawson. Died at Versailles, Ky. 14 miles from Lexington of
Cholera.
National Banner & Nashville Whig. (Fri., Sept. 4, 1835)

Carroll, Miss Mary. Late of New Orleans and family of Lexington, Ky.
Died at St. Louis.
National Banner & Nashville Daily Advertiser. (Mon., July 29, 1833)

Carrol, May Cecilia. Infant daughter of Col. William H. Carrol of
Nashville. Died in Williamson County.
Nashville Whig. (Mon., Sept. 7, 1840)

Carroll, Dr. Richmond. Died on the 11th near Hazlegreen Madison, County, Ala.
National Banner & Nashville Daily Advertiser. (Mon., April 1, 1833)

Carroll, Gen. William. Late Gov. of Tennessee. Died at 8 O'clock
last evening at the age of 56. (Monday, March 26, 1844)
Nashville Whig. (Tues., March 26, 1844)

Carson, Capt. John. Who was shot on Saturday evening January 20th
by Lieut. Smith departed this life about eleven O'clock last night.
The Nashville Whig. (March 12, 1816)

Carson, John. Died in Williamson County.
National Banner. (Feb. 10, 1828)

Carson, Mr. William. Died in Washington County.
National Banner & Nashville Whig. (Sat., July 15, 1826)

Carter, Mr. Daniel Tennessee. Died in Bolivar.
National Banner. (Sat., Aug. 15, 1829)

Carter, Mrs. Eliza. Consort of Mr. Samuel J. Carter. Died in Davidson
County on Saturday 21st inst. after a short illness.
National Banner & Nashville Whig. (Wed., May 25, 1831)

Carter, Mrs. Eliza. Died in Huntingdon.
Nashville Whig. (Tues., May 5, 1846)

Carter, Mr. Garland. Died in Lincoln County, Ky.
National Banner & Nashville Whig. (Sat., Jan. 6, 1827)

Carter, Mr. Goodwin B. For many years a publisher in La. Died in
New Orleans.
National Banner & Nashville Daily Advertiser. (Tues., June 24, 1834)

Carter, Mr. J. T. Of Maine. Died in Washington on the 15th.
Daily Republican Banner. (Thurs., March 22, 1838)

Carter, Dr. James Augustus. Recently from New York. Died in St. Louis, Mo.
National Banner & Nashville Whig. (Wed., Dec. 3, 1834)

Carter, John P. Esq. Died at Huntsville, Ala.
National Banner & Nashville Whig. (Fri., Jan. 22, 1830)

Carter, Lieut. Lawrence R. Of the 7th Regiment of the U. S. Infantry. Died at Fort Gibson on the 19th. A native of Virginia.
National Banner & Nashville Whig. (Fri., April 21, 1837)

Carter, Dr. Richard. The celebrated Indian Doctor in the 53rd year of his age. Died in Shelby County, Ky. on the 4th of Aug. last.
Nashville Union. (Fri., Oct. 12, 1838)

Carter, Major Robert. In the 69th year of his age. Died in Franklin on Thursday last.
Nashville Union. (Mon., Sept. 6, 1839)

Carter, Mr. Robert M. Died in Nashville.
National Banner & Nashville Whig. (Mon., Aug. 29, 1831)

Carter, Mr. Robert M. Died at Tyrell's Spring.
Nashville Republican and State Gazette. (Tues., Aug. 30, 1831 No. 47 Vol. 7)

Carter, Mrs. Sarah. Consort of Mr. Burrel Carter, aged 55 years. Died in Rutherford County.
National Banner & Nashville Whig. (Sat., Sept. 16, 1826)

Carteree, Mrs. Congress St. Died the 18th at Cincinnita, Ohio of Cholera.
National Banner & Nashville Daily Advertiser. (Fri., Oct. 26, 1832)

Cartmell, Mrs. Sarah. Wife of Maj. Henry R. Cartmell. Died in Nashville on the 26th Sept.
National Banner & Nashville Whig. (Mon., Sept. 29, 1834)

Cartwright, Mrs. Mary. Consort of Mr. T. N. Cartwright. Died in Nashville on Sunday last.
The Politician and Weekly Nashville Whig. (Fri., April 30, 1847)

Cartwright, Mr. William G. In the 21st year of his age. Died in Nashville on the 24th inst. He had been a volunteer in the Army and had served under Capt. Foster in the 1st Regiment of Tennessee Regiment.
The Christian Record. (Sat., May 27, 1848)

Caruthers, Edman. Thomas H. Caruthers, age 7, son of Joseph Caruthers, died in Huntsville, Ala. in the same house an hour before Edman Caruthers age 7, brother of Joseph died.
National Banner & Nashville Whig. (Sept. 7, 1831)

Caruthers, Mr. Hugh. Aged 76 years. Died in Madison County, Ala.
National Banner & Nashville Whig. (Mon., Jan. 5, 1835)

Caruthers, Mr. Joseph. Aged 67 years. Died in Henry County.
National Banner & Nashville Whig. (Thurs., Oct. 28, 1830)

Caruthers, Mrs. Sarah. Died at Huntsville, Ala. Wife of Mr. Robert Caruthers.
National Banner & Nashville Whig. (Sat., July 15, 1826)

Caruthers, Mr. Thomas H. Age 7 son of Joseph Caruthers. Died in Huntsville, Ala. In the same house that an hour before Endman Caruthers age 7, brother of Joseph Caruthers died.
National Banner and Nashville Whig. (Vol. 19 No. 1310 Wednesday, Sept. 7, 1831)

Cary, James K. Esq. Died at Columbus, Ohio.
National Banner & Nashville Whig. (Sat., Jan. 20, 1827)

Caseday, Mrs. Araminta. Wife of Mr. Alexander A. Casaday. Died in
this town last evening.
National Banner. (Sat., July 25, 1829)

Casedy, Mrs. Sarah. Wife of Mr. Martin Casedy. Died in McMinn County.
National Banner & Nashville Whig. (Fri., July 15, 1831)

Casey, Mrs. Eliza J. Age 39 years and 11 months. Died in Williamson
County. Consort of Mr. Thomas Casey.
Daily Republican Banner. (Wed., Feb. 19, 1840)

Cash, F. A. Esq. Attorney at Law. Died in Florida, formely of Anson
County, N. C.
National Banner & Nashville Daily Advertiser. (Sat., Aug. 10, 1833)

Cashon, Mr. David. In the 78th year of his age. Died in Weakly County
on the 24th of June. A soldier of the Revolution.
National Banner & Nashville Whig. (Wed., July 8, 1835)

Casner, Frederick. Died 15th at Cincinnita, Ohio of Cholera.
National Banner & Nashville Daily Advertiser. (Wed., Oct. 24, 1832)

Cass, Mrs. Mary. Mothter of the Hon. Lewis Cass. Secretary of War.
Died Muskingum County, Ohio on the 13th of Sept.
National Banner & Nashville Whig. (Mon., Oct. 20, 1834)

Cassedy, Mrs. A. S. Wife of Mr. Alexander A. Casedy. Died in this
town on Thursday the 21st of July. Mr. Alexander A. Cassedy.
National Banner. (Sat., Aug. 1, 1829)

Cassedy, Mrs. Emeline S. Wife of A. A. Cassedy Esq. Aged 33 years.
Died in Nashville on Sunday 6th inst.
Nashville Whig. (Tues., Aug. 8, 1843)

Cassidy, Captain Micheal. Died in Fleming County, Ky.
National Banner. (Sat., April 25, 1829)

Casso, Mr. F. P. J. Died at Tuscaloosa, Ala.
National Banner & Nashville Whig. (Sat., Feb. 10, 1827)

Casteel, ___. Died lately at Capt. Taylor's in Alabama Territory
12 miles south of the Military Ferry. ___ Casteel of Roan County,
Tenn.
The Nashville Whig. The Tenn. Advertiser. (Aug. 8, 1818)

Castis, Mrs. Eliza Park. Granddaughter of the late Mrs. Gen. Washington
aged 55. Died at Richmond, Va.
National Banner & Nashville Daily Advertiser. (Mon., Jan. 23, 1832)

Castleman, Andrew. Died on Sunday the 11th inst. at his residence
in Davidson County. He was 79 years old.
Nashville Whig. (Thurs., Aug. 15, 1844)

Catlett, R. P. Esq. Editor of the Mississippian. Died at Clinton,
Miss.
National Banner & Nashville Daily Advertiser. (Sat., July 6, 1833)

Cauts, Archbald, Esq. Died in Rutherford County on the 3rd inst.
National Banner & Nashville Daily Advertiser. (Thurs., Nov. 14,1833)

Cavette, Mr. Thomas. Died in Madison County, Va.
National Banner & Nashville Daily Advertiser. (Wed., March 7, 1832)

Cavitt, Miss Sophronia. Niece of Mr. W. H. Binkley. Died in Nashville
on the 4th inst. in the 18th year of her age.
The Politician and Weekly Nashville Whig. (Wed., Aug. 11, 1847)

Cawd, Mr. Joshua. D. Died on the 2nd of Aug.
National Banner & Nashville Whig. (Wed., Sept. 7, 1836)

Cawdrew, Mr. Killan. Of Kentucky age 23. Died Hamburg, S. C.
National Banner & Nashville Whig. (Sat., Aug. 26,1826)

Cayce, Mrs. Hannah. Consort of Mr. Ambrose Cayce of Davidson County.
Died in Davidson County at & O'clock Thursday evening the 62nd year of
her age.
National Banner & Nashville Whig. (Wed., July 27, 1831)

Cayce, Mr. James. Aged 64 years. Died in Nashville on the 27th of
Sept.
National Banner & Nashville Whig. (Fri., Sept. 30, 1831)

Cayce, Mr. James M. Son of Mr. Shadrack Cayce. Died at Lawrenceburg.
National Banner & Nashville Whig.(Mon., Nov. 8, 1830)

Caycey, Mr. Shadrack Sr. Aged about 57 years. Died in Friday 13th
inst. near Lawrenceburg, Tenn.
The Western Weekly Review. (Fri., April 13, 1832 Franklin, Tenn.)

Caycey, Mr. Shadrack was 57 years old. Died on Friday the 13th inst.
near Lawrenceburg, Tenn. formerly of this County.
National Banner & Nashville Daily Advertiser. (Mon., April 23, 1832)

Cazelles, Mr. Peter. Died Cincinnati.
National Banner (May 13, 1826)

Cerre, Mrs. Therese L. Died in St. Louis, Mo.
National Banner & Nashville Daily Advertiser. (Mon., Aug. 26, 1833)

Chadwell, Mr. Valantine B. Died in Williamson County on Thursday
last Dec. 30th.
Nashville Republican and State Gazette. (Tues., Jan. 4, 1831 No. 72
Vol. 6)

Chadwell, Mr. Valantine B. On Thursday last Dec. 30th of Consumption.
Died in Williamson County.
National Banner & Nashville Whig. (Vol. 18 No. 1201 Wed., Jan. 5, 1831)

Chaffin, Mrs. Ruth M. Consort of Mr. Edward H. Chaffin of Columbia.
Died on the evening of the 12th inst. in Columbia.
The Politician and Weekly Nashville Whig. (Fri., May 21, 1847)

Chalmers, Mr. James R. Died at Lebanon on the 23d ult. in the 25th
year of his age. Attorney at Law.
Nashville Whig. (Sept. 6, 1824)

Champ, Mr. Robert. Died in Columbia.
National Banner & Nashville Whig. (Sat., Aug. 26, 1826)

Chambers, Mr. Rawland Jr. Died in Woodford County, Ky.
National Banner (April 7, 1826)

Chambers, Mr. Andrew. Died at Florence, Ala. On the 12th ult.
National Banner. (Jan. 6, 1826)

Chambers, Mrs. Elizabeth. Died in Knoxville, Tenn.
Daily Republican Banner. (Sat., Sept. 22, 1838)

Chambers, Dr. Henry. Senator in Congress from Ala. Died in
Dinwiddil, Va. on his way to Washington.
National Banner (Feb. 24, 1826)

Chambers, Mr. John. Died in Maysville, Ky.
National Banner & Nashville Whig. (Sat., Sept. 20, 1828)

Champagney, M. De. Duke de Cadare. Died at Paris recently, Minister of the Interior and of Foreign affairs to Napoleon.
National Banner & Nashville Daily Advertiser. (Sat., Sept. 6, 1834)

Chancellor, Thomas. A soldier of the Revolution. Age 81 years. Died in Rockingham County, Va.
National Banner & Nashville Daily Advertiser. (Tues., Aug. 19, 1834)

Chandler, Mr. David. Died in Bedford County.
National Banner & Nashville Daily Advertiser. (Mon., May 6, 1833)

Chandler, Mr. John. Aged 86. Died in Knox County.
National Banner & Nashville Whig. (Mon., Oct. 31, 1831)

Chaney, Elizabeth Cancilla. Infant daughter of Charles J. Chaney of Louisana. Died in Nashville.
Nashville Whig. (Sat., Aug. 5, 1843)

Chaney, Miss Frances Ann E. Died in Purday, Tenn.
Nashville Republican and the State Gazette. Vol. 7 Saturday, October 29, 1831 No. 73)

Channel, James. Died by throwing himself in the Cumberland below Clarksville and was drowned.
Nashville Whig. (Mon., April 16, 1838)

Channing, Rev. William Ellery. Died at Bennington, Vt. last Sunday evening. (Boston Atlas)
Nashville Whig. (Tues., Oct. 18, 1842)

Chapluin, William R. Cahsier of the bank of Virginia at Danville. Died at Sweet Springs in Va.
National Banner & Nashville Daily Advertiser. (Mon., Sept. 2, 1833)

Chapouil, Peter. In this place on Sunday last, Peter Chapouil a native of Mass.
Nashville Republican. (Tues., Sept. 13, 1836)

Chapman, Charles. Son of Rev. Robert H. Chapman. Age 15. Died in Covington.
National Banner & Nashville Whig. (Mon., Sept. 12, 1831)

Chapman, Miss Elizabeth. Died in Shelbyville.
National Banner & Nashville Daily Advertiser. (Mon., April 29, 1833)

Chapman, Rev. Robert H. D. D. aged 62. Formely President of the University at Chapel Hill, N. C. Died in Winchester, Va.
National Banner & Nashville Daily Advertiser. (Wed., July 3, 1833)

Chapman, Rev. Robert H. D. D. Died at Winchester, Va. on Tuesday the 18th inst. in the 63rd year of his age. He was a native of New Jersey.
National Banner & Nashville Daily Advertiser. (Sat., July 20, 1833)

Chapman, Mr. Samuel. Aged 70 years. Died in this County last Thursday.
National Banner & Nashville Whig. (Sat., Sept. 23, 1826)

Chapman, Mrs. Sarah P. Wife of Dr. John L. Chapman. Died at the residence of her father L. P. Cheatham. Post Master of Nashville on the 19th inst.
Nashville Whig. (Sat., Feb. 28, 1846)

Chapouil, Charlotte S. Of Nashville. Died on last evening, she was the daughter of Mr. Peter Chapouil.
National Banner & Nashville Whig. (Wed., Oct. 14, 1835)

Chapouil, Peter - See above.

Chapouil, Peter. A native of Massachusetts. Died in Nashville on
Sunday last.
Nashville Republican. (Tues., Sept. 13, 1836)

Chapouil, Mr. Peter. A native of Boston, Mass. Died in Nashville
on Sunday 11th.
National Banner & Nashville Whig. (Fri., Sept. 16, 1836)

Charles, Miss Mildred S. In the 15th year of her age. Died on the
16th inst.
National Banner & Nashville Whig. (Mon., Oct. 3, 1836)

Chaudoin, James. In the 43rd year of his age. Died near Jasper on
Sunday the 29th Oct.
Daily Republican Banner. (Thurs., Oct. 16, 1837)

Chauncy, Catherine Maria. Only daughter of Comm. and Mrs. Catherine
Chauncy. Died on Saturday 15th in Washington City.
Nashville Republican Banner. (Thurs., April 27, 1837)

Chauvin, William. Aged upward of 75 years. Died in Nashville on the
29th.
National Banner & Nashville Daily Advertiser. (Thurs., April 3, 1834)

Chears, V. T. Aged 26 formerly of Anson County, N. Carolina. Died
at his residence at La Grange, Tennessee on the 12th inst.
Nashville Whig. (Mon., Dec. 27, 1841)

Cheatham, Mrs. Ann. Consort of John A. Cheatham Esq. of Nashville.
Died at Nashville on the 25th of Feb.
Nashville Republican. (Thurs., March 3, 1836)

Cheatham, Mrs. Ann. Consort of John A. Cheatham, Esq. of Nashville,
departed this life on the 25th of February, after a protracted illness
of several months, her disease was of the pulmonary character. She
lived the Christian faith for many years, she seemed to have anticipated
her approaching dissolution, and met it with usual firmness and
confidence. Indeed her confidence was so great that she seemed to
have no terrors, no dread, buy simply the pain of death. In her last
moments all bodily pain and with her usual confidence and faith
apparently free from all pain, she departed in this place.
Nashville Republican. (Thurs., March 3, 1836)

Cheatham, Mr. George W. Died in Nashville on the 24th inst. He was
buried on his 40th Birthday.
Nashville Whig. (Thurs., Feb. 29, 1844)

Cheatham, Capt. John L. Died in Springfield, Robinson County on the
12th inst.
National Banner & Nashville Daily Advertiser. (Sat., Oct. 19, 1833)

Cheatham, Dr. L. M. Died in Carthage.
Natioanl Banner & Nashville Whig. (Sat., Aug. 26, 1826)

Cheatham, Mrs. P. Of Nashville. Wife of Peter Cheatham. Died at
Randolph, Tennessee.
Nashville Whig. (Fri., Jan. 11, 1839)

Cheatham, Miss Frances A. Daughter of the late Col. A. Cheatham in
the 18th year of her age. Died in Robinson County. On the 24th
ult.
National Banner & Nashville Whig. (Sat., June 2, 1827)

Cheatham, Mrs. Sarah. Consort of Mr. A. Cheatham. Died on the 14th
inst.
Nashville Republican. (Mon., Dec. 19, 1836)

Cheatham, Mrs. Sarah. Consort of Mr. A. Cheatham died on the 14th inst.
National Banner & Nashville Whig. (Dec. 19, 1836)

Cheatham, Mrs. Susannah. Consort of Col. Archer Cheatham. Died at Springfield on the 12th inst. leaves a husband and five children.
Impartial Review and Cumberland Repository. (Feb. 25, 1808 Thurs.)

Cherry, Mrs. Frances E. P. Consort of Col. W. W. Cherry in the 24th year of her age. Died in Rankin Holmes County, Miss. on the 9th of Sept.
National Banner & Nashville Daily Republican Advertiser. (Monday, September 23, 1833)

Cherry, Jeremiah. (Printer) Son of J. Cherry Esq. Postmaster at Columbia, Tenn. Died in Nashville on Sunday the 16th inst. (Obituary, April 29th)
The Christian Record. (Sat., April 22, 1848)

Cherry, John C. In the 28th year of his age. Died in Monroe County, Mi. On Friday the 13th day of June at 6 O'clock.
National Banner & Nashville Daily Advertiser. (Sat., July 5, 1834)

Cherry, Mr. Kenneth. Died in Maury County.
National Banner & Nashville Whig. (Sat., Jan. 10, 1829)

Chester, Mr. John. Aged 60 years. Died in Hawkins County.
National Banner & Nashville Daily Advertiser. (Mon., Nov. 5, 1832)

Chester, Mr. Richard M. Died in Jackson.
National Banner. (April 7, 1826)

Chesnut, Mr. Samuel. Died at Manchester, Ky. Was killed at a fight at a horse race.
National Banner & Nashville Daily Advertiser. (Thurs., Feb. 23, 1832)

Cheves, Mr. Willie. Died in Nashville on Tuesday night last, formerly of Dinwiddle County, Va.
National Banner & Nashville Whig. (Fri., Jan. 22, 1830)

Chew, Dr. Thomas S. Aged 28 years. Died in Natchez.
National Banner & Nashville Whig. (Sat., Aug. 26, 1826)

Chilcutt, Peter. Died in Shelbyville, Tenn. of Cholera.
National Banner & Nashville Daily Advertiser. (Thurs., July 11, 1833)

Child, George. Of Stonington, Commander. Died in the wreck of the Steamboat Lexington.
Daily Republican Banner. (Friday, Jan. 31, 1840)

Childs, Miss Mary Ann. Late of Lynn, Mass. Died at Jackson, Western District.
National Banner & Nashville Daily Advertiser. (Thurs., Aug. 16, 1832)

Childers, Hasten M. Esq. Died on the 12th day of Dec. last of the Parish of Carrol, Louisana.
National Banner & Nashville Whig. (Wed., June 17, 1835)

Childress, Capt. Anderson. Died at Murfreesborough on Wednesday evening last.
National Banner & Nashville Whig. (Sat., May 12, 1827)

Childress, Mrs. Emily. Wife of Edward Childress, age 44 years. Died in the vicinity of Nashville on Wednesday the 18th inst.
Nashville Whig. (Thurs., Sept. 19, 1844)

Childress, Mrs. Drusilla. Wife of Dr. Stephen Childress age 19. Died in Brownsville.
National Banner & Nashville Whig. (Fri., July 18, 1828)

Childress, George. Son of George C. Childress Esq. Age 15 months. Died in the vicinity of Nashville on the 22nd inst.
National Banner & Nashville Daily Advertiser. (Thurs., July 24, 1834)

Childress, Col. George C. Formerly of Nashville. Died in Galveston, Texas Oct. 9th.
Nashville Whig. (Fri., Oct. 29, 1841)

Childress, John Esq. Marshall of this district. Died on yesterday.
Nashville Gazette. (Sept. 11, 1819)

Childress, John. Only child of John C. Childress Esq. Died in Nashville on the 27th ult. in the 4th year of his age.
National Banner & Nashville Daily Advertiser. (Mon., April 1, 1833)

Childress, John A. Died at Florence, Ala. On Sat. the 6th inst.
National Banner & Nashville Whig. (Thurs., Nov. 11, 1830)

Childress, John Albert. Only son of Thomas Childress Esq. Formely of this City. Died at Florence, Ala. on the Sat. Nov. 6th in the 22nd year of his age.
National Banner & Nashville Whig. (Monday, Nov. 15, 1830)

Childress, Mrs. Margaret. Consort of George E. Childress Esq., editor of the Nashville Banner. Died in Nashville on Monday, July 27th.
National Banner & Nashville Whig. (Wed., July 29, 1835)

Childress, Mrs. Martha. Consort of Thomas Childress Esq. Formely of Nashville. Died in Florence, Ala.
Nashville Republican. (Tues., July 19, 1836)

Childress, Mrs. Martha. Consort of Mr. Thomas Childress. Died on the 9th inst. in Florence, Ala. Age 51 years 5 months and 24 days. (Obituary)
Nashville Union. (Tues., July 19, 1836)

Childress, Mrs. Martha. Consort of Mr. Thomas Childress. Died in Florence, Ala. on the 9th July, age 51 years. 5 months and 24 days.
National Banner & Nashville Whig. (July 20, 1836)

Childress, Mrs. Mary G. Consort of Rufus Childress Esq. Died in Maury County on the 24th ult. in the 23rd year of her age. (Obituary)
National Banner & Nashville Daily Advertiser. (Fri., Nov. 2, 1832)

Childress, Mrs. Nancy. Died at the residence of M. S. Pitcher, Summer Street.
Nashville Whig. (Monday Oct. 26, 1840)

Childress, Mrs. Rebecca. Daughter of the Rev. Obadiah Jennings, deceased formely of Nashville. Died at Tuscumbia, Ala. on the 16th in the 30th year of her age.
The Christian Record. (Sat., Jan. 22, 1848)

Childress, Mr. Reps O. Age 50 years. Died in Lincoln County.
National Banner & Nashville Whig. (Sat., Sept. 16, 1826)

Childress, Mr. Stephen. Late of Williamson. Died in Tipton County. Aged 64 years.
National Banner & Nashville Whig. (Sat., Sept. 13, 1828)

Childress, Col. William G. Aged about 55 years. Died in Williamson County on the 22nd inst.
Nashville Whig. (Thurs., June 25, 1846)

Chilton, Rev. John. In the thirty-sixth year of his age. Died in Overton County on the 5th day of Sept. 1840.
Daily Republican Banner. (Sat., Sept. 26, 1840)

Chilton, Rev. John. A resident of Jackson, Tenn. Died in Overton
County, aged 36 years.
Nashville Whig. (Oct. 16, 1840)

Chinn, Mr. David. Died in Bourbon County, Ky.
National Banner & Nashville Whig. (Sat., May 19,1827)

Chinn, Miss Jane. Daughter of R. H. Chinn Esq. Died at Lexington,
Ky. of Cholera.
National Banner & Nashville Daily Advertiser. (Wed., July 3, 1833)

Chisnam, Mr. Isaac. In the 28th year of his age. Died in Bedford
County, Tenn.
National Banner & Nashville Whig. (Fri., Oct. 31, 1834)

Chisolm, Mr. John. Aged 91 years. A native of Va. Died in Lauderdale
County, Ala.
National Banner & Nashville Whig. (Sat., Oct. 25, 1828)

Chisum, Mr. John. Died in Hardeman County, Tenn.
National Banner & Nashville Whig. (Wed., Oct. 22, 1834)

Chitton, Mrs. Sarah W. Consort of William Chitton Jun. Esq. Died
on the 22nd of April of Overton County.
The Union. (Tues., July 4, 1837)

Choffin, John. Died in Amelia City.
Nashville Republican and State Gazette. (Sat., August 13, 1831
No. 40 Vol. 7)

Cholera. List of deathin Cincinnati from Cholera on Page 2.
National Banner & Nashville Daily Advertiser. (Mon., Oct. 29, 1832)

Cholera. List of death in Cincinnati from Cholera on Page 3.
National Banner & Nashville Daily Advertiser. (Tues., Oct. 30, 1832)

Cholera. List of Death in Cincinnati from Cholera on page 2.
National Banner & Nashville Daily Advertiser. (Wed., Oct. 31, 1832)

Cholera. List of death in Cincinnati from Cholera on Page 2.
National Banner & Nashville Daily Advertiser. (Tues., Nov. 6, 1832)

Cholwell, Mr. Jacob. Aged 70 years. Died on the 12th July in Red
Hook Dutchess County, New York.
National Banner & Nashville Whig. (Fri., Aug. 21, 1835)

Cholwell, Robert. Son of the late Jacob Cholwell. Aged 21. Died
at Red Hook Dutchess County, N. Y.
National Banner & Nashville Whig. (Fri., Feb. 3, 1837)

Choteau, Mr. Lewis P. Sub agent formely of St. Louis, Mo. Died at
the Western Creek Agency.
National Banner & Nashville Whig. (Monday, July 4, 1831)

Chrisman, Mr. Louis. Died in Tazewell.
National Banner & Nashville Daily Advertiser. (Fri., March 29, 1833)

Christian, Mr. Aaron. Aged 36 years. Died in this County on Sunday
last.
National Banner (May 20, 1826)

Christian, Gilbert Col. Died on the 14 instant, Col. Gilbert Christian, of Sullivan County, of a fever which he contracted while with
Gen. Sevier, in the Cherokee nation; and on the next day was interred
with military and masonic honors. He was a citizen of unblemished
character, and a brave, prudent steady officer. A grateful country
will long retail a sense of his worth, and lament his loss.
Knoxville Gazette. (Sat., Nov. 24, 1793)

Christian, Dr. Wyatt. Died in Memphis on the 15th inst.
Nashville Whig. (Tues., Sept. 22, 1846)

Christmas, Mrs. Abigail. In her 70th years. Died on the 1st of
June in Williamson County.
National Banner & Nashville Whig. (Sat., Aug. 2, 1828)

Christopher, Mr. Ebenezer. Died at Louisville, Ky.
National Banner & Nashville Whig. (Sat., Dec. 9, 1826)

Christopher, Henry. Died at Versilles, Ky. 14 miles from Lexington
of Cholera.
National Banner & Nashville Whig. (Friday, Sept. 4, 1835)

Christy, John. Died was shot dead in the street of Smithland by
John T. Wooldridge.
Daily Republican Banner. (Thurs., July 30, 1840)

Christy, Miss Louisa. Daughter of Major William Christy age 11 years.
Died St. Charles, Mo.
National Banner & Nashville Daily Advertiser. (Sat., Aug. 24, 1833)

Chunn, Mrs. Martha. Aged 54. Died in Morgan County, Ala.
National Banner & Nashville Whig. (Sat., Sept. 2, 1826)

Clack, Mr. James. Aged 78 years and 4 months. Died on the 30th of
Oct. 1834 at the residence of Dr. Wm. F. Smith in Lincoln County, Tenn.
A soldier in the Revolutionary war.
National Banner & Nashville Whig. (Wed., Nov. 19, 1834)

Clack, Maj. John. A Soldier of the Revolution. Died in Giles County.
National Banner & Nashville Daily Advertiser. (Tues., Jan. 22, 1831)

Clack, Spencer Esq. Aged 86 years. Died near Sevierville on the 9th
inst.
National Banner & Nashville Daily Advertiser. (Mon., July 23, 1832)

Clark, Spencer Esq. Died near Seviersville, Tenn. Aged 86.
Nashville Republican and State Gazette. (Vol. 8 Monday, July 30,
1832 No. 34)

Claiborne, Anastasia. Second daughter of Thomas Claiborne Esq.
Died in Nashville on Thursday 14th inst.
Nashville Whig. (Sat., July 16, 1842)

Claiborne, Wm. C. C. Late governor of Louisiana. Died lately at
New Orleans when he died was a senator in congress.
The Nashville Whig and Tenn. Advertiser. (Dec. 15, 1817)

Clairborne, Mrs. Hannah. Consort of Thomas Claiborne, Esq. of
Davidson County. Died on Thursday evening the 31st March.
Impartial Review and Cumberland Repository. (Thurs., April 7, 1808)

Claiborne, Mrs. Isabella Charlotte. The consort of Doct. Thomas
Augustine Claiborne, late of the navy of the United States. Died on
Wednesday the 12th inst. Age 26 years near Natchez.
The Nashville Whig. (July 2, 1816)

Claiborne, Mr. William F. L. Died in Nashville.
National Banner and Nashville Whig. (Vol. 19 No. 1275 Monday,
June 20, 1831)

Claiborne, Mr. William F. L. Died near this place.
Nashville Republican and State Gazette. (Tues., June 21, 1831)

Clapp, Mr. Barney. Died at New Orleans.
National Banner & Nashville Daily Advertiser. (Feb. 2, 1832)

Clark, Mr. Barhan A. (Broker) Died near Boston by drowning when the Steamboat Bunker Hill was wrecker by the wind.
National Banner & Nashville Daily Advertiser. (Sat., June 30, 1832)

Clark, Mrs. C. Aged 100 years. Died in Granville County, N. C.
National Banner & Nashville Daily Advertiser. (Tues., Feb. 11, 1834)

Clark, Dr. Cains F. Died in Henry County, Tenn. Late of Denwiddle County, Va.
National Banner & Nashville Whig. (Fri., April 10, 1835)

Clark, Capt. Daniel. Died on Thursday night last at Talbots Hotel.
The Nashville Gazette. (Sat., March 31, 1821)

Clark, Edwin T. Esq. Attorney at Law. Died a Helena A. T. Was killed in a fight with a knife.
National Banner & Nashville Whig. (Fri., Jan. 1st.1836)

Clark, Mrs. Elizabeth. Died in Lexington, Ky.
National Banner (Sat., May 16, 1829)

Clark, Mr. George S. Died in Robinson County.
National Banner & Nashville Daily Advertiser. (Tues., June 11, 1833)

Clark, Mrs. Harriet. Wife of Gen. William Clark. Died in St. Louis.
National Banner & Nashville Daily Advertiser. (Sat., Jan. 7, 1832)

Clark, Mrs. Harriet J. Consort of Mr. Edward T. Clark. Esq. Died at Helena, Ark.
National Banner & Nashville Whig. (Mon., Dec. 29, 1834)

Clark, His Excellency James. Governor of Kentucky. Died on Tuesday the 27th inst. He was about 55 or 56 years old.
Daily Republican Banner. (Mon., Sept. 2, 1839)

Clark, James. Governor of the State of Kentucky. Died at his residence in Frankfort on Tuesday the 27th inst.
Nashville Union. (Wed., Sept. 4, 1839)

Clark, Gen. John. Died at Pensacola, Ha. on the 12th inst. Formerly the Governor of Georgia.
National Banner & Nashville Daily Advertiser. (Sat., Nov. 24, 1832)

Clark, Hon. Joshua G. Chancellor of the State of Mississippi. Died at Natchez.
National Banner & Nashville Whig. (Sat., Aug. 9, 1828)

Clark, Rev. L. F. Professor of Chemistry at East Tennessee University Died in Knoxville on the 25th inst.
Nashville Whig. (Fri., Sept. 4, 1840)

Clark, Miss Margaret. Died in Nashville.
National Banner & Nashville Daily Advertiser. (Tues., Jan. 22, 1833)

Clark, Matthew Esq. Aged 70 years. Died in Franklin County, Ky.
National Banner & Nashville Whig. (Mon., Nov. 29, 1830)

Clark, Nathan. Forman of the Coining department of the branch Mint. Died in New Orleans of Yellow Fever.
Daily Republican Banner. (Wed., Sept. 11, 1839)

Clark, Mr. Newton C. Cashier of the Branch bank of the State in Shelbyville. Died in Shelbyville on Tuesday night last 16th.
The Christian Record. (Sat., March 20, 1847)

Clark, Mr. Thomas. Died near Campbell's Station East Tennessee.
National Banner & Nashville Daily Advertiser. (Mon., April 1833 the 22nd.)

Clark, Thomas Esq. Aged 61 years. Died in Lincoln County, Tenn. on Monday the 26th ult.
National Banner & Nashville Whig. (Wed., March 9, 1836)

Clark, Mr. Thomas. Father of James P. Clark of Nashville. Died recently at his residence in Kingston, East Tennessee.
The Christian Record. (Sat., Oct. 30, 1847)

Clark, Mr. William. Died in Madison County, Ky.
National Banner. (March 24, 1826)

Clark, William B. Late of Paris, Tenn. Died at Vicksburge, Miss.
National Banner & Nasvhille Daily Advertiser. (Wed., Feb. 8, 1832)

Clark, Dr. Welma. Died at New Orleans.
National Banner & Nashville Daily Advertiser. (Thurs., Sept. 12, 1833)

Clarke, Mr. James. Died in Nashville on Sunday the 20th inst.
National Banner & Nashville Daily Advertiser. (Mon., May 21, 1832)

Clarke, Dr. Uselma. Died in New Orleans.
National Banner & Nashville Daily Advertiser. (Sat., Aug. 24, 1833)

Clarkson, Mrs. Wife of Peter Clarkson Esq. Died in Bourbon County, Ky.
National Banner & Nashville Whig. (Sat., May 19, 1827)

Clauncey, Commodore Isaac. One of the Senior Officers of the Navy. Died his death announced by the Washington Papers.
Daily Republican Banner. (Wed., Feb. 12, 1840)

Clay, Mrs. Bethenia H. Consort of Mr. Joseph W. Clay. Died near Nashville Aug. 31st. (Obituary)
Nashville Whig. (Wed., Sept. 12, 1838)

Clay, Gen. Green. Died in Madison County, Ky.
National Banner & Nashville Whig. (Sat., Nov. 29, 1828)

Clay, Henry M. Son of J. W. Clay. Died this morning at 2 O'clock.
Daily Republican Banner. (Tues., May 12, 1840)

Clay, Mrs. Julia. Wife of Henry Clay, Jr. Esq. of Lexington. Died in Louisville at the residence of her mother Mrs. Prather.
Nashville Whig. (Fri., Feb. 21, 1840)

Clay, Mathew Esq. Died in Lawrence County, Ala.
National Banner & Nashville Whig. (Sat., Feb. 24, 1827)

Clay, Mrs. Sophia. Wife of Porter Clay Esq. Died at Frankfort, Ky.
National Banner. (Sat., Oct. 3, 1829)

Clay, Mrs. Sophia M. Consort of Mr. Henry M. Clay, Esq. Died in Nashville on Thursday evening.
Nashville Whig. (Sat., Oct. 12, 1844)

Clay, Mr. Woodson. Died on Tuesday evening last, at the residence of Nathan Ewing Esq. in this town Mr. Woodson Clay. A native of Lunenburg County, Va. aged 27 years.
Nashville Whig. (Aug. 23, 1824)

Claypoole, Abraham G. Esq. Died in Natchez.
National Banner. (Sat., Sept. 12, 1829(

Clayton, Mrs. Caroline. Wife of Mr. David Clayton. Died at Columbia, Tenn.
Nashville Whig. (Mon., Sept. 21, 1840)

Clayton, Mrs. Elizabeth. Wife of Rev. Sampson Clayton. Died near
Jasper, aged 28 years.
National Banner & Nashville Daily Advertiser. (Mon., Nov. 12, 1832)

Clayton, Mrs. Mary W. Wife of Alexander M. Clayton, Esq. Died at
Clarksville, Montgomery County on the 20th inst.
National Banner & Nashville Daily Advertiser. (Sat., July 28, 1832)

Clayton, Sam'l, Esq. Died near Lynchburg, Va.
Nashville Republican and State Gazette. (Thurs., Oct. 6, 1831 No. 63
Vol. 7)

Clements, Mr. Eprham. Died in CinCinnati.
National Banner & Nashville Whig. (Sat., May 12, 1827)

Clements, Mr. Jeremiah. Died at Danville, Ky.
National Banner & Nashville Whig. (July 1st, 1826)

Clements, Mr. Joshua. Died in Mobile, Ala.
National Banner & Nashville Daily Advertiser. (Fri., Sept. 20, 1833)

Clemm, Mr. James. Died in Franklin.
National Banner & Nashville Whig. (June 24, 1826)

Clemments, Joel B. M. D. Died at Marianna, Jackson County, Florida
on the 19th ult, in the 23rd year of his age. He was the son of
Maj. Benjamin Clemments of Fayetteville, Tenn.
National Banner & Nashville Whig. (Mon., Oct. 27, 1834)

Cleveland, Mrs. Mary. Died in Fayettville County, Ky. Wife of Mr.
Eli Cleveland.
National Banner & Nashville Whig. (June 17, 1826)

Cliborn, Mr. Shelton. Age 41 years. Died Knox County.
National Banner & Nashville Daily Advertiser. (Mon., Feb. 27, 1832)

Clifford, Mr. Patrick. Died yesterday in this town suddenly.
National Banner & Nashville Whig. (Sat., Oct. 4, 1828)

Clinton, Hon. Dewitt. Governor of the State of New York. Died in
his residence at New York.
National Banner & Nashville Whig. (Sat., March 11, 1828)

Clopper, Mr. James. Aged 22. Died in this town on Tuesday 25th ult.
A native of Philadelphia.
National Banner & Nashville Whig. (Sat., Dec. 6, 1828)

Clopton, Mr. James W. Formerly a citizen of Nashville. Died in Memphis
on the 29th ulto.
Nashville Whig. (Tuesday, Aug. 9, 1842)

Cloud, Mrs. Polly. Wife of Rev. Dr. Cloud. Died in Lexington, Ky.
National Banner & Nashville Whig. (Tues., Feb. 2, 1830)

Clowes, Rev. Timothy L. L. D. Aged 60 years. Died at Hempstead, L.I.
on the 16th inst.
The Politician & Weekly Nashville Whig. (Fri., July 16, 1847)

Cluis, Colonel J. J. A native of France in the 61st year of his age.
Died in Mobile, Ala.
National Banner & Nashville Daily Advertiser. (Thurs., Oct. 31, 1833)

Coalter, Mrs. Mary. Died at Florence, Ala. Wife of Col. George
Coalter.
National Banner, March 10, 1826)

Cobb, Mr. David. Died in Florence, Ala.
National Banner & Nashville Whig. (Sat., July 14, 1827)

Cobb, Mrs. Elizabeth. Died at Tuscumbia, Ala.
National Banner & Nashville Daily Advertiser. (Tues., Nov. 19, 1833)

Cobb, Mrs. Mary. Wife of Mr. O. B. Cobb. Died at Millkins Bend, La.
National Banner & Nashville Daily Advertiser. (Wed., Aug. 20, 1834)

Cobb, Lieut, Samuel K. Of the U. S. Infantry. Died in New Orleans
on the 11th ult.
National Banner & Nashville Daily Advertiser. (Mon., Feb. 17, 1834)

Cobb, Sarah. Wife of Harvey Cobb, aged 30 years. Died in Nashville.
National Banner & Nashville Whig. (Wed., June 24, 1835)

Cobb, Hon. Thomas W. Died in Georgia. Judge of the Ocumles Circuit
and the late Senator in the Congress of the United States.
National Banner & Nashville Whig. (Tues., March 2, 1830)

Cobbs, Mr. Jas. Died in McMinn County.
National Banner & Nashville Whig. (Wed., March 16, 1831)

Cocke, Mrs. Elizabeth. Only daughter of John Pope late Governor of
Arkansas. Died near Springfield, Ky. on the 1st of May.
National Banner & Nashville Whig. (Fri., July 3, 1835)

Cocke, Mrs. Mary. Wife of John W. Cocke Esq. Died in Little Rock,
Ark. at the residence of Judge Ringo on the 5th of Feb. daughter of
Maj. W. Armstrong, formely of Nashville, Tenn. (Obituary)
The Christian Record. (Sat., March 13, 1847)

Cocke, Stephen Esq. Died in Montgomery County.
National Banner. (Sat., May 30, 1829)

Cocke, Mr. Thomas W. Died in Louisville, Ky.
National Banner & Nashville Whig. (Monday, Sept. 26, 1831)

Cockerill, John. Aged 80 years. Died in Nashville on the 10th inst
April.
Nashville Republican. (Thurs., May 10, 1837)

Cockerill, William N. Died in Nashville on Thursday last. aged 42
years.
Daily Republican Banner. (Wed., Dec. 27, 1837)

Cockran, Mr. Jacob. Aged 46 years. Died in Giles County.
National Banner & Nashville Whig. (Mon., Oct. 4, 1830)

Cockran, William Edward. Infant son of Capt. E. A. Cochran. Died
in Murfreesboro.
National Banner & Nashville Daily Advertiser. (Mon., March 31, 1834)

Cockrane, Mr. David Y. Died at Little Rock, Ark.
National Banner & Nashville Whig. (Sat., March 10, 1827)

Cockrell, Mrs. Elizabeth B. Died on Wednesday the 7th inst. at the
residence of Mr. R. R. Royal, Tuscumbia, Ala. Mrs. Elizabeth B.
Cockrell consort of Mr. John Cockrell in the 41st year of her age.
Nashville Whig. (Jan. 26, 1824)

Cockrell, Mrs. Harriet. Consort of Maj. John Cockrell. Died on the
6th inst. near Tuscumbia, Ala.
Daily Republican Banner (Wed., March 13, 1839)

Cockrill, Mr. James. Died in Madison County, Tenn.
National Banner & Nashville Whig. (Sat., Sept. 9, 1826)

Cockrill, John. Aged 80 years. Died at Nashville on the 10th April.
He was born near Winchester, Virginia.
National Banner & Nashville Whig. (Wed., May 10, 1837)

Cockrum, Mr. Jesse. Died in Hardeman County, Tenn.
National Banner & Nashville Whig. (Wed., Nov. 19, 1834)

Cockrum, John Y. Esq. Died in Hardeman County.
National Banner & Nashville Whig. (Fri., Nov. 18, 1831)

Coe, Gen. Levin H. Died at Memphis on the 10th inst.
Nashville Tree Whig and Weekly Commercial Register. (Fri., Aug. 23, 1850 Page 328)

Coffee, Private B. F. With Company D. Died - was killed in the battle of Montrey with the Mexicans on Sept. 21.
Nashville Whig. (Sat., Oct. 24, 1846)

Coffee, Gen. John. A Distinguished officer in the last war. Died near Florence, Ala.
National Banner & Nashville Daily Advertiser. (Thurs., July 11, 1833)

Coffee, John Charles. Infant son of Mr. Joshua D. Coffee. Died in Florence, Ala.
National Banner & Nashville Whig. (Fri., Nov. 14, 1834)

Coffee, Mrs. Mary. Wife of Thomas Coffee. Died in Lauderdale County, Ala.
National Banner & Nashville Daily Advertiser. (Mon., Aug. 27, 1832)

Coffey, Miss Elizabeth. Wife of Rev. Elijah Coffey. Died in Memphis.
National Banner & Nashville Daily Advertiser. (Mon., June 17, 1833)

Coffin, Mr. Robert S. The Boston Bard. Died in Rawley, Mass. On the 7th ult.
National Banner & Nashville Whig. (Sat., June 9, 1827)

Coffman, Mr. Amos E. Died in Logan County, Ky.
National Banner & Nashville Whig. (Mon., Jan. 5, 1835)

Coffman, George. Died of Cholera at the residence of Dr. Green four miles from Florence, Ala. He was from Logan County, Ky.
National Banner & Nashville Whig. (Wed., Oct. 1, 1834)

Coffman, Mr. Jefferson, Died in Logan County, Ky.
National Banner & Nashville Whig. (Mon., Aug. 22, 1831)

Coffman, Mrs. M. Died in Logan County, Ky. Wife of Mr. Adam Coffman.
National Banner & Nashville Whig. (Sat., Feb. 23, 1828)

Coghill, Mrs. Susan Jane. Consort of Frederick Coghill. Died at Hernando, Miss. on the 6th inst.
Nashville Whig. (Fri., July 23, 1841)

Cohea, Mr. Alexander. Died at Monticello.
National Banner & Nashville Whig. (Sat., Sept. 1, 1827)

Cohen, E. A. Of Md. Died in New Orleans of Yellow Fever.
Daily Republican Banner. (Wed., Sept. 27, 1837)

Coker, Mr. William. Aged 19 years. son of Mr. Joel Coker. Died near Knoxville.
National Banner & Nashville Whig. (Mon., Dec. 12, 1830)

Colbert, Levi. One of the eldest and most influential of the Chicasaw Chiefs. Died in the Chickasaw Nation.
National Banner & Nashville Daily Advertiser. (Thurs., Aug. 14, 1834)

Colbert, Martin. Wealthy and influential member of the Chickasaw tribe of Indians. Died in De Soto County, Miss. Aged 45 years.
Nashville Whig. (Wed., Sept. 16, 1840)

Colby, Mr. Z. Died at Batavia, Ohio.
National Banner, (March 24, 1826)

Colden, Cadwaller D. Esq. Died in New York in the 65th year of his age.
National Banner & Nashville Daily Advertiser. (Mon., Feb. 24, 1834)

Coldwell, Mrs. Mary. Consort of Mr. Thomas H. Coldwell. Died in Shelbyville.
Nashville Whig. (Thurs., May 7, 1846)

Coldwell, N. E. Died in Shelbyville, Tenn. of Cholera.
National Banner & Nashville Daily Advertiser. (Thurs., July 11, 1833)

Cole, Mr. Supt. of the Steamboat Mohawk lying at the landing. Died of Cholera in Memphis.
National Banner & Nashville Daily Advertiser. (Wed., Nov. 14, 1832)

Cole, David. From Lincoln County. Died at the Tenn. State Prison of Cholera.
National Banner & Nashville Whig. (Fri., Aug. 14, 1835)

Cole, Mr. John. Well known as an enterprising dealer in books. Died at New Orleans on the 25th of March.
National Banner & Nashville Whig. (Tues., May 11, 1830)

Cole, Mr. Jonas. Firm of Cole & Snow. Died near Boston by drowning when the Boat Bunker Hill was wrecked by the wind.
National Banner & Nashville Daily Advertiser. (Sat., June 30, 1832)

Colelough, Caesar Esq. of Montgomery, Ala. Died in Knoxville, Tenn.
National Banner & Nashville Daily Advertiser. (Mon. Aug. 26, 1833)

Coleman, Mrs. Elizabeth. Aged 60 years. Died in Nashville on last Saturday evening. she came from Cincinnati about 18 months ago.
The Union. (Sat., Aug. 20, 1836)

Coleman, Mrs. Elizabeth. Died recently in Nashville. Aged 60 years.
National Banner & Nashville Whig. (Mon., Aug. 22, 1836)

Coleman, Mr. John. Aged 28 late of Kentucky. Died in Limestone County, Ala.
National Banner & Nashville Whig. (Sat., Sept. 2, 1826)

Coleman, John Thomas. Infant son of George W. Coleman. Died in Nashville on the 6th inst.
National Banner & Nashville Daily Advertiser. (Fri., Dec. 6, 1833)

Coleman, Mr. John W. Aged 30. Died in Woodford County, Ky.
National Banner & Nashville Daily Advertiser. (Wed., Sept. 12, 1832)

Coleman, Mrs. Mary. Died in Madison County, Ala.
Republican and State Gazette. (Thursday, May 19, 1831 No. 3 Vol. 7)

Coleman, Mrs. Mary. Aged 64. Died in Madison County.
National Banner & Nashville Whig. (Fri., May 20, 1831)

Coleman, Mrs. Sarah. Died in Woodford County, Ky.
National Banner & Nashville Whig. (Sat., Oct. 6, 1827)

Coleman, Thomas Esq. Died in Washington, Ala.
National Banner & Nashville Whig. (Sat., April 14, 1827)

Coleman, William Henry Esq. Died in New York one of the properitors of the evening Post and son of the late editor aged 33.
National Banner & Nashville Whig. (Thurs., Aug. 12, 1830)

Coles, Col. Isaac A. of Va. He was a member elect to the next
Legislature. Died on the 21st in the County of Albermarle.
Nashville Whig. (Mon., Aug. 9, 1841)

Colladay, J. W. Aged 33. Died last evening.
Nashville Whig. (Tues., Oct. 3, 1843)

Colland, Mr. George W. Died at Port Gibson, Miss.
National Banner & Nashville Whig. (Sat., Dec. 9, 1826)

Collier, Mr. James. Aged 76. Died near Triana, Ala.
National Banner & Nashville Daily Advertiser. (Mon., Sept. 10, 1832)

Collier, Mrs. Mary. Consort of John C. Collier Esq. Died at Charlotte
on Saturday 27th of March of Consumption.
Nashville Whig. (Mon., April 5, 1841)

Collier, Mary B. Infant daughter of Joseph T. Collier. Died in
Covington, Tenn.
National Banner & Nashville Whig. (Wed., Nov. 14, 1834)

Collier, Mrs. Mary W. Consort of Mr. Thomas Collier, aged 66. Died
in Charlotte, Dickson County on the 22nd inst.
National Banner & Nashville Daily Advertiser. (Wed., Jan. 30, 1833)

Collier, Mr. Micheal. Died in Shelby County, Ky.
National Banner, (June 10, 1826)

Collier, Mrs. Sarah W. Age 24. Wife of Dr. Jas. B. Collier. Died in
Limestone County, Ala.
National Banner & Nashville Whig. (Aug. 5, 1826)

Collier, Mr. Robert. Aged 26 years. Died in Dickson County near
Charlotte on the 17th inst.
National Banner & Nashville Whig. (Fri., May 29, 1835)

Collier, Mrs. Susannah. Aged 80. Died in McMinn County.
National Banner & Nashville Daily Advertiser. (Wed., Nov. 28, 1832)

Collier, Mr. Thomas. In the 73rd year of his age. Died near Charlotte
Dickerson County, Tenn.
Nashville Whig. (Fri., Oct. 5, 1838)

Collier, Mr. Thomas W. In the 39th year of his age. Died in
Charlotte on the 12th inst.
Nashville Whig. (Sat., Feb. 18, 1843)

Collin, Rev. Nicholas D. D. Rector of the Swedish Churches in
Pennsylvania. Died in Philadelphia.
National Banner & Nashville Whig. (Fri., Oct. 21, 1831)

Collins, Mr. Dillard. For many years the Doorkeeper for the House of
Representatives. Died in Wilkinson County, Mi. on the 27th.
National Banner & Nashville Whig. (Thurs., Aug. 19, 1830)

Collins, Private Henry. Company H. First Regiment, Tenn. Volunteers.
Died was killed in the Battle of Monterey with the Mexicans on Sept.
21st, 1846.
Nashville Whig. (Sat., Oct. 24, 1846)

Collins, Mrs. Margeret. In the 60th year of her age. Died in Washington of Apoplexy.
National Banner & Nashville Daily Advertiser. (Mon., April 2, 1832)

Collins, Mrs. Martha. Consort of Brother E. T. Collins of Franklin.
Died on the evening of the 14th inst.
The Western Weekly Review. (Fri., April 26, 1833 Franklin, Tenn.)

Collins, Mr. Peter. In the 73rd year of his age. Died in Henderson
County.
Nashville Whig. (Tues., April 21, 1846)

Collins, Mrs. Virginia W. Consort of Mr. John Collins. Died in
Nashville Yesterday (Monday)
Nashville Whig. (Tues., May 21, 1844)

Collins, Mr. William. Died in Louisville, Ky.
National Banner & Nashville Whig. (Monday, Aug. 16, 1830)

Colquhoun, John. Died in Sullivan County, Mr. John Colquhoun of
Richmond, Virginia.
Knoxville Gazette. (Thurs., Jan. 16, 1794)

Coltart, Mrs. Janet. Wife of John Coltart of Columbia and daughter
of Capt. James Maxwell. Died at the residence of her father in the
County.
National Banner. (March 24, 1826)

Colville, Col. Samuel. Died at Athens, Tenn.
National Banner & Nashville Whig. (Thurs., Sept. 16, 1830)

Colville, Mr. Silas C. Died at Shawneetown Bend, Fanin County, Texas
on the 9th of July.
Nashville Whig. (Tues., Aug. 20, 1844)

Colville, Young Esq. Died at Athens. Aged 34 years.
National Banner & Nashville Whig. (Sat., Dec. 16, 1826)

Colvin, Mr. John R. Died at Washington City.
National Banner. (April 28, 1826)

Combs, Mrs. Elizabeth. Died in Bedford, County, Tenn.
Republican Banner (Wed., April 11, 1832)

Combs, John. Died in Louisville, Ky. On the 18th of Cholera.
National Banner & Nashville Daily Advertiser. (Mon., Oct. 22,1832)

Comestock, Jesse. Of Providence, Clerk. Died in the wreck of the
Steamboat Lexington.
Daily Republican Banner. (Friday, Jan. 31, 1840)

Comfort, Mrs. Martha Ann. Wife of the Rev. Daniel Comfort. President
of the Mississippi College. Died in Clinton, Mississippi.
National Banner & Nashville Daily Advertiser. (Mon., July 21, 1834)

Compton, Mr. Thomas. Died in New Orleans.
National Banner & Nashville Daily Advertiser. (Fri., May 16, 1834)

Condon, Mrs. Barbara. Wife of James Condon Esq. of this County.
Died on Tuesday last of a few days illness (Cholera)
Nashville Whig. (Aug. 30, 1824)

Condon, Elizabeth Adams. Daughter of James Condon, esq. of this
County. Died in the 10th year of her age on Tuesday last.
Nashville Whig. (Sept. 27, 1824)

Condon, Mr. James Junior. 1815. Died on the afternoon of the 27th
inst. (May 27, 1815) Mr. James Condon Junior of this town (Nashville)
age 22 years.
Whig. (May 30, 1815)

Condon, Mr. James. In the 70th year of his age. Died in Davidson
County on the 30th.
Daily Republican Banner. (Tuesday, Sept. 5, 1837)

Condon, Mr. Tully Edward. Died in this town.
National Banner & Nashville Whig. (Sat., Feb. 9, 1828)

Conger, Mr. Felix. Son of Rev. Isaac Conger. Aged 22 years. Died
in Lincoln County, Tenn.
National Banner & Nashville Whig. (Wed., Nov. 19, 1834)

Conger, Mr. Felix. Aged 22, son of Rev. Isaac Conger. Died in
Lincoln County.
National Banner & Nashville Whig. (Wed., Nov. 26, 1834)

Conn, Mrs. Frances. Died Bourbon County, Ky. Aged 49.
National Banner & Nashville Whig. (Sat., Oct. 7, 1826)

Connally, Mrs. Mary. Consort of Mr. John Connally. Died in Madison
County, Ala.
National Banner & Nashville Daily Advertiser. (Mon., Sept. 9, 1833)

Connell, Giles. Fatal effect of lighting. On the 30th inst. about
3 O'clock P.M. a fatal accident occured in Robertson County. Mr.
Giles Connell, while in the act of giving salt to a cow was struck
by lighting and instantly killed. (The cow was knocked down and
remained prostrate about 15 minutes after which she gradually
recovered.)
National Banner & Nashville Whig. (July 28, 1827 Vol 2 No. 84)

Connell, Oliver. A resident of Turnersville, Robertson County. Died
at the residence of C. Lanier in the vicinity of Nashville on the 10th
inst. aged 42 years.
Nashville Whig. (Tues., July 16, 1844)

Conner, Mr. James S. Died in Giles County.
National Banner & Nashville Whig. (Fri., Oct. 20, 1826)

Conner, Mr. Samuel Thompson. Died in Clinton, Miss. on the 7th ult.
in the bloom of Youth. In the town of Elkton, Ky. he left a father,
mother, brother and sister.
National Banner & Nashville Whig. (Mon., June 7, 1830)

Conway, Mr. Benj. Of Knox County. Died on Board the Steamboat Atlantic
near Memphis.
National Banner & Nashville Daily Advertiser. (Wed., June 12, 1833)

Coodnaugh, Mr. Isaiah of Nashville. Died on the 21st inst. at the
residence of Mr. Jacob Dickerson.
The Nashville Gazette. (Sat., July 22, 1820)

Cook, Mr. Died in Bedford County.
National Banner & Nashville Advertiser (Vol. 20 Fri., July 6, 1832
No. 1531)

Cook, Benjamin. Aged 104. Died at Wittingdam N. H. His wife died
last year age 95. See paper for obituary.
National Banner and Nashville Daily Advertiser. (Fri., June 1, 1832)

Cook, Daniel P. Died in Scott County, Ky. on the 15th ult. Late
representative in Congress from the State of Illinois.
National Banner & Nashville Whig. (Sat., Nov. 3, 1827)

Cook, Duval P. Attorney at law and formely of Bowling Green, Ky.
Died on the 1st inst. in Canton, Miss.
Daily Republican Banner. (Monday, Jan. 13, 1840)

Cook, Mr. George. Aged 22 years formely of Boston, Mass. Died in
New Orleans.
National Banner & Nashville Daily Advertiser. (Sat., Aug. 24, 1833)

Cook, Mr. Henry. Aged 77 years. Died in Williamson County.
National Banner & Nashville Daily Advertiser. (Mon., June 17, 1833)

Cook, Isaac S. W. Died at Paris, Henry County.
National Banner & Nashville Whig. (Sat., Sept. 27, 1828)

Cook, Lieut. John A. U. S. Navy aged 38 years. Died at Charleston,
S. C. on the 7th of Feb.
National Banner & Nashville Daily Advertiser. (Sat., March 22, 1834)

Cook, John L. Esq. One of the editors of the Richmond Enquirer.
Died in Richmond, Va.
Nashville Republican. (Tues., May 10, 1836)

Cook, John L. The partner of Mr. Richie in the publication of the
Richmond Enquirer. Died in Richmond on the 29th April in the 53rd.
year of his age.
The Union. (Tues., May 24, 1836)

Cook, Leander. Died 19th at Cincinati. Ohio of Cholera.
National Banner & Nashville Daily Advertiser. (Oct. 26, 1832)

Cook, Mrs. Lucy Ann. In the 23 year of her age. Died at the residence
of her father Rev. E. Jones in Madison County, Tenn. widow of the
late Dr. Marcus Cook.
National Banner & Nashville Daily Advertiser. (Tues., Aug. 19, 1834)

Cook, Miss Mary. Died at Tuscaloosa, Ala.
National Banner & Nashville Whig. (June 14, 1826)

Cook, Mrs. Tabitha M. Widow of the late Valentine Cook. Died in
Logan County, Ky.
National Banner. (Sat., April 18, 1829)

Cooke, Hon. John W. Late of Tennessee. Died in Paducah, Ky.
Daily Republican Banner. (Tues., Oct. 9, 1838)

Cooke, Wilds Kotzebue Esq. of Paris, Tenn. Died at Clinton, Ky.
On the morning of the 25th of July.
National Banner & Nashville Whig. (Mon., Aug. 2, 1830)

Cooke, William. Died at Lancaster, Ky. of Cholera.
National Banner & Nashville Daily Advertiser. (Wed., July 3, 1833)

Cooley, Hon. James. Of the State of Ohio. U. S. Charged Affairs at
Peru. Died in Lima.
National Banner & Nashville Whig. (Fri., June 20, 1828)

Cooley, Mrs. Wm. Died in Henry County.
National Banner & Nashville Whig. (Sat., Sept. 27, 1828)

Coons, Mr. Geo. Died in Fayette County, Ky.
National Banner & Nashville Whig. (Sat., March 17, 1827)

Coons, William. Died at Versailles, Ky. 14 miles from Lexington of
Cholera.
National Banner & Nashville Whig. (Fri., Sept. 4, 1835)

Cooper, Mr. David. Died in Beford County.
National Banner & Nashville Daily Advertiser. (Wed., June 27, 1832)

Cooper, Edward L. Of New York. Died in New Orleans of Yellow Fever.
Daily Republican Banner. (Wed., Sept. 27, 1837)

Cooper, Mr. James. In the 60th year of his age. Died in Bedford
County.
National Banner and Nashville Daily Advertiser. (Thurs., Jan. 19, 1832)

Cooper, James. Infant son of Washington B. Cooper Esq. Died in
Nashville on Tuesday the 7th inst.
Nashville Whig. (Tues., March 14, 1843)

Cooper, Mrs. M. D. Of Consumption. Died recently in Columbia, Tenn.
Nashville Whig. (Mon., Nov. 5, 1838)

Cooper, Mrs. Mary. Aged 101 and 9 days. Died in Roane County, Tenn.
National Banner & Nashville Daily Advertiser. (Tues., Aug. 27, 1833)

Cooper, Mrs. Mary Agnes. Consort of Mathew D. Cooper. Died in
Nashville on the 20th of May.
National Banner and Nashville Daily Advertiser. (Sat., May 24, 1834)

Cooper, Miss Mary Ann. Daughter of Mr. John Cooper. Died in
Christian County, Ky.
National Banner & Nashville Daily Advertiser. (Tues., Oct. 9, 1832)

Cooper, Martha D. Died in Columbia.
Nashville Republican & State Gazette. (Fri., Sept. 14, 1832)

Cooper, Mrs. Polly. Late of Simpson County, Ky. Her death was
occasioned by the bite of a snake. Died at Vandalia, Ill.
National Banner. (Sat., Aug. 22, 1829)

Cooper, Dr. Thomas. In the 80th year of his age. Died in Columbia,
S. C. on May 11th.
Daily Republican Banner. (Fri., May 25, 1839)

Cooper, Dr. Thomas. Of South Carolina, late President of Columbia
College. Died at Columbia, S. C. on the 11th inst. at the advanced
age of 80 years.
Nashville Whig. (Mon., May 27, 1839)

Cooper, Mr. W. B. Of Rutherford County aged 23 years. Died in
Franklin Co.
National Banner & Nashville Daily Advertiser. (Thurs., June 19, 1834)

Cooter, Mr. Andrew. Aged 23. Died at Little Rock, Ark.
National Banner & Nashville Whig. (Sat., Aug. 26, 1826)

Coots, Miss Elizabeth. Aged 38. Died in this County on Sunday.
National Banner. (May 10, 1826)

Cope, Jacob. Died 13th at Cincinnati, Ohio of Cholera.
National Banner & Nashville Daily Advertiser. (Tues., Oct. 23, 1832)

Copeland, Newton W. In the 23rd year of his age. Died near Memphis
on the 28th ulto.
Nashville Whig. (Sat., Oct. 3, 1846)

Coppage, Mrs. Mary Turner. In the 25th year of her age. Died at
Paducah, Ky.
National Banner & Nashville Whig. (Mon., May 4, 1835)

Corbitt, Mr. Elbridge. Age 20. Died in Nashville.
Nashville Whig. (Tues., July 14, 1846)

Corley, J. Providence. Died in the wreck of the steam boat Lexington.
Daily Republican Banner. (Fri., Jan. 31, 1840)

Cormick, J. R. of Virginia. Died in the explosian of the steamboat
Lucy Walker about 5 miles below New Albany.
Nashville Whig. (Tues., Oct. 29, 1844)

Cornelious, Rev. Dr. Secretary of the American Board of Foreign
Missions. Died at Hartford Con.
National Banner & Nashville Daily Advertiser. (Sat., March 3, 1832)

Cosby, Dabney C. Esq. Died at Port Gibson, Missis. Formely lived in Kentucky.
National Banner & Nashville Whig. (Mon., Oct. 4, 1830)

Cosby, Dr. J. Died in Brownville T.
National Banner & Nashville Whig. (Sat., Sept. 9, 1826)

Cosby, John. Of Providence. Died in the wreck of the steamboat Lexington.
Daily Republican Banner. (Fri., Jan. 31, 1840)

Cosby, Miss Mary Ann. Daughter of Thomas W. Cosby. Died in Smith County on the evening of the 20th ult.
National Banner & Nashville Whig. (Fri., May 7, 1830)

Cossitt, Dr. Epaphroditus. Died in Bowling Green, Ky.
National Banner & Nashville Daily Advertiser. (Mon., June 30, 1834)

Cotes, Mr. Jas. T. Aged 31 years. Died at Athens.
National Banner & Nashville Whig. (Sat., Sept. 8, 1827)

Cotton, Mr. John O. Died in Louisville, Ky.
National Banner & Nashville Whig. (Sat., July 8, 1826)

Cotton, Mr. William. Aged about 16 years. Died in Nashville on Saturday last.
Nashville Whig. (Tues., Aug. 1, 1843)

Cotton, Maj. Willie. Died in Jackson County, Ala.
National Banner & Nashville Whig. (Fri., Jan. 22, 1830)

Cottrell, Mr. John. Died in Bedford County.
National Banner & Nashville Whig. (Sat., Oct. 6, 1827)

Coulter, Mr. Robert. A native of New York. Died in Nashville on Sunday 18th inst.
Nashville Whig. (Tues., Sept. 20, 1842)

Council, Mr. Tho. C. Late of North Carolina. Died on Saturday last at the farm of Judge Overton.
Impartial Review and Cumberland Repository. (Aug. 23, 1806)

Covalt, Mr. Isaac. Died at Cincinnati, Ohio 12th of Cholera.
National Banner & Nashville Daily Advertiser. (Sat., Oct. 20, 1832)

Covington, Mrs. Nancy. Consort of William A. Covington. Died on the 31st ultimo in the vicinity of Springfield Robertson County.
Nashville Whig & Tenn. Advertiser. (April 11, 1818)

Cowan, Mrs. Ann. Relict of the late James Cowan Esq. of Lexington. Died Frankfort, Ky.
National Banner and Nashville Daily Advertiser. (Wed.,July 9, 1834)

Cowan, D. G. Esq. Died in Danville, Ky. of Apoplexy.
National Banner & Nashville Daily Advertiser. (Mon., Aug. 5, 1833)

Cowan, David G. Esq. Died at Danville, Ky.
National Banner & Nashville Daily Advertiser. (Sat., July 27, 1833)

Cowan, Mr. Joseph. Died in Rowan County, N. C.
National Banner & Nashville Daily Advertiser. (Thurs., Jan. 2, 1834)

Cowan, Margaret. Daughter of V. D. Cowan Esq. Aged 8 years. Died in Rutherford County on the 11th inst.
National Banner & Nashville Daily Advertiser. (Fri., Feb. 15, 1833)

Cowan, Mr. Nathaniel. Aged 97. Died at Salem, Franklin County.
National Banner and Nashville Whig. (Mon., Aug. 16, 1830)

Cowan, Col. Thos. Died in Wilmington, N. C.
Nashville Republican and State Gazette. (Tues., May 3, 1831)

Cowardian, Oscar. Infant son of Mr. Collin M. Cowardian. Died in
Nashville.
National Banner & Nashville Whig. (Fri., June 10, 1836)

Cowardin, Mr. John V. A Printer. Died in Nashville of Cholera on the
evening of the 18th inst.
National Banner and Nashville Whig. (Fri., June 19, 1837)

Cowerdian, Mrs. Mary. Formely of Virginia. Died in Sangamun County,
Illinois on the 4th of Sept. last was about 80 years.
National Banner & Nashville Whig. (Fri., Oct. 31, 1834)

Cowgill, John Milton. Aged 15, killed in a saw mill. Died in this
County.
National Banner and Nashville Whig. (June 24, 1826)

Cowing, Mr. Samuel K. Formely of Providence, R. I. Died in Louisville, Ky.
National Banner & Nashville Daily Advertiser. (Tues., Feb. 19, 1833)

Cox, Mrs. Consort of Dr. Robert Cox. Died in Sparta.
National Banner & Nashville Daily Advertiser. (Fri., Dec. 27, 1833)

Cox, Mrs. Burthunia P. Consort of Presley T. Cox and second daughter
of Peter P. Smith Esq. of Chatham County, N. C. Died in Marshall
County near Lewisburg on the 8th inst.
Nashville Republican. (Thurs., July 27, 1837)

Cox, Mrs. Elizabeth. Wife of Mr. Samuel Cox. Died in Williamson
County.
National Banner & Nashville Whig. (Fri., July 11, 1828)

Cox, Rev. John. Died near Savannah, Tenn. Formely of this place.
Nashville Republican and State Gazette. (Tues., Oct. 25, 1831)

Cox, Mary Mrs. Died on the 12th ult. in Jefferson County, Mrs.
Mary Cox, the wife of William Cox, Esquire.
Knoxville Gazette. (Thurs., April 10, 1794)

Cox, Mrs. Sarah. At an advanced age. Died at Murfreesborough on the
3rd inst.
Nashville Whig. (Thurs., March 12, 1846)

Cox, Mr. Thomas. In the 69th year of his age. Died in Davidson
County on Monday the 13th inst.
National Banner & Nashville Whig. (Mon., Dec. 20, 1830)

Cox, Mr. Thomas. Aged 69 years. Died in Davidson County on Monday
13th inst.
Nashville Republican and State Gazette. (Dec. 21, 1830)

Cox, William. From Bedford County. Died at the Tennessee State
Prison of Cholera.
National Banner and Nashville Whig. (Fri., Aug. 14, 1835)

Cox, Mr. William R. Died at Natchez.
National Banner & Nashville Whig. (Wed., Oct. 12, 1831)

Cox, Dr. William R. Died at Natchez.
National Banner & Nashville Whig. (Mon., Oct. 31, 1831)

Coxe, Mr. William. Died in Bennington, New Jersey.
Nashville Republican and State Gazette. (Thurs., March 24, 1831)

Cozens, Mr. Horatio Esq. Died in St. Louis.
National Banner & Nashville Whig. (Sat., July 29, 1826)

Crabb, Dr. Francis T. Died in Belleville, Illinois on the 23rd of
December.
National Banner & Nashville Whig. (Sat., Jan. 24, 1829)

Crabb, Hon. Henry. Judge of the Supreme Court of Tenn. Died at his
residence in this vicinity on Thursday morning.
National Banner & Nashville Whig. (Sat., Dec. 1, 1827)

Crabb, Gen. Thomas D. Died in Morgan County, Ala. on the 19th ult.
Aged 37 years.
National Banner. (Sat., April 11, 1829)

Craddock, Mr. M. R. Formely of Franklin, Tenn. Died at Tallahassee,
Florida.
National Banner & Nashville Daily Advertiser. (Mon., June 30, 1834)

Crafton, Nathan. Of Baltimore aged 47 years. Died in Louisville, Ky.
National Banner & Nashville Daily Advertiser. (Sat., Aug. 10, 1833)

Crafts, William Esq. Of Charleston, S. C. Died at Lebanon Springs.
National Banner & Nashville Whig. (Sat., Oct. 7, 1826)

Craig, Henry. Of the House of Maitland, Kennedy & Co. Died in the
wreck of the Steamboat Lexington.
Daily Republican Banner (Fri., Jan. 31, 1840)

Craig, John Esq. Acting Commissioner of the board of Tennessee Canal
Commissioner. Died at Florence, Ala.
The Union. (Sat., June 18, 1836)

Craig, Mrs. Martha. Aged 93. Died in Williamson County on the 5th
inst.
National Banner & Nashville Daily Advertiser. (Sat., Aug. 10, 1833)

Craig, Mrs. Mary Eliza. Aged 22 years. Consort of James T. Craig.
Daily Republican Banner. (Mon., Aug. 12, 1839)

Craig, Mrs. Mary Eliza. Consort of James T. Craig and daughter of
Nathaniel L. Robertson. Died in Davidson County, on Thursday last.
Nashville Union. (Mon., Aug. 12, 1839)

Craig, Mrs. Mary Eliza. Age 22 years. Died in Davidson County on the
8th inst.
Nashville Whig. (Mon., Aug. 12, 1839)

Craig, Mrs. Nancy. Wife of David Craig, Esq. Died in Columbia.
National Banner & Nashville Whig. (Sat., Feb. 16, 1828)

Craig, Mr. Robert. Died in Memphis.
National Banner & Nashville Daily Advertiser. (Wed., May 22, 1833)

Craig, Captain Robert. Aged 90. Died in Washington County, Va. on
the 4th inst. He was a soldier of the revolution.
National Banner and Nashville Daily Advertiser. (Mon., Feb. 17, 1834)

Craighead, Alexander Esq. Died at Sparta on the 14th inst. Attorney
at Law.
National Banner and Nashville Whig. (Sat., Jan. 20, 1827)

Craighead, David. Formely of Nashville. Died on the 6th inst at
Memphis.
The Christian Record. (Sat., Jan. 20, 1849)

Craighead, Elizabeth. Eldest daughter of David Craighead, Esq. of
Nashville. Died at the residence of Judge James Rucks in the 20th
year of her age.
Nashville Whig. (Thurs., April 13, 1843)

Craighead, Miss Jane. Daughter of the late Rev. Thomas B. Craighead.
Died at Memphis, Tenn. on the 10th inst. (Obituary)
The Christian Record. (Sat., Feb. 27, 1847)

Craighead, Mr. John. Aged 44 years. Died in Knoxville.
National Banner and Nashville Whig. (Sat., Aug. 5, 1826)

Craighead, Maj. Joh. Died near Knoxville.
National Banner & Nashville Whig. (Sat., Oct. 6, 1827)

Craighead, Mrs. Temperance. Relict of John Craighead, Esq. Aged 55
years 2 months and 18 days. Died in Knoxville, Tenn. on the 13th inst.
Nashville Whig. (Thurs., Dec. 22, 1842)

Craighead, Rev. Thomas B. Died at his residence near Haysborough in
this County on the morning of the 11th inst.
Nashville Whig. (Sept. 13, 1824)

Craighead, William Esq. Aged 57 years. Died in Knox County, Tenn.
National Banner & Nashville Whig. (Fri., April 10, 1835)

Craigmiles, Miss Eliza C. Died in Green County, Tenn.
National Banner & Nashville Daily Advertiser. (Mon., Aug. 25,1834)

Crane, Capt. Waterman. Died near Port Gibson, Miss.
National Banner (March 10, 1826)

Craven, Thomas. Aged about 57 years. Died on the 14th of Jan. 1840
in Gibson County, Tenn.
Daily Republican Banner. (Sat., April 4, 1840)

Cravens, Capt. Benj. Died in Henry County.
National Banner & Nashville Whig. (Sat., Aug. 25, 1827)

Crawford, Mr. Alexander. Died at Montgomery, Ala.
National Banner & Nashville Whig. (Sat., April 14, 1827)

Crawford, Catherine. Infant daughter of Catherine and Andrew Crawford.
Died the 8th inst. at 6 O'clock P.M. Aged 6 months.
Nashville Whig. (Sat., Oct. 10, 1846)

Crawford, Mr. David. Aged 38. Died in Dixon County on the 7th inst.
Nashville Republican and State Gazette. (Mon., July 23, 1832)

Crawford, Mr. Hugh. Died at Jonesborough.
National Banner. (April 21, 1826)

Crawford, Mr. James. Merchant of Philadelphia. Died on the 28th of
March.
Nashville Whig. (May 24, 1824)

Crawford, Mr. Peter Esq. A Distinguished citizen of that State. Died
in Georgia.
National Banner and Nashville Whig. (Mon., Nov. 15,1830)

Crawford, William. Aged 15. Died in Jonesborough, East Tenn.
Daily Republican Banner. (Wed., July 29, 1840)

Crawford, Hon. William H. Died at Mr. Valentine Merewether on his
way to Court at Ebert. of a heart attack. Death note from Lexington,Ky
National Banner & Nashville Whig. (Wed., Oct. 8, 1834)

Crawley, Mr. C. P. Aged 32 years. Died at Reynoldsburgh.
National Banner & Nashville Whig. (Sat., Jan. 12, 1828)

Crew, Mrs. Margaret. Wife of Capt. Pleasant Crew. Aged 35 years.
Died in Knoxville, Tenn.
National Banner & Nashville Whig. (Fri., Jan. 23, 1835)

Crews, David. Died in Madison County, Ky of Cholera.
National Banner & Nashville Daily Advertiser. (Sat., Aug. 10, 1833)

Criddle, Col. John. In the 51st year of his age. Died on the 5th
inst near this place.
National Banner (Sat., Nov. 7, 1829)

Critten, Mr. John Sr. Aged 75 years. Died in Amelia County, Va. on
the 28th ult.
Daily Republican Banner (Tues., Nov. 20, 1838)

Crittenden, Henry Esq. Died in Shelby County, Ky. A prominent
citizen of Ky.
National Banner & Nashville Whig. (Fri., Jan. 9, 1835)

Crittenden, Hon. Martin. Formely a member of Congress from Vt. Died
at Williston, Vt. 5th inst.
Nashville Whig. (Fri., Sept. 25, 1840)

Crittenden, Robert Esq. Of Little Rock, Arkansas. Died in Vicksburgh,
Mi.
National Banner and Nashville Whig. (Wed., Jan. 14, 1835)

Crocket, Mr. David. Died in this town on Sunday last.
National Banner & Nashville Whig. (Sat., Oct. 4, 1828)

Crocket, Capt. Samuel. Died in Williamson County.
National Banner & Nashville Whig. (Sat., Feb. 10, 1827)

Crockett, Mr. Andrew Jun. Died in Williamson County.
Daily Republican Banner. (Tues., Oct. 9, 1838)

Crockett, George. Clerk of the probate Court of Yazoo County and
brother of Mr. Richard Crockett of Nashville. Died in Benton, Miss.
Nashville Whig. (Tues., July 16, 1844)

Crockett, Granville. Died at Versailles, Ky. 14 miles from Lexington
of Cholera.
National Banner & Nashville Whig. (Fri., Sept. 4, 1835)

Crockett, Mr. John. Died at Huntington, Tenn. on Sunday the 16th inst.
in the 50th year of his age.
National Banner and Nashville Whig. (Mon., Aug. 3, 1835)

Crockett, Col. Joseph. Died in Woodford County, Ky. Formerly of
U. S. Marshall for the District of Ky.
National Banner. (Sat., Dec. 19, 1829)

Crockett, Mrs. Martha. Wife of Mr. Samuel Crockett age 44. Died in
Sumner County, Tenn.
National Banner and Nashville Daily Advertiser. (Tues., Aug. 5, 1834)

Crockett, Mrs. Rachel. Consort of Capt. Newhold Crockett in the 52nd
year of his age. Died in Fayette County, Ky. of Dysentary.
National Banner & Nashville Daily Advertiser. (Sat., Aug. 10, 1833)

Croes, Right Rev. John D. D. Bishop of the Protestant Episcopal for
the Diocese of New Jersey in the 70th year of his age. Died in New
Brunswick, N.J.
National Banner & Nashville Daily Advertiser. (Thurs., Aug. 16, 1832)

Cromwell, Mrs. Ann. Died at St. Louis.
National Banner & Nashville Daily Advertiser. (Fri., Sept. 7, 1832)

Cromwell, Mrs. Ann Eliza. Died in St. Louis.
National Banner & Nashville Advertiser. (Fri., Sept. 7, 1832)

Cromwell, Mrs. Eliza. Died in St. Louis.
National Banner and Nashville Daily Gazette. (Mon., Sept. 10, 1832)

Cromwell, Mrs. Rachel. Died in Fayette County, Ky. Aged 70.
National Banner & Nashville Whig. (Sat., Jan. 10, 1829)

Crooks, Mary Ann. Infant daughter of John Crooks aged 1 year. Died
in Nashville on Monday the 17th inst.
National Banner & Nashville Daily Advertiser. (Tues., June 18, 1833)

Cross, Alfred Hennen. Son of Prof. Nathaniel Cross. Died on Sat.,
last aged about 9 years.
Nashville Whig. (Tues., Feb. 28, 1843)

Cross, Maj. John. Died in Todd County, Ky.
National Banner & Nashville Whig. (Thurs., Sept. 16, 1830)

Cross, Mr. John. On Sunday 3rd inst. Died in Robertson County, Tenn.
See Paper for Obituary.
National Banner and Nashville Advertiser. (Wed., June 6, 1832)

Cross, Mr. John. Of Montgomery County, Tenn. Died in Russellville,
Ky. on the 3rd inst.
National Banner & Nashville Daily Advertiser. (Wed., June 13, 1832)

Cross, Mr. Richard C. Died in Hickman County on the 16th ult. age 23
formely of this town. (Nashville).
Nashville Whig. (July 7, 1823)

Cross, Mrs. Rosannah. Mother of Nathaniel Cross of the Nashville
University. Died on the 15th of June at Basking Ridge, New Jersey
having completed her four score years.
The Christian Record. (Sat., July, 1848)

Cross, William Brownlee. Son of Mr. & Mrs. Nathaniel Cross. Died
funeral at 11 O'clock this morning.
Daily Republican Banner (Wed., Feb. 24, 1838)

Crosthewait, Nancy. Infant Child of V. Crosthwait. Died in Bowling
Green, Ky.
National Banner & Nashville Daily Advertiser. (Mon., June 4, 1832)

Crosthwait, Mr. Samuel. An aged and respectable citizen. Died in
Elizabethtown, Ky.
National Banner & Nashville Daily Advertiser. (Tues., July 15, 1834)

Crosthwait, Mr. Thomas. Died on the morning of the 26th November.
Aged 88 years, brother of Shelton Crosthwait Esq. both formely of
Albermarle County in the State of Virginia. He died in the town near
Jefferson on the Plantation of his brother in the County of Rutherford.
The Nashville Whig. (Tues., Dec. 20, 1815)

Crouch, Mr. Joseph. Of Washington County. Died in Knoxville.
National Banner & Nashville Whig. (Wed., March 2, 1831)

Crouch, Mr. Joseph. Of Washington County. Died in Knoxville.
National Banner & Nashville Whig. (Mon., March 7, 1831)

Crouch, Mrs. Martha. Wife of Mr. Richard Crouch. Died in Todd
County, Ky.
National Banner & Nashville Whig. (Sat., Nov. 22, 1828)

Crouch, Mrs. Virginia. Died in Mathew City, Va.
Nashville Republican and State Gazette. (March 8, 1831)

Crozier, Mrs. Hannah. Widow of the late Capt. John Crozier. Died in
this vicinity on Thursday morning last. In the 63rd year of her age.
Daily Republican Banner. (Sat., Oct. 20, 1838)

Crozier, Dr. Hugh. Son of Maj. Arthur Crozier aged 32 of Clinton,
Tenn. Died at Cane Hill, Ark.
National Banner & Nashville Whig. (Wed., Dec. 3, 1834)

Crozier, Robert C. Of Knoxville, Tenn. Died at Key West E. Florida.
National Banner & Nashville Daily Advertiser. (Fri., Dec. 27, 1833)

Crumbaugh, Mrs. Ellen. Wife of Mr. Eli Crumbaugh of Elkton, Ky.
Died in Mercy County, Ky.
National Banner. (Sat., May 9, 1829)

Crutcher, Edmund Esq. Aged 72 years. Died in Davidson County on
Thursday the 2nd inst.
Nashville Whig. (Sat., July 4, 1846)

Crutcher, Mrs. Ester I. Departed this life on Saturday the 13th inst.
in the 17th year of her age. Wife of Leo. B. Crutcher, editor of the
Weekly Messenger, Russellville, Kentucky.
The Nashville Whig. Tenn. Advertiser. (June 20, 1818)

Crutcher, Miss Martha F. Died in Elizabethtown, Ky. Daughter of
Isaac Crutcher Esq.
National Banner (Jan. 13, 1826)

Crutcher, Thomas Jr. Formely of Lebanon, Tenn. Died at Covington,
Tenn. On the Wednesday 2nd inst.
Nashville Republican. (Tues., Aug. 15, 1837)

Crutcher, Thomas. Son of Edmond Crutcher of Davidson County. Died
in Covington, Tenn. on the 2nd inst.
National Banner & Nashville Whig. (Wed., Aug. 16, 1837)

Crutcher, Thomas. An old and much respected citizen. Died yesterday
afternoon at the Nashville Inn. In the 85th year of his age.
Nashville Whig. (Tues., March 2, 1844)

Crutcher, Mr. Thomas H. Of the house of Crutcher and Wood of this
town. Died at Tyrees Springs 17th inst.
National Banner. (Sat., Aug. 8, 1829)

Crutchfield, Tho. of Fincastle. Attorney at law. Died near Richmond,
Va.
National Banner & Nashville Daily Advertiser. (Wed., March 5, 1834)

Cryer, Mrs. Elizabeth L. Consort of Rev. H. M. Cryer. Died at Gallatin
on Friday the 16th inst. at her home.
National Banner & Nashville Daily Advertiser. (Mon., Aug. 26, 1833)

Cryer, Rev. Hardy M. Died in Sumner County on the 8th inst.
Nashville Whig. (Tues., Feb. 17, 1846)

Cryer, Miss Martha Ann D. Age 13 years. Died in Sumner County.
National Banner & Nashville Daily Advertiser. (Mon., Oct. 15, 1832)

Culbertson, Mr. Joseph. Died at Shawneetown.
National Banner. (March 10, 1826)

Culp, Rev. Daniel. Died in Trenton, Gibson County.
National Banner and Nashville Daily Advertiser. (Sat., May 18, 1833)

Culp, Mrs. Sarah. Died in Trenton.
National Banner and Nashville Daily Advertiser. (Wed., April 25, 1832)

Cummens, Mr. Charles. Formely of Lexington, Ky. Died at Jefferson-ville, Ind.
National Banner & Nashville Whig. (Tues., May 11, 1830)

Cumming, Mr. Andrew. Aged 75 years. Died in Blount, County, Tenn.
National Banner & Nashville Whig. (Wed., Dec. 17, 1834)

Cummings, Rev. Hooper. Of New York. Died in Charleston, S. C.
National Banner. (Jan. 13, 1828)

Cummings, Mrs. Isabella D. S. Aged 3 years. Died in Rutherford County.
National Banner & Nashville Whig. (Sat., Aug. 30, 1828)

Cummings, Mrs. Margaret. Wife of Uriah Cummings. Died at Murfreesborough.
National Banner & Nashville Whig. (Sat., Dec. 16, 1826)

Cummins, Rev. Dr. Francis. Age 81. A Revolutionary Patriot. Died in Green County, Ga. On the 22nd ult. See paper for Obituary.
National Banner and Nashville Advertiser. (Fri., March 23, 1832)

Cummins, Mrs. Grizzle T. Consort of Alexander G. Cummins. Died on the 22d day of Dec. last of Obion County, Tenn.
Daily Republican Banner (Thursday, Jan. 4, 1838)

Cummins, Miss Harriet A. Daughter of John Cummins Esq. of Jackson County, Aged 28. Died at the residence of Col. John J. Hinton in this vicinity.
Nashville Whig. (Monday, Aug. 26, 1839)

Cuningham, Mrs. Wife of Mr. James Cuningham. Died in Gallatin.
National Banner & Nashville Whig. (Sat., Oct. 4, 1828)

Cuningham. Infant son of Jeremiah Cuningham. Died at Shelbyville, Tenn. of Cholera.
National Banner and Nashville Daily Advertiser. (Thurs., July 11, 1833)

Cuningham, Mr. James. Died in Knox County.
National Banner & Nashville Whig. (Friday, Oct. 20, 1826)

Cuningham, Mr. James B. Died in Madison County, Ala.
National Banner and Nashville Whig. (Sat., Dec. 27, 1828)

Cuningham, Capt. John. Died at Cincinnati. Of the steamboat Boliver. Aged 27 years.
National Banner. (April 21, 1826)

Cuningham, John M. Son of Alexander Cuningham. Died in Nashville on the 24th July.
National Banner & Nashville Daily Advertiser. (Thurs., July 25, 1833)

Curd, Spencer Esq. Died in Russelville, Ky.
National Banner & Nashville Daily Advertiser. (Tues., Sept. 25, 1832)

Curle, Mr. Archibald. Died in Madison County, Ky.
National Banner & Nashville Daily Advertiser. (Fri., Jan. 27, 1832)

Curren, Thomas Esq. Died at St. Louis.
National Banner. (April 28, 1826)

Currey, Mr. Robert B. In the 75th year of his age. Died during the night of the 8th at his residence near Nashville.
The Christian Record. (Sat., Dec. 23, 1848)

Currey, William Hume. Infant son of Mr. Robert Currey. Died in
Davidson County.
National Banner and Nashville Whig. (Fri., Feb. 11, 1831)

Currin, Mr. John. Aged 59. Died in Davidson County.
National Banner & Nashville Whig. (Mon., Nov. 1, 1830)

Curry, William Hume. Infant son of Robert B. Curry. Died this
morning.
Nashville Republican and State Gazette. (Thurs., Feb. 10, 1831)

Curry, William Hume. Infant son of Mr. Robert B. Curry. Died in
Davidson County.
National Banner & Nashville Whig. (Fri., Feb. 11, 1831)

Curtis, Captain James. Of Providence, R. I. Died in New Orleans, La.
National Banner & Nashville Daily Advertiser. (Sat., Sept. 13, 1834)

Cutler, Charles. Died in Nashville of Cholera on Sat. the 1st day
of June. He was a native of Mass. and the last 9 months a resident of
Nashville.
National Banner & Nashville Daily Advertiser. (Tues., June 4, 1833)

Cutright, Mr. John Sen. In the 83rd year of his age. Died in
Springfield, Ohio.
National Banner and Nashville Whig. (Mon., Jan. 17, 1831)

Cutts, Mrs. Wife of Hon. Richard Cutts and Sister of Mrs. Madison.
Died at Washington.
National Banner and Nashville Daily Advertiser. (Wed., Aug. 29, 1832)

Dabbs, Mr. Thomas C. Aged 36 years. Died near Huston, Texas on the
16th inst. Oct. (Obituary)
Nashville Union. (Wed., Nov. 26, 1839)

Dabney, Miss Emily. Daughter of John Dabney Esq. Died in Giles
County on the 27th Feb.
Nashville Republican. (Thurs., March 3, 1836)

Dabney, Dr. John T. Of Montgomery County. Died on the 27th May of
Cholera on board the Steamboat Companion between Louisville and West
Port.
National Banner & Nashville Daily Advertiser. (Wed., June 5, 1833)

Dade, Major. 4th Infantry. Died - was killed in the battle by the
Indians in Florida.
The Union. (Sat., January 23, 1836)

Daffey, Susan Eleanor. Eldest daughter of Col. Francis and Pemela
Daffey. Died in Hartsville on the 27th inst. at the age of 3 years
and 4 months.
Nashville Republican. (Tues., June 16, 1836)

Daily, Major Richard. Member of the Bar and useful citizen. Died in
Montgomery County.
National Banner & Nashville Advertiser. (Fri., March 9, 1832)

Daily, Major Richard. Died in Montgomery County.
National Banner & Nashville Daily Advertiser. (Fri., March 9, 1832)

Dale, Mrs. Annie L. Wife of Edward W. Dale Esq. Died in Maury
County.
National Banner & Nashville Whig. (Sat., March 1, 1828)

Dale, Mrs. Elizabeth. Widow of the late Mr. Thomas Dale, aged 84.
Died in Smith County on the 13th inst.
National Banner & Nashville Whig. (Sat., Jan. 24, 1829)

Dale, Mr. John H. Died - was killed by lighting in the vicinity of
Sparta, Tenn.
The Politician and Weekly Nashville Whig. (Fri., July 23, 1847 pg 237)

Dale, Com. Richard. Of the U. S. Navy to the 70th year of his age.
Died at Philadelphia.
National Banner (March 24, 1826)

Dale, Mr. William J. H. Aged 19 years. Died in Nashville.
National Banner & Nashville Whig. (Tues., April 20, 1830)

Daley, Mr. John H. Died in Knoxville.
National Banner & Nashville Whig. (Fri., Jan. 1st 1830)

Dallam?, Mrs. Jane. Relict of the late Col. Richard Dallam. Died
in Russelville, Ky. Aged 81 years.
National Banner & Nashville Daily Advertiser. (Mon., May 28, 1832)

Dallam, Mrs. Jane. Relict of the late Col. Richard Dallam. Age 81
years. Died in Russelville, Ky.
National Banner and Nashville Daily Advertiser. (Mon., May 28, 1832)

Dally, Capt. Joseph G. Died at his residence in Nashville on the 18th
inst.
Nashville Whig. (Thurs., Oct. 26, 1843)

Dalton, Mr. James Madison. In the 27th year of his age. Died in
Hawkins County, Tenn. on the 4th inst.
National Banner & Nashville Daily Advertiser. (Thurs., Sept. 11, 1834)

Dalton, Miss Mary Gentry. Daughter of Capt. John Dalton. Died in
Williamson County on the 25th of Sept. 1833.
National Banner and Nashville Daily Advertiser. (Mon., Feb. 17, 1834)

Daly, Major Richard. Of Montgomery County, Tenn. Died ___ (Obituary)
National Banner & Nashville Daily Advertiser. (Fri., May 25, 1834)

Damerson, George B. Late receiver of Public Monies. Died in Monticello on the 13th ult. In the land office of Clinton.
National Banner and Nashville Daily Advertiser. (Tues., Oct. 22, 1833)

Dana, Dr. James Felman. Professor of Chemistry. Died at New York.
National Banner and Nashville Whig. (Sat., May 19, 1827)

Dance, Mrs. Mary P. Of Nashville Consort of Maj. Russell Dance.
Died in Davidson County.
Nashville Republican. (Tues., June 27, 1837)

Dance, Maj. Russel. Died on Wednesday last at the residence of Mrs.
Thomas Martin in the neighborhood of Nashville.
Nashville Union. (Fri., Oct. 5, 1838)

Dance, Maj. Russell. Merchant. Died at Mrs. Martha four miles north
of Louisville, Ky. On Wednesday last. Formely of Murfreesboro and
more recently of the House of Nichol-Dance & Co., Nashville.
Nashville Whig. (Fri., Oct. 5, 1838)

Dancy, Mrs. Frances M. Consort of Col. David Dancy. Died in Limestone
County, Ala.
National Banner and Nashville Daily Advertiser. (Sat., June 28, 1834)

Dandridge, Mr. Larkin. Died in Lincoln County, Ky.
National Banner & Nashville Whig. (Sat., Jan. 6, 1827)

Daniel, Rev. John J. Died in Henry County on the 13th.
National Banner and Nashville Whig. (Mon., Oct. 6, 1834)

Daniel, Mr. Thomas. Died in Greenville City, N. C.
Nashville Republican and State Gazette. (Thurs., Oct. 6, 1831)

Daniel, William W. Formely of Maury County, Tenn. Died in Vernon,
Miss.
National Banner and Nashville Daily Advertiser. (Fri., Sept. 20, 1833)

Daniels, Mr. Archibald. Died near Port Gibson, Miss.
National Banner and Nashville Whig. (Dec. 30, 1826)

Darby, Mr. Richard. Died near Bellview, Ala.
National Banner and Nashville Whig. (Wed., Feb. 4, 1835)

Darby, Mr. William. Geographer and Taxographical engineer.
Died in Frederick Co., Maryland.
National Banner and Nashville Whig. (Sat., Sept. 8, 1827)

Darden, Mrs. Amelia. Consort of Jesse Darden. Died in Robertson
County on the 12th of Oct. in the 26th year of her age.
National Banner and Nashville Whig. (Mon., Oct. 27, 1834)

Darden, Mrs. Louise W. Late consort of David Darden. Died in Springfield, Robertson County, Tenn. in about the 40th year of her age.
Nashville Whig. (Sat., Aug. 17, 1844)

Dargen, Mrs. Claire M. Died at St. Louis.
National Banner and Nashville Whig. (Sat., July 28, 1827)

Daron, William Esq. Aged 65 years. Died at his residence in Rutherford County on the 27th Sept.
National Banner and Nashville Whig. (Wed., Oct. 22, 1834)

Darragh, John Esq. Died at Pittsburgh. Aged 55 President of the
Bank of Pittsburgh and late Mayor of the City.
National Banner and Nashville Whig. (Sat., June 7, 1828)

Dashiell, Mrs. Ester. Wife of Rev. George Dashiell. Died in Louisville, Ky.
National Banner and Nashville Daily Advertiser. (Tues., July 15, 1834)

D'Auderville De Baulingy. Madam. Died in New Orleans, on the 23rd
of April.
National Banner and Nashville Daily Advertiser. (Fri., May 16, 1834)

Daughty, Mr. George. Died in Nashville.
Nashville Whig. (Tues., April 14, 1846)

Daune, Thos. Died in Jefferson County.
Daily Republican Banner. (Sat., Sept. 22, 1838)

Davall, Mr. Died in Lexington, Ky. from the Cholera.
National Banner and Nashville Daily Advertiser. (Mon., June 10, 1833)

Davejac, Jules Esq. Died at New Orleans.
National Banner and Nashville Whig. (Mon., Feb. 21, 1831)

Davejac, Jules Esq. Died at New Orleans.
National Banner and Nashville Whig. (Mon., Feb. 21, 1831)

Davenport, H. H. Shawneetown. Died in the loss of the Steamboat
Brandywine.
National Banner and Nashville Daily Advertiser. (Mon., April 23, 1832)

Davenport, Mr. Isaac. Died at Round Away Bayon.
National Banner and Nashville Daily Advertiser. (Wed., March 26, 1834)

Davenport, Mr. Thomas M. Died at Tuscaloosa.
National Banner and Nashville Whig. (Sat., Jan. 12, 1828)

Davenport, William Esq. Of Morgan County, Ga.
National Banner and Nashville Whig. (Sat., Oct. 11, 1828)

David, Sampson Esq. Died at Jacksbaraugh.
National Banner and Nashville Whig. (June 17, 1826)

Davidge Henry, Esq. Age 63. Died in Gallatin County, Ky.
National Banner and Nashville Whig. (Wed., Dec. 7, 1831)

Davidge, Henry Esq. Age 63. Died in Gallatin County, Ky.
National Banner and Nashville Whig. (Wed., Dec. 7, 1831)

Davidge, Dr. John Beal. Died at Baltimore.
National Banner. (Sat., Sept. 19, 1829)

Davidson, Mrs. Died at Versailles, Ky. 14 miles from Lexington of
Cholera.
National Banner and Nashville Whig. (Fri., Sept. 4, 1835)

Davidson, Mrs. Elizabeth. Wife of Maj. James Davidson. Died on
the 20th inst. in Wilson County.
Nashville Republican. (Sat., Oct. 1st 1836)

Davidson, George. Age about 16. Died in Shelbyville.
Nashville Whig. (Tues., July 21, 1846)

Davidson, Mrs. George. Died in Shelbyville, Tenn. of Cholera.
National Banner and Nashville Daily Advertiser. (Thurs., July 11, 1833)

Davidson, George N. Aged 31 late of Tennessee. Died recently in
Pontotoc, Miss.
Nashville Whig. (Monday, Jan. 6, 1840)

Davidson, James. Died in Shelbyville, Tenn. of Cholera.
National Banner and Nashville Daily Advertiser. (Thurs., July 11, 1833)

Davidson, Miss Mary Ann. Daughter of Major James H. Davidson. Died
in Logan County, Ky.
National Banner and Nashville Whig. (Mon., Nov. 8, 1830)

Davidson, Mrs. Nancy. Wife of Mr. Thomas Davidson. Died in Dyer
County.
National Banner and Nashville Whig. (Sat., Aug. 16, 1828)

Davidson, Mrs. Susan. Wife of Jesse Davidson of this Place. Died
at Murfreeborraugh.
The Nashville Whig and Tennessee Advertiser. (Oct. 20, 1817)

Davidson, Mr. Thomas. Merchant of Pulaski. Died on steamboat
Cumberland on her trip from New Orleans.
Nashville Whig. (Thurs., March 24, 1842)

Davies, Mr. John. Died at Cincinati. Aged 84.
National Banner. (Sat., Aug. 29, 1829)

Davis, Mr. A. Died in Paris, Tenn.
National Banner and Nashville Whig. (Fri., May 1, 1835)

Davis, Hon. Amas. Died in Owingsville, Ky. on the 11th inst.
National Banner and Nashville Whig. (Wed., July 1, 1835)

Davis, Ann. Died at Cincinnati, Ohio on the 11th inst.
National Banner and Nashville Daily Advertiser. (Thurs., Oct. 18, 1832)

Davis, Mr. Benj. Died in Jefferson County.
National Banner and Nashville Whig. (Sat., Feb. 7, 1829)

Davis, Mr. Cornelious. Age 71. Died in New York very suddenly on
Friday, April 29, 1831.
National Banner and Nashville Whig. (Mon. June 13, 1831)

Davis, Darthula D. Daughter of John Davis Esq. Aged 17. Died in
Davidson County on the 11th inst.
National Banner and Nashville Daily Advertiser. (Thurs., Sept. 12, 1833)

Davis, Mr. Edward R. Died in Limestone County, Ala.
National Banner and Nashville Daily Advertiser. (Mon., July 8, 1833)

Davis, Elisha. For 25 years a citizen of Williamson County. Died
at Natchez, Miss. on the 11th June.
National Banner and Nashville Whig. (Wed., July 8, 1835)

Davis, Mrs. Elizabeth. Consort of Mr. Theophilus Davis. Died in
Shelby County, Ky. in the 22nd year of her age.
National Banner and Nashville Daily Advertiser. (Sat., Feb. 11, 1832)

Davis, Mrs. Elizabeth. Consort of Mr. Theophilus Davis. Age 22.
Died in Shelby County, Ky. on June 22nd
National Banner and Nashville Advertiser. (Sat., Feb. 11, 1832)

Davis, Mrs. Elizabeth. Aged 32. Wife of Capt. Benjamin Davis and
daughter of Thomas Spragin Esq. Died in Dresden on Sunday the 2nd
inst.
National Banner and Nashville Daily Advertiser. (Tues., Feb. 11, 1834)

Davis, Mrs. Elizabeth. Wife of Mr. Nathaniel Davis. Died in Wilson
County, Tenn. on the 21st inst.
National Banner and Nashville Daily Advertiser. (Wed., Sept. 25, 1833)

Davis, Elizabeth A. Formely Mrs. Claiborn West. Originally of Buckingham Co., Va. Died in Christian County, Ky. where she had been
a resident for many years.
Nashville Whig. (Monday, July 20, 1839)

Davis, Mr. Fredrick. Died in Williamson County. Aged 84.
Nashville Republican and State Gazette. (Tues., Nov. 1, 1831)

Davis, Fredrick. Son of James Davis Esq. of White County. Died at
the residence of his father on the 3rd inst. in the 27th year of his
age.
The Union. (Tues., May 30, 1837)

Davis, Mr. Fredrick. In the 84th year of his age. Died on
Monday 17th inst at the residence of Owen T. Watkins, Esq. (Obituary)
The Western Weekly Review. (Fri., Oct. 28, 1831 Franklin, Tenn.)

Davis, Mrs. Wife of Mr. Harrison Davis. Died in Logan County, Ky.
National Banner (April 14, 1826)

Davis, Mrs. Gerusha. Age 51. Wife of Luckett Davis, Esq. Died in
Rutherford County, Tenn. on the 19th inst. Friday, June 24, 1831
National Banner and Nashville Whig. (Fri., June 24, 1831)

Davis, Mrs. Gerusha. Consort of Luckett Davis Esq. Died in
Rutherford County, Tenn. on the 19th inst. Age about 51 years she
has left a husband and six children.
National Banner and Nashville Whig. (Fri., June 24, 1831)

Davis, Isaac. Of Boston. Died in the wreck of the Steamboat Lexington
Daily Republican Banner. (Fri., Jan. 31, 1840)

Davis, Mr. Isam Fielding. Age about 71 years. Died in Gibson County.
Nashville Whig. (Tues., March 31, 1846)

Davis, Jane. Age 3. Daughter of Mr. James E. Davis. Died in
Lexington, Ky.
National Banner and Nashville Advertiser. (June 26, 1832)

Davis, Jane. Aged 3 years daughter of James E. Davis. Died in Lexington, Ky.
National Banner and Nashville Daily Advertiser. (Tues., June 26, 1832)

Davis, Mrs. Jane. Relict of the late William Davis of Nashville.
Died in Nashville on Tuesday night the 3rd inst.
Nashville True Whig and Weekly Commercial Register. (Fri., Dec. 13,1850)

Davis, Dr. John. Died in Jackson.
National Banner and Nashville Whig. (Thurs., May 20, 1830)

Davis, Col. John. Died in Franklin County, Ala.
National Banner and Nashville Daily Advertiser. (Fri., Aug. 17, 1832)

Davis, Col John. Died in Franklin County, Ala.
National Banner and Nashville Advertiser. (Fri., Aug. 17, 1832)

Davis, Mrs. Julin E. Died at Augusta, Ky.
National Banner and Nashville Whig. (Sat., Dec. 16, 1826)

Davis, Dr. Kindall. Died in Montgomery County.
National Banner and Nashville Whig. (Fri., Oct. 3, 1834)

Davis, Lucinda. Daughter of Mr. Richard Davis. Died in Shelbyville, Tenn. of Cholera.
National Banner and Nashville Daily Advertiser. (Thurs., July 11, 1833)

Davis, Miss Lucy M. Late of Batavia, New York. Died in Memphis, Tenn.
Nashville Whig. (Tues., March 31, 1846)

Davis, Mrs. Malinda. Consort of Maj. R. J. Davis. Died in Sevier Co.
Nashville Whig! (Thurs., June 25, 1846)

Davis, Mrs. Margeret. Aged 67. Died in Knoxville.
National Banner and Nashville Whig. (Tues., April 20, 1830)

Davis, Mrs. Nancy. Wife of Mr. Oran Davis. Died in Courtland, Ala.
National Banner and Nashville Whig. (Mon., March 21, 1831)

Davis, Mrs. Nancy. Died in Logan County, Ky.
National Banner and Nashville Whig. (Sat., June 16, 1827)

Davis, Mrs. Nancy. Wife of Mr. Oran Davis. Died in Courtland, Ala.
National Banner and Nashville Whig. (Mon., March 21, 1821)

Davis, Miss Nancy. Daughter of Mr. Harrison Davis. Died in Logan Co.
National Banner and Nashville Whig. (Sat., Sept. 30, 1826)

Davis, Mr. Philip. Died in Limestone County, Ala.
National Banner and Nashville Whig. (Sat., Nov. 3, 1827)

Davis, Mrs. Rachel. Died in Logan County, Ky.
National Banner. (May 13, 1826)

Davis, Susan Amanda. Infant daughter of Elisha Davis. Died on Sunday evening 3rd inst.
The Western Weekly Review. (Fri., Feb. 8, 1833)

Davis, Susan Eliza A. M. Eldest daughter of Sophia E. Davis. Died in Elkton, Tenn. of scarlet fever on the 1st of June. Age 5 years.
Nashville Union. (Mon., June 17, 1839)

Davis, Sylvester P. In the 22nd year of his age. Died in Nashville on the 30th ult.
Nashville Whig. (Thurs., Feb. 5, 1846)

Davis, Thomas Esq. Died at Shelbyville on the 9th inst. for many
years Post Master at that place.
Nashville Whig. (Tues., Sept. 15, 1846)

Davis, William. Died at Cincinnati, Ohio on the 12th of Cholera.
National Banner and Nashville Daily Advertiser. (Sat., Oct. 20, 1832)

Davis, Mr. Wm. Died in Montgomery County, Ky. Killed by lighting.
National Banner and ____. (Sat., May 16, 1829)

Davis, Mr. William C. Former proprietor of the Nashville Race Course.
Died in Smithland on the Wednesday May 26th.
National Banner and Nashville Whig. (Mon., May 31, 1830)

Dawning, Mary Eliza. Daughter of Mr. Richard Dawning, age 7. Died
in Fayette County, Ky.
National Banner and Nashville Advertiser. (Mon., June 18, 1832)

Dawson, Dr. George. Died in Pittsburgh, Pa.
Nashville Republican and State Gazette. (Thurs., April 19, 1831)

Dawson, Moses. Ex-member of the Cincinnati Press. Died in Cincinnati
on Tuesday last.
Nashville Whig. (Tues., Dec. 10, 1844)

Deadrick, Mrs. Wife of Thomas Deadrick, Esq. of this Place. Died
on the 2d inst.
Impartial Review and Cumberland Repository. (Thurs., April 7, 1808)

Deadrick, Mrs. Adelaide. The amiable consort of Mr. David A. Dead-
rick merchant at that place. Died at the cross roads Hawkins, County,
Tenn. on the 10th inst.
Nashville Whig & Tenn. Advertiser. (Dec. 29, 1817)

Deadrick, Captain Davis S. Of Mine-aw-Barton and formely of this
town (Nashville). Died lately at St. Louis.
Nashville Whig. (July 28, 1823)

Deadrick, Mr. Edward D. Age 26 late of this town. Died at Little
Rock, Ark.
National Banner and Nashville Advertiser. (Sat., July 7, 1832)

Deadrick, Mr. Edward D. Late of Nashville age 26. Died at Little
Rock, Ark.
National Banner and Nashville Daily Advertiser. (Sat., July 7, 1832)

Deadrick, George Michael Esq. Died on the 23rd inst. after a short
indisfasetion. President of the Nashville Bank.
Nashville Whig. (Nov. 26, 1816)

Deadrick, John Esq. Died in Shelby County.
National Banner and Nashville Advertiser. (Wed., Jan. 4, 1832)

Deaderick, John Esq. Died in Shelby County.
National Banner and Nashville Daily Advertiser. (Wed., Jan. 4, 1832)

Deadrick, Mr. Thomas. Died in Nashville.
National Banner and Nashville Whig. (Wed., Nov. 16, 1831)

Deadrick, Mr. Thomas. Died in Nashville.
National Banner and Nashville Whig. (Wed., Nov. 16, 1831)

Deagle, Rev. Mathew. Died in Washington City.
Nashville Republican and State Gazette. (Tues., Oct. 25, 1831)

Deake, Wm. Henry. On the 23rd inst. sonof Wm. Deake age 13 years
after an illness of but 4 days; during which time he suffered great
distress, which he bore with Christian fortitude and firmness.
Nashville Republican. (Thurs., Feb. 4, 1836)

Dean, John A. From Campbell County. Died at the Tennessee State
Pentintiary of Cholera.
National Banner and Nashville Whig. (Fri., Aug. 14, 1835)

Deanes, Mr. Davis D. Printer for some time a workman in his office.
Died this morning.
National Banner and Nashville Whig. (Mon., July 5, 1830)

Deanes, Mrs. Martha Jane. Wife of Mr. David D. Deanes. Died at
Columbia.
National Banner. (Sat., Aug. 22, 1829)

Dearborn, Maj. Gen. Henry. Aged 78. Died at Roxbury, Mass.
National Banner. (Sat., July 4, 1829)

Dearing, Mr. Asa. Late of Georgia. Died in Lawerence County, Ala.
National Banner and Nashville Whig. (Sat., Oct. 7, 1826)

Dearmond, Mr. James. Age 60. Died in Roan County.
National Banner and Nashville Whig. (Wed., March 23, 1831)

Dearmond, Mr. James. Aged 60. Died in Roane County.
National Banner and Nashville Whig. (Wed., March 23, 1831)

De Bow, Dr. Sol'n. Formely of Orange County, N. C. Died in New
Orleans.
Nashville Republican and State Gazette. (Sat., September 24, 1831)

De. butts, Dr. Proffessor of Chemistry in the University of Maryland.
Died in Baltimore.
Nashville Republican and State Gazette. (Thurs., April 19, 1831)

Decherd, Mrs. Elizabeth. Died in Franklin County.
National Banner. (April 14, 1826)

Decker?, Mr. John. In the 72d year of his age. Died in Nashville
on Monday last.
Nashville Union. (Wed., May 8, 1839)

Decker, Mr. John. Aged 72 years. Died in Nashville on the 6th inst.
Daily Republican Banner. (Thurs., May 9, 1839)

Declary, Dr. John P. Died in Louisville, Ky. In a fit of derangement
he put an end to his own life.
National Banner and Nashville Daily Advertiser. (Tues., July 15, 1834)

Decutar, Col. John P. Died at Port Gibson early in Nov. last.
Nashville Republican and State Gazette. (Fri., Dec. 7, 1832)

De Ende, Henry Esq. Died in New Orleans.
National Banner and Nashville Advertiser. (Mon., June 11, 1832)

De Ends, Henry Esq. Died in New Orleans.
National Banner and Nashville Daily Advertiser. (Mon., June 11, 1832)

Deery, Elizabeth. Daughter of William Deery Esq. Died in Bloutville
on the 2nd inst.
National Banner and Nashville Daily Advertiser. (Fri., Feb. 15, 1833)

De Genlis, Madame. Aged 89. Died in France.
Nashville Republican and State Gazette. (Thurs., Feb. 24, 1831)

Degraffenried, Dr. Thomas L. Died in Maury County.
Nashville Republican and State Gazette. (Wed., Aug. 8, 1832)

Dehanne, Mr. J. V. A native of Paris and late of New York. Died at
New Orleans.
National Banner and Nashville Daily Advertiser. (Fri., Sept. 20, 1833)

De Hart, Capt. Cyrus. An officer of the revolutionary Army.
Nashville Republican and State Gazette. (Thurs., Oct. 6, 1831)

Deison, Mr. Charles. Died in Florence, Ala. Formely of Lynchburg.
National Banner. (Jan. 20, 1826)

Delano, Dr. Amara. Died at Chillicathe.
National Banner and Nashville Whig. (Thurs., Sept. 9, 1830)

Delano, Dr. Ira. Died at Chillicothe.
National Banner and Nashville Whig. (Sat., July 14, 1827)

Delooch, Coxen C. Esq. Died in Tipton County, Tenn. He had been
married only three weeks to the daughter of Col. Allen of Sommerville.
National Banner and Nashville Whig. (Fri., March 27, 1835)

Delooch, Miss Elizabeth F. Died in Holmes County, Miss. on Sat.
morning Sept. 14th aged 31 years 3 months and 8 days.
National Banner and Nashville Daily Advertiser. (Mon., Sept. 23, 1833)

Delooch, Mr. John M. Of the Merchantile House of S. S. Dean & Co.
of Wesley, Tenn. Aged 21 years. Died in Marshall Co., Miss.
National Banner and Nashville Whig. (Wed., Sept. 7, 1836)

Deming, Mr. City Hotel. Died in Natchez of Yellow Fever.
Daily Republican Banner. (Wed., Oct. 18, 1831)

Deming, Hon. Benjamin F. A Representative in Congress from Vermont.
Died at Saratoga, Spring, New York.
National Banner and Nashville Daily Advertiser. (Fri., Aug. 1, 1834)

Demond, Mr. James. Died near Little Rock, Ark.
National Banner and Nashville Whig. (Sat., May 12, 1827)

Demoss, Hannah. Consort of Lewis Demoss, deceased late of Davidson
County. Died in Sabine County, Mo.
Daily Republican Banner. (Sat., Dec. 7, 1839)

Demoss, Mr. William. In the 68th year of his age. Died in Carroll
County, Tenn. on the 18th Feb. last.
National Banner and Nashville Whig. (Mon., March 21, 1836)

Demumbrane, Capt. Timothy. Died in this town on Monday last. A
venable citizen of Nashville.
National Banner and Nashville Whig. (Sat., Nov. 4, 1826)

Demoubille, Peter. Aged 46 years. Died in Nashville of Cholera.
National Banner and Nashville Whig. (Fri., June 19, 1835)

De Neckere, The Right Reverend. Bishop of New Orleans. Died at
New Orleans of the Prevailing Malady.
National Banner and Nashville Daily Advertiser. (Fri., Sept. 10, 1833)

Deneson, Mr. Patrick, Died in Smith County.
National Banner and Nashville Whig. (Mon., Jan. 31, 1831)

Deneston, Mr. Patrick. Died in Smith County.
National Banner and Nashville Whig. (Mon., Jan. 31,1831)

Denham, Daniel A. Esq. Late of Covington, Tenn. Died in Ark. on his
way to Texas.
Nashville Republican. (Sat., Jan. 28, 1837)

Denham, Daniel A. Esq. Late of Covington, Tenn. Died in Ark. on his
way to Texas.
Nashville Republican. (Sat., Jan. 28, 1837)

Dennis, Mrs. Charity. Died in Nashville, funeral this day at one
o'clock P.M. from the residence of Mrs. A. Goodwin.
National Banner and Nashville Daily Advertiser. (Wed., Jan. 9, 1833)

Dennis, Hon. Littiton P. A Representative in Congress from the state
of Maryland.
National Banner and Nashville Daily Advertiser. (Thurs., May 1, 1834)

Dennis, Mrs. Susan. Aged 54 formely of James City County, Virginia.
Died in Nashville.
Nashville Republican & State Gazette. (Tues., Jan. 17, 1832)

Dennis, Mrs. Susan. Aged 54 years formely of James County, Va. Died
in Franklin, Tenn. on the 5th inst. after illness of four or five
weeks.
National Banner and Nashville Advertiser. (Tues., Jan. 17, 1832)

Dennis, Mrs. Susan. Died in Franklin, Tenn. on the 5th inst. formely
of James City County, Virginia in the 54th year of her age.
The Western Weekly Review. (Fri., Jan. 13, 1832 Franklin, Tenn.)

Denny, Mrs. Adeline. Wife of Mr. A. R. Denny. Died on Sunday last
in the 26th year of her age.
Nashville Whig. (Wed., Sept. 2, 1840)

Denny, Major Jas. W. Of Louisville. Died suddenly at Versailles, Ky.
National Banner and Nashville Daily Advertiser. (Mon., Feb. 11, 1833)

Denny, Mrs. Louisa (For 1. Mi) Wife of Col. Wm. H. D. Denny. Died
at the Grindstone.
National Banner and Nashville Whig. (Sat., Sept. 8, 1827)

Denton, James. From Perry County, Died at the Tennessee State Prison
of Cholera.
National Banner and Nashville Whig. (Fri., Aug. 14, 1835)

Desfarges, Mr. Stephen H. Died at Lexington, Ky. For some time a
resident of Nashville.
National Banner and Nashville Daily Advertiser. (Tues., July 3, 1832)

Desforges, Mr. Stephen H. For some time a resident of Nashville.
Died in Lexington, Ky.
National Banner and Nashville Advertiser. (Mon., July 2, 1832)

Deshazo, Mr. William. (Native of Virginia). Died in Nashville on
Friday the 5th inst.
National Banner and Nashville Daily Advertiser. (Sat., April 6, 1833)

Deshazo, Mr. William. Died in Nashville on Friday the 5th inst. He
was a native of Virginia.
National Banner and Nashville Daily Advertiser. (Sat., April 6, 1833)

Dew, Mrs. Martha. Wife of Mr. Joseph J. Dew and daughter of Major
Sam Greenleaf of Cincinnati. Died at Bolivar.
National Banner and Nashville Whig. (Fri., Nov. 18, 1831)

Dew, Mrs. Martha. Wife of Mr. Joseph J. Dew and daughter of Maj.
Sam Greenleaf. Died at Bolivar.
National Banner and Nashville Whig. (Fri., Nov. 18, 1831)

De Witt, Rev. John, D. D. Died in New York. Eulogy.
Nashville Republican and State Gazette. (Tues., Nov. 8, 1831)

De Witt, Simeon. Surveyor General of this State. Died Ithoca, N.Y.
on the 3rd inst. Aged 78 years 11 months and 7 days.
National Banner and Nashville Whig. (Mon., Jan. 5, 1835)

Dews, Mrs. Sol. Died in Shelbyville, Tenn. of Cholera.
National Banner and Nashville Daily Advertiser. (Thurs., July 11, 1833)

Dews, Mr. Soloman. Aged 48 years. Died in Shelbyville.
National Banner and Nashville Daily Advertiser. (Thurs., June 19, 1834)

Dexter, Hon. Samuel. Of Massachusetts. Died at Athen, in New York
on his way from this city with his family, his illness was very short.
The Nashville Whig. (May 28, 1816)

Dial, Esq. Jeremiah. A Revolutionary Soldier in the 75th year of his
age. Died in Bedford County, Tenn.
National Banner and Nashville Whig. (Fri., Oct. 17, 1834)

Dial, Esq. Jeremiah. A revolutionary soldier in the 7th year of his
age. Died in Bedford County, Tenn.
National Banner and Nashville Whig. (Fri., Oct. 31, 1834)

Dibdens, Esq. Charles. For many years author and manager at many
Theatres. Died at London 25th Jan.
National Banner and Nashville Daily Advertiser. (Mon., April 1, 1833)

Dibrell, Col. Charles. At the advance age of 84. Died on the 15th
inst. of Stockwood, Obion County at the resident of Gen. Gibbs. A
soldier of the Revolution.
Nashville Whig. (Fri., July 31, 1840)

Dick, Col. Nathaniel. Of the firm of N & J Dick & Co. Died in New
York on the 5th inst.
Daily Republican Banner. (Mon., March 11, 1839)

Dickason, James Hartwell. Infant son of H. S. and C. Dickason. Died
in Sommerville.
Nashville Whig. (Sat., April 11, 1846)

Dickenson, Mr. Appleton. Died in Knoxville. Aged 21
National Banner. (Sat., June 27, 1829)

John Dickenson. Died. The funeral will be preached by the Rev'd
Mr. Henderson at the Court House in Nashville on Sunday next.
The Clarion and the Tennessee Gazette. (Dec. 12, 1815 Vol ? No. 122)

Dicker, John. Aged 72 years. A native of Strasburg in Germany.
Died in Nashville on Monday last a citizen of Nashville for the
past 24 years.
Nashville Whig. (Wed., May 8, 1830)

Dickerson, Mrs. Eliza. Consort of Hon. D. W. Dickerson Esq. Died
near Murfreesboro on the 5th inst. in the 22nd year of her age.
Daily Republican Banner. (Sat., Oct. 6, 1838)

Dickey, John Esq. Age 60. Formerly of South Carolina. Died in
Williamson County on the 11th inst.
Impartial Review and Cumberland Repository. (Thurs., Dec. 24, 1807)

Dickinson, Mrs. C. R. Relict of the late Dr. William C. Dickinson.
Died in Nashville on Sunday last.
The Politican and Weekly Nashville Whig. (Fri., March 17, 1848)

Dickinson, Mrs. C. R. Relict of Dr. William G. Dickinson. Died in
Nashville on Sunday last.
The Christian Record. (Sat., March 18, 1848)

Dickinson, John. Died on Friday last, July 7, 1815 after a lingering
indisposition John Dickinson, Esq. Atty at Law and for many years
a citizen of this town, Nashville.
Whig. (July 11, 1815)

Dickinson, John. The funeral of John Dickinson will be preached at the Court House in Nashville on Sunday next (December 17, 1815) Nashville Whig. (Dec. 13, 1815)

Dickison, Mrs. Eliza. Consort of William Dickison Esq. Died in Greenville, Tenn. on the 30th of Oct. in the 71st year of her age. National Banner and Nashville Whig. (Mon., Dec. 19, 1836)

Dickson, Mrs. Catherine. Consort of Maj. E. D. Dickson. Died in Dreston T. on the 19th inst. in the 40th year of her age. National Banner & Nashville Whig. (Mon., Sept. 29, 1834)

Dickson, Hon. David. A Representative in Congress from the State of Mississippi. Died at Little Rock, Ark. Nashville Republican. (Tues., Aug. 30, 1836)

Dickson, Mr. David. Late of Pittsburgh. Died at Florence, Ala. National Banner. (Jan. 27, 1826)

Dickson, Mrs. Eliza. Consort of William Dickson Esq. Died at Greenville, Tenn. on the 30th Oct. in the 71st year of her age. National Banner and Nashville Whig. (Fri., Nov. 25, 1836)

Dickson, Mrs. Eliza. Consort of William Dickson Esq. Died at Greenville, Tenn. on the 30th Oct. in the 71st year of her age. Nashville Republican. (Fri., Nov. 25, 1836)

Dickson, Capt. James E. Of Florence, Ala. Died at the Nashville Hotel last evening April 21, 1832) National Banner and Nashville Advertiser. (Sat., April 21, 1832)

Dickson, Capt. John E. Of Florence, Ala. Died at the Nashville City Hotel last evening. National Banner and Nashville Daily Advertiser. (Sat., April 21, 1836)

Dickson, John P. Esq. In his 22nd year. Died in the neighborhood of Nashville, Feb. 28th. National Banner and Nashville Whig. (Mon., March 14, 1836)

Dickson, Mr. Joseph. Late of North Carolina. Died at Jackson. National Banner and Nashville Advertiser. (Fri., Jan. 27, 1832)

Dickson, Doct. Joseph A. Died on Tuesday the 18th Inst. in Dickson County, Tenn. National Banner and Nashville Whig. (Wed., Aug. 26, 1835)

Dickson, Miss Lucretia. Died on the 27th ult. killed by Lighting. National Banner. (March 10, 1826)

Dickson, Mrs. Margaret. Aged 23 years. Died in Nashville on the 22nd inst. Nashville Whig. (Tues., July 25, 1843)

Dickson, Ja. Moulton. Aged 51 years. Died near Charlotte, Dickson County on the 4th Nov. Formely a member of the Legislature from Dickson County. National Banner and Nashville Whig. (Mon., Nov. 9, 1835)

Dickson, Mr. Thomas. Died in Nashville yesterday. National Banner and Nashville Daily Advertiser. (Sat., Aug. 24, 1833)

Dickson, Dr. William. Formely a member of Congress from this State. Died on Sunday last. Nashville Whig. (Tues., Feb. 20, 1816)

Dickson, William E. Died on the 30th Oct. National Banner and Nashville Whig. (Fri., Nov. 4, 1836)

Dickson, Mr. Wm. M. Died in Madison County, Ala.
National Banner and Nashville Whig. (Sat., July 8, 1826)

Diffey, Lucy. Aged 20. Died in Nashville of Cholera.
National Banner and Nashville Daily Advertiser. (Thurs., June 6, 1833)

Dill, Mr. Newton C. To Miss Narcissa Kerr. Died in Rutherford Co.
National Banner and Nashville Whig. (Sat., Feb. 24, 1827)

Dillahunty, Major Lewis. Died in Hardeman County.
National Banner and Nashville Whig. (July 1, 1826)

Dillahunty, Thomas Esq. Formely of this place. Died in Lawrence
County, Ala.
National Banner and Nashville Whig. (Sat., Sept. 27, 1828)

Dillahunty, Maj. Thomas. Died in Lawrence County, Ala.
National Banner & Nashville Whig. (Sat., Sept. 6, 1828)

Dillon, Maj. Edward. Died in Giles County.
National Banner and Nashville Whig. (Fri., Oct. 20, 1826)

Dillon, Sarah Matilda. Infant daughter of Mrs. Frances A. Dillon.
Died in Columbia, Tenn.
National Banner and Nashville Whig. (Fri., Jan. 9, 1835)

Dishman, Mrs. Mary and in 6 hours afterwards her husband Mr. John
Dishman. In Warren Co., Ky.
National Banner and Nashville Whig. (Sat., Aug. 18, 1827)

Dismuke, Ann. Daughter of Col. John T. Dismuke. Died on the 19th
in Davidson County. Age 4 years 8 months and 19 days.
Nashville Republican. (Sat., July 22, 1837)

Dismuke, Miss Ann T. Daughter of Mr. Paul Dismuke of this County.
Died on Sunday the 18th inst. after a illness which she bore with
a christian fortitude.
The Nashville Whig. (Aug. 27, 1816)

Dismuke, Mrs. Harriet N. Wife of George E. Dismuke. Died on the
4th inst. in Sumner County in the 44th year of her age.
Nashville Free Whig. and Weekly Commercial Register. (Friday, Aug.
30, 1850)

Dismuke, John T. Esq. Aged 54 years. Died at his residence in Davidson County on the 15th inst.
Nashville Whig. (Tues., Sept. 22, 1846)

Dismuke, Sarah. Daughter of Mr. Paul Dismuke. Died in Davidson
County on Wed. 11 inst.
National Banner and Nashville. (Sat., July 14, 1832)

Dismukes, Sarah. Daughter of Mr. Paul Dismukes. Died in Davidson
County on Wednesday 11th inst.
National Banner and Nashville Daily Advertiser. (Sat., July 14, 1832)

Dittmore, Elizabeth Emma. Daughter of Mr. Jacob Dittmore. Died
in Nashville on the 24th ult.
The Christian Record. (Sat., March 4, 1848)

Dittmore, Mr. Jacob. Died in Nashville on the 25th ult.
The Christian Record. (Sat., March 4, 1848)

Dittmore, Mr. Jacob. Aged 43 years. Died in Nashville on the 25th
ult.
The Politician and Weekly Nashville Whig. (Fri., March 17, 1848)

Divine, Mr. Patrick. Died last Tuesday of (consumption) a citizen of this place. (Nashville)
Impartial Review and Cumberland Repository. (Sat., April 25, 1807)

Dixon, Mr. Ezekiel. Of Rutherford County, T. aged 25. Died in Florence, Ala.
National Banner and Nashville Whig. (Sat., Sept. 9, 1826)

Dixon, John C. Of Capt. Jones Company of Giles County. Died on board the Steamboat Memphis on their return from the Seminole war.
National Banner and Nashville Whig. (Fri., Feb. 3, 1837)

Dixon, Mr. Joseph. Late of North Carolina. Died at Jackson.
National Banner and Nashville Daily Advertiser. (Fri., Jan. 27, 1832)

Dixon, Nathaniel Henderson. Youngest son of Dr. M. L. Dixon. Died in Winchester, Tenn. on the 11th Nov. 1833 in the fifth year of his age.
National Banner and Nashville Daily Advertiser. (Tues., Nov. 19, 1833)

Dixon, Colonel Philip. Died near the Mississippi Spring on the 25th May. Aged about 45 years.
Daily Republican Banner. (Wed., June 12, 1839)

Dixon, Mrs. Polly. Age 39. Consort of Maj. Tilmon Dixon. Died on Tuesday 26 inst. at Dixon Springs.
Impartial Review and Cumberland Repository. (Sat., Aug. 30, 1806)

Doak, Mary Weakly Miss. Departed this life on the 22nd ultimo, Miss Mary Weakly Doak, daughter of Capt. Samuel Doak of Knox County.
Knoxville Gazette. (Fri., Feb. 3, 1795)

Doak, Rev. Samuel. Of the Presbytery of Knoxville. Died ___.
The Christian Record. (Sat., May 20, 1848)

Doak, Rev. Samuel D. D. Late President of Washington College. Died in Green County.
National Banner and Nashville Whig. (Mon., Jan. 3, 1831)

Doak, Samuel D. D. Late President of Washington College. Died in Green County.
National Banner and Nashville Whig. (Mon., Jan. 3, 1831)

Dobbins, Mrs. An aged and Respectable lady. Died in Sumner County.
National Banner and Nashville Daily Advertiser. (Tues., Aug. 5, 1834)

Dobbins, Mary Susan. Daughter of Capt. John Dobbins. Died on the 29th Sept. at the residence of Maj. Aaron Wells of Lincoln County. Aged 17 years.
Nashville Union. Wed., Oct. 16, 1839)

Dobbins, Mrs. Nancy. In the 78th year of her age. Died on the 1st ult. at the residence of her daughter in Sumner County.
The Christian Record. (Sat., June 17, 1848)

Dobbs, Mr. John R. Died suddenly on the 5th inst at his residence in Davidson County.
Nashville Whig. (Sat., Nov. 7, 1846)

Doddridge, Hon. Philip. Congress man from Virginia. Died at Washington City, No. 19, 1832. See paper for obituary.
National Banner and Nashville Advertiser. (Sat., Dec. 1st, 1832)

Doddridge, Hon. Philip. Member of Congress from Virginia. Died suddenly at Washington City. Nov. 19th.
National Banner and Nashville Daily Advertiser. (Sat., Dec. 1st, 1832)

Dodge, Pickering Esq. An eminent merchant. Died at Salem, Mass.
National Banner & Nashville Daily Advertiser. (Thurs., Sept. 12, 1833)

Doggrt, Mr. Wm. Aged 28. Died in Shelby County, Ky.
National Banner and Nashville Whig. (Sat., Oct.7, 1826)

Donaho, Miss Martha E. Daughter of the late Dr. E. Donaho of Rutherford
County, Aged 15 years. Died in Smith County, Tenn.
National Banner and Nashville Daily Advertiser. (Tues., Aug. 5, 1834)

Donald, John Sevier. Infant son of John T. and Eliza M. Donald. Died
on Wednesday the 13th ult. Aged 21 months. (Copyed from the N. O.
Pecayune)
Nashville True Whig and Weekly Commercial Register. (Fri., April 17,
1850)
Donaldson, Mrs. K. Died in Bowling reen, Ky.
National Banner and Nashville Whig. (Fri., April 10, 1835)

Done, Judge. Died in Annapolis, Md.
Nashville Republican and State Gazette. (Tues., Oct. 25, 1831)

Donelly, Mr. James. A native of Ireland aged about 85. Died in
Davidson County near Nashville on the 30th Aug.
National Banner and Nashville Whig. (Thurs., Oct. 21, 1830)

Donelson, Alexander, Sen. Died on the 23rd ult, in this county at his
residence in Jones Bend, age 83 yrs. The deceased was the eldest
brother of the late Mrs. Jackson, wife of Gen. Jackson and the last
but one of the numerous family of children of Col. John Donelson,
sen'r one of the Pioneers of the West, who emigrated to Tennessee,
as early as the year 1780. The deceased was an honest man and a
virtuous citizen. He was esteemed and respected by all who knew him.
National Banner and Daily Advertiser. Nashville, Tenn. (Mon., June 2,
1834)

Donelson, Alexander, sen. Died on the 23 ult, in this county at his
residence in Jones Bend. The deceased was the eldest brother of the
late Mrs. Jackson, wife of Gen Jackson and the last but one of the
numerous family of children of Col John Donelson, sen'r one of the
Pioneers of the West, who emigrated to Tennessee, as early as the
year 1780. The deceased was an honest man and a virtuous citizen. He
was esteemed and respected by all who knew him.
Nashville Republican Nashville, Tenn. (Thurs., June 5, 1834)

Donelson, Andrew J. Lieut. United States Corps of Engineers. Died
at the residence of his father, the Hon. A. J. Donelson near Memphis,
Tenn. on Thursday the 20th of October 1859. Born June 6th, 1826 in
Davidson County, Tennessee. He graduated at West Point in 1848.
Obit.
Nashville Patriot Nashville, Tenn. (Thurs., Oct. 27, 1859)

Donelson, Mrs. E. Widow of the late Mr. Lemuel Donelson. Died in
Williamson County.
National Banner and Nashville Whig. (Mon., Dec. 17, 1832)

Donelson, Mrs. E. Died in Williamson County on the 6th inst.
Nashville Republican and State Gazette. (Mon., Dec. 17, 1832)

Donelson, Mrs. E. Consort of the late Lemuel Donelson. Died in
Williamson County on Thursday 6th inst.
The Western Weekly Review. (Fri., Dec. 14, 1832 Franklin, Tenn.)

Donelson, Mrs. E. Consort of the late Lemuel Donelson. Died in
Williamson County on the Thursday 6th inst.
The Western Weekly Review. (Fri., Dec. 14, 1832 Franklin, Tenn.)

Donelson, Mrs. E. Widow of the late Mr Lemuel Donelson. Died in
Williamson County.
National Banner and Nashville Daily Advertiser. (Mon., Dec. 17, 1832)

Donelson, Mrs. Eliza E. Consort of Dr. Samuel Donelson of Shelby
County. Died in Shelby County, Tenn. on the 20th inst.
Nashville Union. (Mon., June 3, 1839)

Donelson, Mrs. Elizabeth. Wife of William Donelson, Esq. Died in the
vicinity of Nashville on the 8th ult. in the 32 year of her age.
Nashville Whig. (Fri., Nov. 5, 1841)

Donelson, Mrs. Elizabeth. The amiable and pious wife of Wm. Donelson
Esq. "We record with feeling of sorrow mingled with submission" (con-
cludes an obituary notice of this lamented lady in the Methodist
Advocate of this city) the untimely death etc. Nov. 5th 1841. Died
in this vicinity on the 8th ult. in the 32nd year of her age.
Whig.

Donelson, Mrs. Emily. Aged 29 years. Died at the home of her husband
Major Andrew Donelson near the Hermitage.
National Banner and Nashville Whig. (Mon., Jan. 16, 1837)

Donelson, Mrs. Emily. Aged 29 years. Died on the 19th inst. at the
seat of her husband Major Andrew Jackson Donelson near the Hermitage.
(Obituary)
The Union. Tues., Jan. 3, 1837)

Donelson, Capt. John. Died in Davidson County on the 21st inst. At
the age of 75.
National Banner and Nashville Whig. (Tues., April 27, 1830)

Donelson, Capt. Jno. Died at the residence at Bainbridge, Ala. of
Apoplexy.
Daily Republican Banner. (Tues., May 5, 1840)

Donelson, Mrs. Laura M. Daughter of Mr. William P. Lawerence of
Nashville. Died on the 4th inst. at the residence of husband in
Shelby County, West Tennessee.
Nashville Whig. (Tues., April 30, 1844)

Donelson, Mr. Lemuel. Aged 42 years. Died on Wednesday the 20th inst.
near Franklin, Tenn.
The Western Weekly Review. (Fri., June 22, 1832 Franklin, Tenn.)

Donelson, Mr. Lemuel. Died near Franklin, Williamson County. On
Wednesday evening 20th inst.
National Banner and Nashville Daily Advertiser. (Thurs., June 21, 1832)

Donelson, Mr. Levin. Died at his residence in Davidson County on
Friday evening the 23rd inst. age 57.
Nashville Banner and Daily Advertiser. (Tues., Aug. 27, 1833)

Donelson, Mr. Levin. Aged about 57 years. Died at his residence in
Davidson County on Friday evening the 23rd inst.
National Banner and Nashville Daily Advertiser. (Tues., Aug. 27, 1833)

Donelson, Mrs. Mary. In the 86h year of her age. Died in Davidson
County on the 16th inst. at the residence of her son Stockley Donelson.
(Obituary Dec. 2)
The Christian Record. (Sat., Nov. 25, 1848)

Donelson, Miss Mary I. Only daughter of the late Capt. John Donelson
of Ala. and Mrs. Eliza E. Donelson of Ala. Died at Hunter Hill,
Davidson County on Saturday the 13th of May in the 19th year of her
age.
Nashville Whig. (Sat., May 20, 1843)

Donelson, Mrs. Phila Ann Lawrence. Wife of Capt. Stockley Donelson
and daughter of Dr. William P. Lawrence. Died at Cleverland the
residence of Capt. Stockley Donelson. Aged 41 years.
Nashville True Whig and Weekly Commerical. (Fri., March 7, 1851)

Donelson, Mrs. Laura M. Daughter of Dr. William P. Lawrence of
Nashville. Died on the 4th inst. at the residence of husband in
Shelby County, West Tennessee.
Nashville Whig. (Tues., April 30, 1844)

Donelson, Mrs. Mary. In the 86th year of her age. Died in Davidson
County on the 16th inst. at the residence of her son. Stockly Donelson
(Obituary Dec. 2)
The Christian Record. (Sat., Nov. 25, 1848)

Donelson, Mrs. Rachel. Died on the 16th inst. Wife of Mr. William
Donelson of this County.
Whig. (Sept. 27, 1824)

Donelson, Mrs. Rachel. Died on the 16th of September, 1824 in Davidson County, Tennessee. Wife of William Donelson.
Whig. (Sept. 27, 1824)

Donelson, Rachel. Wife of Mr. William Donelson of Davidson County
on Sept. 16, 1824. Was daughter of Col. Seven Donelson, brother of
Capt. John.
Whig. (Sept. 27, 1824)

Donelson, Mrs. Rachel. Wife of Mr. William Donelson of this County.
Died on the 16th inst.
Nashville Whig. (Sept. 27, 1824)

Donelson, Mrs. Rachel. Wife of Mr. William Donelson
Sept, 1824

Donelson, Col. William. One of the earlest settlers of this County.
Died on the 13th inst. at his residence in this County. (Davidson)
The Nashville Gazette. (Wed., April 26, 1820)

Donelson, Capt. Wm. One of the earliest settlers of this County.
He was Universily esteemed as an honest man and a good citizen. Col.
Donelson has left a large family and numerous relations and friends
to deplore his loss. Died on the 13th inst. at his residence in
this County.
The Nashville Gazette (April 26, 1820)

Donelson, William. In the 17th year of his age and son of Col. Wm.
Donelson. Died in Rutherford County.
National Banner and Nashville Whig. (Sat., Nov. 17, 1827)

Donho, Mr. Lynch B. Died at Hartsville.
National Banner and Nashville Whig. (Mon., Jan. 31, 1831)

Donho. Lynch B. Died at Hartsville.
National Banner and Nashville Whig. (Mon., Jan. 31, 1831)

Donly, Maj. John. Died on yesterday 10th Sept.
National Banner and Nashville Whig. (Fri., Sept. 11, 1835)

Donne, Charles. Of Louisville. Died in the explosion of the Steamboat Lucy Walker.
Nashville Whig. (Tues., Oct. 29, 1844)

Donnel, Rev. Samuel. Of the Presbyterian Church. Died in Wilson
County lately.
Nashville Whig. (Sept. 13, 1824)

Donnell, Mrs. Mary Jane. Died in Sumner County.
National Banner and Nashville Daily Advertiser. (Tues., Nov. 19, 1833)

Donnell, Mr. Persus. Died in Sumner County.
National Banner and Nashville Daily Advertiser. (Mon., Oct. 15, 1832)

Donnell, Mr. Persus. Died in Sumner County.
National Banner and Nashville Daily Advertiser. (Mon., Oct. 15, 1832)

Donnelly, Peter. Died in Shelbyville, Tenn. of Cholera.
National Banner and Nashville Daily Advertiser. (Thurs., July 11, 1833)

Donnison, William Jr. Is no more this Gentlemen. Was a native of Boston, Mass. He died at New Madrid, Mo. on the 17th of January 1823.
Nashville Whig. (March 12, 1823)

Dooley, Mr. James. Aged 44 years. Died in Lost Prairie, Ark.
National Banner and Nashville Whig. (Fri., Sept. 6, 1833)

Dooley, Mr. Nathaniel. Aged 16 years. Died in Los Prairie, Ark.
National Banner and Nashville Daily Advertiser. (Fri., Sept. 6, 1833)

Doolin, Mr. Lleevellin. Died in this town.
National Banner. (Sat., June 27, 1829)

Dooly, Paris F. Died in Maury County.
National Banner and Nashville Whig. (Fri., April 16, 1830)

Dormenor, Hon. Pierre. Judge of the Perish. Died at Point Coupee, Miss.
National Banner and Nashville Daily Advertiser. (Mon., July 29, 1833)

Dorring, Miss Martha Jane. Died in Coffee County.
Nashville Whig. (Tues., July 21, 1846)

Dorris, Mrs. Elizabeth. In the 69th year of her age. Died in Nashville on Sunday night last.
Nashville Whig. (Tues., March 12, 1844)

Dorris, N. William. Son of William D. and Rebecca Dorris. Died in Nashville on the 25th ult. in the 15th year of his age.
The Politician and Weekly Nashville Whig. (Fri., Dec. 10, 1847)

Dorsey, Mr. Caleb. Died Chillicothe.
National Banner and Nashville Whig. (Thurs., Sept. 9, 1830)

Dorsey, Dr. John L. Aged 26. Died in Cincinnati O.
National Banner and Nashville Daily Advertiser. (Sat., Aug. 10, 1833)

Dorsey, Dr. Resin H. Aged 23. Died in Louisville.
National Banner and Nashville Whig. (Sat., Sept. 9, 1826)

Dortch, Mr. Baker. Died near Poet Royal. A Highly respectable citizen of Robinson County.
National Banner and Nashville Whig. (Mon., Oct. 20, 1834)

Dortch, William H. Esq. Died at Charlotte, Dickerson County on the 12th inst.
National Banner and Nashville Whig. (Fri., Aug. 14, 1835)

Dortch, William H. Died in the town of Charlotte on the 12th inst. in the 31st year of his age.
National Banner and Nashville Whig. (Wed., Aug. 19, 1835)

Douglas, Mrs. Louisa E. Wife of Mr. Hugh Douglas and daughter of the late William Hamilton of Woodford County, Ky. Died at Fayetteville, Tenn. on Feb. 29th (Obituary)
Nashville Whig. (Thurs., March 7, 1844)

Douglass, Mr. E. A member of the thealogical school. Died in Lexington, Ky.
National Banner and Nashville Daily Advertiser. (Tues., July 2, 1833)

Douglass, Mrs. Eliza. Wife of Dr. Elmore Douglas. Died at Gallatin
on Saturday last by being struck by lighting.
National Banner and Nashville Whig. (Mon., May 25, 1835)

Douglass, Mrs. Martha. R. Consort of B. Douglas of Nashville. Died
on the 10th inst at Harrisburg, Pa. in the 30th year of her age.
(Obituary)
The Christian Record. (Sat., July 22, 1848)

Douglass, Matilda Malvina. Daughter of J. C. Douglass Esq. Died in
Sumner County, Tenn. in the 7th year of her age.
National Banner and Nashville Daily Advertiser. (Thurs., Sept. 11, 1834)

Douglass, Mr. Roben G. Died on the 25th of April at his residence
in Barren County, Ky.
Nashville Whig. (Sat., June 25, 1842)

Douglass, Mr. Samuel. Died at Memphis.
National Banner. (Sat., Sept. 5, 1829)

Douglass, Rev. Thomas L. Died on Sunday last at his residence in
Williamson County. Funeral was preached by Rev. A. L. P. Green.
Nashville Whig. (Tues., April 18, 1843)

Douglass, Capt. Wm. Of Louisville, Ky. Who had been appointed by
the President a Commioner to value and sell the cattle belonging to
the Choctaw Indians. Died on the 8th inst. at Columbus, Miss.
National Banner and Nashville Whig. (Mon., Sept. 16, 1831)

Douglass, Capt. Wm. Of Louisville. Who had been appointed by the
President a Commissioner to value and sell the cattle of the Choctaw
Indians. Died at Columbus, Miss. on 8th inst.
National Banner and Nashville Whig. (Mon., Sept. 19, 1831)

Douglass, Mr. William H. Aged 54 years. Died in Sumner County,
Tenn.
National Banner and Nashville Daily Advertiser. (Tues., Aug. 5, 1834)

Douglass, Mrs. Zuritha. Wife of Col. Harris L. Douglas of Wilson
County. Died on the 11th inst in the 19th year of her age.
The Nashville Gazette. (Wed., March 1, 1820)

Douring, Mr. Francis. Died at Lexington, Ky.
National Banner and Nashville Whig. (Wed., Jan. 19, 1831)

Dow, Lorenzo. Died in Georgetown, D. C. on the 2nd inst. He was
a Native of Coventry, Con.
National Banner and Nashville Daily Advertiser. (Thurs., Feb. 20, 1834)

Dow, R. W. Firm of Dow & Co. New York. Died in the wreck of the
Steamboat Lexington.
Daily Republican Banner. (Fri., Jan. 31, 1840)

Downing, Mr. Francis. Died in Lexington, Ky.
Wednesday, Jan. 19, 1831

Downing, Mr. John. Died in Lexington, Ky.
National Banner and Nashville Daily Advertiser. (Sat., Feb. 4, 1832)

Downing, Mr. John. Died in Lexington, Ky.
National Banner and Nashville Advertiser. (Sat., Feb. 4, 1832)

Downing, Mary Eliza. Daughter of Mr. Richard Downing. Died in
Fayette County, Ky. Aged 7 years.
National Banner and Nashville Daily Advertiser. (Mon., June 18, 1832)

Downs, Mr. Cincinnati. Died in the loss of the Steamboat Brandywine.
National Banner and Nashville Daily Advertiser. (Mon., April 23, 1832)

Doxey, Mr. Thomas. In the 74th year of his age. Died at Forrest
Hill, Sumner County on Saturday the 11th inst.
Nashville True Whig and Weekly Commerical Register. (Fri., Aug. 16,
1850)

Doyle, Micheal. Aged 52 years. Died at Franklin on Monday 30th ult.
a native of Ireland.
Nashville Whig. (Tues., Feb. 7, 1843)

Dozier, Mrs. America. Wife of James I. Dozier. Died in Louisville,
Ky. late of Nashville.
National Banner and Nashville Whig! (Wed., Nov. 26, 1834)

Drake, Col. Abraham S. Died in Lexington, Ky.
National Banner and Nashville Whig. (Wed., Sept. 14, 1831)

Drake, Col. Abraham S. Died in Lexington, Ky.
National Banner and Nashville Whig. (Wed., Sept. 14, 1831)

Drake, Mr. Alexander. The celebrated comedian. Died at Cincinnati.
National Banner and Nashville Whig. (Fri., Feb. 26, 1830)

Drake, Brittian Esq. Died at his residence in Wilson County, Tenn.
on the 2nd inst. in the 69th year of his age.
Nashville Whig. (Tues., July 7, 1846)

Drake, Mr. B. W. Died at his residence in Davidson County on Friday
last July 31st.
Daily Republican Banner. (Mon., Aug. 3, 1840)

Drake, Mr. Elijah H. Of the firm Drake and Frazer. Died in Lexington,
Ky. of Cholera at the house of his Brother-in-Law Clifton Thompson.
National Banner and Nashville Daily Advertiser. (Tues., July 2, 1833)

Drake, Miss Elizabeth Adeline. Daughter of Col. Samuel Drake. Died
in Pawhatan County, Va. on the 12th May.
National Banner and Nashville Whig. (Fri., June 10, 1836)

Drake, Mr. Ephraim. Died on the 6th of Dec. last. The son of Mr.
Benj. Drake of this County.
The Nashville Whig. (Jan. 1st 1817)

Drake, Mr. Isaac. Died at Cincinnita, Ohio on the 14th of Cholera.
National Banner and Nashville Daily Advertiser. (Tues., Oct. 23, 1832)

Drake, Mr. Samuel. Died in Cincinnati.
National Banner and Nashville Whig. (Sat., Aug. 5, 1826)

Drake, Mr. Thomas Sen. Died in Bedford County, Tenn. Aged 85 years.
National Banner and Nashville Whig. (Mon., March 30, 1835)

Drake, William Henry. Aged 13 years. Died on the 30th son of William
Drake.
Nashville Republican. (Thurs., Feb. 4, 1836)

Draper, Mr. C. L. Of the house of Cotton, Draper & Co. of Natchez.
Died in Louisville, Ky.
National Banner and Nashville Daily Advertiser. (Mon., Aug. 19, 1833)

Draper, Jas. Esq. Formely a member of Congress from the Wythe
District. Died at Wythe C. H. Va.
National Banner and Nashville Daily Advertiser. (Wed., July 16, 1834)

Drewry, Mary Ann. Only daughter of Mr. John Drewry. Died in this place on Thursday last.
The Nashville Whig and the Tenn. Advertiser. (May 2, 1818)

Driver, Delilah. Infant daughter of William Driver. Died in Nashville on the 14th inst. Aged 22 months.
Nashville Whig. (Tues., June 18, 1844)

Driver, Henry. Second son of Henry and Elizabeth Driver. Died in Nashville on the 23rd inst.
Nashville Whig. (Mon., Sept. 27, 1841)

Dromgoole, Gen. Died at his residence in Brunswick County, Va. He had been relected to Congress, only a few days before his death.
The Politician and Weekly Nashville Whig. (Page 75 Fri., May 14, 1847)

Drummond, Mrs. Sarah. Died in Randolph T.
National Banner and Nashville Daily Advertiser. (Tues., July 15, 1834)

Dryden, Mr. Samuel. Died Cincinnati.
National Banner and Nashville Whig. (Sat., Feb. 10, 1827)

Dubois, Andrew. Died 19th at Cincinnati, Ohio of Cholera.
National Banner and Nashville Daily Advertiser. (Mon., Oct. 29, 1832)

Du Base, Mrs. Francis Eliza. Wife of Dr. A. B. C. Du Base. Died in Shelby County.
National Banner and Nashville Daily Advertiser. (Wed., Jan. 4, 1832)

Du Base, Mrs. Francis Eliza. Wife of Dr. A. B. C. Du Base. Died in Shelby County.
National Banner and Nashville Advertiser. (Wed., Jan. 4, 1832)

Dudley, Miss Caroline E. Daughter of Col. Guilford Dudley. Died on Friday last, in the 30th year of her age. (Obituary)
The Western Weekly Review. (Fri., Jan. 20, 1832) Franklin, Tenn.

Dudley, Miss Carolina E. Daughter of Col. Guilford Dudley. Died in Williamson County.
National Banner and Nashville Advertiser. (Fri., Jan. 27, 1832)

Dudley, Miss Caroline E. Daughter of Col. Guilford Dudley. Died in Williamson County on Friday 13th inst.
National Banner and Nashville Daily Advertiser. (Fri., Jan. 27, 1832)

Dudley, Col. Guilford. A soldier of the revolutionar in the 78th year of his age. Died in Franklin, Tenn. on the 3rd inst.
National Banner and Nashville Daily Advertiser. (Mon., Feb. 11, 1833)

Dudley, Mrs. Maria Annie. Wife of Dr. B. W. Dudley. Died at Lexington, Ky.
National Banner and Nashville Whig. (Sat., Nov. 3, 1827)

Dudley, Mrs. Rebecca. Wife of Jephtha Dudley and daughter of George Trotter. Died at Frankfort, Ky.
National Banner. (Feb. 3, 1826)

Dudley, Mr. Thomas. Died in Nashville on the 18th.
National Banner and Nashville Whig. (Mon., Sept. 19, 1836)

Dufaur, Mr. John James. Died at Vevay, Ind.
National Banner and Nashville Whig. (Sat., April 14, 1827)

Duff, Robert L. Aged 40. Died in Nashville of Cholera on June 5.
National Banner and Nashville Daily Advertiser. (Thurs., June 6, 1833)

Duffy, Susan Eleanor. Eldest daughter of Col. Francis and Mrs. Pamela Duffy. Died at Hartsville, Sumner County on the 27th ult. Gallatin Union.
The Union. (Sat., June 18, 1836)

Duffy, Susan Ellenor. Eldest daughter of Col. Francis and Pamela Duffy. Died in Hartsville on the 27th ult.
National Banner and Nashville Whig. (Wed., June 15, 1836)

Dugan, William. Died 18th at Cincinnati, Ohio of Cholera.
National Banner and Nashville Daily Advertiser. (Fri., Oct. 26, 1832)

Dugger?, Miss Nancy. Daughter of Mr. David Dugger. Died in Maury County.
National Banner and Nashville Whig. (Wed., March 16, 1831)

Dugger, Miss Nancy. Daughter of David Duggar. Died in Maury County.
National Banner and Nashville Whig. (Wed., March 16, 1831)

Duke, Dr. Basil. An old and eminent physician. Died in Washington, Ky.
National Banner and Nashville Whig. (Sat., June 14, 1828)

Duke, Mrs. Nancy. Died in Texas, wife of Thomas Duke, formely of Kentucky.
National Banner and Nashville Whig. (Dec. 2, 1826)

Duke, Mrs. Nancy. Wife of Mr. Thomas Duke formely of Kentucky. Died in Texas.
National Banner and Nashville Whig. (Sat., Dec. 2, 1826)

Dulany, Dr. E. R. Died in Blauntsville, East Tenn.
Daily Republican Banner. (Wed., July 29, 1840)

Dulany, Mr. John R. Aged 22. Died in Sullivan County on the 3d inst.
National Banner and Nashville Daily Advertiser. (Fri., Feb. 15, 1833)

Dumb, William. 51 years. Died in Louisville, Ky on the 18th of Cholera.
National Banner and Nashville Whig. (Mon., Oct. 22, 1832)

Dumeste, Lieut. J. A. Of the U. S. Corps of Topographical Engineers, a Scientist of Worth. Recently surveyed the Tennessee River. Died at Baltimore on the 10th inst.
National Banner and Nashville Whig. (Mon., Oct. 24, 1831)

Dumeste, Lieut. J. A. Died at Baltimore, on the 10th inst.
National Banner and Nashville Whig. (Mon., Oct. 24, 1831)

Dunbar, Mr. James. Aged 52. Died in Stewart County.
National Banner and Nashville Whig. (Thurs., Oct. 14, 1830)

Dunbar, Mr. Robert. Aged 77. Died in Adams County, Miss.
National Banner. (March 31, 1826)

Duncan, Mr. Abner. Died in Logan County, Ky.
National Banner and Nashville Whig. (Mon., Sept. 20, 1830)

Duncan, Abner L. Esq. Distinguished lawyer of that place. Died at New Orleans on the 27th ult.
Nashville Whig. (Jan. 12, 1824)

Duncan, Mr. Addison. Died at Wall Springs, Sumner County, Tenn.
National Banner and Nashville Daily Advertiser. (Mon., Aug. 25, 1834)

Duncan, Benjamin. Died in Philadelphia, former Sheriff of Philadelphia County.
Nashville Whig. (Mon., Aug. 31, 1840)

Duncan, Miss Eliza. E. Died at East Baton Rouge, La.
National Banner and Nashville Daily Advertiser. (Tues., Sept. 10, 1833)

Duncan, Mrs. Eliza L. Consort of Mr. Samuel Duncan. Died in Maury
County.
National Banner and Nashville Whig. (Wed., March 4, 1835)

Duncan, Mrs. Jane McKenzie. Consort of Lucuis Campbell Duncan. Esq.
Counsellor at Law. Died at New Orleans.
National Banner and Nashville Daily Advertiser. (Fri., May 16, 1834)

Duncan, Mrs. Joicy. Consort of James Duncan. Died in the town of
Illinois. (Ill.)
National Banner and Nashville Daily Advertiser. (Mon., May 12, 1834)

Duncan, Mrs. Olivia. Wife of Mr. Lemuel H. Duncan. Died in Shelbyville.
National Banner and Nashville Whig. (Sat., July 22, 1826)

Duncan, Mr. Thomas. Died at Maysville, Ky.
National Banner. (March 24, 1826)

Duncan, Thomas A. Esq. Of Nashville, Tenn. Died on the morning of
Dec. 29 about 90 miles above New Orleans.
National Banner and Nashville Whig. (Tues., Feb. 23, 1830)

Duncan, Pasty. Wife of Garnett Duncan Esq. Died in Lexington, Ky.
National Banner. (Sat., May 16, 1829)

Duncan, Mr. William D. Died at Shakertown, Logan County, Ky. of
the house of Duncan, Forsyth and Riddle of Pittsburgh.
National Banner and Nashville Whig. (Dec. 2, 1826)

Duncan, Mr. William A. Of the house of Duncan, Forsyth and Riddle
of Pittsburg. Died at Shakertown Logan County, Ky.
National Banner and Nashville Whig. (Sat., Dec. 2, 1826)

Duncan, Wm. F. A member of the bar at St. Louis. Died at St. Louis.
National Banner and Nashville Daily Advertiser. (Sat., Aug. 10, 1833)

Dunham, Mr. Elijah. Aged 50. Died at Natchez.
National Banner and Nashville Whig. (Sat., Oct. 7, 1826)

Dunham, Mr. William H. Son of Daniel A. Dunham Esq. Died in this
County on the 1st inst.
National Banner. (Feb. 10, 1826)

Dunlap, Anna Maria. Infant daughter of Gen. H. W. Dunlap of Louisiana.
Died in Franklin County, Alabama at the residence of B. M'Kiernan,
Esq.
Nashville Whig. (Thurs., March 19, 1846)

Dunlap, Mr. Charles G. Died at Paris, Henry County.
National Banner and Nashville Whig. (Sat., Oct. 6, 1827)

Dunlap, Devereaux Esq. Died in Paris, Tenn.
National Banner and Nashville Whig. (Sat., Sept. 9, 1826)

Dunlap, Col. James A. Lately appointed U. S. Attorney for the Middle
District of Florida. Died in New York.
National Banner and Nashville Whig. (Fri., Nov. 25, 1831)

Dunlap, Col. James A. Lately appointed U. S. Attorney for the Middle
District of Fla. Died in New York.
National Banner and Nashville Whig. (Fri., Nov. 25, 1831)

Dunlap, Miss Nancy. Daughter of Mr. James Dunlap. Died in Blout County.
National Banner and Nashville Daily Advertiser. (Thurs., July 4, 1833)

Dunlap, Mr. Robert. Aged about 50 years. Died on the 21st Sept. He was a native of South Carolina but resided for the last twenty years in Stewart County, Tenn.
Nashville Union. (Fri., Oct. 5, 1838)

Dunley, Gilford. A soldier of the revolutionar in the 78th year of his age. Died on Sunday evening 3rd inst.
The Western Weekly Review. (Fri., Feb. 8, 1833) Franklin, Tenn.

Dunn, Mrs. Wife of Mr. James Dunn. Died at Hartsville, Sumner County, she was a daughter of Moses Lawson Esq. of Smith County.
National Banner and Nashville Daily Advertiser. (Mon., Oct. 29, 1832)

Dunn, Mrs. Elizabeth. Wife of Dr. Dudley Dunn. Died in Shelby County.
National Banner and Nasville Whig. (Mon., Sept. 12, 1831)

Dunn, John R. Esq. Died in New Orleans on the 25th (29th?) Sept. a native of Nashville, Tenn.
Nashville Republican. (Sat., Oct. 15, 1836)

Dunn, Mrs. Mary. Wife of Maj. David Dunn. Died in Shelby County.
National Banner and Nashville Daily Advertiser. (Wed., March 13, 1833)

Dunn, Mrs. M. C. Consort of Col. Thomas Dunn. Died in Weakley County, Tenn. on the 22nd inst.
Nashville Republican. (Thurs., April 27, 1837)

Dunn, Michael C. Esq. Notice of his death.
Republican Banner and Nashville Whig. (No. 213 Wed., Aug. 31, 1853)

Dunn, Samuel. Died in Knoxville.
Daily Republican Banner. (Sat., Sept. 22, 1838)

Dunn, Susanna. Daughter of Michael Dunn, aged 14. Died in Davidson County on the 24th inst.
National Banner and Nashville Whig. (Sat., June 30, 1827)

Dunn, Thomas Sergent. At Arms of the House of Representative of the United States, at Middletown in the state of Maryland. Died on the 6th inst.
Nashville Whig. (Oct. 25, 1824)

Dunn, Mr. William. In the 90th year of his age. Died in Knoxville, Tenn. on the 19th inst. a soldier of the Revolution.
Daily Republican Banner. (Fri., Jan. 6, 1838)

Eastin, Mr. Wm. Died in this county on Sunday last. (Aug. 23, 1829) Merchant of Florence, Ala.
National Banner. (Sat., Aug. 29, 1829)

Dunn, Mr. Wilson. Aged 18 years. Died in Rutherford County, Tenn.
National Banner and Nashville Whig. (Fri., Oct. 31, 1834)

Dunnavan, Davis. Died in Princeton, Ky. of Cholera.
National Banner and Nashville Daily Advertiser. (Wed., July 9, 1834)

Dunnaven, John R. Died 19th at Cincinnati, Ohio of Cholera.
National Banner and Nashville Daily Advertiser. (Fri., Oct. 26, 1832)

Dunning, Edward Esq. Died on the 4th inst. at Blountsville on his way from Nashville to Mobile.
National Banner and Nashville Whig. (Fri., Nov. 4, 1836)

Dunning, Mrs. Elizabeth. Aged 75 years. Died in Hickman County, Tenn.
National Banner and Nashville Whig. (Fri., April 10, 1835)

Dunton, Mr. William. Of Clinton, Hinds County, Miss. Died in Davidson County.
National Banner and Nashville Whig. (Monday, Sept. 6, 1830)

Dupont, Eleuthere Irene. An emenint and much lamented citizen of Delaware. Died in Philadelphia.
National Banner and Nashville Whig. (Fri., Nov. 2, 1834)

Dupont, Victor Esq. of Delaware. Died at Philadelphia.
National Banner and Nashville Whig. (Sat., Feb. 24, 1827)

Durrer, Mrs. Rhoda of Nashville. Died on Friday 14th.
Nashville Whig. (Sat., March 16, 1844)

Dutton, Private Booker H. With Company F. First Reg. Tenn. Volunteer. Died - was killed in the Battle of Monterey with the Nexicans on Sept. 21st.
Nashville Whig. (Sat., Oct. 24, 1846)

Duty, Capt. William. Aged 70. Died in Madison County, Tenn. A soldier of the Revolutionar .
National Banner and Nashville Whig. (Thurs., Sept. 30, 1830)

Duval, Brook Esq. Aged 45. Died in Robertson County on 21st ult.
Nashville Republican and State Gazette. (January 1, 1831)

Duval, Brook Esq. Aged 45. Died in Robertson County.
National Banner and Nashville Whig. (Mon., Jan. 3, 1831)

Duval, Col. Edmund B. Of Maryland. Died in Philadelphia.
Nashville Republican and State Gazette. (Sat., Feb. 26, 1831)

Dwight, Rev. Nathaniel. M. D. of Norwich, Conn. Aged 62. Died at Orange, N.Y.
National Banner and Nashville Whig. (Fri., July 29, 1831)

Dwight, Rev. Nathaniel M. D. Age 62 of Norwick, Conn. Died at Oswego, N.Y. A brother of the late president of Yale College.
National Banner and Nashville Whig. (Fri., July 29, 1831)

Dwyer, Mrs. Wife of Mr. Wm. Dwyer. Died in Nashville.
National Banner and Nashville Whig. (Fri., March 19, 1830)

Dwyer, Mrs. Daniel. Died in Shelbyville, Tenn. of Cholera.
National Banner and Nashville Daily Advertiser. (Thurs., July 11, 1833)

Dwyer, Daniel. Aged 67 years. Formely of Franklin, Tenn. Died in Louisville, Ky.
Nashville Whig. (Mon., Nov. 30, 1840)

Dwyer, Mrs. Elizabeth. Died in this town.
National Banner. (Sat., Sept. 19, 1829)

Dwyer, Mr. James. A Louisville Merchant. Died at Rankin Holmes, Co. Mi. late of Lincoln Co., Tenn.
National Banner and Nashville Daily Advertiser. (Tues., July 18, 1834)

Dwyer, Mr. Jeremiah. Youngest son of Daniel Dwyer formely of Franklin, Tenn. Died in Nashville on the 24th ult. in the 28th year of his age. (Obituary)
Nashville Whig. (Fri., Oct. 5, 1838)

Dwyer, Mr. John. Died on the 29th Dec. at Satartian, Miss. formely a merchant of Fayetteville.
Nashville Whig. (Wed., Jan. 16, 1839)

Dwyer, Joseph. Doctor of that city. Died at New Orleans on the 7th inst.
Nashville Whig. (Sept. 27, 1824)

Dwyer, Joseph T. A native of Ireland but for many years a resident of Nashville. Died Yesterday about 9 O'clock A.M.
Nashville Whig. (Thursday, Feb. 1, 1844)

Dwyer, Miss Lucinda. Daughter of Mr. W. Dwyer. Died in Bedford Co., Tenn.
National Banner and Nashville Daily Advertiser. (Thurs., June 19, 1834)

Dye, Rev. George W. Died at his residence in Montgomery County. on the 7th inst. An aged and beloved minister of the M. E. Church.
Nashville True Whig and Weekly Commercial Register. (Fri., Oct. 25, 1850)

Dyer, Mrs. Elizabeth. Died at the residence of Isham Dyer Esq. in Nashville.
Daily Republican Banner. (Sat., Oct. 20, 1838)

Dyer, Harriet. Infant daughter of Mr. Isham and Mrs. Harriet Dyer. Died in Nashville on the 11th inst.
National Banner and Nashville Daily Advertiser. (Tues., Aug. 12, 1834)

Dyer, Hazer. Aged 3. Died in Nashville, June 8th of Cholera.
National Banner and Nashville Daily Advertiser. (Mon., June 10, 1833)

Dyer, John Decker. Infant son of Mr. Isham Dyer. Died in Nashville on Thursday evening July 29th.
National Banner and Nashville Whig. (Mon., Aug. 2, 1830)

Dyer, Matthew B. In the 44th year of his age formely of Dinwiddle County, Ala. Died in Fayette County, Tenn. on the 20th inst.
Nashville Republican. (Thurs., July 27, 1837)

Dyer, Matthew B. In the 48th year of his age. Died on the 20th in Fayette County, Tenn.
National Banner and Nashville Whig. (Fri., July 28, 1837)

Dyer, Miss Sophia. Daughter of the late Col. R. H. Dyer. Age 14. Died in Madison County, Tenn.
National Banner and Nashville Whig. (Sat., Sept. 9, 1826)

Dyer, Major William H. Died in Madison County.
National Banner. (Feb. 17, 1826)

Dykeman, Margaret. Died 19th at Cincinnati, Ohio of Cholera.
National Banner and Nashville Daily Advertiser. (Fri., Oct. 26, 1832)

Dysart, Mrs. Elizabeth H. Consort of John Dysart Esq. Died in Bedford County, Tenn.
National Banner and Nashville Whig. (Fri., Nov. 14, 1834)

Dysart, Col. Johnson. Died in Rockcastle County, Ky.
National Banner and Nashville Whig. (Sat., Aug. 26, 1826)

Eades, Mr. John. Aged 21. Died in Madison County.
National Banner and Nashville Whig. (Sat., Aug. 5, 1821)

Eagan, Mr. Hugh Senr. In the 56th year of his age. Died in Wilson County on Thursday morning 4th ult.
National Banner & Nashville Whig. (Fri., Aug. 7, 1835)

Eagleton, Miss Elizabeth. Died in Blount County, Tenn.
National Banner & Nashville Advertiser. (Tues., June 26, 1832)

Eagleton, Mrs. Rachel. Wife of Mr. Alexander Eagleton. Died in
Vigo County, Ind.
National Banner & Nashville Whig. (Fri., Oct. 20, 1826)

Eakin, Felix Grundy. Son of William & Felicia C. Eakin. Died in
Nashville on the 16th inst.
Nashville Whig. (Sat., June 20, 1846)

Eakin, Rev. George, Jun. Died in Jonesborough, Tenn. of the
Methodist Church.
Nashville Republican & State Gazette. (Tues., May 24, 1831)

Eakin, Moses. Died in this place on last Thursday.
The Nashville Whig & Tenn. Advertiser. (March 7, 1818)

Eakin, Spencer. Of the firm of S. & T. Eakin of Nashville. Died
suddenly in Shelbyville while on a visit.
Daily Republican Banner. (Tues., June 30, 1840)

Earl, Francis Virginia. Age 1 year & 7 months and 19 days. Youngest
daughter of S. C. Earl. Died in Nashville on Monday 19th inst.
Nashville Whig. (Fri., Aug. 23, 1839)

Earl, Mr. R. E. B. Died on the 16th inst at the residence of Ex-
President Jackson.
Nashville Union. (Wed., Sept. 19, 1838)

Earle, Austin. Died in this town on Friday the 10th inst. A native
of Mass.
Nashville Whig. (Sept. 13, 1824)

Earthman, Mr. Lewis. Died in this county on Friday last.
National Banner and Nashville Whig. (Fri., July 11, 1828)

Easley, Mr. Miller W. Died near Rutledge, E. T.
National Banner & Nashville Whig. (Sat., Feb. 21, 1829)

Eason, Mr. George. Died in Lincoln County.
National Banner & Nashville Whig. (Sat., Oct. 6, 1827)

Eason, John G. Merchant of Jonesboro. Died in Jonesboro, Tenn.
Daily Republican Banner. (Thurs., Aug. 24, 1837)

East, Mr. Addison. An old and respectable citizen. Died in
Nashville on Tuesday, Dec. 31st.
National Banner & Nashville Daily Advertiser. (Mon., Jan. 6, 1834)

Eastland, Maj. Joseph. Age 48. Died in Lincoln County on the 18
ult at the residence of E. Eastland.
National Banner & Nashville Advertiser. (Thurs., March 1, 1832)

Eastland, Josephine. Infant daughter of E. W. Eastland. Aged 1
year, 3 months. Died in Smith County.
National Banner & Nashville Daily Advertiser. (Wed., July 17, 1833)

Eastland, Mr. Nancy. Died on Thursday morning last. The beloved
consort of Col. Thomas Eastland of Franklin County. Leaving to
lament the irreparable loss, a husband and 6 children. Thurs.,
October 27, 1814.
The Nashville Whig. (Tues., Nov. 1, 1814)

Eastman, William J. In the 28th year of his age. Died on the 7th
inst. on board the Steamboat Mohawk, near Paducah.
Nashville True Whig & Weekly Commercial Register. (Fri., Aug. 23, 1850)

Eastram, Capt. William. of Kenhawa. Died in Nashville.
National Banner & Nashville Daily Advertiser. (Mon., Sept. 1, 1834)

Eatin, John. Died 13th at Cincinnati, Ohio of Cholera.
National Banner & Nashville Daily Advertiser. (Tues., Oct. 23, 1832)

Eaton, Private A. J. Company K. First Regiment Tenn. Volunteers.
Died - was killed in the Battle of Monterey with the Mexicans on
Sept. 21st. 1846.
Nashville Whig. (Sat., Oct 24, 1846)

Eaton, Mr. H. H. Assistant Professor of Chemistry in Transylvania
University. Died at Lexington, Ky. on the 15th ult.
National Banner & Nashville Advertiser. (Tues., Sept. 4, 1832)

Eaton, Mrs. Myra. Died on the 5th inst. at the seat of the late
William T. Lewis near this place, Nashville. Mrs. Myra Eaton the
young consort of John H. Eaton Esq., Attorney at Law.
Whig. (June 20, 1815)

Eaton, Col. Rufus. Died at St. Charles, Missouri on the 5th inst. of
Cholera.
National Banner & Nashville Daily Advertiser. (Wed., Sept. 3, 1834)

Eaton, Mr. William B. Of Franklin. Died at Fiarfield near this place,
the seat of Mrs. Mary Lewis on the 19th inst.
The Nashville Whig. (Tues., Dec. 26, 1815)

Eavidson, Mr. Samuel. Of Bedford County, Tenn. Died in Philadelphia
on the 2d of May in the 25th year of his age.
National Banner & Nashville Whig. (Fri., June 10, 1836)

Eberle, Dr. John. Professor of the Theory and Practice of medicine
in the medical Department of Transylvania College. Died in Lexington
yesterday evening of Feb. 3.
Daily Republican Banner. (Thurs., Feb. 8, 1838)

Edgar, Henry. Son of Mr. Andrew Henry Edgar. Died at Gallatin on
the 31st inst. in his third year.
The Politician & Weekly Nashville Whig. (Wed., Sept. 8, 1847)

Edgar, Henry. Infant son of Mr. Andrew Henry Edgar. Died at Gallatin,
Tenn. on the 31st ult. in his third year.
The Christian Record. (Sat., Sept. 4, 1847)

Edgar, General John. Died at Kaskaskia.
National Banner & Nashville Whig. (Mon., Jan. 10, 1831)

Edgar, Dr. Samuel D. Of Livingston, Miss. Died at Wheeling, Va. on
21st Dec. He was the last brother of Rev. John T. Edgar D. D.
Nashville Whig. (Mon., Jan. 3, 1842)

Edgar, Thomas Wharton. Infant son of Rev. Dr. Edgar. Died yesterday
morning in his 6th year.
Nashville Whig. (Sat., Oct. 21, 1843)

Edmiston, Mrs. Agatha. Consort of Major Thomas Edmiston. Died in
this county on the 20th inst. in the 44th year of his age.
National Banner. (Sat., Sept. 26, 1829)

Edmonds, Miss Ann Virginia. In the 16th year of her age. Died in
Knoxville.
National Banner & Nashville Whig. (Fri., Nov. 21, 1834)

Edmonds, Robert Esq. Of this county. Died on Friday last.
Nashville Whig. (Tues., Feb. 20, 1816)

Edmondson, Capt. J. N. Died at St. Louis.
National Banner & Nashville Whig. (Sat., Nov. 3, 1827)

Edmondson, Mr. Thomas. Died on the 2d inst. in this county. An early settler of this county.
Nashville Whig. (Aug. 23, 1824)

Edmondson, Major William. In the 58th year of his age. Died in Pontotoc, Miss. on the 4th inst.
Daily Republican Banner. (Fri., March 2, 1838)

Edmonson, Mrs. Polly. Died in Madison County, Ala.
National Banner & Nashville Whig. (Sat., Aug. 18, 1827)

Edmunds, Mr. Henry C. Of Lauderdale County. Died in Madison County, Ala.
National Banner & Nashville Whig. (Sat., Aug. 12, 1826)

Edrington, Mr. Joseph. Aged 56. Died in Columbus, Ky.
National Banner & Nashville Whig. (Sat., Sept. 9, 1826)

Edwards, Major B. W. Formerly of Pulaski. Died in Florence, Ala. on the 3d inst.
Nashville Republican. (Tues., Sept. 13, 1836)

Edwards, B. W. Formerly of Pulaski, Tenn. Died in Florence, Ala. on the 3d Sept.
National Banner & Nashville Whig. (Fri., Sept. 16, 1836)

Edwards, Major Benjamin W. A candidate for Governor of Miss. Died on the 18th of Aug. in Holmes County.
The Union. (Tues., Sept. 5, 1837)
Nashville Republican, (Tues., Sept. 13, 1836?)

Edwards, Mr. David. Died in Tuscaloosa.
National Banner & Nashville Whig. (Sat., Sept. 16, 1826)

Edwards, Mrs. Margaret. Wife of Mr. Benjamin Edwards. Aged 69. Died in Elkton, Ky.
National Banner & Nashville Whig. (Sat., July 29, 1826)

Edwards, Mr. Mellen. Printer, aged 36 years. Died in New Orleans formerly of Cincinnati. Ohio.
National Banner & Nashville Whig. (Wed., Oct. 22, 1834)

Edwards, Mrs. Nancy. Died at Pontiac, Michigan.
National Banner. May 20, 1826)

Edwards, Hon. Ninian. Formerly Governor of Illinois. Died at Belleville.
National Banner & Nashville Daily Advertiser. (Sat., Aug. 3, 1833)

Edwards, Hon. Pierpoint. U. S. Judge for the District of Con. Died at Bridgeport, Con.
National Banner. (April 28, 1826)

Edwards, Mr. Thomas. Age 27. Died at Carthage.
National Banner & Nashville Daily Advertiser. (Wed., April 24, 1833)

Edwards, Mr. Wm. Died in Sumner County, aged 76.
National Banner & Nashville Whig. (Sat., Feb. 2, 1828)

Eggers, Mrs. Elizabeth. Died 18th at Cincinnati, Ohio of Cholera.
National Banner & Nashville Daily Advertiser. (Thurs., Oct. 25, 1832)

Eggleston, Mr. E. M. Late of Mississippi formerly of Virginia. Died in Nashville.
National Banner & Nashville Whig. (Mon., Sept. 29, 1834)

Egnew, Jesse W. Formerly of Columbia, Ten. Died at New Orleans of Yellow Fever, on 30th ult.
National Banner & Nashville Advertiser. (Wed., Nov. 14, 1832)

Eichbaum (An infant child.) of Mr. William A. Eichbaum. Died in this town yesterday.
National Banner. (Sat., Aug. 22, 1829)

Eichbaum, Adeline. Daughter of William A. & Catharine Eichbaum. Died in Nashville on Tuesday morning last.
Nashville Whig. (Thursday, March 12, 1846)

Eichbaum, Thomas Crutcher. Infant son of William A. & Catharine M. Eichbaum. Died in Nashville July 19th.
Nashville Whig. (Thursday, July 20, 1843)

Elam, Mrs. Widow of the late Mr. Daniel Elam. Died in Rutherford County.
National Banner & Nashville Advertiser. (Fri., Jan. 27, 1832)

Eldridge, Maj. Eli. Died in Lawrence County, Ala.
National Banner & Nashville Whig. (Sat., May 31, 1828)

Elgin, Mr. James. Aged 29. Died in Smith County.
National Banner & Nashville Whig. (Dec. 2, 1826)

Elgin, Mrs. Nancy E. Died in Hardeman County.
National Banner & Nashville Whig. (Wed., Sept. 14, 1831)

Elgin, Dr. Wm. D. In the Merdian of his life and usefulness. Died in Hardeman County, Tenn.
National Banner & Nashville Daily Advertiser. (Sat., Sept. 6, 1834)

Ellicott, Henry Esq. Late a member of the Maryland Legislature. Died in Anne Arundel County, Md.
National Banner & Nashville Daily Advertiser. (Fri., Aug. 30, 1833)

Elliot, Georgiana. Infant daughter of Col. George Elliot. Died at Wall-Springs, Sumner County, Tenn.
National Banner & Nashville Daily Advertiser. (Mon., Aug. 25, 1834)

Elliott, Henry. A soldier of West Tenn. Bregade. Died at Fort Mitchell, Ala. on the 17th.
National Banner & Nashville Whig. (Mon., Dec. 19, 1836)

Elliott, Henry W. A soldier of the West Tenn. Brigade. Died at Fort Mitchell, Ala. on the 17th ult.
National Banner & Nashville Whig. (Fri., Nov. 25, 1836)

Elliott, Henry W. A soldier of the West Tenn. Brigade. Died at Fort Mitchell, Ala. on the 17th ult.
Nashville Republican. (Fri., Nov. 25, 1836)

Elliott, Isaac Inman, Private. Company G. First Regiment Tenn. Volunteers. Died - was killed in the Battle of Monterey with the Mexicans on Sept. 21st.
Nashville Whig. (Sat., Oct. 24, 1846)

Elliot, Mr. J. C. Aged 39. Died in New Orleans.
National Banner & Nashville Daily Advertiser. (Tues., June 24, 1834)

Elliot, John. A native of Scotland, and brother of Hugh Elliot, Esq. of Philadelphia. Died at Tuscumbia, Ala.
Nashville Whig. (Fri., Sept. 4, 1839)

Elliott, John Hon. Late Senator in Congress from Ga. Aged 55. Died at Savannah.
National Banner & Nashville Whig. (Sat., Sept. 8, 1827)

Elliot, John Mr. Died at Baltimore on the 8th ultimo in the 105th year of his age.
National Banner. (Jan. 6, 1826)

Elliott, Jonathan. Known as the author of the American Diplomatic. Died in Washington City.
Nashville Whig. (Tues., March 24, 1846)

Elliot, Dr. J. T. Aged 21. Died in Madison County, T.
National Banner & Nashville Whig. (Sat., Sept. 9, 1826)

Elliott, Mr. Patrick. Aged 80. Died in Washington County.
National Banner and Nashville Whig. (Mon., June 13, 1831)

Ellis, Mrs. Amanda. Wife of Mr. Elijah Ellis. Died in Franklin, Ohio.
National Banner & Nashville Whig. (Sat., Aug. 26, 1826)

Ellis, Mrs. Amanda. Aged 23. Died in Jackson, Ohio.
National Banner & Nashville Whig. (Sat., Aug. 26, 1826)

Ellis, Mrs. Elizabeth M. Consort of Nathaniel D. Ellis. Age 16 years. Died near the Spanish Bluff Red River, at the residence of Hon. R. Ellis.
National Banner & Nashville Daily Advertiser. (Mon., Sept. 8, 1834)

Ellis, Mr. James M. In his 17th year. Died in Williamson County at the residence of Marcus Boyd on Sunday the 29th Dec. His parents live in Carroll County, Miss.
Daily Republican Banner. (Fri., Jan. 3, 1840)

Ellis, Rev. Joseph. In the 71st year of his age. Died in Madison County, Ky.
National Banner & Nashville Whig. (Mon., June 7, 1830)

Ellis, Robert Esq. In the 53rd year of his age. Died in Todd County, Ky. on Wed., the 28th of July.
National Banner & Nashville Whig. (Thurs., Aug. 5, 1830)

Ellis, Mrs. Susannah. Wife of Capt. Josiah Ellis. Died in M'Nairy County.
National Banner & Nashville Whig. (Sat., May 19, 1827)

Elliston, Mrs. Elizabeth. Consort of Joseph T. Elliston Esq. Died on Tuesday 24th inst. of Davidson County.
Nashville Whig. (Sat., Feb. 28, 1846)

Elliston, Mr. John. Died in this town on Saturday evening last.
Nashville Whig. (Jan. 29, 1823)

Ely, Mr. Ralph. Died at Cincinnati.
National Banner & Nashville Whig. (July 1, 1826)

Embree, Mr. Elihu. Died on Monday the 4th inst. in Jonesboro Editor of the Emancipator.
The Nashville Gazette. (Sat., Dec. 23, 1820)

Emerson, James. Died on Ohio River when steamboat boiler collapsed scalded to death.
National Banner & Nashville Daily Advertiser. (Wed., Nov. 20, 1833)

Emerson, Mr. William. Firm of Emerson & Nones. Died near Boston by drowning when the Steamboat Bunker Hill was wrecked by the wind.
National Banner & Nashville Daily Advertiser. (Sat., June 30, 1832)

Emmerson, Mrs. Rachel. Died in Knox County.
National Banner & Nashville Advertiser. (Tues., May 8, 1832)

Emmerson, Hon. Thomas. In the 64th year of his age. Died on Saturday last in Nashville.
National Banner & Nashville Whig. (Friday, Aug. 4, 1837)

Emmitt, Mrs. Catherine. Died in Russellville, Ky.
National Banner & Nashville Whig. (Fri., Feb. 12, 1830)

Emmitt, Mr. Josiah. Aged 32. Died in Montgomery, Ala.
National Banner & Nashville Whig. (Sat., Sept. 30, 1826)

Emmons, Dr. Richard. Died at Washington City on the 15th inst.
National Banner & Nashville Daily Advertiser. (Mon., March 3, 1834)

England, W. With the second Tenn. Regiment. Died - was killed in
the Battle of Sierra Gorda with the Mexicans.
The Politician & Weekly Nashville Whig. (Fri., May 21, 1847)

Engle, Mrs. Martha S. Daughter of George & Martha Dillard, late of
Henry County, Va. Consort of Henry A. Engle, Esq. Died near
Batesville on the 17th.
Daily Republican Banner. (Tues., Dec. 12, 1837)

English, Mr. George Bethune. A native of Boston, aged 39. Died in
Washington City. on Saturday the 20th ult.
National Banner & Nashville Whig. (Sat., Oct. 18, 1828)

Enness, Mrs. Susan. Died at Cincinnati.
National Banner & Nashville Whig. (June 24, 1826)

Ensley, Mr. Edward. Died in Bedford County.
National Banner. (March 17, 1826)

Ensor, Mrs. Matilda. Wife of Mr. John K. Ensor. Died at Elizabethton.
National Banner & Nashville Whig. (Mon., Nov. 29, 1830)

Eppes, Hon. John W. For many years a distinguished Member of Congress
from that State. Died lately in Virginia.
Nashville Whig. (Oct. 6, 1823)

Epps, Gen. Richard. Died in Sussex County, Va.
Nashville Republican & State Gazette. (Mon., Aug. 20, 1832)

Ernest, Mrs. Catherine. Died in Lexington, Ky.
National Banner & Nashville Whig. (Fri., July 11, 1828)

Ernest, Mr. James H. Died in Louisville.
National Banner & Nashville Whig. (Wed., Sept. 7, 1831)

Ernest, Mr. James H. Died in Louisville, Ky.
National Banner & Nashville Whig. (Wed., Sept. 7, 1831)

Erskine, Rev. G. Of Ten. Died in Caldwell, Liberia.
Nashville Republican & State Gazette. (Tues., March 29, 1831)

Erskine, Rev. G. Late of Tennessee. Pastor of the Presbyterian
Church in the colony. Died at Caldwell, Liberia.
National Banner & Nashville Whig. (Mon., March 28, 1831)

Erwin, Ann Mrs. Died in Lexington, Ky. Consort of James Erwin, Esq.
and daughter of the Hon. Henry Clay. Mrs. E. has been long known as
possessing a kind, humane and benevolent disposition. In the discharge
of the social and domestic relations of life she was all that could
be desired. The death of this accomplished and amiable lady has made
a void in society that will long long be felt. To her surviving
family her loss in irreparable.
Nashville Republican. (Nashville, Tenn. Tues., Dec. 22, 1835)

Ervin, James Esq. Formerly a Representative in Congress from the
Pedee District, S. C. Died recently at Darlington Court House, S. C.
Nashville Whig. (Wed., Nov. 14, 1838)

Ervin, Mr. William. In the 32nd year of his age. Died in Nashville
on the 9th formerly a citizen of Baltimore.
Daily Republican Banner. (Fri., Jan. 19, 1837)

Erwin, Mr. Isaac. Aged 84. Died in Gipson County. A soldier of the revolution.
National Banner & Nashville Whig. (Thurs., Aug. 12, 1830)

Erwin, Col. Andrew. In the 61st year of his age. Died in Bedford County on the 19th inst.
National Banner & Nashville Daily Advertiser. (Mon., April 21, 1834)

Erwin, Mrs. Elvira Julia. Wife of Mr. Andrew Erwin. Died this morning
Daily Republican Banner. (Fri., July 6, 1838)

Erwin, Emma. Infant daughter of John P. Erwin Esq. Died in Nashville on the 24th inst.
National Banner & Nashville Daily Advertiser. (Mon., Aug. 25, 1834)

Erwin, Hugh B. Infant son of Hugh Erwin. Died in this vicinity on the 27th ult.
Nashville Whig. (Wed., July 4, 1838)

Erwin, John P. Jr. In the 26th year of his age. Died on the 3rd inst. at the residence of his father, John P. Erwin Esq. his only son.
Nashville Whig. (Tues., May 12, 1843)

Erwin, Juliet. Daughter of James Erwin Esq. Died in Nashville on Sunday morning aged 5 years.
Nashville Whig. (Tues., Oct. 8, 1844)

Erwin, Mrs. Lavinia. Consort of the late Capt. Joseph Erwin. Died at Plaquimine, La. on the 12th of Feb.
Nashville Republican.(Tuesday, March 1, 1836)

Erwin, Mrs. Mary. Wife of Mr. Isaac Erwin. Died on the 9th Sept. near Plaquemine, Louisiana daughter of Capt. John Nichols, of Davidson County.
National Banner & Nashville Daily Advertiser. (Wed., Oct. 3, 1832)

Erwin, Mrs. Mary. Wife of James Erwin Esq. Died near Farmington, Bedford County.
National Banner & Nashville Whig. (Fri., July 25, 1828)

Erwin, Robert W. Son of Erwin, John P. Aged one year. Died on Saturday 19th instant.
National Banner & Nashville Whig. (Aug. 26, 1826)

Erwin, Thomas Yeatman. Third son of Andrew Erwin Esq. in his 18th year. Died in Nashville at the residence of the Hon. John Bell. on the 26th inst.
The Christian Record. (Sat., May 1, 1847)

Erwin, Thomas Yeatman. Son of Andrew Erwin age 18 years. Died on the evening of the 25th inst. at the residence of Hon. John Bell.
The Politician & Weekly Nashville Whig. (Fri., April 30, 1847)

Erwin, Mr. William. In the 32nd year of his age. Died in this place, Nashville on the 9th inst. A citizen of Baltimore, Md.
Nashville Union. (Thurs., Jan. 18, 1838)

Eskridge, Dr. Ionatius P. Of Virginia. Died in Batesville, Arkansas Territory.
National Banner & Nashville Daily Advertiser. (Mon., June 30, 1834)

Essex, Mr. Thomas. Bookseller. Died at St. Louis.
National Banner & Nashville Whig. (Sat., Jan. 12, 1828)

Este, Mrs. Wife of D. K. Este. Died at Cincinnati.
National Banner. (April 28, 1826)

Estell, John. Died yesterday morning by the rupture of a blood
vessel.
The Union. (Tues., April 19, 1836)

Estell, Mr. John. Died in Nashville Monday, April 18th.
National Banner & Nashville Whig. (Wed., April 20, 1836)

Estell, Joseph. Lately a Dry goods merchant of Nashville. Died at
Clinton, Mississippi. on the 10th inst.
Nashville Whig. (Thurs., Dec. 28, 1843)

Estes, Barkley. Died by Committing suicide in Davidson County
by hanging himself.
The Union. (Thurs., May 19, 1836)

Estes, Joel Esq. Of Haywood County. Died in Stewart County, T. on
the 10th inst.
National Banner & Nashville Daily Advertiser. (Fri., Sept. 20, 1833)

Estes, Mrs. Sarah. Wife of Mr. John Estes. Died in Madison County,
Ala.
National Banner & Nashville Whig. (Mon., Sept. 13, 1830)

Estill, Mrs. Jane. Wife of Wallis Estill, Esq. Died in Franklin
County.
National Banner. (Sat., July 4, 1829)

Estill, Capt. Willis. Died in Winchester, Ten. in the 77th year of
his age.
National Banner & Nashville Whig. (Fri., Feb. 13, 1835)

Estin, John. Died 13th at Cincinnati. Ohio of Cholera.
National Banner & Nashville Daily Advertiser. (Tues., Oct. 23, 1832)

Ethridge, Mr. Eli. Of Lawrence County. Died on Sat. the 19th of
April.
National Banner & Nashville Whig. (Sat., May 3, 1828)

Ethridge, Dr. Elisha. Age 43. Died in Pulaski on June 16th of
Cholera.
National Banner & Nashville Daily Advertiser. (Wed., June 19, 1833)

Eustage, Rev. Thomas. One of the associate editors of the St. Louis
Herald of Religious Liberty. Died on Sunday morning the 25th inst.
The Christian Record. (Sat., July 15, 1848)

Evans, Miss Ann Maria. Formerly of Frankfort, Ky. Died in the
neighborhood of Nashville.
National Banner & Nashville Whig. (Wed., Sept. 28, 1836)

Evans, Miss Ann Maria. of Frankfort, Ky. Died in this vicinity at
the residence of John McIntosh.
Nashville Republican. (Tues., Sept. 27, 1836)

Evans, Ashley. Of Capt. M'Coin Company of Sumner County. Died at
Sea, in Oct. last on board the U. S. Steamer, American.
Nashville Republican. (Tues., Nov. 1, 1836)

Evans, Mr. Evan. Died at Frankfort, Ky.
National Banner & Nashville Whig. (Sat., April 12, 1828)

Evans, Mr. Joh. Jailer of Jefferson County. Died in Louisville, Ky.
National Banner. (Jan. 6, 1826)

Evans, Mary Eliza. Daughter of Samuel W. Evans of Miss. Died in
Davidson County.
National Banner & Nashville Whig. (Wed., July 8, 1835)

Eve, Hon. Joseph. Late Charge d'affaris of the U. S. to Texas. Died
at Galveston on the 13th ult.
Nashville Whig. (Sat., July 15, 1843)

Everett, John Esq. Formerly professor in Transylvania University.
Died at Boston.
National Banner. (March 17, 1826)

Everly, Mr. Jacob. Aged about 37 years. Died in Franklin, Tenn. on
Thursday 2d inst.
National Banner & Nashville Whig. (Fri., July 10, 1835)

Everyt, Alexander Esq. Died lately in Johnston County a soldier of
the revolution.
National Banner & Nashville Daily Advertiser. (Sat., March 24, 1832)

Eves, Mrs. M. Consort of Mr. Joseph Eves. Died in New Orleans.
National Banner & Nashville Whig. (Sat., Aug. 26, 1826)

Evins, Mrs. Hannah. Wife of E. M. Evins Esq. Aged 30. Died in
Bledsoe.
Nashville Union. (Mon., Dec. 2, 1839)

Ewell, Dr. James. Author of the Medical Companion. Late of New Orleans
& formerly of Washington City. Died in Covington, Lou.
National Banner & Nashville Advertiser. (Thurs., Nov. 15, 1832)

Ewin, Mrs. Elvira Julia Ewin. Wife of Andrew Ewin Esq. Died in
Nashville this morning.
Nashville Whig. (Fri., July 6, 1838)

Ewing, A. C. Esq. Aged 37. Died in Williamson County, Tenn.
National Banner and Nashville Daily Advertiser. (Mon., June 30, 1834)

Ewing, Mr. Alexander C. In the 37th year of his age. Died in
Williamson County, Tenn.
National Banner and Nashville Daily Advertiser. (Tues., June 24, 1834)

Ewing, Col. Andrew in the 61st year of his age. Died in Bedford
County on the 19th inst. at Pleasant Retreat.
National Banner and Nashville Daily Advertiser. (Thurs., May 1, 1834)

Ewing, Mr. Andrew B. Died in Madison County.
National Banner and Nashville Whig. (Sat., Aug. 11, 1827)

Ewing, Elizabeth. Only daughter of Martin W. Ewing of Yazoo County,
Miss. Died on the Steamboat Freeman descending the river from
Louisville on the 18th of Cholera.
National Banner and Nashville Daily Advertiser. (Sat., Aug. 17, 1833)

Ewing, Mr. James C. Died in Bedford County. Died in Bedford County.
National Banner. (Jan. 27, 1826)

Ewing, Doctor John O. In the 26 year of his age. Died on Tuesday
morning last.
National Banner (March 3, 1826)

Ewing, Major J. W. Died in Hopkinsville, Ky.
National Banner and Nashville Whig. (Fri.,.Jan. 23, 1835)

Ewing, Maj. J. W. Died in Hopkinsville, Ky.
National Banner and Nashville Whig. (Fri., March 6, 1835)

Ewing, Mrs. Margaret. Wife of Andrew Ewing, Esq. daughter of Col.
Andrew Haynes. Died last evening. (Obituary in Jan. 11, 1841, Whig)
Nashville Whig. (Fri., Jan. 8, 1841)

Ewing, Mary Louisa. Daughter of Mr. Wm. B. Ewing, aged 5 years 9 months. Died in Davidson County on the 12th inst.
National Banner and Nashville Daily Advertiser. (Fri., Sept. 13, 1833)

Ewing, Nathan Esq. Died in Nashville on Saturday last in the 55th of his age. Was clerk of Davidson County Court.
National Banner and Nashville Whig. (Tues., May 4, 1830)

Ewing, Mrs. Rebecca. Wife of Edwin H. Ewing, Esq. Attorney at law. Died at Mile End in the Nashville Vicinity on Sat. 27th inst. Aged 27 years.
Nashville Whig. (Tues., July 30, 1844)

Ewing, Gen. Robert. Died in Logan County, Ky.
Nashville Republican and State Gazette. (July 23, 1832)

Ewing, Mrs. Sally. Wife of Dr. Urban Ewing, aged 26. Died in Louisville, Ky.
National Banner and Nashville Daily Advertiser. (Sat., Aug. 10, 1833)

Ewing, Mr. Thomas. Late editor of the Mississippi Watchman. Died in Vickburg, Miss.
National Banner and Nashville Daily Advertiser. (Wed., May 22, 1833)

Ewing, Wm. J. Infant son of Mr. Wm. B. Ewing. Died in Davidson County on Thurs., the 7th inst.
National Banner and Nashville Daily Advertiser. (Mon., March 11, 1833)

Ewing, Mr. William N. Died in Blount County, Tenn.
National Banner and Nashville Daily Advertiser. (Tues., June 26, 1832)

Ewing, Col. Young. Died in Lagrange, Tenn. on the 5th ult.
National Banner and Nashville Daily Advertiser. (Mon., Nov. 23, 1833)

Exum, Mr. William. Aged 60 years. Died in Sumner County, Tenn.
National Banner and Nashville Whig. (Fri., March 13, 1835)

Fairbanks, Mr. Elijah. In the 27th year of his age. Died at Pleasant Exchange Hunderson County on the 6th ult. of consumption.
National Banner & Nashville Daily Advertiser. (Sat., March 3, 1832)

Fairchild, Mr. Alpheus. Died in Cincinnati.
National Banner. (Feb. 24, 1826)

Fairfax, Mrs. Cecilia. Died in Nashville on Wednesday last.
National Banner and Nashville Whig. (Fri., Dec. 3, 1830)

Fairman, Mr. Gideon. An eminent engraver. Died at Philadelphia.
National Banner & Nashville Whig. (Sat., April 7, 1827)

Falconer, Mr. Edward P. In the 28th year of his age. Died at Lebanon on Friday the 22d inst.
The Union. (Tues., April 26, 1836)

Fallon, Miss Terressa. Daughter of the late Andrew Fallon, Esq. of New York. Died in Mobile, Ala. of Yellow Fever.
Daily Republican Banner. (Tues., Oct. 1, 1839)

Falls, Mr. James. Died in Davidson County.
National Banner & Nashville Daily Advertiser. (Fri., June 14, 1833)

Fannill, Mrs. Dorothy B. Died in Bedford County.
National Banner & Nashville Whig. (Thurs., July 22, 1830)

Fansworth, James Fuller. Son of E. D. Fansworth. Died in Nashville on the 27th inst. aged three years and 2 months.
The Christian Record. (Sat., Sept. 4, 1847)

Farley, D. Rivers Woodyard. Died in the loss of the Steamboat
Brandywine.
National Banner & Nashville Daily Advertiser. (Mon., April 23, 1832)

Farley, Mr. Michael. Aged 25. Died in Washington, Ala.
National Banner & Nashville Whig. (Sept. 2, 1826)

Farley, Mr. Owen. Died at Tuscaloosa.
National Banner & Nashville Whig. (Sat., July 22, 1826)

Farmer, Mr. Holt. Aged 27. Died at Covington on the 26th ult.
National Banner. (Sat., May 16, 1829)

Farmer, Rev. Nathan. Died in Giles County on the 3d inst. Minister
of the Cumberland Presbyterian Church.
National Banner & Nashville Daily Advertiser. (Wed., Dec. 12, 1832)

Farmer, Susan. Infant daughter of Mr. Bailey Farmer. Died in
Murfreesborough.
National Banner & Nashville Daily Advertiser. (Tues., May 27, 1834)

Farnham, John H. Esq. Died in Salem, Ind.
National Banner & Nashville Daily Advertiser. (Thurs., July 25, 1833)

Farnham, Mr. William H. Aged 69, a native of Newburyport, Mass.
Died in Salem, Ind.
National Banner. (Sat., Oct. 3, 1829)

Farnsworth, James Fuller. Son of E. D. Farnsworth. Died in Nashville
on the 27th inst. aged 3 years and 2 months.
The Politician & Weekly Nashville Whig. (Wed., Sept. 1st. 1847)

Farrar, Mrs. Jane. Wife of Mr. Field Farrar. Died on the 19th Sept.
last of Charlotte, Dickson County, Tenn.
National Banner & Nashville Whig. (Wed., Oct. 22, 1834)

Farrar, Miss Laura. Daughter of Field Farrar. Aged 12 years. Died
in Charlotte, Dickson County on the 7th Aug.
National Banner & Nashville Whig. (Wed., Aug. 19, 1835)

Farrar, Mrs. Martha. Died in Claiborne County, Miss.
National Banner & Nashville Whig. (Sat., Nov. 3, 1827)

Farrar, Miss Mary P. Daughter of Mr. Cyprian Farrar. Died in Madison
County.
National Banner & Nashville Whig. (Wed., Sept. 7, 1831)

Farrell, Norman. Infant son of John Farrell M.D. of N. Orleans.
Died on the 12th inst.
Nashville Whig. (Fri., Oct. 18, 1839)

Farress, Miss Elizabeth A. Died at Covington, Tenn.
National Banner & Nashville Whig. (Wed., Oct. 1, 1834)

Farrington, Richard B. Esq. Died in Triana, Ala.
National Banner. (Sat., Oct. 10, 1829)

Farris, Rev. James W. Died at his residence in Hardeman County, West
Tenn. on the 27th ult. a member of the Tennessee Annual Conference.
National Banner & Nashville Daily Advertiser. (Wed., Nov. 14, 1832)

Farris, Mrs. Matilda. Aged 19. Died in Pittsburgh.
National Banner & Nashville Whig. (Sat., July 29, 1826)

Fartner, Mrs. Keziah. Died in Humphreys County on the 20th ult. in
the 50 years of her age.
National Banner & Nashville Whig. (Sat., Sept. 13, 1828)

Faul, Mr. Algemon S. Died in Clark County, Ky. Aged 21.
National Banner. (May 13, 1826)

Faulk, Jehu M. Esq. Attorney & Counsellor at law. Died in Monroe,
Louisiana from a wound inflicted by the hand of an unknown person.
Daily Republican Banner. (Thurs., April 12, 1838)

Faulkes, Thomas A. Of this County who died on the 8th inst. The
Funeral will be preached on 30th inst. at his late dwelling by the
Rev. Mr. Craighead.
The Nash. Whig & Tenn. Advertiser. (Nov. 24, 1817)

Fay, Mrs. Sarah. Wife of Mr. Andrew Fay of Pulaski, age 26. Died in
Franklin on the 1st inst.
National Banner & Nashville Whig. (Sat., July 15, 1826)

Fearn, Mr. Edward. Died in Madison County, Ala.
National Banner. (March 24, 1826)

Feeney, Mrs. Rosanna. Aged 73. Died at Huntsville, Ala.
National Banner & Nashville Whig. (Sat., April 7, 1827)

Felch, Dr. Cleever. Late editor of Corams Champion. Died at New York.
National Banner & Nashville Whig. (Sat., April 21, 1827)

Felt, J. Porter. Of Salem. Died in the wreck of the Steamboat Lexington.
Daily Republican Banner. (Fri., Jan. 31, 1840)

Fendlay, Mrs. Mary Anne. Died at New Orleans on the 26th.
National Banner & Nashville Daily Advertiser. (Tues., Sept. 10, 1833)

Fenner, Mrs. Mary. Died in Halifax, N. Carolina.
Nashville Republican & State Gazette. (Thurs., April 7, 1831)

Fentress, Mrs. Nancy. The amiable consort of the Hon. Speaker of the
House of Representative. Died at the residence of the Hon. James
Fentress of Montgomery County, Ten. on the 27th ult.
The Nash. Whig & Tenn. Advertiser. (Nov. 17, 1817)

Fenwick, The Right Rev. Edward. Roman Catholic Bishop of the Diocese
of Cincinnati. Died at Wooster Wayne County, Ohio on the 27th Sept.
in the 64th year of his age.
National Banner & Nashville Daily Advertiser. (Wed., Oct. 10, 1832)

Ferguson, Henry G. Of N. Y. Died in New Orleans of Yellow Fever.
Daily Republican Banner. (Wed., Sept. 27, 1837)

Ferguson, Mrs. Isabella. Died in Smith County.
Nashville Republican & State Gazette. (Mon., Dec. 17, 1832)

Ferguson, Mrs. Catherine. Died at Louisville, Ky. Wife of Wm. Ferguson, Esq. Aged 30.
National Banner & Nashville Whig. (Sat., Sept. 20,1828)

Ferguson, Mr. John. Died in Wilson County.
National Banner & Nashville Whig. (Wed., July 27, 1831)

Ferguson, Mr. John K. Formerly of Kentucky. Died - drowned near
the mouth of Yazoo River.
National Banner & Nashville Whig. (Mon., Nov. 29, 1830)

Fernandis, Mr. William. Died near Vicksburg, Mi.
National Banner & Nashville Daily Advertiser. (Sat., Aug. 17, 1833)

Ficklin, Rev. John H. Aged 54. Died in Scott County, Ky.
National Banner & Nashville Whig. (Sat., Sept. 9, 1826)

Field, Col. Abner. Aged 33. Late clerk of the Circuit Court. Died
at Vandalia, Illinois.
National Banner & Nashville Whig. (Thurs., July 1, 1830)

Field, Mrs. Elizabeth. Wife of Mr. J. Field, Died in Franklin.
National Banner & Nashville Whig. (Mon., Aug. 9, 1830)

Field, Hume R. Esq. Died at Tuscaloosa, Ala.
National Banner & Nashville Whig. (Mon., Dec. 19, 1831)

Field, Mary. Aged 91 years and nine months. Died on the 21st October
in Madison County, Va. Wife of Capt. Henry Field Jr.
National Banner & Nashville Whig. (Wed., Nov. 24, 1830)

Field, Michael. Printer. Died in New Orleans.
National Banner & Nashville Daily Advertiser. (Sat., Sept. 21, 1833)

Fields, Mr. Eli. Of Nashville. Died in Davidson County on Sunday 6th
of April. Suddenly.
National Banner & Nashville Daily Advertiser. (Mon., April 7, 1834)

Fields, Mrs. Sarah. Consort of Maj. William Fields. Died in Maury
County on the 2nd inst. in the 54th year of her age.
National Banner & Nashville Daily Advertiser. (Wed., June 19, 1833)

Fifth, Mrs. Nye. Widow of John Fifth. Died 16th at Cincinnati,
Ohio of Cholera.
National Banner & Nashville Daily Advertiser. (Wed., Oct. 24, 1832)

Figg, Catharine. Aged 9 years. Died 16th at Cincinnati, Ohio of
Cholera.
National Banner & Nashville Daily Advertiser. (Wed., Oct. 24, 1832)

Files, William Wallace. Aged 19. Son of the late Col. David Files.
Died in Mobile, Ala.
National Banner & Nashville Daily Advertiser. (Fri., May 16, 1834)

Finch, Mr. Edmund. Died in Davidson County on the 31st ult.
National Banner & Nashville Daily Advertiser. (Wed., April 4, 1832)

Fine, Maj. Peter. Aged 73. Died in Cocke County. A soldier of the
revolution.
National Banner & Nashville Whig. (Sat., Aug. 26, 1826)

Finley, Mrs. Died in Danville, Ky. of Cholera.
National Banner & Nashville Daily Advertiser. (Mon., Aug. 5, 1833)

Finley, Mrs. Mary. Aged 65. Died in Lebanon, Tenn. on the 10th inst.
at 2 o'clock a.m.
National Banner & Nashville Whig. (Thurs., Oct. 11, 1830)

Finley, Mrs. Mary. Wife of Col. Obadiah G. Finley. Died in Lebanon.
National Banner & Nashville Whig. (Fri., Feb. 19, 1830)

Finn, Anna. Daughter of James & Elizabeth Finn. Died in Nashville
on Saturday 13th inst. aged four years and five months.
The Christian Record. (Sat., March 20, 1847)

Finn, Mrs. Elizabeth. Wife of Mr. R. F. Finn. Died at Cincinnati.
National Banner & Nashville Whig. (Friday, March 18, 1831)

Finn, H. S. Of Newport, the comedian. Died in the wreck of the
Steamboat Lexington.
Daily Republican Banner. (Fri., Jan. 31, 1840)

Finn, Mr. John. Of Nashville. Died in Louisville on Wednesday the
4th inst. on board the Steamboat E. W. Stephens.
Nashville True Whig & Weekly Commercial Register. (Fri., Dec. 13, 1850)

Finn, Lawrence Thales. Son of John Finn. Aged 4 years. Died in Franklin, Ky. on the 24th inst.
National Banner. (Sat., May 30, 1829)

Finn, Mr. Thomas. Aged 36 years. Died in Nashville after a long and painful sickness.
National Banner & Nashville Daily Advertiser. (Tues., Jan. 22, 1833)

Finnerty, Mr. John. Native of Ireland and for many years a respectable merchant of N. Orleans. Died in New Orleans.
National Banner & Nashville Daily Advertiser. (Fri., Sept. 20, 1833)

Finney, Mrs. Jane. Aged 64. Died in Robinson County, Tenn.
Nashville Republican & State Gazette. (Tues., Jan. 31, 1832)

Fischel, Miss Sarah. Daughter of Dr. & Mrs. Mary A. Fischel. Died in Nashville on the 23d inst. in the 8th year of her age.
The Christian Record. (Sat., May 27, 1848)

Fiser, Dr. J. C. Died in Dyersburg.
Nashville Whig. (Tues., July 14, 1846)

Fisher, James. Died 15th at Cincinnati, Ohio of Cholera.
National Banner & Nashville Daily Advertiser. (Wed., Oct. 24, 1832)

Fisher, Miss Mary Ann. Died at Cincinnati.
National Banner. (March 24, 1826)

Fisher, Mr. Robert W. Died at Tennessee Rolling Works on Cumberland River on the 28th ult. He was a native of Baltimore but for several years has lived in Nashville.
The Christian Record. (Sat., April 10, 1847)

Fisher, Miss Sophia. Died at Cincinnati.
National Banner & Nashville Whig. (Sat., March 10, 1827)

Fisk, Rev. Dr. E. Died in Philadelphia.
National Banner & Nashville Daily Advertiser. (Thurs., Jan. 2, 1834)

Fisk, Mr. Marion. Aged 27. Died at Spring Hill, Ala.
National Banner & Nashville Whig. (Sept. 2, 1826)

Fisk, Mrs. Mary. From Framingham, Mass. in her society has lost one of its brightest ornaments. Died in Smith County on the 23rd of Feb.
Imp. Rev.,(Mch. 1, 1806)

Fisk, Moses, Esq. Late resident of Hilham, Tenn. Died Sunday the 26th July, aged 80 years 1 month and 14 days.
Daily Republican Banner. (Wed., Aug. 5, 1840)

Fisk, Mr. Nathaniel. Formerly of Northampton, Mass. Died in New Orleans.
National Banner & Nashville Daily Advertiser. (Mon., Aug. 19, 1833)

Fite, Leonard Sr. Esq. A soldier of the revolution. Died at Alexandria, Dekalb County 22nd March in his 82nd year.
Nashville Whig. (Thurs., Apirl 14, 1842)

Fite, Mrs. Sarah Ann. Consort of Col. William C. Fite. Died in Gibson County.
Nashville Whig. (Tues., April 21, 1846)

Fitzhugh, Mrs. Ann Eliza. Consort of Dr. Fitzhugh. Died in Hardeman County.
National Banner & Nashville Daily Advertiser. (Wed., April 25, 1832)

Fitzhugh, Dr. Edmund. Formerly of Virginia. Died in Hardeman County, Tenn.
National Banner & Nashville Advertiser. (Wed., May 23, 1832)

Fitzhugh, Mr. Samuel Sen. Aged 67. Died in Davidson County on 12th Aug.
Nashville Republican & State Gazette. (Thurs., Aug. 25, 1831)

Fitzhugh, Mr. Samuel T. Died at Louisville, Ky.
National Banner. (March 10, 1826)

Fitzhugh, Mr. William H. Of Fahfax, Va. Died in Cambridge, Md.
National Banner & Nashville Whig. (Mon., June 7, 1830)

Fitzgerald, John. Died on the 4th inst. after a short and painful illness. Copied from Ball. Chronicle June 15th.
National Banner & Nashville Daily Advertiser. (Thurs., June 26, 1834)

Flanagan, Philip. Died in Huntsville, Ala. on the 14th inst. He was from Winchester, Ten.
National Banner & Nashville Daily Advertiser. (Mon., March 26, 1832)

Fleming, Samuel Esq. Died in Knox County.
National Banner & Nashville Daily Advertiser. (Mon., April 8, 1833)

Flemming, James M. Infant son of William M. and Caroline S. Flemming. Died in Jonesborough.
Nashville Whig. (Tues., May 5, 1846)

Flemming, Richard Esq. Died in Giles County, Tenn.
National Banner and Nashville Whig. (Wed., March 4, 1835)

Fleshhart, Mrs. Elizabeth. Died in Knoxville.
National Banner & Nashville Whig. (Sat., Dec. 20, 1828)

Fletcher, Charlotte. and Brother of England Deck Passengers. Died on the Steamer George Collier about 80 miles below Natchez. Scalded to death.
Daily Republican Banner. (Tues., May 14, 1839)

Fletcher, Mr. John. A native of Pennsylvania. Died at his residence in Neville, Clearmont County, Ohio.
National Banner & Nashville Whig. (Mon., May 11, 1835)

Fletcher, Mrs. Martha. Wife of John Fletcher, Esq. Died in Rutherford County.
National Banner & Nashville Whig. (Sat., Dec. 27, 1828)

Fletcher, Mary. Youngest child of Thomas H. Fletcher Esq. of Nashville. Died in Arkansas Co., Ark. on the 13th Aug. at the residence of Joseph W. Clay Esq. in the 11th year of her age.
Nashville Whig. (Thurs., Aug. 27, 1846)

Fletcher, Sarah. Wife of Thomas H. Fletcher Esq. Died suddenly on Sunday afternoon in Nashville.
Nashville Whig. (Mon., June 25, 1838)

Fletcher, Mrs. Sarah. Consort of Thomas H. Fletcher. Died yesterday in Nashville.
Daily Republican Banner. (Mon., June 25, 1838)

Fletcher, Mrs. Susan. Died in Madison County. Wife of Mr. Benton Fletcher.
National Banner & Nashville Whig. (Sat., Aug. 11, 1827)

Fletcher, Gen. Thomas. Died in Bath Co., Ky member of the Ky legislature
National Banner. (March 21, 1826)

Flewellen, Captain William. A native of Halifax County, N. C. Died in Carroll County in the 81st year of his age. A soldier of the revolution.
National Banner & Nashville Whig. (Wed., Sept. 24, 1834)

Flint, Mrs. T. G. Died in Shelbyville, Tenn. of Cholera.
National Banner & Nashville Daily Advertiser. (Thurs., July 11, 1833)

Flint, Timothy Esq. Died in Salem, Mass.
Nashville Whig. (Fri., Sept. 4, 1840)

Flournoy, Mrs. Ann. Died in Arkansas. Late of Limestone County, Ala.
National Banner & Nashville Whig. (Fri., April 10, 1835)

Flournoy, Francis Esq. Aged 64 years. Died in Scott County, Ky.
National Banner & Nashville Whig. (Wed., March 4, 1835)

Flournoy, Rev. Robert. Aged 37 years. Minister of the Methodist Episcopal Church. Died at Perry, Houston County, Geo.
National Banner & Nashville Daily Advertiser. (Fri., May 16, 1834)

Flournoy, Samuel Esq. Died in Princeton, Ky.
National Banner & Nashville Whig. (Fri., July 25, 1828)

Flournoy, William C. Attorney at law. Died in Pulaski on the 23d inst.
Nashville Whig. (Fri., Sept. 28, 1838)

Flournoy, William C. Attorney at law. Died in Pulaski on the 22d inst.
Daily Republican Banner. (Thurs., Sept. 27, 1838)

Flower, Mr. Richard. One of the proprietors & founders of this town. Died at Albion, Illinois.
National Banner. (Sat., Sept. 18, 1829)

Floyd, Hon. Jas. Age 61 of Philadelphia. Died in New York on the 5 inst. formerly a member of the U. S. Senate from Massachusetts.
National Banner & Nashville Whig. (Mon., April 25, 1831)

Floyd, General John. Late Governor of Virginia. Died recently at the sweet Sulphur Springs, in Virginia. He was a native of Kentucky.
The Union. (Sat., Sept. 9, 1837)

Floyd, The Hon. John. Late Governor of Virginia. Died at the Sweet Springs on the 16th inst.
Daily Republican Banner. (Wed., Aug. 30, 1837)

Floyd, Samuel. With the second Tennessee Regiment. Died - was killed in Mexico in the Battle of Sierra Gorda with the Mexicans.
The Politician & Weekly Nashville Whig. (Fri., May 21, 1847)

Fluger, Mr. Henry (Fleeger?) Died at Pittsburgh.
National Banner & Nashville Whig. (July 1, 1826)

Fly, Mrs. Jane. Died in Madison County. Wife of Mr. John Fly.
National Banner. (Sat., May 16, 1829)

Fogg, Miss Elizabeth. The Friends and acquaintances of Mr. & Mrs. are invited to attend the funeral tomorrow 11 a.m.
National Banner & Nashville Advertiser. (Mon., March 19, 1832)

Fogg, Ellen. Infant daughter of Godfrey M. Fogg Esq. Died Suddenly on Sunday last.
Nashville Whig. (Thurs., Nov. 7, 1844)

Fogg, Francis B. Jr. Eldest son of Francis B. Fogg Sr. Died on the 12th inst at the residence of his father in Nashville in the 23rd year of his age.
The Politician & Weekly Nashville Whig. (Fri., Feb. 18, 1848)

Fogg, Francis B. Jr. Esq. Died on Saturday night last.
The Christian Record. (Sat., Feb. 10th 1848)

Fogg, Mrs. Martha. Consort of Mr. James G. Fogg. Died in Giles County on the 6th inst.
National Banner & Nashville Daily Advertiser. (Wed., Jan. 30, 1833)

D. Follen and Lady. Died in the wreck of the steamboat Lexington. He was formerly professor of German literature at Harvard University.
Daily Republican Banner. (Fri., Jan. 31, 1840)

Foltz, Mrs. Catharine C. Consort of Mr. Reuben M. Foltz. Youngest daughter of Mr. Geary of Pittsburgh, Pa. Died in Nashville at the residence of her sister Mrs. Dally on the 6th inst.
The Christian Record. (Sat., June 18th 1847)

Folwell, J. A. Infant son of Mr. Jos. & Catharine Folwell. Died in Franklin, Tenn. on Sunday, June 28th.
National Banner & Nashville Whig. (Fri., July 10, 1835)

Fonte, Mr. Jacob. Aged 62. Died in Roane County.
National Banner & Nashville Whig. (Mon., Oct. 31, 1831)

Foote, Philip A. Esq. Died in Huntsville, Ala.
Nashville Republican & State Gazette. (Thurs., June 16, 1831)

Foote, Philip A. Esq. Age 38. Died in Huntsville, Ala.
National Banner & Nashville Whig. (Wed., June 15, 1831)

Forbes, James G. Died 15th at Cincinnati, Ohio of Cholera.
National Banner & Nashville Daily Advertiser. (Tues., Oct. 24, 1832)

Forbes, Jno. Murray Esq. Died in Buenos Ayres, U.S. Charge d'affaires at that place.
Nashville Republican & State Gazette. (Tues., Aug. 30, 1831)

Ford, Bartlett Esq. Died in Franklin County, Miss.
National Banner & Nashville Whig. (Sat., March 10, 1827)

Ford, Joseph. Washington, Ky. Died in the loss of the Steamboat Brandywine.
National Banner & Nashville Daily Advertiser. (Mon., April 23, 1832)

Ford, Capt. Lewis. A soldier of the Revolution, aged 76. Died in Smith County.
National Banner & Nashville Daily Advertiser. (Fri., Feb. 22, 1833)

Ford, Mrs. Louisa. Died at Vicksburgh, Miss.
National Banner. (March 17, 1826)

Ford, Mrs. Mary. Consort of Captain Daniel Ford and daughter of the Rev. John Fite. Died in Cannon County, Tenn. on 25th March of consumption.
National Banner & Nashville Whig. (Fri., April 1, 1836)

Ford, Miss Nancy. Daughter of Mr. Zachariah Ford. Died in Smith County.
National Banner & Nashville Daily Advertiser. (Thurs., Jan. 19, 1832)

Miss Nancy Ford. Daughter of Mr. Zachariah Ford. Died in Smith County.
National Banner and Nashville Advertiser. (Thurs., Jan. 19, 1832)

Ford, Mrs. Nancy B. Wife of Mr. Walter Ford. Died at Florence, Ala.
National Banner. (Sat., Nov. 7, 1829)

Ford, Nicholas. Formerly of Nashville. Died in the explosion of the
Steamboat, Lucy Walker.
Nashville Whig. (Tues., Oct. 29, 1844)

Ford, Mr. Pain. Aged about 25 years. Died in Fayette County at the
residence of his father on Monday evening the 5th inst.
National Banner & Nashville Daily Advertiser. (Sat., Aug. 17, 1833)

Ford, Mr. Patrick H. Formerly editor of the St. Louis Enquirer. Died
in St. Louis.
National Banner. (Sat., Feb. 10, 1827)

Foreman, Mr. Howard, A native of Hyde Park, New York. Died in Davidson
County on the 4th inst.
National Banner & Nashville Whig. (Thurs., Aug. 12, 1830)

Formwalt, Mrs. Evelina. Aged 93 years. Died in Knoxville.
National Banner & Nashville Whig. (Fri., Oct. 3, 1834)

Formwalt, Mr. Henry. Died in Pulaski.
National Banner & Nashville Whig. (Sat., Aug. 18, 1827)

Forrest, De Capt. Died on board the Steamboat Scotland near the
mouth of Salt River.
National Banner & Nashville Daily Advertiser. (Mon., July 14, 1834)

Forster, Mrs. Altona H. Died in Raleigh, N. C. Widow of the late
Rev. A. Forster.
National Banner & Nashville Whig. (Sat., Dec. 15, 1827)

Forsyth, Mr. George R. A worthy citizen of Nashville. Died on
Tuesday night.
Nashville Whig. (Thurs., March 28, 1844)

Forsythe, Mr. John. Of Brown County, Ohio. Died - drowned in the
Ohio River.
National Banner & Nashville Whig. (Sat., Aug. 5, 1826)

Fort, Mrs. Consort of Mr. Isaac Fort. Died in Lawrence County, Ala.
National Banner & Nashville Whig. (Sat., Oct. 7, 1826)

Fort, Mr. Daniel. Aged 25. Died near Bowling Green, Ky.
National Banner & Nashville Daily Advertiser. (Sat., Aug. 2, 1834)

Fort, Mrs. Dorothy. Died in Robinson County.
National Banner & Nashville Whig. (Sat., March 10, 1827)

Fort, Doctor Joseph H. Aged 40 years. Died in Hinds County, Miss.
formerly of Robinson County, Tenn.
National Banner & Nashville Daily Advertiser. (Sat., Jan. 25, 1834)

Fort, Rev. Sugg. Died near Port Royal on Sat. the 21st in Robinson
County.
National Banner & Nashville Whig. (Sat., March 28, 1829)

Fort, Virginia C. Consort of Mr. Eppa L. Fort. Died in Montgomery
County, Tenn. on the 21st inst.
National Banner & Nashville Whig. (Fri., Jan. 6, 1837)

Fortson, Mr. John. Aged 39 years. Died in Montgomery County, Tenn.
National Banner & Nashville Daily Advertiser. (Sat., June 2, 1832)

Foster, Miss Ann. Aged about 19 years. Died at the residence of her
father James H. Foster Esq.
Nashville True Whig & Weekly Commercial Register. (Fri., Sept. 6,1850)

Foster, Mr. Backer. Aged 47. Died in Maury County.
National Banner & Nashville Whig. (Wed., March 16, 1831)

Foster, Charles B. Son of Mr. George Foster. Died in Nashville.
National Banner & Nashville Daily Advertiser. (Wed., April 25, 1832)

Foster, Mrs. Eleanor. Wife of Anthony Foster Esq. of this place,
Nashville. Died on Tuesday evening last.
Nashville Whig. (June 17, 1823)

Foster, Mr. George G. Died in Logan Cty, Ky.
National Banner & Nashville Whig. (Wed., Feb. 25, 1835)

Foster, James C. H. Esq. Died in Dyer County.
National Banner & Nashville Advertiser. (Wed., April 25, 1832)

Foster, Mrs. Jane M. Consort of Ephraim H. Foster Esq. Died at
Mansfield the residence of her husband in the vicinity of Nashville
on Friday last.
The Politician & Weekly Nashville Whig. (Fri., Nov. 19, 1847)

Foster, Mrs. Jane M. Consort of the Hon. Ephraim H. Foster. Aged
55 years. Died at Mansfield the residence of her husband in the
vicinity of Nashville on Friday the 12th inst.
The Christian Record. (Sat., Nov. 20, 1847)

Foster, Louisa. Infant daughter of Robert C. Foster Esq. Died at
Franklin, T.
National Banner. (Sat., April 25, 1829)

Foster, Mrs. N. E. Consort of J. W. Foster Esq. and only daughter of
Rev. Thomas Calhoun of Wilson County. Died at Columbus, Miss. on
Sat. evening 1st inst. at the residence of Col. A. J. Calhoun.
Nashville Whig. (Mon., May 17, 1841)

Foster, Rebecca. Daughter of A. J. Foster of Greenville, Va. Died
in the explosion of the Steamboat Lucy Walker.
Nashville Whig. (Tues., Oct. 29, 1844)

Foster, Robert C. Sen. Aged 75 years. Died at Mansfield the residence
of his son, Hon. E. H. Foster.
Nashville Whig. (Tuesday, Oct. 1, 1844)

Foster, Mr. Septimus. Merchant. Died in Nashville on Tuesday the 19th.
Daily Republican Banner. (Sat., March 23, 1839)

Foster, Mr. Septimus. Merchant. Died in Nashville on Tuesday 19th
inst.
Nashville Whig. (Fri., March 22, 1839)

Foster, Rev. Stephen. Professor of languages in the East Tenn. College
Died in Knoxville, Tenn.
National Banner & Nashville Whig. (Fri., Jan. 23, 1835)

Foster, Mrs. Susan. Died in Logan County, Ky.
National Banner & Nashville Whig. (Sat., Oct. 28, 1826)

Foster, Mr. William. Died in Louisville, Ky.
National Banner & Nashville Whig. (Wednesday, Aug. 3, 1831)

Fountain, Mr. Jefferson. Died at Frankford, Ky.
National Banner. (March 17, 1826)

Fowle, Jonathan Esq. Attorney at law. Died in Philadelphia on the
30th ult.
National Banner. (Sat., Sept. 19, 1829)

Fowler, Mr. Jacob. Died at Natchez.
National Banner. (Jan. 20, 1826)

Fowler, John. Former Post Master of Lexington. Died at Lexington, Ky.
Nashville Whig. (Mon., Aug. 31, 1840)

Fowler, Mrs. Milliscent. Wife of Captain John Fowler. Died at
Lexington, Ky.
National Banner & Nashville Daily Advertiser. (Thurs., July 25, 1833)

Fowler, Mr. Zachariah. Died in Madison County, Ky. aged 30.
National Banner & Nashville Whig. (Sat., Sept. 9, 1826

Fowlkes, Mrs. Mary G. Wife of Doctor Jeptha Fowlkes. Died in the
vicinity of Nashville on the 4th inst. in the 27th year of her age.
Nashville Whig. (Fri., Nov. 19, 1841)

Fowlks, Jephtha Pendleton. Aged 2 years and 3 months. Son of Dr.
Jephtha Fowlks. Died in Memphis on Thursday night, the 22nd inst.
Nashville Whig. (Fri., Dec. 7, 1838)

Fox, Mr. James. Of Warren County, Tenn. Aged 76 years. Died in
Athens, Ala.
National Banner & Nashville Whig. (Fri., Nov. 14, 1834)

Fox, Mr. Lark. Died in Clinton, Mi.
National Banner & Nashville Daily Advertiser. (Fri., Sept. 20, 1833)

Fox, Miss Mary. Died near Bowling Green, Ky.
National Banner & Nashville Whig. (Fri., Feb. 6, 1835)

Foxall, Mr. Thomas. Died in Sumner County on the 17th March in the
44th year of his age.
National Banner & Nashville Whig. (Wed., April 15, 1835)

Frances, Woodson, Son of Miller Frances Esq. Died in Nashville on
the 28th inst.
Daily Republican Banner. (Mon., July 30, 1838)

Frances, Woodson. Son of Miller Frances Esq. Died in Nashville on
the 28th inst.
Nashville Whig. (Mon., July 30, 1838)

Francis, Mrs. Sally. Wife of Hugh Francis Esq. Died in Roane County.
National Banner. (Feb. 17, 1826)

Francisco, Peter. A revolution Hero and sergeant at arms, to the House
of Delegates. Died at Richmond, Va. aged about 70 years on 16th ult.
Nashville Republican & State Gazette. (Tues., Feb. 1, 1831)

Franklin, Mr. Edward. Died in M'Minn County.
National Banner & Nashville Whig. (Wed., Sept. 7, 1831)

Franklin, Mrs. Elizabeth B. Wife of Major Lawson D. Franklin. Died
in Jefferson County near the mouth of Nolichucky.
Nashville Whig. (Tues., May 5, 1846)

Franklin, Isaac Esq. Of Sumner County, Tenn. Died on the 27th ult.
on his plantation in Louisiana.
Nashville Whig. (Thurs., May 7, 1846)

Franklin, Mr. James R. A native of Tennessee. Died in New Orleans.
National Banner & Nashville Daily Advertiser. (Tues., June 24, 1834)

Franklin, Mr. John. Died near Gallatin, T. An old and respectable
citizen of Sumner County.
National Banner & Nashville Daily Advertiser. (Mon., July 14, 1834)

Franklin, Walter S. Esq. Clerk of the House of Representative. Died at Lancaster, Pennsylvania.
Daily Republican Banner. (Mon., Oct. 8, 1838)

Franklin, Walter S. Late Clerk of the House of Representative. Died at Lancaster, Pennsylvania on the 20th ulto.
Nashville Union. (Monday, Oct. 8, 1838)

Fraser, Mr. Arthur. Aged 24 years. Died in Bedford County, Tenn.
National Banner & Nashville Daily Advertiser. (Thurs., June 19, 1834)

Fraser, Capt. U. 3d Artiller. Died - killed in Battle with the Seminoles Indians, in Florida.
The Union. (Sat., Jan. 23, 1836)

Frashee, Miss Rachel. Died in Monroe County.
National Banner & Nashville Whig. (Sat., Sept. 15, 1827)

Frazer, Mrs. Philadelphia. Died in Fayette County, Ky.
National Banner & Nashville Whig. (Mon., Sept. 20, 1830)

Frazier, Mr. George W. Aged 23. Died in Rhea County.
National Banner & Nashville Whig. (Mon., Oct. 4, 1830)

Frazier, Maj. James. Aged 75. Died in Sumner County.
National Banner & Nashville Daily Advertiser. (Sat. July 13, 1833)

Frazier, Miss Lucinda. Daughter of Thomas Frazier Esq. Died in Knox County, Tenn. Aged 17 years.
National Banner & Nashville Whig. (Mon., Nov. 10, 1834)

Frazier, Mrs. Rebecca. Died in Knoxville.
Daily Republican Banner. (Sat., Sept. 22, 1838)

Free, Polly. Died 15th at Cincinnati, Ohio of Cholera.
National Banner & Nashville Daily Advertiser. (Wed., Oct. 24, 1832)

Freeland, Edward H. Assistant Surgeon. Died at Mahon of the U. S. Schr. Shark.
National Banner & Nashville Whig. (Mon., Jan. 5, 1835)

Freeman, Mr. James. Died in Blount County.
National Banner & Nashville Whig. (Sat., Sept. 15, 1827)

Freeman, Mr. Joshua. Died in Knox County.
National Banner & Nashville Advertiser. (Sat., Sept. 22, 1832)

Freeman, Mrs. Lurany. Died in Bedford County, Tenn.
National Banner & Nashville Whig. (Fri., Oct. 17, 1834)

French, Allen L. Of the late firm of Smith and French. Died in Knoxville on Thursday the 31st ult.
The Christian Record. (Sat., Jan. 23, 1847)

French, Joseph. Aged about 18 years. Died in Hickman County, Ky.
National Banner & Nashville Whig. (Fri., Jan. 9, 1835)

French, Mrs. Mary. Died in Christian County, Ky.
National Banner & Nashville Daily Advertiser. (Mon., April 29, 1833)

French, Miss Mary Reed. Late of Virginia. Aged 20 years. Died at Moscow, Ky.
National Banner & Nashville Whig. (Mon., Jan. 5, 1835)

French, Mr. Wm. P. Formerly of Boston, aged 33 years. Died in New Orleans.
National Banner & Nashville Daily Advertiser. (Tues., June 24, 1834)

Frick, John. Died 16th at Cincinnati, Ohio of Cholera.
National Banner & Nashville Daily Advertiser. (Wed., Oct. 24, 1832)

Friend, Mr. Died in Elkton, Giles County.
Nashville Republican & State Gazette. (Thurs., July 14, 1831)

Friend, Mr. John. Died in Madison County, Ala.
National Banner & Nashville Whig. (Mon., June 7, 1830)

Frierson, Mr. David. Died in Maury County.
National Banner & Nashville Whig. (Sat., March 22, 1828)

Frisby, Dr. Gideon. Died in New Orleans.
Nashville Republican & State Gazette. (Sat., May 14, 1831)

Frith, Mr. Archibald. Died on Oct. 8th at Rome. Smith County, Ten.
He was distinguished as a merchant.
National Banner & Nashville Whig. (Fri., Dec. 12, 1834)

Frith, Mr. Wm. 25. Died in Mobile.
National Banner & Nashville Whig. (September 2, 1826)

Fritzlen, John. Died at Versailles, Ky. 12 miles from Lexington
of Cholera.
National Banner & Nashville Whig. (Fri., Sept. 4, 1835)

Frost, Mr. Pleasant C. Aged 21, formerly of White County. Died in
Brownsville.
National Banner & Nashville Whig. (Wed., March 16, 1831)

Frost, Pleasent C. Died in Brownsville, Ten.
Nashville Republican & State Gazette. (Thurs., March 17, 1831)

Fry, James H. Infant son of James H. Fry. Died this morning 8th
inst. of the scarlet fever.
The Western Weekly Review. (Franklin, Tenn. Fri., Feb. 8, 1833)

Fry, James H. Infant son of Joseph H. Fry. Died in Franklin, Tenn.
National Banner & Nashville Daily Advertiser. (Mon., Feb. 11, 1833)

Fry, Mr. Nathan. Formerly of Philadelphia. Died in Cincinnati, O.
National Banner & Nashville Daily Advertiser. (Thurs., Aug. 8, 1833)

Fulkes, John D. Of Rutherford County, Died in Huntsville, Ala. by
committing suicide.
Nashville Whig. (Sat., Feb. 18, 1843)

Fuller, Mr. Lycurgus. Died in Lexington, Tenn.
Nashville Whig. (Tuesday, July 21, 1846)

Fuller, William Sanders. Infant son of Mr. Charles A. Fuller. Died
in Nashville on Sunday night Sept. 5th aged 22 months.
The Christian Record. (Sat., Sept. 11, 1847)

Fullerton, Mrs. Wife of Mr. James Fullerton. Died in Lauderdale
County, Ala.
National Banner & Nashville Daily Advertiser. (Mon., Aug. 27, 1832)

Fullerton, Humphrey Esq. Died at Chillicothe. Clerk of the Supreme
Court and Court of Common Pleas . Aged 52.
National Banner & Nashville Whig. (Mon., May 31, 1830)

Fulton, Mrs. Elizabeth. Wife of David Fulton. Died at Florence, Ala.
in the 65th year of her age.
National Banner. (Sat., Dec. 19, 1829)

Fulton, Mr. James. Died in Maury County on the 22d ult.
National Banner. (Jan. 13,1826)

137

Fultz, Mrs. Wife of Mr. Andrew Fultz. Died in M'Minn County.
National Banner. (Sat., Aug. 15, 1829)

Funnelly, Mr. Winthrop H. Aged 27. Died in Mobile.
National Banner & Nashville Whig. (Sat., Sept. 16, 1826)

Furtwaengler, Mr. L. E. A native of Baden Germany. Died in Nashville
on the 7th April aged nearly 22 years.
National Banner & Nashville Whig. (Mon., April 13, 1835)

Fyffe, Isaac W. Esq. Postmaster & County surveyor. Died in Athens, T.
National Banner. (Sat., Aug. 15, 1829)

Gadsden, Mr. Joh. Died in Charleston, S. C.
Nashville Republican & State Gazette.(Tues., February 22, 1831)

Gaillard, Hon. John. Senator in Congress from South Carolina. Died
in Washington City.
National Banner. (March 24, 1826)

Gainer, James C. Formerly Sheriff of Henry County. Died on Monday
the 25th ult. at the time of death was a Director of the Branch Bank
of Tennessee at Trenton.
Nashville Whig. (Sat., Aug. 13, 1842)

Gaines, Mrs. Barbary Blount. Wife of Major Gen. Edmund P. Gaines.
Died at the residence of James G. Lyon Esq. (Mobile Com. Adv.)
National Banner & Nashville Whig. (Mon., Dec. 19, 1836)

Gaines, Mrs. Barbary Blount. Wife of Major Gen. Edmund P. Gaines.
Died at the residence of James G. Lyon. (Mobile Com.)
Nashville Republican. (Monday, Dec. 19, 1836)

Gaines, Susan. Sister of Gen. Gaines. Died in Kingsport, at an
advanced age.
Daily Republican Banner. (Wed., July 29,1840)

Gaines, Mr. Wm. Aged 69. Died in Mercer County, Ky.
National Banner & Nashville Whig. (Sat., March 31, 1827)

Gainus, Mrs. Nicy. Wife of Mr. Robert L. Gainus. Died at Knoxville.
National Banner. (Sat., May 9, 1829)

Gaither, Dr. Abner. Died in Shelbyville, Tenn. of Cholera.
National Banner & Nashville Daily Advertiser. (Thurs., July 11, 1833)

Gaither, Mr. B. Died in Bedford County.
National Banner & Nashville Advertiser. (Sat., Aug. 4, 1832)

Gaither, Mr. James Esq. Died in Nelson County, Ky.
National Banner. (Sat., Aug. 1, 1829)

Gaither, Mrs. Jane L. and her infant daughter. Died in Springfield
Ky. on the 9th of July from the effects of Cholera. The decesaed was
the wife of Dr. Edward B. Gaither.
National Banner & Nashville Daily Advertiser. (Wed., Aug. 21, 1833)

Galbraith, William Esq. Clerk of Jackson County Court. Died in
Jackson County.
National Banner & Nashville Whig. (Fri., Oct. 10,1834)

Galbreath, John. Infant son of William Galbreath. Died in Shelbyville, Tenn.
National Banner & Nashville Whig. (Fri., Jan. 23, 1835)

Galbreath, Miss Partenia. Died in Christian County, Ky.
National Banner & Nashville Advertiser. (Fri., June 8, 1832)

Gales, Mrs. Winfred. Consort of Joseph Gales Esq. of Nashville late
of North Carolina. Died on Wednesday afternoon in the 79th year of
her age.
Nashville Whig. (Wed., July 10, 1839)

Gallespie, Davidella. Daughter of David and Mary L. Gallespie late
of Nashville. Died at the residence of Mrs. Tyrees near Lexington,
Mo. on the 5th April aged 5 months and 27 days.
Nashville Union. (Mon., April 29, 1839)

Galloway, Benjamin. Died in Hagertown, Maryland.
Nashville Republican & State Gazette. (Sat., Sept. 17, 1831)

Gallaway, Mr. James. In the 35th year of his age. Died in Maury
County, Tenn. on Wednesday the 19th inst.
National Banner & Nashville Daily Advertiser. (March 5, 1834)

Galloway, Mrs. Nancy. Wife of Mr. Samuel Galloway. Died in Nashville.
National Banner & Nashville Whig. (Fri., June 10, 1831)

Gamble, Mrs. Catherine. Relick of the late Col. Robert Gamble. Died
at Richmond, Va.
National Banner & Nashville Daily Advertiser. (Mon., Jan. 9, 1832)

Gamble, Mrs. Died in Bedford County.
National Banner & Nashville Advertiser. (Wed., April 11, 1832)

Gamble, Captain Edmund. An Officer of the revolutionary war and for
many years a resident of this county. Died on Wednesday last.
Nashville Whig. (Aug. 9th, 1824)

Gamble, Col. Geo. Aged 45. Died in Hamilton County.
National Banner & Nashville Whig. (Sat., Sept. 9, 1826)

Gamble, Mr. James C. Of the house of Gamble and Byrd. Died at Mobile.
National Banner. (May 13, 1826)

Gamble, Maj. William. Aged 78. An officer of the revolutionary army.
Died in Washington City.
National Banner & Nashville Daily Advertiser. (Mon., Feb. 4, 1833)

Gammon, Mrs. Leviey. Died in Knox County.
National Banner. (April 21, 1826)

Gammon, Miss Minerva J. Daughter of Mr. Dozier B. Gammon. Died in
Kingston.
National Banner & Nashville Whig. (December 2, 1826)

Gammon, Richard Esq. Died in Sullivan County.
National Banner & Nashville Daily Advertiser. (Tues., Jan. 22, 1833)

Ganaway, Robert B. Infant son of Samuel L. and Margaret J. Ganaway.
Died near Cherryville, Haywood County.
Nashville Whig. (Tues., April 21, 1846)

Gano, Rev. Stephen. For 30 years pastor of the Baptist Church in that
town. Died in Providence, R. I.
National Banner & Nashville Whig. (Sat., Sept. 13, 1828)

Gardiner, Capt. G. W. 2d Artillery. Died was killed in battle with
the Seminols Indians in Florida.
The Union. (Sat., Jan. 23, 1836)

Gardner, Mrs. Emily. Died in Dresden, Tenn.
Nashville Republican & State Gazette. (Mon., July 30, 1832)

Gardner, Mr. John. Aged 70 died in Sumner County.
National Banner & Nashville Whig. (Sat., Feb. 2, 1828)

Garland, Mrs. Mary C. Wife of Professor L. C. Garland of Randolph
Macon College. Died in Mecklenburg Co., Va.
National Banner & Nashville Daily Advertiser. (Tues., July 15, 1834)

Garland, Mr. Rufus K. Formerly of Tipton County, Tenn. Died in
Last Prairie, Ark.
National Banner & Nashville Daily Advertiser. (Wed., Aug. 7, 1833)

Garner, Dan. H. Printer. Son of William Garner Esq. Died in
Nashville on the 3rd inst.
The Christian Record. (Sat., Nov. 6, 1847)

Garner, Mr. James. At the age of 105 years. Died at the residence
of Mr. Lewis Garner on the 15th inst. He was born in Virginia and
served in the Revolutionary war. (Flor. Ala. Gaz.)
National Banner & Nashville Daily Advertiser. (Wed., June 27, 1832)

Garner, William Archibald. Son of John E. Garner aged 9 months.
Died in Springfield Robertson Co. on the 27th ult.
Nashville Whig. (Tues., April 4, 1843)

Garnett, Thos. Esq. Aged 61. Died in King and Queen City, Va.
Nashville Republican & State Gazette. (Thurs., March 3, 1831)

Garrard, Mr. Edward H. A student of Transylvania University. Died in
Bourbon County, Ky.
National Banner (May 10, 1826)

Garrard, Mrs. Nancy. Wife of Mr. Wm. W. Garrard. Died at
Florence, Ala.
National Banner & Nashville Whig. (Sat., Aug. 18, 1827)

Garret, Ambrose. Died - scalded to death on Ohio River when steamboat
boiler collapsed.
National Banner & Nashville Daily Advertiser. (Wed., Nov. 20, 1833)

Garret, Mr. William. A native of Wales. Died in Nashville on Sunday
the 29th ult.
Nashville Whig. (Tues., Oct. 1, 1844)

Garrett, Miss Elizabeth. Daughter of William Garrett. Died in the
vicinity of Nashville on Monday the 13th inst.
Nashville Whig. (Thurs., July 16, 1846)

Garrett, Mrs. Elizabeth. Wife of Mr. C. Garrett. Died in Franklin.
National Banner & Nashville Daily Advertiser. (Mon., June 3, 1833)

Garrett, Mrs. Elizabeth. Aged 72 years. Died on the 16th inst.
Consort of William Garrett Recorder of Nashville.
Nashville True Whig & Weekly Commercial Register. (Fri., July 19, 1850)

Garrett, Mr. George Jun. Of Sumner County. Died in Giles County.
National Banner & Nashville Advertiser. (Thurs., Feb. 4, 1832)

Garrett, Mrs. Wife of Gray Garrett. Died in Jefferson County.
National Banner. (May 13, 1826)

Garrett, Col. Henry A. Died on the 12th ult. at his plantation on
Second Creek. In Adams County, Miss. Formerly of Tenn.
Nashville Whig. (Thurs., March 7, 1844)

Garrett, Mr. James. Died at Louisville, Ky.
National Banner. (Sat., April 25, 1829)

Garrett, Mrs. R. P. Formerly of this town. Died in Robinson County.
National Banner. (Sat., July 18, 1829)

Garripney, Mons. G. Aged about 56 years. Died in Mobile, Ala. of
yellow fever.
Daily Republican Banner. (Tues., Oct. 1, 1839)

Garrish, Francis B. Aged 63 years. Died 13th at Cincinnati, Ohio
of Cholera.
National Banner & Nashville Daily Advertiser. (Tues., Oct. 23, 1832)

Garrison, Mrs. Charlotte. Wife of Moses F. Garrison. age 35. Died
in Madison County on the 13th Oct.
National Banner & Nashville Whig. (Mon., Oct. 17, 1836)

Gentry, J. H. Of Mo. Died in New Orleans of Yellow Fever.
Daily Republican Banner. (Fri., Sept. 29, 1837)

Gentry, Tabitha W. Infant daughter of the Hon. M. P. Gentry. Died
on Monday the 4th inst. at the residence of Dr. James W. Hoggatt, in
Wilson County, aged about 19 months.
Nashville Whig. (Tues., Feb. 27, 1844)

Garrard, Mrs. Elizabeth. Widow of the late Col. James Garrard Ex-
Governor of Ky. Died in Bourbon County, Ky.
National Banner & Nashville Advertiser. (Wed., Sept. 12, 1832)

Garrison, Mrs. Wife of Mr. John Garrison. Died in Madison County.
National Banner & Nashville Daily Advertiser. (Wed., July 2, 1833)

Garvin, James A. Professor of Chemistry in East Tennessee University.
Died in Knoxville on the 29th inst.
Nashville Whig. (Tues., July 7, 1846)

Garvin, Mrs. Mary. Wife of John Garvin. Died in Green County.
National Banner. (Sat., Dec. 5, 1829)

Gassaway, Mr. John. Died in Shelby County, Ky.
National Banner. (June 10, 1826)

Gates, Mr. Elom B. A native of Tennessee. Died at Port Gibson, Miss.
National Banner & Nashville Daily Advertiser. (Tues., July 17, 1832)

Gates, Hon. Horatio. A native of Barre, Mass. Died at Montreal,
Canada a member of the Legislative Council of Lower Canada.
National Banner & Nashville Daily Advertiser. (Fri., May 16, 1834)

Gayle, John. Principal of the academy in that place. Died in
Clarksville.
Nashville Republican & State Gazette. (Thurs., March 3, 1831)

Gayle, Mrs. Lucy. Wife of Mr. John Gayle. Died at Clarksville.
National Banner & Nashville Whig. (Mon., Aug. 30, 1830)

Gaylord, H. H. Died of Cholera. Copyed from Maysville Eagle &
Monitor.
National Banner & Nashville Daily Advertiser. (Thurs., June 6, 1833)

Gee, Mrs. Wife of Mr. Benjamin Gee. Aged 26. Died at Knoxville.
National Banner. (March 17, 1826)

Gee, Mrs. Mary. Consort of W. W. Gee, deceased. Died - the friends
are requested to attend her funeral at 2 P.M. today, May 17.
Daily Republican Banner. (Fri., May 17, 1839)

Geise, L. Of Baltimore, died in New Orleans of yellow fever.
Daily Republican Banner. (Wed., Oct. 4, 1837)

Genet, E. C. Esq. He came to this country as Minister of the French
Republic, soon after the Revolution. He married a daughter of the late

Gov. George Clinton. Died at his residence Rensselner County,
New York.
National Banner & Nashville Daily Advertiser. (Tues., July 29, 1834)

George, Rev. Enoch. Bishop of the Methodist Church, age 60. Died
at Staunton, Virg. on the 23rd ult.
National Banner & Nashville Whig. (Sat., Sept. 20, 1828)

German, Mrs. Sarah. Died on Sunday night last, after a long and
lingering illness for many years a resident of this town.
Impartial Review and Cumberland Repository. (Thurs., June 9, 1808)

Gettys, Mrs. Wife of Mr. James Gettys. Died at Athens, E. T.
National Banner & Nashville Daily Advertiser. (Wed., July 17, 1833)

Gibbes, Mr. Edwin. Aged 31. Died at Charleston, S. C.
National Banner & Nashville Whig. (Mon., July 18, 1831)

Gibbes, Wm. Hasell Esq. Counseller at law. Died at Charleston, S.C.
National Banner & Nashville Daily Advertiser. (Mon., March 10, 1834)

Gibbes, Mrs. Louisa Maria. Wife of William H. Gibbes Jr. Died in
Haynesville, Lowndes County, Ala.
National Banner & Nashville Daily Advertiser. (Wed., Jan. 18, 1832)

Gibbes, Mr. William Hasell. Formerly of Charleston, S. C. Died in
Haynesville, Ala.
National Banner & Nashville Whig. (Mon., Feb. 23, 1835)

Gibbs, Alphonso. Oldest son of Gen. George W. Gibbs in the 22nd year
of his age. Died yesterday in this vicinity.
National Banner & Nashville Whig. (Fri., Oct. 3, 1834)

Gibbs, Col. Joseph S. Died at Port Gibson, Miss.
National Banner & Nashville Whig. (December 2, 1826)

Gibbs, Mrs. Polly. Relict of Mr. Smith Gibbs, dec'd. Died in Logan
County, Ky.
National Banner & Nashville Whig. (Wed., Feb. 25, 1835)

Gibsen, Mrs. Jane. Wife of Robert Gibsen, merchant of Nashville.
Died in the vicinity of Nashville.
Nashville Republican. (Sat., Sept. 24, 1836)

Gibson, Private A. J. Company K. First Regiment, Tenn. Volunteers.
Died - was killed in the Battle of Monterey with the Mexicans on
Sept. 21st, 1846.
Nashville Whig. (Sat., Oct. 24, 1846)

Gibson, James M. Postmaster of Randolph, Tenn. Died in Randolph,
Tenn.
Nashville Republican & State Gazette. (Thurs., March 24, 1831)

Gibson, Mr. James M. Postmaster. Died in Randolph on the 10th inst.
National Banner & Nashville Whig. (Wed., March 23, 1831)

Gibson, Mrs. Jane. Wife of Robert Gibson. Merchant of Nashville.
Died on the 21st inst.
National Banner & Nashville Whig. (Wed., Sept. 28, 1836)

Gibson, Mr. John. Died in Montgomery County.
National Banner & Nashville Whig. (Sat., Aug. 9, 1828)

Gibson, Mary. Aged 2 years, 10 months and 10 days. Daughter of
Joseph F. Gibson. Died in Nashville on Monday 2d inst.
Daily Republican Banner. (Thurs., July 5, 1838)

Gibson, Mary. Infant daughter of Joseph F. Gibson, Merchant. Died on Sunday 1st inst.
Nashville Whig. (Wed., July 4, 1838)

Gibson, Philander. Late of Tennessee. Died at Pine Bluff, Arkansas.
Nashville Whig. (Mon., Oct. 5, 1840)

Gibson, Maj. Samuel. Died at the creek agency, Miss.
National Banner. (March 17, 1826)

Gibson, Mrs. Sarah Goff. Wife of Col. D. C. Gibson. Died at Look-out Mountain on the 10th day of Jan. 1835.
National Banner & Nashville Whig. (Mon., April 1, 1835)

Gibson, Mrs. Sophia W. Wife of Joseph F. Gibson and daughter of Elihu S. Hall. Died on yesterday morning.
Daily Republican Banner. (Tues., Dec. 17, 1839)

Gibson, Miss Susan. Aged 17. Died in Logan County, Ky.
National Banner & Nashville Whig. (Sat., Sept. 20, 1828)

Gibson, Mr. William. Died in this town on the 2nd inst.
National Banner & Nashville Whig. (Sat., May 17, 1828)

Gibson, Dr. Wm. C. Died in Madison County, Ala.
National Banner & Nashville Whig. (Sat., March 17, 1827)

Gibson, William C. Age 29. Died in New Orleans on 25 April a native of Ohio.
National Banner & Nashville Advertiser. (Thurs., May 10, 1832)

Gifford, Wm. Translator of Juvenal. Died in London.
National Banner & Nashville Whig. (Sat., March 31, 1827)

Gilbert, Mrs. Nancy. Wife of Capt. Thomas Gilbert. Died this morning in Nashville.
Nashville Whig. (Fri., May 24, 1839)

Gilbert, Mrs. Sally. Died in Vevay, Ind.
National Banner & Nashville Whig. (Sat., Feb. 17, 1827)

Gildart, Mrs. Sophia. Died in Wilkinson County, Mississippi in 64 year, on Wednesday 27th of October.
Nashville Republican & State Gazette. (Thurs., March 31, 1831)

Giles, William B. Esq. Died in Amelia County, Va. for 40 years he was in public life.
National Banner & Nashville Whig. (Mon., Dec. 27, 1830)

Gilford, William. Died - was drowned in the Tennessee River near Decatur, Ala. in the 20th year of his life. From the Jonesboro Sentinel.
The Union. (Sat., May 27, 1837)

Gill, Mrs. Betsey. Wife of Mr. James Gill. Died in Knoxville.
National Banner & Nashville Daily Advertiser. (Mon., July 15, 1833)

Gill, Lieut. C. G. With the Second Tenn. Regiment. Died - was killed in the Battle of Sierra Gorda with the Mexicans.
The Politicians & Weekly Nashville Whig. (Fri., May 21, 1847)

Gill, Doctor J. V. Died in Lancaster, Ky. of Cholera.
National Banner & Nashville Daily Advertiser. (Wed., July 3, 1833)

Gill, Mrs. Mary. Died 15th at Cincinnati, Ohio of Cholera.
National Banner & Nashville Daily Advertiser. (Wed., Oct. 24, 1832)

Gill, Dr. William. Died at Lancaster, Ky. of Cholera.
National Banner & Nashville Daily Advertiser. (Wed., July 3, 1833)

Gillaspie, Alexander. A soldier of the revolution. Died in Copiah
County, Miss. on Thursday the 28th Nov. in the 9th year of his age.
Nashville Union. (Fri., Dec. 27, 1839)

Gillespie, Mr. State driver. Died in Memphis of Cholera.
National Banner & Nashville Daily Advertiser. (Mon., June 3, 1833)

Gillespie, Mr. George Senr. Died in Washington County.
Knoxville Gazette. (Thurs., Jan. 2, 1794)

Gillespie, Geo. T. Died in Greene County.
Daily Republican Banner. (Sat., Sept. 22, 1838)

Gillespie, Mr. W. A cot-freeghter from Tennessee. Died in New Orleans
on the 2d of July.
National Banner & Nashville Whig. (Thurs., July 29, 1830)

Gillespie, William. Infant son of Dr. Allen Gillespie aged 11 months.
Died in Sumner County, Tenn.
National Banner & Nashville Whig. (Wed., Nov. 19, 1834)

Gilliam, Mrs. William. Died in Murfreesborough, Tenn. of consumption.
National Banner & Nashville Whig. (Wed., July 8, 1835)

Gilman, Hon. John T. Formerly Governor of the State. Died at Exeter,
N.H.
National Banner & Nashville Whig. (Sat., Sept. 27, 1828)

Gilman, Mrs. Mary. A native of England at an advanced age. Died at
Lexington, Ky. at the residence of John Peck Esq. her son-in-law.
National Banner & Nashville Daily Advertiser. (Wed., March 6, 1833)

Gilman, Miss Mary Susanna. Daughter of T. W. Gilman. Died in Nashville on the 31st Dec. in the 14th year of her age.
National Banner & Nashville Whig. (Mon., Jan. 18, 1836)

Gilman, Miss Mary Susanna. Daughter of Mr. T. Gilman. Died in
Nashville on the 31st ult. in the 14th year of her age.
The Union. (Tues., Jan. 19, 1836)

Gilman, Miss Mary Susanan. Daughter of Mr. T. Gilman. Died in
Nashville on the 31st ult. in the 14th year of her age.
Nashville Republican. (Sat., Jan. 16, 1836)

Gilman, Miss Mary Susanna. Daughter of Mr. T. Gilman, in this city on
the 31st ult., in the 14th year of her age.
Nashville Republican. (Sat., Jan. 16, 1836)

Gilmer, Mrs. Elizabeth. Widow of the late R. H. Gilmer Esq. Died
at Clinton, Miss.
National Banner & Nashville Daily Advertiser. (Thurs., June 19, 1834)

Gilpin, Mr. Israel. A soldier of the Revolution, aged 93 years.
Died in Boone County, Ky.
National Banner & Nashville Daily Advertiser. (Wed., Aug. 20, 1834)

Gingry, Mrs. Elizabeth. Wife of Capt. James Gingry. Died in
Rutherford County.
National Banner. (Sat., Aug. 22, 1829)

Gingry, Harriet. Second daughter of Joseph and Ann Gingry. Died
suddenly of Fever, aged 13 years.
Daily Republican Banner. (Tues., Aug. 25, 1840)

Gipson, William C.   Printer, aged 29 years.   Died at New Orleans on 25th April.   A native of Ohio.
National Banner & Nashville Daily Advertiser. (Thurs., May 10, 1832)

Girard, Stephen.   Died
National Banner & Nashville Daily Advertiser. (Wed., Feb. 1, 1832)

Gist, Mr. Levi I.   Of Courtland, Ala.   Died at Lexington, Ky.
National Banner & Nashville Whig. (Mon., Oct. 11, 1830)

Gist, Mrs. Martha.   Age 60.   Died in Washington Rhea County.
National Banner & Nashville Whig. (Mon., Sept. 12, 1831)

Glascock, Mrs. Ann H.   Wife of Dr. Glascock and daughter of the late Col. Sandford of Maury Co.   Died in Madison County, Ala.
National Banner & Nashville Daily Advertiser. (Tues., Aug. 7, 1832)

Glascock, Mrs. Ann H.   In the 19th year of her age.   Died on Sunday evening the 29th ult. in Madison Co., Ala.   She was the wife of Dr. Glascock and daughter of the late Col. Sanford, formerly a member of Congress from Maury County. (Huntsville Democrat)
National Banner & Nashville Daily Advertiser. (Sat., Sept. 22, 1832)

Glascock, Mary Ann.   Infant daughter of Dr. Glascock.   Died in Maury County at the residence of Mr. James Holland on the 10th inst.
National Banner & Nashville Daily Advertiser. (Sat., Sept. 22, 1832)

Glascock, Mrs. Olivia.   Wife of Mr. Edwin R. Glascock.   Died inNashville on the 3d inst.
Daily Republican Banner. (Mon., Nov. 6, 1837)

Glasgow, Col. James.   Of Davidson County, formerly Sec. of the State of North Carolina.   Died on Wednesday the 17th inst.
The Nashville Gazette. (Sat., Nov. 20, 1819)

Glasgow, Mr. Jesse.   In the 77th year of his age.   Died in Davidson County on the 1st day of March.
Daily Republican Banner. (Sat., March 10, 1838)

Glass, Mrs. Hannah.   Wife of Capt. Jesse Glass.   Died in Monroe County.
National Banner & Nashville Whig. (Mon., April 4, 1831)

Glass, Miss Ann G.   Died in Henderson, Ky.
National Banner & Nashville Whig. (Sat., Sept. 30, 1826)

Gleason, Michael.   Son of William Gleason of Philadelphia.   Died in Tuscaloosa, Ala.
Nashville Whig. (Fri., Sept. 11, 1840)

Gleaves, Absalom Esq.   Died in Davidson County.
National Banner & Nashville Whig. (Wed., Sept. 24, 1834)

Gleaves, James M.   Died at the residence of his brother in law M. H. Gleaves on the 29th inst.
Nashville Whig. (Mon., July 5, 1841)

Gleaves, Martha Caroline.   Infant daughter of Michael Gleaves Esq. Died in this county on 16th inst.
National Banner & Nashville Whig. (Fri., July 25, 1828)

Gleaves, Mr. Michael.   Died in Davidson County on the 24th inst.
National Banner & Nashville Daily Advertiser. (Thurs., Jan. 30, 1834)

Gleaves, Capt. Thomas.   Aged 38 years.   Died at his residence in Davidson County on the 16th inst.
Nashville Republican & State Gazette. (Thurs., Feb. 24, 1831)

Gleaves, William D. Youngest son of the late Michael Gleaves, Esq.
Died at Franklin, Robertson County, Texas, July 29th.
Nashville Whig. (Wed., Sept. 30, 1840)

Gleeson, Mrs. Amelia. Late consort of William W. Gleason of Gibson
County. Died on the 25th of August of consumption.
National Banner & Nashville Whig. (Mon., Sept. 8, 1835)

Gleeves, Capt. Thomas. Age 37. Died in Davidson County on the 16 inst
National Banner & Nashville Whig. (Fri., Feb. 25, 1831)

Glenn, Miss Eliza S. H. Died at Columbia, Tenn. An accomplished
instructress in the Columbia Female Academy.
National Banner & Nashville Daily Advertiser. (Mon., June 9, 1834)

Glenn, Robert. Died at Cincinnati, Ohio of Cholera.
National Banner & Nashville Daily Advertiser. (Tues., Oct. 24, 1832)

Glisan, Mr. Thomas. Formerly of Washington City, aged about 28 years.
Died in Paris, Tenn. on the 17th May by a fall from the second story
of the Jackson Hotel.
National Banner & Nashville Whig. (Fri., June 10, 1836)

Glover, Miss Marcianna. Died at Clarksville.
National Banner & Nashville Whig. (Thurs., May 20, 1830)

Glover, Private Tinsley. Company K. First Regiment Tenn. Volunteers
Died - was killed in the Battle of Monterey with the Mexicans on Sept.
21st 1846.
Nashville Whig. (Sat., Oct. 24, 1846)

Glover, Capt. William. Died in Sumner County.
National Banner & Nashville Whig. (Mon., July 19, 1830)

Gobert, Dr. Paul M. Died at St. Louis.
National Banner & Nashville Whig. (Sat., Dec. 9, 1826)

Godfrey, Mrs. Elizabeth. Died in Washington County, Ala.
National Banner. (May 13, 1826)

Godman, Dr. John D. In the 32nd year of his age. Died in Philadelphia
on the 17th ult.
National Banner & Nashville Whig. (Fri., May 7, 1830)

Goff, Capt. Andrew. Died in Williamson County.
National Banner & Nashville Whig. (Wed., Oct. 12, 1831)

Goggins, Col. Pleasent M. Died in Lynchburg, Va.
Nashville Republican & State Gazette. (Tues., Feb. 22, 1831)

Goldsborough, Mrs. Henrieta Maria. Relict of the late Hon. Robert H.
Goldsborough. Died at Myrtle Grove, Md.
Nashville Whig. (Fri., June 1st 1838)

Goneke, Mrs. Eliza. Wife of Mr. John F. Goneke. Died in Columbia.
National Banner & Nashville Whig. (Wed., July 6, 1831)

Gooch, Capt. John A. Died in Centerville on the 7th inst of a Pistol
ball shot by Robert Trimble.
Impartial Review and Cumberland Repository. (Sat., March 21, 1807)

Good, Dr. J. Mason. Died at Shepporton, Eng.
National Banner & Nashville Whig. (Sat., April 14, 1827)

Goodall, Col. Wm. Died in Smith County.
National Banner & Nashville Whig. (Sat., Aug. 5, 1826)

Goodgion, Capt. William F. Died in Maury County, Tenn. on the 29th
Aug. in the 36th year of his age.
Nashville Whig. (Wed., Sept. 4, 1839)

Goodhue, Dr. Wm. S. Died in Sommerville, Ala.
National Banner & Nashville Whig. (Sat., Nov. 18, 1826)

Goode, Mr. Campbell. Age 83, a revolutionary soldier. Died in
Carrollton, Ill.
National Banner & Nashville Whig. (Wed., June 8, 1831)

Goodlett, Dr. Adam G. For over 30 years a physician of Nashville.
Died in Rutherford County on the 17th inst. in the 69th year of his
age.
Nashville True Whig & Weekly Commercial Register. (Fri., April 26, 1850)

Goodloe, Mrs. Elizabeth. The companion of Mr. John M. Goodloe. Died
on the 22d. inst. of this neighborhood.
Impartial Review and Cumberland Repository. (Sat., June 27, 1807)

Goodman. Of Capt. Battles Company. Died at the encampment of the
Brigade of Tennessee Volentees in the Creek Nation.
Nashville Republican. (Thurs., Aug. 25, 1836)

Goodrich, Mrs. Elizabeth. Age 82. Died in Davidson County. On the
12 inst. consort of Mr. John Goodrich.
National Banner & Nashville Advertiser. (Wed., Aug. 22, 1832)

Goodrich, Albert W. Esq. Aged 24. Died at the residence of his father
in Davidson County on the morning of the 15th.
Nashville Union. (Wed., Nov. 27, 1839)

Goodrich, Mrs. Betty. Died in this county, aged 82.
Nashville Republican & State Gazette. (Wed., Aug. 22, 1832)

Goodrich, Mrs. Elizabeth. Consort of Mr. John Goodrich. Died in
Davidson county on the 12th inst., aged 82.
National Banner & Nashville Daily Advertiser. (Wed., Aug. 22, 1832)

Goodrich, Mary Maria. Infant daughter of E. W. Goodrich Senr. Died
in Davidson County on Wed. 25, inst.
National Banner & Nashville Advertiser. (Thurs., July 26, 1832)

Goodrich, Miss Oliva P. Daughter of Mr. Harvey Goodrich. Died in
Middleburg.
National Banner & Nashville Whig. (Wed., Sept. 7, 1831)

Goodrich, Rhoda. Infant daughter of E. M. & Lucy Ann Goodrich.
Died on the 4th inst., aged one year and five months.
Nashville Union. (Fri., July 5, 1839)

Goodwin, Mr. A. T. Of Nashville, Tenn. Died in Rutherford County
on Tuesday the 21st inst.
National Banner & Nashville Whig. (Wed., July 29, 1835)

Goodwin, Mr. Frederick H. Formerly of Plymouth, Mass. and late of
New York. Died in New Orleans.
National Banner & Nashville Daily Advertiser. (Thurs., Aug. 8, 1833)

Goodwin, Mr. James S. Of the house of J. S. Goodwin & Co. of Chula,
Mi. Died in Coffeeville, Mi.
National Banner & Nashville Whig. (Fri., Oct. 2, 1835)

Goodwin, Hon. Peterson. Member of Congress. Died at his seat in
Virginia on the 22d ult.
The Nashville Whig & Tenn. Advertiser. (March 14, 1818)

Goodwin, T. With the Second Tenn. Regiment. Died - was killed in
the battle of Sierra Gorda with the Mexicans.
The Politician & Weekly Nashville Whig. (Fri., May 21, 1847)

Goodwin, William W. In the 26th year of his age. Died on the 24th
inst.
Nashville True Whig & Weekly Commercial Register. (Fri., July 26, 1850)

Goodwin, Mr. William W. In the 38th year of his age. Died in Nashville
this morning the 24th inst. of a lingering illness.
National Banner & Nashville Daily Advertiser. (Tues., Jan. 24, 1832)

Goolsby, Mr. William. Died in Albermarle, Va. the 22d March. A man
who had reached the age of 108 years.
The Nashville Whig. & Tenn. Advertiser. (May 2, 1818)

Gordon, Miss Catheline. Aged 16 years. A native of Philadelphia.
Died in New Orleans.
National Banner & Nashville Daily Advertiser. (Thurs., Aug. 7, 1834)

Gordon, Mr. Fielding L. Of Tennessee. Died at St. Louis.
Nashville Republican. (Sat., April 2, 1836)

Gordon, Mrs. Died in this place Monday night last. Consort of Mr.
Jos. Gordon and daughter of Hugh Bell.
The Nashville Whig. & Tenn. Advertiser. (March 14, 1818)

Gordon, Captain John. Died in Maury County on Wednesday last at his
residence.
Nashville Gazette. (June 23, 1819)

Gordon, Mrs. Leonora. Wife of Col. George Gordon formerly of Tennessee.
Died at Woodville, Miss.
National Banner & Nashville Daily Advertiser. (Wed., Sept. 25, 1833)

Gordon, Nicholas. Tobaconist. Died in Nashville yesterday evening.
Daily Republican Banner. (Thurs., Oct. 11, 1838)

Gordon, Capt. Wm. L. Of the U. S. Navy. Died in Baltimore, Md.
National Banner & Nashville Daily Advertiser. (Thurs., June 19, 1834)

Gore, Hon. Christopher. Died in Waltham, Massachusetts, aged 69.
National Banner & Nashville Whig. (Sat., March 31, 1827)

Gorham, Dr. John. Died at Boston an emiment physician of that city.
National Banner. (Sat., April 25, 1829)

Gorin, Gladin A. Infant son of H. H. Gorin, P.M. at Indian Mound.
Died in Stewart County on the 11th March, aged one year and 10 months.
National Banner & Nashville Whig. (Wed., April 29, 1835)

Gorin, Col. Gladdin. After a long illness. Died in Stewart County,
Tenn. on 1st inst. Age 60.
National Banner & Nashville Advertiser. (Fri., Feb. 24, 1832)

Gould, Ann Rebecca. Infant daughter of Mr. & Mrs. James Gould. Died
on the 30th ult. in Nashville.
The Christian Record. (Sat., July 10, 1847)

Gould, Ann Rebecca. Infant daughter of Mr. & Mrs. James Gould. Died
on the 30th ult. in Nashville.
The Politician & Weekly Nashville Whig. (Fri., July 9, 1847)

Gould, Rev. Daniel. Of the Presbyterian Church, aged 44. Died in
Slatesville, N. S.? a native of New Hampshire.
National Banner & Nashville Daily Advertiser. (Thurs., June 19, 1834)

Gould, Edwin. Printer, late of New York. Died in New Orleans.
National Banner & Nashville Daily Advertiser. (Tues., June 24, 1834)

Gould, The Hon. James. Died at his residence in Litchfield, Con. on
the 11th inst.
Nashville Whig. (Fri., June 1, 1838)

Gould, Mr. Silas. Died in Elizabethtown, Ky.
National Banner & Nashville Daily Advertiser. (Mon., Nov. 19, 1832)

Goulding, Rev. Thomas D. D. Pastor of the Presbyterian Church at
Columbus, Ga. Died suddenly last night the 21st ult. of a heart
attack, was 62 years of age.
The Christian Record. (Sat., July 22, 1848)

Gooan, Andrew R. Esq. Died in Marshall County, Miss. on Sat. 28th ult.
Nashville Whig. (Mon., July 12, 1841)

Gowdey, Margaret. Youngest daughter of Thomas Gowdey of Nashville.
Died last evening.
Nashville Whig. (Fri., Oct. 19, 1838)

Gowen, Mr. John Sen. Died near Nashville in the 61st year of his age.
National Banner & Nashville Whig. (Fri., April 17, 1835)

Gowen, John J. Formerly of Davidson County, Tenn. Died at his
residence in Holmes County, Mississippi on the 6th inst.
Nashville Whig. (Thurs., Aug. 17, 1843)

Gowen, John Esq. Died in Baltimore. In a fit of derangement he committed suicide.
National Banner & Nashville Daily Advertiser. (Fri., May 16, 1834)

Grady, Mr. Burrell. Died at Knoxville.
National Banner & Nashville Whig. (Sat., Nov. 3, 1827)

Grady, S. Y. Died in Shelbyville, Tenn. of Cholera.
National Banner & Nashville Daily Advertiser. (Thurs., July 11, 1833)

Graham, Mrs. Elizabeth K. Consort of Capt. John Graham. Died of
consumption in the 32nd year of her age on Sat. 8th inst. at the
residence of her sister.
Nashville Whig. (Sat., June 15, 1844)

Graham, George Esq. Died at Washington on the 8th inst. Commissioner
of the General Land Office.
National Banner & Nashville Whig. (Mon., Aug. 23, 1830)

Graham, Mr. James. Aged 26. Died at Jackson, Tenn.
National Banner & Nashville Whig. (Sat., Aug. 25, 1827)

Graham, Mr. John. Aged 45. Died in Franklin, Tenn. of Cholera.
National Banner & Nashville Whig. (Fri., July 10, 1835)

Graham, Mrs. Mary. Aged 84. Died in Blount County.
National Banner & Nashville Whig. (Sat., Feb. 9, 1828)

Graham, Mr. Michael. Died in Bedford County, Va.
National Banner & Nashville Daily Advertiser. (Mon., June 9, 1834)

Graham, Miss. Daughter of Mr. Robert Graham. Died in Warren County,Ky.
National Banner. (Sat., Sept. 5, 1829)

Graham, Mrs. Susan. Died in Sumner County.
Nashville Republican & State Gazette. (Thurs., April 14, 1831)

Grainger, Francis of Ky. Died in New Orleans of Yellow Fever.
Daily Republican Banner. (Wed., Sept. 27, 1837)

Grammer, Mrs. Levina. Consort of Jacob Grammer, aged 63. Died in
Williamson County on the 24th of Sept.
National Banner & Nashville Whig. (Sat., Oct. 18, 1828)

Grant, A. S. Died at St. Louis, Misso'.
National Banner & Nashville Whig. (Sat., June 16, 1827)

Grant, Col. James. Comptroller of Public Accounts for the State.
Died in Raleigh, N. C.
National Banner & Nashville Whig. (Fri., Nov. 21, 1834)

Grantham, Mr. Richard. Died in Grainger County in the 93rd year of
his age.
Nashville Whig. (Tues., July 21, 1846)

Graves, George C. Died in Knoxville, Tenn. of Fever.
Daily Republican Banner. (Sat., Oct. 13, 1838)

Graves, Geo. C. Infant son of D. C. Graves. Died in Knoxville, Tenn.
Daily Republican Banner. (Sat., Sept. 22, 1838)

Graves, Mr. John P. A native of Virginia and nephew of Capt. W. F.
White. Died in Nashville on Friday last aged 19 years.
Nashville Whig. (Mon., July 30, 1838)

Graves, Lua E. Aged 25 years. Died in Edgefield on Saturday 11th
inst. Wife of Rev. J. R. Graves.
Nashville True Whig & Weekly Commercial Register. (Fri., Jan. 17, 1851)

Graves, Mrs. Wife of William Graves. Died in Knoxville, Tenn.
Daily Republican Banner. (Sat., Sept. 29, 1838)

Graves, Mr. William Henry. Died in St. Louis was shot by Mr. Mitchell.
National Banner & Nashville Daily Advertiser. (Sat., Oct. 20, 1832)

Graves, Zwinglius. Infant son of Rev. James R. and Lua Graves. Died
on Tuesday night last.
Nashville Whig. (Sat., Sept. 12, 1846)

Gray, Mrs. Anna. Aged 71 years. Consort of the late John Gray.
Died in Williamson County on the 16th.
Daily Republican Banner. (Fri., June 22, 1838)

Gray, Benajah Esq. Died at his residence in Davidson County, on the
10th June in the 61st year of his age.
The Union. (Tues., July 5, 1836)

Gray, Cornelia W. Daughter of Dr. James Gray of LaGrange, Tenn.
Died at the residence of John W. Walker Esq. In Nashville last
evening.
Nashville Whig. (Mon., Aug. 5, 1839)

Gray, Mrs. Elizabeth. Consort of Major Gray. Died in Elkton, Todd
County, Ky on Tuesday 29th ult.
National Banner & Nashville Daily Advertiser. (Sat., Feb. 9, 1833)

Gray, Maj. Henry L. Died in Haywood County, Tenn.
National Banner & Nashville Advertiser. (Wed., April 4, 1832)

Gray, Mr. Jacob. Formerly of Williamson County, Tenn. Died in
Davidson County, Tenn. on Tuesday last, aged 29 years 1 month and
7 days.
National Banner & Nashville Whig. (Fri., April 21, 1837)

Gray, Major John. Died in Elkton, Todd County, Ky. on the 18th inst.
National Banner & Nashville Daily Advertiser. (Fri., Nov. 22, 1833)

Gray, Mr. John. Aged 78 years. Died in Williamson County, on the 8th inst.
Daily Republican Banner. (Fri., June 22, 1838)

Gray, Miss Margaret. Died in Wilson County on Tuesday 14th ulto.
National Banner & Nashville Whig. (Fri., Aug. 7, 1835)

Gray, Mrs. Margaret. Died at the mouth of Sandy, Ten.
Nashville Republican & State Gazette. (Sat., Oct. 29, 1831)

Gray, Miss Mary. Died at Frankfort, Ky. of Cholera on Nov. 6th 1832.
National Banner & Nashville Daily Advertiser. (Tues., Nov. 13, 1832)

Gray, Mrs. Rachel. Died at Frankford, Ky.
National Banner. (March 17, 1826)

Gray, Mr. Samuel B. Died in Wilson County just one week after his sister died.
National Banner & Nashville Whig. (Fri., Aug. 7, 1835)

Gray, Sarah. In the 19th year of her age. Died in Davidson County on the 25th June, daughter of the late Benajah Gray.
The Union. (Tues., July 5, 1836)

Gray, Tabitha. Infant daughter of Price Gray. Died near Franklin on the 12th inst.
National Banner & Nashville Whig. (Mon., Sept. 22, 1834)

Gray, Col. Thomas. Died in Cocke County. Aged 84, Counsellor at Law.
National Banner. (Sat., Oct. 3, 1829)

Gray, Mrs. Z. B. Wife of Mr. Price Gray, aged 39 years. Died on Friday last 19th inst.
The Western Weekly Review. (Fri., April 26, 1833 Franklin, Tenn.)

Grayson, Benjamin Esq. Clerk of the Nelson County Court. in the 69th year of his age. Died in Bardstown, Ky. on Thursday the 22d ult.
National Banner & Nashville Whig. (Tues., May 11, 1830)

Green, Mr. Charles. Age 67 years. Died in Davidson County on the 2nd inst. One of the early settlers of this county.
National Banner & Nashville Whig. (Fri., Jan. 29, 1830)

Green, Mr. Christopher. Aged 82 years. The last brother of General Nathaniel Green. Died in Warwick, Rhode Island.
Nashville Republican & State Gazette. (Tues., Feb. 14, 1831)

Green, Mr. Elisha. Died at Plumb Point on the Mississippi on the 4th inst. formerly of Davidson County. Aged about 70.
National Banner & Nashville Whig. (Thurs., July 22, 1830)

Green, Mrs. Eliza. Consort of Mr. William C. Green. Died on Friday the 27th ult. at the residence of Mr. Myal Green of Fayette County.
National Banner & Nashville Daily Advertiser. (Mon., Jan. 21, 1833)

Green, Mr. Ezekiel. Died at Louisville, Ky. in consequence of an injury rec'd. from falling off a warf.
National Banner & Nashville Whig. (Fri., May 6, 1831)

Green, James I. Died at the Fountain of Health on his way to Roane County from the Convention in Nashville.
National Banner & Nashville Daily Advertiser. (Mon., Sept. 1, 1834)

Green, Dr. John M. Died in Carrollsville on the 27th ult. of a wound received in a conflict with Edward Sandford Esq.
National Banner. (Jan. 13, 1826)

Green, Hon. John W. Late a Judge of The Supreme Court of Appeals. Died in Virginia.
National Banner & Nashville Daily Advertiser. (Wed., Feb. 26, 1834)

Green, Mrs. Judith. Died in Nashville on Wednesday the 18th aged about 85 years. Mother of the Rev. A. L. P. Green.
Nashville Whig. (Thurs., March 19, 1846)

Green, Rev. Lemuel. Died in Philadelphia an old respectable Minister of the Methodist Church aged 80 years.
Nashville Republican & State Gazette. (Sat., June 4, 1831)

Green, Mr. Lewis. Of Davidson County. Died on Saturday the 18th inst. he left a wife and several children.
Impartial Review and Cumberland Repository. (Sat., Oct. 25, 1806)

Green, Col. Liberty. Aged 49. Died in Green County, Ky.
National Banner & Nashville Whig. (Sat., Dec. 2, 1826)

Green, Miss Lucy Ann. Died at Chariton, Mo.
National Banner & Nashville Whig. (Sat., Nov. 3, 1827)

Green, Miss Mary. Daughter of Sherwood Green, Esq. Aged 14. Died on the 16th in Williamson County.
National Banner & Nashville Whig. (Sat., June 7, 1828)

Green, Mrs. Mary. Wife of Mr. Edmund Green. Died in Sumner County.
National Banner & Nashville Whig. (Mon., Sept. 6, 1830)

Green, Mrs. Mary. Wife of Mr. Edmund Green. Died in Bedford County.
National Banner & Nashville Whig. (Wed., Dec. 14, 1831)

Green, Mary Roane. Wife of Thomas Green Esq. and the second daughter of Thomas and Isabella Ritchie all of Nashville. Died on 9th of Oct. she was 31 years of age.
Nashville Whig. (Thurs., Oct. 27, 1842)

Green, Mrs. Patsy. In her 44th year. Died in Williamson County on the 24th of July.
National Banner & Nashville Whig. (Sat., Aug. 2, 1828)

Green, Robert W. Company I. First Regiment, Tenn. Volunteers. Died from wounds received in the Battle of Monterey with the Mexicans on Sept. 21, 1846.
Nashville Whig. (Sat., Nov. 21, 1846)

Green, Miss Sarah L. Died in Lincoln County.
National Banner & Nashville Whig. (July 1, 1826)

Green, Mrs. Saral Angelica. Wife of Maj. Thomas Jefferson Green and daughter of the late Hon. Jesse Wharton of Tennessee. Died in Davidson County on the 11th April aged 23 years.
National Banner & Nashville Whig. (Mon., April 13, 1835)

Green, Sherwood Sr. Esq. Died near Nolensville in Williamson County. Tuesday 2nd inst.
Daily Republican Banner. (Sat., June 6, 1840)

Green, William Esq. Died in East Greenwich, R. I. Aged 83. Brother of Gen. Nathaniel Green.
National Banner & Nashville Whig. (Sat., Oct. 28, 1826)

Green, William A. Firm of Allen & Green. Died in the wreck of the steamboat, Lexington.
Daily Republican Banner. (Fri., Jan. 31, 1840)

Green, Wm. M. Esq. Of Jefferson. Died in Hinds County, Miss.
National Banner. (Sat. Aug. 22, 1829)

Greene, Mrs. Consort of J. B. Greene. Died in Clarksville, Tenn.
National Banner & Nashville Daily Advertiser. (Mon., June 30, 1834)

Greene, Willis. Aged 25 years. Died in Louisville, Ky. of consumption on 13th.
National Banner & Nashville Daily Advertiser. (Fri., Oct. 19, 1832)

Greenfield, Mrs. Wife of Mr. Wm. Greenfield. Died in Elkton, Ky.
National Banner & Nashville Whig. (Sat., May 19, 1827)

Greenfield, Mrs. Keren T. Consort of Dr. G. T. Greenfield. Died in
Maury County.
National Banner & Nashville Advertiser. (Wed., June 27, 1832)

Greenfield, Fanny Alice. Daughter of Wesley & Rebecca Greenfield.
Died on the morning of the 6th inst. in Nashville in her 8th year.
The Christian Record. (Sat., Nov. 20, 1847)

Greenfield, Mr. William. Of the house of Wm. Greenfield Cromwell &
Co. Died in Clarksville, Tenn. of Cholera.
National Banner & Nashville Whig. (Wed., July 8, 1835)

Greenup, Christopher. Died in Kentucky late governor of that State.
The Nashville Whig & Tenn. Advertiser. (May 9, 1818)

Greer, Mr. John. In his 52nd year. Died in Nashville on the 25th
ult.
The Politician & Weekly Nashville Whig. (Wed., Oct. 6, 1847)

Greer, Mrs. Aged 48. Wife of the late Vance Greer, of Fayetteville.
Died in Nashville on Tuesday night.
Nashville Whig. (Fri., Feb. 8, 1839)

Greer, Joseph Esq. Age 74. Died in Lincoln County.
National Banner & Nashville Whig. (Wed., March 16, 1831)

Greer, Mrs. Sarah. Wife of Joseph Greer, Esq. of this place. Died
at Knoxville, the 29 ult.
Impartial Review and Cumberland Repository. (Sat., June 13, 1807)

Gregg, Maj. John. Died in Bourbon County, Ky.
National Banner. (Jan. 20, 1820)

Gregg, Mr. Samuel. A native of Baltimore. Died on Monday evening.
Nashville Whig. (Thurs., Aug. 3, 1843)

Gresham, Mr. A. A citizen of Nashville. Died on the 6th inst. at
M'Minnville.
Nashville Republican. (Tues., Sept. 13, 1836)

Gresham, Mr. Austin. A citizen of Nashville. Died in M'Minnville on
the 6th Sept.
National Banner & Nashville Whig. (Fri., Sept. 10, 1836)

Gresham, Mrs. Eliza C. Consort of Mr. Austin Gresham. Died at the
residence of Mr. James Condon on Tuesday evening last.
National Banner & Nashville Daily Advertiser. (Sat., June 21, 1834)

Grey, Mr. Sampson. Aged 38 years. Died near Little Rock, Ark.
National Banner & Nashville Whig. (Wed., Nov. 26, 1838)

Griffin, Edward. Of Montgomery County. Died on the 28th at West
Port, Ky. of Cholera.
National Banner & Nashville Daily Advertiser. (Wed., June 5, 1833)

Griffin, Mr. Samuel. Died at the Fountain of Health in Davidson
County.
Daily Republican Banner. (Tues., March 13, 1838)

Griffin, Thomas. With the Second Tenn. Regiment. Died - was killed
in the Battle of Sierra Gorda with the Mexicans.
The Politician & Weekly Nashville Whig. (Fri., May 21, 1847)

Griffith, Mr. Lately elected to Harrison County in the Kentucky
legislature. Died in Cynthiana.
National Banner & Nashville Whig. (Sat., Sept. 9, 1826)

Grimes, Mr. James. Died in Fayette County, Ky.
National Banner & Nashville Whig. (Fri., July 11, 1828)

Grimke, Thomas S. Esq. Of South Carolina. Died near Columbus, Ohio.
while traveling through that state.
National Banner & Nashville Whig. (Wed., Oct. 22, 1834)

Grimme, Mr. Alexander D. Died at Gallatin.
National Banner & Nashville Daily Advertiser. (Mon., Oct. 29, 1832)

Gringer, Mrs. Agness. Died at Natchitoches.
National Banner & Nashville Whig. (Sat., Nov. 3, 1827)

Grinter, Mrs. Elizabeth. Wife of Mr. John Grinter. Died in Logan
County, Ky.
National Banner & Nashville Whig. (Mon., Aug. 23, 1830)

Grinter, Mr. John. Age 76. Died in Logan County, Ky.
National Banner & Nashville Whig. (Mon., June 13, 1831)

Grisham, Mr. A. On the 6th inst. at McMinnville, Mr. A. Grisham,
a citizen of this place.
Nashville Republican, Tues., Sept. 13, 1836)

Grizzard, James. Aged six years. Died on Thurs. morning last and on
Sat. morning last, Eleanora Adeline aged 3 years children of James
and Charlotte Grizzard.
National Banner & Nashville Daily Advertiser. (Tues., Feb. 5, 1833)

Grizzard, Mr. Jerimiah. Died in Davidson County on Thursday night last
in the 80th year of his age.
National Banner & Nashville Whig. (Sat., Dec. 17, 1831)

Groe, Dederick. Of Germany, a passenger. Died on the Steamer George
Collier about 80 miles below Natchez, scalded to death.
Daily Republican Banner. (Tues., May 14, 1839)

Grofton, Nathan Esq. Of Baltimore. Died at Louisville, Ky. of Cholera.
National Banner & Nashville Daily Advertiser. (Wed., July 31, 1833)

Grooms, Mrs. Cynthia Ann. Aged 24. Died at Frankfort, Ky.
National Banner & Nashville Whig. (Thurs., July 29, 1830)

Grooms, Mrs. Mary. Wife of Wm. Grooms. Died at Frankfort, Ky.
National Banner. (Sat., May 16, 1829)

Grove, William B. Died lately at Fayetteville, N. C. President of
the U. S. Bank at that place.
The Nashville Whig & Tenn. Advertiser. (April 25, 1818)

Groves, Mr. Frederick A. Died at St. Louis.
National Banner. (Sat., Aug. 1, 1829)

Grub, Mr. Jonas. Died in Louisville, Ky.
National Banner & Nashville Daily Advertiser. (Thurs., Jan. 2, 1834)

Grubbs, Mr. James. Of Estill County. Died in Madison County, Ky.
National Banner & Nashville Whig. (Sat., Aug. 12, 1826)

Grubbs, Mr. John Y. Died in Logan County, Ky.
National Banner & Nashville Advertiser. (Mon., Sept. 17, 1832)

Grundy, Mrs. Ann. Wife of Hon. Felix Grundy. Died on the evening of
the 27th inst.
The Christian Record. (Sat., Feb. 6, 1847)

Grundy, James P. Formerly of Nashville. Died at his residence in
Trenton on the 6th inst.
Nashville Whig. (Tues., May 14, 1844)

Grundy, John R. Esq. Attorney at law. Died at Columbus, Mississippi
on the 6th inst. Eldest son of Hon. Felix Grundy of Nashville.
Nashville Republican. (Sat., June 25, 1836)

Grundy, John R. Esq. Eldest son of the Hon. Felix Grundy of Nashville.
Died at Columbus, Mississippi on the 6th inst. in the 33d year of his
age.
The Union. (Tues., June 16, 1836)

Grundy, Samuel Esq. Father of the Rev. R. C. Grundy of Nashville.
Died in Washington County, Ky. on Wednesday 14th inst. He was a
brother of the Hon. Felix Grundy.
Nashville Whig. (Wed., July 28, 1841)

Guest, Maj. Joshua. Died at Columbia.
National Banner & Nashville Whig. (Fri., Feb. 11, 1831)

Guice, Mr. Jonathan. Died in Franklin County, Miss.
National Banner & Nashville Whig. (Sat., Dec. 16, 1826)

Gunn, Mrs. Clarissa H. Wife of Dr. John C. Gunn of Louisville. Died
on the 26th inst. in the 41st year of her age.
Nashville True Whig & Weekly Commercial Register. (Fri., March 7, 1851)

Gunn, Sarah. Corner of Elm and 6th Street. Died in Cincinnati of
the Cholera on the 10th inst.
National Banner & Nashville Daily Advertiser. (Wed., Oct. 17, 1832)

Gunning, Major John. Died in Nashville from the kick of a horse in
the stable of Mr. Thomas Alderson.
National Banner & Nashville Whig. (Fri., April 15, 1831)

Gunning, Major John. His death were truly distressing. He was kicked
down and trampled and mangled by a horse. Died in Nashville.
National Banner & Nashville Whig. (Fri., April 15, 1831)

Gunter, J. G. With the Second Tenn. Regiment. Died - was killed in
the Battle of Sierra Gorda with the Mexicans.
The Politician and Weekly Nashville Whig. (Fri., May 21, 1847)

Guthrie, Ellen Tennessee. Daughter of Henry C. & Lucinda T. Guthrie
of Nashville. Died on Thursday the 29th age 1 year, 8 months & 16 days.
The Politician & Weekly Nashville Whig. (Fri., May 7, 1847)

Guthrie, Henry Sr. A revolutionary soldier, aged 82 years and 24 days.
Died in Davidson County on the 4th of Jan. last.
Nashville Republican. (Tues., April 11, 1837)

Guthrie, Mr. John. A native of England and late of East Tennessee,
aged about 60. Died in Columbia, Tenn. on the 21st Sept. Also on
the same day his son F. Guthrie, aged 18.
Nashville Whig. (Tues., Oct. 1, 1844)

Guthrie, John Chevallie. Son of John & Minerva Guthrie. Died on the
23rd at Columbia, Tenn. aged 5 years 10 months & 15 days.
Nashville Whig. (Tues., Dec. 5, 1843)

Guy, Mrs. Mary Harriett. Died in Roane County, wife of Mr. Joseph
Guy of Franklin County, Ala.
National Banner & Nashville Whig. (Sat., Aug. 26, 1826)

Gwin, Mrs. Caroline M. J. Consort of Dr. Wm. M. Gwin aged 26 years
and 11 months. Died at Clinton, on the 14th.
National Banner & Nashville Daily Advertiser. (Tues., Oct. 29, 1833)

Gwin, Mrs. Edith. Consort of Colonel Samuel Gwin. Died at Clinton,
Miss. Nov. 13, 1837. She was born August 22d 1800.

Gwin, Mrs. Edith. Consort of Col. Samuel Gwin. Died on the 13th
inst. near Clinton, Miss.
Nashville Union. (Thurs., Nov. 23, 1837)

Gwin, Colonel Edward. A soldier of the revolution. Died in Carroll
County, Tenn. on the 8th inst.
National Banner & Nashville Whig. (Wed., Oct. 12, 1831)

Gwin, James. Youngest child of Major Thomas Gwin. Died in Washington
County, Miss.
National Banner & Nashville Daily Advertiser. (Sat., Aug. 24, 1833)

Gwin, Mary Frances. Youngest child of Dr. William M. Gwin. Died in
Benton, Miss.
National Banner & Nashville Daily Advertiser. (Sat., Aug. 24, 1833)

Gwin, Mrs. Nancy. Wife of Mr. Samuel Gwin. Died in Clinton, Miss.
National Banner & Nashville Daily Advertiser. (Tues., Nov. 13, 1832)

Gwin, Samuel. Aged 5 years 5 months & 15 days, only child of Dr.
William M. Gwin. Died in the vicinity, Natchez, on 20th of Aug. last.
The Union. (Sat., Oct. 1, 1836)

Gwin, Major Thomas W. Of Washington County, Miss. late of Sumner
County, Tenn. Died at Clinton on the 10th inst. aged 31 years.
National Banner & Nashville Daily Advertiser. (Tues., Oct. 29, 1833)

Gwinn, Miss Elizabeth. Died in Williamson County, Tenn.
National Banner & Nashville Daily Advertiser. (Mon., Aug. 26, 1833)

Hackett, Baron. Of Hacketts Town, a native of Holland. Died in New
Orleans of Yellow Fever.
Daily Republican Banner. (Thurs., Sept. 5, 1839)

Hackney, Mrs. Mary. Consort of Fielding Hackney and eldest daughter
of Samuel McManus Esq. Died on the 11th inst. (from Lagrange Whig)
Nashville Union. (Wed., Oct. 16, 1839)

Hackney, Mrs. Mary W. Wife of George W. Hackney Esq. Died in Maury
County.
National Banner. (Sat., June 27, 1829)

Haden, Mr. George. Died at Clarksville, formerly of Christian County,
Ky.
National Banner & Nashville Daily Advertiser. (Thurs., Jan. 10, 1833)

Hadley, Augusta William. Son of Doctor John D. Hadley. Died on the
19th inst. in the 3d year of his age.
The Nashville Gazette. (Sat., Oct. 30, 1819)

Hadley, Maj. William. Died at his residence in Davidson County on
30th ulto.
Nashville Whig. (Tues., Aug. 2, 1842)

Hadly, Amelia. Daughter of Doctor John L. and Amelia Hadly. Died on
the 4th inst in the 17th year of her age. (Communicated)
Daily Republican Banner. (Tues., April 7, 1840)

Hadly, Capt. Joshua. In the 77 year of his age. Died in Williamson
County on the 8th inst.
National Banner & Nashville Whig. (Tues., Feb. 23, 1830)

Hadwin, Mr. Henry. Died at Danville, Ky.
National Banner & Nashville Whig. (Sat., Feb. 10, 1827)

Hagar, Mr. Jonathan. Died in Davidson County of Cholera on the 1st
inst.
National Banner & Nashville Daily Advertiser. (Wed., June 5, 1833)

Haggard, Mrs. Rachel. Consort of Capt. James Haggard of Dover, Stewart County, age 23. Died on the 5th inst.
Impartial Review and Cumberland Repository. (Thurs., May 26, 1808)

Hagen, J. Dick Hill. Infant son of Henry Hagen. Died in Nashville
yesterday.
Nashville Whig. (Fri., April 19, 1839)

Haggerty, Mr. Michael. A native of Ireland. Died in New Orleans.
National Banner & Nashville Daily Advertiser. (Tues., June 24, 1834)

Hague, Mr. John. Aged 93 years. Died in Nashville on Tuesday night
the 13th inst. He was a native of Germany, come to America and
fought through the Revolutionary War.
Nashville Whig. (Mon., July 26, 1841)

Haile, Leonard. In the prime of life. Son of Col. B. Haile. Died
in Jefferson County, Tenn.
National Banner & Nashville Whig. (Fri., Jan. 23, 1835)

Haile, Mrs. Martha. Consort of Mr. Dudley Haile. Aged 67. Died in
Bedford County, Ten. on the 25th ult.
National Banner. (Sat., Oct. 17, 1829)

Hales, William. Of East Tenn. Died - fell overboard in the Miss.
River at New Orleans and drowned.
Nashville Whig. (Fri., July 6, 1838)

Hale, Mr. Claiborne D. Aged 20 years, son of Mr. Alexander Hale.
Died in Blount County, Tenn.
National Banner & Nashville Daily Advertiser. (Tues., Aug. 27, 1833)

Halford, John R. Died at Carthage, Miss. on the 27th ult.
Daily Republican Banner. (Mon., Nov. 16, 1840)

Hall, Private Benjamin. With the Fourteenth Regiment Infantry under
Gen. Pillow. Died - was killed in the Battle before Mexico City.
The Nashville Politician and Weekly Nashville Whig. (Fri., Oct. 29, 1847)

Hall, Private Benjamin. With the 14th regiment, part of the third
Division, commanded by Gen. Pillow. Died - killed in the Battle before
the City of Mexico.
The Christian Record. (Sat., Oct. 30, 1847)

Hall, Mr. Charles M. Aged 78. Died in this County.
National Banner & Nashville Whig. (Sat., Oct. 7, 1826)

Hall, Major Clement. Died on the 4th inst. in the 71st year of his age.
A venerable soldier of the revolution in which he performed an honor-
able part.
Nashville Whig. (Aug. 16, 1824)

Hall, Mr. Elisha L. Formerly of Franklin, Tenn. Died near Martinsville, Lou.
National Banner & Nashville Whig. (Mon., Nov. 8, 1830)

Hall, Lieut. James V. A distinguished officer of the U. S. Army.
Died lately in Orleans.
The Nash. Whig & Tenn. Advertiser. (March 14, 1818)

Hall, Mrs. Jane. Wife of Dr. E. S. Hall. Died in Bedford County.
National Banner & Nashville Whig. (Sat., Sept. 30, 1826)

Hall, Mr. John. Formerly of Nashville in the 18th year of his age.
Died at Dover, Mason County, Ky.
Nashville Whig. (Wed., July 28, 1841)

Hall, John A. Son of J. H. M. and Ann Rebecca Hall. Died in Davidson County on Friday the 11th inst. Aged two years and 7 months.
The Politician and Weekly Nashville Whig. (Fri., Feb. 18, 1848)

Hall, John E. Esq. Died at Philadelphia late editor of the Port
Folio Aged 34.
National Banner. (Sat., July 4, 1829)

Hall, John H. Aged 75 years. Died Thursday last at the residence of
his son Allen A. Hall.
The Union. (Sat., Aug. 26, 1837)

Hall, Capt. Joseph C. Of the U. S. Marine Corps. Died in New York.
National Banner & Nashville Daily Advertiser. (Wed., June 5, 1833)

Hall, Miss Lucy. Daughter of Dr. Hall. Died in Louisville, Ky.
National Banner & Nashville Whig. (Wed., Sept. 14, 1831)

Hall, Mrs. Lucy R. Wife of Dr. B. H. Hall. Resident Physician of
the Marine Hospital. Died in Louisville.
National Banner & Nashville Daily Advertiser. (Thurs., Feb. 21, 1833)

Hall, Mrs. Mary. Wife of A. A. Hall Esq. Editor of the Nashville
Republican & daughter of Dr. John Newnan. Died in this town on Sunday
morning last.
National Banner. (Sat., Nov. 21, 1829)

Hall, Miss Martha C. Died on Monday morning the 22nd inst. May 22,
1815, after a long and lingering pulmonary complaint, age 18 years.
Nashville.
Nashville Whig. (May 23, 1815)

Hall, Mrs. Mary P. Wife of the Hon. James Hall. Died at Vandalia.
National Banner & Nashville Advertiser. (Mon., Sept. 17, 1832)

Hall, Miss Nancy. Died in Deerfield, Ohio.
National Banner & Nashville Whig. (Sat., Oct. 28, 1826)

Hall, Robert P. Esq. Of North Carolina. Died on the 7th.
National Banner & Nashville Whig. (Sat., July 15, 1826)

Hall, Mr. Samuel. Son of the Rev. N. H. Hall. Died at Lexington,
Ky.
National Banner & Nashville Daily Advertiser. (Wed., Aug. 7, 1833)

Hall, Mrs. Sophia. Consort of Elihu S. Hall, Merchant of this town.
Died on Sunday morning last of pulmonary complaint.
The Nashville Whig. (Tues., Jan. 23, 1816)

Hall, William Hon. Died at Bellows Falls, Vt.
Nashville Republican & State Gazette. (Tues., March 8, 1831)

Hall, Wm. Lee. Died at Washington City. on the 29th ult. A Representative in Congress from the State of Virginia.
Nashville Whig. (March 22, 1824)

Hallett, Ann M. Infant daughter of Mr. James & Ann M. Hallett of
Nashville. Aged 17 months & 4 days. Died on Wednesday morning 23d
inst.
The Christian Record. (Sat., June 26, 1847)

Hallett, Ann M. Infant daughter of Mr. James and Ann M. Hallett
aged 17 months & 4 days. Died on Wednesday 23rd inst.
The Politician & Weekly Nashville Whig. (Fri., June 25, 1847)

Halley, Mrs. Elizabeth. Wife of Mr. Joshua Halley. Died Fayette
County.
National Banner & Nashville Whig. (Mon., Sept. 12, 1831)

Hallum, Mr. Carteus. Aged 21 years. Died in Carthage, Ten.
National Banner & Nashville Daily Advertiser. (Tues., Feb. 5, 1833)

Hallum, Mrs. W. Died in Nashville at the Washington Hotel this
morning.
Nashville Whig. (Wed., April 10, 1839)

Hallum, Mrs. W. Died in Nashville at the Washington Hotel this
morning.
Daily Republican Banner. (Fri., April 12, 1839)

Hamblen, Mary Donelson. Wife of Dr. Hamblen of Virginia. Died about
February 1819. (Letter March 12, 1819 said about a month ago, would
be Feb.)

Hamilton, Mr. Andrew. Died in Jackson.
National Banner & Nashville Whig. (Sat., Sept. 27, 1828)

Hamilton, Mr. Charles. Died in Claiborn County, Miss.
National Banner & Nashville Whig. (Sat., Feb. 10, 1827)

Hamilton, Edward H. Of this place. Died on the 15th inst.
Nashville Whig. (June 21, 1824)

Hamilton, Eli B. Chancellor at law. Died at Westfield, Mass.
National Banner & Nashville Daily Advertiser. (Thurs., Sept. 12, 1833)

Hamilton, Mrs. Eliza. Died at Parish, Henry County. Wife of Maj.
Alexander Hamilton and daughter of Hugh Dunlap Esq.
National Banner & Nashville Whig. (Sat., Oct. 6, 1827)

Hamilton, Miss Elizabeth. Died in Williamson County.
National Banner & Nashville Advertiser. (Mon., July 2, 1832)

Hamilton, Miss Elizabeth. Aged 15 years. Died at the residence of
her father near Franklin, Ten. Tuesday last.
The Western Weekly Review. (Franklin, Tenn. Fri., June 29, 1832)

Hamilton, Elizabeth Hannah. Daughter of James W. and Mary E. Hamilton
aged 5 years. Died in Murfreesborough on the 3rd inst.
Nashville Whig. (Thurs., March 12, 1846)

Hamilton, Capt. Harry. In the 46th year of his age. Died on Saturday the 20th of May, in Sumner County, Tenn.
Nashville Republican. (Tues., June 13, 1837)

Hamilton, Mr. Henry. Aged 56. Died at Jackson.
National Banner & Nashville Whig. (Sat., Sept. 20, 1828)

Hamilton, James Esq. Died near the post of Arkansas.
National Banner. (March 10, 1826)

Hamilton, Hon. John C. Judge of the Circuit Court. Died at Charlotte,
Suddenly.
National Banner & Nashville Daily Advertiser. (Mon., March 11, 1833)

Hamilton, Rev. Jno. T. Died in Nicholasville, Ky. Pastor of the Presbyterian Church in that city.
Nashville Republican & State Gazette. (Thurs., Sept. 1, 1831)

Hamilton, Joseph. Died on 2d of July at Rural Mount, Jefferson County, Ten. A soldier of the Revolution.
National Banner & Nashville Daily Advertiser. (Thurs., Sept. 11, 1834)

Hamilton, Leonard. Washington, Ky. Died in the loss of the Steamboat Brandywine.
National Banner & Nashville Daily Advertiser. (Mon., April 23, 1832)

Hamilton, Miss Margaret J. B. Died in Knox County.
National Banner & Nashville Whig. (Sat., Oct. 6, 1827)

Hamilton, Mrs. Mary. Wife of Col. H. Hamilton and last sister of Judge McNairy, deceased. Died at her residence in Giles Co. on the 16th inst. aged 78.
Nashville Whig. (Thurs., Oct. 20, 1842)

Hamilton, Mrs. Mary. Aged 61. Died in Rutherford County.
National Banner & Nashville Whig. (Thurs., Sept. 23, 1830)

Hamilton, Mrs. Mary. Wife of Mr. John C. Hamilton. Died in Cynthiana, Ky.
National Banner & Nashville Whig. (Sat., Sept. 9, 1826)

Hamilton, Capt. Pliny. Died in Prince George's County, Md.
Nashville Republican & State Gazette. (Sat., March 19, 1831)

Hamilton, Dr. Robert. Died in Jefferson County.
National Banner & Nashville Daily Advertiser. (Mon., June 24, 1833)

Hamilton, Mr. Robert H. Son of Hon. John C. Hamilton. Died - drowned on the 17th ult. in the Mississippi 40 miles below Memphis.
National Banner & Nashville Whig. (Fri., Aug. 19, 1831)

Hamilton, Sarah F. Wife of James Hamilton. Died on the 29th in Mill Creek Neighborhood in the 37th year of her age.
Nashville Whig. (Tues., Oct. 22, 1844)

Hamilton, Mr. William S. Died in Williamson County.
National Banner & Nashville Whig. (Sat., Sept. 20, 1828)

Hamlin, Mary Catherine. Infant daughter of Dr. & Mrs. T. B. Hamlin. Died in Nashville on Sunday 19th inst. aged three years and 10 months.
The Politician & Weekly Nashville Whig. (Wed., Sept. 22, 1847)

Hammond, Charles Esq. Late editor of the Cincinnati Gazette. Died in Cincinnati, Ohio aged 61 years.
Daily Republican Banner. (Wed., April 8, 1840)

Hammond, Mr. Henry A. A native of England. Died in Randolph T.
National Banner & Nashville Daily Advertiser. (Tues., July 15, 1834)

Hammond, Mr. J. D. Of the firm of J. D. & C. B. Hammond. Died in Mobile, Ala. of Yellow fever.
Daily Republican Banner. (Tues., Oct. 1st, 1839)

Hammond, Mrs. Sally C. Died in Cincinnati. Wife of Mr. C. Hammond.
National Banner & Nashville Whig. (Sat., Aug. 12, 1826)

Hammond, Timothy Esq. Died in Cincinnati, Ohio.
National Banner & Nashville Daily Advertiser. (Fri., Aug. 1, 1834)

Hammond, Mr. William L. Died in Madison County, Ala.
National Banner. (May 4, 1826)

Hammons, Mr. Aged 58 years. Died in Bedford County, Ten.
National Banner & Nashville Whig. (Wed., Feb. 25, 1835)

Hampton, Hon. J. P. Died in Wilkinson County, Missis. Judge of the
3d judicial district.
National Banner & Nashville Whig. (Sat., Feb. 24, 1827)

Hampton, General Wade. Died at his residence in Columbia, S. C. on
the 4th inst. in the 81st year of his age. The most extensive
planted in the U. S.
National Banner & Nashville Whig. (Wed., March 4, 1835)

Hanby, Gen. Gabriel. Died in Blount County, Ala.
National Banner. (April 7, 1826)

Hancock, Mr. John. Died in Madison County, Ala.
National Banner. (Sat., May 2, 1829)

Hancock, Rev. Robert. Aged 76. Died in Madison County, Ala.
National Banner & Nashville Whig. (Mon., April 25, 1831)

Hand, Mrs. Sarah. Died in Wayne County, Miss.
National Banner. (May 13, 1826)

Handy, Mrs. Margaret Frances. Wife of Edward Smith Handy of Philadelphia. Died in Philadelphia on the 22nd March of Consumption in the 24th
year of her age. Eldest daughter of Mr. James Woods, of Nashville.
Nashville Whig. (Sat., April 4, 1846)

Handy, Theora Jane. Wife of Edward Smith Handy, Esq. Of Philadelphia
and second daughter of Robert Woods Esq. Died at West Wood at the
residence of her father in this vicinity on 16th inst.
Nashville Whig. (Thurs., May 19, 1842)

Handy, William B. Of the House of G. G. Jenkins & Co. Died in New
Orleans of Yellow Fever.
Daily Republican Banner. (Wed., Sept. 27, 1837)

Haney, Mrs. Consort of Mr. Haney. Died suddnely on the 8th inst. in
Nashville.
Impartial Review and Cumberland Repository. (Sat., June 14, 1806)

Hankinson, John Esq. Died at Natchez.
National Banner (March 10, 1826)

Hanna, Mr. James. Aged 65. Died in Sumner County.
National Banner & Nashville Daily Advertiser. (Tues., April 9, 1833)

Hanna, Mr. James. Merchant of this town. Died on Thursday last. He
has left an amiable wife and six small children on Friday his remains
were interred with Masonic Honors.
The Nashville Whig. (June 9, 1817)

Hanna, Mr. John D. Died in Sumner County.
National Banner & Nashville Daily Advertiser. (Sat., April 13, 1833)

Hanna, Miss Mary Ann. Oldest daughter of Mr. James Hanna of this
place. Died yesterday morning after a long and painful illness.
The Nashville Whig. (April 16, 1817)

Hanna, Mrs. Sarah. In the 74th year of her age. Died on Wednesday
15th inst. at her residence in the Parish of Thibodeaux, La.
(N. O. Bulletin)
Nashville Whig. (Sat., Oct. 7, 1843)

Hannah, Mr. John M. Died at Beach Point, in Smith County on the 27th
of March in the 31st year of his age.
National Banner & Nashville Whig. (Wed., May 4, 1831)

Hannum, Mrs. Martha. Wife of Mr. W. L. Hannum. Died in Memphis.
National Banner & Nashville Daily Advertiser. (Tues., June 11, 1833)

Hansbough, Mrs. Martha. Died in Logan County, Ky.
National Banner & Nashville Advertiser. (Tues., Nov. 27, 1832)

Hansbrough, Mr. Alfred S. Died in Marion, Ark.
National Banner & Nashville Whig. (Sat., Sept. 9, 1826)

Hanson, Hugh C. Of Baltimore, died in New Orleans of Yellow Fever.
Daily Republican Banner. (Fri., Sept. 29, 1837)

Hanson, Jehu. Aged 70 years. Died in Davidson County on the 12th
inst.
Daily Republican Banner. (Tues., Sept. 16, 1837)

Haralson, Mr. James M. Clerk of Humphreys Circuit Court. Died at
Reynoldsburg.
National Banner & Nashville Whig. (Thurs., Oct. 14, 1830)

Harbison, Susan Eliza. Daughter of James Harbison aged 8 months and
10 days. Died in Maury County on the 10th inst.
National Banner & Nashville Daily Advertiser. (Thurs., April 18, 1833)

Hardaway, Mrs. Sarah. Died on the 5th inst. In Robinson County
Consort of Maj. Joseph Hardaway and on the following day her brother
died Major James Payne.
The Nashville Whig & Tenn. Advertiser. (Dec. 15, 1817)

Hardeman, Mrs. Ann. Aged 23. Wife of Thomas Hardeman Esq. Died at
Franklin.
National Banner. (March 17, 1826)

Hardeman, Hon. Bailey. Secretary of the Treasury. Died at Caney
Creek, Texas.
Nashville Republican. (Sat., Nov. 12, 1836)

Hardeman, Nicholas Perkins Esq. of Williamson County Court. Died
in Franklin on the 27th inst.
Nashville Whig & Tenn. Advertiser. (May 30, 1818)

Hardeman, Col. Thomas. Aged 37 years. Died in Williamson County,
Sept. 16th.
National Banner & Nashville Whig. (Mon., Sept. 19, 1836)

Hardeman, Thomas Esq. In the 84th year of his age. Died in Williamson
County.
National Banner & Nashville Daily Advertiser. (Tues., July 2, 1833)

Hardeway, Mr. Joseph. A soldier of the Revolution. Died in Memphis,
Ten. in the 75th year of his age.
National Banner & Nashville Whig. (Wed., Feb. 25, 1835)

Hardeway, Mr. Joseph Sen. Of Robinson County. Died in Memphis, Ten.
a soldier of the Revolution.
National Banner & Nashville Whig. (Fri., March 6, 1835)

Harding, Cassandra. Died 16th at Cincinnati, Ohio. of Cholera.
National Banner & Nashville Daily Advertiser. (Wed., Oct. 24, 1832)

Harding, Nathaniel M'Nairy. Infant son of Mr. William G. Harding.
Died in Davidson County.
National Banner & Nashville Daily Advertiser. (Tues., Nov. 13, 1832)

Harding, Nathaniel McNairy. Youngest son of Gen. William G. Harding
of Davidson County. Died suddenly in Nashville on the 5th inst. in
the 10th year of his age.
Nashville Whig. (Tues., June 13, 1843)

Harding, Mr. William. Died in Union County, Ky.
National Banner. (Feb. 24, 1826)

Harding, Mr. William Sen. Died in Nashville, Sunday 13th May he lived
on Stone's River.
National Banner & Nashville Daily Advertiser. (Mon., May 14, 1832)

Hardwick, Rev. Benjamin. Died in Dickson County on the 2d Sept.
A native of Buckingham County, Va. in the 69th year of his age.
National Banner & Nashville Whig. (Fri., Sept. 11, 1835)

Hardy, Mr. Madison. Of Lunenburg County, Va. In the 21st year of his
age. Died in Madison County, Ala.
National Banner & Nashville Whig. (Mon., Aug. 1, 1831)

Hare, Capt. Henry. Died on Friday the 8th at the residence of Mr.
O. T. Watwins from a wound occasioned by the kick of a horse.
The Western Weekly Review. (Thurs., April 21, 1831) Franklin, Tenn.

Hare, Capt. Henry. Died in Franklin.
National Banner & Nashville Whig. (Mon., April 25, 1831)

Hargrove, Maj. Francis. Aged 85. Died in this county.
National Banner & Nashville Whig. (Sat., Aug. 9, 1828)

Harkreader, Capt. James H. Died in Humphrey County on the 16th March.
National Banner & Nashville Daily Advertiser. (Wed., March 20, 1833)

Harkrider, Mrs. Rebecca. Died in Humphrey County on the 28th.
Consort of John Harkrider, aged 57 years.
National Banner & Nashville Daily Advertiser. (Sat., June 14, 1834)

Harmon, Capt. Joseph. Died near Port Gibson, Mi.
National Banner & Nashville Daily Advertiser. (Mon., July 28, 1834)

Harney, Maj. Thomas. Of this County. His death was occasioned by
the bite of a mad-dog. Died on Friday last.
The Clarion & Tennessee Gazette. (July 20, 1813)

Harpale, Adam. A soldier of the revolutionary war. Died in Wilson
County, age 81 years.
Daily Republican Banner. (Wed., Jan. 24, 1838)

Harper, Mr. Berryman. Of Lawrence County, Ala. Died at Florence, Ala.
National Banner & Nashville Whig. (Mon., Nov. 28, 1831)

Harper, Charles Carroll. Of Baltimore. Died at Paris, France on 26th
June. Eldest son of the late Gen. Robert Goodloe Harper.
National Banner & Nashville Whig. (Fri., Aug. 18, 1837)

F. J. Harper. Member of Congress Elect. From the County of Philadephia
Pa. Died Lately at his residence in Frankford.
The Union. (Sat., April 8, 1837)

Harper, James Esq. Cashier of the Branch bank of the United States
at Lexington. Died at Lexington, Ky. on the 25th ult. in the 46
year of his age.
National Banner & Nashville Whig. (Wed., Nov. 2, 1831)

Harper, Robert Goodloe. Youngest son of the late General R. G.
Harper of Baltimore. Died at sea on his voyage from Havre to New York.
National Banner & Nashville Daily Advertiser. (Mon., June 30, 1834)

Harper, Mr. Thomas. Formerly of Williamson County, Tenn. Died in
Lawrence County, Ala.
National Banner & Nashville Whig. (Mon., Oct. 31, 1831)

Harrel, Mrs. Nancy. Died at Russellville, Ky.
National Banner & Nashville Whig. (Thurs., Oct. 28, 1830)

Harris, Adam G. A native of Germany in the 66 year of his age.
Died at his residence, 4 miles from Nashville on Sat., Oct. 10th.
Nashville Whig. (Fri., Oct. 16, 1840)

Harris, Hon. Alfred M. Died in Pulaski, Ten. on Thursday, Feb. 21st.
Judge of the circuit court.
National Banner & Nashville Whig. (Sat., March 1, 1828)

Harris, Mrs. Ann. Aged 69. Died in Gallatin.
National Banner & Nashville Whig. (Mon., Nov. 15, 1830)

Harris, Archibald Esq. Died in Orange County, Ala.
National Banner & Nashville Whig. (Fri., Nov. 21, 1834)

Harris, Dr. A. W. A young physician, aged 21 years 10 months. Died
in Nashville on the 10th inst.
Nashville Whig. (Tues., Oct. 13 & 15th 1846)

Harris, Carey A. Esq. Formerly Superintendent of Indian Affairs.
Died at the residence of Dr. F. T. Reid in Franklin on the 18th inst.
in the 36th year of his age.
Nashville Whig. (Tues., June 28, 1842)

Harris, Miss Christiana. Daughter of Auther Harris Esq. Died in
Wilson County, Tenn.
National Banner & Nashville Daily Advertiser. (Tues., Aug. 5, 1834)

Harris, Mr. Davi Sen. Died in Woodford County, Ky.
National Banner & Nashville Whig. (Mon., June 7, 1830)

Harris, Mr. David. Aged 46 years. Died in Hardeman County on the
22d inst.
National Banner & Nashville Daily Advertiser. (Thurs., March 22, 1832)

Harris, Mrs. Eliza. Wife of Thomas J. Harris, of Pittsburgh, Pa.
Died her funeral from the residence of Mr. Robt. A. Cole, Sumner St.
Daily Republican Banner. (Tues., June 4, 1839)

Harris, Elizabeth Sophronia. Infant daughter of William and Elizabeth
Harris. Died in Nashville on Wednesday 29th ult.
National Banner & Nashville Daily Advertiser. (Mon., Feb. 3, 1834)

Harris, Mr. Frederick. Engineer, formerly of Nashville. Died in
New Orleans on the 16th of March last.
Nashville Republican. (Thurs., April 14, 1836)

Harris, Mr. George S. Late of Bedford County, Va. Died in Davidson
County on Sunday 10th inst.
National Banner & Nashville Whig. (Fri., July 15, 1831)

Harris, Gwynn Esq. Died at Annapolis, Md.
Daily Republican Banner. (Mon., Oct. 28, 1837)

Harris, Howell G. Esq. Formerly a member of the Senate of Tennessee.
Died at Paris, Henry County in the 41st year of his age.
National Banner & Nashville Whig. (Mon., June 7, 1830)

Harris, James. From Maury County did at the State Prison of Tenn. of
Cholera.
National Banner & Nashville Whig. (Fri., Aug. 14, 1835)

Harris, Mr. John. Aged 23. Died in Madison County, Ala. in consequence of a fall from his horse.
National Banner. (Feb. 3, 1826)

Harris, 1st Lieut. Joseph W. 3d Artillery. Died May 18th in the
U. S. Army.
National Banner & Nashville Whig. (Monday, July 31, 1837)

Harris, Josephine. Daughter of George W. and Emeline Harris. Died in
Knoxville on the 28th ult.
Nashville Whig. (Thurs., March 12, 1846)

Harris, Mrs. Lucinda. Consort of Col. George Harris. Purser in the
U. S. Navy and daughter of the late James McGavock, of Nashville.
Died on the 23rd inst. near Nashville.
The Christian Record. (Sat., June 26, 1847)

Harris, Mrs. Lucinda. Consort of Col. J. George Harris. Purser in
the U. S. Navy. Died on the morning of the 23d near Nashville.
The Politician & Weekly Nashville Whig. (Fri., June 25, 1847)

Harris, Mrs. Mary. In the 67th year of her age. Died in Rutherford
County, Ten. on the 28th ult. consort of the late Simpson Harris and
sister of the late John Coffee, of Ala.
Daily Republican Banner. (Fri., May 3, 1839)

Harris, Mrs. Mary C. Died in Jackson.
Nashville Whig. (Tues., July 21, 1846)

Menora F. Harris. Infant daughter of William Harris. Died in
Nashville on Thursday last.
Nashville Republican. (Sat., March 11, 1837)

Harris, Mr. Moses B. Aged about 26 years. Died in Davidson County
on the 4th inst. had but recently returned from Mexico.
The Christian Record. (Sat., July 10, 1847)

Harris, Mr. Moses B. Aged about 26 years. Died in Davidson County
on the 4th inst. He was a volunteer in Capt. Fosters company and had
but recently returned from Mexico.
The Politician & Weekly Nashville Whig. (Fri., July 9, 1847)

Harris, Mr. Oram A. Died in Randolph, T.
National Banner & Nashville Daily Advertiser. (Tues., July 15, 1834)

Harris, Peter Esq. A soldier of the Revolution, aged 82. Died in
Marion County.
National Banner & Nashville Daily Advertiser. (Sat., June 1, 1833)

Harris, Rev. Thomas. Died 19th at Cincinnati, Ohio of Cholera.
National Banner & Nashville Daily Advertiser. (Mon., Oct. 29, 1832)

Harris, Capt. Thomas A. Died in Rutherford County.
National Banner. (Sat., Aug. 8, 1829)

Harris, Thomas J. Esq. Died in Mobile, aged 23.
National Banner & Nashville Whig. (Sat., Sept. 30, 1826)

Harris, Thomas J. Formerly of Pittsburgh. Died on Tuesday night
March 29th.
Nashville Whig. (Sat., April 2, 1842)

Harris, General Thomas K. Died on the 18th inst. of the wounds which
he received in the recounter with Colonel Simpson.
The Nashville Whig. (Tues., March 26, 1816)

Harris, West Esq. Aged 57 years. Died in Hardeman County, Tenn.
National Banner & Nashville Whig. (Fri., Jan. 23, 1835)

Harrison, Mrs. Consort of Mr. John Harrison. Died in Nashville on
Saturday morning last of (consumption).
Impartial Review and Cumberland Repository. (Sat., April 12, 1806)

Harrison, Mrs. Russells Alley, N. of 4th St. Died 19th at Cincinnati, Ohio of Cholera.
National Banner & Nashville Daily (Fri., Oct. 26, 1832)

Harrison, The Hon. A. G. Died at his residence in Fulton, Missouri on the 7th inst. He was a member of Congress from that State.
Nashville Union. (Fri., Oct. 18, 1839)

Harrison, Ainsworth Sr. Died in Wilson County, on the 3rd Dec. in the 71st year of his age. A soldier of the Revolution.
National Banner & Nashville Whig. (Fri., Dec. 12, 1834)

Harrington, Mr. Giles C. Died in Newark, O.
National Banner & Nashville Whig. (Sat., Aug. 26, 1826)

Harrison, Hon. Albert G. Member elect to the Congress from Missouri. Died in St. Louis on the 7th inst.
Daily Republican Banner. (Fri., Sept. 20, 1839)

Harrison, Mrs. Ann. Widow of Nicholas Harrison deceased formerly of Lynchburg, Virginia. Died in Wilson County, at the home of her son-in-law the Rev. M. C. Henderson.
National Banner and Nashville Daily Advertiser. (Sat., March 3, 1832)

Harrison, Dr. Benjamin, 34. Died at the residence of his father in North Bend, was a son of Gen. Harrison.
Daily Republican Banner. (Fri., July 3, 1840)

Harrison, Mrs. Cynthia. In the 75 year of her age. Died in Sumner County on the 15th of Feb.
National Banner & Nashville Whig. (Sat., March 17, 1827)

Harrison, George E. Of Brandon. Died Obituary Sketch.
Nashville Union. (Mon., Feb. 25, 1839)

Harrison, James Washington. Infant son of James B. and Eliza Harrison. Died in Nashville on Saturday of the 4th.
The Christian Record. (Sat., June 10, 1848)

Harrison, John. Died at sea, on board the U. S. Steamer Major Dade in Capt. M'Cains Company.
Nashville Republican. (Tues., Nov. 1, 1836)

Harrison, John Volunteer in Capt. McCoin Company of Tenn. Troop. Died at sea on board the steamer Major Dade.
National Banner & Nashville Whig. (Wed., Nov. 2, 1836)

Harrison, John Ward. Son of Wm. and Susan Harrison. Died in Nashville on Sat. the 27th aged 11 years 6 months and 11 days.
National Banner and Nashville Whig. (Mon., Oct. 6, 1834)

Harrison, Mr. Joshua. Died in Murfreesborough. Aged 30 years.
National Banner. (Jan. 6, 1826)

Harrison, Patrick. Died at Cincinnati, Ohio on 14th of Cholera.
National Banner and Nashville Daily Advertiser. (Tues., Oct. 23, 1832)

Harrison, Dr. Richard. Died in Greenville, S. C.
Nashville Republican and State Gazette. (Tues., April 12, 1831)

Harrison, Romulus S. Died at the residence of his half-brother, Mr. John T. Hill, on the night of the 27th inst. (Obituary)
The Christian Record. (Sat., July 31, 1847)

Harrison, Romulus S. Died at the residence of his half brother Mr. John L. Hill, on the night of the 27th inst. in the 27 year of his age.
The Politician and Weekly Nashville Whig. (Wed., Aug. 4, 1847)

Harrison, William Henry. Late President of the United States. Died
at the Presidents House in Washington, the 4th day of April.
Nashville Whig. (Mon., April 12, 1841)

Hart, Mr. Joseph. Died at Columbia.
National Banner & Nashville Daily Advertiser. (Wed., July 3, 1833)

Hart, Mr. Joseph. Died in Columbia.
National Banner & Nashville Daily Advertiser. (Thurs., June 20, 1833)

Hart, Mrs. Ann Eliza. Wife of John T. Hart. Died in Madison County,
Ala.
National Banner, (March 17, 1826)

Hart, Mr. H. Formerly from New York. Died was accidentally knocked
from the warf and drowned in New Orleans.
Nashville Union. (Fri., March 1, 1839)

Hart, Mr. Jacob. A native of Chestnut Hill near Philadelphia. Died
in New Orleans.
National Banner & Nashville Whig. (Fri., June 10, 1836)

Hart, John Holman. Eldest sone of the late Capt. Oliver Hart in the
26th year of age. Died in Nashville on the 28th June.
Nashville Whig. (Fri., July 2, 1841)

Hart, Miss Nancy. Daughter of Mr. Henry Hart. Died in Robertson Co.
National Banner & Nashville Daily Advertiser. (Mon., Oct. 1, 1832)

Hart, Capt. Oliver. Died on board the Steamboat, Memphis on her passage
from New Orleans to Nashville.
Nashville Republican. (Sat., June 4, 1836)

Hart, Rev. Robert. In the 60th year of his age. Died at his residence at M'Lemoresville on Sunday the 26th Dec. in Carroll County.
Nashville Whig. (Thurs., Jan. 6, 1842)

Hart, Mrs. Sally. Wife of Mr. Thomas P. Hart. and daughter of
John Postlethwait Esq. Died at Lexington, Ky.
National Banner & Nashville Whig. (Mon., Feb. 7, 1831)

Hart, Seaborn Jones. In the 22nd year of his age. Died near Carthage
on the 21st Aug.
Daily Republican Banner. (Sat., Sept. 8, 1838)

Hart, Mrs. Susannah. Widow of the late Col. Thomas Hart. Died at
Lexington, Ky. Aged 85.
National Banner & Nashville Daily Advertiser. (Mon., Sept. 17, 1832)

Hart, Mr. Thomas. Son of the late Capt. N. G. S. Hart. Died in
Lexington, Ky.
National Banner & Nashville Whig. (Sat., Sept. 9, 1826)

Hartsfield, Miss Candis. Died in Tipton County.
National Banner. (Sat., Sept. 5, 1829)

Harvie, Lewis, Esq. Of Richmond. Died at Norfolk on his way to France.
Son of Col. John Harvie, dec. was a member of the Executive Council
of Va.
Impartial Review and Cumberland Repository. (Sat., May 23, 1807)

Hartwick, Mrs. Of the Nashville Theatre. Died in this town on Friday
last.
National Banner. (Jan. 6, 1826)

Harwell, Mrs. Julia. Wife of Mr. Hartwell Harwell. Died in Giles
County.
National Banner & Nashville Advertiser. (Thurs., Jan. 19, 1832)

Harwell, Raleigh. Aged 73 years. Died in Giles County.
Nashville Republican. (Sat., Aug. 27, 1836)

Harwood, Mrs. Emily E. C. Died in Madison County, Ala.
National Banner & Nashville Whig. (Sat., July 8, 1826)

Hasbrook, Mrs. Mary. Died in Louisville, Ky.
National Banner & Nashville Whig. (Sat., Jan. 31, 1829)

Haskell, Hon. Joshua. Died on the 13th in Jackson in the 54th year of
his age.
Daily Republican Banner. (Mon., Jan. 6, 1840)

Haskell, Mrs. Nancy. Consort of Hon. Joshua Haskell. Died in
Jackson on Sat. 8th inst.
Nashville Republican. (Tues., Oct. 18, 1836)

Haskell, Mrs. Nancy. Consort of Hon. Joshua Haskell. Died in Jackson,
Tenn. on the 8th Oct.
National Banner & Nashville Whig. (Mon., Oct. 17, 1836)

Haskew, Mr. Wm. Died in Knox County.
National Banner & Nashville Whig. (Sat., Oct. 6, 1827)

Haskins, Mr. Edward M. Died in Powhatan, Virginia.
Nashville Republican & State Gazette. (Sat., Sept. 17, 1831)

Haskins, Mrs. Sarah. Wife of Mr. John Haskins. Died in Knox County.
National Banner & Nashville Whig. (Sat., Aug. 26, 1826)

Haslerigg, Mr. Richard. Died in Rhea County, aged 58.
National Banner & Nashville Whig. (Sat., Feb. 24, 1827)

Hatchett, Mr. Edward. Died in this town (Nashville)
Nashville Republican & State Gazette. (Thurs., Aug. 11, 1831)

Hatchett, Mr. Tilman. In the 23d year of his age. Died in Rutherford
County, Tenn. son of Mr. Archer Hatchett of Franklin County, Ten.
National Banner & Nashville Whig. (Fri., Oct. 31, 1834)

Hathaway, Mrs. Elizabeth. Wife of Mr. W. L. Hathaway. Died in
Huntsville, Ala.
National Banner & Nashville Daily Advertiser. (Fri., May 3, 1833)

Hatton, Capt. John M. Died in Scott County, Ky.
National Banner & Nashville Whig. (Mon., March 7, 1831)

Haven, Nathaniel A. Esq. Died at Portsmouth, N.H.
National Banner & Nashville Whig. (July 1, 1826)

Havens, Mr. Died in Louisville, Ky. of New York.
National Banner & Nashville Whig. (Sat., Aug. 5, 1826)

Hawkins, Mrs. Catherine. Wife of Mr. Cleon Hawkins and daughter of
Mr. Elisha Craig. Died in Georgetown, Ky.
National Banner & Nashville Daily Advertiser. (Wed., Aug. 7, 1833)

Hawkins, Miss Catherine V. Aged 20 years. Died in Hardin County.
Daily Republican Banner. (Tues., Sept. 3, 1839)

Hawkins, Mr. James Wood. Former Post Master in that place. Died at
Frankfort, Ky.
National Banner & Nashville Whig. (Mon., May 31, 1830)

Hawkins, Mr. John. Died in Bourbon County, Ky.
National Banner & Nashville Whig. (Sat., Sept. 9, 1826)

Hawkins, Capt. John. Died at Elkton, Giles County.
National Banner & Nashville Daily Advertiser. (Tues., July 17, 1832)

Hawkins, Mr. John T. Died in Fayette County, Ky.
National Banner. (Feb. 17, 1826)

Hawkins, Col. Joseph H. Attorney at law. Resident of New Orleans,
formerly a member to Congress from Lexington, Ky. Died at
Madisonville, Louisa. on the 1st inst.
Nashville Whig. (Oct. 20, 1823)

Hawkins, Mr. Martin. Died in Scott County, Ky.
National Banner & Nashville Whig. (Mon., Nov. 29, 1830)

Hawkins, Mrs. Mary. Wife of Littleberry Hawkins Esq. Died in Louisville, Ky.
National Banner & Nashville Whig. (Mon., Dec. 1, 1834)

Hawkins, Mr. Nathanial. Late of North Carolina. Died in Courtland,
Ala.
National Banner. (Jan. 13, 1826)

Hawkins, Mrs. Rachel. The mother of Capt. James Scantland of Nashville.
Died in Oldham County, Ky. On the 20th March, in the 73 year of her
age.
Nashville Whig. (Thurs., April 2, 1846)

Hawkins, Mr. Robert. Died at Courtland, Ala.
National Banner. (Sat., Dec. 5, 1829)

Hawkins, Stephen M. Esq. Aged 25. Died in Grainger County on the
13th inst.
National Banner. (Sat., Aug. 29, 1829)

Hawks, Mr. Asahel A. Died at Chillicothe.
National Banner & Nashville Whig. (Sat., Sept. 8, 1827)

Hawley, Mr. Francis W. Aged 21 years. Died in St. Louis, Mo.
National Banner & Nashville Daily Advertiser. (Mon., Aug. 26, 1833)

Hawley, Mr. Francis W. Age 21 years. Died in St. Louis.
National Banner & Nashville Daily Advertiser. (Tues., Sept. 10, 1833)

Haxall, Mr. Philip. Died at Richmond, Va.
National Banner & Nashville Daily Advertiser. (Mon., Jan. 9, 1832)

Hay, George. Eldest son of Preston and Sarah Hay. Died on the 11th
inst. in the 13th year of his age.
Nashville Whig. (Sat., July 18, 1846)

Hay, Hon. Geo. U. S. Judge for the eastern District of Va. and son-
in-law of James Monroe, late President U. States. Died Albermarle, Va.
National Banner & Nashville Whig. (Thurs., Oct. 7, 1830)

Hay, Mr. John. Of this town (Nashville). Died on Tuesday last of a
lingering illness.
Impartial Review and Cumberland Repository. (Thurs., Oct. 6, 1808)

Hay, John G. Esq. Aged 26 years. Died in Nashville.
National Banner & Nashville Whig. (Mon., June 29, 1835)

Hayden, Major. Paymaster for the U. S. Army. Died at Hampstead,
C. H. Ark.
National Banner & Nashville Whig. (Sat., July 8, 1826)

Hayden, Mr. Benj. Died in Cincinnati.
National Banner & Nashville Whig. (Thurs., June 17, 1830)

Hayden, James Esq. A clerk in the store of G. M. Willing & Co.

169

Died - was burned to death in St. Louis, Mo. on Saturday morning
on Aug. 31st.
Daily Republican Banner. (Mon., Sept. 9, 1839)

Haydock, William. Aged 52. Died in Philadelphia, July 30th.
National Banner & Nashville Whig. (Wed., Aug. 16, 1837)

Hayes, Mrs. Mary C. Wife of Dr. R. P. Hayes. Died on Sunday night.
National Banner & Nashville Whig. (Sat., Feb. 9, 1828)

Hayes, Richard, H. Attorney at law. Died - in Columbia on last
Monday was killed by William Polk, Esq.
Daily Republican Banner. (Wed., Dec. 5, 1838)

Hayes, Dr. R. P. Died Saturday afternoon 8th inst. from the effects
of posing by a negro servant. (Cin. Whig)
National Banner & Nashville Whig. (Mon., April 17, 1837)

Hayes, Mr. William P. Aged 40 years. Died in Franklin, Tenn. of
Cholera.
National Banner & Nashville Whig. (Friday, July 10, 1835)

Haylton, Mrs. Sarah. Died in Richmond, Va.
Nashville Republican & State Gazette. (Tues., Dec. 13, 1831)

Haynes, Mrs. Died in Richmond, Va.
Nashville Republican & State Gazette. (Tues., Dec. 13, 1831)

Haynes, Col. Andrew. Died at his residence near Nashville, on Sunday
the 21st inst.
The Christian Record. (Sat., Jan. 27, 1849)

Haynes, Mr. Anderson. Died in Williamson County.
National Banner & Nashville Whig. (Wed., Oct. 12, 1831)

Haynes, Mrs. Ann E. Consort of Col. Andrew Haynes. Died in this
vicinity. (Sat., Feb. 18, 1837)

Haynes, Mrs. Letitia. Wife of Richard Haynes. Died in Knoxville,
Tenn.
Daily Republican Banner. (Sat., Sept. 29, 1838)

Haynes, Mrs. Mary. In the 60th year of her age. Died at Woodville,
Mi.
National Banner & Nashville Daily Advertiser. (Thurs., March 22, 1832)

Haynes, General Robert Y. Of South Carolina. Died at Ashville, N.C.
while attending the railroad convention.
Daily Republican Banner. (Thurs., Oct. 3, 1839)

Haynie, Miss Mary H. Died in Tuscumbia, Ala.
National Banner & Nashville Daily Advertiser. (Tues., July 2, 1833)

Hays, Mrs. Mary W. Wife of Mr. W. P. Hays. Died at Franklin, T.
National Banner. (Sat., April 25, 1829)

Hays, Stokley D. Col. Register of the Land Office in Clinton, Miss.
Died at Jackson, Tenn. on the 18th inst.
Nat. Ban.(Mon. Sept. 12, 1831)

Hayter, Jefferson Esq. Of Memphis, Tenn. Died at New York.
Nashville Republican. (Thurs., April 27, 1837)

Hays, Mr. Adam. Aged 75. Died in Rutherford County.
National Banner & Nashville Daily Advertiser. (Mon., Oct. 8, 1832)

Hays, Col. Andrew. Died on Sun. morning 10th inst at Jackson, Miss.
Nashville Whig. (Sat., Sept. 23, 1843)

Hays, Mrs. Ann. Aged 55. Died in Davidson County.
Nashville Republican & State Gazette. (Tues., July 12, 1831)

Hays, Mrs. Ann. Died July 12, 1831.

Hays, Mrs. Ann. Wife of Charles Hays. Died in Davidson County on
the 8th inst.
National Banner & Nashville Whig. (Mon., July 11, 1831)

Hays, Blackman. Aged about 41 years. Died in Davidson County on
the 30th ult.
The Christian Record. (Sat., April 10, 1847)

Hays, Clemment Washington. Aged three weeks and 4 days. Died in this
county on the 15th inst.
National Banner & Nashville Whig. (Sat., May 19, 1827)

Hays, Mrs. Elizabeth. Wife of Mr. John Hays. Died in Huntsville,
Ala.
National Banner & Nashville Whig. (Fri., June 27, 1828)

Hays, Jacob. Of New York, in his 79th year. Died at his residence
in New York City on the 21st inst. The Oldest Police Officer in the
United States.
Nashville True Whig & Weekly Commercial Register. (Fri., July 5, 1850)

Hays, James C. Esq. Died in Texas on his way home from Mexico.
National Banner & Nashville Whig. (Sat., Nov. 4, 1826)

Hays, Mrs. Jane. Aged 68. Died in Madison County, Tennessee.
National Banner & Nashville Daily Advertiser. (Thurs., Feb. 13, 1834)

Hays, Jane Mrs. Departed this life on the 1st instant, at her late
residence in this vicinity, age 68 years. This venerable lady was a
daughter of Capt. John Donelson one of the pioneers of Tennessee.
The grave had long since deprived her of her companion, and she has
now followed him to the world of spirits, leaving her family to lament
her absence, and to cherish her memory with that affection which her
many virtues inspired -- Jackson Statesman.
Nashville Republican Nashville, Tenn. (Thurs., Feb. 13, 1834)

Hays, Mr. John. Eldest son of Charles Hays Esq. Died in Davidson
County on Sat. 30th May.
Nashville Whig. (Mon., June 1, 1840)

Hays, Mary Elizabeth. Infant daughter of O. B. Hays Esq. Died in
Davidson County on the 17th inst.
National Banner & Nashville Whig. (Mon., Sept. 29, 1834)

Hays, Miss Mary S. Died - April 29, 1815. Daughter of Colonel Robert
Hays of this (Davidson County). She died after an illness of 36
hours in the 18th year of her age.
Nashville Whig. (May 23, 1815)

Hays, Mrs. Martha. Consort of John Hays, in the 38th year of her age.
Died on Sunday the 3d inst.
Nashville Republican. (Tues., July 11, 1837)

Hays, Mr. William. In the 45th year of his age. Died in Davidson
County. on the 21st inst.
National Banner & Nashville Whig. (Wed., Sept. 30, 1835)

Hayward, Mrs. Eliza. Consort of E. Hayward Esq. Commissioner of
the General Land Office. Died in Washington City.
National Banner & Nashville Daily Advertiser. (Thurs., June 19, 1834)

Haywood, Mrs. Elizabeth. Relict of John Haywood Esq. Late Treasurer
of that State, Died in Raleigh, N. C.
Nashville Republican & State Gazette. (Mon., Aug. 20, 1832)

Haywood, John Esq. Age 72. Died in Raleigh, N. C. Treasurer of that
State for 40 years.
National Banner & Nashville Whig. (Sat., Dec. 15, 1827)

Haywood, Hon. John. Judge of the supreme Court of Tenn. in the 66th
year of his age. Died last night at his residence in this county.
National Banner & Nashville Whig. (Sat., Dec. 23, 1826)

Haywood, Robert. Age 14, son of John Haywood, Esq. of Davidson County
Died in Franklin County, N. C. about the 1st. inst.
Impartial Review and Cumerland Repository. (Thurs., July 28, 1808)

Hazard, Benjamin. Of Newport. Died on Wednesday last.
Nashville Whig. (Mon., March 29, 1841)

Hazle, Mr. Samuel K. Died in Nashville.
National Banner & Nashville Daily Advertiser. (Fri., Dec. 14, 1832)

Hazlerigg, John. At an advanced age. Died in Bourbon County, Ky
of Cholera.
National Banner & Nashville Daily Advertiser. (Sat., Aug. 10, 1833)

Heard, Major Morgan A. Died in Logan County, Ky.
National Banner & Nashville Daily Advertiser. (Mon., Sept. 9, 1833)

Hearn, Col. N. G. Aged 32. Died in Henderson County.
Nashville Whig. (Mon., Sept. 7, 1840)

Heartle, Dr. Ozeas. In the 22nd year of his age. Died in New Orleans.
National Banner & Nashville Daily Advertiser. (Sat., Aug. 24, 1833)

Heathcock, Mr. John. Died in Knox County.
National Banner. (March 24, 1826)

Hedenburgh, Ann Matilda. Infant daughter of Charles J. and Mary
E. Hedenburgh. Died in Nashville on the 14th inst.
Nashville Whig. (Sat., Sept. 16, 1843)

Hegeman, Jane, Emily and Juliet. Daughters of Dr. J. W. Hegeman.
Died at Vicksburg, Miss. on Tuesday the 7th May.
National Banner & Nashville Daily Advertiser. (Mon., May 20, 1833)

Heggins, Williams. Died 14th, At Cincinnati, Ohio of Cholera.
National Banner & Nashville Daily Advertiser. (Tues., Oct. 23, 1832)

Heister, Gen. Joseph. In the 82nd year of his age. Died at Reading,
Pa. on the 10th inst. formerly Governor of Penn.
National Banner & Nashville Daily Advertiser. (Tues., June 26, 1832)

Hellen, David H. Son of Mr. David Hellen. Died in Mobile, Ala.
National Banner & Nashville Whig. (Wed., Nov. 19, 1834)

Hemphill, Miss Esther. Died in Nashville on the 14th inst. at the
residence of Mr. W. R. McAlister. Obituary June 24, 1848
The Christian Record. (Sat., June 17, 1848)

Henderliter, Mr. Jesse. Aged 47 years. Died in Little Rock, Ark.
National Banner & Nashville Daily Advertiser. (Tues., Aug. 5, 1834)

Henderson, Mrs. Ann M. H. Died at Mount Pinson wife of Col. Thomas
Henderson.
National Banner. (Sat., Aug. 22, 1829)

Henderson, Mr. Archibald. Died at Pittsburgh.
National Banner & Nashville Whig. (Sat., Jan. 13, 1827)

Henderson, Mrs. Eliza J.   Consort of Mr. William T. Henderson of Sumner
County. Died on the 18, inst.
Impartial Review and Cumberland Repository. (Feb., 28, 1807)

Henderson, Mrs. Elizabeth. Wife of Thomas Henderson Esq. Died in
M'Minn County.
National Banner & Nashville Whig. (Thurs., Sept. 16, 1830)

Henderson, Lieut. John Eaton. Of the 2d U. S. Artillery. Died at
Washington, D. C. on the 4th of July.
National Banner & Nashville Whig. (Mon., July 18, 1836)

Henderson, Hon. Leonard. Chief Justice of the state. Died in Granville
County, N. C.
National Banner & Nashville Daily Advertiser. (Mon., Sept. 2, 1833)

Henderson, Mrs. Margaret M. Wife of Dr. James M. Henderson. Died in
Carroll County.
National Banner. (Sat., Dec. 19, 1829)

Henderson, Pleasant Esq. Died in McMinnville on the 28th inst. by a
shock of lighting formerly of North Carolina.
Nashville Republican. (Thurs., July 6, 1837)

Henderson, Lieut R. 2d Artillery. Died was killed in Battle with
the Seminole Indians in Florida.
The Union. (Sat., Jan. 23, 1836)

Henderson, Rev. Robert. D. D. of the Presbyterian Church. Died in
Williamson County, Ten.
National Banner & Nashville Daily Advertiser. (Mon., Aug. 25, 1834)

Henderson, Col. Thomas. A native of Rockingham County, N. C. Died
in Sumpter County, Ala. on the 22d June, aged 60 years.
National Banner & Nashville Whig. (Wed., July 20, 1836)
Nashville Republican. (Tues., July 17, 1836)

Henderson, Col. Thoas. Late of Madison County, Tenn. Died in
Sumpter County, Ala.
Nashville Republican. (Tues., July 19, 1836)

Henderson, Col. William. Of Sumner County. Died on 18th inst. he was
an officer in the Revolutionary War.
Impartial Review and Cumberland Repository. (Feb., 28, 1807)

Hendley, Miss Letitia. Died in Lexington, Ky.
National Banner & Nashville Whig. (Tues,, Feb. 2, 1830)

Hendman, Mrs. Sarah. Aged 76. Died in Knoxville.
National Banner & Nashville Advertiser. (Sat., Sept. 22, 1832)

Hendricks, Mr. Harman. President of the Manhatten Fire Insurance Co.
Died in New York on the 4th inst. at his residence No. 61
Greenwich Street.
Nashville Whig. (Wed., April 11, 1838)

Hendrickson, Mrs. and three children. Died scalded to death on Ohio
River when boiler exploded.
National Banner & Nashville Daily Advertiser. (Wed., Nov. 20, 1833)

Hening, Wm. W. Esq. Clerk of the Chancry court. Died at Richmond, Va.
National Banner & Nashville Whig. (Sat., April 19, 1828)

Henley, Miss Eliza Jane. Died in Rutherford County.
National Banner & Nashville Whig. (Sat., Dec. 30, 1826)

Henley, Leonard. Died in Williamsburg, Va.
Nashville Republican & State Gazette. (Thurs., Feb. 24, 1831)

Henley, Patrick H. Infant son of Mr. T. B. Henley. Died in Rutherford County.
National Banner & Nashville Whig. (Sat., Jan. 13, 1827)

Henley, Mrs. Susan. Wife of Mr. T. B. Henley. Died in Rutherford County.
Nashville Whig. (June 4, 1823)

Henne, Doctor James. Formerly of Nashville, aged 54 years. Died in New Orleans on the 5th ult.
The Nashville Gazette. (Sat., May 20, 1820)

Henning, Mr. George. Died in Gainesville, Ala. on the 21st ult. formerly of Nashville and for the past 7 years residing in Mobile, Ala.
Nashville Whig. (Wed., Aug. 5, 1840)

Henry, A. I. England. Died in the wreck of the steam boat Lexington.
Daily Republican Banner. (Fri., Jan. 31, 1840)

Henry, Mrs. Ann. Wife of Dr. Stephen Henry. Died at Detroit.
National Banner & Nashville Whig. (Sat., May 12, 1827)

Henry, Isaac N. Esq. One of the Editors of the St. Louis Enquirer in the twenty-fourth year of his age. The deceased was a native of Tennessee.
The Clarion and Tennessee Gazette. (Jan., 23, 1821)
(From the St. Louis Enquirer of Jan. 6)

Henry, John J. Esq. Died in Williamson County.
National Banner. (Feb. 10, 1826)

Henry, Maj. M. W. Aged 48 years. Died in Bowling Green, Ky. on the 30th ult.
Daily Republican Banner. (Sat., Aug. 4, 1838)

Henry, Maj. Robert P. M. C. Died in Christian County, Ky.
National Banner & Nashville Whig. (Sept. 2, 1826)

Henry, Mr. William. Aged 36 years. Died in Circleville, Ohio on the 27th ult.
National Banner & Nashville Daily Advertiser. (Fri., Feb. 15, 1833)

Hensley, James. Aged 42. Died yesterday morning.
Nashville Whig. (Sat., Feb. 19, 1842)

Here, Capt. Henry. Died in Franklin.
National Banner & Nashville Whig. (Mon., April 25, 1831)

Hereford, John W. Esq. Aged 42. Died at Memphis on 13th of August.
National Banner & Nashville Advertiser. (Thurs., Oct. 4, 1832)

Herman, Joseph Esq. Aged 40 years. Died in Claiborne County, Mo.
National Banner & Nashville Daily Advertiser. (Tues., Aug. 5, 1834)

Herndon, Mrs. Ann. Wife of Mr. George R. Herndon. Died in Logan County, Ky.
National Banner & Nashville Whig. (Sat., Sept. 13, 1828)

Herndon, Mr. Elisha. Died in Logan County, Ky.
National Banner & Nashville Whig. (Sat., July 22, 1826)

Herndon, Mrs. Louisa A. Wife of John B. Herndon. Died at Russellville, Ky.
National Banner & Nashville Whig. (Mon., June 6, 1831)

Herndon, Miss Sally. Daughter of Mr. Geo. R. Herndon. Died in Logan County, Ky.
National Banner & Nashville Whig. (Sat., March 10, 1827)

Herndon, Mr. William. Died in Nashville his funeral will take place
with Masonic honors this afternoon.
National Banner & Nashville Whig. (Mon., July 26, 1830)

Herndon, Zachariah. Died in Georgetown, Ky.
National Banner & Nashville Whig. (Sat., Oct. 7, 1826)

Heron, James. Aged 45 years. Died in N. York on 29th ult.
Daily Republican Banner. (Mon., Oct. 12, 1840)

Heron, James Mathew. At the residence of Col. J. G. Williams on the
9th inst. Infant son of W. M. Heron of Athens, Tenn. aged 2 years,
2 months and 20 days.
Nashville Republican. (Sat., Feb. 13, 1836)

Heron, James Matthews. Infant son of W. M. Heron of Athens, Tenn.
Died at the residence of Col. J. G. Williams. on the 9th aged 2 years,
2 months.
National Banner & Nashville Whig. (Fri., Feb. 12, 1836)
Nashville Republican. (Sat., Feb. 13, 1836)

Heron, Mr. John E. Of Hardeman County, Tenn. formerly of the U. S. Navy
Died in Fayette County, Ky.
National Banner & Nashville Advertiser. (Fri., Feb. 24, 1832)

Herring, Crissian. Of Germany, a passenger. Died on the steamer George
Collier, scalded to death on the 6th.
Daily Republican Banner. (Tues., May 14, 1839)

Hervey, James. Died 14th Cincinnati, Ohio of Cholera.
National Banner & Nashville Daily Advertiser. (Tues., Oct. 23, 1832)

Hester, Gen. Gabriel. His age 56 years. Died in Pittsburgh, Pa.
National Banner & Nashville Whig. (Mon., Oct. 20, 1834)

Hewitt, Caleb Esq. Sheriff of Davidson County. Died on Monday the
9th inst. of a wound he received from James Maxwell, on Thursday last.
who struck him with an adze while he was in the act of serving a
writ on him.
The Nashville Whig. (Sept. 10, 1816)

Hewlett, McHenry. Infant son of W. E. and Jane A. M. Hewlett. Died
on Wednesday 4th inst.
Daily Republican Banner. (Thurs., July 5, 1838)

Hewlett, Mrs. Mary. Died in Nashville on Tuesday last.
National Banner & Nashville Whig. (Thurs., July 22, 1840)

Hewlett, Col. Reuben G. Age 27. Died in Madison County, Ala.
National Banner & Nashville Advertiser. (Mon., Feb. 27, 1832)

Hewley, Alfred A. Aged 35 years and 8 months. Died in Wilson County
on Friday the 1st inst.
The Politician and Weekly Nashville Whig. (Fri., Oct. 8, 1847)

Hewston, Mrs. Mary G. Wife of Mr. Charles Hewston and daughter of
Edward B. Roche of Clarksville, Montgomery Co., Tenn. Died at
Tennessee Iron Works on the 14th inst.
Nashville Whig. (Mon., Sept. 21, 1840)

Heyser, George B. Son of William Heyser of Chambersburgh. Died in
that borough on the 25th ult. of Cholera.
(Pittsburgh Gazette)
National Banner & Nashville Daily Advertiser. (Sat., Oct. 13, 1832)

Heysham, Mr. Alexander Hamilton. Son of the late Capt. Heysham. Died
at Philadelphia on Sat. morning July 24th in the 26th year of his age.
National Banner & Nashville Whig. (Thurs., Aug. 12, 1830)

Hickey, Mr. John T. Formerly of Rutledge, Tenn. Died in Huntsville, Ala. on the 13th inst.
National Banner & Nashville Whig. (Wed., Oct. 22, 1834)

Hickey, Mr. John T. A native of Rutledge, Ten. aged 21 years. Died in Huntsville, Ala.
National Banner & Nashville Whig. (Fri., Nov. 21, 1834)

Hickey, Mrs. Paulina. Wife of Thomas M. Hickey Esq. Died in Lexington Ky.
National Banner. (March 24, 1826)

Hicklise, Mr. Hugh. Died in Bourbon County, Ky.
National Banner. (March 24, 1826)

Hickman, Mrs. Wife of James Hickman. Died in Knoxville, Tenn.
Daily Republican Banner. (Sat., Sept. 29, 1838)

Hickman, Ashbell Brunson. Infant son of Edwin W. and Penelope Hickman. Died on Thursday, August 8th, aged 3 months and 23 days.
Nashville True Whig & Weekly Commercial Register. (Fri., Aug. 16, 1850)

Hickman, Benjamin Esq. Died at Frankford, Ky.
National Banner & Nashville Daily Advertiser. (Mon., Jan. 7, 1833)

Hickman, Mr. John. A soldier of the revolution at a very advanced age . Died in Logan County, Ky.
National Banner & Nashville Whig. (Mon., Jan. 5, 1835)

Hickman, Major John P. Died yesterday at his place in the vicinity of Nashville.
Daily Republican Banner. (Thurs., Feb. 6, 1840)

Hickman, Mrs. Narcissa. Relict of the late Maj. John P. Hickman and daughter of Col. Robert Weakley, deceased. Obituary Jan. 13. Died in the vicinity of Nashville on the 4th inst.
The Christian Record. (Sat., Jan. 6, 1849)

Hickman, Mr. William. Died in Shelby County.
National Banner & Nashville Whig. (Mon., Nov. 29, 1830)

Hickox, Doct. Horace. Died in Athens, Tenn.
National Banner & Nashville Whig. (Fri., Nov. 21, 1834)

Hicks, Ann H. C. Daughter of Mr. Allen W. Hicks. Died in Madison County.
National Banner & Nashville Daily Advertiser. (Wed., Aug. 7, 1833)

Hicks, Elias. In the 82nd year of his age. Died in Jericho Long Island on the evening of the 27th ult. An eminent minister of the Gospel.
National Banner & Nashville Whig. (Tues., March 23, 1830)

Hicks, Mrs. Nancy. Wife of Mr. Edward D. Hicks and daughter of John Davis Esq. of Davidson County. Died in Nashville last night.
National Banner & Nashville Daily Advertiser. (Wed., March 14, 1832)

Hicky, Mr. Cornelieus Jun. Died in Knox County.
National Banner. (May 4, 1826)

Higginbotham, Mrs. Lucretia. Consort of Doctor R. A. Higginbotham of this town. Died on Wednesday last.
Nashville Whig. (July 12, 1824)

Higginbotham, Dr. Ralph A. Died in Nashville.
National Banner & Nashville Whig. (Mon., Aug. 29, 1831)

Higginbotham, Dr. Reuben A.   Died in this place.
Nashville Republican & State Gazette. (Tues., Aug. 30, 1831)

Higgins, Mr. Joseph.   Died in Lexington, Ky.   A native of Ireland.
National Banner & Nashville Whig. (Sat., Sept. 9, 1826)

High, John.   Of Philadelphia.   Died in New Orleans of Yellow Fever.
Daily Republican Banner. (Wed., Oct. 4, 1837)

Hight, Mr. Richard H.   Died in Madison, Ten.
Nashville Republican & State Gazette. (Thurs., April 7, 1831)

Hightower, Miss Harriet.   Died in Nashville on Friday the 17th inst.
at the residence of Dr. Berry.   She was the daughter of Hardy Hightower Esq. of Ala.
National Banner & Nashville Daily Advertiser. (Mon., Jan. 20, 1833)

Hightower, Mr. John.   Died in Sommerville, Fayette County on the
18th inst.
National Banner & Nashville Whig. (Sat., July 29, 1826)

Hightower, Mr. Joseph B.   In the 26th year of his age.   Died in Tipton
County, Tenn.
National Banner & Nashville Daily Advertiser. (Fri., Aug. 1, 1834)

Hightower, Miss Mary.   Died in Lauderdale County, Ala.
National Banner & Nashville Daily Advertiser. (Mon., Aug. 19, 1833)

Hill, Hon. Aaron.   Died at Boston, former Post Master of that place.
National Banner & Nashville Whig. (Mon., Dec. 27, 1830)

Hill, Francis M'Alister.   Infant child of H. R. W. Hill Esq.   Died in
Nashville on Saturday 10, inst.
National Banner & Nashville Advertiser. (Tues., Nov. 13, 1832)

Hill, The Hon. Isaac.   Died on Saturday the 22, ult.   Senator from
New Hampshire.   Died at the age of 63.
Nashville True Whig & Weekly Commercial Register. (Fri., April 4, 1850)

Hill, Mr. James C.   Formerly Merchant.   Died at his residence in Franklin on Tuesday last.
The Western Weekly Review. (Fri., June 24, 1831) Franklin, Tenn.

Hill, Col. James J.   Died in Henderson County.   Formerly of Franklin
County, N. C.
National Banner & Nashville Whig. (Sat., July 14, 1827)

Hill, Mrs. Jane Ann.   Wife of Samuel Hill, Esq.   Died in Nashville on
the 21st ult. in the 26th year of her age.
Nashville Whig. (Thurs., Aug. 3, 1843)

Hill, Mr. John.   Aged about 123 to 127.   Died near St. Thomas in the
County of Franklin, Penn.
National Banner & Nashville Whig. (Mon., April 25, 1831)

Hill, Mr. Jno.   Age 123 or 127.   Died near Pittsburgh, Pa.
Nashville Republican & State Gazette. (Thurs., April 19, 1831)

Hill, Mr. John.   Age somewhere about 123 or 127, according to a army
discharge.   Born in England, served in Army 28 years, under George 1.
Died in Franklin County, Pa. near St. Thomas on 23 ult.
National Banner & Nashville Whig. (Mon., April 25, 1831)

Hill, 2nd. Sergent John A.   With Company D.   Died - was killed in
the Battle of Monterey, with the Mexicans on Sept. 21st.
Nashville Whig. (Sat., Oct. 24, 1846)

Hill, Rev. Joshua C. Died on the 12th day of May after an illness of more than 12 months.
National Banner & Nashville Whig. (Sat., June 9, 1827)

Hill, Mrs. Mary C. Wife of Mr. William G. Hill and daughter of Elihu S. Hall, Esq. Died in this County yesterday.
National Banner (Sat., Aug. 22, 1829)

Hill, Mrs. Rachel. Died at Knoxville.
National Banner & Nashville Whig. (Sat., May 26, 1827)

Hill, Mr. Samuel. Died in Logan County, Ky.
National Banner & Nashville Advertiser. (Sat., Oct. 16, 1832)

Hill, Sarah Branch. Daughter of H. R. W. Hill Esq. Died in Nashville on Friday the 9th inst.
National Banner & Nashville Daily Advertiser. (Tues., Nov. 13, 1832)

Hill, Mr. Solon. Attorney at law. Aged about 28 years. Died at New Orleans on Sunday the 1st inst.
National Banner & Nashville Daily Advertiser. (Fri., Sept. 20, 1833)

Hill, Mr. Thomas. Merchant of this town (Nashville) Died on Sunday night the 30th ult.
Nashville Whig. (Sept. 8, 1823)

Hill, William. Died in Knoxville, Tenn. with the fever.
Daily Republican Banner. (Sat., Oct. 13, 1838)

Hillard, Mrs. Mildred. Died in Williamson County, wife of Mr. Thomas Hillard.
National Banner & Nashville Whig. (Sat., Oct. 6, 1827)

Hilliard, Mr. Isaac. Died at his residence near Nashville on Wednesday last.
National Banner & Nashville Daily Advertiser. (Mon., April 23, 1832)

Hilliard, Mr. Isaac. Died at his residence near Franklin, Tenn. on Wednesday last. The Western Weekly Review. (Friday, April 13, 1832) Franklin, Tenn.

Hilliard, J. H. Of Williamson County. Died in the loss of the Steam Boat Brandywine.
National Banner & Nashville Advertiser. (Mon., April 23, 1832)

Hilliard, Mrs. Lavinia. Daughter of Daniel Lineau of Murfreesboro. Died at Bersheba in Warren County, Friday 11th inst.
National Banner & Nashville Whig. (Fri., Aug. 18, 1837)

Hilliard, Mrs. Lovinia. Daughter of Daniel Leinau of Murfreesboro. Died at Bershaba Springs in Warren County the 11th inst.
Nashville Republican. (Thurs., Aug. 17, 1837)

Hilliard, Mrs. Mary Moore. Relict of the late Isaac Hilliard, Esq. of Williamson County, Tenn. and daughter of Col. Hardy Murfree of the Army of the Revolution. Died at the residence of her son-in-law William Hardeman, Esq. near Jackson, Miss on the 1st inst.
The Christian Record. (Sat., March 18, 1848)

Hilliard, Mrs. Mary Moore. Relict of the late Isaac Hilliard Esq. of Williamson County. Died at the residence of her son-in-law William Hardeman Esq. near Jackson, Miss. on Wednesday the 1st inst.
The Politician & Weekly Nashville Whig. (Fri., March 17, 1848)

Hilson, Mr. ___. One of the most distinguished Comedians in the United States. Died at Louisville, Ky.
National Banner & Nashville Daily Advertiser. (Mon., Aug. 25, 1834)

Hindman, Mrs. Sarah. Age 76. Died in Knoxville.
National Banner & Nashville Advertiser. (Sat., Sept. 22, 1832)

Hinkle, Mrs. Catharine. Died at Louisville, Ky. Wife of Mr. John
Hinkle.
National Banner & Nashville Whig. (Sat., Feb. 23, 1828)

Hinkle, Mr. John. Died at Louisville, Ky.
National Banner & Nashville Whig. (Sat., April 26, 1828)

Hinson, Mrs. Eliza. Consort of Thos. H. Hinson and daughter of John
Stanfield. Died in Dickson County, Tenn. in the 23d year of her age.
Nashville Republican. (Sat., Sept. 10, 1836)

Hinson, Mrs. Eliza. Consort of Thos. H. Hinson. Died in Hickman
County, Tenn. 1st Sept. in the 23rd year of her age.
National Banner & Nashville Whig. (Mon., Sept. 12, 1836)
Nashville Republican. (Sat., Sept. 10, 1836?)

Hinson, Jane. Second daughter of Mr. Harbert Hinson. Aged 2 years
7 months. Died in Henry County.
National Banner & Nashville Daily Advertiser. (Sat., May 18, 1833)

Hinton, Mrs. Candace B. Consort of Col. Wm. Hinton. Died in Wake
County, N. C.
Nashville Republican & State Gazette. (Thurs., Oct. 6, 1831)

Hinton, Mrs. Martha A. Consort of Col. John J. Hinton. Died in
Davidson County on the 17th inst. in the 40th year of her age.
Nashville Whig. (Sat., July 22, 1843)

Hitchcock, Andrew E. Son of the late Judge Henry and Mrs. Ann Hitchcock. Died on Sunday morning the 8th inst. Aged 17 years.
The Christian Record. (Sat., Oct. 14, 1848)

Hitchcock, Andrew Erwin. Son of the late Judge Henry and Mrs. Ann
Hitchcock. Died in Nashville on Sat. the 8th inst. in the 18th
year of his age.
The Christian Record. (Sat., Oct. 21, 1848)

Hitchcock, Hon. Henry. In the 48th year of his age. Died in Mobile,
Ala. on the 11th of Aug.
Daily Republican Banner. (Thurs., Aug. 22, 1839)

Hitchcock, Hon. Henry. Late Judge of the Supreme Court of Alabama.
Died at his residence in Mobile, Ala. on Sunday Aug. 11, 1839.
Nashville Union. (Fri., Sept. 6, 1839)

Hitchcock, Hon. Henry. In the 48th year of his age. Died at his
residence in Mobile, Ala. on Aug. 11.
Nashville Whig. (Fri., Aug. 30, 1839)

Hitchcock, Mr. James H. Died in Columbia.
National Banner & Nashville Daily Advertiser. (Wed., April 24, 1833)

Hite, Capt. Abraham. Aged 71 years. Died in Jefferson County, Ky.
An officer of the revolution.
National Banner & Nashville Daily Advertiser. (Tues., July 17, 1832)

Hite, Mary Ann Eliza Virginia. Infant daughter of Mr. Z and Mrs.
Mary Hite. Died at 4 P.M. on the 26th ult.
National Banner & Nashville Whig. (Fri., May 8, 1835)

Hiter, J. Y. Esq. Aged 63. Died in Clarksville.
Nashville Whig. (Thurs., April 30, 1846)

Hixon, Mrs. Rachel. Mother. Died in short Mountain Township Crawford
County, Ark.
National Banner & Nashville Whig. (Fri., March 27, 1835)

Hixon, Miss Sally. Died in Short Mountain Township, Crawford City, Ark. Feb. 17, 1835.
National Banner & Nashville Whig. (Fri., March 27, 1835)

Hixon, Mr. Samuel. Son. Died Feb. 26, in Short Township, Crawford County, Ark.
National Banner & Nashville Whig. (Fri., March 27, 1835)

Hixon, Mr. Thomas. Father. Died in Short Mountain Township, Crawford County, Ark. Feb. 23.
National Banner & Nashville Whig. (Fri., March 27, 1835)

Hixon, Mr. Thomas Jr. Son. Died in Short Mountain Township, Crawford County, Ark. Feb. 22.
National Banner & Nashville Whig. (Fri., March 27, 1835)

Hixon, Mr. William. Son. Died Feb. 23 in Short Mountain Township, Crawford County, Ark.
National Banner & Nashville Whig. (Fri., March 27, 1835)

Hoard, Mr. Stanwix. Died in Washington County.
National Banner & Nashville Whig. (Sat., Dec. 23, 1826)

Hobbs, C. S. Died in Nashville.
Nashville Republican & State Gazette. (Tues., March 29, 1831)

Hobbs, Mr. Colin S. Died in Nashville this morning.
National Banner & Nashville Whig. (Fri., March 25, 1831)

Hobbs, Ensign Oliver G. Died in Nashville last evening of a wound received in the late Seminole Campaign.
Nashville Republican. (Tues., March 28, 1837)

Hobbs, Ensign Oliver C. Late of Nashville State Guards. Died in Nashville on Monday last of a wound received in the Florida campaign.
The Union. (Thurs., March 30, 1837)

Hobbs, Sergeant Oliver G. Died from wound received in the war with the Indians in Florida. National Banner & Nashville Whig. (Mon., April 17, 1837)

Hobbs, Mr. Thomas. Ranger of Bedford County. Died in Shelbyville on the 16th inst.
The Christian Record. (Sat., March 20, 1847)

Hobbs, Mr. Warren. Aged 26. Of Danvers, Mass. Died on the 11th inst.
National Banner & Nashville Whig. (Sat., July 29, 1826)

Hobbs, William H. In the 22nd year of his age. Died in Nashville yesterday morning.
Daily Republican Banner. (Mon., Nov. 12, 1838)

Hobbs, William H. Printer. Died yesterday morning Nov. 11, funeral this afternoon at 2 O'clock from the residence of Mr. P. W. Moxey.
Nashville Union. (Mon., Nov. 12, 1838)

Hobbs, William H. Printer aged 24. Died yesterday morning, funeral this afternoon at 2 O'clock from the residence of the Mother of the deceased, Broad Street.
Nashville Whig. (Mon., Nov. 12, 1838)

Hobson, John. In the 52d year of his age. Died near Nashville on the first day of Oct. He was a native of Virginia.
National Banner & Nashville Whig. (Fri., Oct. 7, 1836)

Hobson, John. A native of Boston, Mass. Died in Pensacola, Fla.

He was found death in the market about day light on the morning of
the 8th of July.
National Banner & Nashville Daily Advertiser. (Thurs., Aug. 8, 1833)

Hobson, Joseph. In the 23d year of his age. Died on Sat. last while
out hunting, he accidently shot himself.
Nashville Whig. (Tues., Nov. 22, 1842)

Hobson, Mrs. Susanna A. Consort of Mr. Nichols Hobson of this county.
Died on Friday morning last the 7th inst.
Nashville Whig. (Feb. 26, 1823)

Hobson, Master William. Youngest son of the late Captain Wm. Hobson
of this County. Died on Wednesday morning.
Nashville Whig. (July 12, 1824)

Hodge, Mr. Joseph H. Aged 40. Died in Pulaski on June 5 of Cholera.
National Banner & Nashville Daily Advertiser. (Wed., June 19, 1833)

Hodge, Mrs. Letitia. Consort of Dr. William Hodge. Died in Gallatin,
Tenn.
Nashville Republican & State Gazette. (Sat., April 23, 1831)

Hodge, Maj. Samuel M. Died in Rutherford County.
Nashville Whig. (Sat., April 11, 1846)

Hodgen, Rev. Isaac. Died in Green County, Ky.
National Banner. (April 28, 1826)

Hodges, Miss Cecilia. Died in Logan County, Ky.
National Banner & Nashville Daily Advertiser. (Sat., April 13, 1833)

Hodges, Warren. Died at the residence of Dr. Green four miles from
Florence. He was from Logan County, Ky. Died of Cholera.
National Banner & Nashville Whig. (Wed., Oct. 1, 1834)

Hodsden, Mrs. Elizabeth. Consort of Dr. Robert H. Hodsden. Died in
Maryville, E. Tenn.
Nashville Whig. (Sat., Aug. 6, 1842)

Hoffman, Hon. Isaiah Ogden. One of the Judges of the Superior Court
on New York. Died in New York on the 24th Jan.
National Banner & Nashville Whig. (Mon., Feb. 13, 1837)

Hogan, Thomas Esq. One of the proprietors and late editor of the
Nashville Union. Died on Saturday night last.
Nashville Whig. (Tues., May 14, 1844)

Hoge, Edward. Aged 59. Died in Warren County.
Nashville Whig. (Fri., Sept. 11, 1840)

Hoge, Miss Elizabeth Lacy. Daughter of the late Rev. Samuel Davis
Hoge of Virginia. Died in Clarksville on Sat. last.
The Politician & Nashville Weekly Whig. (Fri., April 16, 1847)

Hoge, Rev. Samuel D. Died at Athens, Ohio.
National Banner & Nashville Whig. (Sat., Jan. 20, 1827)

Hogg, Mr. Harvey Mr. Merchant of Carthage, Ten. Died at the
Castatian Springs in Sumner County, Sat. the 28th Nov.
Daily Republican Banner. (Fri., Dec. 4, 1840)

Hogg, James B. Son of Dr. Samuel Hogg. Died in Nashville of Cholera.
National Banner & Nashville Daily Advertiser. (Wed., June 5, 1833)

Hogg, Maj. John B. Of Trenton. Died in Dickson County on Friday last
in the 49th year of his age.
National Banner & Nashville Daily Advertiser. (Tues., June 4, 1833)

Hogg, Dr. Samuel. Formerly of Nashville. Died in Rutherford on the 28th inst.
Nashville Whig. (Tues., May 31, 1842)

Hogg, Mr. Samuel E. Jr. Second son of Dr. Samuel Hogg of Nashville. Died on Sunday morning 6th inst. in the 25th year of his age.
Nashville Whig. (Tues., Feb. 8th, 1842)

Hogg, Doct. T. T. Aged 26 years, 8 weeks and 14 days. Died at Port Gibson on the 28th inst. formerly from Tennessee.
Daily Republican Banner. (Mon., Nov. 16, 1840)

Hogg, Dr. T. T. In the 27th of his age. Died at Port Gibson, Miss on the 28th ult. formerly of Nashville and son of Dr. Samuel Hogg.
Nashville Whig. (Mon., Nov. 16, 1840)

Hoggatt, Abram S. Esq. Of this County in the 27th year of his age. Died on the same day (Tuesday last).
Nashville Whig. (Aug. 30, 1824)

Hoggatt, Mrs. Diana. In the 62 year of her age. Died on the 10th inst. in this county.
National Banner & Nashville Whig. (Fri., July 25, 1828)

Hoggatt, Captain John. An Officer in the Revolutionary War. Died on Wednesday last.
Nashville Whig. (Aug. 2, 1824)

Hogshead, Wm. Esq. Died in Anderson County.
National Banner & Nashville Whig. (Sat., May 24, 1828)

Hogue, Mr, David. Of Indiana. Died at Maryville.
National Banner & Nashville Whig. (Mon., June 6, 1831)

Holcombe, Hon. George. Died at Allenton, N. J. Member of Congress from New Jersey.
National Banner & Nashville Whig. (Sat., Feb. 9, 1828)

Holcombe, Col. Philomel. Aged 72 years. Died in Fayette County, Ten. A patriot of the revolutionary army.
National Banner & Nashville Whig. (Wed., Nov. 26, 1834)

Holder, Ezera Esq. Editor of the Philadelphia Courier. Died in Washington City.
Nashville Whig. (Tues., March 31, 1846)

Holderman, Mr. Jacob. Died in Hart County.
National Banner & Nashville Whig. (Sat., Oct. 6, 1827)

Holeman, James T. Esq. Attorney at law. Died suddenly near Nashville on Saturday last.
Nashville Whig. (Mon., Feb. 18, 1839)

Holland, Mr. Alexander G. Aged 28 years. Died at his residence on Bradleys Creek, Wilson County on the morning of 21st of May.
National Banner & Nashville Daily Advertiser. (Wed., May 29, 1833)

Holland, Mrs. Elizabeth L. Wife of Dr. R. C. Holland and daughter of Mr. Nelson & Mrs. Sarah Turner. Died in Louisville, Ky. Oct. 12th 1850. The deceased was born in Lexington, Ky. Feb. 14th 1825.
Nashville True Whig & Weekly Commercial Register. (Wed., Dec. 25, 1850)

Holland, John. Aged 92. Died in Yalabusha County, Miss. He was born and raised in Bedford County, Virginia and fought in the Revolutionary War.
Nashville Union. (Mon., Dec. 9, 1839)

Holland, Mr. Joseph. A native of Baltimore. Died in Mobile, Ala of Yellow Fever, aged 45.
Daily Republican Banner. (Tues., Oct. 1, 1839)

Hollett, Collingwood. Son of James & Ann Hollett. Died in Nashville on Monday 23rd, aged 5 weeks.
The Politician & Weekly Nashville Whig. (Wed., Sept. 1st. 1847)

Holley, Rev. Horrace, D. D. Late president of Transylvania University. Died at Sea on passage from New Orleans to Liverpool.
National Banner & Nashville Whig. (Sat., Sept. 1, 1827)

Holliman, Mrs. Consort of Mr. Joel Holliman. Died in Smith County, Ten.
National Banner & Nashville Advertiser. (Fri., June 22, 1832)

Hollingsworth, Mrs. Eliza. Wife of Henry Hollingsworth, Esq. Mayor of Nashville, aged 21. Died in Nashville yesterday.
Nashville Union. (Mon., May 20, 1839)

Hollingsworth, Mrs. Rachel. Relict of the late John Hollingsworth Esq. Died at Pittsburgh, Penn. on Saturday the 7th inst. in the 77th year of her age. She was the daughter of John Wilkins Esq. a captain in the revolutionary war.
Nashville Whig. (Thurs., Sept. 19, 1844)

Hollism Mr. Jesse. Died in Wilson Co., Ten.
National Banner & Nashville Daily Advertiser. (Mon., Aug. 25, 1834)

Holloway, Miss Clara. Died at Louisville, Ky.
National Banner & Nashville Whig. (Mon., April 4, 1831)

Holloway, Miss Clara. Died in Louisville, Ky.
National Banner & Nashville Whig. (Mon., April 11, 1831)

Holloway, Mr. Jesse H. Died near Athens, Ala.
National Banner & Nashville Whig. (Sat., Feb. 19, 1828)

Holloway, Mary. The daughter of Betsey Holloway, aged 8 years. Died in Fayetteville.
National Banner & Nashville Whig. (Sat., Sept. 8, 1827)

Hollowa-, Mrs. Mary Jane. Consort of Mr. George Holloway. Died in Franklin City, Ky.
National Banner & Nashville Daily Advertiser. (Mon., May 21, 1832)

Holman, Mr. Daniel H. Aged 21. Died in Lincoln County, on the 26th ult.
National Banner & Nashville Whig. (Sat., Sept. 8, 1827)

Holman, G. Esq. Late manager of the Charleston Theatre in the 53d year of his age. Died at the watering place Rockaway, Long Island on Sunday morning, the 24th ult.
The Nashville Whig. (Sept. 29, 1817)

Holman, Col. James T. A member of the Nashville Bar. Died in the vicinity of Nashville on Saturday.
Daily Republican Banner. (Mon., Feb. 18, 1839)

Holmes, Mrs. Aged 40 years. Longworth Street. Died in Cincinnati. of Cholera on Oct. 11th.
National Banner & Nashville Daily Advertiser. (Wed., Oct. 17, 1832)

Holmes, David Esq. Late Governor of Mississippi and United States Senator from Miss. Died at Duvalls, Sulphur Springs near Winchester in Frederick County, Va. on Monday the 20th inst.
National Banner & Nashville Daily Advertiser. (Sat., Sept. 8, 1832)

Holmes, Hon. Gabriel. Died in Sampson County, North Carolina. Member of Congress elect and late Governor the State.
National Banner. (Sat., Oct. 24, 1829)

Holmes, Mrs. Hannah. Died in Nashville.
National Banner & Nashville Whig. (Tues., Feb. 2, 1830)

Holmes, Capt. R. Of the U. S. Dragoons. Died on the 4th inst. at Jefferson Barracks.
National Banner & Nashville Daily Advertiser. (Fri., Nov. 15, 1833)

Holmes, Robert. Infant son of Mr. Jas. Holmes. Died in Murfreesborough
National Banner & Nashville Daily Advertiser. (Sat., Sept. 6, 1834)

Holt, Isaac W. M. H. Age about 8 years son of Dr. Holt. Died in Bedford County.
National Banner & Nashville Whig. (Wed., Feb. 4, 1835)

Holt, Mrs. Jane. Died in Bourbon County, Ky.
National Banner. (March 24, 1824)

Holt, Mr. John. Died in Maury County.
National Banner & Nashville Whig. (Sat., May 19, 1827)

Holt, Mr. John C. Died in Florence, Ala.
National Banner & Nashville Daily Advertiser. (Tues., Dec. 18, 1832)

Holt, Mr. John C. Died in Florence.
Nashville Republican & State Gazette. (Mon., Dec. 17, 1832)

Holt, William C. Esq. Died in Norfolk, Va. For many years speaker of the Senate of Va.
Nashville Republican & State Gazette. (Wed., Dec. 12, 1832)

Holyoke, Dr. Edward Augustus. Aged 100. Died at Salem, Mass.
National Banner. (Sat., April 18, 1829)

Hood, Mrs. Isabella. Wife of Mr. John B. Hood. Died at Athens.
National Banner & Nashville Whig. (Wed., March 9, 1831)

Hood, Mrs. Isabella. Died in Athens, Ten.
Nashville Republican & State Gazette. (Thurs., March 3, 1831)

Hood, Mr. James. Formerly a Merchant of Nashville. Died at Florence, Ala.
Nashville Whig. (Wed., Oct. 9, 1839)

Hooe, William Fitzhugh. Passed Midhsipman of the U. S. Navy. Died in King George County, Va.
National Banner & Nashville Daily Advertiser. (Fri., Aug. 30, 1833)

Hook, Dr. John. Lately from Virginia. Died in Nashville on Monday last.
Impartial Review and Cumberland Repository. (Thurs., Oct. 1, 1807)

Hooper, Infant daughter of Mr. J. Hooper. Died in Wilson County, Louisiana.
National Banner & Nashville Daily Advertiser. (Mon., March 31, 1834)

Hooper, Mr. Age 50. Died in Blount County, Ten.
National Banner & Nashville Advertiser. (Tues., June 26, 1832)

Hooper, Mr. Daniel. Died in Knox County.
National Banner & Nashville Whig. (Sat., Oct. 6, 1827)

Hooper, Mrs. Elizabeth. Aged 63 years. Died in Davidson County on the 10th June relict of the late Capt. Joseph Hooper.
National Banner & Nashville Daily Advertiser. (Tues., June 12, 1832)

Hooper, Mrs. Mary Ann. Consort of C. Y. Hooper Esq. Died in the
vicinity of Nashville March 28th in the 35th year of her age.
Daily Republican Banner. (Thurs., April 2, 1840)

Hooper, Mrs. Mary Ann. Consort of C. V. Hooper Esq. Died in
Davidson County, March 28th in the 25th year of her age.
Nashville Whig. (Wed., April 1, 1840)

Hoover, Andrew Jackson Esq. A Representative in General Assembly.
Died in Murfreesborough on Saturday the 11th inst.
The Nashville Union. (Tues., Nov. 14, 1837)

Hope, Mr. Benjamin. A soldier of the Revolution. Died at Williams-
boro, N. C.
National Banner & Nashville Daily Advertiser. (Tues., Feb. 11, 1834)

Hoover, Mr. Philip. Late of Nashville. Died in Hickman County on the
18th inst.
National Banner & Nashville Whig. (Wed., June 22, 1831)

Hoover, James Priestly. Age 11 months. Infant son of Philip Hoover.
Died in Hickman County on the 5th inst.
National Banner & Nashville Whig. (Wed., April 27, 1831)

Hoover, Mr. Philip. Late of this place. Died in Hickman County on
18th inst.
Nashville Republican & State Gazette. (Thurs., June 23, 1831)

Hope, John Esq. Formerly member of the legislature of Tennessee.
Died at New Orleans of the prevailing fever.
National Banner. (Sat., Sept. 19, 1829)

Hope, Mrs. Mary. Aged 70 years. Consort of Adam Hope, Esq. Died
in Davidson County on the 22d ult.
Nashville Union. (Thurs., April 5, 1838)

Hope, Mr. Ralph I. Died at Knoxville.
National Banner & Nashville Whig. (Sat., Jan. 19, 1828)

Hopkins, Benjamin. Died at Cincinnati, Ohio on 13th of Cholera.
National Banner & Nashville Daily Advertiser. (Sat., Oct. 20, 1832)

Hopkins, Miss Catherine P. In the 16th year of her age. Departed
this life at Carthage on the 26th ult.
Nashville Whig. (Jan. 15, 1823)

Hopkins, Mrs. Cynthia. Aged 32 years. Died in Williamson County of
consumption.
National Banner & Nashville Daily Advertiser. (Mon., May 26, 1834)

Hopkins, Edward. Died at Cincinnati, Ohio of Cholera.
National Banner & Nashville Daily Advertiser. (Tues., Oct. 23, 1832)

Hopkins, Mr. Francis H. Died in St. Louis.
National Banner & Nashville Whig. (Sept. 2, 1826)

Hopkins, Mrs. Jane E. Died in Christian County, Ky.
National Banner & Nashville Advertiser. (Tues., June 26, 1832)

Hopkins, Lacy Esq. Died in Madison County, Ala.
Nashville Republican & State Gazette. (Thurs., Feb. 24, 1831)

Hopkins, Miss Mary. Died at Cincinnati, Ohio on 13th of Cholera.
National Banner & Nashville Daily Advertiser. (Tues., Oct. 23, 1832)

Hopkins, Mr. Samuel. Formerly of Powhatan County, Va. Died in this
town on Sunday last.
National Banner & Nashville Whig. (Sat., April 28, 1827)

Hopkins, Miss Sophronia. Aged 20. Died in Chillicothe.
National Banner & Nashville Whig. (Sat., Aug. 19, 1826)

Hopkins, Mr. Thomas. In the 73rd year of his age. Died in Warren
County on the 30th March.
National Banner & Nashville Whig. (Fri., April 1, 1836)

Hopkins, Mr. Thomas. In the 73d year of his age. Died on the 20th
inst. at the house of Mr. Routon, 30 or 35 miles from Nashville.
The Union. (Sat., April 9, 1836)

Hopkins, Mr. W. D. Died in Williamson County, Tennessee.
National Banner & Nashville Daily Advertiser. (Wed., Aug. 20, 1834)

Hopson, Mr. William. Died in Christian County, Ky.
National Banner & Nashville Daily Advertiser. (Fri., Nov. 23, 1832)

Horn, Mrs. Charity. Died in Sumner County.
National Banner & Nashville Whig. (Wed., Feb. 16, 1831)

Hornbeak, Mrs. Sarah. Died in Hickman County, Tennessee.
Nashville Republican & State Gazette. (Thurs., Oct. 6, 1831)

Horton, Col. Daniel. Aged 39. Died in Madison County, T.
National Banner & Nashville Whig. (Sat., Sept. 9, 1826)

Horton, John D. Infant son of Joseph W. Horton Esq. Died in Davidson
County on 19th inst.
National Banner & Nashville Daily Advertiser. (Wed., June 20, 1832)

Horton, Joseph W. Esq. Cashier of the Bank of the State of Tenn.
Died on the morning of the 1st inst. at his residence near Nashville.
The Christian Record. (Sat., Nov. 14, 1846)

Horton, Joseph W. Cashier of the Bank of the State of Tennessee.
Died on the morning of the 1st inst. at his residence near Nashville.
Nashville Whig. (Tues., Nov. 3, 1846)

Horton, Josiah Esq. Formerly Sheriff of this County. Died in this
county on Tuesday last.
National Banner & Nashville Whig. (Sat., July 14, 1827)

Horton, Mrs. Lavinia. Relict of the late Col. D. Horton. Died in
Madison County.
National Banner & Nashville Whig. (Sat., Sept. 16, 1826)

Horton, Miss Leticia Ann. Daughter of William Horton Esq. Died near
Huntingdon in Carroll County on 29th Oct. in the 19th year of her
age.
National Banner & Nashville Daily Advertiser. (Wed., Nov. 7, 1832)

Hoskins, James G. Esq. Died in Montgomery County, Ten.
Daily Republican Banner. (Wed., Jan. 17, 1838)

Hosmer, Hon. Stephen Titus. Died in Middletown, Conn. late Chief
Justice of the Supreme Court of that state.
National Banner & Nashville Daily Advertiser. (Sat., Sept. 6, 1834)

Hoss, Capt. John. Died in Jonesborough, East Tenn.
Daily Republican Banner. (Wed., July 29, 1840)

Houlsowser, Mr. Michael. Died in Lauderdale County, Ala.
National Banner & Nashville Whig. (Sat., July 22, 1826)

House, James Hamilton. Son of Mr. & Mrs. George W. House. Died -
funeral this morning at 10 o'clock Dec. 21, 1844 by Dr. Edgar.
Nashville Whig. (Sat., Dec. 21, 1844)

Houston, Mrs. Elizabeth. Mother of the former Governor of Ten.
Age 73. Died in Blount County on the 8th inst.
National Banner & Nashville Whig. (Mon., Sept. 19, 1831)

Houston, Mrs. Elizabeth. Mother of Gen. Sam Houston. Died in Blount
County, Ten. Age 73 years.
The Western Weekly Review. (Fri., Sept. 23, 1831) Franklin, Tenn.

Houston, Mr. James B. For many years an industrious citizen of this
place. Died on Saturday last.
Nashville Whig. (May 31, 1824)

Howard, Abraham. Of the firm of Howard & Merry Baston. Died in the
wreck of the steamboat Lexington.
Daily Republican Banner. (Fri., Jan. 31, 1840)

Howard, Mrs. Ann. In the 94 year of her age. Died in Bardstown, Ky.
National Banner & Nashville Whig. (Wed., Nov. 12, 1834)

Howard, Dr. Asa. Aged 25. Died at Reynoldsburg.
National Banner & Nashville Whig. (Sat., Nov. 18, 1826)

Howard, Hon. Daniel. Died in West Bridgewater, Mass.
National Banner & Nashville Daily Advertiser. (Fri., Sept. 20, 1833)

Howard, Mrs. Henreittta. Wife of Thomas Howard Esq. One of the
representative from Franklin County. Died in Franklin County.
Nashville Whig. (Mon., Nov. 11, 1839)

Howard, Horton. His wife and daughter. Died in Columbus, O.
National Banner & Nashville Daily Advertiser. (Tues., Sept. 3, 1833)

Howard, Miss Jane Elizabeth. Died in Henry County.
National Banner & Nashville Daily Advertiser. (Wed., July 24, 1833)

Howard, Mr. Robert R. Firm Howard and Manning. Died near Boston by
drowning when the Steam Boat, Bunker Hill was wrecked by the wind.
National Banner & Nashville Daily Advertiser. (Sat., June 30, 1832)

Howard, Mrs. Sally. Wife of Mr. George Howard. Died in Cincinnati, O.
National Banner & Nashville Daily Advertiser. (Thurs., Aug. 22, 1833)

Howard, Dr. William. Died in Baltimore.
National Banner & Nashville Daily Advertiser. (Sat., Sept. 6, 1834)

Howell, Charles Trabue. Youngest son of Rev. R. B. C. Howell. Aged
2 years and 9 months.
Daily Republican Banner. (Wed., July 24, 1839)

Howell, Charles Trabue. Infant son of Rev. R. B. C. Howell. Died on
Monday night aged 2 years and 9 months.
Nashville Whig. (Wed., July 24, 1839)

Howell, Mr. Courtland. Died at Louisville, Ky. Formerly of Philadelphia.
National Banner & Nashville Whig. (Thurs., May 20, 1830)

Howell, Dr. James. Died in Clarksville.
Nashville Whig. (Tues., July 14, 1846)

Howell, Major John. Died lately in New Orleans. Major John Howell
of Robertson County very suddenly.
Nashville Whig. (April 18, 1815)

Howell, Richard Crawford. Second son of Rev. R. B. C. Howell. Died at
4 o'clock on the morning of Thursday 15th May.
National Banner & Nashville Whig. (Wed., May 20, 1835)

Howell, Mrs. Sophia. Consort of John J. Howell Esq. Died in Newport, Tenn. Aged about 46 years.
National Banner & Nashville Whig. (Mon., Nov. 24, 1834)

Howell, Mr. Wm. Aged 35. Died in Mobile.
National Banner & Nashville Whig. (Sat., Sept. 30, 1826)

Howell, Col. William S. Died in Knoxville, Tenn. with the Fever.
Daily Republican Banner. (Sat., Oct. 13, 1838)

Howerton, Ann C. Daughter of Wm. Howerton, dec'd. Died in Shelby County, Tenn. of Cholera.
National Banner & Nashville Whig. (Wed., Aug. 5, 1835)

Howerton, Rufus Y. Son of Wm. Howerton, Dec'd. Died in Shelby County, Tenn. of Cholera.
National Banner & Nashville Whig. (Wed., Aug. 5, 1835)

Howerton, William. Died in Shelby County, Tennessee on the 6th of July of Cholera.
National Banner & Nashville Whig. (Wed., Aug. 5, 1835)

Howlett, Isaac Grandeson. Son of Maj. Isaac H. and Elizabeth M. Howlett. Died in Madison County, Tenn. on the 27th June at his brothers, Dr. G. C. Howlett.
Nashville Whig. (Tues., July 7, 1846)

Howlett, Maj. Isaac H. In the 47th year of his age. Died in Davidson County on Monday morning last. A native of Virginia.
National Banner & Nashville Daily Advertiser. (Thurs., Aug. 22, 1833)

Howlett, Mr. William. Died in Davidson County.
Nashville Republican & State Gazette. (Thurs., April 19, 1831)

Howlett, Mr. William. Died in Davidson County on Monday morning 11th April in the 56th year of his age.
National Banner & Nashville Whig. (Mon., April 18, 1831)

Hoyle, Mrs. Sarah. Died in M'Minn County.
National Banner & Nashville Whig. (Mon., Nov. 15, 1830)

Hoyt, Mrs. Adeline F. Wife of Mr. David Hoyt, Bookseller and daughter of Mr. Ephraim Mason of Hubbardstown, Mass. Died in Rochester, N.Y.
National Banner & Nashville Whig. (Wed., Sept. 14, 1831)

Hubbard, Adolphus Frederick, Esq. Formerly Lieut. Governor of Ill. Died in Quincy, Illinois.
National Banner & Nashville Daily Advertiser. (Thurs., Oct. 4, 1832)

Hubbard, Thomas Esq. Died in Mobile.
National Banner & Nashville Whig. (Sat., Sept. 30, 1826)

Hubbell, Capt. William. An aged and respectable citizen. Died in Georgetown, Ky.
National Banner & Nashville Whig. (Mon., May 23, 1831)

Hubble, Mr. Peter. Died at New Orleans on the 25th.
National Banner & Nashville Daily Advertiser. (Tues., Sept. 10, 1833)

Huber, Mrs. Died in Danville, Ky. of Cholera.
National Banner & Nashville Daily Advertiser. (Mon., Aug. 5, 1833)

Hudiburg, Son of Lewis Hudiburg. Died in Knoxville, Tenn.
Daily Republican Banner. (Sat., Oct. 6, 1838)

Hidiburg, Mrs. Wife of Lewis Hudiburg, Died in Knoxville, Tenn.
Daily Republican Banner. (Sat., Sept. 29, 1838)

Hudiburg, Lewis. Died in Knoxville, Ten. of Fever.
Daily Republican Banner. (Sat., Oct. 13, 1838)

Child of Mr. C. Hughes. Died in Danville, Ky. of Cholera.
National Banner & Nashville Daily Advertiser. (Mon., Aug. 5, 1833)

Hughes, A. M. Late clerk of the Senate of this state. Died in Dresden
Daily Republican Banner. (Wed., Sept. 3, 1838)

Hughes, Beverly Esq. Died near Vicksburg, Miss.
National Banner & Nashville Whig. (Sat., Feb. 24, 1827)

Hughes, Mr. Abner. Died in Sullivan on the 3d inst. He was a native
of North Carolina and came to Tenn. when a youth.
Nashville Union. (Fri., Dec. 20, 1839)

Hughes, Capt. Blackmore. Aged 23. Died in Blount County.
National Banner & Nashville Whig. (Sept. 2, 1826)

Hughes, Capt. David. Died in Hindastan, Ia.
National Banner & Nashville Whig. (Sat., Sept. 9, 1826)

Hughes, Mr. Henry S. Died in Philadelphia.
National Banner & Nashville Whig. (Wed., Sept. 7, 1831)

Hughes, Mr. Joseph. Aged 50. Died at the Hermitage the residence of
Gen. Jackson.
National Banner & Nashville Whig. (Sat., Sept. 27, 1828)

Hughes, Mrs. Mary. Widow of the late James Hughes of Frankford, Ky.
Died at the residence of her brother Judge Humphreys.
National Banner & Nashville Whig. (Sat., Oct. 13)

Hughes, Olivia. Aged 4 months, youngest child of Oliver H. Hughes.
Died on Wednesday 27th.
Daily Republican Banner. (Sat., June 30, 1838)

Hughes, Olivia. Youngest child of O. H. Hughes. Died on Thursday
28th inst. aged 4 months.
Nashville Whig. (Fri., June 29, 1838)

Hughes, Mr. Robert. Died at Richmond, Va.
National Banner & Nashville Advertiser. (Mon., Jan. 9, 1832)

Hughes, Robert B. Aged 34 years. Died in Marshall County, Tenn. on
the 11th inst.
Daily Republican Banner. (Wed., Sept. 23, 1840)

Hughes, William H. Died in Lawrence County, Ala.
Nashville Republican & State Gazette. (Thurs., July 7, 1831)

Hughes, William R. Aged 39 years. Died in Marshall County, Ten.
Formerly of Henry County, Va.
Daily Republican Banner. (Wed., Sept. 23, 1840)

Hughs, Mr. Edward. Died in Logan County, Ky.
National Banner & Nashville Daily Advertiser. (Mon., June 17, 1833)

Hughs, Mr. Jas. Sr. Aged 60. Died in Franklin, Tenn. on Sat. 4th
inst. of Cholera.
National Banner & Nashville Whig. (Fri., July10, 1835)

Hull, Miss Clarissa M. Daughter of Alexander & Elizabeth Hull. Died
in Russellville, Ky. on the 8th inst. aged 17 years.
The Politician & Weekly Nashville Whig. (Fri., July 23, 1847)

Hull, George W. Aged 22. Died at Russellville, Ky. on Tuesday last.
Daily Republican Banner. (Fri., Dec. 8, 1839)

Hull, Mr. Isaac. Died in Mercer County.
National Banner & Nashville Whig. (Sat., Sept. 1, 1827)

Hull, Rev. J. F. Rector of Christ Church. Died in New Orleans.
National Banner & Nashville Daily Advertiser. (Thurs., June 20, 1833)

Hull, Mr. Peter. Died at Lexington, Ky.
National Banner & Nashville Whig. (Sat., July 28, 1827)

Hull, Gen. William. Aged 72 years. Died at Newton, Mass.
National Banner. (Dec. 23, 1825)

Hulme, Mr. George Esq. Aged nearly 74 years. Died in Williamson
County, Tenn.
National Banner & Nashville Whig. (Wed., April 8, 1835)

Hume, Alfred Esq. Resolutions on his death by the Mayor and Alderman
of the City of Nashville.
Republican Banner and Nashville Whig. (No. 267 Mon., Oct. 29, 1853)

Hume, Rev. William. Died in Nashville on Thursday, May 23.
National Banner & Nashville Daily Advertiser. (Fri., May 24th, 1833)

Humes, Thomas Esq. Aged 54. Died at Huntsville, Ala.
National Banner & Nashville Whig. (Mon., Nov. 15,1830)

Hummel, Mr. Jacob Sen. Aged 67 years and 1 day.
Died on the 22d ult. in Penns. Township, Union County. He was one of
the veterans of the revolution.
National Banner & Nashville Daily Advertiser. (Fri., March 23, 1832)

Humphrey, William Harvey. Infant son of Julius and Eliza Humphrey.
Died near Nashville on the 10th inst.
Nashville Whig. (Mon., Oct. 12, 1840)

Humphreys, Mrs. Wife of Capt. Benj. Humphries of Williamson County.
Died on 22, she left husband and nine children.
Impartial Review and Cumberland Repository. (Thurs., July 28, 1808)

Humphreys, Charles Esq. Counsellor at law. Died at Lexington, Ky.
National Banner & Nashville Whig. (Mon., Oct. 11, 1830)

Humphreys, Gideon P. Infant son of West H. Humphreys, Esq. Died in
Nashville yesterday.
Nashville Whig. (Mon., Sept. 7, 1840)

Humphreys, Martha Adeline. Eldest daughter of Dr. E. Humphreys.
Died in Auburn, N.Y. on the 23d inst. Aged 22 years.
Nashville Whig. (Thurs., Oct. 20, 1842)

Humphreys, Miss Mary. Daughter of Mr. John Humphreys. Died near
Athens, Ala.
National Banner & Nashville Daily Advertiser. (Mon., Feb. 18, 1833)

Humphreys, Hon. Parry W. Died at Hernando, DeSota County on Sat. last.
Formerly a member of Congress from Tenn. Judge of the Supreme Court.
From Marshall Co. (Mi.) Republican.
Nashville Union. (Mon., Feb. 25, 1839)

Humphreys, Hon. Parry W. Late of Tennessee. Died at his residence
in Hermondo, Miss.
Nashville Whig. (Wed., Feb. 27, 1839)

Humphreys, Mr. Wm. Son of Charles Humphreys, Esq. Died at Lexington,
Ky.
National Banner & Nashville Whig. (June 17, 1826)

Hundley, David Mr. In the 25th year of his age. Died in Jonesborough, Tenn.
National Banner & Nashville Whig. (Fri., Jan. 9, 1835)

Hundley, Mr. John W. Died in Jefferson County, Ky.
National Banner & Nashville Whig. (Mon., Oct. 4, 1830)

Hungerford, Gen. J. P. A soldier of the Revolution and formerly a member of Congress. Died in Westmoreland, Va.
National Banner & Nashville Daily Advertiser. (Tues., Feb. 11, 1834)

Hunt, Andrew H. Esq. Died at Natchez, Miss.
National Banner & Nashville Daily Advertiser. (Mon., July 23, 1832)

Hunt, Andrew Jackson. Editor of the Times. Died at Little Rock, Ark.
National Banner & Nashville Whig. (Fri., Oct. 2, 1835)

Hunt, Mr. Caswell. Died in Shelbyville.
Nashville Whig. (Tues., April 21, 1846)

Hunt, Charlton Esq. Aged about 35. Died in Lexington, Ky. yesterday evening.
National Banner & Nashville Whig. (Fri., Jan. 6, 1837)

Hunt, Mr. Henry H. Died at Pensacola on the 17th ult. Aged 30, late of Lexington, Ky. and brother of the editor of this paper.
National Banner & Nashville Whig. (Sat., Oct. 20, 1827)

Hunt, Henry J. Esq. Mayor of the City. Died at Detroit.
National Banner & Nashville Whig. (Sat., Oct. 7, 1826)

Hunt, Mr. James. A Revolutionary Soldier, aged 78 years. Died in Rutherford County, Tenn.
National Banner & Nashville Whig. (Mon., Nov. 10, 1834)

Hunt, Dr. John Wilson. Formerly of Lexington, Ky. Aged 26 years. Died in New Orleans.
National Banner & Nashville Daily Advertiser. (Thurs., Aug. 8, 1833)

Hunt, Miss Mary. Daughter of John Hunt, Esq. Died in Claiborne County
National Banner & Nashville Whig. (Sat., Aug. 5, 1826)

Hunt, Lieut. Samuel Wellington. Of the U. S. Army. Died at St. Louis.
National Banner. (Oct. 3, 1829)

Hunt, Sion Esq. Died in Williamson County.
National Banner & Nashville Whig. (Sat., Oct. 7, 1826)

Hunt, Theodore Esq. For many years recorder of land titles in Missouri. Died in St. Louis, Jan. 21st.
National Banner & Nashville Daily Advertiser. (Sat., Feb. 11, 1832)

Hunt, W. Hasell. A Native of Massachusetts. Died at his residence in Nashville on Saturday morning 3d inst. For many years the publisher and associate editor of the Nashville Banner.
Nashville Whig. (Mon., July 5, 1841)

Hunt, Mr. William. Of the circus. Died at New Orleans.
National Banner & Nashville Whig. (Sat., April 12, 1828)

Hunt, William Gibbes Esq. Editor of this paper, a native of Boston, Mass, aged 42 years 6 months. Died in Nashville at 2 o'clock on the morning of Tuesday 13th Aug.
National Banner & Nashville Daily Advertiser. (Wed., Aug. 14, 1833)

Hunter, Mrs. Agnes F. Wife of the Rev. Hiram A. Hunter. Died in Washington, Ind. on the 28th ult.
National Banner. (Sat., Sept. 12, 1829)

191

Hunter, James Esq. Formerly one of the Editors of the Daily Advertiser and recently of the Daily News. Died in Albany, N.Y.
National Banner & Nashville Daily Advertiser. (Fri., Aug. 1, 1834)

Hunter, Maria. Wife of David M. Hunter. Died in Moulton, Mos.
National Banner & Nashville Whig. (Sat., Jan. 20, 1827)

Hunter, Mrs. Mary. Consort of Capt. Jacob Hunter. Died in Nashville on Friday the 8th inst. of Consumption.
Nashville Whig. (Thurs., Sept. 14, 1843)

Hunter, Old Mrs. Died at Versailles, Ky. 14 miles from Lexington, Ky. of Cholera.
National Banner & Nashville Whig. (Fri., Sept. 4, 1835)

Hunter, Mrs. Patience. Died in Maury County.
National Banner & Nashville Whig. (Thurs., Aug. 19, 1830)

Hunter, Capt. W. S. Died at Versailles, Ky. 14 miles from Lexington, Ky. of cholera.
National Banner & Nashville Whig. (Fri., Sept. 4, 1835)

Huntingdon, Mrs. Maria. Late of Natchez. Died at Cincinnati.
National Banner. (Sat., Sept. 12, 1829)

Huntsman, Miss Malinda. Daughter of Adam Huntsman, Esq. of Madison County. Age 15. Died in Lincoln County.
National Banner & Nashville Whig. (Sat., Aug. 19, 1826)

Hurst, Mr. James H. Of Philadelphia, age 22 years. Died in Nashville at the residence of Dr. B. McNairy, on the 5th inst.
National Banner & Nashville Daily Advertiser. (Sat., Sept. 6, 1834)

Hurt, Bird S. Esq. Of Hurts Cross Roads, Maury County. Died at Hot Spring, Arkansas.
Nashville Republican. (Sat., Nov. 12, 1836)

Hurt, Mr. Floyd. In the 57th year of his age. Died in this vicinity on the 25th inst.
Nashville Whig. (Tues., March 29, 1842)

Hurt, George M. Son of Philip Hurt of Sumner County in the 25th year of his age. Died on the 1st day of April.
The Union. (Tues., April 5, 1836)

Hurt, Mrs. Harriet. Wife of Mr. Alfred Hurt. Died at Lexington, Ky.
National Banner. (Sat., April 18, 1829)

Hurt, Mr. Paul G. Died - drowned in the Appomattox near Petersburg, Va.
National Banner & Nashville Daily Advertiser. (Mon., June 30, 1834)

Huston, Emily. Daughter of Wm. Huston. Died of cholera. Copyed from the Maysville Eagle & Monitor.
National Banner & Nashville Daily Advertiser. (Thurs., June 6, 1833)

Hutchins, Major John. Died lately in Madison County, Alabama Territory
Nashville Whig. (Dec. 1, 1817)

Hutchinson, Miss Isabella. Died in Springfield T. on the 7th inst. Consort of John Hutchinson, Esq.
National Banner & Nashville Whig. (Sat., Sept. 16, 1826)

Hutchinson, Jesse. Died in the City of Boston on Sunday morning last.
Nashville True Whig & Weekly Commercial Register. (Fri., March 7, 1851)

Hutchinson, Mrs. Polly. Wife of Samuel Hutchinson Esq. Died in Logan County, Ky.
National Banner & Nashville Daily Advertiser. (Tues., June 11, 1833)

Hutchinson, Mrs. Sally. Consort of Mr. Wilson Hutchinson. Died on Thursday morning 5th inst. at Springfield, Robertson County.
National Banner & Nashville Whig. (Sat., March 7, 1829)

Hutton, Mr. John M. Died in Williamson County.
National Banner & Nashville Advertiser. (Mon., Sept. 3, 1832)

Hutton, Mr. John M. In the 65th year of his age. Died in Williamson County near Franklin on the 30th inst. The deceased came from Ireland in the year 1784.
The Western Weekly Review. (Frid., Aug. 31, 1832) Franklin, Tenn.

Hyde, Mrs. Lucy. Wife of Maj. Richard Hyde. Died in Williamson County
National Banner & Nashville Whig. (Fri., Sept. 30, 1831)

Hyde, Mrs. Mary D. Consort of Mr. Henry Hyde, dec'd. of Davidson County. Died in Williamsport, Maury Co., Ten. on Friday the 21st Aug. of Cholera.
National Banner & Nashville Whig. (Wed., Aug. 26, 1835)

Hyder, Mrs. Polly. Died in Carter, Tenn.
Nashville Republican & State Gazette. (Fri., Dec. 7, 1832)

Hymes, Mr. George. Died in Bedford County.
National Banner & Nashville Whig. (Wed., Dec. 14, 1831)

Hynes, Ann. Third daughter of Col. A. Hynes. Died on the night of the 12th inst.
National Banner & Nashville Daily Advertiser. (Sat., Dec. 14, 1833)

Hynes, Mrs. Ann E. Consort of Col. Andrew Hynes. Died in this vicinity.
National Banner & Nashville Whig. (Mon., Feb. 20, 1837)

Hynes, Laura. In the 4th year of her age. Died in the neighborhood of Nashville on the 2nd Nov. Daughter of Col. Andrew Haynes.
National Banner & Nashville Daily Advertiser. (Mon., Dec. 16, 1833)

Ideda, John. Of France, a passenger. Died on the Steamer George Collier about 80 miles below Natchez. Scalded to death.
Daily Republican Banner. (Tues., May 14, 1839)

Imes, Miss Minerva. Aged 17 years. Died near Russellville, Ky.
National Banner & Nashville Daily Advertiser. (Mon., Sept. 9, 1833)

Inge, Richard Sen. Esq. Aged 79 years. Died in Tuscaloosa County, Ala. One of the oldest and most respectable citizens.
National Banner & Nashville Advertiser. (Sat., Aug. 24, 1833)

Inge, Col. William M. Of Sumpter County. Died at his residence in Livingston a few days ago.
Nashville Whig. (Mon., Dec. 27, 1841)

Ingersall, Mr. David S. Tragedian, aged about 26 years. Died in Nashville Monday 6th inst.
Nashville Union. (Wed., Aug. 8, 1838)

Ingham, Hon. Sam D. Member of Congress. Died in Bucks County, Penn.
National Banner & Nashville Whig. (Sat., Nov. 29, 1828)

Ingram, Andrew. Died in Knoxville, Tenn. with fever.
Daily Republican Banner. (Sat., Oct. 13, 1838)

Inman, Mr. Henry D. Died in Logan County, Ky.
National Banner & Nashville Whig. (Sat., May 12, 1827)

Innes, Gilbert, Esq. Died at Edinburgh on 26 Feb. Deputy Governor
of the Royal Bank of Scotland.
National Banner & Nashville Advertiser. (Fri., June 1, 1832)

Irby, Mr. John T. Died at Tuscaloosa, Ala.
National Banner & Nashville Whig. (Sat., Nov. 3, 1827)

Irby, Mrs. Sarah. Died near Bowling Green, Ky.
National Banner & Nashville Daily Advertiser. (Wed., July 16, 1834)

Irvine, Mr. Adam. Died Madison County, Ky. Aged 24.
National Banner. (Feb. 10, 1826)

Irvin, Mr. Francis. Died in Campbell County.
National Banner & Nashville Daily Advertiser. (Mon., July 15, 1833)

Irvin, Mrs. Margaret. Wife of the Rev. Mr. Jas. Irvin. Died in
Franklin.
National Banner & Nashville Whig. (Mon., April 11, 1831)

Irvin, Maj. William Sen. Died at Memphis.
National Banner & Nashville Whig. (Sat., Aug. 16, 1828)

Irwin, Adaline B. The only child of the late Joseph M. Irwin of
Nashville. Died at the residence of her grnad-father the Rev. H. F.
Beaumont in Clarksville on the 1st inst.
Nashville True Whig & Weekly Commercial Register. (Fri., Dec. 6, 1850)

Irwin, Mrs. Ann. Wife of Mr. Christopher Irwin. Died in Maury County.
National Banner & Nashville Daily Advertiser. (Wed., Jan. 9, 1833)

Irwin, David. Of Nashville. Died in Pensacola, Florida on the 6th
of Oct.
National Banner & Nashville Whig. (Fri., Oct. 24, 1834)

Irwin, Capt. James. Of Nashville. Died at Paducah, mouth of Tennessee
on Friday last.
National Banner & Nashville Daily Advertiser. (Mon., May 20, 1833)

Irwin, Mr. James H. Died in Clarksville.
National Banner & Nashville Whig. (Sat., Sept. 13, 1828)

Irwin, Capt. Joseph M. In his 38th year. Died in New Orleans on the
2nd of Yellow fever.
The Christian Record. (Sat., Nov. 25, 1848)

Irwin, Mrs. Mary. Died on Wednesday the 18th inst. of a pulmonary
complaint after a long and lingering illness which she bore with
Christian fortitude. The Consort of Mr. David Irwin of this town.
The Nashville Whig. (Dec. 25, 1816)

Irwin, William. Aged 42 years and eleven months. Died in Harden
County, Tenn. on the 18th May.
National Banner & Nashville Daily Advertiser. (Fri., June 13, 1834)

Isaacks, Hon Jacob C. Died in Hardeman County late a representative
in Congress from the mountain District in this state.
National Banner & Nashville Whig. (Fri., Oct. 2, 1835)

Islands, Deacon William. A brother of Joseph Island, aged 26 years.
Died at North Fork in the Creek Nation on the 18th Dec. last.
The Christian Record. (Sat., April 29, 1848)

Isler, Mr. Peter. For many years a printer for the state. Died in
Jackson, Mi.
National Banner & Nashville Daily Advertiser. (Sat., Aug. 24, 1833)

Ivey, James P. From Monroe County. Died at the Tenn. State Prison of Cholera.
National Banner & Nashville Whig. (Fri., Aug. 14, 1835)

Izard, George. Governor of the territory of Arkansas. Died in this place, Little Rock, Ark. on Nov. 22d.
National Banner & Nashville Whig. (Sat., Dec. 13, 1828)

Izard, Ralph. Died in Knoxville.
Daily Republican Banner. (Sat., Sept. 22, 1838)

Jack, Mr. Alexander. Merchant. Died at New Orleans on the 27th ult.
National Banner & Nashville Daily Advertiser. (Tues., Spet. 10, 1833)

Jack, Jeremiah Esq. A revolutionary soldier. Died in Knox County.
National Banner & Nashville Daily Advertiser. (Tues., July 2, 1833)

Jackson, Brice. Of Montgomery County, Tenn. Died in the loss of the Steam Boat Brandywine.
National Banner & Nashville Daily Advertiser. (Mon., April 23, 1832)

Jackson, David. Died in Danville, Ky. of Cholera.
National Banner & Nashville Daily Advertiser. (Mon., Aug. 5, 1833)

Jackson, Mrs. Elizabeth S. Wife of Col. Anthony W. Jackson. Died on yesterday morning.
Daily Republican Banner. (Tues., Dec. 12, 1837)

Jackson, Mr. Hugh. Suddenly on Thursday morning last. Died in Nashville, he left a wife and two children.
Impartial Review and Cumberland Repository. (Sat., June 21, 1806)

Jackson, James Esq. Formerly a merchant of Nashville. Died in Florence, Ala.
Daily Republican Banner. (Wed., Aug. 19, 1840)

Jackson, Mr. John. Died at Pittsburgh.
National Banner & Nashville Whig. (Sat., Jan. 13, 1827)

Jackson, John Esq. Died in Florence, Ala.
National Banner & Nashville Advertiser. (Tues., May 8, 1832)

Jackson, John R. Youngest son of Capt. Joseph Jackson, aged about 17 years. Died on the 11th ulto at Blains & Roads, Granger County, Tenn. (Knox Times)
Nashville Whig. (Mon., July 6, 1840)

Jackson, Mr. John R. Printer. Died in Nashville on Friday Feb. 1st.
National Banner & Nashville Daily Advertiser. (Sat., Feb. 2, 1833)

Jackson, Capt. Joseph D. A native of Wilson County, Tenn. Died in New Orleans on the 29th Aug. aged 28 years.
The Politician & Weekly Nashville Whig. (Wed., Sept. 15, 1847)

Jackson, Mr. Thomas B. A native of Ireland. Died in Mobile, Ala. of Yellow fever.
Daily Republican Banner. (Tues., Oct. 1st. 1839)

Jackson, Mr. William O. In the 29th year of his age. Died on Monday the 4th inst. in Davidson County. of Cholera.
The Western Weekly Review. (Friday, Feb. 8, 1833) Franklin, Tenn.

Jacob, Thomas. Died in Northampton County, Va.
Nashville Republican & State Gazette. (Thurs., April 7, 1831)

Jacobs, Mrs. Sarah. Died in Knoxville.
National Banner & Nashville Whig. (Tues., April 27, 1830)

James, Mrs. Elizabeth Jane. Died in Boliver.
Nashville Republican & State Gazette. (Wed., Oct. 24, 1832)

James, Mr. James. Died at Peubla on his way to Mexico City.
National Banner & Nashville Daily Advertiser. (Fri., June 6, 1834)

James, Lyman Esq. Died at Bellfonte, Ala. on the 16th Dec. Attorney
at Law. Formerly of Massachusetts.
National Banner & Nashville Whig. (Fri., Dec. 31, 1830)

James, Rhoda Goodrich. An interesting and beautiful child, aged 3 yrs
and 3 months, daughter of the late Lyman James. Died in Davidson
County, on the 15th inst.
National Banner & Nashville Daily Advertiser. (Fri., Aug. 17, 1832)

James, Mr. William. Of Giles County, Tenn. Died at Marianna, W.
Florida of Fever.
Nashville Republican. (Mon., Nov. 28, 1836)

Jamison, Mrs. Elizabeth. Consort of David K. Jamison and daughter of
Col. John Witherspoon. Died in Carrollville, Ten. on the 11th inst.
National Banner & Nashville Whig. (Wed., Aug. 31, 1831)

January, Miss Elizabeth, Isabella and Andrew January, three children
of Andrew M. January. Died of Cholera. Copyed from the Maysville
Eagle and Monitor.
National Banner & Nashville Daily Advertiser. (Thurs., June 6, 1833)

January, James B. Esq. Died at Lexington, Ky.
National Banner. (Sat., Nov. 7, 1829)

Jarnagan, Mr. Chesley. Died in Jefferson County.
National Banner. (May 4, 1826)

Jarmon, Ebenezar Bolivar. Son of Col R. B. Jarmon aged 2 years and
4 months. Died in Fayetee County on the 9th inst.
National Banner & Nashville Daily Advertiser. (Wed., May 22, 1833)

Jarmon, Mr. Joseph. Son of Gen. Robert Jarmon. Died in Humphreys
County on the 12th inst.
National Banner & Nashville Whig. (Sat., July 22, 1826)

Jarmon, Gen. Robert. Died at his residence in Humphrey County on
the 7th ult.
National Banner & Nashville Whig. (Sat., March 21, 1829)

Jarmon, Major William. Died at Perryville on the 25th ult. son of the
late Gen. Rob. Jarmon. He ledt a wife and infant child.
National Banner & Nashville Whig. (Fri., March 12, 1830)

Jarnagin, Edward. In the 21st year of his age. Died at Chucky Band,
Jefferson County, Tennessee on 15th September 1834.
National Banner & Nashville Whig. (Wed., Oct. 8, 1834)

Jarrett, Mr. Archibald. Aged 66. Died in Rutherford County on the
19th inst.
National Banner & Nashville Whig. (Mon., Dec. 27, 1830)

Jay, Mr. Joseph. Died near Kaskaskia, Ill.
National Banner & Nashville Whig. (Sat., Aug. 12, 1826)

Jeffers, Capt. Osborne. Died in Port Gibson, Mi.
Nashville Republican & State Gazette. (Sat., June 4, 1831)

Jefferson, Joseph Sr. Age 57. Died at Harrisburg, Pa. Aug. 4.
National Banner & Nashville Advertiser. (Sat., Aug. 18, 1832)

Jefferson, Mrs. Sarah S. In the 57th year of her age. Died in Haywood County, Ten. on the 23d of Aug.
National Banner & Nashville Whig. (Mon., Sept. 8, 1835)

Jeffreys, Dr. Kinchin T. Died in Henderson County.
National Banner & Nashville Daily Advertiser. (Wed., Nov. 7, 1832)

Jenkins, Mr. Aaron. Died in Anderson County.
National Banner. (May 27, 1826)

Jenkins, Mr. David. A native of Ireland in the 24th year of his age.
Died on Tuesday last after an illness of 24 hours.
Nashville Whig. (Fri., May 20, 1840)

Jenkins, Francis M. Of the House of C. C. Jenkins & Co. Died in New
Orleans of Yellow Fever.
Daily Republican Banner. (Wed., Sept. 27, 1837)

Jenkins, George G. Of the House of G. G. Jenkins & Co. Died in
New Orleans of Yellow Fever.
Daily Republican Banner. (Wed., Sept. 27, 1837)

Jenning, Rev. Obadiah D. D. Died in this town (Nashville) this morning
the highly respected and much esteemed Pastor of the Presbyterian
Church.
National Banner & Nashville Advertiser. (Thurs., Jan. 12, 1832)

Jennings, Mrs. Anne G. Died at Charleston, Ind. Wife of the Hon.
Jonathan Jennings aged 33.
National Banner. (April 28, 1826)

Jennings, Mr. Benjamin G. Died in Mt. Pleasant.
National Banner & Nashville Daily Advertiser. (Thurs., June 20, 1833)

Jennings, Ellen Isabella. Youngest daughter of the late Rev. Obediah
Jennings, of Nashville. Died suddenly in Philadelphia.
Nashville Whig. (Fri., June 7, 1839)

Jennings, Dr. J. D. Son of the late Rev. Obadiah Jennings, D. D.
Died in Clinton, Mi. on Friday the 3d inst.
National Banner & Nashville Whig. (Mon., Feb. 20, 1837)

Jennings, Mrs. W. Relict of Rev. Obedia Jennings D. D. Died in
Philadelphia formerly of Nashville.
Nashville Whig. (Sat., April 9, 1842)

Jeoplin, Miss Louisa. Aged 18. Died in Pulaski on June 10 of Cholera.
National Banner & Nashville Daily Advertiser. (Wed., June 19, 1833)

Jeter, Mrs. Polly. Wife of Mr. William Jeter. Died at Knoxville.
National Banner & Nashville Whig. (Mon., Feb. 21, 1831)

Jeter, Richard T. Only 16 years old. Son of Mrs. Jeter, No. 223
Greenwich Street. Died in New York of Hydrophobia.
Daily Republican Banner. (Tues., Sept. 3, 1839)

Jett, John Esq. Died in Sparta, Tenn. President of the Branch bank
of Tennessee in Sparta.
Daily Republican Banner. (Fri., Sept. 18, 1840)

Jetter, Mrs. Polly. Died in Knoxville, Ten.
Nashville Republican & State Gazette. (Thurs., March 3, 1831)

Jetton, John W. Esq. Eldest son of Col. Robert Jetton, of Ruther-
ford and Clerk and Master of the Chancery Court at Murfreesboro.
Died in St. Augustine, Florida.
Nashville Whig. (Mon., Jan. 14, 1839)

197

Jetton, Mrs. Margaret. Wife of John Jetton. Aged 67. Died near Murfreesborough.
National Banner & Nashville Whig. (Sat., July 22, 1826)

Johns, Dr. Died in Logan County, Ky.
National Banner & Nashville Whig. (Sat., May 12, 1827)

Johns, Mr. John Sen. Died in this County.
National Banner. (May 4, 1826)

Johnson, Dr. A. B. Died at Natchez.
National Banner & Nashville Daily Advertiser. (Wed., Aug. 7, 1833)

Johnson, Andrew (Gov.) Appointment of members of his military staff.
Republican Banner and Nashville Whig. (Vol. 39 No. 280 Saturday, Nov. 19, 1853)

Johnson, Mr. Benjamin H. Died at Newcastle, Ky.
National Banner. (April 21, 1826)

Johnson, Hon. C. C. A member of the House of Representative from Virginia. Died in Alexandria on Sunday by falling in the river and drowned (From the Baltimore Gazette)
National Banner & Nashville Daily Advertiser. (Thurs., June 28, 1832)

Johnson, Mr. Cader. Died in Maury County.
National Banner & Nashville Whig. (Fri., April 16, 1830)

Johnson, Mr. Christain A. Died near Huntsville, Ala. was shot from Ambush while on his way home.
National Banner & Nashville Daily Advertiser. (Sat., July 21, 1832)

Johnson, Mr. Edward. Died in Port Gibson, Miss.
National Banner & Nashville Whig. (Sat., Jan. 12, 1828)

Johnson, Mrs. Eliza E. Wife of Mr. Thomas G. Johnson. Died at Memphis
National Banner & Nashville Daily Advertiser. (Wed., July 10, 1833)

Johnson, Mrs. Elizabeth. Wife of Mr. John Johnson. Died in Giles County.
National Banner & Nashville Whig. (Fri., June 17, 1831)

Johnson, Mrs. Elizabeth. Died in Giles County.
Nashville Republican & State Gazette. (Thurs., June 16, 1831)

Johnson, Mrs. Elizabeth. On the 26th of this month, Mrs. Elizabeth Johnson, consort of John Johnson of this County (Davidson), in the sixtieth year of her age - her death was occasioned by the effects of a cancer on her tongue of about 18 months, patience and fortitude; she has lived near here about fifty years. Her anchor of hope was fast in her God; she was a kind and loving wife, an indulgent mother, and kind neighbor. She left a husband and ten children to lament her loss.
Nashville Republican, (Sat., April 30, 1836)

Johnson, Mrs. Elizabeth. Wife of G. J. Johnson Esq., aged 32. Died at Louisville, Ky.
National Banner. (March 31, 1826)

Johnson, Ellen. Infant daughter of John B. & Eliza Ann Johnson. Died in Nashville, on Monday last.
Nashville Whig. (Thurs., July 4, 1844)

Johnson, George Olliver. Youngest son of Col. A. W. Johnson. Died on yesterday.
Nashville Whig. (Sat., June 8, 1844)

Johnson, Gotlif. Died in Knoxville, Tenn.
Daily Republican Banner. (Sat., Oct. 6, 1838)

198

Johnson, Mrs. Harriet. Wife of Joseph H. Johnson. Died in Nashville on the 12th inst.
National Banner & Nashville Whig. (Mon., Jan. 12, 1835)

Johnson, Mr. Henry. A soldier of the Revolution. Died near Decatur, Ala.
National Banner & Nashville Daily Advertiser. (Tues., July 15, 1834)

Johnson, Mr. Isaac. Aged 45. Died in Knox County.
National Banner & Nashville Whig. (June 24, 1826)

Johnson, Col. James. Member of Congress. Died in Scott County, Ky.
National Banner & Nashville Whig. (Sept. 2, 1826)

Johnson, Col. James. Died in Scott County, Ky. Member of Congress.
National Banner & Nashville Whig. (Sat., Sept. 2, 1826)

Johnson, James H. Company I. with First Reg. Tenn. Volunteers. Died was killed in the Battle of Monterey with the Mexicans on Sept. 21st.
Nashville Whig. (Sat., Oct. 24, 1846)

Johnson, Mr. James T. A native of Scotland and formerly a resident of Nashville. Died at Covington, West Ten. on the 12th ult.
National Banner & Nashville Whig. (Mon., Jan. 10, 1831)

Johnson, Mr. John. Of Pittsburgh. Died on board steamboat, Gen. Wayne.
National Banner & Nashville Whig. (Sat., Feb. 9, 1828)

Johnson, Judge John. In the 60th year of his age. Died in St. Francis County, Arkansas.
National Banner & Nashville Daily Advertiser. (Tues., Aug. 19, 1834)

Johnson, Joseph H. Merchant of Nashville. Died in Lynn, Mass. on the 9th inst.
National Banner & Nashville Whig. (Wed., April 26, 1837)

Johnson, Major Lilliton. Aged 45. Died in Bolivar, T.
National Banner & Nashville Daily Advertiser. (Mon., July 14, 1834)

Johnson, Mrs. Louisa. Wife of Wm. Johnson Esq. Died in Williamson County, Ten.
National Banner & Nashville Daily Advertiser. (Mon., Aug. 26, 1833)

Johnson, Miss Louisa M. Died at Maysville, Ky.
National Banner. (March 24, 1826)

Johnson, Miss Lydia. Died at Tuscumbia, Ala.
National Banner & Nashville Whig. (Fri., Feb. 18, 1831)

Johnson, Margaret Louisa. Aged 5 years 1 month and 23 days. Died in Fayette County, Tennessee on the 26th day of Sept. the eldest daughter of Col W. D. Johnson.
Nashville Whig. (Thurs., Oct. 12, 1843)

Johnson, Mrs. Martha. Died in Hardeman County.
National Banner & Nashville Whig. (Sat., Feb. 2, 1828)

Johnson, Mrs. Martha. Oldest daughter of Robert West Esq. and wife of Willie B. Johnson Esq. of Clarksville, Tenn. Died on the 14th inst. in Dickson County.
National Banner. (Sat., Dec. 26, 1829)

Johnson, Miss Mary G. Died in Madison County.
National Banner. (May 13, 1826)

Johnson, Mary Joanna. Infant daughter of William Johnson Esq. Died on Monday last in Franklin.
The Western Weekly Review. (Fri., March 8, 1833) Franklin, Tenn.

Johnson, Miss Parnell. In the 34th year of her age. Died on the morning of the 25th inst.
The Nashville Gazette. (Sat., Jan. 29, 1820)

Johnson, Mrs. Phebe. Died in Limestone County, Ala.
National Banner & Nashville Whig. (Sat., July 8, 1826)

Johnson, Capt. Reuben. Age 53. Died in Liberty, Smith County.
National Banner & Nashville Advertiser. (Fri., March 9, 1832)

Johnson, Robert. Aged 4 years. and on 22d ult. Rachel Johnson aged
12 years, children of Mr. Robert Johnson.
National Banner & Nashville Whig. (Sat., Jan. 13, 1827)

Johnson, Rev. Samuel. Died at Cincinnati on the 23d of May. Rector
of St. Pauls Church of that city.
National Banner & Nashville Daily Advertiser. (Thurs., May 30, 1833)

Johnson, Mrs. Sarah. Consort of Mr. Andrew Johnson of Franklin, Tenn.
Died on Monday evening last.
The Western Weekly Review. (Fri., Sept. 23, 1831) Franklin, Tenn.

Johnson, Mr. Thomas. Died in Shelby County.
National Banner. (Sat., Sept. 19, 1829)

Johnson, Thomas R. Assistant Surgeon of the U. S. Army. Died 11th
July 1837.
National Banner & Nashville Whig. (Mon., July 31, 1837)

Johnson, Dr. Thomas R. U. S. Army in the 36th year of his age. Died
in Baltimore on the 11th.
National Banner & Nashville Whig. (Mon., July 31, 1837)

Johnson, Mr. William. Aged 80 years. Died in Maury County.
National Banner & Nashville Whig. (Fri., Feb. 19, 1830)

Johnson, William Curtis. Only son of William H. Johnson formerly of
Russellville, Ky. Died in Statesville on the 20th of May. of Scarlet
Fever.
National Banner & Nashville Daily Advertiser. (Fri., June 7, 1833)

Johnston, Miss Elizabeth. Daughter of Robert Johnston of this county.
In the 19th year of her age. Died - departed this life Oct. the third
1824.
Nashville Whig. (Oct. 18, 1824)

Johnston, Rufus M. By a "Friend". Dated May 21, 1869. Born in
Lincoln County, N. C. (in 1828). Died in Charlotte, N. C. April 20,
1869. Moved to N. Y. at age of 16 (1854) entered mercantile
business, married Southern Girl and moved to Columbia, S. C. where he
was President of the Exchange Bank, member of Legislature & filled
many other offices of trust. Printed 8½ x 11. single sheet.

Johnston, Samuel Sen. Aged 80 years. Died near Athens, Ala.
National Banner & Nashville Daily Advertiser. (Mon., Feb. 18, 1833)

Johnston, William. Aged 62. Died near Lebanon, Wilson County.
The Union. (Tues., Dec. 13,1836)

Johnston, Mr. William R. Son of Alexander Johnston, Esq. Died in
Maury County.
National Banner & Nashville Whig. (Thurs., Sept. 16, 1830)

Jones, Mrs. Died in Shelbyville, Tenn. of Cholera.
National Banner & Nashville Daily Advertiser. (Thurs., July 11, 1833)

Jones, Amzi. Dry Goods Merchant of Nashville. Late of Rutherford
County. Died on Saturday night 17th inst.
Nashville Whig. (Tues., June 20, 1843)

200

Jones, Mrs. Ann B. (Wife of Jones, John T. Esq.) Died at Cincinnati.
National Banner. (May 20, 1826)

Jones, Col. Benj. B. Died in Lawrence County, Ala.
National Banner & Nashville Whig. (Fri., March 26, 1830)

Jones, Gen. Calvin. In the 73d year of his age. Died in the vicinity
of Bolivar, Tenn. on the 20th ult.
Nashville Whig. (Sat., Oct. 3, 1846)

Jones, Mr. Calvin. Died at Kingston.
National Banner & Nashville Advertiser. (Mon., January 16, 1832)

Jones, Mr. C. M. Of Nashville. Died in Lebanon on Tuesday evening
25th ult. of Consumption.
Nashville True Whig & Weekly Commercial Register. (Fri., July 5, 1850)

Jones, David. In the 74th year of his age. Died on Wednesday 4th inst.
The Christian Record. (Sat., Oct. 21, 1848)

Jones, Col. E. B. W. Of Illinois. Died at Princeton, Ky.
National Banner & Nashville Whig. (Sat., Nov. 18, 1826)

Jones, Mrs. Eliza H. Wife of Mr. A. Jones. Died on the 7th inst. in
Rutherford County. Daughter of the late Rev. Henry Hartwell Marable
member of the Methodist Episcopal Church.
The Union. (Thurs., Nov. 19, 1835)

Jones, Francis Esq. Died in Alabama. Formerly a member of Congress
from this state.
National Banner & Nashville Whig. (Sat., Aug. 26, 1826)

Jones, Mr. Gerard. Died in Evansville.
National Banner & Nashville Whig. (Sat., Sept. 9, 1826)

Jones, H. City Hotel. Died in Natchez of Yellow Fever
Daily Republican Banner. (Wed., Oct. 18, 1837)

Jones, Hugh Lawson White. Son of Gov. James C. Jones. Died in Nashville on Tuesday the 17th inst.
Nashville Whig. (Thurs., Oct. 19, 1843)

Jones, James B. Esq. Aged 54 years. Died in Carroll County, Tenn.
a native of Halifax County, Va.
Daily Republican Banner. (Sat., Nov. 21, 1840)

Jones, Mrs. Jane. Wife of Mr. John W. Jones formerly of this
county. Died in Tipton County on 2d inst. of cholera.
National Banner & Nashville Whig. (Fri., Aug. 14, 1835)

Jones, Mrs. Jane Watson. Consort of Capt. John W. Jones. Died in
Tipton County in the 34th year of her age.
National Banner & Nashville Whig. (Fri., Aug. 28, 1835)

Jones, Mrs. Jane W. Died in Madison County, Ala.
National Banner & Nashville Whig. (Mon., Oct. 4, 1830)

Jones, Mr. Joel W. Died in Madison County, Ala.
National Banner & Nashville Whig. (Sat., Feb. 24, 1827)

Jones, Mr. Laban. Died in Bedford County.
National Banner & Nashville Whig. (Sat., Sept. 30, 1826)

Jones, Mrs. Laury. Died 13th at Cincinnati, Ohio of Cholera.
National Banner & Nashville Daily Advertiser. (Tues., Oct. 23, 1832)

Jones, Mrs. Lucy. Died on Tuesday 7th inst. Consort of Maj. Samuel
Jones of Christian County, Ky.
Nashville Whig. (Sept. 20, 1824)

Jones, Miss Martha B. Died in Jackson, Tenn.
Nashville Republican & State Gazette. (Wed., Aug. 22, 1832)

Jones, Mrs Martha E. Late of Columbus, Georgia. Died in Mobile, Ala.
of Yellow Fever.
Daily Republican Banner. (Tues., Oct. 11 1839)

Jones, Mrs. Martha. W. Lady of Berthier Jones Esq. of Memphis. Died
in Davidson County on the 10th of July.
National Banner & Nashville Daily Advertiser. (Fri., Aug. 1, 1834)

Jones, Mrs. Mary Lacy. Wife of Rev. William D. Jones and only daughter
of Col. William Cocke Lacy of Amelia County, Virginia. Died Nov. 30th
1846 near Hopkinsville, Ky.
The Christian Record. (Sat., Jan. 30, 1847)

Jones, Mrs. Mary S. Died at Huntsville, Ala. Wife of Capt. Irby Jones.
National Banner. (March 31, 1826)

Jones, Mr. Nelson. Died in Maury County.
National Banner & Nashville Daily Advertiser. (Mon., Aug. 25, 1834)

Jones, Miss Prudence E. Daughter of Mr. Benjamin Jones. Died in
Madison County, Ala.
National Banner & Nashville Whig. (Thurs., Sept. 2, 1830)

Jones, Mr. Richard. Died at Franklin, Ky.
National Banner & Nashville Daily Advertiser. (Sat., Feb. 16, 1833)

Jones, Mr. Richard H. Merchant of Nashville. Died at Brownsville,
from a pistol shot fired by Mr. Anderson.
National Banner & Nashville Whig. (Wed., June 14, 1837)

Jones, Mrs. Sarah. Wife of Col. Arthur Jones. Aged 47. Died near
Tuscumbia, Ala.
National Banner & Nashville Whig. (Sat., Sept. 13, 1828)

Jones, Mrs. Sarah Bland. Wife of Dr. Joseph Jones. Died in Haywood
County.
National Banner & Nashville Whig. (Thurs., Sept. 2, 1830)

Jones, Mr. Thomas C. A native of Charleston, S. C. Died in New
Orleans, La.
National Banner & Nashville Whig. (Wed., Dec. 3, 1834)

Jones, Maj. William. Age 51. Died in Madison County, Ala.   Formerly
of Virginia.
National Banner & Nashville Advertiser. (Mon., Oct. 1, 1832)

Jones, Major William. Aged 51. Formerly of Virginia. Died in
Madison County, Ala.
National Banner & Nashville Daily Advertiser. (Mon., Oct. 1, 1832)

Jones, Hon. William. Former Secretary of the Navy, and late collector
for the Port of Philadelphia. Died at Bethleham Penn. on the 6th
inst.
National Banner & Nashville Whig. (Fri., Sept. 23, 1831)

Jones, Mr. Wm. Aged 22. Died in Madison County, Ala.
National Banner & Nashville Whig. (Sat., Sept. 16, 1826)

Jones, Mr. Wm. Died at Bowling Green, Ky.
National Banner. (Sat., May 2, 1829)

Jones, Mr. Wood. Died in Wilson County. on the 29th ult.
National Banner & Nashville Daily Advertiser. (Mon., June 3, 1833)

Jordan, Mr. Buford. A citizen of Liberty, Smith County. Died on 28th Jan. last in Claiborne County, Miss. aged 24 years.
National Banner & Nashville Whig. (Fri., April 16, 1830)

Jordan, Mrs. Elizabeth. Consort of Archer Jordan Esq. of Williamson County. Died on the 10th July, 1832
The Western Weekly Review. (Fri., Aug. 3, 1832) Franklin, Tenn.

Jordan, Fleming, Esq. Died in Madison County, Ala.
National Banner & Nashville Whig. (Mon., Aug. 22, 1831)

Jordan, Mr. Samuel. Died in Barren County, Ky.
National Banner & Nashville Whig. (Sat., Sept. 8, 1827)

Jordan, Mrs. Sarah W. Wife of Mr. Henry E. W. Jordan. Died in Henderson County.
National Banner & Nashville Daily Advertiser. (Wed., Aug. 7, 1833)

Jordan, Mr. Stephen. Died in Humphreys County, T. on the 25th ult. In the 25th year of his age.
National Banner & Nashville Whig. (Sat., Sept. 1826)

Joseph, Mr. Samuel. Died in Cincinnati.
National Banner. (March 17, 1826)

Joslin, Col. Benjamin. Late of this neighborhood. Died near Trenton, Tenn. over 75 years of age.
National Banner & Nashville Whig. (Mon., Nov. 3, 1834)

Jouitt, Mr. Mathew H. Died near Lexington, Ky. an eminent artist.
National Banner & Nashville Whig. (Sat., Aug. 25, 1827)

Jourdan, Capt. Benjamin. Aged 28. Died in Huntsville, Ala.
National Banner & Nashville Whig. (Sat., Aug. 26, 1826)

Jourdan, Mrs. Margaret. Died in Washington County.
National Banner & Nashville Whig. (Mon., Mon., 2, 1831)

Jungman, Mrs. Catherine. Wife of Gottlob Jungman who died yesterday. Died in Louisville, Ky yesterday afternoon at 4 o'clock in the 67th year of her age.
National Banner & Nashville Daily Advertiser. (Fri., June 14, 1833)

Jungmann, Mr. Gottlob. Formerly of Nashville aged 76. Died at Louisville, Ky.
National Banner & Nashville Daily Advertiser. (Thurs., June 14, 1833)

Justis, Matthew. Of Columbus, Georgia. Died in Mobile, Ala. of yellow fever.
Daily Republican Banner. (Tuesday, Oct. 1, 1839)

Kaclspm, Mr. Andrew J. B. In the 21st year of his age. Died in Nashvilleon Wednesday night 5th inst.
Nashville Whig. (Sat., July 8, 1843)

Kain, Mr. John. Died in Knox County.
National Banner & Nashville Whig. (Mon., July 18, 1831)

Kani, Mrs. Mary. Widow of the late Mr. John Kain. Died at Knoxville.
National Banner & Nashville Daily Advertiser. (Wed., May 15, 1833)

Kane, Hon. E. K. A Senator in Congress from Illinois. Died in Washington City on the 11th inst.
The Union. (Sat., Dec. 26, 1835)

Kane, Mr. Joseph K. Formerly of Nashville. Died at Clinton, Mass.
National Banner & Nashville Daily Advertiser. (Sat., Sept. 6, 1834)

Kavanaugh, Mr. Philman. Died in Madison County, Ky.
National Banner. (Sat., April 25, 1829)

Keays, Lieut. J. L. 3d Artillery. Died was killed in battle with the
Seminole Indians in Florida.
The Union. (Sat., Jan. 23, 1836)

Keeble, Mrs. Eliza. Consort of Mr. Walter Keeble. Died on the morning
of the 26th inst. near Jefferson, Rutherford County in the 25th year
of her age. (Obituary) Sat., Feb. 6, 1847)
The Christian Record. (Sat., Jan. 30, 1847)

Keel, Mr. Edward A. Died in Henderson County.
National Banner & Nashville Whig. (Fri., July 18, 1828)

Keel, Mrs. Rosannah. Died in Columbia, Ky.
National Banner & Nashville Whig. (Fri., July 25, 1828)

Keeling, Leonard Esq. Died in Davidson County. for many years a
magisterate of Davidson County.
National Banner & Nashville Daily Advertiser. (Tues., Nov. 6, 1832)

Keels, Major George W. Died in Williamsburg District, S. C.
National Banner & Nashville Daily Advertiser. (Mon., April 7, 1834)

Keen, Mr. William Jun. Died in this town last evening.
National Banner. (Sat., July 25, 1829)

Keenan, John M. Son of John Keenan 17. Died in Pulaski June 14
of Cholera.
National Banner & Nashville Daily Advertiser. (Wed., June 19, 1833)

Keene, Mrs. Ann S. Wife of Dr. A. C. Keene. Died in Scott County,
Ky.
National Banner. (May 27, 1826)

Keep, Samuel Esq. Of Washington, D. C. Died at Baltimore on the
evening of the 10th at the City Hotel, aged 26.
National Banner & Nashville Whig. (Mon., Aug. 30, 1830)

Keer, Mr. John. Aged 26. Died in Natchez.
National Banner & Nashville Whig. (Sat., Oct. 7, 1826)

Kehr. W. Of Germany. Died in New Orleans of Yellow Fever.
Daily Republican Banner. (Wed., Sept. 27, 1837)

Kellar, Mr. John C. Died at Brazoria, Texas on 13th inst.
National Banner & Nashville Daily Advertiser. (Thurs., Jan. 31, 1833)

Mrs. Kellogg. Died on the 28th ult. The house of Mr. Austin Kellogg
in Smithfield, Pennsylvania was destroyed by fire and in it his wife
and only child, about five weeks old. Mrs. Kellogg was hatchelling
flax near the hearth, when a coal snapped from the chimney and set
the flax on fire. The flames spread so rpaidly as to overwhelm Mrs.
K. before she could escape with her infant.
The Clarion and Tennessee Gazette. (March 28, 1820)

Kelly, Mrs. Elizabeth. Consort of Hon. Judge Kelly and sister of the
Hon. John Rowan. Died at Bardstown, Ky of Cholera.
National Banner & Nashville Daily Advertiser. (Sat., Aug. 10, 1833)

Kelly, Mr. Henry. Died in Lexington, Ky.
National Banner & Nashville Daily Advertiser. (Wed., July 31, 1833)

Kelly, William Esq. A member of the Legislature from Green County.
Died at the house of Mr. William D. Baird of Rutherford County.
The Nashville Gazette. (Sat., Jan. 8, 1820)

Kelly, Hon. William. Aged 49. Died in New Orleans, La.
National Banner & Nashville Daily Advertiser. (Sat., Sept. 13, 1834)

Kelton, Mr. David M. Merchant of this city. Died lately in Philadelphia.
The Nashville Whig & Tennessee Advertiser. (June 20, 1818)

The Right Rev. Kemp, James D. D. Died in Baltimore.
National Banner & Nashville Whig. (Sat., Nov. 17, 1827)

Kemper, Caleb. Died 16th at Cincinnati, Ohio of Cholera.
National Banner & Nashville Daily Advertiser. (Wed., Oct. 24, 1832)

Kendall, Mrs. Conny. Died in Logan County, Ky.
National Banner & Nashville Whig. (Sat., Sept. 1, 1827)

Kendall, Mr. James. Died in Franklin County, Ky.
National Banner. (Sat., Aug. 22, 18__)

Kendall, Miss Mary J. Daughter of Mr. James Kendall age 14 yrs. 11 months. Died in Elkton, Ky.
National Banner & Nashville Advertiser. (Mon., January 23, 1832)

Kendall, Miss Mary J. Daughter of Mr. James Kendall. Aged 14 years and 11 months. Died in Elkton, Ky. on the 17th inst.
National Banner & Nashville Daily Advertiser. (Mon., Jan. 23, 1832)

Kendall, Mr. Zebedee. Father of the Postmaster General. Died in Dunstable, Mass. on Wednesday aged 84 years.
Daily Republican Banner. (Fri., Aug. 30, 1839)

Kenley, Mr. Hugh G. Died in Dyer County.
National Banner & Nashville Daily Advertiser. (Wed., Feb. 8, 1832)

Kenneda, William. Revolutionary War Hero. Editorial on his death.
Republican Banner & Nashville Whig. (No. 240, Sat., Oct. 1, 1853)

Kennedy, Mr. Adam M. Of Knox County, Tenn. Died in Greenville, S. C.
National Banner & Nashville Daily Advertiser. (Mon., Jan. 16, 1832)

Kennedy, Mr. Adam M. Of Knox County, Ten. Died in Greenville, S. C.
National Banner & Nashville Advertiser. (Mon., Jan. 16, 1832)

Kennedy, Rev. James. Aged 55. Died in Knox County.
National Banner & Nashville Whig. (Sat., Sept. 16, 1826)

Kennedy, Miss Jane. Aged 15, daughter of Mr. Walter Kennedy. Died in Knox County.
National Banner & Nashville Whig. (Wed., March 2, 1831)

Kennedy, 1st. Kieut. John F. 1st Artillery. Died 18th May 1837. in the U. S. Army.
National Banner & Nashville Whig. (Mon., July 31, 1837)

Kennedy, Lucas Esq. Died at Paris, Henry County.
National Banner & Nashville Whig. (Sat., Jan. 13, 1827)

Kennedy, Stephen. Died at Cincinnati, Ohio of Cholera.
National Banner & Nashville Daily Advertiser. (Sat., Oct. 20, 1832)

Kennedy, Thomas S. Esq. Of New Orleans. Died at Louisville, Ky.
Nashville Whig & National Banner. (Tues., Aug. 10, 1831)

Kennelly, Miss Nancy H. Died in Maury County, Ten. of consumption.
National Banner & Nashville Daily Advertiser. (Wed., Sept. 25, 1833)

Kenner, Doctor Frank S. Aged 27. Died on the 16th of Dec. in the
town of Liberty, Smith County.
National Banner & Nashville Whig. (Tues., Feb. 2, 1830)

Kenney, Thomas Esq. Of New Orleans. Died in Louisville, Ky.
National Banner & Nashville Whig. (Wed., Aug. 10, 1831)

Kennon, Dr. R. R. Of Tuscaloosa, Ala. Died at Columbus, Mississippi.
Nashville Whig. (Sat., Jan. 27, 1838)

Kenny, G. W. With the Second Tenn. Regiment. Died was killed in the
Battle of Sierra Gorda with the Mexicans.
The Politician & Weekly Nashville Whig. (Fri., May 21, 1847)

Kent, Hon. Joseph. Senator in Congress from the State of Maryland.
Died in Baltimore from being thrown from his horse.
Daily Republican Banner. (Thurs., Nov. 30, 1837)

Kenworthy, J. L. The celebrated American Ventriloquist. Died in
Dallas County, Ala. in the 33d year of his age.
Nashville Whig. (Fri., Sept. 11, 1840)

Kerchival, Dr. John. Died at Bardstown, Ky.
National Banner & Nashville Whig. (Sat., June 16, 1827)

Kercheval, Mr. Samuel. A merchant of high standing. Died in Pulaski
on the 25th inst.
Nashville Whig. (Tues., Aug. 1st 1843)

Kerley, Mrs. Sally. Died in Madison County, Ky, aged 23.
National Banner. (March 10, 1826)

Kerley, Maj. Wm. Aged 67. Died in Madison County, Ky.
National Banner & Nashville Whig. (Sat., Jan. 12, 1828)

Kernahan, Mr. Abram. Died in Lauderdale County, Ala.
National Banner & Nashville Daily Advertiser. (Tues., March 19, 1833)

Kerr, Miss Narcissa. To Mr. Newton C. Dill. Died in Rutherford
County.
National Banner & Nashville Whig. (Sat., Feb. 24, 1827)

Kerr, Mrs. Susannah. Wife of Mr. Wiley Kerr. Died in M'Minn County.
National Banner & Nashville Whig. (Fri., July 25, 1828)

Ketchum, Major D. Of the 6th Reg. U. S. Infantry. Died at Jefferson
Barracks, Missouri.
National Banner & Nashville Whig. (Sat., Sept. 27, 1828)

Key, Mrs. Jennette. Aged 84 years. Died at the residence of her
daughter Mrs. Nancy Williamson in Davidson County, on the 9th inst.
(Obituary).
The Christian Record. (Sat., July 29, 1848)

Key, Mr. Job. Died in Madison County, Ala.
National Banner & Nashville Whig. (Sat., Jan. 26, 1828)

Key, Mr. William T. Died in Limestone County, Ala.
National Banner & Nashville Daily Advertiser. Monday, July 8, 1833)

Keyes, Mr. William. From Kentucky. Died at the residence of Mr.
John McAlpin in Green County, Ala. on the 25th ult.
Nashville Whig. (Fri., Sept. 11, 1840)

Keys, Miss. Corner of 2d and Sycamore St. Died 18th at Cincinnati,
Ohio of Cholera.
National Banner & Nashville Daily Advertiser. (Fri., Oct. 26, 1832)

Keys, Mr. William. Saddler, a native of Ireland. Died in Nashville on Sunday morning the 21st aged 37 years.
National Banner & Nashville Whig. (Mon., Sept. 22, 1834)

Kezer, J. H. Aged 11 months. Died at Gastilian Springs, infant son of Mr. T. & Mrs. E. T. Kezer.
The Union. (Sat., July 2, 1836)

Kibby, E. Junior Editor of the Commercial Register. Died in Mobile, Ala. of yellow fever, aged about 27 years.
Daily Republican Banner. (Tues., Oct. 1st. 1839)

Kidd, Mr. Nancy. Aged about 60. Died in Williamson County on the 22d of March.
Nashville Republican & State Gazette. (Thurs., April 7, 1831)

Kidd, Mrs. Patsey C. Wife of Mr. Walter Kidd. Died in Fayette County, Ky.
National Banner & Nashville Whig. (Sat., Oct. 25, 1828)

Kieroff, Mrs. Juliet. Aged about 51 years. Died in Nashville on Wednesday 24th inst.
The Christian Record. (Sat., Jan. 27, 1849)

Kile, Mrs. Mildred. Daughter of Col. William Perkins, dec'd. Died in Buckingham County, Va.
Daily Republican Banner. (Fri., May 17, 1839)

Kilgere, Mrs. Abigail. Died at Glasgow, Ky.
National Banner. (Sat., May 2, 1829)

Killen, Samuel M. Esq. Post Master at La Grange, Ten. Died twenty five miles from La Grange, Ten. Fayette County.
National Banner & Nashville Whig. (Wed., Nov. 11, 1835)

Kilpatrick, Mr. George. Died at Columbia.
National Banner & Nashville Whig. (Fri., June 20, 1828)

Kilpatrick, James. Dated Sept. 5, 1791. Was killed Poor Valley Creek 17 miles from Hawkins County Court house.
Knoxville Gazette. (Nov. 5, 1791)

Kilpatrick, Mrs. Sarah. Consort of Doct. T. J. Kilpatrick. Died in Pulaski.
Nashville Whig. (Tues., April 21, 1846)

Kimbel, Mrs. Eliza. Wife of Capt. John R. Kimbel of New Orleans. Died in Alexandria, La.
National Banner & Nashville Whig. (Sat., Aug. 5, 1826)

Kimble, Ann M. Daughter of Josiah Kimble formerly of Dickson County, Tenn. Died in Texas.
Nashville Whig. (Mon., Nov. 5, 1838)

Kimbrough, Mrs. Elizabeth. Wife of Mr. William Kimbrough. Died in Monroe County.
National Banner & Nashville Whig. (Mon., May 2, 1831)

Kimbrough, Mr. James. Aged 67. Died in Shelby County.
National Banner & Nashville Daily Advertiser. (Mon., April 22, 1833)

Kincannon, Maj. F. L. Formerly a citizen of Fayetteville. Died on the 9th Dec. in M'Minnville in the 33d year of his age.
National Banner & Nashville Whig. (Fri., Dec. 30, 1836)

Kincannon, Mr. Hugh. Died in Fayetteville on the 11th inst.
National Banner & Nashville Daily Advertiser. (Thurs., Aug. 23, 1832)

King, Mr. Alexander. Died in Nashville yesterday.
Daily Republican Banner. (Thurs., May 2, 1839)

King, Mr. Alexander. A native of Ireland. Died at his residence on High Street on Tuesday last.
Nashville Whig. (Fri., May 3, 1839)

King, Charles Esq. Aged 45. Died in Limestone County, Ala.
National Banner & Nashville Whig. (Sat., Sept. 8, 1827)

King, Mr. Elias C. Aged 25. Died in Fayette County, Ky.
National Banner & Nashville Whig. (Fri., Feb. 26, 1830)

King, Mrs. Eliza H. Departed this life on the 27th inst. in the 25th year of her age. Consort of Mr. Thomas S. King, Merchant of this town.
The Nashville Whig. (April 30, 1816)

King, Doct. Frederick G. Died in New York City. Youngest son of the late Hon. Rufus King aged 28.
National Banner (Sat., June 6, 1829)

King, Mr. James B. On the 10 inst. Died in Sumner County.
National Banner & Nashville Whig. (Fri., June 17, 1831)

King, Mr. James B. Died in Sumner County on the 10th inst.
National Banner & Nashville Whig. (Mon., June 30, 1831)

King, Gen. John E. Aged 70. Died in Cumberland County, Ky.
National Banner & Nashville Whig. (Fri., June 27, 1828)

King, Mr. Joseph, Aged 70. Died in Wilcox County, Ala.
National Banner & Nashville Whig. (July 1, 1826)

King, Mr. Madison. Died in Clarksville, Ten. of Cholera.
National Banner & Nashville Whig. (Wed., July 8, 1835)

King, Mrs. Nancy. Wife of Mr. Walter King. Died near Kingston.
National Banner & Nashville Whig. (Thurs., July 29, 1830)

King, Mrs. Patsey. Died in Knoxville.
Nashville Republican & State Gazette. (Tues., June 21, 1831)

King, Mrs. Patsey P. Wife of Mr. Robert King. Died at Knoxville.
National Banner & Nashville Whig. (Mon., June 20, 1831)

King, Mrs. Patsey P. Wife of Mr. Robert King. Died at Knoxville.
National Banner & Nashville Whig. (Mon., June 20, 1831)

King, Mr. Redden B. Of Kingston. Died in Madison County, Ten.
National Banner & Nashville Daily Advertiser. (Wed., Aug. 21, 1833)

King, Richard. A ruling elder in the Presbyterian Church. Died at his residence one mile south Gallatin in the 67th year of his age.
National Banner & Nashville Daily Advertiser. (Tues., Aug. 19, 1834)

King, Robert Esq. Daughtman of the General Land Office. Died in Washington City.
Nashville Republican & State Gazette. (Thurs., Feb. 24, 1831)

King, Rufus. Died in New York, on the 29th ult in the 73d year of his age.
National Banner & Nashville Whig. (Sat., May 19, 1827)

King, Mrs. Sarah K. Died in this vicinity on the 18th inst, age 26.
Nashville Republican & State Gazette. (Thurs., April 19, 1831)

King, Mrs. Sarah K. Late consort of Wm. King. aged 24. Died in Davidson County.
National Banner & Nashville Whig. (Wed., April 20, 1831)

King, Mrs. Sarah R. Wife of Wm. King, aged 24. Died in Davidson County on the 18 inst.
National Banner & Nashville Whig. (Wed., April 20, 1831)

King, Dr. Thomas. Died in Clarksville, Tenn.
Nashville Republican & State Gazette. (Thurs., April 14, 1831)

King, Major Thomas J. In the 26th year of his age. Died at Abingdon, Va. on the 12th ult. late of Nashville.
National Banner & Nashville Daily Advertiser. (Mon., Feb. 20, 1832)

King, Maj. Thos. J. Age 26. late of Nashville. Died in Montgomery County. See paper for obituary.
National Banner & Nashville Advertiser. (Mon., Feb. 20, 1832)

King, Thomas S. Esq. Aged 65 years. Died at his late residence on the Murfreesboro Pike six miles from Nashville on yesterday.
Nashville True Whig. & Weekly Commercial Register. (Fri., Feb. 14, 1851)

King, Col. William. Formerly of Nashville. Died at Saltville, Washington County, Va. the 30th April.
The Politician & Weekly Nashville Whig. (Fri., May 14, 1847)

King, Mr. William R. Died in Rutherford County.
Nashville Whig. (Tues., July 21, 1846)

King, Mrs. W. P. Wife of Mr. Oswin H. King. aged 17 years. Died in Lexington, Henderson County on the 20th ult.
National Banner & Nashville Whig. (Thurs., Nov. 4, 1830)

Kingsburry, 2d Lieut. Charles E. 3d Dragoons in U. S. Army. Died 9th June in Florida.
National Banner & Nashville Whig. (Mon., July 31, 1837)

Kingsley, Capt. Alpha. Died yesterday morning at his residence in Nashville.
Nashville Whig. (Tues., Sept. 29, 1846)

Kinkead, Robert Jr. Died in Versailles, Ky. 14 miles from Lexington, Ky. of Cholera.
National Banner & Nashville Whig. (Fri., Sept. 4, 1835)

Kinnard, Hon. Geo. L. A member of Congress from Indiana. Died of injuries received from the bursting of the boiler on the Steamboat Flora.
Nashville Republican. (Fri., Dec. 9, 1836)

Mr. Thomas Kinnard. Died in Madison County, Ky.
National Banner & Nashville Whig. (Sat., Sept. 15, 1827)

Kirby, Mrs. Ann. Aged 69. Died in Rutherford County.
National Banner & Nashville Whig. (Sat., Aug. 30, 1828)

Kirk, Mr. George. Died at Cincinnati.
National Banner & Nashville Whig. (June 24, 1826)

Kirk, Mr. Lawrence. Of Nashville. Died in Clarksville, Tenn. of Cholera.
National Banner & Nashville Whig. (Wed., July 8, 1835)

Kirkland, Mr. William D. Died in Port Hudson, La.
National Banner & Nashville Daily Advertiser. (Thurs., June 28, 1832)

Kirkham, Mr. John. Aged 39 years. Died in Grainger County, Tenn.
National Banner & Nashville Daily Advertiser. (Fri., Aug. 16, 1833)

Kirkman, Ellen Washington. Daughter of Mr. & Mrs. John Kirkman.
Died on the morning of the 10th aged one year nine months on seven
days.
The Christian Record. (Sat., Jan. 13, 1849)

Kirkman, Miss Mary. Wife of James Kirkman of Florence and oldest
daughter of James Jackson Esq. Died in Lauderdale County, Al. on
Wednesday 13th inst.
National Banner & Nashville Daily Advertiser. (Mon., March 18, 1833)

Kirkman, Sarah. Infant daughter of Hugh and Ellenora C. Kirkman,
aged 39 days.
Nashville Whig. (Tues., June 7, 1842)

Kirkman, Thomas Esq. Died in this town on Friday morning last in the
47th year of his age.
National Banner (April 14, 1826)

Kirkpatrick, Hon. Andrew. Late chief justice of that state. Died
in New Jersey.
Nashville Republican & State Gazette. (Thurs., Feb. 3, 1831)

Kirkpatrick, Mr. John. Died in Nashville on Tuesday last, leaving a
wife and children.
Impartial Review and Cumberland Repository. (Sat., April 19, 1806)

Kitrell, Mr. John A. Died in Maury County.
National Banner & Nashville Whig. (Fri., March 19, 1830)

Kitrell, Doctor Soloman A. A worthy citizen and a gentleman of pro-
fessional merit. Died on Tuesday last in Clarksville.
The Nashville Whig & Tenn. Advertiser. (Feb. 14, 1818)

Kizer, Mr. James. Died in Randolph T.
National Banner & Nashville Daily Advertiser. (Tues., July 15, 1834)

Kloss, Geo. A. Of Germany. Died in New Orleans of Yellow Fever.
Daily Republican Banner. (Fri., Sept. 29, 1837)

Knapp, Col. Samuel C. In the 46th year of his age. Died in Memphis,
Ten.
National Banner & Nashville Whig. (Fri., March 27, 1835)

Kneas, William Esq. Late of the U. States mint. Died in Philadelphia.
Nashville Whig. (Mon., Sept. 7, 1840)

Knight, Mr. James Derby. Died in Nashville on the 12th inst. in the
27th year of his age.
Nashville Whig. (Tues., March 15, 1842)

Knight, Mrs. James D. Died in Nashville on Tuesday the 6th inst.
Funeral services this morning at 10 o'clock from the Episcopal Church
Nashville Whig. (Thurs., Dec. 8, 1842)

Knight, James Wilson. Infant son of James D. and Louisa Knight.
Died on Thursday the 8th inst.
Sat., Sept. 10, 1842

Knight, Doct. John. Aged 87 years. Died on the 12th in Shelby County,
Ky. He was born in Scotland about 1751.
Daily Republican Banner. (Wed., March 21, 1838)

Knot, Mr. Willis. Died in Shelbyville, Ten.
National Banner & Nashville Whig. (Fri., March 13, 1835)

Knott, Mr. Willis. Died in Bedford County, Ten.
National Banner & Nashville Whig. (Fri., March 27, 1837)

Knox, Hugh Esq. Died in Arkansas.
National Banner & Nashville Whig. (Fri., April 10, 1835)

Knox, Mr. James A. Late of New Orleans. Died in Nashville on Tuesday
May 26, at the residence of his father-in-law George Crocket Esq.
Nashville Whig. (Thurs., May 28, 1846)

Knox, Mr. James. Of the house of Anderson Knox & Co. Died in this
town on Sunday morning last.
National Banner. (March 3, 1826)

Knox, John Esq. Formerly of the house of Knox Boggs & Co. of Philadelphia, on 7th inst.
Nashville Whig. (Wed., Aug. 18, 1841)

Knox, Mr. Joseph. Died in Bedford County.
National Banner & Nashville Whig. (Sat., July 22, 1826)

Krepps, Gen. Solomon G. Senator elect in the state legislature.
Died at Bridgeport, Penn. of cholera.
National Banner & Nashville Daily Advertiser. (Wed., July 31, 1833)

Kring, G. C. Of D. C. Died in New Orleans of Yellow Fever.
Daily Republican Banner. (Fri., Sept. 29, 1837)

Kross, Dederick. Of Boston, Mass. a passenger. Died on the Steamer
George Collier about 80 miles below Natchez. Scalded to death.
Daily Republican Banner. (Tues., May 14, 1839)

Kuydendal, Susan S. Daughter of John C. Kuydendal Esq. Died in
Yorkville, Gibson County, in the 17th year of her age.
Daily Republican Banner. (Tues., April 7, 1840)

Kyle, Jonathan Wood. Infant son, Mr. Jas. Kyle. Died near Newmarket,
Ten.
National Banner & Nashville Daily Advertiser. (Fri., Aug. 16, 1833)

Kyle, Mrs. Mildred. Consort of the late representative from Becking-
ham County and daughter of Col. William Perkins. Died in the county
of Buckingham on the 24th inst. (Richmond Whig)
Nashville Whig. (Wed., May 22, 1839)

Labatut, Gen. John B. At the advanced age of 84 years. Died in New
Orleans on the 9th.
Daily Republican Banner. (Sat., March 16, 1839)

Lacaste, Maj. Gen. Pierre. Died at New Orleans.
National Banner & Nashville Daily Advertiser. (Tues., July 29, 1834)

Lackey, Mary Elizabeth. Wife of W. D. Lackey Esq . Merchant of
Fayetteville, aged 16 years. Died at Fayetteville, Tenn.
Nashville Whig. (Mon., April 29, 1839)

Lackey, Mr. Thomas. Aged 70. Died at Jonesborough.
National Banner. (Sat., Aug. 15, 1829)

Lacy, Miss Martha C. Aged 38 years. Died near Bloomfield, Ky. on
the 20th July of cholera at the residence of her mother.
National Banner & Nashville Daily Advertiser. (Wed., Aug. 21, 1833)

Lacy, Hopkins, Esq. Died in Madison County, Ala.
National Banner & Nashville Whig. (Fri., Feb. 25, 1831)

Lacy, Col. Stephen. Died in Madison County.
National Banner & Nashville Whig. (Mon., Aug. 30, 1830)

Lacy, Mr. William. Died in Madison County, Ten.
Nashville Republican & State Gazette. (Thurs., April 7, 1831)

Lacy, William H. Esq. Died on the 28th Dec. on passage from New
Orleans to Pensacola of Harrodsburg, Ky. brother of Thomas J. Lacy,
Esq. of Nashville.
National Banner & Nashville Daily Advertiser. (Thurs., Jan. 23, 1834)

Lagrand, Miss Mary Morton. Aged 16. Died in Lexington, Ky.
National Banner & Nashville Daily Advertiser. (Mon., March 26, 1832)

Laird, Nancy B. Youngest daughter of Mrs. Nancy G. Laird aged five
years. Died in Shelbyville, on Sunday 25th ulto.
The Politician & Weekly Nashville Whig. (Fri., May 14, 1847)

Lajore, Mrs. Aged 107. Died in St. Louis.
National Banner & Nashville Whig. (Thurs., Aug. 19, 1830)

Lamar, Mr. John. In his 64th year. Died in Putnam County, Ga.
National Banner & Nashville Daily Advertiser. (Fri., Sept. 20, 1833)

Lamar, Judge L. Q. C. Died in Georgia on the 4th. He committed
suicide in a fit of mental alienation.
National Banner & Nashville Daily Advertiser. (Thurs., Sept. 11, 1834)

Lamar, Rebecca. Mother of the President of Texas. Died at the
residence of her son in Houston on the 25th ult. in the 65th year of
her age on a visit to her son.
Nashville Union. (Fri., Sept. 13, 1839)

Lamb, Miss Isabella. Daughter of Capt. A. Lamb. Died in Bledsoe
County on the 6th inst. in the 14th year of her age.
National Banner & Nashville Whig. (Sat., Jan. 17, 1829)

Lamkin, Mrs. Elizabeth. Died at Mooresville, Ala.
National Banner & Nashville Whig. (Sat., Feb. 24, 1827)

Lamkin, Mrs. Rosanna. Widow of Mr. William Lamkin. Died in Madison
County, Ala.
National Banner & Nashville Whig. (Mon., June 6, 1831)

Lamons, Mr. Samuel. Died in Monroe County.
National Banner & Nashville Whig. (Sat., Oct. 11, 1828)

Landsdown, John. Aged 35 years. Died in Nashville of a broken blood
vessel.
National Banner & Nashville Whig. (Wed., June 24, 1835)

Lane, Mr. Jerome B. Died yesterday morning in Nashville in the 20th
year of his age.
Nashville Whig. (Thurs., Sept. 19, 1844)

Lane, John F. M. Aged 14. Son of the Dr. Henry L. of St. Genevieve.
National Banner & Nashville Whig. (Sat., July 29, 1826)

Lane, Jonathan. A soldier of the Revolution, aged 78. Died in Cox-
sackie, New York on the 15th.
National Banner & Nashville Whig. (Mon., July 31, 1837)

Lang, John Esq. Editor of the N. Y. Gazette. Died at New York.
Nashville Republican (Sat., April 2, 1836)

Lang, Robert U. Senior editor of the New York Gazette. Died yesterday in New York. (N. Y. Jour. of Com)
Nashville Republican (Sat., July 2, 1837)

Langborn, Mrs. Wife of Major Maurice Langborn died in Mason Co., Ky.
National Banner & Nashville Whig. (Sat., Aug. 5, 1826)

Langham, Col. Elisa. In the 73rd year of his age. Died in Madison County, Ohio on the 3rd of April, an officer of the Revolution and formerly Speaker of the House of Representatives of the State of Ohio.
National Banner & Nashville Whig. (Fri., May 7, 1830)

Langhorne, James G. Of Madison County, Mississippi on a journey to Virginia. Died at the residence of his brother-in-law in Green County, Alabama.
Nashville Whig. (Mon., July 19, 1841)

Lanier, Rev. Edmund. Died in Nashville yesterday morning.
Daily Republican Banner. (Mon., Nov. 16, 1840)

Lanier, Rev. Edmund. Died in Nashville yesterday morning.
Nashville Whig. (Mon., Nov. 16, 1840)

Lanier, Mrs. Eliza Ann. Consort of Capt. R. Lanier. Died in this County on the 9th ult.
National Banner. (Sat., May 2, 1829)

Lanier, Miss Frances. Daughter of the Rev. Edmund Lanier. Died in this town.
National Banner & Nashville Whig. (Sat., April 19, 1828)

Lankin, Mr. William. Carpenter, formerly of Quebec, L. C. Died in New Orleans.
National Banner & Nashville Daily Advertiser. (Thurs., Aug. 8, 1833)

Lankford, Mr. William. In the 29th year of his age. Died in Reynoldsburg, Ten. on the 29th Aug.
National Banner & Nashville Whig. (Mon., Sept. 14, 1835)

Lanning, Mr. Samuel. Aged 34 a native of Moorestown, N. J. Died in New Orleans.
National Banner & Nashville Daily Advertiser. (Tues., June 24, 1834)

Lanphier, R. G. Aged 36. Died in Nashville on Sunday the 4th inst.
Nashville Whig. (Fri., Nov. 9, 1838)

Lantrip, Mr. John. From Virginia. Died at Knoxville.
National Banner. (April 21, 1846)

Lassiter, Mr. Frederick. Died in Sumner County.
National Banner & Nashville Whig. (Mon., Sept. 26, 1831)

Lapsley, Mrs. Catharine R. Wife of the Rev. Robert A. Lapsley. Died last night in the 43rd year of her age.
Nashville Whig. (Tues., March 26, 1844)

Lapsley, Rev. Joseph B. Of the Presbyterian Church. Died on the 25th ult. at his resident near Bowling Green, Ky.
Nashville Whig. (Oct. 6, 1823)

Larkin, John. Aged 75. Died in Dickson County.
National Banner. (April 7, 1826)

Larkins, Mr. Lionel. Died in Louisville, Ky.
National Banner & Nashville Daily Advertiser. (Thurs., Aug. 15, 1833)

Latapie, Anthony. Aged 48 years. Died on 8th Dec. last at Forbes Department of the High Pyrences, France. A citizen of Louisville, Ky. and formerly a merchant of Nashville.
Nashville Republican. (Tues., March 8, 1836)

Latham, Mrs. Catharine. Aged 67 years. Died in Nashville at the residence of her son-in-law Mr. T. B. Macy, on Monday 16th inst.
Nashville Whig. (Thurs., July 13, 1843)

Latham, David Esq. A Senator from Martin County. Died at Raleigh, N. C.
National Banner & Nashville Daily Advertiser. (Thurs., Jan. 2, 1834)

Latham, Hon. James. Indian Agent. Died in Peoria, Ill.
National Banner & Nashville Whig. (Sat., Jan. 6, 1827)

Lathin, John Esq. Died lately in Jefferson County.
Knoxville Gazette. (Thurs., Jan. 16, 1794)

Lathim, John Esq. Died lately in Jefferson County, John Lathim, Esquire
Knoxville Gazette. (Thurs., Jan. 16, 1794)

Lathrop, James W. Esq. Died at Columbus, Ohio.
National Banner & Nashville Whig. (Sat., Feb. 23, 1828)

Latimer, Miss Elizabeth A. Died in Nashville on the 24th ult.
The Christian Record. (Sat., Jan. 1st. 1848)

Latimer, Mrs. Katharine. Aged 23 years. Died in Bedford County.
National Banner. (Jan. 27, 1826)

Lattimer, Mr. George. Of Nashville. Died on Thursday 14th inst.
Nashville Whig. (Sat., March 16, 1844)

Lattimer, Mr. Robert W. Son of Mrs. Jane A. Lattimer. Died in Nashville on Sunday morning last.
Nashville Whig. (Tues., April 14, 1846)

Laughlin, Cora Kezer. Daughter of Col. Samuel H. Laughlin of Mc-
Minnville. Died at the residence of Timothy Kezer in this vicinity
on 3d inst. Aged 3 years old.
Nashville Whig. (Thurs., Sept. 8, 1842)

Laughlin, Isabella. Daughter of Col. S. H. Laughlin. Died at the
residence of her brother-in-law, T. Kezer Esq. Aged 17.
Nashville Whig. (Thurs., June 9, 1842)

Laughlin, Mr. Washington S. Age 20. Died at Murfreesborough on
Friday 7th inst.
National Banner & Nashville Whig. (Fri., Oct. 14, 1831)

Laurence, Mr. John. Aged 40 years. Died in Wilson County on the 2nd
June.
National Banner & Nashville Daily Advertiser. (Wed., July 3, 1833)

Laurens, Levy. Son of -- Laurens of Charleston, S. C. Died in
Houston, Texas on the 25th June.
National Banner & Nashville Whig. (Mon., July 31, 1837)

Lavender, John Esq. Aged 52. Died in Monroe County.
National Banner. (April 21, 1826)

Lawler, The Hon. Joab. A member of the House of Representative.
Died in Washington.
Nashville Whig. (Fri., May 18, 1838)

Lawless, Capt. Levi. Died at Matanzas of Yellow Fever.
National Banner & Nashville Daily Advertiser. (Mon., June 9, 1834)

Lawless, Louisa Maria. Aged 9 months, daughter of L. E. Lawless Esq.
Died in St. Louis, Mo. on Friday the 19th July of Asiatic Cholera.
National Banner & Nashville Daily Advertiser. (Mon., Aug. 12, 1833)

Lawless, William Frederick. Aged 5 years. Son of L. E. Lawless Esq.
Died in St. Louis on Friday the 19th of July, Asiatic Cholera.
National Banner & Nashville Daily Advertiser. (Mon., Aug. 12, 1833)

Lawrence, Dr. Of a Pulmonary affection. Died in Nashville on the 6th inst.
National Banner & Nashville Advertiser. (Mon., Oct. 8, 1832)

Lawrence, Mr. Benjamin. Son of Doctor William Lawrence. Died in Nashville on the 30th Aug.
National Banner & Nashville Whig. (Wed., Aug. 31, 1836)

Lawrence, Banjamin Rush. Eldest son of Dr. William P. Lawrence, aged 19 years and 2 months. Died in Nashville on 30th ulto.
National Banner & Nashville Whig. (Mon., Sept. 5, 1836)

Lawrence, Charles Pease. Age 1 and 10 months. Died in Nashville on the 8th inst. of dropsy of the Brain. Infant son of Dr. Wm. P. Lawrence.
National Banner & Nashville Advertiser. (Fri., Nov. 9, 1832)

Lawrence, Mr. Elias D. Died at Louisville, Ky.
National Banner & Nashville Whig. (Fri., July 11, 1828)

Lawrence, Jennings. Infant child of Thomas P. and Sarah A. Lawrence Died at the residence of Mrs. Sarah Vaughn near Nashville on the 9th inst. aged 9 months and 10 days.
Nashville Whig and Weekly Commercial Register. (Fri., Aug. 16, 1850)

Lawrence, Mrs. Mary. At the advanced age of 81. Died in Nashville on the 27th ultimo.
National Banner. (Sat., Aug. 8, 1829)

Lawrence, Mrs. Mary C. Wife of Mr. John B. Lawrence. Died in Memphis.
National Banner & Nashville Daily Advertiser. (Wed., Jan. 4, 1832)

Lawrence, Lieut. N. C. U. S. Navy. Died in New York on the 12th.
National Banner & Nashville Whig. (Mon., July 31, 1837)

Lawrence, Mrs. N. P. Consort of Dr. William P. Lawrence of Nashville. Died on the 19th inst. in her 55th year. (Obituary)
Nashville Whig. (Sat., March 28, 1846)

Lawrence, Mrs. Sarah. Wife of Mr. Edmund Lawrence in the 62 year of her age. Died in Williamson County on the 1st of Sept.
National Banner & Nashville Whig. (Sat., Sept. 9, 1826)

Lawrence, William Esq. Died at Memphis.
National Banner & Nashville Whig. (Fri., April 23, 1830)

Lawrence, Mr. W. H. In the 23d year of his age. Died in Nashville on the 23d inst.
Daily Republican Banner. (Sat., Aug. 26, 1837)

Lawring, Miss Sarah Jane. Aged 17. Died in Rutherford County, Tenn.
National Banner & Nashville Daily Advertiser. (Mon., April 7, 1834)

Lawry, Judge. Died - lately in North Carolina.
The Nashville Whig. & Tenn. Advertiser. (Feb. 7, 1818)

Laws, Mr. Chas. Jr. Died at Louisville, Ky.
National Banner & Nashville Daily Advertiser. (Mon., Oct. 15, 1832)

Lea, Mrs. Ellen. Wife of Albert Miller Lea Esq. Died in Baltimore of Consumption.
Nashville Whig. (Fri., Feb. 21, 1840)

Lea, Mr. John. Aged 29. Died in Rhea County.
National Banner & Nashville Whig. (Mon., Dec. 27, 1830)

Lea, Mrs. Susan Wills. Wife of the Hon. Luke Lea. Died at the residence of her husband in Cleveland, Tenn. on the 9th day of June. Mrs Lea was the daughter of John and Nancy T. McCormack.
The Christian Record. (Sat., July 1, 1848)

Lear, Benjamin Lincoln Esq. Died in Washington City.
National Banner & Nashville Daily Advertiser. (Mon., Oct. 15, 1832)

Leatherman, Mrs. Felix. Consort of Mr. Charles Leatherman of Giles County. Died in Rutherford County, she was the only daughter of Daniel Alexander Esq.
National Banner & Nashville Whig. (Mon., Aug. 17, 1835)

Ledbetter, Mr. Asa. Died in Shelby County, Illinois, drowned in Kaskaskai River.
National Banner & Nashville Whig. (Sat., Feb. 16, 1828)

Lee, Col. Boswell. Aged 56. Died at Springfield, Mass. For the last eighteen years, Supintendant of the National Armory at that place.
National Banner & Nashville Daily Advertiser. (Thurs., Sept. 12, 1833)

Lee, Charles. Of Boston. Died in the wreck of the Steam boat Lexington.
Daily Republican Banner. (Fri., Jan. 31, 1840)

Lee, D. C. Richard Esq. Died at Washington.
National Banner & Nashville Whig. (Sat., March 31, 1827)

Lee, Mr. Guy. Of Smith County. Died at New Orleans of Cholera.
National Banner & Nashville Daily Advertiser. (Wed., July 10, 1833)

Lee, Gen. Harry. Of Va. A revolutionary patriot. Died on the 25th ult. on Cumberland Island near Savanah.
The Nashville Whig. & Tenn. Advertiser. (April 25, 1818)

Lee, Maj. Henry. The distinguished author of the life of Napolean. Died.
Nashville Republican. (Sat., March 25, 1837)

Lee, Mr. Ralph. Died in Cincinnati.
Nashville Whig. (Mon., Oct. 8, 1838)

Lee, Mr. Wm. P. Died in Louisville, Ky.
National Banner & Nashville Whig. (Sat., July 8, 1826)

Leech, Mr. David. Died in Maury County.
National Banner & Nashville Whig. (Fri., Oct. 20, 1826)

Leetch, Mr. W. C. Died in Bolivar.
National Banner & Nashville Whig. (Sat., Nov. 3, 1827)

Leftwich, Mr. John B. Citizen and Merchant of Florence, Ala. Died on the 16th inst. in the city of New York for many years a citizen of Maury County, Tenn.
Nashville True Whig and Weekly Commercial Register. (Fri., Sept. 6, 1850)

Legare, Mr. Solomon. In his 80th year a soldier of the Revolution. Died in Charleston, S. C.
National Banner & Nashville Daily Advertiser. (Mon., July 14, 1834)

Legate, Mr. Charles. Aged 60 years. Died near Little Rock, Ark.
National Banner & Nashville Whig. (Mon., Jan. 5, 1835)

Leggett, William. In the 39th year of his age. Died - his death announced by the New York Evening Post of the 30th Newly appointed agent to Guatamalia.
Daily Republican Banner. (Sat., June 8, 1839)

Le Grand, Major Peter. Aged 63. Died in Tipton County, Tenn.
National Banner & Nashville Daily Advertiser. (Fri., Aug. 1, 1834)

Leiris, Rev. Carlisle. Pastor of the Evangelical protestant Church
of New Orleans. Died in New Orleans.
National Banner & Nashville Daily Advertiser. (Sat., Sept. 21, 1833)

Lellogg, William. Infant son of Mr. & Mrs. Lellogg. Died in
Clarksville.
Nashville Whig. (Thurs., April 30, 1846)

Lemaster, Mr. Joseph. Died in Columbia. A soldier of the revolution.
National Banner & Nashville Whig. (Sat., Aug. 26, 1826)

Lemay, Mr. John. A soldier of the Revolution. Died at Oxford, N.C.
National Banner & Nashville Daily Advertiser. (Tues., Feb. 11, 1834)

Lemmerick, William. Son of Thomas Lemmerick Esq. Died in Florence,
Ala.
Nashville Whig. (Wed., Sept. 16, 1840)

Lemon, Mr. James. Died in Lexington, Ky.
National Banner & Nashville Advertiser. (Tues., May 8, 1832)

Lemon, Mr. James H. Died in Jessamine County, Ky.
National Banner. (April 7, 1826)

Lennard, W. W. Esq. Died in Hardeman County, Tenn.
National Banner & Nashville Daily Advertiser. (Tues., Sept. 16, 1834)

Lennon, Mr. John. Of Nashville. Died on the 13th inst. Late of the
county Monaghan, Ireland.
The Nashville Gazette. (Wed., Sept. 14, 1819)

Lenox, Hugh. From Haywood County. Died at the Tenn. State Prison
of Cholera.
National Banner & Nashville Whig. (Fri., Aug. 14, 1835)

Leonard, Miss Matilda. Daughter of Mr. Thomas Leonard. Died in
Athens, Ala.
National Banner & Nashville Whig. (Wed., Nov. 12, 1834)

Leonard, Mrs. Perilla. Wife of Mr. S. L. Leonard and daughter of
Moses Fisk Esq. Died at Hilham.
National Banner & Nashville Whig. (Wed., Sept. 24, 1834)

Lester, Mrs. Martha Ann. Wife of Sterling H. Lester Esq. and second
daughter of the late William Wharton Esq. of Davidson County. Died
in Pulaski (Giles County) on the 5th inst. in the 24th year of her age.
National Banner & Nashville Whig. (Thurs., Sept. 30, 1830)

Lester, Col. Nathan. Late junior editor of the Columbus Democrat.
Died at Jackson, Miss. on the 22d inst. aged about 28 years. (Obituary)
Nashville Whig. (Mon., Aug. 5, 1839)

Lesuever, Virginia Caroline. Daughter of Littlebury Lesuever Esq.
aged 13 years 4 months. Died in Lincoln County.
National Banner & Nashville Daily Advertiser. (Wed., Aug. 14, 1833)

Levoy, Miss Ellen. Died in Lexington, Ky.
National Banner & Nashville Daily Advertiser. (Wed., July 31, 1833)

Levine, Mrs. Anne. Consort of L. C. Levin, Esq. Died on Sunday,
Jan. 5th.
National Banner & Nashville Daily Advertiser. (Mon., Jan. 6, 1834)

Lewis, Dr. Charles J. Died at Mobile.
National Banner & Nashville Whig. (Sat., Dec. 9, 1826)

Lewis, Mr. Edward H. A native of Virginia. Died in Limestone County, Ala.
National Banner. (Sat., Aug. 8, 1829)

Lewis, Mrs. Elizabeth. Died in Fayette County, Ky.
National Banner & Nashville Whig. (Sat., April 14, 1827)

Lewis, Fielding Esq. Died at his residence on James River, Va.
National Banner & Nashville Daily Advertiser. (Mon., June 30, 1834)

Lewis, Maj. Henderson. Died in Memphis of Cholera formerly of Carthage.
National Banner & Nashville Daily Advertiser. (Wed., March 26, 1834)

Lewis, Mr. Hickman. Died at the residence of his brother John H. Lewis Esq. in Huntsville, Ala. on Sat. the 5th inst.
Nashville Whig. (Tues., Aug. 15, 1843)

Lewis, Col. Joel. An old and respectable inhabitant of this county died on Friday last.
The Nashville Whig. (Nov. 26, 1816)

Lewis, Mr. John. 40. Died in Pulaski on June 10, of Cholera.
National Banner & Nashville Daily Advertiser. (Wed., June 19, 1833)

Lewis, Mrs. Consort of Mr. John Lewis aged 30. Died in Pulaski on June 6 of Cholera.
National Banner & Nashville Daily Advertiser. (Wed., June 19, 1833)

Lewis, Hon. Joshua. Died in New Orleans.
National Banner & Nashville Daily Advertiser. (Thurs., June 20, 1833)

Lewis, Maj. Lawrence. The nephew and last of Washington near blood relations. Died at Wood Lawn in the County of Fairfax, Virginia in the 73d year of his age in the month of Nov.
Nashville Union. (Fri., Dec. 27, 1839)

Lewis, Miss Margaret. Died in Fayette County.
National Banner & Nashville Whig. (Sat., Oct. 28, 1826)

Lewis, Mrs. Margaret G. The amiable companion of Wm. B. Lewis esq. Died at Fairfield near Nashville.
Nashville Whig. (Tues., Feb. 27, 1816)

Lewis, Mrs. Mary Adelaide. Wife of Maj. William B. Lewis to whome whe left the solace and the care of an infant son and daughter five days old. Died on Friday the 2d inst. Aged __.
Nashville Whig. (May 7, 1823)

Lewis, Gen. Morgan. Formerly Governor of the State of New York. Died on the 7th inst. at the advanced age of ninety years. He was one of the last survivors of the Revolutionary War.
Nashville Whig. (Thurs., April 18, 1844)

Lewis, Mr. Sam W. Died at Potesi, Mo.
National Banner & Nashville Whig. (Sat., June 16, 1827)

Lewis, Mr. Samuel. Died in Sumner County.
National Banner & Nashville Whig. (Mon., Oct. 31, 1831)

Lewis, Mr. Thomas D. Died in Christian County, Ky.
National Banner & Nashville Advertiser. (Fri., Nov. 23, 1832)

Lewis, Major William. Aged 68 years. Died in Franklin County, Ala.
National Banner & Nashville Daily Advertiser. (Wed., Aug. 20, 1834)

Lewis, Mr. William Henry. Only son of William B. Lewis Esq. Died on Tuesday, Aug. 30th at the residence of Mr. Richard Bostick in the

20th year of his age. (Obituary).
Nashville Whig. (Sat., Sept. 3, 1842)

Lewis,Col. Willis. In about the 60th year of his age. Died in
Hardeman County.
National Banner & Nashville Whig. (Thurs., Nov. 4, 1830)

Lightfoot, Thos. Walker. Died at Culpper? Court House, Va. Clerk of
the Superior Court.
Nashville Republican & State Gazette. (Tues., March 29, 1831)

Likins, Mrs. Abel. Of Virginia. Died at Knoxville.
National Banner & Nashville Whig. (Sat., Nov. 18, 1826)

Lilly, Mrs. Elenora A. Nov. 11, 1830. Consort of Mr. Eliakim Lilly,
merchant of Pittsburg, Penn. Youngest daughter of Mrs. Sarah Cooper,
of Nashville. Died at Cincinnatti.
National Banner & Nashville Whig. (Mon., Jan. 10, 1831)

Limerick, Rev. Daniel. Of the Methodist Episcopal Church. Died
Tuesday the 29th of March at Uniontown, Pa.
National Banner & Nashville Whig. (Wed., April 19, 1837)

Linck, Miss Laura. Aged 16 years, daughter of Francis Linck Esq.
Died in Evansville, Ind, formerly of Nashville.
Daily Republican Banner. (Sat., March 10, 1838)

Lincoln, Mrs. Mary. Aged 75 years. Died in Carter County, Tenn.
National Banner & Nashville Daily Advertiser. (Tues., Sept. 16, 1834)

Lindsay, Capt. Anthony. Died in Scott County, Ky.
Nashville Republican & State Gazette. (Tues., May 3, 1831)

Lindsay, Jane Rachel. Consort of Lewis Lindsay. Died in Wilson
County on the 20th of June.
Daily Republican Banner. (Thurs., July 9, 1840)

Lindsay, Mrs. Jane. Aged 77. Died in Frankford, Ky.
National Banner. (Sat., Aug. 22, 1829)

Lindsay, Lafayette. Son of Lewis Lindsay. Died in Wilson County on
the 12th June.
Daily Republican Banner. (Thurs., July 9, 1840)

Lindsay, Victoria. Daughter of Lewis Lindsay. Died in Wilson County
on the 5th July. Daily Republican Banner. (Thurs., July 9, 1840)

Lindsay, Col. William. Of the U. S. Army. Died in Huntsville, on
the 15th inst.
Daily Republican Banner. (Mon., Sept. 25, 18__)

Lindsey, Rev. Eli. Died in Conway Co., Ark.
National Banner & Nashville Daily Advertiser. (Mon., June 9, 1834)

Lindsey, Robert Esq. Died in Knox County.
National Banner. (Sat., July 25, 1829)

Lindsley, John Berrien. Son of A. V. S. and Eliza M. Lindsley.
Died on Thursday Oct. 28th aged 2 years 6 months and 12 days.
The Christian Record. (Sat., Nov. 6, 1847)

Lindsley, Philip. Son of A. V. S. and Eliza M. Lindsley. Died on
Thursday 13th inst. aged 4 years and 7 months and 11 days. Grand-
son of the Rev. Philip Lindsley.
The Politician and Weekly Nashville Whig. (Fri., Oct. 22, 1847)

Lindsley, Philip. Son of A. V. S. and Eliza M. Lindsley and grandson of

the Rev. Philip Lindsley D. D. Died on Thursday, Oct. 14th aged 4 years 7 months and 11 days.
The Christian Record. (Sat., Nov. 6, 1847)

Lindsley, Philip Jr. Died on Tuesday evening Sept. 10th. Aged nine years two months and fourteen days.
Nashville Whig. (Sat., Sept. 14, 1844)

Lineau, Daniel. Merchant of Murfreesboro. Died at Bershaba Springs, Tenn. on the 11th inst.
National Banner & Nashville Whig. (Wed., Aug. 16, 1837)

Linebaugh, Mr. Daniel. Died in Russellville, Ky.
National Banner. (March 31, 1826)

Linn, Mr. Barnabas. Recently from New Orleans. Died at St. Louis.
National Banner. (Sat., Aug. 29, 1829)

Linn, Hon. John. A member of the house of Representative from the State of New Jersey. Died yesterday afternoon, aged about 57 years. (Nat. Intel. 6th inst.)
The Nashville Gazette. (Sat., Jan. 27, 1821)

Linn, Mrs. Consort of Maj. Joseph Linn. Died in Madison County, Tenn.
National Banner & Nashville Whig. (Sat., Sept. 30, 1826)

Linn, Dr. James. Died in Halifax County, Va. on Monday 7 of March.
Impartial Review and Cumberland Repository. (Sat., April 26, 1806)

Linsey, Mr. Caleb. Died in Clark County, Ark.
National Banner & Nashville Whig. (Sat., Jan. 13, 1827)

Linton, John Esq. An eminent merchant of New Orleans and President of the Canal Bank of that city. Died at Sarotoga Springs, N.Y.
National Banner & Nashville Whig. (Mon., Sept. 22, 1834)

Lipscomb, Mr. John. Died at his residence near Salem in Franklin County, Tenn. on the 15th Sept. in the 36th year of his age.
The Politician and Weekly Nashville Whig. (Wed., Oct. 6, 1847)

Litton, Mr. Alexander H. In this place, Mr. Alexander H. Litton, late conductor of the English and Commercial School in this place and a highly worthy citizen.
Nashville Republican. (Sat., May 28, 1836)

Little, Harvey D. Esq. Editor of the Medical Botanist. Died at Columbus, O.
National Banner & Nashville Daily Advertiser. (Mon., Sept. 9, 1833)

Little, Mr. James. In the 20th year of his age. Died in Nashville on Thursday the 10th inst. Formerly of Pulaski, Tenn.
Nashville Whig. (Sat., Sept. 12, 1846)

Little, Rev. Robert. Died in Harrisburgh, Penn. Paster of the First Unitarian Church in Washington.
National Banner & Nashville Whig. (Sat., Sept. 1, 1827)

Littlefield, Mrs. Catherine. Consort of Dr. Littlefield. Died in Maury County.
National Banner & Nashville Daily Advertiser. (Thurs., June 20, 1833)

Littlefield, Edward Esq. Late President of the Bank of Tennessee. Died in Nashville.
National Banner & Nashville Whig. (Wed., Feb. 24, 1836)

Littlejohn, Mrs. Monica. Wife of Rev. John Littlejohn. Died in Logan County, Ky.
National Banner & Nashville Whig. (Sat., Jan. 26, 1828)

Litton, Mr. Alexander H.   Died in Nashville on May 25th.
National Banner & Nashville Whig. (Fri., May 23, 1836)

Litton, Alexander H.   Infant son of Rev. Samuel G. Litton.   Died in
La Grange, Tenn. on Friday June 30th.
Nashville Whig. (Sat., July 8, 1843)

Litton, Mr. Alexander H.   Died in Nashville, late conductor of the
English and Commercial School.
Nashville Republican. (Sat., May 28, 1836)

Litton, Jacob.   Aged 18 years, son of Joseph Litton of Nashville.
Died Franklin, Tenn. of Cholera.
National Banner & Nashville Whig. (Mon., July 20, 1835)

Litton, Mr. Joseph.   Died in Nashville on Tuesday last in the 68th
year of his age.
Nashville Whig. (Thurs., June 25, 1846)

Litton, Joseph Jr.   Son of Joseph Litton Sr.   Died in Nashville on
Monday 16th inst.   He was an active member of the City Fire Department.
Nashville Whig. (Wed., Aug. 18, 1841)

Litton, Miss Margaret.   Youngest daughter of Mr. Alexander H. Litton.
Died in Nashville.
National Banner & Nashville Daily Advertiser. (Sat., Sept. 8, 1832)

Litton, Miss Margaret.   Died in Nashville.   Youngest daughter of
Alexander H. Litton.
National Banner & Nashville Advertiser. (Sat., Sept. 8, 1832)

Livingston, Jon. Brookholst.   Of New York, one of the Judges of the
Supreme Court of the United States.   Died at Washington City.
Nashville Whig. (April 9, 1823)

Livingston, Hon. Edward.   Late minister to France.   Died on the 22nd
of May at his home in Duchess County, New York. (Obituary)
The Union. (Sat., June 12, 1836)

Livingston, Mrs. Eleanor R.   Relict of the late Williamson Livingston
and eldest daughter of John Nichols Esq. of Nashville.   Died last
evening.
Nashville Whig. (Mon., March 29, 1841)

Livingston, Mrs. Elizabeth.   Aged 30.   Wife of Mr. John Livingston.
National Banner & Nashville Daily Advertiser. (Tues., June 24, 1834)

Livingston, Rev. Gilbert R.   Paster of the First reformed Dutch Church,
Crown Street.   Died in Philadelphia on the 9th inst.
National Banner & Nashville Daily Advertiser. (Wed., March 26, 1834)

Livingston, Phoebe Jane.   Infant daughter of Mr. John Livingston
18 months old.   Died in New Orleans.
National Banner & Nashville Daily Advertiser. (Tues., June 24, 1831)

Lloyd, Col. Edward.   Formerly Governor of the State.   Died at Annapolis
Maryland recently a member of the U. S. Senate, aged 56.
National Banner & Nashville Daily Advertiser. (Thurs., June 19, 1834)

Lloyd, Hon. Jas.   Formerly a member of the United States Senate from
Massachusetts, aged 61 years.   Died in New York on the 5th inst.
National Banner & Nashville Whig. (Mon., April 25, 1831)

Lloyd, Mr. John.   Died in Kingston, Roane County.
National Banner. (Sat., Aug. 29, 1829)

Lloyd, Mr. Stephen.   Died in Giles County.
National Banner & Nashville Whig. (Wed., April 27, 1831)

Lloyd, William. In the 74th year of his age. Died in Nashville on the 18th inst.
National Banner & Nashville Whig. (Fri., Jan. 23, 1835)

Locke, Mr. Charles C. Died in New Orleans on the 30th Aug. of Yellow Fever., late of Memphis, Tenn.
Nashville Whig. (Mon., Sept. 23, 1839)

Locke, Mr. Silas. Of Murfreesborough. Died at Tyrees Springs on Monday 9th inst.
National Banner & Nashville Whig. (Mon., Aug. 16, 1830)

Locke, Col. William. Of Rutherford County. Died in Maury County.
National Banner & Nashville Whig. (Mon., Sept. 26, 1831)

Locke, Col. Wm. Of Gainsboro, Jackson County. Died in Henry County of Cholera.
National Banner & Nashville Daily Advertiser. (Sat., June 15, 1833)

Lockelier, Jeffrey. A free man of color, aged 42 years. Died on the 22nd inst. at the residence of Col. Armstrong.
National Banner & Nashville Whig. (Mon., Sept. 27, 1830)

Locke, Capt. Silas. He was a native of Ireland. Died lately at Smith Springs.
National Banner & Nashville Whig. (Mon., Sept. 6, 1830)

Locker, George L. Esq. Died at Hopkinsville, Ky.
National Banner & Nashville Daily Advertiser. (Mon., Sept. 17, 1832)

Lockett, Mrs. Helen A. J. Consort of Henry C. Lockett, and daughter of John D. and Mary A. T. Anthony late of Knoxville, Tennessee. Died on the 25th inst. aged 17 years.
The Politician and Weekly Nashville Whig. (Fri., Dec. 31, 1847)

Lockhart, David Esq. Of the firm of Andrew Lockhart & Co. Died in New Orleans.
National Banner & Nashville Daily Advertiser. (Sat., Sept. 21, 1833)

Lockhart, Maj. James. Died in Nashville, a pioneer of the West and one of the first settlers in Tennessee.
National Banner & Nashville Daily Advertiser. (Wed., Nov. 7, 1832)

Lockhart, Maj. James. Died in Nashville.
National Banner & Nashville Advertiser. (Wed., Nov. 7, 1832)

Lockhart, Mr. Robert. Merchant of Athens, Ala. Died in Philadelphia.
National Banner. (May 13, 1826)

Lockhart, Mr. Samuel. Died at Louisville, Ky.
National Banner. (March 31, 1826)

Lockwood, Edwin. Died 18th at Cincinnati, Ohio of Cholera.
National Banner & Nashville Daily Advertiser. (Thurs., Oct. 25, 1832)

Lodge, Mrs. Susanna. Died at Cincinnati.
National Banner & Nashville Whig. (Sat., Aug. 11, 1827)

Lofland, Mr. Banjamin H. Formerly of Russellville, Ky. Died in Perry County, Tenn.
National Banner & Nashville Whig. (Mon., Nov. 10, 1834)

Logan, Mr. James Walker. Late of Shelbyville, Ky. Died in Little Rock, Ark.
National Banner & Nashville Whig. (Mon., Aug. 3, 1835)

Logan, John Esq. A member of the legislature. Died in Shelby Co.,Ky.
National Banner. (Jan. 20, 1826)

222

Lonas, Willie. Son of Mr. Henry Lonas. Died in Knox County.
National Banner & Nashville Whig. (Sat., Feb. 24, 1827)

London, Doctor William S. Aged about 30 years. Died near Middleburg,
Hardeman County, Tenn. on the 15th Feb. Son of Lavender London, of
Nelson County, Va.
National Banner & Nashville Daily Advertiser. (Fri., March 7, 1834)

London, Elizabeth Campbell. Aged 11 months, only child of Samuel
London Esq. Died in Giles County near Cornersville.
National Banner & Nashville Whig. (Wed., Oct. 8, 1834)

Loner, Mrs. Evelina. Wife of Mr. John Loner. Died at Knoxville,
Nov. 17.
National Banner. (Sat., Dec. 5, 1829)

Long, Col. Armstead. Died in Culpepper City, Va.
Nashville Republican & State Gazette. (Tues., March 8, 1831)

Long, Henry. Died 16th at Cincinnati, Ohio of Cholera.
National Banner & Nashville Daily Advertiser. (Wed., Oct. 24, 1832)

Long, Mr. John. Died at St. Louis.
National Banner. (April 21, 1826)

Long, Joseph Esq. Died at Lynchburg in this State on the 6th inst.
Post Master at that Place.
Nashville Union. (Mon., Sept. 24, 1838)

Long, Joseph Esq. Died in Lynchburg, Tenn. Post Master at that Place
Daily Republican Banner. (Tues., Sept. 25, 1838)

Long, Mrs. Mary P. Wife of M. A. Long Esq. Died in Shelbyville, Ten.
on the 30th ult.
Daily Republican Banner. (Mon., April 7, 1838)

Long, Mr. Michael. Died on Wednesday last in Williamson County.
The Western Weekly Review. (Fri., April 13, 1832) Franklin, Tenn.

Long, Mr. Michael. Died on Wednesday last an old and respectable
citizen.
National Banner & Nashville Advertiser. (Mon., April 23, 1832)

Long, Mr. Mitchael. Died on Wednesday last an old and respectable
citizen of Williamson County.
National Banner & Nashville Daily Advertiser. (Mon., April 23, 1832)

Long, Mrs. Sarah. Wife of Richard Long. Died in Bedford County in
the 71st year of her age. (Obituary)
National Banner & Nashville Daily Advertiser. (Fri., Oct. 19, 1832)

Long, Mrs. Sarah. On the 6 inst. wife of Richard Long a Surviving
Patroit of the American Revolution, age 71. Died in Bedford County.
National Banner & Nashville Advertiser. (Fri., Oct. 19, 1832)

Long, Willis. Died at New Castle of Cholera.
National Banner & Nashville Daily Advertiser. (Sat., Aug. 10, 1833)

Longley, Mrs. Elizabeth. Died in Columbia.
National Banner. (Sat., July 25, 1829)

Longley, Mr. James. Aged 31. Died at Columbia.
National Banner. (Sat., April 25, 1829)

Longstreet, Dr. Wm. S. Died in White County.
National Banner - Nashville Daily Advertiser. (Fri., Dec. 27, 1833)

Looney, Miss Annis L. Daughter of A. Looney Esq. Died in Maury
County, Ten.
National Banner & Nashville Daily Advertiser. (Mon., Feb. 17, 1834)

Looney, Mrs. Mary A. Wife of David Looney Esq. of Maury. Died near
Columbia July 24th, aged 25.
Nashville Whig. (Wed., July 29, 1840)

Looney, Mrs. Sarah. Aged about 89 years. Died near Knoxville on
Wednesday last.
Daily Republican Banner. (Sat., Oct. 20, 1838)

Loper, Mr. Clement. Aged 45. Died at Mobile.
National Banner & Nashville Whig. (Sat., Sept. 30, 1826)

Lord, Col. Thomas. Aged 28. Died at Columbus, Ohio.
National Banner. (April 14, 1826)

Lorimier, Major William. Died in Reynoldsburgh.
National Banner & Nashville Whig. (Fri., Jan. 29, 1830)

Lotspeech, Mr. David. Died at Hopkinsville, Ky.
National Banner & Nashville Daily Advertiser. (Wed., Aug. 22, 1832)

List of Deaths in Louisville, Ky. from Cholera, on Page 2.
National Banner & Nashville Daily Advertiser. (Mon., Oct. 29, 1832)

Love, Col. Charles I. Died at his Iron Works in Perry County on the
28th July.
The Union. (Sat., Aug. 5, 1837)

Love, Col. C. I. Of this vicinity. Died on Sat. last at his Iron
Works, in Perry County, Tenn.
Nashville Republican (Thurs., Aug. 3, 1837)

Love, Mr. David. Died in Maury County.
National Banner & Nashville Whig. (Sat., April 21, 1827)

Love, Mrs. Frances. Consort of Col. Charles I. Love. Died in
Davidson County.
National Banner & Nashville Daily Advertiser. (Wed., June 19, 1833)

Love, Henry I., Esq. Late of Washington City. Died at Mansfield
the residence of Charles I. Love, on the 6th day of October. In the
25th year of his age.
Nashville Whig. (Oct. 11, 1824)

Love, Capt. Joseph. Son of Gen. Thomas Love. of North Carolina, age
23. Died in Madison County.
National Banner & Nashville Whig. (Thurs., June 24, 1830)

Love, Col. Joseph. Died in Rhea County.
Nashville Republican & State Gazette. (Tues., June 21, 1831)

Love, Col. Joseph. Aged 52. Formerly of Knox County. Died in
Rhea County.
National Banner & Nashville Whig. (Mon., June 20, 1831)

Love, Mr. Joseph. Age 80. Formerly of Davidson County. Died at
Little Rock, Ark. on 16 of Aug.
National Banner & Nashville Whig. (Fri., Sept. 2, 1831)

Love, Josiah Esq. Attorney at law. Died lately at Jonesborough.
Knoxville Gazette. (Thurs., Jan. 2, 1794)

Love, Mrs. Lucinda. Wife of Mr. James V. Love. Died in Lawrenceburg,
Ky.
National Banner & Nashville Whig. (December 2, 1826)

Love, Robert Caruthers. Second son of Col. John D. Love, aged 2
years and 5 months. Died in Henry County.
National Banner & Nashville Daily Advertiser. (Sat., May 18, 1833)

Love, Mr. Samuel. Died in Carter County.
Nashville Republican and State Gazette. (Wed., Dec. 5, 1832)

Love, Mr. Samuel. Died in Knox County.
National Banner. (April 21, 1826)

Love, Mrs. Thomas. Aged 31 years. Died in Jefferson County.
National Banner & Nashville Whig. (Mon., Oct. 17, 1831)

Love, Mr. Washington. Died at Frankfort, Ky.
National Banner. (Sat., Aug. 1, 1829)

Loving, Mr. A. B. Aged 18 years formerly of Nashville, Tenn.
Died in Columbus, Mi. on the 12th inst.
Nashville Republican. (Sat., Sept. 24, 1836)

Loving, Mary E. Youngest daughter of Dr. H. T. Loving of Russellville
Died near Bowling Green, Ky.
National Banner & Nashville Whig. (Fri., Oct. 31, 1834)

Loving, Col. William. Nearly 65 years of age. Died near Russellville,
Ky.
National Banner & Nashville Daily Advertiser. (Sat., Aug. 2, 1834)

Lowance, Joseph. Of Park County, Ia.? A Passenger. Died on the Steamer
George Collier, about 80 miles below Natchez. Scalded to death.
Daily Republican Banner. (Tues., May 14, 1839)

Lowe, Thomasine Marvell. Daughter of W. Lowe aged 2 years. Died in
Nashville on 2d inst.
Daily Republican Banner. (Thurs., March 21, 1839)

Lowe, William. Died in Shelbyville, Tenn.
National Banner & Nashville Daily Advertiser. (Thurs., July 11, 1833)

Lowndes, William Esq. Died at sea on the 27th October last. For
many years a distinguished member of Congress from S. Carolina.
Nashville Whig. (Feb. 5, 1823)

Lowery, Martha. Infant daughter of Mr. Lowery. Died at Murfreesborough.
National Banner & Nashville Daily Advertiser. (Mon., Aug. 27, 1832)

Lowrey, Capt. Robert T. Died in Amite County, Mississippi.
National Banner. (Jan. 27, 1826)

Lowry, Mrs. Nancy. Wife of Mr. David Lowry. Died in Monroe County.
Nashville Banner & Nashville Whig. (July 28, 1827)

Lowry, David. Died 14th at Cincinnati, Ohio of Cholera.
National Banner & Nashville Daily Advertiser. (Tues., Oct. 23, 1832)

Lowry, Mr. Gresham L. Died in Jessamine County, Ky.
National Banner. (April 7, 1826)

Lowry,Miss Sarah G. Of N. Y. Died in New Orleans of Yellow Fever.
Daily Republican Banner. (Wed., Oct. 4, 1837)

Loyd, Hon. James. Died in New York City.
Nashville Republican & State Gazette. (Sat., April 23, 1831)

Loyd, Mr. Stephen. Died in Giles County.
Nashville Republican & State Gazette. (Sat., April 23, 1831)

Lucas, Alexander. Died at Raleigh, N. C. senior editor of the Raleigh Minerva.
The Clarion and Tennessee Gazette. (January 23, 1821) (From the St. Louis Enquirer of Jan. 6.)

Lucas, Dr. John R. Of Limestone County. Died in Morgan County, Ala.
National Banner & Nashville Whig. (Wed., Aug. 3, 1831)

Lucas, Dr. John R. Of Limestone County. Died in Morgan County, Ala.
National Banner & Nashville Whig. (Wed., Aug. 3, 1831)

Luckett, Major Craven P. Formerly of Louisville, Ky. Died at Tallahasse, Fla.
National Banner & Nashville Daily Advertiser. (Thurs., July 18, 1833)

Lucky, Eliza Ann. Aged 7 years. Died 17th at Cincinnati, Ohio of Cholera.
National Banner & Nashville Daily Advertiser. (Wed., Oct. 24, 1832)

Luke, Miss Francis Ann. Aged 15 years. Died in Macon County, Ky.
National Banner. (March 3, 1826)

Luke, William. Son of Doctor Lea of this town, aged nearly two years. Died at Winchester on the 9th inst.
Nashville Whig. (Sept. 20, 1824)

Lumpkin, Thomas A. Esq. Died at Claiborne, Ala.
National Banner & Nashville Whig. (Sat., Nov. 3, 1827)

Lumsden, Mrs. Wife of Mr. William Lumsden. Died in Fayetteville, N.C.
National Banner & Nashville Daily Advertiser. (Sat., Aug. 10, 1833)

Lusk, Mr. John. Aged 104 years. Died in Warren County, Tennessee on the 8th of June. A soldier of the Revolution.
Nashville Whig. (Fri., June 29, 1838)

Lusk, Joseph. Infant son of Robert Lusk Esq. Died in Nashville on the 3d inst.
Nashville Whig. (Tues., July 7, 1846)

Lutz, Mr. Samuel H. Died at Cincinnati.
National Banner. (Sat., Aug. 8, 1829)

Lyle, Mr. John K. Died in Montgomery, Ala.
National Banner & Nashville Whig. (September 2, 1826)

Lynch, Mr. John Bowman. Eldest son of Dr. Lynch of S. Carolina. Died in Nashville on the 3d inst. in the 28th year of his age.
Nashville Whig. (Thurs., May 12, 1842)

Lynes, Mrs. Died in this place on the 23d inst.
The Nashville Whig and Tenn. Advertiser. (Feb. 28, 1818)

Lynn, Mrs. Elly. Widow of the late Maj. Stephen Lynn aged 60. Died in Montgomery County.
National Banner & Nashville Whig. (Fri., April 1, 1831)

Lyon, Mrs. Eliza. Wife of Mr. Alpheus Lyons. Died in Nashville on Monday afternoon 28 May. See paper for Obituary.
National Banner & Nashville Advertiser. (Tues., May 29, 1832)

Lyon, Mrs. Eliza. Wife of Mr. Alpheus Lyon a Merchant of Nashville. Died in Nashville on Monday 28th May.
National Banner & Nashville Daily Advertiser. (Tues., May 29, 1832)

Lyon, Mrs. Elly. Died in Montgomery County, Ten.
Nashville Republican & State Gazette. (Thurs., March 31, 1831)

Lyon, Mrs Elly. Age 60, widow of the late Maj. Stephenson Lyon.

Died in Montgomery County.
National Banner & Nashville Whig. (Fri., April 7, 1831)

Lyon, Miss Eliza. Daughter of Mr. James S. and Mrs. Martha Lyon.
Died in Jackson suddenly on the 7th inst. in the 20th year of her age.
Nashville Whig. (Sat., March 21, 1846)

Lyon, Miss Eliza. Daughter of Mr. James S. and Mrs. Martha Lyon.
Died in Jackson suddenly on the 7th inst. in the 20th year of her
age.
Nashville Whig. (Sat., March 21, 1846)

Lyons, Mr. Guthridge. Aged 74. Died in Montgomery County.
National Banner & Nashville Whig. (Sat., March 10, 1827)

Lyons, Mr. John. Died in Nashville on Monday evening last.
Nashville Republican. (Sat., Jan. 31, 1836)

Lyon, Samuel. Infant son of Mr. Alpheus Lyon. Died on Sunday the
18th inst. at the residence of his grandfather, M. C. Dunn, Esq. of
this County.
National Banner & Nashville Daily Advertiser. (Thurs., Nov. 22, 1832)

Lyon, Samuel. Infant son of Mr. Alpheus Lyon Esq. Died at the
residence of his grandfather, M. C. Dunn Esq. of Davidson County
(Obituary).
National Banner & Nashville Daily Advertiser. (Thurs., Nov. 22, 1832)

Lyons, Mr. John. In this place on Monday evening last Mr. John Lyons.
Nashville Republican. (Sat., Jan. 30, 1836)

Lytle, William Esq. Aged 60 years. Died in Nashville yesterday for
many years a member of the Legislature from Davidson County. His
funeral today from the Methodist E. Church at 2 o'clock.
Nashville Union. (Fri., Jan. 18, 1839)

Mabon, Miss Elizabeth. Age 90. Died in Knoxville.
National Banner & Nashville Whig. (Mon., Oct. 31, 1831)

Mabry, General Joseph A. Of Tennessee. Died in Tuscaloosa, Ala.
Nashville Republican. (Sat., April 29, 1837)

Mabry, Gen. Joseph A. Of Knox County this State. Died in Tuscaloosa,
Ala. on the 19th April for many years a member of the Legislature of
Tennessee.
The Union. (Sat., May 6, 1837)

Mabry, Mr. Seth. Died in Wilson County.
National Banner & Nashville Whig. (Sat., Dec. 9, 1826)

McAdams, ___. The great road maker. Died lately at Moffat, aged 81.
The Union. (Tues., March 14, 1837)

McAdams, John Loudon Esq. Died recently at Moffat in Scotland.
Nashville Republican. (Sat., Feb. 11, 1837)

McAffry, William P. Died at Knoxville, Ten. Aug. 28.
National Banner & Nashville Daily Advertiser. (Mon., Sept. 9, 1833)

McAdoo, Mr. John. Age 73. Died in Anderson County.
National Banner & Nashville Whig. (Mon., Jan. 10, 1831)

McAffee, Mr. Thomas. Died at Florence, Ala.
National Banner & Nashville Daily Advertiser. (Wed., Aug. 7, 1833)

M'Affrey, Joseph. Son of T. M'Affrey. Died in Knoxville, Ten.
Daily Republican Banner. (Sat., Oct. 27, 1838)

M'Affry, Maj. Terence. Died at Knoxville.
National Banner & Nashville Whig. (Tues., April 20, 1830)

McAlister, Mrs. Frances. Relict of the late John McAlister of Franklin
and Mother of James McAlister of Nashville. Died in Nashville at the
residence of her son-in-law, Mr. H. R. W. Hill, on the 11th inst.
Nashville Whig. (Sat., July 15, 1843)

McAlister, James Akin. Infant son of W. K. and Mrs. Frances R.
McAlister. Died in Nashville on the 22nd ult, aged three years and
four days.
The Christian Record. (Sat., Jan. 1st. 1848)

M'Alister, Mr. John. Of Franklin, T. Died near Bowling Green, Ky.
Drowned in Green River.
National Banner & Nashville Whig. (Sat., April 7, 1827)

McAllister, Mrs. Frances. Aged 89. Died in Washington County suddenly.
National Banner & Nashville Daily Advertiser. (Wed., April 3, 1833)

M'Allister, J. A Soldier of the Revolution. Died at M'Allister Cross
roads, Montgomery County.
National Banner. (Feb. 10, 1826)

McAlpin, Mrs. Rebecca. Consort of R. C. McAlpin. Died on Thursday
the 9th inst. at the residence of Mr. John Burgess.
National Banner & Nashville Daily Advertiser. (Tues., Jan. 14,1834)

M'Amy, James Esq. Died in Athens, T.
National Banner & Nashville Whig. (Sat., Oct. 7, 1826)

McAulay, Mrs. Margaret. Consort of Dan'l M'Aulay. Died at Gallatin
on the 17th ult.
National Banner & Nashville Whig. (Sat., March 10, 1827)

M'Bath, Mrs. Caroline D. Wife of Mr. James M'Bath. Died at Knoxville.
National Banner & Nashville Whig. (Sat., April 21, 1827)

M'Bee, Mr. William. Aged 70 years. Died in Knox County.
National Banner. (Feb. 10, 1826)

McBroom, William Esq. Of Huntsville. Died in Florence, Ala.
National Banner & Nashville Whig. (Sat., April 26, 1828)

McCabe, Bryan. Died on the morning of Wednesday the 28th ult. at Mrs.
Bell's in Hawkins County, Mr. Bryan McCabe of Philadelphia, of the
small-pox. He took the infection at Bladensburg, on his way to this
place. Mr McCabe was a valuable citizen, highly esteemed by his
acquaintances.
Knoxville Gazette. (Thurs., June 5, 1794)

M'Cabe, Mr. Hugh. Died in Mount Pleasant.
Nashville Republican & State Gazette. (Mon., Dec. 17, 1832)

McCabe, Mr. Hugh. Formerly of Williamson County. Died on Wednesday
5th inst. in Mt. Pleasant, Maury Co.
The Western Weekly Review. (Fri., Dec. 14, 1832) Franklin, Tenn.

M'Caleb, Rev. James. Died in Hickman County.
National Banner & Nashville Whig. (Sat., June 7, 1828)

McCall, Fanny. Aged 15 years. Second daughter of Dr. Alexander
McCall. Died on Sunday night 20th inst. on consumption.
Nashville Whig. (Thurs., March 24, 1842)

McCall, Mr. Hugh. Formerly of Williamson County. Died in Mount
Pleasant, Maury County.
National Banner & Nashville Advertiser. (Mon., Dec. 17, 1832)

McCalla, Dr. Andrew. Died in Lexington, Ky.
National Banner & Nashville Advertiser. (Mon., Dec. 3, 1832)

M'Callie, Mr. John Sen. Died in Blount County.
National Banner & Nashville Whig. (Mon., April 4, 1831)

M'Callie, Mr. Jno. Died in Blount County, Ten.
Nashville Republican & State Gazette. (Tues., April 5, 1831)

McCampbell, Mr. Eli S. In his 21st year. Died in Nashville on the
22d inst. A pupil in the Tennessee Institute for the Blind.
The Politician & Weekly Nashville Whig. (Fri., July 2, 1847)

McCampbell, Mr. Eli S. In his 21st year. Died in Nashville on the
morning of the 22d inst. (Obituary).
The Christian Record. (Sat., June 26, 1847)

McCampbell, Mr. J. C. Died in Knoxville, Tenn.
Daily Republican Banner. (Sat., Sept. 29, 1838)

M'Campbell, Maj. John. Died on Sunday night last aged about 39 years.
(Knoxville Reg. Feb. 13)
The Nashville Gazette. (Sat., Feb. 17, 1821)

McCanless, Mr. John. In the 87th year of his age. Died in Maury
County on the 15th October. A Revolutionary soldier.
Nashville Republican. (Fri., Nov. 11, 1836)

McCanless, Mr. John. In the 87th year of his age. Died in Maury
County, Tenn. on the 15th Oct. A Revolutionary soldier. He lived
for many years in East Tenn.
National Banner & Nashville Whig. (Fri., Nov. 11, 1836)

McCann, Mr. Hezekiah. Died in Fayette County, Ky.
National Banner & Nashville Whig. (Fri., March 6, 1835)

McCann, Sarah. Aged 12 months. Died in Nashville.
National Banner & Nashville Daily Advertiser. (Thurs., June 6, 1833)

M'Carkle, Mr. Wm. Formerly editor of the Freemans Journal. Died
in Philadelphia.
National Banner. (March 3, 1826)

M'Carley, Mrs. Martha. Wife of Mr. Wm. M'Carley. Died in Logan
County, Ky.
National Banner. (Sat., April 18, 1829)

McCarpin, Francis. From Maury County. Died at the Tenn. State Prison
of Cholera.
National Banner & Nashville Whig. (Fri., Aug. 14, 1835)

M'Cartney, James Esq. Aged 47. Died in Madison County, Ala.
National Banner & Nashville Whig. (Mon., Aug. 1, 1831)

McCartney, Dr. Joseph. Age 60. Died at Louisville, Ky.
National Banner & Nashville Advertiser. (Mon., Nov. 5, 1832)

M'Cartney, Mrs. Maria. Wife of Mr. Joseph M'Cartney. Died in Louisville, Ky.
National Banner & Nashville Whig. (Mon., April 4, 1831)

M'Cartney, Mrs. Maria. Wife of Mr. Joseph M'Cartney. Died at Louisville, Ky.
National Banner & Nashville ___(Mon., April 11, 1831)

McCauley, Lilias Arnot. Infant daughter of Capt. C. S. McCauley.
Died in Philadelphia on 28th June.
Nashville Whig. (Wed., July 17, 1839)

McCauley, Maria Louisa. Infant daughter of Capt. C. S. McCauley.
Died at Philadelphia 25th June.
Nashville Whig. (Wed., July 17, 1839)

M'Cheaney, Mr. John. Died in Warren County, Ky.
National Banner. (Sat., July 25, 1829)

McChenney, Mr. David. Died in Frankfort, Ky. on the 24th inst.
Daily Republican Banner. (Wed., Aug. 28, 1839)

McClain, Mrs. Betsey. Died at Knoxville.
National Banner & Nashville Advertiser. (Tues., July 17, 1832)

McClain, Mr. Joseph. Died at Athens.
National Banner & Nashville Whig. (Sat., Sept. 1, 1827)

McClanahan, James W. Late Lieut. in the Mexican War. Died on the
2nd inst. at his residence at Dixons Springs, Smith County.
Nashville True Whig & Weekly Commercial Register. (Fri., July 19,
1850)

M'Clellan, Miss Jane. Aged about 19 years. Died in Sullivan County.
National Banner & Nashville Daily Advertiser. (Mon., March 18, 1833)

McClellan, Samuel. Son of Mr. & Mrs. Samuel A. McClellan. Died in
Nashville on Thursday morning 14th inst. aged 2 years 8 months and nine
days.
Nashville Whig. (Sat., May 16, 1846)

M'Clellen, Mrs. Elizabeth. Died in Jonesborough.
National Banner & Nashville Whig. (Tues., April 27, 1830)

McClew, Mrs. Sarah. Died in Florence, Ala.
National Banner & Nashville Daily Advertiser. (Mon., May 12, 1834)

M'Cluer, Lieut. James. Of the 1st Infantry, U.S.A. Died at Fort
Brooke, Tampa Bay.
Nashville Whig. (Mon., May 14, 1838)

McCluer, Mr. John. Died in Bedford County.
National Banner & Nashville Whig. (Fri., Oct. 20, 1826)

M'Clung, Mr. Charles Jun. Died in White County near Sparta.
National Banner & Nashville Whig. (Sat., Jan. 12, 1828)

M'Clung, Mr. Charles Jun. Died near Sparta.
National Banner & Nashville Whig. (Sat., Jan. 19, 1828)

McClung, James. Infant son of James W. McClung Esq. Died at Huntsville
National Banner & Nashville Advertiser. (Fri., July 6, 1832)

M'Clung, John A. Of the firm of Keenan & M'Clung. Died in Tuscumbia
on the 18th inst. his wife Mrs. Susan M'Clung on the 16th.
National Banner & Nashville Daily Advertiser. (Fri., Sept. 29, 1832)

McClung, Lawson Smith. Infant son of Col. Matthew McClung. Died
in Knoxville, Tenn.
National Banner & Nashville Daily Advertiser. (Mon., May 28, 1832)

M'Clung, Mrs. Malvina L. B. Daughter of Pleasant M. Miller Esq.
Died in Nashville at the residence of Gen. Gaines.
National Banner & Nashville Whig. (Mon., Dec. 6, 1830)

M'Clung, Mrs. Margaret. Aged 56. Died in Knox County.
National Banner & Nashville Whig. (Sat., Sept. 8, 1827)

McClung, Col. Matthew. In the 49th year of his age. Died at his
residence in the vicinity of Knoxville on the 5th inst.
Nashville Whig. (Tues., Oct. 15, 1844)

M'Clung, Mrs. Susan. Died in Tuscumbia on the 16th inst.
National Banner & Nashville Daily Advertiser. (Sat., Sept. 29, 1832)

McClure, Mr. James A. Aged 29. Died in Blount County on the same
day his father Mr. John McClure died at the same house.
National Banner & Nashville Daily Advertiser. (Tues., Nov. 19, 1833)

M'Clure, Mr. James W. Aged 27. Died in Paris, T.
National Banner & National Whig. (Sat., March 31, 1827)

M'Clure, Col. John. Died in Lexington, Henderson County.
National Banner & Nashville Whig. (Mon., March 28, 1831)

M'Clure, Col. Jno. Died in Lexington, Ten.
Nashville Republican & State Gazette. (Tues., March 29, 1831)

McClure, Mr. John. Aged 63. Died in Blount County, Ten.
National Banner & Nashville Daily Advertiser. (Tues., Nov. 19, 1833)

M'Clure, Miss Julia Ann. Daughter of Mrs. Mitchell. Died at Clarksville, Tenn. of Cholera.
National Banner & Nashville Whig. (Wed., July 8, 1835)

M'Clure, Mr. William. Died in Palmyra on Thursday April 21st.
National Banner & Nashville Whig. (Fri., April 29, 1831)

M'Clure, Mr. Wm. Died in Palmyra on April 21st.
National Banner & Nashville Whig. (Fri., April 29, 1831)

McClutchan, The Rev. John S. The pastor of Bethany Church, and clerk
of Concord Prebyterry. Died at Salem, Va. on Saturday morning the
24th June.
The Christian Record. (Sat., July 22, 1848)

McComick, Mr. Ansley. Died in Lincoln County, Ky.
National Banner & Nashville Whig. (Sat., Jan. 13, 1827)

M'Conathy, Mr. Jacob. Died at Lexington, Ky.
National Banner & Nashville Whig. (Sat., April 14, 1827)

M'Connell, Mrs. Jane. Died in this town on Saturday last very
suddenly.
National Banner & Nashville Whig. (Sat., Feb. 21, 1829)

McConnell, Col. John. A lawyer of distinguish talent. Died at his
residence in Greenup Co., Ky.
National Banner & Nashville Daily Advertiser. (Fri., July 18, 1834)

McConnico, Rev. Garner. An aged and distinguished minister of the
Baptist Church. Died in Williamson County, Tenn.
National Banner & Nashville Daily Advertiser. (Mon., Aug. 26, 1833)

M'Cord, Major David. Receiver of public money for the Cahabwa
district. Died in Dallas County, Ala.
National Banner & Nashville Whig. (Sat., April 12, 1828)

McCord, Mrs. Elizabeth. Wife of William McCord of Illinois and
daughter of David Rice of Greenville, Tennessee. Died in the vicinity
of Paris, Edgar County, Illinois, aged 26 years and 7 months.
The Politician and Weekly Nashville Whig. (Fri., July 2, 1847)

McCord, Mrs. Elizabeth. Wife of William McCord of Illinois. Died
in the vicinity of Paris, Edgar County, Illinois on the 30th of April.
Daughter of David Rice of Greenville, Tenn. aged 26 years and 7
months. (Obituary)
The Christian Record. (Sat., June 26, 1847)

M'Corkle, Mr. Albert M. Formerly of Nashville. Died in Randolph on the 10th inst.
Daily Republican Banner. (Thurs., Aug. 23, 1838)

McCorkle, Mr. Alexander. Died in Henry County.
National Banner & Nashville Daily Advertiser. (Wed., Feb. 27, 1833)

McCorkle, Mr. Alexander. Died in Henry County.
National Banner & Nashville Daily Advertiser. (Thurs., Aug. 16, 1832)

McCormack, James. Late of Davidson County, Tenn. Died at Vineyard Washington County, Ark. Ter. on the 29th Aug. aged 29 years, only son of George McCormack.
National Banner & Nashville Whig. (Fri., Oct. 2, 1835)

McCormack, Mrs Minerva. Aged about 28 years, wife of Mr. William McCormack. Died in Lincoln County, Ten.
National Banner & Nashville Whig. (Fri., Jan. 23, 1835)

McCormack, Capt. John. Died at Elkton, Ten.
National Banner & Nashville Whig. (Thurs., Aug. 12, 1830)

McCown, Alexander Sr. Died in Nashville on Saturday 11th inst. in the 60th year of his age.
The Politician and Weekly Nashville Whig. (Fri., March 17, 1848)

McCown, Alexander Sr. In the 60th year of his age. Died in Nashville on Sat. 11th inst. at the residence of his son.
The Christian Record. (Sat., March 18, 1848)

M'Coy, Dr. Cummings. Aged 28. Died at New Philadelphia, E. Tenn. on the 14th.
National Banner & Nashville Whig. (Sat., Nov. 3, 1827)

McCoy, Daniel. An old Revolutionary soldier, in the 94th year of his age. Died in Winchester, Tennessee on the night of the 6th inst.
Nashville Union. (Tues., Feb. 13, 1838)

M'Coy, Mrs. Eliza. Aged 23. Died at New Philadelphia, E. Tenn. on the 6th ult.
National Banner & Nashville Whig. (Sat., Nov. 3, 1827)

McCoy, Mr. James D. Aged 28 years. Died in Alexandria, La. formerly of Georgetown, Ky.
National Banner & Nashville Whig. (Fri., Oct. 31, 1834)

McCoy, John. Died 14th at Cincinnati, Ohio of Cholera.
National Banner & Nashville Daily Advertiser. (Tues., Oct. 23, 1832)

McCrab, Mrs. Louisa. In the 78th year of her age. Died on the 29th Oct. at the residence of her daughter Mrs. Mary S. Lanier. (Obituary)
Nashville Whig. (Sat., Nov. 28, 1846)

McCracken, Alexander D. Esq. Died at Reynoldsburg on the 14th inst. He was Post Master at that place.
Daily Republican Banner. (Mon., Sept. 25, 1838)

McCracken, Mr. Seneca. Died in Franklin County, Ky.
National Banner. (Sat., Oct. 3, 1829)

McCraken, Mr. E. Died in Huntingdon, Tenn.
The Union. (Sat., June 18, 1836)

M'Craskey, Miss Lucinda Ann. Wife of Mr. John M'Craskey. Died in Rockville, Monroe County.
National Banner & Nashville Daily Advertiser. (Mon., April 15, 1833)

McCraw, William. Died was killed in White County, Ark. on the 20th ult. by Alfred Baker.
Nashville Union. (Fri., Dec. 27, 1839)

McCrearey, Mrs. F. J. Died in Robinson County.
National Banner & Nashville Daily Advertiser. (Mon., Aug. 5, 1833)

McCreary, Dr. Andrew. Of Natchez, Mississippi. Died at Louisville, Ky. on the 14th inst.
Nashville Whig. (Thurs., Sept. 21, 1843)

McCreary, Mrs. Lucy. Aged 67. Died in Robinson County on the 6th inst.
Nashville Republican. (Thurs., March 16, 1837)

M'Crory, Mrs. Sary Leforce. Eldest daughter of M. M. Johnson. Died in Williamson County on Tuesday the 26th ult.
National Banner & Nashville Whig. (Thurs., June 3, 1830)

McCullen, Mr. James. Died in Scott County, Ky.
National Banner & Nashville Daily Advertiser. (Wed., Aug. 14, 1833)

McCullock, Major Benjamin. Long a residence in Rutherford County near Murfreesboro. Died in McMinnville on the 10th inst.
The Christian Record. (Sat., Aug. 21, 1847)

McCullock, Maj. Benjamin. In the 64th year of his age. Died at McMinnville, Tenn. on the 10th inst.
The Political & Weekly Nashville Whig. (Wed., Sept. 1, 1847)

McCullock, Mr. Henry. Died in Nashville at the residence of Mr. William Nichol on the 26th inst. aged 17 years. Son of Benjamin and Sarah McCullock.
National Banner & Nashville Whig. (Wed., March 30, 1831)

McCulloch, Henry. Age 17. Son of Benj. and Sarah McCulloch of Rutherford County. Died at Nashville was a student of Nashville University.
National Banner & Nashville Whig. (Wed., March 30, 1831)

McCulloch, Mr. Henry. Student of the University of Nashville from Murfreesborough.
Nashville Republican & State Gazette. (March 29, 1831)

McCulloch, James H. Collector of the port of Baltimore. Died on the border of Baltimore on Thursday evening.
National Banner & Nashville Whig. (Fri., Nov. 25, 1836)

McCulloch, James H. Collector of the Port of Baltimore. Died on the borders of Baltimore.
Nashville Republican. (Fri., Nov. 25, 1836)

McCullough, Mr. William. Of Carthage. Died on the steam boat, Uncle Sam on her passage from New Orleans to Louisville.
National Banner & Nashville Advertiser. (Sat., April 21, 1832)

M'Cullough, Mrs. Eliza. Died at Carthage. Wife of Mr. William M'Cullough, Merchant.
National Banner & Nashville Whig. (Mon., Nov. 8, 1830)

M'Cully, John. About 90 years old. Died recently in Plum in Davidson County an old resident and a soldier of the Revolution.
National Banner & Nashville Whig. (Mon., Oct. 20, 1834)

McCurdy, Mr. John L. Merchant in Nashville. Died in Davidson County on Monday last.
National Banner & Nashville Whig. (Wed., July 13, 1831)

McDaniel, Alfred W. Aged 32. Son of Collin M'Daniel of Williamson
County. Died in St. Francisville, La. on the 16th.
Daily Republican Banner. (Wed., Nov. 29, 1837)

M'Daniel, Mrs. Harriett. Wife of Dr. George M'Daniel. Died in Clarksville.
National Banner & Nashville Whig. (Mon., Nov. 29, 1830)

McDaniel, Mr. John. Aged about 25 years. Died in Hardeman County
2 miles north of Middleburgh on the 10th inst. He was a citizen of
Bedford County.
National Banner & Nashville Daily Advertiser. (Thurs., Dec. 19, 1833)

Macdonald, Alexander Esq. Merchant of Baltimore. Died in that city
on the 27th.
National Banner & Nashville Whig. (Mon., Aug. 22, 1836)

M'Donald, Duncan. Died in Raleigh, N. C.
Nashville Republican & State Gazette. (Tues., May 3, 1831)

M'Donald, Jno. Esq. Died in Pittsburg, Pa.
Nashville Republican & State Gazette. (Sat., June 4, 1831)

M'Donald, Lieut. S. Aged 105 years. He has left three children under
10 years of age. Died in Isle of Tikes, N. York.
Nashville Republican & State Gazette. (Thurs., March 10, 1831)

M'Donald, Maj. William. Died in Lauderdale County, Ala.
National Banner & Nashville Whig. (Friday, July 25, 1828)

McDonough, Thomas. Of the U. S. Navy. Died at sea, on his passage
from the Mediterranean Com.
National Banner. (Dec. 23, 1825)

McDougal, Mr. Charles A. Died at New Orleans on the 28th.
National Banner & Nashville Daily Advertiser. (Tues., Sept. 10, 1833)

M'Dougal, Mrs. Eleanor. Aged 43. Died in Chillicothe.
National Banner & Nashville Whig. (Sat., Aug. 26, 1826)

McDowell, Mrs. Amanda. Died in Fleming County, Ky.
National Banner & Nashville Whig. (Sat., Jan. 20, 1827)

M'Dowell, Dr. Ephraim. Died in Danville, Ky.
National Banner & Nashville Whig. (Mon., July 12, 1830)

M'Duffie, Mrs. Mary R. Wife of Hon. Geo. M'Duffie and daughter of
R. Singleton Esq. Died near Manchester, S. C.
National Banner & Nashville Whig. (Mon., Oct. 11, 1830)

Mace, Mr. Absalom T. Died in Smith County.
National Banner & Nashville Whig. (Fri., Nov. 21, 1834)

McEfee, M. H. Esq. Senior. Editor of the Initial and Telegraph. Died
in New Market, Tenn.
National Banner & Nashville Daily Advertiser. (Fri., Oct. 18, 1833)

M'Elmurry, Maj. John. Died at Little Rock, Ark.
National Banner & Nashville Whig. (Sat., March 10, 1827)

M'Elwee, Mr. James M. Aged 25, late of Roan County.
National Banner & Nashville Whig. (Sat., Sept. 9, 1826)

M'Ewen, Mr. James. Died in Williamson County.
National Banner & Nashville Whig. (Sat., Aug. 18, 1827)

McEwen, Mrs. Jane. Wife of James McEwen Esq. Died in McMinnville in the 75th year of her age.
National Banner & Nashville Whig. (Fri., March 20, 1835)

M'Ewen, Mr. John. Aged 75 year. Died in Davidson County on the 4th inst.
National Banner & Nashville Whig. (Sat., June 20, 1828)

McEwen, Mrs. Sophia Elizabeth. Wife of Joseph H. McEwen Esq. Died yesterday. Her funeral to be at 9 o'clock July 15th at the Methodist Church.
Nashville Whig. (Sat., July 15, 1843)

M'Ewen, Mrs. Susan. Wife of Mr. Cyrus M'Ewen. Died in Williamson County.
National Banner & Nashville Whig. (Sat., Dec. 20, 1828)

M'Fall, Dr. David. Died in Paris, Ky.
Nashville Republican & State Gazette. (Thurs., April 19, 1831)

McFarland, Mrs. Margaret. Relict of the late Mr. Thomas McFarland. Died in this county on the 22d ult.
National Banner. (Jan. 13, 1826)

McFarland, Mary C. Daughter of Benjamin McFarland, Esq. Died in Weakley County, Tenn. on the 17th.
Nashville Republican. (Thurs., Sept. 22, 1836)

McFarland, Mary C. Infant daughter of Benjamin M. McFarland of Weakley County, Tenn. Died on the 17th inst.
Nashville Republican. (Sat., Sept. 24, 1836)

McFarland, Mr. Of Versailles, Ky. Died in Lexington, Ky. See paper for Obituary.
National Banner & Nashville Advertiser. (Mon., March 26, 1832)

McFarland, Rev. John. Died in Paris, Ky.
National Banner & Nashville Whig. (Sat., Aug. 9, 1828)

M'Farland, Mr. John. Died at Pittsburgh. Editor of the Alleghany Democrat.
National Banner & Nashville Whig. (Sat., Sept. 1, 1826)

MacFarlane, Col. Stephen. Age 61. Died in Cincinnati.
National Banner & Nashville Advertiser. (Mon., Nov. 19, 1832)

M'Farland, Mr. Wm. Cashier of the Bank of Orleans. Died at New Orleans suddenly.
National Banner. (Sat., Aug. 22, 1829)

M'Ferrien, Rev. James. Aged 56. Died in Tipton County on the 3d inst. A Methodist Minister.
Daily Republican Banner. (Fri., Sept. 18, 1840)

McGarvey, Mr. John. Died in Hopkinsville, Ky on the 31st ult.
National Banner & Nashville Daily Advertiser. (Tues., Feb. 5, 1833)

M'Gavock, Albert T. In his 22nd year. Died in this vicinity on the 28th Oct. at the residence of his father, Mr. David M'Gavock.
National Banner & Nashville Whig. (Fri., Nov. 4, 1836)

McGavock, Mary Caroline. In the ninth year of her age. Died on Saturday the 7th inst. Eldest daughter of Dr. David T. and Caroline E. McGavock.
Nashville Whig. (Tues., Oct. 10, 1843)

McGavock, Mrs. Cynthia. Died - yesterday. The amiable consort of

Mr. John M'Gavock of this County. The friends are invited to attend her burial at Mr. David M'Gavock's at 12 o'clock this day.
The Nashville Whig & Tenn. Advertiser. (Oct. 20, 1817)

M'Gavock, David Esq. Aged 75 years. Died at his residence near Nashville on the 7th inst.
Nashville Union. (Fri., Aug. 10, 1838)

McGavock, David Sr. A citizen of Davidson County. Died yesterday at the residence near Nashville.
Nashville Whig. (Wed., Aug. 9, 1838)

McGavock, David Sr. Died yesterday near Nashville. An old and respectable citizen.
Daily Republican Banner. (Thurs., Aug. 9, 1838)

McGavock, Mrs. Elizabeth. Consort of D. McGavock, Esq. of this neighbor hood. Died in Rockbridge County, Virginia on 23d of Oct. whilst on a visit to friends.
Impartial Review and Cumberland Repository. (Thurs., Dec. 3, 1807)

McGavock, Mrs. Mary. Wife of Mr. David McGavock. Died in this vicinity at 9 o'clock this morning (16th inst.) aged 48.
National Banner & Nashville Daily Advertiser. (Wed., July 16, 1834)

McGavock, Randal Sen. One of the early pioneers of Tennessee. Died at his residence near Franklin on Thursday last.
Nashville Whig. (Sat., Sept. 30, 1843)

M'Gee, Mrs. Elizabeth. Died in Shelbyville.
National Banner & Nashville Daily Advertiser. (Mon., June 3, 1833)

McGee, Doct. William. Died on Thursday the 15th inst. of Williamson County.
The Western Weekly Review. (Fri., June 15, 1832) Franklin, Tenn.

McGee, Doctor William. Died in Williamson County, Ten.
National Banner & Nashville Daily Advertiser. (Tues., June 26, 1832)

M'Gehee, George W. Died on the 24th Sept. at Judge Martins Coosa-watie, in the 28th year of his age.
National Banner. (Sat., Oct. 17, 1829)

M'Ghee, Mrs. Betsy. Wife of John M'Ghee Esq. Died in Monroe County.
National Banner. (Sat., April 25, 1829)

M'Gilvray, Mr. William. An old respectable citizen. Died at Franklin.
National Banner & Nashville Whig. (Mon., Jan. 24, 1831)

M'Gilvery, Mrs. Consort of Wm. M'Gilvery. Died at Franklin.
National Banner & Nashville Whig. (Sat., Jan. 20, 1827)

McGimpsey, Mrs. Mary. Aged about 38 years. Died in Shelbyville, Ten.
National Banner & Nashville Whig. (Wed., Dec. 17, 1834)

McGouegal, Mr. Daniel. Merchant of this place, a native of Ireland. Died in Courtland, Ala.
The Nashville Republican & State Gazette. (Thurs., Dec. 16, 1830)

McGowan, Mr. Reuben. Died at Mobile, Ala. on the 19th of Oct. formerly of Tennessee in the 36th year of his age.
National Banner & Nashville Whig. (Fri., Dec. 10, 1830)

M'Graw, Mr. Samuel K. Died in Huntsville, Ala.
National Banner. (Sat., Sept. 19, 1829)

M'Gregor, Gen. John. Died in Rutherford County of Cholera.
National Banner & Nashville Whig. (Wed., July 15, 1835)

McGregor, Mrs. Mildred M. Relict of the late Gen. John McGregor.
Died in Rutherford County on Sun. last.
The Union. (Thurs., Jan. 7, 1836)

M'Guire, Mr. John R. Aged 26. Died in Haywood County.
National Banner & Nashville Whig. (Fri., May 7, 1830)

M'Guire, Mrs. Patrick. Died in Jefferson County.
National Banner & Nashville Whig. (Mon., Nov. 28, 1831)

M'Guire, Mr. Patrick. Died in Jefferson County.
National Banner & Nashville Whig. (Mon., Nov. 28, 1831)

M'Guire, Mr. Thomas J. Printer. Died at St. Louis.
National Banner & Nashville Whig. (Thurs., Aug. 19, 1830)

McGunnegle, Mr. Wilson. Died at St. Louis.
National Banner. (Sat., July 11, 1829)

M'Henry, Mr. Archibald. Formerly of Tennessee. Died in Arkansas.
National Banner & Nashville Whig. (Fri., April 10, 1835)

McHenry, Mr. George W. Aged about 26 years. Died near Little Rock,
Ark.
National Banner & Nashville Whig. (Mon., Jan. 5, 1835)

M'hoon, Miss Frances. Formerly of Rutherford County. Died at Randolph
Ten.
National Banner & Nashville Daily Advertiser. (Wed., March 12, 1834)

McIlvaine, Joseph Esq. Died at Harrisburg. He was found dead in bed
on the morning of the 16th inst.
Daily Republican Banner. (Wed., Jan. 24, 1838)

McIndoe, Mr. Robert. Aged 25 years. Died in Nashville on the 11th
inst. formerly of Newberry, Virginia.
Nashville Whig. (Fri., Feb. 13, 1838)

M'Indoe, Mr. Robert. Aged about 30 years. Died in Nashville, yesterday
Daily Republican Banner. (Tues., Feb. 12, 1839)

M'Intire, Charles. Died in New Orleans on the 24th May. of Russellville (Ky.) Volunteers lately with Gen. Jackson a worthy young man.
The Nashville Whig and Tenn. Advertiser. (June 13, 1818)

McIntosh, Albert Gallatin. Son of Daniel McIntosh. Died in Nashville
on the 28th inst. in the 7th year of his age.
National Banner & Nashville Daily Advertiser. (Thurs., Jan. 30, 1834)

M'Intosh, Dr. Donald. Died in Knoxville on the 6th.
Daily Republican Banner. (Wed., Oct. 11, 1837)

McIntosh, Mrs. Sally. In her 75th year. Died in Nashville on the 9th
inst. at the residence of her son-in-law, Mr. Samuel D. Morgan.
(Obituary)
The Christian Record. (Sat., Aug. 19, 1848)

McIver, Mrs. Eliza N. Daughter of William Williams Esq. Died in this
County on Tuesday last.
National Banner. (March 31, 1826)

M'Iver, Mr. Evander. Aged 32. Died in Rutherford County.
National Banner & Nashville Whig. (Sat., Sept. 27, 1828)

M'Iver, Mrs. Margaret. Wife of Col. John M'Iver of this neighborhood.
Died on Monday morning last the 8th inst.
Nashville Whig. (Nov. 15, 1824)

McKay, Alexander. Died at Cincinnati, Ohio on the 13th of Cholera.
National Banner & Nashville Daily Advertiser. (Sat., Oct. 20, 1832)

M'Kay, Mrs. Sarah M. Wife of H. B. M'Kay Esq. Died in St. Louis,
Mo. on the 1st inst. she was a sister of Dr. Thomas R. Jennings of
Nashville.
Nashville Whig. (Sat., July 13, 1844)

McKeag, Robert. Died at Cincinnati, Ohio on the 11th inst. of Cholera.
National Banner & Nashville Daily Advertiser. (Thurs., Oct. 18, 1832)

McKean, Mrs. Margaret. Died in Bolivar on the evening of the 11th
inst. Consort of John McKean, Esq.
National Banner & Nashville Daily Advertiser. (Thurs., April 4, 1833)

McKee, Rev. James. Died in Trenton, Gibson County, age 25.
National Banner & Nashville Whig. (Fri., Jan. 1st, 1830)

McKee, Col. John. Age 64. Died in Green County, Ala.
National Banner & Nashville Advertiser. (Sat., Aug. 25, 1832)

McKee, Mrs. Lucy Ann. Wife of Rev. D. D. McKee and daughter of the
late Rev. John Rice Kerr of Danville, Ky. Died in Newport, Pa. on
the 25th ult. (Obituary)
The Christian Record. (Sat., Sept. 11, 1847)

M'Kee, Col. Samuel. Died near the mouth of the Ohio.
National Banner & Nashville Whig. (Sat., Dec. 23, 1826)

M'Kee, Mr. Samuel. In the 61st year of his age. Died in Carroll
County on the 3rd inst.
National Banner & Nashville Whig. (Mon., May 24, 1830)

M'Kendrick, Mr. Wm. Died in Gibson County.
National Banner & Nashville Whig. (Sat., Oct. 28, 1826)

McKenney, Maj. R. T. Died in St. Louis, Mo.
National Banner & Nashville Daily Advertiser. (Tues., July 15, 1834)

Mackenzie, Marshall. Youngest son of Kenneth and Mary Mackenzie.
Died in St. Louis, on Thursday Oct. 28th.
The Politician & Weekly Nashville Whig. (Fri., Nov. 19, 1847)

McKenzie, Mr. James. A native of South Carolina. Died at Port
Gibson, Mi.
National Banner & Nashville Daily Advertiser. (Mon., July 28, 1834)

Mackey, Mr. James. Died in Washington County.
National Banner & Nashville Whig. (Sat., Dec. 23, 1826)

Mackey, Capt. William. In the 42nd year of his age. Died in Warren
County, Ten.
National Banner & Nashville Whig. (Fri., Jan. 23, 1835)

McKim, Hon. Isaac. A Representative in Congress. Died in Washington
on Sunday at ten o'clock, April 1st.
Daily Republican Banner. (Sat., April 7, 1838)

McKim, Hon. Isaac. Of Maryland. Died in Washington on Sunday the
1st inst. He was one of the Representatives from Baltimore.
Nashville Whig. (Mon., April 9, 1838)

McKin, Elex, Esq. Died in Baltimore.
Nashville Republican & State Gazette. (Sat., Feb. 4, 1832)

M'Kingsley, Mr. Henry. Died at Memphis.
National Banner & Nashville Whig. (Sat., Sept. 15, 1827)

McKinley, James. Aged 1 year. Died in Nashville.
National Banner & Nashville Whig. (Fri., July 17, 1835)

McKinly, William Green. Infant son of Mr. John McKinly. Died in
Murfreesborough.
National Banner & Nashville Daily Advertiser. (Tues., May 27, 1834)

McKinne, Michael Esq. Died in Hardeman County on the 9th Sept. in
the sixtieth year of his age.
Daily Republican Banner. (Sat., Oct. 3, 1840)

McKinney, Mrs. Wife of Gerard McKinney. Died in Lexington, Ky.
National Banner & Nashville Daily Advertiser. (Tues., July 2, 1833)

McKinzey, Mr. John. Aged 28 years. A native of Edenburgh. Died
at New Orleans.
National Banner & Nashville Daily Advertiser. (Fri., Sept. 20, 1833)

M'Kinzie, Caleb Phifer. In the 21st year of his age. Died in Hardeman County on the 17th.
Daily Republican Banner. (Wed., Sept. 3, 1838)

McKissack, James. United States agent for the Cherokees. Died at
Fort Gibson, Arkansas on the 12th ult.
The Politician & Weekly Nashville Whig. (Fri., Feb. 11, 1848)

Macknett, Charles Esq. An officer of the Revolution, aged 76. Died
in Germantown, Pa. he died in the house in which he was born.
National Banner & Nashville Daily Advertiser. (Thurs., Feb. 13, 1834)

M'Knight, Mrs. Eleanor. Died in Rutherford County.
National Banner & Nashville Whig. (Sat., Feb. 2, 1828)

M'Knight, Mrs. Fanny. Died in St. Louis. Consort of Mr. Thomas
M'Knight.
National Banner. (Jan. 6, 1826)

M'Knight, William A. M. A teacher in Centreville Academy. A native
of N. Carolina. Died in Rutherford County on the 13th May.
Daily Republican Banner. (Sat., June 20, 1840)

M'Knight, William. Died in Rutherford City.
Nashville Republican & State Gazette. (Tues., March 8, 1831)

McKnight, Mr. William. Age 78. Died in Rutherford County.
National Banner & Nashville Whig. (Wed., March 9, 1831)

M'Lane, Mr. Joseph. Age 60. Died in Knox County.
National Banner & Nashville Whig. (Sat., Aug. 5, 1826)

M'Laran, Mrs. Susan E. Wife of Mr. James M'Laran. Died in Madison
County, Ala.
National Banner & Nashville Whig. (Tues., Feb. 2, 1830)

McLaughlin, Mrs. Elizabeth. Died in Marion County, Missis.
National Banner & Nashville Whig. (Sat., Feb. 24, 1827)

M'Laughlin, Mr. J. J. Late of Hopkinsville, Ky. Died in Nashville
on Sat. 7th inst.
National Banner & Nashville Whig. (Fri., Feb. 13, 1835)

M'Lean, Mr. Charles. One of the settlers of that County. Died in
Rutherford County.
National Banner. (Jan. 6, 1826)

McLean, Fergus. Father of the Hon. Judge McLean, of the United States
Supreme Court aged 91. Died in Clear Creek Township, Warren County,
Ohio.
Nashville Republican. (Thurs., March 2, 1837)

McLean, Mr. Hector. Age 45. Native of Ky. Died at New Orleans suddenly.
National Banner & Nashville Advertiser. (Sat., Feb. 11, 1832)

M'Lean, Mr. Hector. Aged about 45 years. A native of Kentucky. Died at New Orleans suddenly.
National Banner & Nashville Daily Advertiser. (Thurs., Feb. 9, 1832)

McLean, Hon. J. Member of Congress from Ohio. Died at Washington since the adjournment of Congress.
The Union. (Sat., April 8, 1837)

M'Lean, Hon. John. Senator in Congress from the State of Illinois. Died at Shawneetown, Ill.
National Banner & Nashville Whig. (Mon., Oct. 25, 1830)

M'Lean, Miss Mary Ann. Died at Jackson, Ten.
National Banner. (Sat., April 25, 1829)

M'Lean, Mrs. Sarah. Widow of the late Dr. Lachan M'Lean. Died at Jackson.
National Banner & Nashville Whig. (Fri., July 18, 1828)

McLean, Hon. William. The brother of Judge McLean. Died at Cincinnati on the 12th inst. aged 45 years. He was a native of Ky.
Nashville Union. (Mon., Oct. 21, 1839)

McLemore, Mrs. Consort of John C. McLemore Esq. Died in LaGrange, Tenn. on the 2nd inst.
Nashville Republican. (Thurs., July 7, 1836)

McLemore, Mrs. Elizabeth. Wife of John C. McLemore of Nashville. Died in LaGrange, Tenn. on the 2nd inst.
National Banner & Nashville Whig. (Mon., July 11, 1836)

McLemore, Nathaniel Mr. Late of North Carolina. Died departed this life at his residence in Davidson County on the 4th inst.
Nashville Whig. (Jan. 26, 1824)

McLemore, Mr. Robert. Died in Williamson County.
Nashville Whig. (Jan. 29, 1823)

McLeod, ___. Infant son of Rev. Mc McLeod. Died in Murfreesborough on the evening of the 9th inst.
National Banner & Nashville Daily Advertiser. (Mon., March 31, 1834)

M'Leod, Rev. Alexander. Senior pastor of the first Reformed Presbyterian Congregation in that city. Died in New York on the 17th ult.
National Banner & Nashville Daily Advertiser. (Mon., March 11, 1833)

M'Lin, Alexander Esq. Died in Lincoln County, T.
National Banner & Nashville Whig. (Sat., Sept. 30, 1826)

M'Llvain, Bloomfield Esq. Aged 29, and a few hours afterwards at the same place his father. Hon. Joseph M'Llvain of the U. S. Senate, aged 57. Died in Burlington, N. J. on the 18th ult.
National Banner & Nashville Whig. (Sat., Sept. 9, 1826)

McMahon, William. A native of Ireland, father of John V. L. McMahon Esq. of Baltimore. Died at Cumberland, Md.
Nashville Whig. (Wed., Sept. 16, 1840)

McManes, Mr. Was shot sitting in the House of M. Long on Thursday evening last, by a negro man.
Impartial Review and Cumberland Repository. (Sat., Oct. 18, 1806)

M'Means, Mrs. Margaret R. Consort of James R. M'Means Esq. Died
in Henry County.
National Banner & Nashville Daily Advertiser. (Wed., Oct. 16, 1833)

McMillan, Andrew. Cashier of the branch of the Union Bank of Tenn.
Died in Knoxville.
Daily Republican Banner. (Fri., Sept. 28, 1838)

M'Minn, Joseph Esq. Late Governor of this State. Died at the Cherokee
Agency on the 17th ult.
Nashville Whig. (Dec. 20, 1824).

M'Minn, Mrs. Wife of Mr. Robert M'Minn. Died in this town.
National Banner & Nashville Whig. (Sat., Aug. 26, 1826)

M'Mullen, Mrs. Christen. Died in Knox County.
National Banner & Nashville Whig. (Sat., Oct. 6, 1827)

McMurphy, Daniel. Died in Augusta, Ga. of Yellow Fever.
Daily Republican Banner. (Fri., Oct. 4, 1839)

M'Murry, Hosea Esq. Died in Henry County, T. on the 7th inst.
National Banner & Nashville Whig. (Sat., Sept. 30, 1826)

McMurry, Mr. John. In the 34th year of his age. Died on the 31st
Oct. at the residence of his father, Samuel McMurry Gallatin, Nov.
15th, 1847. (Obituary)
The Christian Record. (Sat., Nov. 20, 1847)

McMurry, Mrs. Martha. Consort of Mr. William McMurry. Died on the
28th ult. near Nashville.
The Christian Record. (Sat., Feb. 13, 1847)

McMurry, Mr. Washington. On the 1st inst. Died at the residence of
Dr. John H. Marable in Montgomery County. (Student of Medicine)
National Banner & Nashville Daily Advertiser. (Mon., Oct. 15, 1832)

McMurtry, John Esq. Aged 89. Died at his residence in Sumner County
on the 16th inst. A soldier of the Revolution.
Nashville Whig. (Fri., March 19, 1841)

McNair, Mr. Sub-agent and son of the late Governor of Missouri,
killed by a stroke of lighting. Died at the Osage Agency.
National Banner & Nashville Whig. (Mon., July 4, 1831)

M'Nair, Alexander Esq. Late governor of Missouri.
National Banner. (April 21, 1826)

M'Nairy, Mrs. Consort of the Hon. John M'Nairy. Died in Nashville
yesterday 27th inst. in the 68th year of her age. (Obituary).
National Banner & Nashville Daily Advertiser. (Sat., May 3, 1832)

M'Nairy, Daniel Webster. Aged one year and 8 months. Died on last
night 18th inst. son of Dr. Boyd M'Nairy.
National Banner & Nashville Daily Advertiser. (Thurs., Dec. 19, 1833)

McNairy, Mrs. Elizabeth H. Wife of John N. McNairy Esq. Died on
Sunday last at the residence of her father-in-law N. A. McNairy Esq.
Nashville Whig. (Tues., May 31, 1842)

Judge John McNairy. Age 75 years. Died at his residence near the
City on Friday evening. Judge of the Circuit Court of the U. States
for the District of Tennessee.
Daily Republican Banner. (Mon., Nov. 13th, 1837)

M'Nairy, Hon. John. Formerly Judge of Circuit Court. Died at his
residence near Nashville on Friday last in the 75th year of his age.
Nashville Union. (Tues., Nov. 14, 1837)

M'Nairy, Mrs. Mary. Aged 87. Died in Davidson County on Monday last
Mother of the Hon. Judge M'Nairy.
National Banner & Nashville Whig. (Thurs., July 1, 1830)

M'Nairy, Mrs. Mary. Consort of the Hon. John M'Nairy. Died on
Friday the 27th ult.
National Banner & Nashville Daily Advertiser. (Thurs., May 3, 1832)

McNairy, Nathaniel. Infant son of Mr. William H. McNairy of Nashville.
Died on the morning of the 17th inst.
The Christian Record. (Sat., Feb. 29, 1847)

M'Nairy, Mr. Robert. Of Giles County. Died in this vicinity at the
residence of his brother, Nath. A. M. M'Nairy.
National Banner & Nashville Whig. (Mon., Sept. 5, 1831)

M'Neal, Capt. Tho. Died in Hardeman County.
National Banner & Nashville Whig. (Thurs., July 29, 1830)

M'Neal, Mr. Alexander. Died at Claiborne, Ala.
National Banner. (May 13, 1826)

McNeely, William. From Campbell County. Died at the Tenn. State
Prison of Cholera.
National Banner & Nashville Whig. (Fri., Aug. 14, 1835)

M'Neil, Loueza Matilda, Aged 5 and Mary Elizabeth, aged 3 years.
Both daughter of Archibald M'Neil. Died in Huntsville, Ala.
National Banner & Nashville Whig. (Sat., Aug. 26, 1826)

M'Neil, Mr. L. H. Printer. Died in Tuscaloosa, Alabama.
Nashville Republican & State Gazette. (Thurs., April 7, 1831)

McNeil, Mr. L. H. Age 36. of consumption. Died in Tuscaloosa.
National Banner & Nashville Whig. (Fri., April 7, 1831)

McNeil, Mrs. Mary. Wife of Dr. William McNeil. Died in Nashville
on Saturday morning 30th ult.
Nashville Whig. (Wed., July 4, 1838)

McNeil, Sarah Ann. In the 21st year of her age. Died in Smith
County on Monday 29th ulto.
Nashville Whig. (Mon., Aug. 12, 1839)

McNeil, Dr. William. Aged 79. Died on Thursday 21st inst. A native
of Massachusetts.
Nashville Whig. (Sat., March 23, 1844)

McNeill, Mr. John. Aged 90. Died in Knox County.
National Banner & Nashville Daily Advertiser. (Mon., Aug. 5, 1833)

McNeill, Sarah Ann. Daughter of Archibald McNeill. Died in Smith
County on Monday 29th in the 21st year of her age.
Daily Republican Banner. (Tues., Aug. 13, 1839)

McNeill, William Esq. Post Master at Hico. Died in Carroll County.
Nashville Republican. (Thurs., Feb. 16, 1837)

McNeil, Mrs. Sarah P. Consort of Dr. William McNeil. Died in Nashville on the evening of the 27th inst. In the 50th year of her age.
Nashville Whig. (Thurs., Feb. 1, 1844)

McNeill, William L. Esq. Postmaster at Hico. Died at Hico, Carroll
County, Tennessee on the 7th inst.
National Banner & Nashville Whig. (Wed., Feb. 15, 1837)

McNitt, Mr. James M. Died at Liexington, Ky son of Mr. Robert M'Nitt.
National Banner & Nashville Advertiser. (Thurs., March 15, 1832)

M'Nitt, Mr. Robert H. Jr. Died in Lexington, Ky.
National Banner & Nashville Advertiser. (Fri., March 30, 1832)

M'Nitt, Mrs. Wife of Robert M'Nitt. Died in Lexington, Ky.
National Banner & Nashville Whig. (Wed., Mar. 2, 1831)

M'Nutt, Mr. Alexander. Died in Fayetteville.
National Banner & Nashville Whig. (Sat., Oct. 6, 1827)

McNutt, Mrs. Malinda N. Relict of George McNutt. Died at her residence 3 miels east of Knoxville on the 8th inst.
The Christian Record. (Sat., cec. 16, 1848)

Macomb, Anna Matilda. Daughter of Maj. General Macomb, aged 21 years. Died on Friday morning at the residence of Col. Stanon Narrows, Long Island.
National Banner & Nashville Whig. (Mon., Oct. 6, 1834)

Macon, Major John. Aged 76. Died in Maury County.
National Banner & Nashville Whig. (Sat., March 1, 1828)

Macon, Mrs. Mary J. Age 73. Died at Columbia.
National Banner & Nashville Whig. (Fri., Feb. 25, 1831)

Macon, Hon. Nathaniel. Died at his residence in North Carolina on the 29th June in the 82d year of his age.
The Union. (Tues., July 19, 1837)

M'Peters, Scott Esq. Died in Grainger County.
National Banner. (Sat., Aug. 8, 1829)

M'Phearson, Mr. Alexander. Died in Roane County.
National Banner & Nashville Whig. (Fri., Oct. 20, 1826)

Macpherson, Mrs. Elizabeth. Widow of the late Gen. Macpherson and daughter of Bishop White. Died in Philadelphia.
National Banner & Nashville Whig. (Wed., Nov. 23, 1831)

McPheters, Mrs. Martha. Died in Fayette County, Ky.
National Banner & Nashville Whig. (Wed., Aug. 17, 1831)

MacQuillan, Cynthia Holland. Consort of Capt. Joseph MacQuillen, aged 37 years. Died at Lake Providence, La. on Sat. 14th of August 1836.
National Banner & Nashville Whig.(Mon., Sept. 12, 1836)

McQuiston, Malinda D. Wife of William McQuiston of New Orleans. Died at the residence of her father Solomon Clark at Pontotoc, Miss. on the 31st March. (Obituary).
Nashville Whig. (Sat., April 30, 1842)

M'Rae, Allan Esq. Member of the Virginia Legislature. Died in Richmond, Va.
National Banner. (Jan. 6, 1826)

McRae, Rev. Mr. Of the Methodist Episcopal Church. Died was killed by the Indians within three miles of Mickanopy.
Daily Republican Banner. (Sat., April 11, 1840)

M'Ready, Mr. James. Aged 35 years. Died in New Orleans.
National Banner & Nashville Daily Advertiser. (Tues., June 24, 1834)

M'Rhea, Dr. Wilson. Died in Sumner County on the 22nd inst.
National Banner. (Sat., Oct. 3, 1829)

McRoberts, Hon. Samuel. Senator in Congress from Illinois. Died in Cincinnati, aged about 40 years.
Nashville Whig. (Sat., April 1st. 1843)

M'Spedding, Mr. Alexander A. Died in Sommerville, T.
National Banner & Nashville Whig. (Sat., Sept. 30, 1826)

Macurdy, John F. Late secretary of State under Governor Metcalf.
Died at Frankfort, Ky. on the 6th inst.
National Banner & Nashville Daily Advertiser. (Sat., July 13, 1833)

M'Whirter, Mrs. Mary P. Wife of Dr. Samuel McWhirter. Died in Wilson
County.
National Banner & Nashville Advertiser. (Fri., Aug. 10, 1832)

McWhirter, Mrs. Mary P. Wife of Dr. Samuel McWhirter. Died in
Wilson County.
National Banner & Nashville Daily Advertiser. (Fri., Aug. 10, 1832)

Madearis, Capt. John. One of the officers of the Revolution aged 90.
Died in Bedford County, Tennessee.
National Banner & Nashville Daily Advertiser. (Mon., April 7, 1834)

Madeira, Jacob Esq. Died at Cincinnati.
National Banner & Nashville Whig. (Tues., Feb. 2, 1830)

Madison, Mrs. Age 80. The last sister of Patrick Henry. Died in
Bollinggreen, Ky.
National Banner & Nashville Whig. (Wed., Sept. 7, 1831)

Madison, Mrs. Eleanor. Aged 98. Mother of the ex-president. Died
at Montpelier, Va.
National Banner & Nashville Whig. (Sat., March 7, 1829)

Madison, Ex President James. Died at Montpelier, Va. on the 28th
June.
The Union. (Tues., July 12, 1836)

Mael, Mr. Absalom T. Aged 27. Died in Smith County.
National Banner & Nashville Whig. (Fri., Oct. 10, 1834)

Magnie, Mr. Wm. Died at Claiborne, Ala.
National Banner & Nashville Whig. (Sat., Feb. 10, 1827)

Maguire, Walter B. Infant son of Edward and Fanny Maguire. Died on
Friday the 25th inst. at the City Hotel.
Nashville Whig. (Tues., Sept. 29, 1846)

Mahard, Mrs. Ann. Consort of John Mahart sen. Esq. Died in
Cincinnati, O.
National Banner & Nashville Daily Advertiser. (Sat., Aug. 10, 1833)

Mahon, Mrs. Sarah P. Consort of Dr. Martin H. W. Mahon. Died in
Harden County, Ten. on the 21st of Aug.
National Banner & Nashville Whig. (Sat., Sept. 6, 1828)

Major, Mr. George. Died in Taylorsville, Ky.
National Banner & Nashville Whig. (Thurs., Sept. 2, 1830)

Mallory, Mrs. Elizabeth. Died near Sparta.
National Banner & Nashville Whig. (June 24, 1826)

Mallory, Hon. Robert C. Died in Baltimore. Member of Congress from
Mass.
Nashville Republican & State Gazette. (Tues., May 3, 1831)

Mandell, Joseph. Died 17th at Cincinnati, Ohio of Cholera.
National Banner & Nashville Daily Advertiser. (Wed., Oct. 24, 1832)

Maney, Charles Carroll. Infant son of William Maney, Esq. Died on
Saturday 9th inst. in Franklin.
The Western Weekly Review. (Fri., March 15, 1833) Franklin, Tenn.

Maney, Fanny M. Relict of the late Thomas Maney of Murfreesboro, and daughter of Hon. John Bell of Nashville. Died at the residence of Dr. James Maney, on the 21st inst. in Rutherford County.
The Christian Record. (Sat., Oct. 30, 1847)

Maney, Miss Francis E. Died in Rutherford County.
National Banner & Nashville Whig. (Sat., Feb. 3, 1827)

Maney, Mrs. Jane. Died - will be buried from the residence of Mr. and Mrs. Philip Callaghan at 3 o'clock this afternoon.
Daily Republican Banner. (Tues., Jan. 9, 1838)

Mangee, Mr. Louis. Aged 53. Died in Natchez.
National Banner & Nashville Whig. (Sat., Oct. 7, 1826)

Mangum, Joseph Sen. In the 67th year of his age. Died in Lawrence County, Ala.
National Banner & Nashville Daily Advertiser. (Thurs., June 21, 1832)

Manifee, Mr. Reuben. Died at Memphis.
National Banner & Nashville Whig. (Sat., Aug. 25, 1827)

Mann, Mr. Benj. J. Aged 75. Died in Campbell County, Ky.
National Banner. (March 31, 1826)

Mann, Hon. Ephraim. Died in Raleigh, N. C. The Senator from Tyrrall County.
National Banner & Nashville Whig. (Wed., Dec. 17, 1834)

Manning, Ann Maria. Aged 13 months. Died in Rutherford County.
National Banner & Nashville Whig. (Sat., Aug. 30, 1828)

Manning, Private H. R. With the 14th Regiment part of the third Division commanded by Gen. Pillow. Died - was killed in the last Battle before the City of Mexico.
The Christian Record. (Sat., Oct. 30, 1847)

Mansfield, Col. Jared L. L. D. Aged 71. Died in New Haven, Conn. on the 3d ult.
National Banner & Nashville Whig. (Tues., March 2, 1830)

Mansfield, Mr. James. Of Todd County, Ky. Died at Hopkinsville, Ky. On Sunday last, from a pistol shot wound received about a month ago.
National Banner & Nashville Daily Advertiser. (Fri., Dec. 28, 1832)

Manton, Charles Esq. Lately a citizen of this town. Died at Providence, R. I. on the 20th of February last.
The Nashville Whig. (Tues., April 16, 1816)

Marable, Rev. Henry Hartwell. Aged 80 years and 3 months. Died at his residence in Rutherford County, on the 26th inst., has been for 56 years a member of the Methodist Episcopal Church.
National Banner & Nashville Daily Advertiser. (Tues., Oct. 29, 1833)

Marable, Isaac M. In the 25th year of his age. Died at his residence in Rutherford County on the 25th inst.
The Nashville Gazette. (Wed., July 28, 1819)

Marable, Mrs. Nancy. Wife of Dr. Henry Marable. Died in Dickson County.
National Banner & Nashville Whig. (Thurs., Oct. 14, 1830)

March, Mrs. Sarah. Wife of Jesse D. March. Died in Nashville on Saturday last in the 34th year of her age.
Nashville Whig. (Tues., June 18, 1844)

Mardis, Hon. Samuel W. Died in Talladega County, Ala. on Monday 14th inst.
Nashville Republican. (Fri., Dec. 10, 1836)

245

Marechal, Rev. Ambrose. Roman Catholic Archbishop of Baltimore. Died at Baltimore.
National Banner & Nashville Whig. (Sat., Feb. 23, 1828)

Marie, Francis Anne. Age 102. Died at Ardes, Ruy-de-Dome. Born in 1730, Died in 1832. See paper for Obituary.
National Banner & Nashville Advertiser. (Tues., April 3, 1832)

Marigny, Catharine. Aged 28. Died in Natchez.
National Banner & Nashville Whig. (Sat., Oct. 7, 1826)

Markley, Mrs. Frances. Wife of Mr. John A. Markley. Died in Frankfort, Ky.
National Banner & Nashville Whig. (Thurs., Sept. 2, 1830)

Marks, Mrs. M. Consort of Mr. William Marks. Aged 43. Died in Pulaski of cholera on June 4th.
National Banner & Nashville Daily Advertiser. (Wed., June 19, 1833)

Marl, David. Died at Cincinnati, Ohio of Cholera on 11th.
National Banner & Nashville Daily Advertiser. (Thurs., Oct. 18, 1832)

Marley, Mr. Robert. Of Knox County, Clock pedler. Died at Bellborough, Williamson County of Cholera.
National Banner & Nashville Daily Advertiser. (Sat., July 6, 1833)

Marr, Mrs. Jane. Consort of Maj. G. W. Marr. Died in Obion County.
Nashville Whig. (Thurs., April 30, 1846)

Marr, Maj. Wm. M. For many years a resident of Ten.
Nashville Republican & State Gazette. (Sat., Sept. 17, 1831)

Marrs, Mrs. Died in Shelbyville, Tenn. of Cholera.
National Banner & Nashville Daily Advertiser. (Thurs., July 11, 1833)

Marrs, John A. Jun. Died in Shelbyville, Tenn. of Cholera.
National Banner & Nashville Daily Advertiser. (Thurs., July 11, 1833)

Marry, Gen. Joseph A. Of Tennessee. Died on Wednesday evening last in Tuscaloosa, Ala.
National Banner & Nashville Whig. (Wed., May 3, 1837)

Marsh, Edward. About 17 years old. Died on the 14th at the residence of G. W. Cheatham Esq. in Nashville.
Nashville Whig. (Thurs., Aug. 18, 1842)

Marshall, Infant daughter of John Marshall. Died in Shelbyville, Tenn. of Cholera.
National Banner & Nashville Daily Advertiser. (Thurs., July 11, 1833)

Marshall, Mrs. D. Alexander. Wife of Dr. Alexander Marshall. Died at Danville, Ky.
National Banner & Nashville Whig. (Mon., Sept. 20, 1830)

Marshall, Mrs. Elihu. Aged 56. Died in this town last night.
National Banner. (Sat., Oct. 31, 1829)

Marshall, Eliza Jane. Daughter of Mr. Joseph H. Marshall. Died in Nashville.
National Banner & Nashville Daily Advertiser. (Mon., March 18, 1833)

Marshall, Mrs. Elizabeth. Widow of the late Rev. Robert Marshall of Ky. Died on the 13th of November last at the residence of her son in the 78th year of her age.
The Christian Record. (Sat., Jan. 6th 1849)

Marshall, Mrs. John. Died in Shelbyville, Tenn. of Cholera.
National Banner & Nashville Daily Advertiser. (Thurs., July 11, 1833)

Marshall, John Esq. Aged 35 years. Died at his seat in Farquier
Co., Va. Third son of Chief Justice Marshall.
National Banner & Nashville Daily Advertiser. (Fri., Dec. 27, 1833)

Marshall, Mrs. Maria. Wife of L. R. Marshall Esq. Died in Natchez,
Mi.
National Banner & Nashville Daily Advertiser. (Sat., Aug. 24, 1833)

Marshall, Mrs. Mary Ann. Wife of Mr. William Marshall. Died this
morning.
Daily Republican Banner. (Sat., July 14, 1838)

Marshall, Mrs. Mary W. Wife of Chief Justice Marshall, aged 65 years.
Died at Richmond, Va.
National Banner & Nashville Daily Advertiser. (Mon., Jan. 9, 1832)

Marshall, Rob. B. Esq. Died at Tuscumbia, Ala.
National Banner & Nashville Whig. (Sat., Oct. 11, 1828)

Marshall, Rev. Robert. Age 72. Died in Lexington, Ky.
National Banner & Nashville Advertiser. (Tues., June 26, 1832)

Marshall, Mr. Samuel. Died at Shawneetown.
National Banner & Nashville Whig. (Mon., July 19, 1830)

Marshall, Mr. William. Aged 69. Died in Williamson County.
National Banner. (Feb. 10, 1826)

Marshall, Mr. William M. Formerly of Nashville. Died at Natchez on
June 8th of Cholera.
National Banner & Nashville Daily Advertiser. (Fri., June 21, 1833)

Martin, Mrs. Consort of James G. Martin Esq. Died at Clifton the
seat of her husband in Davidson County on the 15th inst.
The Union. (Thurs., April 21, 1836)

Martin, Mrs. Wife of Mr. Hugh Martin. Died in Jefferson County.
National Banner & Nashville Whig. (Thurs., May 20, 1830)

Martin, Colonel Barkley. Died on the 16th inst. of the County of
Bedford. He was violently attacked whilst superintending the opening
of the road from West Tenn. to Augusta, Georgia reached here in a
wagon on the 15th and expired the day following.
The Nash. Whig. (Tues., Nov. 28, 1815)

Martin, Major Brice F. Died at the residence of his father Col.
William Martin of Smith County on the 18th day of Dec. 1843. (Obituary)
Nashville Whig. (Sat., Jan. 13, 1844)

Martin, Mrs. Catharine B. Wife of John L. Martin Esq. Died in
Lexington, Ky.
National Banner & Nashville Whig. (Mon., Aug. 30, 1830)

Martin, Cornelia. Youngest daughter of Mr. Thomas Martin. Died in
Pulaski on Sunday 12th inst.
National Banner & Nashville Daily Advertiser. (Thurs., Aug. 23, 1832)

Martin, Mrs. Cornelia Frances. Wife of Mr. Charles E. H. Martin.
Died in Nashville very suddenly on Saturday last.
Nashville True Whig & Weekly Commercial Register. (Fri., Jan. 3, 1851)

Martin, His Excellency Daniel. Governor of Maryland. Died in Talbot
County, Md.
National Banner & Nashville Whig. (Mon., July 25, 1831)

Martin, Mr. David. Of Columbia. Died in Paris, Henry County.
National Banner & Nashville Whig. (Wed., Aug. 17, 1831)

Martin, Dr. Edward B.   Died in Warren County, Ky.
National Banner & Nashville Whig. (Fri., March 6, 1835)

Martin, Mrs. Elizabeth.   Died in Lynchburg, Va.
Nashville Republican & State Gazette. (Tues., April 12, 1831)

Martin, Dr. George.   Died on Sunday morning 29th inst at the residence
of his son Dr. Robert Martin.
Nashville Whig. (Tues., May 31, 1842)

Martin, George Walker.   Infant son of John W. and Margaret J. Martin.
Died in Nashville yesterday aged about 16 months.
The Politician and Weekly Nashville Whig. (Fri., July 9, 1847)

Martin, Gideon.   Infant son of G. W. Martin of Nashville.   Died on
Thursday 22d inst. of Whooping cough.
Nashville Republican. (Tues., June 27, 1837)

Martin, James.   In the 106th year of his age.   Died at Knoxville he
was a soldier of the American Revolution.
National Banner & Nashville Daily Advertiser. (Mon., July 22, 1833)

Martin, Col. James.   In the 94th year of his age.   Died in Stokes
County, North Carolina.
National Banner & Nashville Whig. (Wed., Nov. 26, 1834)

Martin, Mr. James H.   Died in Conway County, Ark. Ter.
National Banner. (March 24, 1826)

Martin, Mrs. Jane.   Consort of A. Martin Esq.   Attorney at Law.
National Banner & Nashville Whig. (Sat., Jan. 24, 1829)

Martin, Mr. Jeremiah.   Died at Natchez, Miss.
National Banner & Nashville Daily Advertiser. (Mon., Jan. 9, 1832)

Martin, John.   Formerly of Caroline County, Virginia.
Died in Wilson County, on April 10.
Nashville Republican. (Thurs., May 10, 1837)

Martin, Mr. Joseph W.   Of White Plains, Miss., aged 20 years.   Student
of Lagrange College.   Died at Lagrange, Ala.
National Banner & Nashville Whig. (Fri., June 3, 1831)

Martin, Hon. Luther.   Of Maryland, aged 81, died in New York.
National Banner & Nashville Whig. (Sat., Aug. 5, 1826)

Martin, Martha H.   Wife of William P. Martin Esq.   Died at Columbia,
Tenn.
Nashville Whig. (Mon., Sept. 21, 1840)

Martin, Capt. Mathew.   Of Wilson County.   Died on Monday last, his
death was occasioned by a fall from a window in the third story of
Talbot Hotel.
The Nashville Whig. (June 16, 1817)

Martin, Norval D.   Son of Col. William Martin of Smith Co.   Died on
Tuesday morning last at the Residence of Dr. Shelby.
Nashville Republican. (Thurs., Feb. 2, 1837)

Martin, Patrick.   Died lately on his way home, after having been
engaged in his country's service, through out the recent glorious
campaign in the south.   Patrick Martin Esq., Attorney at law, formerly
of this town (Nashville)
Nashville Whig. (April 4th, 1815)
Nashville Whig. (April 18, 1815)

Martin, Private Peter H.   Company G. First Regiment Tenn. Volunteers.
Died was killed in the Battle of Monterey with Mexicans on Sept. 21st
1846.   Nashville Whig. (Sat., Oct. 24, 1846)

Martin, Mr. R. H. Died on the 19th inst at the residence of Mr. W.
N. Hawkins 7 miles from Nashville.
Daily Republican Banner. (Sat., July 21, 1838)

Martin, Miss Rachel Jackson. Died on the 8th inst at the residence
of her father near the Hermitage.
The Christian Record. (Sat., Jan. 15, 1848)

Martin, Mr. Robert S. Died at Hopkinsville, Ky.
National Banner & Nashville Daily Advertiser. (Mon., April 29, 1833)

Martin, Mrs. Sarah B. Wife of Col. P. Martin. Died at Russellville,
Ala.
National Banner & Nashville Whig. (Fri., Feb. 18, 1831)

Martin, Thomas D. Died was drowned while going from Nashville to his
home in Sumner County. (Obituary)
The Christian Record. (Sat., March 4, 1848)

Martin, Doctor Thomas J. Died in Smith County on the 18th at the
residence of his father in the 27th year of his age. Son of Col.
William Martin.
National Banner & Nashville Daily Advertiser. (Mon., Aug. 12, 1833)

Martin, Colonel William. In the 81st year of his age. Died at his
residence in Smith Co. on the 4th inst. (Obituary)
Nashville Whig. (Thurs., Nov. 19, 1846)

Mardis, Hon. Samuel W. Of Alabama formerly a member of Congress.
Died in Taladega County, on the 14th ult.
The Union. (Sat., Dec. 10, 1836)

Mashulatubbee, Mingo. Aged about 60 years. Died near the Choctaw
Agency on the 30th ult. He was for many years Chief of the Lower
Towns District.
Daily Republican Banner. (Thurs., Oct. 4, 1838)

Mason, Col. Daniel. Died on Friday the 13th inst. In Humphreys
County, formerly of Northampton County, N. C.
National Banner & Nashville Daily Advertiser. (Mon., April 23, 1832)

Mason, Dr. David H. Aged 27. Died near Athens, Ala.
National Banner & Nashville Daily Advertiser. (Mon., July 14, 1834)

Mason, Isaac. In the 63rd year of his age. Died at Barren Plains,
Robertson County on Monday the 14th inst.
Nashville Whig. (Sat., Sept. 19, 1846)

Mason, Mr. James. Late of Halifax County, North Carolina. Died on
the 27th June near Jefferson.
The Nashville Whig. (July 2, 1816)

Mason, Hon. Jonathan. Age 75. Formerly a Member of Congress from
Mass.
National Banner & Nashville Whig. (Fri., Nov. 18, 1831)

Mason, Jonathan. A soldier of the Revolution. Died recently in New
Hampshire aged 74 years.
Nashville Union. (Fri., July 5, 1839)

Mason, Hon. Jonathan. Aged 75, formerly member of Congress from
Massachusetts. Died at Boston.
National Banner & Nashville Whig. (Fri., Nov. 18, 1831)

Mason, Joseph B. Died in Shelbyville, Tenn. of Cholera.
National Banner & Nashville Daily Advertiser. (Thurs., July 11, 1833)

Mason, General R. B. Died suddenly in St. Louis of Cholera on the 26th ult.
Nashville True Whig. & Weekly Commercial Register. (Fri., Aug. 9, 1850)

Massengill, Mrs. Dorcas. Wife of Mr. Michael Massengill. Died in Grainger County.
National Banner & Nashville Whig. (Mon., Dec. 6, 1830)

Massengill, Mr. John. On Wednesday 3d inst. Died at the residence of Alexander Porter Esq. in Nashville.
National Banner & Nashville Whig. (Fri., Aug. 5, 1831)

Massengill, Mr. Jno. Died in this town.
Nashville Republican & State Gazette. (Sat., Aug. 6, 1831)

Massey, Ephriam M. Esq. In the 47th year of his age. Died at Cornersville, Giles County, Tennessee on Feb. 27th.
Nashville Republican. (Thurs., March 10, 1836)

Masterson, Ann Eliza. Infant daughter of W. W. Masterson Esq. Died at Lebanon, Wilson County.
Nashville Whig. (Mon., Sept. 7, 1840)

Mathews, Hon. George. Judge of the Supreme Court, of La. Died on Monday the 14th Nov. near St. Francisville, in the Parish of W. Feliciana.
National Banner & Nashville Whig. (Mon., Dec. 5, 1836)

Mathews, Capt. John. Died in Franklin County on the 30th June.
National Banner & Nashville Whig. (Wed., Aug. 17, 1831)

Mathis, Miss Catherine. Died in Limestone County, Ala.
National Banner & Nashville Whig. (Mon., Oct. 4, 1830)

Matlock, Mr. James. In the 23d year of his age. Died in Nashville on the 24th Feb.
Nashville Whig. (Thurs., Feb. 26, 1846)

Matthew, Julia Augusta. Daughter of Mr. J. P. & Mrs. E. A. Matthews Died in Nashville on Sunday 12th inst. aged about two years and ine months.
The Politician and Weekly Nashville Whig. (Wed., Sept. 22, 1847)

Matthews, Cornelius Scott. Infant son of Mr. J. P. and Mrs. E. A. Matthews. Died in Nashville on Saturday 4th inst.
The Christian Record. (Sat., Sept. 11, 1847)

Matthews, Mr. Edward. A baker, formerly of Cincinnatti, Ohio. Died in Memphis, Tenn.
National Banner & Nashville Whig. (Mon., Aug. 3, 1835)

Matthews, Eudora Adelina. Infant daughter of Mr. J. P. and Mrs. Eudora Matthews of Nashville. Died on the 30th ult. in her 5th year. (Obituary)
The Christian Record. (Sat., Sept. 4, 1847)

Matthews, Capt. John. Died on the 30th of June near Winchester, Franklin County, Ten.
The Western Weekly Review. (Fri., Aug. 13, 1831) Franklin, Tenn.

Matthews, Mr. John. Died in Franklin County on the 30th of June.
National Banner & Nashville Whig. (Wed., July 6, 1831)

Matthews, Mr. Soloman. Died in Tuscumbia, Ala.
National Banner & Nashville Whig. (Sat., Nov. 18, 1826)

Matthis, Mrs. Fanny. Died in Elizabethtown, Ky.
National Banner & Nashville Daily Advertiser. (Tues., July 15, 1834)

Maugh, John. Died 14th at Cincinnati, Ohio of Cholera.
National Banner & Nashville Daily Advertiser. (Tues., Oct. 23, 1832)

Maulton, Col. Michael. Died on the 31st August at his resident in
Meridianville M. T. Col. M. was a N. Carolinian. He accompanied
general Jackson in an expedition against the southern Indians and
fought bravely in the ever memorable battle of Orleans.
The Nashville Whig. (Sept. 15, 1817)

Maultrie, Mrs. Wife of Mr. Wm. Moultrie. Died in Lauderdale County,
Ala.
National Banner & Nashville Whig. (Sat., Aug. 26, 1826)

Maupin, Miss Matilda A. Died at Louisville, Ky.
National Banner & Nashville Whig. (Fri., July 11, 1828)

Maury, Hon. A. P. Died at his residence in Williamson County, Tenn.
near Franklin on the 22nd of July. (Obituary)
The Christian Record. (Sat., July 12, 1848)

Maury, Lieut. Abram. Of Franklin County. Died on the 8th inst.
(April 8, 1815) after a long and lingering indisposition, Lieut.
Abram Maury of Franklin County, late of Capt. Hammond's Company of
Rangers.
Nashville Whig. (April 18, 1815)

Maury, Alfred Esq. Died at Helena, Ark. Formerly of Tennessee.
National Banner & Nashville Whig. (Sat., March 7, 1829)

Maury, Col. Thomas T. and Mr. John Sample. Both of Franklin. Died
at sea in April last. These gentlemen were afflicted with a pulmonary
disease and were on a voyage for the purpose of repairing their
health.
The Nashville Whig. (June 16, 1817)

Maxey, Mrs. Sarah. Consort of Mr. Zenas Maxey. Died in Powhatan
County, Va. on the 10th May.
National Banner & Nashville Whig. (Fri., June 10, 1836)

Maxwell, Capt. James. Died in this county, an old and highly respectable citizen.
National Banner. (April 7, 1826)

Maxwell, James. The melter and refiner of the Branch Mint. Died in
New Orleans of Yellow Fever.
Daily Republican Banner. (Wed., Sept. 11, 1839)

Maxwell, Mr. James J. Died in Rutherford County.
National Banner & Nashville Whig. (Sat., Jan. 10, 1829)

Maxwell, Mr. Nathaniel Sen. Aged 94. Died in Washington County, Va.
on the 24th ult.
National Banner & Nashville Daily Advertiser. (Mon., Feb. 17, 1834)

May, Miss Anne F. Eldest daughter of Judge May. Died at Petersburg,
Va.
National Banner & Nashville Daily Advertiser. (Thurs., March 6, 1834)

May, Mr. James F. In the 32nd year of his age. Died killed when his
horse ran away about five miles on Franklin Pike, and through him
from his vehicle. (Obituary)
Nashville Whig. (Tues., Oct. 17, 1843)

May, Mrs. Ann. Wife of Hon. William L. May of Springfield, Illinois.
Died on Friday night last. (Obituary) from Illinois Republican.
The Union. (Sat., Aug. 6, 1836)

May, Powhatan Esq. Attorney at law of Jackson and late of Virginia. Died in Nashville about one o'clock this morning.
National Banner & Nashville Whig. (Mon., Aug. 9, 1830)

May, Doctor Francis. An eminent Physician in the death of this gentleman, Society has lost a valuable member. Died in this place on Wednesday 28th inst.
The Nashville Whig & Tenn. Advertiser. (Dec. 1, 1817)

May, Mr. Baily. Died in Sumner County.
National Banner & Nashville Whig. (Sat., Oct. 4, 1828)

Mayberry, Mr. Charles. Died in Warren County on the 17th ult.
National Banner & Nashville Whig. (Thurs., June 3, 1830)

Maybin, Mr. William A. Aged 37. Died in Philadelphia.
National Banner & Nashville Whig. (Sat., Feb. 7, 1829)

Mayfield, Avery. From Warren County. Died at the Tenn. State Prison of Cholera.
National Banner & Nashville Whig. (Fri., Aug. 14, 1835)

Mayfield, Mr. Jno. Died in Warren County, N. C.
Nashville Republican & State Gazette. (Sat., March 19, 1831)

Mayfield, John Esq. Died in Hardeman County.
National Banner & Nashville Whig. (Sat., Oct. 6, 1827)

Mayfield, Mr. Milton G. 30. Died in Pulaski on June 10, of Cholera.
National Banner & Nashville Daily Advertiser. (Wed., June 19, 1833)

Maylin, Rev. Jos. Of the Baptist denomination. Died at Medford, N.J.
National Banner & Nashville Daily Advertiser. (Fri., May 16, 1834)

Mayo, Col. John. Died lately in Richmond.
The Nashville Whig. & Tenn. Advertiser. (June 27, 1818)

Mays, Mr. Hiiton I. Died in Cairo.
National Banner & Nashville Whig. (Sat., Dec. 2, 1826)

Mays, Mrs. Susan Moriah. Consort of Drury Mays Esq. and daughter of Capt. Beverly Williams. in the 22d year of her age. Died in Gibson County, Tenn. on the 24th April.
National Banner & Nashville Daily Advertiser. (Thurs., May 16, 1833)

Maysey, Mrs. Jane. Wife of Maj. Charles Maysey and daughter of Col. Hugh Montgomery. Died near Pikeville.
National Banner & Nashville Whig. (Tues., Feb. 2, 1830)

Mayson, C. C. Esq. Treasurer of the State. Died at Jackson on the 30th ult.
Daily Republican Banner. (Mon., Oct. 16, 1837)

Meacham, John. Son of Mr. B. Meacham. Died in Knox County.
National Banner & Nashville Whig. (Mon., May 2, 1831)

Mead, Rev. Stith. Of the Methodist Episcopal Church, age 68 years. Died in Amherst County, Va. near Lynchburg.
National Banner & Nashville Daily. (Tues., Aug. 19, 1834)

Meade, Mr. Nicholas. Died in Bedford County, Va.
Nashville Republican & State Gazette. (Thurs., April 19, 1831)

Meade, Richard Kidder. In the 50th year of his age. Died at Lucky hit farm, Frederick County, Va. on Tuesday the 20th.
National Banner & Nashville Daily Advertiser. (Tues., March 19, 1833)

Mease, Mrs. Sarah. Wife of James Mease, M. D. Died in Philadelphia.
Nashville Republican & State Gazette. (Thurs., March 10, 1831)

Mechar, Mr. Peter. A resident of that vicinity for 30 years. Died at
Memphis.
National Banner & Nashville Whig. (Fri., July 18, 1828)

Medley, Boswell, Aged 43 years. Died in Nashville of Cholera.
National Banner & Nashville Whig. (Wed., July 15, 1835)

Meek, Mr. Samuel. Formerly of Washington County, Va. Died in Carroll
County, Miss. on the 14th July.
National Banner & Nashville Whig. (Fri., July 29, 1836)
Nashville Republican. (Sat., July 30, 1836)

Meigs, Col. Return J. Agent of the United States for the United
States for the Cherokee Indians.
Nashville Whig. (Feb. 5, 1823)

Melanephy, Constantine. Died 19th at Cincinnati, Ohio of Cholera.
National Banner & Nashville Daily Advertiser. (Fri., Oct. 26, 1836)

Melish, Mr. John. Geographer. Died in Philadelphia.
Nashville Whig. (Jan. 29, 1823)

Mellen, The Hon. Prentiss, L. L. D. In the 77th year of his age.
Died this morning at 1 o'clock. Late Chief Justice of the Supreme
Court of Tennessee.
Nashville Whig. (Fri., Jan. 15, 1841)

Melville, Maj. Thomas. Age 82. A Revolutionary hero. Concerned in
the destructionof tea, in Boston harbor. Died in Boston.
National Banner & Nashville Advertiser. (Mon., Oct. 8, 1832)

Mendenhall, Mr. Mordecai. Aged 58 years. Died in Jefferson County.
National Banner & Nashville Daily Advertiser. (Fri., Aug. 16, 1833)

Meneer, Mr. John. In the 77th year of his age. Died in Neeleys
Bend, Davidson County on the 13th inst.
Nashville Whig. (Thurs., Sept. 17, 1846)

Menefee, Richard H. Esq. Died at Lexington on Saturday night. One
of the ablest men in Ky.
Nashville Whig. (Wed., March 3, 1841)

Menefee, Mr. Wm. B. Formerly of Culpepper County, Va. aged 24 years.
Died in Vernon, Mi.
National Banner & Nashville Daily Advertiser. (Tues., Aug. 5, 1834)

Menifee, Major William N. In the 27th year of his age. Died on Tues.
17th inst at his late residence.
Nashville Whig. (Aug. 23, 1824)

Menziers, Mr. Duncan. A native of Perth, Scotland. Died in Mobile,
Ala. of Yellow fever.
Daily Republican Banner. (Tues., Oct. 1, 1839)

Meredith, John J.. Esq. Late editor of the Knoxville Enquirer, aged
25. Died near Bolivar.
National Banner. (Sat., Sept. 26, 1829)

Meredith, Thomas H. and his wife within two or three weeks of each
other. Died lately at their residence in Giles County.
Nashville Whig. (March 12, 1823)

Meritt, Mr. Hansel. Formerly of Nashville. Died in Jackson, Miss.
National Banner & Nashville Whig. (Fri., Sept. 23, 1836)

Meriweather, Mrs. Mary. Died in Madison County. Wife of Maj. James Meriwether.
National Banner & Nashville Advertiser. (Thurs., Aug.16, 1832)

Meriwether, Mr. Charles. Died in Louisville, Ky.
National Banner & Nashville Whig. (Sat., Feb. 7, 1829)

Meriwether, Mrs. Mary. Wife of Maj. James Meriwether. Died in Madison County.
National Banner & Nashville Daily Advertiser. (Thurs., Aug. 16, 1832)

Merrett, Mrs. Mary Ann. Consort of Mr. Hansell Merritt. Died in Nashville on the 22nd inst. in the 20th year of her age. She was a daughter of Zachariah Noell, of Davidson County, Tenn.
National Banner & Nashville Daily Advertiser. (Thurs., April 25, 1833)

Merrick, Miss Lydia F. Died at Natchez, Miss.
National Banner & Nashville Whig. (Mon., Oct. 17, 1831)

Merrie, Mr. William. Died at Cincinnati.
National Banner. (March 31, 1826)

Merrill, Mrs. Mary B. Wife of Col. Benj. Merrill. Died in Fayette County, Ky.
National Banner & Nashville Whig. (Thurs., Oct. 21, 1830)

Merriman, Mr. Francis. Died in Knox County.
National Banner & Nashville Whig. (Sat., Aug. 12, 1826)

Merritt, Mr. Hansel. Formerly of Nashville, Tenn. Died at Jackson, Mi. on the 6th was about 25 years of age.
Nashville Republican. (Thurs., Sept. 22, 1836)

Merriweather, Mrs. Jane. Wife of Henry W. Merriweather Esq. Died in Montgomery County.
National Banner & Nashville Whig. (Sat., Sept. 6, 1828)

Merriwether, Mrs. Elizabeth. Wife of Capt. William Merriweather of Jefferson County, Ky. Died in Lexington, Ky.
National Banner. (Sat., July 18, 1829)

Merry, Mrs. Prisecilla. Age 45. Died in Memphis.
National Banner & Nashville Whig. (Wed., March 2, 1831)

Merryman, Mr. Thomas. Died in the County of Powhatan Sate of Virginia, on the 11th Jan.
National Banner & Nashville Whig. (Fri., Feb. 10, 1837)

Messengill, Mr. John. Died in Nashville on Wed. 3d inst. At the residence of Alexander Potter Esq.
National Banner & Nashville Whig. (Fri., Aug. 5, 1831)

Metcalf, Ilai. Died in Robinson County on the 21st inst. formerly of this town.
Nashville Whig. (April 26, 1824)

Metcle, Miss Elizabeth. Formerly of New York. Died at the residence of her nephew. A Van Wyck, in Nashville.
National Banner & Nashville Daily Advertiser. (Tues., Oct. 1, 1833)

Mezick, Jesuah and George H. Brothers from Baltimore. Died at New Orleans of Yellow fever.
National Banner & Nashville Daily Advertiser. (Fri., Sept. 20, 1833)

Middleton, Mrs. Sophia Western wife of E. J. Middleton, Esq. aged 26. Died in Washington City.
National Banner & Nashville Daily Advertiser. (Wed., July 9, 1834)

Mikels, Joseph. Died in Knoxville, Tenn. of the Fever.
Daily Republican Banner. (Sat., Oct. 13, 1838)

Milam, Mrs. Wife of Mr. Benjamin Milam. Died in Logan County, Ky.
National Banner & Nashville Whig. (Mon., Aug. 22, 1831)

Miler, C. C. Died 14th at Cincinnati, Ohio of Cholera.
National Banner & Nashville Daily Advertiser. (Wed., Oct. 24, 1832)

Miles, Mr. Israel. Died at Hendersonville. Sumner County, by suicide.
National Banner. (Feb. 3, 1826)

Miles, John. Aged 92. Died at Greenburgh, Ky. A soldier of the
revolution.
National Banner & Nashville Whig. (Sat., April 7, 1827)

Milford, Mr. James. A native of Boston, Mass., aged 34. Died at
Cincinnati, Ohio.
National Banner & Nashville Daily Advertiser. (Sat., Aug. 2, 1834)

Millar, Mr. Alexander. A native of Ireland aged 27 years. Died in
Nashville on 22d Oct.
National Banner & Nashville Whig. (Mon., Oct. 24, 1836)

Millard, Mrs. Aged 28. Wife of Maj. Henry Millard. Died in New
Orleans.
National Banner & Nashville Daily Advertiser. (Tues., June 24, 1834)

Milledge, Hon. John. Aged 61 years. Formerly governor of Georgia,
Senator in Congress.
The Nashville Whig & Tenn. Advertiser. (March 7, 1818)

Miller, Mrs. Wife of Mr. Thomas Miller. Died at Knoxville.
National Banner & Nashville Whig. (Sat., March 10, 1827)

Miller, Mrs. Wife of Mr. Anderson Miller. Died in Logan County, Ky.
National Banner & Nashville Advertiser. (Mon., June 18, 1832)

Miller, Dr. Benjamin P. Died at Jacksonville, Illinois.
National Banner & Nashville Whig. (Mon., July 19, 1830)

Miller, Branch W. Esq. Died in New Orleans.
National Banner & Nashville Daily Advertiser. (Tues., June 24, 1834)

Miller, Hon. Daniel. Died in Philadelphia.
Nashville Republican & State Gazette. (Tues., May 10, 1831)

Miller, Daniel H. Esq. Late Representative in Congress from the third
Congressional district of Pennsylvania in the 48 year of his age.
Died at Philadelphia.
National Banner & Nashville Whig. (Mon., May 23, 1831)

Miller, F. With the second Tenn. Regiment. Died - was killed in the
Battle of Sierra Garda with the Mexicans.
The Politician and Weekly Nashville Whig. (Fri., May 21, 1847)

Miller, Col. Garland B. Died in Franklin County.
National Banner & Nashville Advertiser. (Mon., Dec. 24, 1832)

Miller, Henry M. Esq. Aged 83. Formerly of Virginia. Died at
Red Sulphur Springs, Va. for a number of years past a resident of
Raleigh, N. C.
National Banner & Nashville Daily Advertiser. (Sat., Aug. 10, 1833)

Miller, H. W. At Richardson Hotel. Died in New Orleans of Yellow
Fever.
Daily Republican Banner. (Fri., Sept. 29, 1837)

Miller, Mr. Jacob. Died in Giles County.
National Banner & Nashville Daily Advertiser. (Wed., Dec. 12, 1832)

Miller, Mr. James O. Died in Madison County, Ala.
National Banner & Nashville Whig. (Sat., Nov. 3, 1827)

Miller, John. Died in Shelbyville, Tenn. of Cholera.
National Banner & Nashville Daily Advertiser. (Thurs., July 11, 1833)

Miller, John Esq. Died in Jefferson County, Ky.
National Banner & Nashville Whig. (Sat., Aug. 25, 1827)

Miller, John Jun. Son of John Miller, Esq. Died in Maury County.
National Banner & Nashville Whig. (Mon., Oct. 4, 1830)

Miller, Mr. John. Silver Smith, formerly of this place. Died in
Huntsville, Alabama on Wednesday the 7th inst.
Nashville Whig. (April 19, 1824)

Miller, Col. John. Formerly of Tennessee, aged 58.
National Banner. (Feb. 24, 1826)

Miller, Mrs. John A. Died in Georgetown, Ky.
National Banner & Nashville Whig. (Sat., Oct. 7, 1826)

Miller, John C. Esq. Cashier of the office of the planters Bank of
Tennessee. Died in Clarkesville on the 4th inst.
Nashville Whig. (Mon., Feb. 11, 1839)

Miller, Mr. Jonathan A. Died in Shelby County, Ky.
National Banner. May 27, 1826)

Miller, Mrs. Mary. Aged 58. Died in Gibson County. Wife of Mr.
Andrew Miller late of Rutherford County.
National Banner. (Sat., Sept. 12, 1829)

Miller, Miss Mary Jane. Of Madison. Died at Tarborough, N. C.
National Banner & Nashville Whig. (Mon., May 31, 1830)

Miller, Pleasant M. Jr. Son of Hon. P. M. Miller of Jackson, Tenn.
Died in Texas.
Nashville Whig. (Mon., Sept. 7, 1840)

Miller, Rev. Robert Johnson. Of the Episcopal Church aged 76. Died
in Burke County, North Carolina. A native of Scotland, a whig of the
Revolution.
National Banner & Nashville Daily Advertiser. (Thurs., June 19, 1834)

Miller, Mrs. Sarah. Wife of Rev. Andrew Miller. Died in Monroe
County.
National Banner & Nashville Daily Advertiser. (Wed., July 17, 1833)

Miller, Mrs. Sarah A. Wife of Mr. Pitser Miller. of Hawkins County.
Daughter of Wm. Lyons Esq. of Hawkins County. Died at Bolivar.
National Banner & Nashville Whig. (Wed., Dec. 14, 1831)

Miller, Mr. Thomas B. Died in Henry County.
Nashville Whig. (Tues., March 31, 1846)

Miller, Thomas Jefferson Esq. Died in St. Louis on the 15th ult.
One of the proprietors and publishers of the St. Louis Times in the
28th year of his age.
National Banner & Nashville Daily Advertiser. (Sat., Feb. 2, 1833)

Miller, William. From Roan County. Died at the Tenn. State Prison
of Cholera.
National Banner & Nashville Whig. (Fri., Aug. 14, 1835)

Miller, Mr. William A. Formerly of Virginia. Died in Tipton County, Tenn.
National Banner & Nashville Daily Advertiser. (Wed., April 4, 1832)

Millermew, John. Son of Thos. Millermew. Died in Knoxville, Tenn.
Daily Republican Banner. (Sat., Sept. 22, 1838)

Mills, Benj. Esq. Late Judge of the Court of Appeals, and one of the most eminent lawyers in Kentucky. Died in Frankfort, Ky.
National Banner & Nashville Whig. (Tues., Dec. 13, 1831)

Mills, Hon. Elijah H. Died at Northampton, Mass. Formerly Senator in Congress from that state.
National Banner. (Sat., June 6, 1829)

Mills, Mr. Isham. In the 80th year of his age. Died in Hawkins County.
National Banner & Nashville Daily Advertiser. (Wed., Jan. 18, 1832)

Mills, Mr. Otheniel C. Printer, a native of Kentucky. Died on his passage from New Orleans to New York, aged 34.
National Banner & Nashville Daily Advertiser. (Thurs., Aug. 8, 1833)

Millwood, John. Died at the residence of Benj. Bondurant, in Dresden, Tenn. on 18th July, said he was from Clay County, Illinois.
National Banner & Nashville Whig. (Fri., Aug. 7, 1835)

Milstead, Mrs. Wife of Mr. John Milstead. Died in Lincoln City, Ten.
National Banner & Nashville Whig. (Mon., Oct. 20, 1834)

Mimms, John Esq. Came to his death by freezing, Pulaski, Tenn.
National Banner & Nashville Daily Advertiser. (Fri., Feb. 3, 1832)

Minner, Mr. Peter. Died in Hardeman County, Ten.
National Banner & Nashville Whig. (Wed., Oct. 22, 1834)

Minor, Lt. C. L. C. Quarter Master U. S. Army. Died at Fort Towson on the 31st Oct.
National Banner & Nashville Daily Advertiser. (Fri., Dec. 27, 1833)

Minor, Henry Esq. Clerk of the Supreme Court of Alabama. Died at Tusculoosa, Ala. Formerly of Montgomery County, Tenn.
Nashville Whig. (Sat., Jan. 27, 1838)

Minor, Mrs. Mary Jane. Wife of Charles Minor, Esq. Died in Montgomery County on the 17th ult.
National Banner & Nashville Whig. (Sat., Dec. 20, 1828)

Minor, Col. Thomas. A soldier of the Revolution. Died in Fredericksburg, Va. age 82.
National Banner & Nashville Daily Advertiser. (Thurs., Aug. 14, 1834)

Mitchel, Mrs. Elizabeth. Wife of Wm. Mitchel Esq. Died in Rutherford County, on the 7th inst.
National Banner & Nashville Whig. (Sat., April 19, 1828)

Mitchell, Contantine P. Merchant of Nashville, aged 32 years. Died on July 16th in Smith County, near Dixon Springs.
Daily Republican Banner. (Thurs., July 26, 1838)

Mitchell, C. W. Died in Grainger County at the residence of Capt. Jacksons.
Daily Republican Banner. (Sat., Oct. 6, 1838)

Mitchell, Dr. Daniel L. The Distinguished Naturalist. Died in New York, on 7th inst.
National Banner & Nashville Whig. (Wed., Sept. 21, 1831)

Mitchell, Mr. J. W. Of Rodney, Mi. Died in Nashville.
National Banner & Nashville Advertiser. (Fri., Oct. 12, 1832)

Mitchell, Hon. James C. Aged about 55 years. Died on the 17th ult.
at his residence in Hines County near Jackson. He was a native of
Augusta County, Virginia but removed at an early age to Tennessee.
Nashville Whig. (Thurs., Sept. 14, 1843)

Mitchell, Mr. James. Aged 80. Father of the Hon. James C. Mitchell.
Died at Athens, Ten.
National Banner & Nashville Whig. (Thurs., Sept. 16, 1830)

Mitchell, James. Aged 80 years, six months and one day. Died on
the 18th May in Robertson County in his youth he fought in the Revolution War.
National Banner & Nashville Whig. (Fri., May 29, 1835)

Mitchell, Hon. James C. Formerly a member of Congress from Tennessee.
Died on Thursday the 17th near Jackson, Mississippi.
Nashville Whig. (Thurs., Aug. 31, 1843)

Mitchell, Mr. John. Steward of the University. Died in Nashville
last night.
National Banner & Nashville Daily Advertiser. (Sat., Feb. 25, 1832)

Mitchell, Mrs. John. Died in Shelbyville, Tenn. of Cholera.
National Banner & Nashville Daily Advertiser. (Thurs., July 11, 1833)

Mitchell, Capt. Marcus. Died in Giles County. An old citizen of said
county.
Nashville Republican. (Thurs., Oct. 6, 1836)

Mitchell, Mrs. Margaret. Consort of Robert B. Mitchell. Died in
Robertson County.
Nashville Whig. (Thurs., April 30, 1846)

Mitchell, Mr. Mark. Age 65. Late of Rutherford County. Died in
Dyer County.
National Banner & Nashville Whig. (Wed., March 16, 1831)

Mitchell, Martha. Daughter of Mr. John Mitchell. Died in Bedford
County, Tenn.
National Banner & Nashville Advertiser. (Wed., April 11, 1832)

Mitchell, Mrs. Mary. Aged 73. Wife of Mr. Mark Mitchell. Died
in Rutherford County.
National Banner. (Sat., Sept. 12, 1829)

Mitchell, Miss Nancy. Aged 18. Died in Columbia, T.
National Banner & Nashville Whig. (Sat., Oct. 7, 1826)

Mitchell, Dr. Samuel L. The distinguished naturalist, died in New
York, on the 7th inst.
National Banner & Nashville Whig. (Wed., Sept. 21, 1831)

Mitchell, Mr. Samuel. Aged 60 years. Died in Knox County, Tenn.
National Banner & Nashville Daily Advertiser. (Mon., May 28, 1832)

Mitchell, Mr. Samuel. Died at Huntsville, Ala.
National Banner & Nashville Whig. (Sat., June 2, 1827)

Mitchell, Mrs. Sarah. Wife of Dr. Ira S. Mitchell. Died in Randolph.
National Banner & Nashville Daily Advertiser. (Wed., March 6, 1833)

Mitchell, Sophronia. Daughter of John Mitchell. Died in Shelbyville,
Tenn. of Cholera.
National Banner & Nashville Daily Advertiser. (Thurs., July 11, 1833)

Mitchell, Mrs. Susannah M. Wife of Mr. Thomas C. Mitchell. Died in Rutherford County on 27th ult.
National Banner & Nashville Whig. (Fri., Nov. 4, 1831)

Mitchell, Col. William. Died in Marion County.
National Banner & Nashville Whig. (June 2, 1827)

Mitchell, Capt. William N. A native of Richmond, Va. aged 24. Died in Paris, Henry County, on the 6th inst.
National Banner & Nashville Daily Advertiser. (Fri., Feb. 1, 1833)

Moaman, Mr. John. Died in Warren County, Ky.
National Banner. (Sat., July 25, 1829)

Moberly, Mrs. Frances. Wife of Mr. John Moberly Sr. Died in Madison County, Ky.
National Banner. (Sat, April 25, 1829)

Moberly, Mr. John Sen. Died in Madison County, Ky.
National Banner & Nashville Daily Advertiser. (Sat., Aug. 10, 1833)

Mock, John. Harrison County, Indiana. Died in the loss of the Steam Boat Brandywine.
National Banner & Nashville Daily Advertiser. (Mon., April 23, 1832)

Moffit, W. M. Esq. A Member of the Ala. Legislature. Died at Greensborough, Ala.
National Banner & Nashville Daily Advertiser. (Thurs., Jan. 2, 1834)

Molton, Mr. James K. Of Dickson County. Son of Col. M. Molton. Died on the 14th inst.
The Nashville Whig. (Feb. 28, 1816)

Moneypenny, Private James M. With the 14th Regiment part of the third Division commanded, by Gen. Pillow. Died was killed in the last Battle before the City of Mexico.
The Christian Record. (Sat., Oct. 30, 1847)

Mongin, Mr. Daniel W. Died in Green County.
National Banner & Nashville Advertiser. (Tues., Sept. 25, 1832)

Monks, Mr. Richard. Died in Lexington, Ky.
National Banner & Nashville Whig. (Sat., May 31, 1828)

Monohan, Mr. Charles Tiernan. Died at Havannah on the 27th of June of Yellow Fever. A native of Hagertown, Md. in the 23d year of his age.
National Banner. (Sat., Aug. 15, 1829)

Monroe, Mrs. Wife of the Ex-President Monroe. Died in Loudon County, Va.
National Banner & Nashville Whig. (Mon., Oct. 11, 1830)

Monroe, Mr. Andrew. Died at Milton, Va . Brother of the late president of the United States.
National Banner & Nashville Whig. (Sat., Dec. 30, 1826)

Monroe, David P. Esq. Died in Lincoln County.
National Banner & Nashville Whig. (Sat., Feb. 16, 1828)

Monroe, James. Died at the residence of his son-in-law in New York on the 4th inst.
The Western Weekly Review. (Fri., July 22, 1831) Franklin, Tenn.

Montague, Mr. Clement. Of Paris, Ten. Died in Barren County, Ky. on the 14th.
National Banner & Nashville Whig. (Mon., Dec. 19, 1836)

Montague, Mrs. Mary M. Wife of Mr. A. G. Montague. Died on the morning of the 22nd inst. aged about 33 years.
Nashville Whig. (Tues., May 26, 1846)

Montgomery, Mrs. Ann M. Wife of Mr. Andrew C. Montgomery. Died in Blount County.
National Banner & Nashville Advertiser. (Mon., Feb. 27, 1832)

Montgomery, Mr. Hugh. Died in Rutherford County.
National Banner. (April 14, 1826)

Montgomery, Col. Hugh. Died near Jacksborough.
National Banner & Nashville Daily Advertiser. (Tues., July 2, 1833)

Montgomery, Mrs. John. Died in Danville, Ky. of Cholera.
National Banner & Nashville Daily Advertiser. (Mon., Aug. 5, 1833)

Montgomery, Lucius Polk. Only son of Benj. B. & Matilda W. Montgomery. Died on the 12th inst., aged 2 years 7 months and 7 days. at Ross Landing, Tenn.
Daily Republican Banner. (Sat., Nov. 25, 1837)

Montgomery, Mr. Samuel. Died in Hardeman County.
National Banner & Nashville Whig. (Wed., July 6, 1831)

Montgomery, Mr. Thomas. Formerly of Franklin, Tenn. Died in Tuscumbia.
National Banner & Nashville Daily Advertiser. (Mon., June 24, 1833)

Montgomery, Hon. Thomas. Formerly member of Congress. Died in Lincoln County, Ky.
National Banner & Nashville Whig. (Sat., April 19, 1828)

Montgomery, Rev. William. Died at his residence near Fayette, Jefferson County, Miss. at the advanced age of 80 years.
The Christian Record. (Sat., April 15, 1848)

Montgomery, Mr. Wm. Aged 60. Died in Franklin County, Ky.
National Banner & Nashville Whig. (Mon., Aug. 2, 1830)

Montgomery, Mrs. Mary. Died in Lexington, Ky.
National Banner & Nashville Daily Advertiser. (Wed., May 7, 1834)

Mooda, John. A workman in the Branch Mint. Died in New Orleans about the 10th inst. of Yellow Fever.
Daily Republican Banner. (Wed., Sept. 11, 1839)

Moore, Mrs. Consort of Mr. Eli Moore. Died in Lincoln County, Ten.
National Banner & Nashville Whig. (Mon., Jan. 5, 1835)

Moore, Mr. Andrew. Aged 45. Died in Lincoln County on Tuesday the 28th.
National Banner & Nashville Whig. (Sat., Sept. 8, 1827)

Moore, Mrs. Araminta. Mother of William H. Moore, aged 60 years. Died on Thursday.
National Banner & Nashville Whig. (Sat., Aug. 26, 1837)

Moore, Capt. Benjamin. Died in Christian County, Ky.
National Banner & Nashville Whig. (Fri., Sept. 30, 1831)

Moore, Miss Charlotte. Died in Knox County.
National Banner & Nashville Whig. (Sat., Aug. 16, 1828)

Moore, David Milton. Son of Mr. David M. Moore, of the Planters Hotel. Died in Nashville.
National Banner & Nashville Daily Advertiser. (Mon., Aug. 26, 1833)

Moore, Miss Emily S. H.   Daughter of the late Col. William Moore.
Died in Carthage at the residence of Mr. James Beck.
National Banner & Nashville Whig. (Wed., March 16, 1831)

Moore, Mr. F. A.   Merchant.   Died in Centerville, Franklin County,
Tenn.   In the 26th year of age.
National Banner & Nashville Whig. (Fri., Oct. 31, 1834)

Moore, Mr. Gully.   In the 88th year of his age.   Died in Montgomery
County.
National Banner & Nashville Whig. (Sat., March 10, 1827)

Moore, Mrs. Harriet.   Wife of Dr. David Moore, and daughter of the
late Hon. John Haywood, Judge of the Supreme Court of Tenn.   Died in
Madison County, Ala.
National Banner & Nashville Whig. (Mon., Nov. 7, 1831)
Nashville Republican and State Gazette. (Thurs., Nov. 10, 1831
p. 3, col. 4)

Moore, Capt. Henry.   Aged 46 years.   Died in Hopkins County, Ky.
National Banner & Nashville Daily Advertiser. (Tues., Aug. 27, 1833)

Moore, Mr. Holly.   Son of Mr. Lawson Moore.   Died in the neighborhood
of Danville, Ky.
National Banner & Nashville Daily Advertiser. (Mon., Aug. 5, 1833)

Moores, Mr. Isaac M.   Died in Hardeman County.
National Banner & Nashville Whig. (Wed., Oct. 12, 1831)

Moore, Mrs. Isabella C.   Wife of Robert I. Moore.   Died in Nashville
on Saturday last.
National Banner & Nashville Whig. (Mon., April 25, 1831)

Moore, James Esq.   Died near Natchez.
National Banner. (Sat., June 27, 1829)

Moore, James.   Died in Bedford County, Ten. on the evening of the
1st inst. formerly from Greenville County, N. C. aged about 50 years.
National Banner & Nashville Whig. (Mon., Nov. 15, 1830)

Moore, James.   In the 88th year of his age.   Died on Thursday 14th
inst. near Murfreesboro.   He was a soldier of the Revolution.
Daily Republican Banner. (Wed., March 20, 1839)

Moore, Mrs. Jane Eliza.   Consort of Co. William L. Moore and daughter
of Logan Henderson of Rutherford County.   Died in Columbia on the
8th Jan. in the 21st year of her age.
National Banner & Nashville Daily Advertiser. (Tues., Feb. 4, 1834)

Moore, Mr. John.   Died in this town on Tuesday last.
National Banner & Nashville Whig. (Sat., April 21, 1827)

Moore, John.   Died at Cincinnati, Ohio of Cholera.
National Banner & Nashville Daily Advertiser. (Wed., Oct. 24, 1832)

Moore, Mr. John F.   Aged 52 years.   Died in Limestone County, Ala.
National Banner & Nashville Whig. (Fri., March 6, 1835)

Moore, Dr. John Patrick.   Aged 34 years.   Died at Mills Point, Ky. on
the 20th of March.
National Banner & Nashville Whig. (Fri., March 27, 1835)

Moore, Mr. John T.   Died in Columbia.
National Banner & Nashville Whig. (Fri., June 3, 1831)

Moore, John W.   Editor of the Red River Whig.   Died was murdered on
the 6th inst.
Daily Republican Banner. (Tues., July 23, 1839)

Moore, Mrs. Kindness. Aged 30. Died in Lincoln County on the 30th of the prevailing fever.
National Banner & Nashville Whig. (Sat., Sept. 8, 1827)

Moore, Mrs. Martha. Consort of R. L. Moore, Merchant. Died in Nashville on Thursday last.
National Banner & Nashville Whig. (Mon., Jan. 26, 1835)

Moore, Miss Mary. Of Murfreesboro. Died at Columbia.
National Banner & Nashville Whig. (Fri., Feb. 25, 1831)

Moore, Miss Mary T. Daughter of Mr. James Moore of Rutherford County. Died at Columbia.
National Banner & Nashville Whig. (Wed., March 9, 1831)

Moore, Narcissa. Daughter of Willis Moore, dec'd. Died in Shelbyville, Tenn. of Cholera.
National Banner & Nashville Daily Advertiser. (Thurs., July 11, 1833)

Moore, The Rev. Nathaniel. Aged 75. Died in Maury County.
National Banner. (Sat., July 4, 1829)

Moore, Mr. Reilson. Died in St. Clair County, Ill.
National Banner & Nashville Whig. (Fri., July 11, 1828)

Moore, Mr. Robert I. In his 58th year. Died on the evening of the 19th inst. at his residence in Nashville.
The Christian Record. (Sat., Dec. 23, 1848)

Moore, Robert R. Son of Mr. William H. Moore. Died in Nashville on Wednesday 13th inst.
Nashville Whig. (Sat., March 16, 1844)

Moore, Sterling B. Aged 8 years, son of John and Polly Moore. Died on the 1st July in Davidson County.
Nashville Republican (Thurs., July 7, 1836)

Moore, Thomas C. Died in Shelbyville, Tenn.
National Banner & Nashville Daily Advertiser. (Thurs., July 11, 1833)

Moore, Mr. Thos. J. Aged about 30 years. Died in this County on Tuesday morning last.
National Banner & Nashville Whig. (Sat., Dec. 27, 1828)

Moore, Mr. William Jun. Died in Madison County, Ala.
National Banner & Nashville Advertiser. (Wed., March 7, 1832)

Moore, Col. William. In the 82d year of his age. Died on the 3rd inst. at his reisdence in Carthage.
Nashville Whig. (Nov. 24, 1823)

Moore, Mr. William Jun. Died in Madison County, Ala.
National Banner & Nashville Daily Advertiser. (Wed., March 7, 1832)

Moore, William. Died at Versailles, Ky. 12 miles from Lexington of Cholera.
National Banner & Nashville Whig. (Fri., Sept. 4, 1835)

Moore, William C. Died on Sunday the 7th inst. at the City Hotel.
Nashville Whig. (Sat., Jan. 13, 1844)

Moore, Mr. Willis. Killed by lighting on the 30th ult. Died in Shelbyville, Ten.
National Banner & Nashville Daily Advertiser. (Sat., Aug. 24, 1833)

Moorefield, Mr. Thomas. Died in this town.
National Banner & Nashville Whig. (Sat., March 10, 1827)

Moorehead, William. Died 18th at Cincinnati, Ohio of Cholera.
National Banner & Nashville Daily Advertiser. (Fri., Oct. 26, 1832)

Moores, Mrs. Winnifred. Died at the residence of L. B. Fite in Nashville on Saturday last.
Nashville Whig. (Tues., Dec. 6, 1842)

Moran, Mr. Louis. Died at Detroit.
National Banner. (March 17, 1826)

More, Mrs. Harriet. Wife of Dr. David More, daughter of the late Hon.
John Haywood Judge of the Supreme Court of Tenn.
National Banner & Nashville Whig. (Mon., Nov. 7, 1831)

Morehead, Mrs. and child. Died at Versailles, Ky. 12 miles from
Lexington, of Cholera.
National Banner & Nashville Whig. (Fri., Sept. 4, 1835)

Morehead, Mrs. Alvina. Died in Mobile, Ala. of Yellow Fever.
Daily Republican Banner. (Tues., Oct. 1, 1839)

Morehead, Mrs. Amanda. Wife of Charles S. Morehead, Esq. Died at
Hopkinsville, Ky.
National Banner (Sat., July 18, 1829)

Morehead, Maj. Armstead. Died in Bowling Green.
National Banner & Nashville Whig. (Sept. 2, 1826)

Morehead, Charles. Infant son of James T. Morehead. Died in Logan
County, Ky.
National Banner & Nashville Advertiser. (Mon., June 18, 1832)

Morehead, Major Charles. Died in Logan County, Ky.
National Banner & Nashville Whig. (Sat., Dec. 20, 1828)

Morehead, Mrs. Mary A. Late of Warren County, Ky. Died in Nashville
on yesterday aged 60 years.
Daily Republican Banner. (Mon., May 21, 1838)

Morford, Anna M. Aged 21, daughter of the late Edward Morford of
Princeton. Died at Edgehill, N. Jersey 31st May.
Nashville Whig. (Wed., June 26, 1839)

Morgan, Mrs. Celia. Wife of James Morgan. A native of Hertford
County, N. C. Died in New Washington, Texas.
Daily Republican Banner. (Fri., Nov. 27, 1840)

Morgan, Mrs. Frances. In the 76th year of her age. Died on the 15th
in Davidson County at the residence of David Ralston Esq.
Nashville Whig. (Thurs., Oct. 20, 1842)

Morgan, Frank Armstrong. Son of Samuel D. Morgan. Died in Nashville
on Thursday the 14th inst.
National Banner & Nashville Daily Advertiser. (Fri., Nov. 15, 1833)

Morgan, Mr. Gideon. Aged 79. Died in Roane County.
National Banner & Nashville Whig. (Mon., Nov. 29, 1830)

Morgan, John Sen. A soldier of the Revolution, in the 82d year of
his age. Died in Warren County on the 8th Jan.
National Banner & Nashville Whig. (Fri., March 6, 1835)

Morgan, Mrs. Mary. Consort of Lewis Morgan. Died in this County on
the 6th.
Daily Republican Banner. (Mon., April 9, 1838)

Morgan, Mrs. Mary Thomas. Wife of William Morgan. Died in Nashville on the 25th ulto. (Obituary)
The Christian Record. (Sat., Jan. 6, 1849)

Morgan, Peter. Died in Shelbyville, Tenn. of Cholera.
National Banner & Nashville Daily Advertiser. (Thurs., July 11, 1833)

Morgan, Rufus Col. Died in Roane County aged 45.
National Banner & Nashville Whig. (Sept. 2, 1826)

Morgan, Rufus Grant. Samuel St. Clair Morgan. Both children of Samuel D. Morgan of Nashville. Died in Nashville the former in sixth and the latter in eighth year of his age.
National Banner & Nashville Daily Advertiser. (Tues., Nov. 5, 1833)

Morgan, Hon. Thomas Nicholson. For the last 10 years an associate Judge of the City Courts of New Orleans. Died in Nashville on the 3rd inst. of Consumption in the 35th year of his age.
Nashville Whig. (Sat., Oct. 5, 1844)

Morison, Mrs. Elizabeth. Died on Friday evening last. Wife of Mr. Andrew Morison of this town.
Nashville Whig. (June 21, 1824)

Morris, Maj. Granville Rodgers. Aged 48 years. Died recently on his plantation near Chocchuma, Miss.
The Politician & Weekly Nashville Whig. (Fri., June 25, 1847)

Morris, Hon. Mathias. Late a representative in Congress, from Bucks County, Pa. Died at Doylestown on the 9th inst.
Daily Republican Banner. (Mon., Nov. 23, 1839)

Morris, Richard, Esq. Died in Hanover County, Va.
Nashville Republican & State Gazette. (Tues., Aug. 30, 1831)

Morris, Mr. Richard. Aged 37. Died in Pulaski on June 15 of Cholera.
National Banner & Nashville Daily Advertiser. (Wed., June 19, 1833)

Morris, Tabbitha. Died on Monday Aug. 12th in the 70th year of her age.
Nashville True Whig and Weekly Commercial Register. (Fri., Aug. 16, 1850)

Morrison, Mr. Andrew. Died in Nashville, Funeral this afternoon at 4 o'clock.
National Banner & Nashville Daily Advertiser. (Thurs., Sept. 20, 1832)

Morrison, Andrew Esq. In the 24th year of his age. Died in Bedford County aon the 17th ult.
National Banner & Nashville Daily Advertiser. (Wed., March 6, 1833)

Morrison, Mr. David. Died in Cynthiana, Ky.
National Banner & Nashville Whig. (Sat., July 22, 1826)

Morrison, DeWitt Clinton. Aged 2 years 6 months. Son of Mr. David Morrison. Died in Nashville on Tuesday last.
National Banner & Nashville Whig. (Mon., Sept. 6, 1830)

Morrison, Mr. William. Died in Arkansas County, Ark.
National Banner & Nashville Whig. (Sat., May 12, 1827)

Morrison, William. Merchant of the firm of Clark and Morrison. Died on Monday the 9th inst. 22 miles west of Nashville in the 36th year of his age.
Daily Republican Banner. (Tues., Oct. 17, 1837)

Morriss, Rev. Edward. In the 74th year of his age. Died on Wednesday evening the 10th inst. in Wilson County.
National Banner & Nashville Whig. (Fri., Feb. 26, 1830)

Morrow, Mr. George. Died at St. Louis.
National Banner & Nashville Advertiser. (Wed., March 7, 1832)

Morrow, Mr. James. Died in Knoxville, Tenn. on Saturday last.
Daily Republican Banner. (Sat., Sept. 29, 1838)

Morrow, Mr. Robert. Engineer of Steam Boat, St. Louis. Died in
St. Louis.
National Banner & Nashville Whig. (Thurs., Aug. 19, 1830)

Morrow, Mr. William. Near 70 years old. Died in Christian County,
Ky.
National Banner & Nashville Daily Advertiser. (Tues., June 26, 1832)

Morse, Rev. Jedediah, D. D. Aged 65 years. Died at New Haven, Con.
National Banner & Nashville Whig. (July 1, 1826)

Morse, Mrs. Kesiah. Wife of Eliza Morse. Aged 37. Died in Knoxville, Ten.
National Banner & Nashville Whig. (Mon., Nov. 24, 1834)

Mortimer, B. Of Maysville, Ky. Died in the loss of the Steam Boat
Brandywine.
National Banner & Nashville Daily Advertiser. (Mon., April 23, 1832)

Mortimer, Mr. George H. In the 21st year of his age. Died in Henry
County, Ky.
National Banner & Nashville Daily Advertiser. (Sat., Aug. 10, 1833)

Mortimer, John. Of Maysville, Ky. Died in the loss of the Steam
Boat, Brandywine.
National Banner & Nashville Daily Advertiser. (Mon., April 23, 1832)

Morton, Dr. A. B. Died in Shelbyville, Tenn. of Cholera.
National Banner & Nashville Daily Advertiser. (Thurs., July 11, 1833)

Morton, Mrs. Eliea. Wife of Mr. John Morton. Died in Logan County,
Ky.
National Banner. (Sat., May 9, 1829)

Morton, Miss Elizabeth. Died at Bolivar.
National Banner & Nashville Whig. (Thurs., Aug. 19, 1830)

Morton, Mrs. Elizabeth. Wife of William R. Morton Esq. and grand
daughter of the late John Bradford. Died at Lexington, Ky.
National Banner & Nashville Daily Advertiser. (Wed., Aug. 7, 1833)

Morton, Gen. Jacob. Died suddenly in New York.
National Banner & Nashville Whig. (Fri., Dec. 23, 1836)
Nashville Republican. (Tues., December, 1836)

Morton, Mrs. Louisa. Wife of William I. Morton, Esq. Died at
Russellville, Ky.
National Banner & Nashville Whig. (Thurs., July 29, 1830)

Morton, Mrs. Mary A. Aged 19 years, wife of Mr. Elijah Morton. Died
in Nashville on the 25th inst. daughter of Dr. E. Humphreys of
Auburn, N.Y.
Nashville Whig. (Wed., Sept. 30, 1840)

Morton, Mrs. Sarah. Wife of Wm. Morton Esq. aged 76. Died in
Lexington, Ky.
National Banner & Nashville Whig. (Mon., Aug. 2, 1830)

Mosby, Mr. John W. Died at Columbia.
National Banner & Nashville Daily Advertiser. (Wed., July 3, 1833)

Moseley, Agnes F. Wife of Mr. Henry Moseley and daughter of William E. J. Armstrong of Maury County, Tennessee in the 30th year of her age. Died near College Church, Lafayette County, Miss. Jan. 6th, 1848. (Obituary)
The Christian Record. (Sat., Feb. 19, 1848)

Moseley, Mr. William F. Died near Courtland, Ala.
National Banner & Nashville Advertiser. (Thurs., June 28, 1832)

Mosely, Mr. Henry W. Died at Memphis.
National Banner & Nashville Advertiser. (Wed., Feb. 8, 1832)

Mosley, Mrs. Jemina. Wife of Mr. William Mosley. Died in Wilson County.
National Banner & Nashville Daily Advertiser. (Mon., Nov. 19, 1832)

Mosley, Tho. Formerly of this place. Died on the 27th ult. at Natchez (Miss.)
The Nashville Whig. & Tenn. Advertiser. (Nov. 24, 1817)

Moss, Mrs. Wife of Mr. Reuben Moss. Died at Raleigh, N. C. by being struck by lighting, while in bed.
Daily Republican Banner. (Fri., Oct. 19, 1838)

Moss, Mr. Philip. Died in Woodford County, Ky.
National Banner & Nashville Whig. (Sat., Nov. 3, 1827)

Moss, Dr. Samuel S. Of New Kent, Co. Va. Died in Nashville on the 7th inst.
The Union. (Sat., June 18, 1836)

Motley, Mr. A. Age 20. Died in Smith County.
National Banner & Nashville Advertiser. (Wed., April 25, 1832)

Motto, Mrs. Jane K. In the 70th year of her age. Died in Baltimore County, Maryland on the 21st Dec. 1845. Mother of John D. Grass of Nashville.
Nashville Whig. (Sat., Jan. 3, 1846)

Mowry, John. From Monroe County. Died at the Tenn. State Prison of Cholera.
National Banner & Nashville Whig. (Fri., Aug. 14, 1835)

Moyers, Mr. Frederick. Died in Grainger County.
National Banner. (Sat., Aug. 8, 1829)

Mudge, Lieut. 3d Artillery. Died was killed in Battle with the Seminole Indians in Florida.
The Union. (Sat., Jan. 23, 1836)

Muhlenburg, Hon. Henry A. Democratic candidate for Gov. of Penn. Died at Reading on Sunday the 11th inst.
Nashville Whig. (Thurs., Aug. 22, 1844)

Muirhead, Mr. Robert. In the 30th year of his age. Died in Holmes County, Miss. a native of Lanarkshire, Scotland.
Nashville Whig. (Wed., Sept. 16, 1840)

Mulherrin, Mr. James. An early settler. Died in this county, on Sunday night last.
National Banner. (May 4, 1826)

Mullendore, Abraham, Mr. Age 69. Died in Sevier County.
National Banner & Nashville Whig. (Mon., March 21, 1831)

Mullett, George W. Aged 61. Died in Salem, Mass. born without eyes.
The Union. (Sat., June 18, 1836)

Munroe, Mr. George. Son of L. F. and Adeline Monroe. Died in
Nashville on the 27th ult. Aged about 19 years.
The Politician & Weekly Nashville Whig. (Fri., July 2, 1847)

Munroe, Colonel Israel. Died in New York of Cholera on the 20th Aug.
National Banner & Nashville Daily Advertiser. (Wed., Sept. 3, 1834)

Munroe, Mr. John L. Printer. Died in Nashville on Tuesday last.
He served 12 months in the army as a Volunteer under Capt. R. C.
Foster, 3rd.
The Christian Record. (Sat., Jan. 15, 1848)

Munscroft, Henry F. Aged 18. Died at Cincinnati, Ohio on the 12th
inst. of Cholera.
National Banner & Nashville Daily Advertiser. (Thurs., Oct. 18, 1832)

Murden, Jeanette. Infant daughter of Edward G. and Jeanette Murden.
Died in Nashville on the 17th ult.
The Christian Record. (Sat., May 27, 1848)

Murfree, Mrs. Elizabeth. Wife of William H. Murfree Esq. Died at
Franklin.
National Banner & Nashville Whig. (Sat., July 22, 1826)

Murphey, William. In the 68th year of his age. Died on the 6th inst.
5 miles East of Nashville, a citizen of Davidson County for the past
35 years.
Nashville Whig. (Mon., Oct. 8, 1838)

Murphy, Enoch Esq. County Surveyor. Died in Overton County.
National Banner & Nashville Daily Advertiser. (Mon., Aug. 25, 1834)

Murphy, Rev. G. D. Died at Bankstons Springs near Clinton, Miss.
National Banner & Nashville Daily Advertiser. (Fri., Sept. 20, 1833)

Murphy, Hugh. Died in the vicinity of Knoxville.
Daily Republican Banner. (Sat., Oct. 6, 1838)

Murphy, Capt. Peter. Died at Cincinnati.
National Banner & Nashville Whig. (Sat., Dec. 30, 1826)

Murphy, Major William. One of the oldest settlers. Died in this
neighborhood on Sat. the 6th inst.
Nashville Union. (Fri., Oct. 12, 1838)

Murpo, Mrs. Wife of Mr. B. Murpo. Died in Nashville on the night
of the 10th inst.
National Banner & Nashville Daily Advertiser. (Tues., March 11, 1834)

Murray, Mrs. Catharine. Wife of Thomas P. Murray. Died at the
residence of her mother, Mrs. Elizabeth Wilson in Williamson County.
Obituary.
The Christian Record. (Sat., Sept. 2, 1848)

Murray, Miss Cynthia. Daughter of Mr. Ephriam Murray. Died in
Washington County.
National Banner & Nashville Whig. (Mon., June 13, 1831)

Murray, Mrs. Hadessa. Wife of Major Robert Murray. Died in Huntingdon
on the 4th inst. in the 25th year of her age. Obituary.
National Banner & Nashville Daily Advertiser. (Wed., April 11, 1832)

Murray, Lieut. John Wilkins. Age 20 of Pittsburg, Pa. Graduate of
the Military Academy at West Point. Died at Contonment Gibson on
the 13 Feb.
National Banner & Nashville Whig. (Mon., April 4, 1831)

Murray, Mr. Robert. Died in Knox County.
National Banner & Nashville Whig. (Sat., Feb. 7, 1829)

Murray, Mr. William. Aged 111 years and 6 months. Died in the
vicinity of Jonesborough, Tenn.
National Banner & Nashville Whig. (Mon., July 25, 1836)

Murrell, John A. The notorious land Pirate. Died in Pikeville, Bledsoe County on Sunday the 3d inst.
Nashville Whig. (Thurs., Nov. 21, 1844)

Murrill, Benjamin. Of Nashville, Tenn. Died in the loss of the
Boat Brandywine.
National Banner & Nashville Daily Advertiser. (Mon., April 23, 1832)

Murry, Lieut. John Wilkins. Died at Cantonment Gibson on the 13th
of February in the 20th year of his age. A recent graduate of Military Academy at West Point.
National Banner & Nashville Whig. (Wed., April 6, 1831)

Murrystone, Right Rev. William D. D. Bishop of the Protestant Epis-
copal Church in Maryland. Died on the 26th ult. near Salisbury
Somerset County, Md.
Daily Republican Banner. (Thurs., March 15, 1838)

Myers, Mr. James T. Aged 18. Died in Sumner County, Tenn.
National Banner & Nashville Daily Advertiser. (Tues., Aug. 5, 1834)

Mygatt, Mr. Lemuel C. Of the firm of Messrs Mygatt & Edwards. Died
in New Orleans on the 24th Sept.
The Christian Record. (Sat., Nov. 20, 1847)

Mynatt, Miss Ciby. Aged 14. Daughter of Mr. John Mynatt, sen.
National Banner & Nashville Whig. (Sat., Oct. 7, 1826)

Mynatt, Mr. Aged 18. Son of Mr. John Mynatt, sen. Died in Knox
County.
National Banner & Nashville Whig. (Sat., Oct. 7, 1826)

Mynatt, Mr. John. Aged 53. Died in Knox County.
National Banner & Nashville Whig. (Sat., Jan. 20, 1827)

Mynatt, Mr. Richard. Died in Knox County.
National Banner & Nashville Whig. (December 2, 1826)

Myratt, Mr. E. Esq. Of Knoxville. Died in Kingston, Tenn.
Nashville Republican. (Sat., March 25, 1837)

Myrick, Mrs. Elizabeth. Wife of Howell Myrick Esq. Died in Hardeman
County.
National Banner & Nashville Whig. (Tues., March 16, 1830)

Myrick, Capt. Howell. Of Hardeman County. Died in Nashville on the
21st inst.
National Banner & Nashville Daily Advertiser. (Mon., June 24, 1833)

Nailor, Mr. E. Front St. near corporation line. Died at Cincinnati,
Ohio of Cholera.
National Banner & Nashville Daily Advertiser. (Fri., Oct. 26, 1832)

Nance, William H. Esq. Aged 58 years 6 months. Died in Davidson
County on the 5th inst.
Daily Republican Banner. (Tues., Oct. 10, 1837)

Nantz, Mr. Thomas W. Died at Russellville, Ky.
National Banner & Nashville Daily Advertiser. (Mon., Sept. 17, 1832)

Napier, Doct. Elias W. In the 65th year of his age. Died at his
residence at White Bluff Forge, in Dickson County, Tenn. on the 7th
of August 1848.
The Christian Record. (Sat., Sept. 2, 1848)

Npaier, Mr. James R. Eldest son of Col. R. C. Napier. Died in
Nashville from an injury received while diving into shallow water.
Obit.
National Banner & Nashville Daily Advertiser. (Wed., July 18, 1832)

Napier, Col. R. C. Died at Laural Furnace, Dickson County.
National Banner & Nashville Daily Advertiser. (Sat., March 22, 1834)

Nash, Miss Amandfi. Died in Memphis.
National Banner & Nashville Whig. (Mon., Aug. 9, 1830)

Nash, Mrs. Betsey. Wife of Mr. William Nash. Died in Warren County,
Ky.
National Banner & Nashville Whig. (Thurs., Aug. 5, 1830)

Nash, Martha. Consort of William Nash, dec'd. Died in Dyer County
aged about 69 years.
National Banner & Nashville Whig. (Fri., March 13, 1835)

Nash, William Jr. Aged 77 years 7 months 7 days. Died in Dyer County,
a soldier of the Revolution.
National Banner & Nashville Whig. (Fri., March 13, 1835)

Nashee, Mr. George. Editor of the State Journal. Died at Columbus,
Ohio.
National Banner & Nashville Whig. (Sat., June 9, 1827)

Neal, Mrs. Anna. Wife of C. W. Neal. Died at Alexandria, Smith
County, on the 5th Feb.
Nashville Republican. (Tues., March 14, 1837)

Neal, Mr. John. Died in Logan County, Ky.
National Banner. (Sat., May 16, 1829)

Neal, Joseph C. Esq. Died in Philadelphia on Saturday evening last
in the 40th year of his age.
The Politician & Weekly Nashville Whig. (Wed., Aug. 4, 1847)

Neal, Thomas D. Aged about 33 years. Died in Hartsville, Sumner
County, on Sunday the 4th Aug.
Nashville Whig. (Fri., Aug. 9, 1839)

Neal, Mr. William. In the 62d year of his age. Died in Franklin,
Tenn. on Sunday night last.
The Western Weekly Review. (Franklin, Tenn., Fri., Aug. 24, 1832)

Neal, Mr. William. Aged 61. Died at Franklin.
National Banner & Nashville Daily Advertiser. (Wed., Aug. 29, 1832)

Neeley, Mrs. Henriette. Wife of Rev. P. P. Neeley. Died in Columbia
on the 6th inst.
The Christian Record. (Sat., March 20, 1847)

Neely, Mr. Charles. Died in Simpson County, Ky.
National Banner. (May 4, 1826)

Neely, Mrs. Mary. Died on Wednesday the 27th inst.
The Western Weekly Review. (Fri., March 1, 1833) Franklin, Tenn.

Neely, Mary Elizabeth. Infant daughter of Geo. W. Neely. Died on
Wednesday morning last aged 2 years and 5 months.
The Western Weekly Review. (Fri., Feb. 22, 1833) Franklin, Tenn.

Neely, William Esq. Aged 66 years. Died in this vicinity on 27th
ulto. was a native of South Carolina, moved to this county in 1801.
Nashville Whig. (Sat., June 4, 1842)

Negrin, Miss Adel. Infant daughter of Mr. Paul Negrin. Died in
Nashville at 9 o'clock yesterday morning.
National Banner & Nashville Whig. (Wed., Aug. 10, 1831)

Neill, Mrs. Levina. Wife of Mr. John Neill. Died in this town.
National Banner & Nashville Whig. (Sat., Sept. 27, 1828)

Neill, Maj. Samuel W. Late of Henderson County, Ten. Died in Clinton,
La.
National Banner & Nashville Whig. (Fri., Sept. 23, 1831)

Neill, Capt. Wm. Aged 90 years, a soldier of the Revolution. Died in
Henderson County, Ten.
Nashville Republican & State Gazette. (Thurs., March 3, 1831)

Neill, Capt. William. Died in Henderson County.
National Banner & Nashville Whig. (March 14, 1831)

Neilson, Mrs. Catherine. Consort of Mr. Charles B. Neilson, Merchant
of Franklin. Died at Warm Springs, North Carolina on 24 of May.
Impartial Review and Cumberland Repository. (Thurs., June 9, 1808)

Neilson, William Esq. Age 85. Post Master. Died at Warm Springs,
N. C.
National Banner & Nashville Advertiser. (Mon., Feb. 27, 1832)

Neilson, William Esq. Died at his residence at Warm Springs, N. C.
on the 31st Jan. 1832 about 90 years. Obit.
National Banner & Nashville Daily Advertiser. (March 3, 1832)

Nelson, Lieut. With the Second Tenn. Regiment. Died was killed in
the Battle of Sierra Gorda with the Mexicans.
The Politician & Weekly Nashville Whig. (Fri., May 21, 1847)

Nelson, Miss Charlotte S. Daughter of Hugh Nelson Esq. Died in
Albermarle County, Va.
National Banner & Nashville Daily Advertiser. (Thurs., Aug. 22, 1833)

Nelson, Mr. Daniel. In the 47th year of his age. Died near New
Market, Jefferson County, Tennessee on the 2nd inst. He was the father
of Mr. Anson Nelson of Nashville.
The Christian Record. (Sat., Jan. 9, 1847)

Nelson, Elijah Esq. Aged 60 years. Died in Knox County.
National Banner & Nashville Daily Advertiser. (Mon., Jan. 30, 1832)

Nelson, Mrs. Eliza. Consort of the Hon. H. Nelson. Died in
Albemarie County, Va.
National Banner & Nashville Daily Advertiser. (Mon., June 30, 1834)

Nelson, Hon. Hugh. Died at Belvoir in Albemarle, Va. on the 18th.
Nashville Republican. (Tues., April 12, 1836)

Nelson, Hon. Hugh. At Belvoir, his seat, Albemarle, (Virginia) on
the 18th ult., the Hon. Hugh Nelson, after a short but severe illness.
Mr. Nelson had spent too large a portion of his life in conspicuous
public station, not to be well known throughout his country. He was
successively a member of the Legislature of Virginia, Speaker of the
house of Delegates, a Judge of the Gen. Court, a member of the House
of Representatives of the U. S. and Minister Plenipotentiary near
the Court of Spain.
Nashville Republican. (Tues., April 12, 1836)

Nelson, Mr. James L. Died at Bolivar.
National Banner & Nashville Whig. (Sat., Feb. 2, 1828)

Nelson, Col. John. In the 42d year of his age. Died in Murfrees-
borough on Wednesday evening the 3rd inst. On his way home to
Washington County.
National Banner & Nashville Whig. (Fri., Feb. 12, 1830)

Nelson, Louisa. Aged one year and 5 months. Died in Henry County
on the 24th June last. She was the daughter of Major Samuel Nelson.
National Banner & Nashville Whig. (Mon., Sept. 22, 1834)

Nelson, Mr. S. M. Of the commercial house of Nelson & Titus. Died
at Memphis on Sunday last.
Nashville Whig. (Tues., April 4, 1843)

Nelson, Mrs. Sarah. Died in Overton County.
National Banner & Nashville Whig. (Mon., Oct. 25, 1830)

Nelson, Miss Susan. Of Danville, Ky. Daughter of the late Rev. Sam'l
K. Nelson. Died in Jonesborough.
National Banner. (Sat., June 13, 1829)

Nelson, Rev. Thomas H. Pastor of the First Presbyterian Church. Died
in Knoxville on the 25th ult.
Daily Republican Banner. (Wed., March 13, 1839)

Nelson, Mr. William Sen. Died in Montgomery County.
National Banner & Nashville Whig. (Thurs., Sept. 23, 1830)

Nesbit, Nathan Esq. Aged 29. Died in Sommersville, T.
National Banner & Nashville Whig. (Sat., Sept. 30, 1826)

Nesbit, Thomas. Printer, in the 63d year of his age. Died in
Philadelphia on the 6th inst.
The Politician & Weekly Nashville Whig. (Fri., April 23, 1847)

Nesbit, Thomas. Printer in the 63d year of his age. Died in
Philadelphia on the 6th inst.
The Christian Record. (Sat., April 24, 1847)

Netson, Rev. Thomas. Pastor of the first Presbyterian Church. Died
in Knoxville, Tenn. on Monday last.
Daily Republican Banner. (Sat., Sept. 29, 1838)

Nettles, Major John A. Died near Statesville, Wilson County on the
10th Aug. last.
National Banner & Nashville Daily Advertiser. (Tues., Aug. 9, 1834)

New, Gen. Richard B. Died in Elkton, Todd County, Ky. on Monday 12th
inst. Late Speaker of the House of Representative in Ky. Legislature.
National Banner & Nashville Daily Advertiser. (Wed., May 21, 1834)

New, Col. Robert A. Died at Louisville, Ky.
National Banner & Nashville Daily Advertiser. (Tues., July 2, 1833)

Newby, Mr. John. Died in Logan County, Ky.
National Banner & Nashville Daily Advertiser. (Sat., Oct. 13, 1832)

Newell, Mr. Benj. Died in Cincinnati.
National Banner & Nashville Whig. (Sat., May 12, 1827)

Newell, Joseph Dally. Son of Thomas & Jane Newell. Died in Nashville
on the 29th ult. aged 7 years and two months.
Nashville Whig. (Tues., March 5, 1844)

Newman, Eliza. Aged 11 years. Daughter of Mr. G. Newman. Died in
Rutherford County, Tenn.
National Banner & Nashville Daily Advertiser. (Wed., May 7, 1834)

Newman, Miss Polly. Died in Knox County.
National Banner & Nashville Whig. (Sat., Oct. 28, 1826)

Newnan, Dr. John. One of the oldest physicians of Nashville. Died
in Nashville on Sunday morning.
Nashville Whig. (Mon., Dec. 31, 1838)

Newnan, Dr. John. Died in Nashville on Sunday morning last.
Daily Republican Banner. (Tues., Jan. 1, 1839)

Newsom, Mr. E. Died in this County, Davidson.
Nashville Republican & State Gazette. (Tues., March 29, 1831)

Newsom, Mrs. Eliza. Died in Davidson County at the home of her father,
John Davis Esq.
National Banner & Nashville Daily Advertiser. (Fri., April 26, 1833)

Newson, Elridge Esq. Died in Madison County, aged 57.
National Banner & Nashville Whig. (Sat., Sept. 16, 1826)

Newsom, Mr. William E. Died in Davidson County on the 21st inst. in
his 32nd year. He left a wife and one child to mourn his loss.
National Banner & Nashville Whig. (Mon., March 28, 1831)

Newsom, Mr. William E. Aged 32. Died at his residence this County, on
21st ulto.
Nashville Republican & State Gazette. (Thurs., April 21, 1831)

Newton, Mr. Frederick. Died in Nashville on Thursday 21st inst.
Nashville Whig. (Sat., Dec. 23, 1843)

Newton, Mr. Ignatius. Died in Georgetown, D. C.
National Banner & Nashville Daily Advertiser. (Fri., Sept. 20, 1833)

Niblet, Hiram. Formerly of South Carolina. Died at Hazelgreen, on
the night of the 5th inst. Huntsville Adv.
National Banner & Nashville Whig. (Mon., Jan. 17, 1831)

Nichol, Mrs. Harriet. Wife of Mr. John Nichol. Died in Nashville on
the 28th inst.
National Banner & Nashville Daily Advertiser. (Thurs., Jan. 30, 1834)

Nichol, Mr. Joseph. In this place, last evening, Mr. Joseph Nichol,
age 23 years.
Nashville Republican. (Thurs., Dec. 15, 1836)

Nichol, Mr. Joshua. Aged 23 years. Died in Nashville last evening.
Nashville Republican. (Thurs., Dec. 15, 1836)

Nichol, Josiah Esq. President of the Nashville Branch of the United
States Bank. Died in Nashville of Cholera on Friday, May 31st.
National Banner & Nashville Daily Advertiser. (Sat., June 1, 1833)

Nichol, Mr. Josiah D. Second son of John Nichol Esq. of Nashville.
Died on Thursday evening last.
Nashville Whig. (Sat., April 2, 1842)

Nichol, Mrs. Martha Eliza. Consort of Mr. James Nichol, of Nashville.
Died on the 27th inst at the residence of her brother, Mr. E. S.
Edmunds near Hopkinsville, Ky. (Obituary)
The Christian Record. (Sat., May 6, 1848)

Nichol, Thomas W. Infant son of Alexander R. Nichol Esq. Died in
Nashville on Sunday 29th inst.
The Politician & Weekly Nashville Whig. (Wed., Sept. 1, 1847)

Nichol, Thomas W. Infant son of Alexander R. Nichols Esq. Died in
Nashville on Sunday 29th inst.
The Christian Record. (Sat., Sept. 4, 1847)

Nichol, Mr. William. Died at Nashville, Tenn. on the 26 inst. Saturday.
National Banner & Nashville Whig. (Wed., March 30, 1831)

Nichol, Surgeon Wm. H. Of the U. S. Army. Died at Jefferson Barracks,
Mo.
Nashville Republican & State Gazette. (Sat., March 26, 1831)

Nicholas, Major Cary. Died at Tallahassee, Fla.
National Banner. (Sat., June 6, 1829)

Nicholas, Nelson Esq. Died at Lexington, Ky. Editor of the Kentucky
Whig.
National Banner & Nashville Whig. (Sat., July 15, 1826)

Nichols, Mrs. Wife of John Nichols Esq. Died in Davidson County.
Daily Republican Banner. (Thurs., Aug. 9, 1838)

Nichols, Mrs. Wife of John Nichols Esq. Of Davidson County. Died
yesterday in this vicinity.
Nashville Whig. (Wed., Aug. 9, 1838)

Nichols, Capt. John. A citizen of Davidson County. Died on Sunday
18th inst.
Nashville Whig. (Tues., Sept. 20, 1842)

Nichols, Margery. Second daughter of John Nichols Esq. Died on Monday
night 21st inst. of Consumption.
Nashville Whig. (Thurs., March 24, 1842)

Nichols, Miss Mary. Died in Danville, Ky. of Cholera.
National Banner & Nashville Daily Advertiser. (Mon., Aug. 5, 1833)

Nichols, Mrs. Rachel. Wife of Mr. John Nichols, Merchant of this place.
Died on the 9th inst.
Nashville Whig. (Aug. 16, 1824)

Nicholson, Mr. Joseph J. Died at Jackson.
National Banner. (Sat., July 25, 1829)

Nicholson, Mrs. Mary B. Died in Maury County.
Nashville Republican & State Gazette. (Thurs., June 16, 1831)

Nicholson, Mrs. Mary B. Wife of Mr. Calvin H. Nicholson. Died in
Maury County.
National Banner & Nashville Whig. (Fri., June 17, 1831)

Nicholson, Mr. Samuel. Age 69. Died in Knoxville.
National Banner & Nashville Whig. (Mon., March 7, 1831)

Niles, Hezekiah. Editor of the Niles Weekly Register. Died at
Wilmington, Delaware, on the 2nd inst.
Daily Republican Banner. (Thurs., April 11, 1839)

Niles, Hezekiah Esq. The Veteran Editor of the Weekly Register. Died
at Wilmington, Delaware a few days since.
Nashville Whig. (Fri., April 12, 1839)

Nimmo, Judge Mathew. Died in Franklin, La.
Nashville Republican & State Gazette. (Sat., June 4, 1831)

Nixon, Henry. President of the Bank of North America, Philadelphia.
Died in Albany, New York.
Nashville Whig. (Mon., Aug. 31, 1840)

Nixon, Mary Ann. In the 1st Ward. Died in Lexington, Ky of Cholera.
National Banner & Nashville Daily Advertiser. (Tues., July 2, 1833)

Nixon, Col. Richard. Died at his residence near Brownsville, Western Dist.
Nashville Republican & State Gazette. (Thurs., Feb. 10, 1831)

Nixon, Col. Richard. Died near Brownsville. A native of North Carolina and one of the first settlers of Haywood County.
National Banner & Nashville Whig. (Fri., Feb. 11, 1831)

Nixon, Wm. F. Son of Capt. Wm. Nixon, age 16. Died in Maury County.
National Banner & Nashville Whig. (Thurs., Dec. 1, 1831)

Noble, Gen. James. Senator in Congress, from Indiana. Died in Washington on 26 ult.
National Banner & Nashville Whig. (Mon., March 14, 1831)

Noble, Hon. James. Senator from the state of Indiana. Died in Washington City.
Nashville Republican & State Gazette. (Tues., March 15, 1831)

Noble, Capt. William. Died at Cincinnati.
National Banner & Nashville Whig. (Sat., June 9, 1827)

Noel, Mrs. Eliza. Wife of Mr. Beverly Noel, aged 19. Died in Frankford, Ky.
National Banner (June 10, 1826)

Noke, Mrs. Catharine. Consort of Wm. C. Noke, late of the city of York England, in the 22d year of her age. Died on Saturday evening 10th instant.
Nashville Whig. (July 12, 1824)

Nolen, Mr. James Sen. Aged between 90 and 100 years. Died in Madison County, Ten. a native of South Carolina and a soldier of the Revolution.
National Banner & Nashville Whig. (Wed., Dec. 17, 1834)

Nolen, Mrs. Olive. Wife of Mr. James Nolen. Died in Montgomery County.
National Banner. (Sat., May 2, 1829)

Norfleet, Mr. Thomas. Died on the 18th ult. of Cholera. Late of Person County, North Carolina.
National Banner & Nashville Whig. (Wed., Aug. 19, 1835)

Norman, Mr. James. In the 76th year of his age. Died on Saturday morning 27th April, in Davidson County.
Nashville Whig. (Tues., May 7, 1844)

Norman, Mary. Aged 45. Died in Nashville of Cholera.
National Banner & Nashville Whig. (Fri., June 19, 1835)

Norman, Capt. Thomas. Died in Rutherford County.
National Banner & Nashville Whig. (Sat., Feb. 2, 1828)

Norman, Mr. Thomas. A soldier of the Revolution. Died in Nashville on the 17th inst.
National Banner & Nashville Whig. (Thurs., May 20, 1830)

Norment, Mary Ann. Wife of Rev. John H. Norment. Died at Athens, Tenn. on Tuesday the 19th inst., in the 31st year of her age.
National Banner & Nashville Daily Advertiser. (Thurs., Nov. 28, 1833)

Norment, Mr. William T. Died in this County.
National Banner & Nashville Whig. (Sat., March 10, 1827)

Norris, Mrs. Mary. Wife of Mr. Tho's L. Norris. Died in Jefferson County, Miss.
National Banner. (June 10, 1826)

North, Mrs. Rhoda. Wife of Mr. E. North Sr. Died in Williamson
County.
National Banner & Nashville Daily Advertiser. (Mon., May 13, 1833)

Norton, Capt. Abner P. Died in the Pacific Ocean, Sept. 28, 1830.
National Banner & Nashville Whig. (Fri., March 25, 1831)

Norton, Mr. John, Jun. Aged 20, son of Mr. George Norton. Died in
Lexington, Ky.
National Banner & Nashville Daily Advertiser. (Thurs., Feb. 28, 1833)

Norton, Mr. Stephen P. Died at Lexington, Ky.
National Banner & Nashville Whig. (Sat., May 3, 1828)

Norvell, Caleb C. Infant son of C. C. Norvell. Died yesterday
afternoon.
Nashville Whig. (Wed., Nov. 3, 1841)

Norvell, Hendrick. Passed Midshipman of the U. S. Navy, aged 28
years. Died on Sat. morning 18th at the residence of his brother
Joseph Norvell.
National Banner & Nashville Whig. (Mon., March 27, 1837)

Norvell, Joseph Jr. Son of Hon. John Norvell of Michigan. Died at
Pontiac, Michigan, aged 22 years.
Nashville Whig. (Fri., Sept. 4, 1840)

Norvell, Maj. Joseph. Died of appoplexy on Thursday of last week in
the 54th year of his age.
The Christian Record. (Sat., Jan. 16, 1847)

Norvell, Lipscomb, Senior. An officer in the Army of the Revolution,
aged 87 years. Died in Nashville at the residence of his son-in-law
James Walker Esq.
Nashville Whig. (Sat., March 4, 1843)

Norvell, Miss Martha. In the 19th year of her age. Died in Nashville
on Tuesday morning last.
National Banner & Nashville Whig. (Thurs., May 27, 1830)

Norvell, Moses, Esq. Editorial on his death.
Republican Banner & Nashville Whig. (No. 85 Tues., April 12, 1853)

Norvell, Moses, Esq. Adjournment of Davidson County Criminal Court
to attend funeral.
Republican Banner & Nashville Whig. (No. 86 Wed., April 13, 1853)

Norvell, Mrs. Polly. Died in Lynchburg, Va.
Nashville Republican & State Gazette. (Tues., March 8, 1831)

Norvell, Doctor Thomas. In the 39th year of his age. Died on the 23rd
of August in the Parish of St. Johns the Baptist, La.
Nashville Whig. (Tues., Sept. 19, 1843)

Norvill, John L. Died at sea in Oct. last. on board the U. S. Steamer
American, of Capt. Henry's Company, Sumner County.
Nashville Republican. (Tues., Nov. 1, 1836)

Norville, John L. A Volunteer of the Tenn. Brigade. Died at sea in
Oct. on board the U. S. Steamer American, of Captain McCoins Co. of
Sumner County.
National Banner & Nashville Whig. (Wed., Nov. 2, 1836)

Nott, Mrs. Consort of Capt. William Nott. Died in Maury County, Ten.
National Banner & Nashville Whig. (Fri., April 10, 1835)

Nourse, Mrs. Rebecca. Died near Russellville, Ky. After being confined to her bed for about fourteen years.
National Banner & Nashville Daily Advertiser. (Sat., Feb. 16, 1833)

Nowland, Andrew Jackson. Aged 16 months. Died in Nashville on the
17th inst. only child of Capt. Edward W. B. Nowland.
National Banner & Nashville Daily Advertiser. (Sat., Aug. 18, 1832)

Nowland, Mrs. Rebecca. Mother in-law, Wm. S. Fulton, Sec. of this
Territory in the 65th year of her age. Died on board the Steamboat,
Little Rock on the Arkansas River.
National Banner & Nashville Daily Advertiser. (Wed., Jan. 22, 1833)

Nowlin, Bryant Ward Esq. Aged 67 years. Died in Bedford County, Tenn.
on the 3d day of June.
National Banner & Nashville Whig. (Wed., Sept. 2, 1835)

Nowlin, John S. Aged 28. Died in Henry County, Tenn. on the 1st day
of July.
National Banner. (Sat., Sept. 12, 1829)

Noyes, Mrs. Abigail. Died at Franklin. Wife of Mr. O. J. Noyes.
National Banner & Nashville Whig. (Sat., June 7, 1828)

Noyes, Mrs. Catherine. Widow of the late Dr. Levi Noyes, of Springfield
Tenn. Died in Washington.
National Banner & Nashville Daily Advertiser. (Wed., Aug. 29, 1832)

Nuckolls, Mrs. Temperance. Wife of Dr. Richard Nuckolls, aged 70.
Died at her residence in Robinson County, Ten. on the 21st Jan., 1834.
National Banner & Nashville Daily Advertiser. (Feb. 15, 1839)

Nugent, Col. John T. Died in Nashville on the 17th Jan.
National Banner & Nashville Whig. (Wed., Jan. 21, 1835)

Nuttall, Col. William B. Died near Tallahassee on April 20.
National Banner & Nashville Whig. (Fri., May 27, 1836)

Nye, Ann Green. Daughter of N. G. Nye Esq. Died in Pulaski.
Nashville Republican. (Sat., Aug. 27, 1836)

Nye, Mr. David L. Died in Pulaski on the 14th inst.
National Banner & Nashville Whig. (Mon., Sept. 20, 1830)

Nye, Ichobod. In the 78th year of his age. Died at Marietta, Ohio
on the 27th.
Daily Republican Banner. (Tues., Dec. 29, 1840)

Nye, Mrs. Sarah. Widow of the late Mr. Nathan Nye, aged 84 years.
Died in Sandwich, Mass. on Feb. 23d.
National Banner & Nashville Whig. (Fri., April 17, 1835)

Nye, Doctor Shadrach. Died in Carracas, South America, on the 27th
Oct. last. For many years a citizen of Nashville.
Nashville Whig. (Thurs., Dec. 28, 1843)

Obrien, John and Wife. Of New Orleans, Passengers. Died on the
Steamer George Collier, about 80 miles below Natchez. Scalded to
death.
Daily Republican Banner. (Tues., May 14, 1839)

Oden, Mr. Thomas A. Died in Rutherford County.
National Banner & Nashville Whig. (Sat., Feb. 17, 1827)

O'Fallon, Mrs. Harriet. Wife of Col. John O'Fallon. Died at St.
Louis.
National Banner. (March 10, 1826)

O'Farlin, Mr. John. Died at Vandalia.
National Banner & Nashville Whig. (Fri., July 11, 1828)

Ogden, Col. Aaron. Aged 82 years. Died at Elizabethtown on Friday evening. He has been Governor of New Jersey and Senator in Congress.
Daily Republican Banner. (Mon., April 29, 1839)

Ogden, David Esq. Late of New York aged 26 years. Died in New Orleans, La.
National Banner & Nashville Whig. (Wed., Dec. 3, 1834)

Ogden, Doct. James R. Of New York. Died in Woodville, Mis.
National Banner & Nashville Whig. (Sat., Aug. 19, 1826)

Ogden, Mr. Titus. Of this town (Knoxville). Died a valuable and much esteemed citizen.
Knoxville Gazette. (Sat., Nov. 23, 1793)

Ogle, Hon. Charles. A member of Congress. Died at his residence in Somerset County, Pennsylvania on 12th inst.
Nashville Whig. (Fri., May 21, 1841)

O'Harrow, Mr. Martin. Died in Florence, Ala.
National Banner & Nashville Daily Advertiser. (Wed., March 26, 1834)

Oldham, Mr. Thomas. Died at Lexington, Ky.
National Banner & Nashville Whig. (Sat., Sept. 15, 1827)

Oldham, Mr. William. Died at Louisville, Ky.
National Banner. (March 31, 1826)

Oliver, Col. Alexander. Died at Cincinnati.
National Banner & Nashville Whig. (Fri., July 18, 1828)

Oliver, Mrs. Sarah M. Wife of Mr. Robert Oliver. Died in Cincinnati.
National Banner & Nashville Whig. (Sat., Feb. 16, 1828)

Oliver, Thomas Esq. Died at St. Genevieve. Judge of probate and clerk of the Circuit Court.
National Banner. (Jan. 20, 1826)

Olliver, Mr. Willy B. Aged 21. Of Anderson County, T. Died in Alabama.
National Banner & Nashville Whig. (Sat., Oct. 7, 1826)

Olmsted, Mrs. Elizabeth. Consort of Chas G. Olmsted. Died on Sunday morning 9th inst.
The Western Weekly Review. (Fri., Dec. 14, 1832) Franklin, Tenn.

Olmsted, Mrs. Elizabeth. Wife of Charles G. Olmsted, Esq. Died in Franklin.
National Banner & Nashville Daily Advertiser. (Mon., Dec. 17, 1832)

O'Neale, William Esq. Aged 86 years. Died in Washington City on the 24th ult.
Daily Republican Banner. (Sat., Nov. 4, 1837)

B. Openiser. City Hotel. Died in Natchez of Yellow Fever.
Daily Republican Banner. (Wed., Oct. 18, 1837)

O'Reilly, Mrs. Mary. Wife of Dr. James C. O'Reilly. Died in Columbia.
National Banner & Nashville Whig. (Sat., Feb. 17, 1827)

Orgain, Mr. James. Aged 22. Died in Henry County.
National Banner & Nashville Daily Advertiser. (Wed., Oct. 3, 1832)

Orgain, Mr. James. Died in Montgomery County.
Nashville Republican & State Gazette. (Wed., Oct. 3, 1832)

Organ, Mr. Samuel. Aged 22. Died in Montgomery County.
National Banner & Nashville Whig. (Sat., June 2, 1827)

O'Riley, Thomas Troost. Aged 22. Died in Nashville yesterday morning.
Nashville Union. (Mon., Dec. 2, 1839)

O'Riley, Thomas Troost. Died on Tuesday last at the residence of Pro.
Troost, his step father.
Daily Republican Banner. (Wed., Dec. 4, 1839)

Oris, Captain Isaac. Aged 87. An Officer of the Revolutionary War.
Died at Otisville, Orange County, N. York.
Nashville Whig. (Mon., Nov. 19, 1838)

Ormond, Mrs. Wife of Mr. David Ormond. Died in Sumner County.
National Banner & Nashville Advertiser. (Mon., Dec. 3, 1832)

Orr, Dr. Charles. From Chester district, S. C. Died in Lexington, Ky.
National Banner & Nashville Whig. (Sat., Feb. 17, 1827)

Orr, Hugh Read. Died on the 7th inst. at the house of Maj. William
Edmiston, in Davidson County. (Obituary)
The Christian Record. (Sat., Nov. 13, 1847)

Orr, James. Died 15th at Cincinnati, Ohio of Cholera.
National Banner & Nashville Daily Advertiser. (Wed., Oct. 24, 1832)

Orr, William. Died in Russellville, Ky.
National Banner & Nashville Daily Advertiser. (Mon., May 13, 1833)

Ormsby, Miss Elizabeth. Died in Louisville on Monday evening 8 inst.
National Banner & Nashville Whig. (Mon., Aug. 15, 1831)

Orton, Capt. Richard. Died on the 3d instant. One of the first
settlers of the town of Franklin.
Nashville Whig. (July 12, 1824)

Osborne, Abraham. Of Ohio. Died in the loss of the Steam Boat
Brandywine.
National Banner & Nashville Daily Advertiser. (Mon., April 23, 1832)

Osborn, Seleck Esq. Died in Philadelphia, a poet of eminence and
editor of several popular papers.
National Banner & Nashville Whig. (December 2, 1826)

Oseola, Chief. Died at Sullivans Island on Tuesday night last.
Daily Republican Banner. (Mon., Feb. 12, 1838)

Ostrander, Mrs. Henlen A. C. Wife of Dr. F. W. Ostrander of New
York. Died in Louisville, Ky.
National Banner & Nashville Whig. (Wed., Sept. 14, 1831)

Otey, Capt. John H. Aged 62. Died in Bedford County, Va.
National Banner & Nashville Whig. (Mon., Dec. 27, 1830)

Otey, Lucy. Infant daughter of Jno. H. Otey. Died this morning 8th
inst. of the scarlet fever.
The Western Weekly Review (Fri., Feb. 8, 1833) Franklin, Tenn.

Otey, Lucy. Infant daughter of Jno. H. Otey. Died in Franklin, Ten.
National Banner & Nashville Daily Advertiser. (Mon., Feb. 11, 1833)

Otey, Sarah C. Infant daughter of John H. Otey. Died on Thursday
21st inst.
The Western Weekly Review. (Fri., Feb. 22, 1833) Franklin, Tenn.

Otis, William. Formerly of Barnstable, Mass. Died in Washington on
the 7th of April for many years a clerk in the General Land Office.
Nashville Republican (Thurs., April 27, 1837)

Outlaw, Maj. Alexander. Age 49. Died at Cahawba, Ala. on 13th July.
Formerly of Jefferson County, Ten.
National Banner & Nashville Advertiser. (Fri., Aug. 10, 1832)

Outlaw, Mr. Joseph. Age 75. A soldier of the revolution. Died in
Knox County.
National Banner & Nashville Advertiser. (Mon., Jan. 30, 1832)

Outlaw, Mrs. Sarah. Aged 28 years, consort of J. B. Outlaw Esq.
Died in Moscow, Ky. Daughter of Rev. Samuel Gibson formerly of Sumner
County, Tenn.
Nashville Republican (Sat., Feb. 11, 1837)

Overall, Rev. Lorenzo D. Died in Columbia of Cholera. A Minister of
the Methodist Church.
National Banner & Nashville Daily Advertiser. (Sat., Sept. 6, 1834)

Overstreet, Mr. Albert G. Aged 25 years. Died on the 28th ult. in
Jefferson County.
National Banner & Nashville Daily Advertiser. (Sat., Feb. 9, 1833)

Overton, Mr. James. Son of Gen. Thomas Overton. Died at Alexander,
La. on the 27th February.
National Banner & Nashville Whig. (Sat., March 29, 1828)

Overton, Hon. John. Formerly one of the judges of the supreme Court
of this state. Died in Davidson County.
National Banner & Nashville Daily Advertiser. (Sat., April 13, 1833)

Overton, Judge. The Late Judge Overton (Married to the widow of the
late Dr. Francis May and sister of Hon. Hugh L. White).
The Nashville Republican and State Gazette. (April 17, 1833, p. 3
col. 4) (Not in TSL collection)

Overton, Mrs. Rachel N. Consort of Mr. John Overton. Died on Thurs-
day evening last, funeral at 10 o'clock from First Presbyterian
Church by Rev. Dr. Edgar.
Nashville Whig. (Sat., Sept. 23, 1843)

Overton, Mr. Richard. A young man of considerable promise from
Virginia. Died in Clarksville.
National Banner & Nashville Advertiser. (Mon., Feb. 6, 1832)

Overton, Major Samuel. Died at Pensacola on the 31st of August.
National Banner & Nashville Whig. (Sat., Oct. 27, 1827)

Owen, Mr. Town Constable. Died in Mephis on Tuesday last, of Cholera.
National Banner & Nashville Daily Advertiser. (Wed., Nov. 14, 1832)

Owen, Catharine Howard. Infant daughter of Dr. B. R. and Catharine K.
Owen. Died at Lebanon on the 4th inst.
Nashville Whig. (Thurs., March 12, 1846)

Owen, Mrs. Elizabeth. Wife of James Owen of this county. Died
yesterday about 1 o'clock P.M.
National Banner & Nashville Whig. (Sat., Aug. 25, 1827)

Owen, Col. George W. Died on Aug. 18th near Mobile. Ala. The deceased
was an Alumnus of the University of Nashville.
Daily Republican Banner. (Fri., Sept. 8, 1837)

Owen, Mr. Ira H. Age about 30. Died Sunday 4th in Davidson County.
National Banner & Nashville Whig. (Mon., Sept. 19, 1836)

Owen, Mrs. Margaret. Consort of Col. William E. Owen. Died in the
vicinity of Memphis on Friday last, 2nd inst. in the 35th year of her
age.
Nashville Whig. (Tues., Aug. 13, 1844)

Owen, Mrs. Rebecca. Died in Scott County, Ky.
National Banner & Nashville Whig. (Sat., May 19, 1827)

Owen, Mr. Robert C. Died in Davidson County on the 17th inst.
National Banner & Nashville Whig. (Sat., Oct. 27, 1827)

Owen, Mr. Samuel. Aged about 40 years. Died at the residence of his
brother J. C. Owen in Williamson County.
Nashville Union. (Wed., Oct. 31, 1838)

Owen, Sandy Esq. Died in this town on Tuesday last.
National Banner. (Sat., Oct. 10, 1829)

Owen, William. Aged 12 years. Died in Nashville of Measles.
National Banner & Nashville Whig. (Fri., June 19, 1835)

Owens, Miss Amanda. Daughter of Wm. Owens, Died in Russellville, Ky.
National Banner & Nashville Advertiser. (Mon., July 2, 1832)

Owens, Jabez Esq. Died in Williamson County on Tuesday last the 20th
inst.
Nashville True Whig and Weekly Commercial Register. (Fri., Aug. 30, 1850

Packett, Mr. Reuben. Age 69. Died in Knox County.
National Banner & Nashville Advertiser. (Thurs., Aug. 23, 1832)

Page, Mr. Overseer for Boswell and Ater. Died in Lexington, Ky. of
Cholera.
National Banner & Nashville Daily Advertiser. (Tues., July 2, 1833)

Page, Mr. Jas. R. Of the New Orleans and Western Theatres. Died at
Cincinnati, O.
National Banner & Nashville Daily Advertiser. (Mon., Sept. 9, 1833)

Page, Benjamin. Aged 68. For many years an esteemed and respected
inhabitant of Pittsburgh. Died at his Farm near Cincinnati.
National Banner & Nashville Daily Advertiser. (Tues., June 24, 1834)

Page, Mr. Edward Le. Died in Cincinnati.
National Banner & Nashville Whig. (Sept. 2, 1826)

Page, James. Died at the residence of Ebenezer Barclay in the town of
Leesburg, County of Washington, Tenn. on the 17th of April last.
National Banner & Nashville Daily Advertiser. (Wed., June 13, 1832)

Page, Dr. James. Aged 49 years. Died in Baltimore, Surgeon in the
U. S. Navy.
National Banner & Nashville Daily Advertiser. (Mon., April 2, 1832)

Page, Mr. Joel. Of Haywood County. Died on Sunday the 19th in Haywood County, Tenn.
Daily Republican Banner. (Sat., Feb. 1, 1840)

Page, Julia. Infant daughter of Mr. Thos. Page. Died in Frankfort,
Ky. on the 4th inst.
National Banner & Nashville Daily Advertiser. (Sat., Aug. 10, 1833)

Page, Miss Sophia. Wife of Mr. Thomas Page. Died in Frankford,
Ky.
National Banner. (May 13, 1826)

Page, Mrs. Susannah. Died in Logan County.
National Banner & Nashville Whig. (Mon., Sept. 26, 1831)

Page, William Boyd. Died in Pagebrook, Va.
National Banner & Nashville Whig. (Sat., Sept. 27, 1828)

Page, Mr. William J. Died in Logan County, Ky.
National Banner & Nashville Whig. (Sat., July 29, 1826)

Padgett, John D. From Overton County. Died at the Tenn. State Prison
of Cholera.
National Banner & Nashville Whig. (Fri., Aug. 14, 1835)

Paine, Mrs. Susannah G. Consort of Rev. Robert Paine. President of
Lagrance College, Ala. Died in the vicinity of Nashville.
Nashville Republican. (Tues., June 28, 1836)

Palmer, Mrs. Charlotte C. Died at Maysville, Ky.
National Banner. (Feb. 24, 1826)

Palmer, Mr. James W. Book seller and publisher of the Louisville
Price Current. Died in Louisville, Ky. on the 18th inst.
National Banner & Nashville Daily Advertiser. (Tues., Jan. 22, 1833)

Palmer, Mrs. Mary W. Relict of the late J. W. Palmer. Died on the
3d inst.
Nashville Republican. (Thurs., June 22, 1837)

Pamplin, Mrs. Frances. Aged 60. Died in Lincoln County on the 11th
inst.
National Banner & Nashville Whig. (Thurs., May 27, 1830)

Paradise, Mr. William. Aged 89. Died in Davidson County.
National Banner & Nashville Daily Advertiser. (Thurs., Aug. 30, 1832)

Parham, Mrs. Martha L. Wife of Lewis A. Parham. Died in Knoxville,
Tenn.
Daily Republican Banner. (Sat., Oct. 6, 1838)

Paris, Mr. William. Died at Statesville, Ten.
National Banner & Nashville Whig. (Mon., Sept. 12, 1831)

Paris, Mr. William. Wool carder formerly of Kentucky. Died at
Statesville, Ten.
National Banner & Nashville Whig. (Mon., Setp. 12, 1831)

Parish, Mrs. Mary M. Wife of Mr. C. D. Parish. Died in Williamson
County, Tenn.
National Banner & Nashville Daily Advertiser. (Wed., Aug. 20, 1834)

Park, Andrew. Aged 32 years. Died in Memphis on the 22nd inst.
Nashville Whig. (Tues., June 30, 1846)

Park, Mr. Asa. Painter. Died in Lexington, Ky.
National Banner & Nashville Whig. (Sat., Feb. 10, 1827)

Park, James B. Oldest son of David and Jane Park. Died in Memphis.
Nashville Whig. (Tues., April 21, 1846)

Park, Margaret Naomi. Daughter of Mr. William Park. Died at Knoxville, Ten.
National Banner & Nashville Whig. (Fri., Oct. 3, 1834)

Parker, Maj. Alexander. An early settler in Lexington and a soldier
of the revolution. Aged 75. Died at Frankfort, Ky. on the 27th ult.
National Banner & Nashville Whig. (Mon., June 28, 1830)

Parker, Mrs. Ann. In her 30th year. Died in this town on Friday
morning last.
National Banner & Nashville Whig. (Sat., Oct. 28, 1826)

Parker, Elvira and Susan. Daughters of William Parker, late of
Maury County. Died - they both died on the 4th within 1 hour of
each other and were interred in the same coffin.
National Banner & Nashville Daily Advertiser. (Thurs., Jan. 19, 1832)

Parker, Mr. Fielding. Age 114. Died at Winchester, Ky. on the 12th ult.
National Banner & Nashville Advertiser. (Sat., Feb. 6, 1832)

Parker, Mr. Fielding. In the 114th year of his age. Died at Winchester Ky on the 12th ult.
National Banner & Nashville Daily Advertiser. (Sat., Feb. 4, 1832)

Parker, Mrs. Frances Elizabeth. Wife of Mr. Edward T. Parker. Died in Madison County, Ala. daughter of Capt. Justin Dyer.
National Banner. (Sat., Setp. 19, 1829)

Parker, Mr. John. About 30 years old. Died in Nashville a native of Bedford County.
National Banner & Nashville Whig. (Mon., July 27, 1835)

Parker, Mrs. Mary. Aged 78 years. Died in Davidson County on the 4th February.
National Banner & Nashville Daily Advertiser. (Fri., Feb. 22, 1833)

Parker, Mrs. Mary A. Consort of the late James W. C. Parker of Williamson County. Died in Nashville on Saturday the 15th inst.
The Christian Record. (Sat., April 22, 1848)

Parker, Judge Richard E. Of the Court of Appeals. Died in Clark County, Virginia.
Nashville Whig. (Mon., Sept. 28, 1840)

Parker, Mr. Robert H. Jr. Died at New Orleans.
National Banner & Nashville Whig. (Sat., Feb. 23, 1828)

Parker, Mrs. Sally. Consort of Mr. Aaron Parker. Died in McMinn County.
National Banner & Nashville Daily Advertiser. (Wed., July 10, 1833)

Parker, Mrs. Susan. Wife of Mr. Samuel Parker and daughter of Mr. David C. Snow of Nashville. Died in Sumner County on Thursday morning 1st. inst.
National Banner & Nashville Whig. (Mon., Sept. 5, 1831)

Parker, Mrs. Susan. Consort of Thomas Parker. Died at the residence of Mr. John Hibbitt on Wednesday the 24th Oct. while on a visit in the 66th year of her age.
Nashville Union. (Wed., Nov. 7, 1838)

Parker, Miss Susan Ann. Daughter of Mr. Thomas Parker. Died in Sumner County.
National Banner & Nashville Whig. (Wed., Feb. 16, 1831)

Parker, Mr. W. G. Formerly of Boston. Died in Baton Rouge, La.
National Banner & Nashville Daily Advertiser. (Fri., May 16, 1834)

Parks, Belinda Dickinson. Daughter of Elizabeth and Thomas Parks. Died in Franklin.
Nashville Whig. (Thurs., April 30, 1846)

Parks, Mr. Joseph. Died in Nashville on the 20th.
National Banner & Nashville Daily Advertiser. (Sat., March 22, 1834)

Parks, Miss Nancy Elvira. Aged 15 years. Daughter of James Parks. Died in Wilkes City, N. C.
National Banner & Nashville Daily Advertiser. (Sat., Aug. 10, 1833)

Parks, Mrs. Polly. Wife of Mr. David Parks. Died in Butler County, Ky.
National Banner. (May 13, 1826)

Parmentier, Mr. Andrew. Died on Friday last at Brooklin, near New York.
National Banner & Nashville Whig. (Wed., Dec. 22, 1830)

Parmantier, N. S. Aged 59 years. Died in Nashville.
National Banner & Nashville Whig. (Fri., July 17, 1835)

Parmlee, Mr. Sulvanus. Died in St. Louis.
National Banner. (Sat., Sept. 19, 1829)

Parrish, Mr. Abraham. Died near Franklin.
National Banner & Nashville Whig. (Sat., Feb. 2, 1828)

Parrish, Mr. James C. Of the firm of Parris Lockhart & Kelly. Died in Mobile, Ala. of Yellow fever.
Daily Republican Banner. (Tues., Oct. 1st. 1839)

Parrish, Mr. James M. Died in Lexington, Ky.
Nashville Republican & State Gazette. (Tues., March 29, 1831)

Parrish, Col. Joel. Died in Nashville on the 4th inst. formerly Cashier of the Bank of the State of Tennessee.
National Banner & Nashville Daily Advertiser. (Sat., April 5, 1834)

Parrish, Mr. Jonathan. Died in Fayette County, Ky.
National Banner & Nashville Whig. (Fri., July 11, 1828)

Parrish, Miss P. Aged 18 years. Died at the residence of Col. B. S. Tappan in Franklin, Tenn. of Cholera.
National Banner & Nashville Whig. (Fri., June 10, 1835)

Parrish, Mr. Robert. Died in Williamson County.
National Banner & Nashville Whig. (Sat., Sept. 8, 1827)

Parrish, Mrs. Sophia. Wife of Col. Joel Parrish. Died in this town on Friday night last.
National Banner & Nashville Whig. (Sat., Feb. 9, 1828)

Parrish, Mr. William G. In the 21st year of his age. Died in Nashville, Tenn.
National Banner & Nashville Daily Advertiser. (Mon., Oct. 1, 1832)

Parrish, Mr. Woodson. Died in Nashville on Thursday night, Nov. 22 very suddenly.
National Banner & Nashville Daily Advertiser. (Sat., Nov. 24, 1832)

Parron, Mrs. Nancy. Died in Shelby County, Ten.
Nashville Republican & State Gazette. (Tues., March 29, 1831)

Parrott, Mr. L. D. In the 25th year of his age. Died on the 21 st inst. A native of Knoxville, Tennessee.
National Banner & Nashville Whig. (Mon., Oct. 3, 1836)

Parshall, Dr. John. Aged about 57 years. Died in Nashville on Sunday the 16th inst. at the residence of Mrs. Cockrell.
The Christian Record. (Sat., April 22, 1848)

Parson, Julia Todd. Aged 3 years and 6 months. Daughter of Mr. Benj. S. Parsons. Died in Brownville, Ten. on the 11th inst.
National Banner & Nashville Daily Advertiser. (Wed., Aug. 28, 1833)

Parsons, Mrs. Louisa. Aged 25, wife of B. L. Parsons and daughter of Gen. C. Hawkins of Florence, Ala. Died at Christmasville, 3d inst.
National Banner & Nashville Daily Advertiser. (Mon., July 16, 1832)

Partlow, William A. Aged 20 years. Died at Rural Hill, Wilson County on the 14th inst. Son of F. P. Partlow, Esq.
Daily Republican Banner. (Thurs., May 28, 1840)

Pascales, Dr. Felix A. O. An eminent and learned physician. Died at New York.
National Banner & Nashville Daily Advertiser. (Sat., Aug. 3, 1833)

Pasey, General Thomas. Died at Shawneetown on the 8th ult.
The Nashville Whig & Tenn. Advertiser. (April 25, 1818)

Pastlethwaite, Mrs. Mary. Died in Wodford County, Ky. Aged 61.
National Banner. (March 17, 1826)

Pate, John Esq. Died in Obion County.
National Banner & Nashville Whig. (Fri., May 7, 1830)

Path, White. A distinguished Indian Chief of the Cherokee Tribe. Died near Hopkinsville, Ky. a few days since, aged 75 years.
Nashville Whig. (Fri., Nov. 9, 1838)

Patin, Mr. J. Aged 104 years. Died lately at St. Martinsville, Louisiana.
The Union. (Sat., Feb. 18, 1837)

Paton, Mr. William. Postmaster, aged 70. Died at Paris, Ky.
National Banner. (March 17, 1826)

Pattello, Mr. Harrison. Age 27. Died in Rutherford County.
National Banner & Nashville Advertiser. (Nov. 20, 1832)

Patterson, Mr. Andrew. Died at Cincinnati.
National Banner & Nashville Whig. (Sat., Sept. 1, 1827)

Patterson, Catharine. Infant daughter of Alex and Isabella Patterson. Died on the 10th in Nashville.
Nashville Whig. (Tues., Oct. 13, 1846)

Patterson, Mrs. Catherine. Died in Lexington, Ky.
National Banner & Nashville Daily Advertiser. (Wed., May 9, 1832)

Patterson, Commodore Daniel T. Of the U. S. Navy. Commander of the Navy Yards and Station in Washington. Died on Sunday the 25th inst. at his residence in Washington.
Daily Republican Banner. (Tues., Sept. 3, 1839)

Patterson, Mr. George B. Died in Lawrence County, Ala.
National Banner & Nashville Whig. (Sat., May 31, 1828)

Patterson, Mrs. Isabella. Consort of Dr. A. J. Patterson. Died in Fayette County on the 3d of May. She was a daughter of Capt. James Hays, dec'd.
National Banner & Nashville Daily Advertiser. (Fri., June 6, 1834)

Patterson, Jno. Died in Buckingham County, Va.
Nashville Republican & State Gazette. (Sat., Aug. 13, 1831)

Patterson, Mrs. Margaret. Aged 24 years. Died at the residence of her father, Mr. John Miller near Whites Creek.
National Banner. (May 27, 1826)

Patterson, Mary. Aged 26 years. Died in Nashville, July 3d of Cholera.
National Banner & Nashville Whig. (Wed., July 8, 1835)

Patterson, Mr. Saml. A native of Downpatrick Co. Down, Ireland. Died at St. Louis, Mo. on Monday 5th inst.
Daily Republican Banner. (Fri., Oct. 16, 1840)

Patterson, Mr. Thomas. Aged 76. A soldier of the revolution. Died in this vicinity.
Nashville Republican. (Thurs., Aug. 11, 1837)

Patton, Mrs. Ann. Wife of John Patton. Died in Coffee County on the morning of the 7th inst.
Daily Republican Banner. (Thurs., Jan. 10, 1839)

Patton, Archibald. Age 28. Died in Bedford County on the 22 ult.
National Banner & Nashville Whig. (Fri., April 22, 1831)

Patton, James Esq. Died at his residence on Thursday Aug. 9th in Bedford County.
National Banner & Nashville Whig. (Sat., Sept. 1, 1827)

Patton, Col. John. Died in Buncomb County, N. C.
National Banner & Nashville Whig. (Wed., April 27, 1831)

Patton, Mr. John. Died in St. Louis.
National Banner & Nashville Whig. (Sat., Dec. 20, 1828)

Patton, Mr. M. B. Died at Randolph, Ten. in a few hours after landing from the Tobacco Plant on the 10th inst. has been residing at Vixburg, Miss.
National Banner & Nashville Daily Advertiser. (Fri., July 25, 1834)

Patton, Mrs. Samuel. Died in Murfreesborough, Tenn. on July 1st of Cholera.
National Banner & Nashville Whig. (Fri., July 3, 1835)

Patton, Mr. Samuel. Died in Bedford County.
National Banner & Nashville Whig. (Sat., Jan. 10, 1829)

Patton, Mr. Thomas. Age 43. Died in Washington County.
National Banner & Nashville Whig. (Mon., April 11, 1831)

Patton, Mr. William Sen. Died at Hopkinsville, Ky.
National Banner & Nashville Whig. (Wed., Sept. 21, 1831)

Paul, James M. Aged 13 months. Son of Mr. Isaac Paul. Died in Nashville on the 19th inst.
National Banner & Nashville Whig. (Mon., Sept. 22, 1834)

Paul, Hon. John W. Judge of the 8th Judicial Circuit of Ala. Died in Montgomery, Ala.
National Banner & Nashville Whig. (Wed., Nov. 12, 1834)

Paul, Rev. Thomas. A black man. Died at Boston.
National Banner & Nashville Whig. (Fri., May 6, 1831)

Paulding, John. Died on the 20th ult. at his resident in Yorktown, N. York.
The Nashville Whig. & Tenn. Advertiser. (March 21, 1818)

Pavatt, Doctor Orville H. Died at Pekin, Illinois on the 19th July last, of Cholera.
National Banner & Nashville Daily Advertiser. (Fri., Aug. 22, 1834)

Payne, Mrs. Alvira. Wife of Zachariah Payne. Died in Nashville on Sunday 27th leaving a husband and seven children.
The Politician and Weekly Nashville Whig. (Fri., July 2, 1847)

Payne, Doctor Cleveland C. In the 24th year of his age. Died at the residence of Doctor M. D. Mitchell in the town of Shelbyville on the 22d ult.
Nashville Whig. (Nov. 8, 1824)

Payne, Col. Duval. Died in Mason County, Ky.
National Banner & Nashville Whig. (Mon., July 12, 1830)

Payne, Mrs. Eliza. Wife of Thos. J. Payne, Esq. Died in Woodford County, Ky.
National Banner & Nashville Whig. (Sat., Sept. 20, 1828)

Payne, Col. George. Died in Goochland County, Virginia.
Nashville Republican & State Gazette. (Thurs., May 26, 1831)

Payne, Major James. Died on the 6th inst.
The Nashville Whig. & Tenn. Advertiser. (Dec. 15, 1817)

Payne, Col. James B. Died near Lexington, Ky.
National Banner & Nashville Daily Advertiser. (Wed., July 16, 1834)

Payne, Mrs. Margaret. Died in Giles County.
Nashville Republican & State Gazette. (Wed., July 18, 1832)

Payne, Mr. Robert B. In the 33d year of his age. Died at his
residence on the Lost Branch, Carroll County on the 4th inst. of
consumption.
National Banner & Nashville Daily Advertiser. (Tues., May 21, 1833)

Payne, Rueben W. Died at the residence of his fathers, near Nashville
on Wednesday 9th inst. in the 18th year of his age.
The Politician and Weekly Nashville Whig. (Fri., Feb. 11, 1848)

Payne, Mr. Zebediah. Died in Bedford County.
National Banner & Nashville Whig. (Sat., Oct. 6, 1827)

Payson, Mr. Thomas. Died in Maury County.
National Banner & Nashville Whig. (Sat., March 22, 1828)

Peale, Mr. Chs. W. Founder of the Museum. Died in Philadelphia.
National Banner & Nashville Whig. (Sat., March 31, 1827)

Peale, James Esq. Aged 82. A distinguished painter and the first
proprietor of the Museum of Philadelphia. Died in Philadelphia.
National Banner & Nashville Whig. (Fri., June 17, 1831)

Pearce, William. Died at Cincinnati, Ohio on the 12th of Cholera.
National Banner & Nashville Daily Advertiser. (Thurs., Oct. 18, 1832)

Pearl, Mrs. Clarinda. In the 49th year of her age. Consort of Mr.
Dyer Pearl of Nashville. Died on the 14th on her way to England.
Daily Republican Banner. (Fri., May 25, 1838)

Pearon, Thomas. A native of Ireland. Died in New Orleans.
National Banner & Nashville Daily Advertiser. (Fri., Sept. 20, 1833)

Pears, Mrs. Sarah. Aged 45 years. Died near Pittsburgh, Pa. on the
21st April.
National Banner & Nashville Daily Advertiser. (Tues., May 8, 1832)

Pears, Mrs. Sarah. Age 45. Died near Pittsburgh, Pa. on 21st April,
her husband, Thomas Pears on the 26th April, age 46.
National Banner & Nashville Advertiser. (Tues., May 8, 1832)

Pears, Mr. Thomas. Age 46. Died near Pittsburgh, Pa. on 26th April.
His wife Mrs. Sarah Pears, age 45 on the 21st of April.
National Banner & Nashville Advertiser. (Tues., May 8, 1832)

Pearson, Dr. Ebenezer H. Died at Cincinnati.
National Banner & Nashville Whig. (Sat., Oct. 25, 1828)

Pearson, Mrs. Elizabeth. Died at Harrodsburgh, Ky.
National Banner & Nashville Whig. (Sat., Jan. 20, 1827)

Pearson, Mr. John. Aged 24. Died in New Orleans.
National Banner & Nashville Daily Advertiser. (Tues., June 24, 1834)

Pearson, Hon. Joseph. Died at Salisbury, North Carolina on the 27th
inst. formerly a representative from that State to Congress.
National Banner & Nashville Whig. (Wed., Nov. 26, 1834)

Pearson, Mr. Parker. Died in Richmond, Ky.
National Banner & Nashville Whig. (Sat., Aug. 12, 1826)

Pearson, William L. Infant son of Capt. M. and Ann J. Pearson. Died
in Fayetteville on the 16th ult.
Nashville Whig. (Thurs., March 12, 1846)

Peck, Mrs. Elizabeth. Age 70 years. Relict of the late Mr. Adam
Peck. Died in Jefferson County, Tenn. aged 77 years and 3 months.
National Banner & Nashville Daily Advertiser. (Mon., May 28, 1832)

Peck, Hon. James H. Judge of the U. S. District Court for the District of Missouri. Died on the 29th at St. Charles.
Nashville Republican. (Tues., May 12, 1836)

Peck, Ruluff, Esq. Died at St. Charles, Mo.
National Banner & Nashville Whig. (Sat., Feb. 9, 1828)

Peck, Mrs. Temperance B. Daughter of the late Maj. Lazarus Crawford.
Died in Weakley County near Dresden on the 17th inst. in the 44th
year of her age.
Nashville Whig. (Sat., April 1st. 1843)

Peckham, Mrs. Died in Danville, Ky. of Cholera.
National Banner & Nashville Daily Advertiser. (Mon., Aug. 5, 1833)

Pederclaux, Philip Esq. Notary public. Died in New Orleans.
National Banner & Nashville Whig. (Sat., Aug. 26, 1826)

Peebles, Mr. Alexander. Aged about 28 years. Died at his residence
in Franklin on Tuesday evening last.
The Western Weekly Review. (Fri., June 10, 1831) Franklin, Tenn.

Peebles, Mr. Daniel. Formerly of Tennessee. Died in Conandia. Louis.
National Banner & Nashville Daily Advertiser. (Mon., July 29, 1833)

Peebles, Miss Martha. Died in Russellville, Ky.
National Banner & Nashville Daily Advertiser. (Fri., April 12, 1833)

Peebles, Mrs. Mary. Died in Franklin, Ten on 9th inst.
National Banner & Nashville Daily Advertiser. (Tues., Nov. 19, 1833)

Peebles, Miss S. Died in Williamson County, Tenn.
National Banner & Nashville Daily Advertiser. (Mon., July 28, 1834)

Peek, Miss Esther. Daughter of Mr. Simons Peek. Died in Rutherford
County.
National Banner & Nashville Daily Advertiser. (Sat., Oct. 13, 1832)

Peel, Hunter Esq. In Madison County, Ala.
Nashville Republican & State Gazette. (Thurs., March 24, 1831)

Peers, Maj. Valentine. Aged 74. Died at Maysville, Ky.
National Banner & Nashville Whig. (Thurs., July 1, 1830)

Peery, Mr. Joshua. Aged 90 years and 10 months. Died on the 9th
ult. at his residence in Williamson County.
The Christian Record. (Sat., Nov. 27, 1847)

Peete, Capt. Banjamin. A native of Sussex County, Virginia, aged
66. Died in Limestone County, Ala.
National Banner & Nashville Daily Advertiser. (Mon., April 7, 1834)

Pegram, Gen. John. U. S. Marshall for the eastern district of Virginia. Died at Petersburgh, Va.
National Banner & Nashville Whig. (Wed., April 27, 1831)

Pegram, Gen. Jno. Died in Va. Marshall of the Eastern District.
Nashville Republican & State Gazette. (Thurs., May 5, 1831)

Pegram, Gen. J. W. Of Richmond, Va. Died in the Explosion of the
Steam Boat Lucy Walker just below New Albany.
Nashville Whig. (Tues., Oct. 29, 1844)

Peirce, Mrs. Ann. Of New York, aged 73. Died at Cincinnati at the
residence of Col. Pendleton.
National Banner & Nashville Daily Advertiser. (Fri., July 18, 1834)

Peirce, George. Died at his residence in Smith County, on the 21st
inst. of July, after a severe illness of two weeks. The deceased
had been recently married and to the partner of his heart this visi-
tation must have been pecula rly afflicting. He was a man who
enjoyed to a great extent, the confidence and esteem of all who knew
him. His intercourse with his fellow men was characterized by a
strict regard for truth and honesty and in the domestic and social
relations, his conduct was kind, liberal and affectionate. Thus has
one who prospects of present bliss were as bright as any been torn
away by the destroyed in the prime of his life, leaving a chasm in
the family of his circle and friends, which time nor circumstances
can easily fill.
National Banner & Nashville Whig. (Sept. 2, 1826)

Pence, Mr. Isaac. Died in Florence, Ala.
National Banner. (Sat., Sept. 26, 1829)

Pendleton, Edmund Gaines. Son of Mrs. Dr. M. B. Sappington in the
14th year of his age. Died at the Exchange Hotel on Sunday last.
Nashville Whig. (Mon., July 12, 1841)

Penington, A. Esq. Died in Baton Rogue.
National Banner & Nashville Whig. (Sat., Sept. 2, 1826)

Penn, John Esq. Died at Stone-park, Bucks. Governor of Portland,
formerly a proprietor and hereditary Governor of Pennsylvania, U.S.A.
National Banner & Nashville Daily Advertiser. (Sat., Sept. 6, 1834)

Penn, S. Jr. Formerly of the Louisville Advertiser. but of late years,
Editor of the Missouri Reporter. Died in St. Louis.
Nashville Whig. (Thurs., June 25, 1846)

Pennington, Mrs. Wife of Graves Pennington Esq. Died in this vicinity
on Monday last.
Nashville Whig. (Fri., April 19, 1839)

Pennington, Martha. Infant daughter of Pennington, Mr. Graves. Died
in this county yesterday.
National Banner. (Sat., Aug. 22, 1829)

Pennington, Mrs. Martha M. In the 49th year of her age. Died in
Davidson County on the 15th inst. The consort of Mr. Graves Pennington.
Nashville Union. (Fri., April 26, 1839)

Penninan, Col. Atherton T. Jr. A printer. Died in New Orleans. A
native of Boston.
National Banner & Nashville Daily Advertiser. (Mon., June 11, 1832)

Penniston, A. Esq. Died in Baton Rouge, La.
National Banner & Nashville Whig. (Sept. 2, 1826)

Pepper, Mrs. Pernecy. Wife of Gen. W. W. Pepper. Died at Springfield
on the 6th inst. in the 25th year of her age.
Nashville Whig. (Thurs., Sept. 14, 1843)

Pepper, Miss Susan. Daughter of Wm. B. & Mary Pepper of Giles County.
Died on the 27th ult. aged about 22 years.
National Banner & Nashville Whig. (Wed., Sept. 23, 1835)

Percy, Ellis Ware. Youngest son of the late Col. Thomas Percy of
Huntsville, aged 7 years. Died at the Nashville Inn yesterday.
Nashville Whig. (Sat., Nov. 28, 1844)

Percy, Mrs. Maria. Relict of the late Col. Percy. Died in Nashville
yesterday afternoon, she was the second daughter of Col. Leroy Pope
of Huntsville, Ala.
The Politician & Weekly Nashville Whig. (Wed., Aug. 4, 1847)

Percy, Mrs. Mary Ann Henrietta. Consort of Charles Percy Esq.and
youngest daughter of the late Mr. Josiah Nichol, in her 29th year.
Died in Nashville on the 9th inst.
The Christian Record. (Sat., Dec. 16, 1848)

Perdue, Isham. Aged 54. Died in Nashville from Cholera.
National Banner & Nashville Daily Advertiser. (Tues., June 11, 1833)

Dr. Charles Perkins. Aged about 36 years. Died in Pulaski, Tenn. on
Saturday evening the 2d inst.
National Banner & Nashville Whig. (Sat., June 23, 1827)

Perkins, Constantine, Esq. In Tuscaloosa, Ala. Constantine Perkins
Esq. formerly of Williamson County, Ten.
Nashville Republican. (Sat., Sept. 24, 1836)

Constantine Perkins, Esq. Formerly of Williamson County, Tenn. Died
in Tuscaloosa, Ala.
Nashville Republican. (Sat., Sept. 23, 1836)

Constantine Perkins. Age 44 years and 1 month. Died Saturday the
17th inst. Communicated, Tuskaloosa, Ala.
National Banner & Nashville Whig. (Mon., Oct. 3, 1836)

Mrs. Eliza Perkins. Aged 25 years. Died in Davidson County on the
8th inst. Consort of Mr. James W. Perkins and daughter of Thomas
Edmiston, Esq.
National Banner & Nashville Whig. (Thurs., June 10, 1830)

Mrs. Grace Perkins. Died in Franklin County.
National Banner. (April 14, 1826)

Grief Perkins, Esq. Died in Logan County, Ky.
National Banner & Nashville Daily Advertiser. (Mon., June 17, 1833)

Perkins, Mrs. Martha Ann. Died at Mayslick, Ky.
National Banner & Nashville Whig. (Sat., Sept. 15, 1827)

Perkins, Major Nathaniel. Died at Natches.
National Banner. (Jan. 20, 1826)

Perkins, Nicholas P. Esq. Aged 33. Died at Franklin, Williamson Co.
National Banner & Nashville Daily Advertiser. (Tues., July 23, 1833)

Perkins, Mrs. Wife of Mr. Nichols P. Perkins, and daughter of Pleasant Craddock, Esq. of this place. Died at Pulaski.
The Nashville Whig. and Tenn. Advertiser. (Oct. 13, 1817)

Perkins, Col. Peter. Of Huntsville, M. T. Died on the 22d inst. of
a pulmonary complaint at the house of Major Tho. Edtniston in this
County.
The Nashville Whig. (May 28, 1816)

Perkins, Thomas H. Sen. Aged 83 years. Died in Williamson County
on the 16th inst.
Daily Republican Banner. (Fri., Nov. 23, 1838)

Perkins, Washington Esq. Notary Public. Died on 26th inst. in Nashville.
The Nashville Gazette. (Sat., Jan. 29, 1820)

Perkins, William O. Died in Lauderdale County, Ala.
Daily Republican Banner. (Wed., Nov. 18, 1840)

Perkins, Capt. William. Died in Logan County, Ky.
National Banner & Nashville Whig. (Sat., Sept. 1, 1827)

Perrault, Lieut. Col. P. H. Of the United States Topographical
Engineers. Died at Georgetown, D. C.
National Banner & Nashville Daily Advertiser. (Fri., Feb. 28, 1834)

Perrett, Mr. P. H. Died at Cincinnati.
National Banner (April 28, 1826)

Perry, Mrs. Agnes. Wife of Mr. James M. Perry. Died at Louisville,
Ky.
National Banner (Sat., Sept. 19, 1829)

Perry, Angelina. Died in Pulaski. Infant daughter of James Perry,
Esq.
Nashville Republican & State Gazette. (Thurs., July 7, 1831)

Perry, John. Infant son of John W. Perry. Died in Pulaski.
National Banner & Nashville Advertiser. (Wed., June 27, 1832)

Perry, Capt. Robert S. Died in Paris, Henry County on the 11th inst.
National Banner & Nashville Daily Advertiser. (Thurs., March 22, 1832)

Perry, Col. Simeon. Died in Sevier County, Ky. by the hand of an
assissan.
National Banner & Nashville Whig. (Sat., Oct. 28, 1826)

Perry, Wm. L. Esq. Clerk of the circuit court. Died in Lexington,
Henderson County.
National Banner & Nashville Whig. (Sat., Dec. 16, 1826)

Persley, Mr. William. Died in Knox County, drowned.
National Banner (May 27, 1826)

Person, Col. Thomas. Died in Shelby County.
National Banner & Nashville Whig. (Wed., July 6, 1831)

Person, Col. Thomas. Died in Shelby County.
National Banner & Nashville Whig. (Wed., July 6, 1831)

Peterkin, Mr. John. A native of Scotland. Died in New Orleans.
National Banner & Nashville Whig. (Sat., Sept. 9, 1826)

Peters, Alex. Died at Versailles, Ky. 14 miles from Lexington, Ky.
of Cholera.
National Banner & Nashville Whig. (Fri., Sept. 4, 1835)

Peters, Alex. Died at Versailles, Ky. 14 miles from Lexington, Ky.
of Cholera.
National Banner & Nashville Whig. (Fri., Sept. 4, 1835)

Peters, Hon. John Thompson. Age 69. Died in Hartford Con. on the
28th Aug. One of the associate Judges of the Supreme Court.
National Banner & Nashville Daily Advertiser. (Sat., Sept. 13, 1834)

Peters, Hon. Richard. For many years Judge of the U. S. court for the
eastern district of Penn. Died at Philadelphia.
National Banner & Nashville Whig. (Sat., Sept. 13, 1828)

Peticolas, Adolphua. Infant son of T. V. Peticolas. Died in this town.
National Banner & Nashville Whig. (Sat., Sept. 23, 1826)

Petillo, Mrs. Margaret. Died in Maury County.
National Banner & Nashville Whig. (Sat., Sept. 1, 1827)

Pettibone, Mrs. Louisa A. Died in Pike County, Mo.
National Banner & Nashville Whig. (Sat., Nov. 3, 1827)

Pettit, Mrs. A. W. Died at Frankfort, Ky.
National Banner & Nashville Whig. (Mon., June 7, 1830)

Pettit, Mr. Hugh. Late Sheriff of Franklin Co., Ala. Died in the
Chickasaw Nation.
National Banner & Nashville Daily Advertiser. (Wed., Aug. 20, 1834)

Pettus, Mr. John Iverson. Aged 22. Died in Madison County, Ala.
National Banner & Nashville Whig. (September 2, 1826)

Petty, Mr. Gaden. Aged 56. Died in Limestone County, Ala.
National Banner & Nashville Whig. (Mon., March 7, 1831)

Petway, Mr. Benjamin F. Son of H. Petway Esq. Died at the residence
of his father in Davidson County on the 22nd inst., in the 24th year
of his age.
The Politician and Weekly Nashville Whig. (Fri., June 25, 1847)

Petway, Mr. Benjamin F. Son of H. Petway in the 24th year of his age.
Died at the residence of his father in Davidson County on the 22nd
inst.
The Christian Record. (Sat., June 26, 1847)

Petway, Robert. Aged 20 years, one month and twenty two days. Died
near Nashville yesterday at 5 o'clock.
National Banner & Nashville Daily Advertiser. (Fri., Nov. 8, 1833)

Pew, Mr. Gilbert. Long a resident of Nashville. Died suddenly on
Thursday evening last.
The Nashville Gazette. (Sat., May 26, 1821)

Peyton, Mr. John. A citizen of this Davidson County. Died on Tuesday
the 20th inst. at a very advanced age was one of the first settlers
of this state.
National Banner & Nashville Daily Advertiser. (Mon., Aug. 26, 1833)

Phagan, Mr. James. Died at Russellville, Jefferson County.
National Banner & Nashville Whig. (Sat., Nov. 3, 1827)

Phelps, Charles H. Of Stonington. Died in the wreck of the steam
boat, Lexington.
Daily Republican Banner. (Fri., Jan. 31, 1840)

Phelps, Mr. Thomas H. Died in Fayetteville.
National Banner & Nashville Whig. (Sat., Oct. 6, 1827)

Philips, Mr. Charles. Aged 41. Died in Gibson County.
National Banner & Nashville Whig. (Fri., May 7, 1830)

Philips, Jefferson. Died at Louisville, Ky. on the 15th of Cholera.
National Banner & Nashville Daily Advertiser. (Mon., Oct. 22, 1832)

Phillip, Mr. John. Killed by a fall from his horse. Died in Roane
County.
National Banner & Nashville Whig. (Sat., May 12, 1827)

Phillips, Mr. John D. In the 19th year of his age. Died near Harrisburg, Tenn.
National Banner & Nashville Daily Advertiser. (Tues., Sept. 16, 1834)

Phillips, Mr. Joseph. Nearly 80 years old. Died on Monday the 8th
inst. at his farm in Williamson County. He was in the battle of Kings
Mountain.
The Western Weekly Review. (Fri., April 19, 1833) Franklin, Teen.

Phillips, Julia Ann Lafayette. Eldest daughter of Mr. R. B. Phillips
in her tenth year. Died in Nashville on the 5th inst.
National Banner & Nashville Whig. (Fri., Feb. 13, 1835)

Phillips, Mrs. Margaret H. Consort of Mr. John Phillips. Died at
Centerville, Hickman County, on Sat. 24th Jan. 1836 in the 36th year
of her age. (Obituary)
The Union. (Tues., Feb. 16, 1836)

Phillips, Mrs. Margaret H. Wife of Mr. John Philips, Merchant. Died
in Centreville, Hickman County, Tenn. on the 24th Jan. age 36.
Nashville Republican (Tues., Feb. 16, 1836)

Phillips, Mrs. Rebecca. Wife of Mr. Lemuel Phillips. Died in Columbia
National Banner & Nashville Whig. (Thurs., Aug. 19, 1830)

Phillips, Mr. Richard. Died in Jefferson County, Ky.
National Banner & Nashville Whig. (Thurs., May 27, 1830)

Philips, Sally. On the 21st inst. Infant daughter of Wm. D. Philips
of this County.
Nashville Republican & State Gazette. (Sat., June 25, 1831)

Philips, Mrs. Susan. Died in Kingston.
National Banner & Nashville Whig. (December 2, 1826)

Philips, Mr. William Sen. Age 55. Died in Henry County.
National Banner & Nashville Advertiser. (Wed., Aug. 29, 1832)

Philips, Mr. Wm. Senr. Age 69. Died on Friday the 25 inst. in
Davidson County.
Impartial Review and Cumberland Repository. (Thurs., March 31, 1808)

Philips, Mr. Wm. Died on the third instant. A native of this County.
He had just arrived at manhood.
The Nashville Whig. and Tenn. Advertiser. (Nov. 10, 1817)

Phillip, Hon. William. Died at Boston, Mass. Late Lieut governor of
Mass.
National Banner & Nashville Whig. (Sat., June 23, 1827)

Phillip, Mr. William sen. Aged 55. Died in Henry County.
National Banner & Nashville Daily Advertiser. (Wed., Aug. 29, 1832)

Philpot, Mrs. Delila. Consort of Mr. B. Philpot. Died in Weakley
County, Ten. on the 12th.
National Banner & Nashville Whig. (Mon., Oct. 6, 1834)

The only child of __ Philpot, Esq. Aged 4 years. Died in Hardeman
County, Ten. on Monday 12th Aug.
National Banner & Nashville Daily Advertiser. (Fri., Aug. 30, 1833)

Philpot, Col. John W. Died in Hardeman County.
National Banner & Nashville Whig. (Wed., Oct. 12, 1831)

Philpot, Col. John W. Died in Hardeman County.
National Banner & Nashville Whig. (Wed., Oct. 12, 1831)

Phoebus, Capt. Thos. Publisher of the Memphis Gazette. Died in
Memphis.
Daily Republican Banner. (Thurs., Sept. 20, 1838)

Piatt, Col. William. Formerly of the United States Army. Died at
Philadelphia. He was with Gen. Jackson at the battle of New Orleans.
National Banner & Nashville Daily Advertiser. (Sat., Sept. 6, 1834)

Pickens, Gen. A revolutionary Officer. Died in Pendleton District,
S. C. on the 30th ult.
The Nashville Whig. (Sept. 29, 1817)

Pickens, Hon. Israel. Late governor of Alabama.
National Banner & Nashville Whig. (Sat., June 9, 1827)

Pickering, Hon. Timothy. Aged 84. Died in Salem, Mass. on the 20th
ult.
National Banner & Nashville Whig. (Sat., Feb. 21, 1829)

Pickett, Mr. E. A. Died in Knoxville, Tenn.
Daily Republican Banner. (Sat., Oct. 27, 1838)

Pickett, Miss Julia C. Died at Louisville, Ky.
National Banner & Nashville Whig. (Sat., Jan. 12, 1828)

Pickett, Mr. Reuben. Died in Brownsville, Ten.
National Banner & Nashville Daily Advertiser. (Thurs., Sept. 11, 1834)

Pickett, Mrs. Sarah Ann. Aged 18 years late of New Jersey wife of
Mr. Jas. Pickett. Died in New Orleans.
National Banner & Nashville Daily Advertiser. (Mon., Aug. 26, 1833)

Pierce, Mr. George W. Died in Jackson.
National Banner & Nashville Advertiser. (Wed., Aug. 29, 1832)

Pierce, George. Died at his residence on the 21st of July.
National Banner & Nashville Whig. (Sat., Sept. 2, 1826)

Pigg, Mrs. Anna. On Saturday 3 inst. Died in Davidson County.
National Banner & Nashville Whig. (Wed., Sept. 7, 1831)

Pigg, Mrs. Ann A. Aged 23. Died in Davidson County, on Saturday
3d inst.
National Banner & Nashville Whig. (Wed., Sept. 7, 1831)

Pkke, Mr. James M. In the 43d year of his age. Died at Nashville on
Saturday last.
The Western Weekly Review. (Friday, Jan. 13, 1832) Franklin, Tenn.

Pike, Mr. James M. In this town, Nashville, last night Extensively
known as a broker and lottery agent. The funeral will take place from
his residence on Summer Street, tomorrow at 2 o'clock. Died on
Saturday the 7th at 3 o'clock.
National Banner & Nashville Daily Advertiser. (Sat., Jan. 7, 1832)

Pike, Mr. Job. H. Died at Lexington, Ky.
National Banner. (Sat., Nov. 7, 1829)

Pike, John B. Infant son of Mr. James M. Pike, aged 18 months. Died
in Nashville on Tuesday 16th inst.
National Banner & Nashville Whig. (Fri., Aug. 19, 1831)

Pilcher, Mrs. Catherine. Wife of Mr. Mason Pilcher. Died in this town
on Friday last.
National Banner & Nashville Whig. (Sat., Oct. 18, 1828)

Pilcher, Mrs. Elizabeth. Consort of Mr. Edward Pilcher of Lexington.
Died at Louisville, Ky. on Monday last.
Nashville Whig. (Wed., March 7, 1838)

Pilcher, Mr. Fielding. Late of Nashville. Died at Lake Providence,
La. on the 14th Sept.
National Banner & Nashville Whig. (Fri., Oct. 31, 1834)

Pilcher, James Hensley. Infant son of Capt. and Mrs. Merritt S.
Pilcher, aged 5 years. Died on the night of the 22nd inst.
Nashville Whig. (Thurs., May 25, 1843)

Pilcher, Mrs. Lucretia. Wife of Mason Pilcher, late of Nashville.
Died in Louisana.
Daily Republican Banner. (Sat., Jan. 19, 1839)

Pilcher, Mrs. Lucretia. Wife of Capt. Mason Pilcher, formerly of Nashville. Died in Louisiana.
Nashville Whig. (Mon., Jan. 21, 1839)

Pilcher, Matthew Barrow. Only child of Merritt S. and Nancy Pilcher aged 1 year. Died in Nashville on the 20th Oct.
National Banner & Nashville Whig. (Fri., Oct. 31, 1834)

Pilcher, Merritt S. Infant son of Capt. Merritt S. Pilcher. Died last evening.
Nashville Whig. (Tues., Feb. 7, 1843)

Pilcher, Mr. Presley. Of this place, Nashville. Died lately in St. Louis.
Nashville Whig. (Oct. 6th 1823)

Pilcher, Mrs. Sarah. Formerly of Lexington, Ky. aged 66 years. Died in Nashville on Thursday 10th inst.
National Banner & Nashville Daily Advertiser. (Fri., Oct. 11, 1833)

Pillow, Andrew J. Late of Davidson County. Died in Houston, Texas 24th May.
Nashville Whig. (Wed., July 31, 1839)

Pillow, Andrew J. Died in Houston, Texas on the 24th May. Late of Davidson County, Tennessee.
Daily Republican Banner. (Mon., July 30, 1839)

Pillow, Wm. Carroll. Died in Columbia.
Nashville Republican & State Gazette. (Fri., Sept. 14, 1832)

Pinckney, Edward Esq. Son of the celebrated Wm. Pinckney. Died in Baltimore, Maryland.
National Banner & Nashville Whig. (Sat., May 3, 1828)

Pinckney, Col. Ninian. Of the U. S. Army. Died Baltimore.
National Banner. (Jan. 13, 1826)

Pinckney, Gen. Thomas. An officer of the Revolution aged 70. Died in Charleston, S. C.
National Banner & Nashville Whig. (Sat., Nov. 29, 1828)

Pindall, James Esq. Formerly Representative in Congress. Died in Clarksburg, Va.
National Banner (Jan. 6, 1826)

Pindell, Mrs. Mary E. Wife of Major Thomas H. Pindell. Died at Lexington, Ky.
National Banner (Feb. 17, 1826)

Pindell, Dr. Richard. In the 78th year of his age. Died in Lexington, Ky. on the 20th of March.
National Banner & Nashville Daily Advertiser. (Fri., March 20, 1833)

Pinkard, Mrs. Agnes. Wife of Marshall P. Pinkard. Died in Williamson County, on Sunday Nov. 22d.
National Banner. (Sat., Dec. 5, 1829)

Pinkard, Mr. Hiram. Died in Maury County at the Manual Labor Academy on Wednesday 24th ult. in the 17th year of his age.
National Banner & Nashville Daily Advertiser. (Fri., May 3, 1833)

Pinkard, Martha S. Infant daughter of M. P. Pinkard. Died in Maury County, on the 5th inst.
National Banner & Nashville Daily Advertiser. (Wed., Aug. 14, 1833)

Pinkard, Mr. Thomas. Aged about 31 years. Died on the 18th inst. at
H. Gee's, 8 miles from Nashville. Formerly of Culpepper County,
Virginia.
Nashville Whig. (Tues., May 19, 1846)

Pinkerton, Mr. The geographer, aged 97. Died Paris, Tenn.
National Banner. (May 4, 1826)

Pinkham, David Coffin. A native of Mass. formerly of Louisville, Ky.
Died at Key West.
National Banner & Nashville Daily Advertiser. (Mon., May 13, 1833)

Pinnick, Dr. Joseph P. In the 63d year of his age. Died on 7th inst.
one mile from Nashville at his residence.
National Banner & Nashville Whig. (Mon., May 11, 1835)

Pinson, Miss Narcissa. Daughter of Joel Pinson Esq. Died in Ponto-
loc, Mi. in the 15th year of her age, late of Lincoln County, Tenn.
National Banner & Nashville Whig. (Wed., April 8, 1835)

Pipkin, Harriet S. Aged about 7 years. Died in Williamson County.
National Banner & Nashville Whig. (Wed., Feb. 4, 1835)

Pipkin, Miss Mary. Daughter of Col. Phillip Pipkin in the 22nd year
of her age. Died in this County on 10th inst.
National Banner & Nashville Whig. (Sat., Aug. 30, 1828)

Pipkin, Mr. Stewart. Died in Davidson County on Sunday last.
National Banner & Nashville Whig. (Thurs., Sept. 9, 1830)

Pitcher, Hon. N. Formerly Lieut. Governor of New York. Died in the
State of New York.
The Union. (Sat., June 18, 1836)

Pittman, Mr. Asa. Of the house of Pittman & Wilkinson. Merchant of
Nashville and late of Columbia. Died on Friday evening 5th inst.
National Banner & Nashville Whig. (Mon., May 8, 1837)

Pittman, Mr. Asa. Of the house of Pittman & Wilkinson. Died on
Friday evening last Merchant of Nashville and late of Columbia, Ky.
Nashville Republican. (Tues., May 9, 1837)

Pitts, George Beckham. Was born in Georgetown, Ky. on the 25th Jan.
1805. Died at the residence of his brother F. E. Pitts in Nashville
on the 27th. He was a printer.
National Banner & Nashville Daily Advertiser. (Fri., Feb. 28, 1834)

Pleasant, James Esq. Formerly Governor of Virginia and Senator in
the Congress. Died at Goochland, Va. on the 9th inst.
The Union. (Tues., Dec. 13, 1836)

Plessis, Right Reverend J. O. Bishop. Catholic Bishop. Died at
Quebec suddenly.
National Banner. (Jan. 6, 1826)

Plumley, Stephen. Died in Knoxville, Tenn.
Daily Republican Banner. (Sat., Oct. 27, 1838)

Plumley, Mrs. Theodoria. Died in Knox County.
National Banner & Nashville Whig. (Sat., July 29, 1826)

Plumley, Mr. Wm. Died in Knox County.
National Banner & Nashville Whig. (Sat., Aug. 19, 1826)

Plummer, Mrs. Mary Ann Jane. Wife of Mr. Joseph E. Plummer. Died
at Memphis on the 26th ult.
National Banner & Nashville Daily Advertiser. (Fri., July 6, 1832)

Plummer, Mr. Seymour. Died in Florence, Ala. Merchant and some years since a resident of Nashville.
National Banner & Nashville Whig. (Fri., July 15, 1835)

Pogue, Gen. Robert. Died in Macon County, Ky. An old and useful citizen.
National Banner & Nashville Daily Advertiser. (Sat., Aug. 24, 1833)

Poindexter, Mrs. Susan. Wife of Major John Poindexter. Died in Logan County, Ky.
National Banner & Nashville Whig. (Wed., Jan. 19, 1831)

Polanen, R. G. Van Esq. Aged 77 years. Died at Bridgeport, Conn. Formerly in the employ of the Dutch Government in the East Indies.
National Banner & Nashville Daily Advertiser. (Mon., Sept. 30, 1833)

Polk, Mr. Alexander H. Aged 19. Son of Col. William Polk. Died at Raleigh, N. C.
National Banner & Nashville Whig. (Thurs., Sept. 30, 1830)

Polk, Mrs. Belinda. Consort of William H. Polk Esq. of Columbia. Died at the residence of her father. Dr. W. G. Dickinson in Nashville on Tuesday night.
Nashville Whig. (Thurs., March 28, 1844)

Polk, Caroline Lafayette. Wife of Thomas R. Polk and daughter of Elisha B. Smith. Died at the residence of her father in La Grange on the 18th ult. in the 19th year of her age.
Nashville Whig. (Tues., July 4, 1843)

Polk, John L. Died in Maury County. Son of the late Maj. Sam Polk and the 3d son that has died in 12 months.
Nashville Republican & State Gazette. (Thurs., Oct. 6, 1831)

Polk, Marshall T. Esq. Late of Columbia, Tenn. Died at Charlotte, Mecklenburg County, N. C.
National Banner & Nashville Whig. (Fri., May 6, 1831)

Polk, Marshall T. Esq. Died in Charlotte, N. C. formerly of this state.
Nashville Republican & State Gazette. (Tues., May 3, 1831)

Polk, Mrs. Mary Ann. Wife of Lucius J. Polk and daughter of the late William Eastin in the 30th year of her age. Died at Hamilton Place, Maury County, on the 1st inst.
The Politician and Weekly Nashville Whig. (Wed., Aug. 25, 1847)

Polk, Rufus King. Son of the late Col. William Polk of Raleigh, N. C. Died in Nashville on the 25th inst.
Nashville Whig. (Tues., Feb. 28, 1843)

Polk, Maj. Samuel. In the 56th year of his age. Died on Saturday evening of the 3rd inst. at his residence in Columbia, Tenn. after an unusually long and afflicting illness. A native of Meclinburg County, North Carolina. At an early period of his life he threw himself into the tide of adventure that was setting Westward from his native state and among the enterpizing pioneers of this section of the country, was one of the first and most enterpizing. He came to the country when its primitive forests of cane exhibited scarcely any evidence of the presence of civilized man, or the approach of emprovement, with a young family dependant upon his personal exertions without any other resource than the native rigor of his mind, and unerarying industry, and lived to see the fruits of his enterprize abundant and mature, and the wild features and solitude of a primitive country pass away before the hand of improvement and busy hunt of a dense and intelligent population. Nor was he less distinguished for his social and domestic relations, than in his deaseless activity and adventurous disposition; an ardent attachment to his friends, and high relish for the pleasures of (-?) intersourse rendered him always in the fireside circle an entertaining and instructive companion, alike welcome to the young and the old.

The illness which terminated in his dissolution was of more than two years duration and was doubtless induced by the frequent subjected him in the early part of his life, and indeed throughout the most of it, for at a recent period he was one of the most active and intelligent explorers of the western district of this state. Six or seven months before his decease he professed his belief in and confident reliance upon the promises of divine revelations; and a few hours before his death with a mind unusually serene and rational, he expressed to his friends his consciousness of the approaching event, perfect resignation to the will of providence and freedom from those agonizing apprehensions which sometimes crowd upon that fearful hour. He has left behind him a large family and many relatives and friends who can well appreciate and will long remember his worth and lament the dispensation that has removed him.
National Banner & Nashville Whig. (November 17, 1827)

Polk, Samuel Washington. Died in Columbia, Tenn.
Nashville Union. (Wed., March 13, 1839)

Polk, Samuel Washington. Died in Columbia, Tenn.
Daily Republican Banner. (Wed., March 13, 1839)

Polk, Maj. Samuel. Died in Columbia on the 3d inst. in the 56th year of his age.
National Banner & Nashville Whig. (Sat., Nov. 17, 1827)

Pollard, Doct. Died in Princeton, Ky. of Cholera.
National Banner & Nashville Daily Advertiser. (Wed., Nov. 21, 1832)

Pollard, Isaac Clark. Only son of G. W. Pollard. Died in Maury County, near Columbia aged 13 months and 15 days.
Daily Republican Banner. (Fri., July 3, 1840)

Pollard, Mr. Isaac N. Formerly of Nashville. Died in Carrollton, Miss.
Daily Republican Banner. (Sat., Dec. 30, 1837)

Pollock, Mr. Neil. Died in this town.
National Banner. (Sat., Aug. 1, 1829)

Pollock, Mrs. Rebecca R. Died in Fayette County, Ky.
National Banner & Nashville Whig. (June 24, 1826)

Pollock, Mr. Thomas. A native of Scotland. Died in Lauderdale County, Ala.
 National Banner & Nashville Whig. (Sat., Jan. 12, 1828)

Palmer, Rev. Benjamin F. D. D. Died at Orangeburg on the 9th ult. in the 67th year of his age.
The Christian Record. (Sat., Nov. 13, 1847)

Pondexter, Mrs. Susan C. Wife of Major Pondexter. Died in Logan County, Ky.
National Banner & Nashville Whig. (Wed., Jan. 19, 1831)

Ponsonby, Hon. Mr. Chancellor of the British Exchequer. Died in London on the 8th of July.
The Nashville Whig. (Sept. 29, 1817)

Pool, Mr. John. A revolutionary soldier. Died in Fayette County, Ky.
National Banner (March 17, 1826)

Pope, Mr. Alexander. Son of Col. Leroy Pope of Huntsville, Ala. Died at New Orleans on the 22d of Yellow Fever.
National Banner & Nashville Whig. (Mon., Nov. 10, 1834)

Pope, Alexander Esq.   Died at Louisville, Ky.
National Banner & Nashville Whig. (Sat., Dec. 16, 1826)

Pope, Col. Elias F.   One of the first settlers of Randolph.   Died in
Tipton County, Tenn.
National Banner & Nashville Daily Advertiser. (Fri., Aug. 1, 1834)

Pope, Rev. Harris.   Died in Henry County.
National Banner & Nashville Whig. (Sat., Aug. 25, 1827)

Pope, Mrs. Jane R.   Wife of Mr. H. Pope, and daughter of Mr. William
Patton.   Died at Huntsville, Ala.
National Banner & Nashville Daily Advertiser. (Thurs., Feb. 9, 1832)

Pope, Mrs. Jane R.   Wife of Mr. H. Pope and daughter of Mr. William
Patton.   Died at Huntsville, Ala.
National Banner & Nashville Advertiser. (Sat., Feb. 11, 1832)

Pope, Mrs. Judith.   Wife of Col. Leroy Pope.   Died in Huntsville, Ala.
National Banner & Nashville Whig. (Sat., July 14, 1827)

Pope, L. (Col.).   Editorial on his death by The McMinnville Enterprise,
Sept. 1, 1853.
Republican Banner and Nashville Whig. (No. 216. Sat., Sept. 3, 1853)

Pope, Mr. Minor.   Aged 20.   Died in Louisville, Ky.
National Banner & Nashville Whig. (Sat., May 19, 1827)

Pope, Mr. Wm. F.   Of a wound received in a duel in February last, of
Louisville, Ky.   Died in Little Rock, Ark.
National Banner & Nashville Whig. (Mon., July 4, 1831)

Pope, Mr. Worden.   Clerk of the Jefferson County Court.   Died in
Louisville, Ky.
Nashville Union. (Thurs., April 26, 1838)

Pope, Worden Esq.   Died at Louisville, Ky. on Friday last.
Nasvhille Whig. (Wed., April 25, 1838)

Popham, John.   Of N. Y.   Died in New Orleans of Yellow Fever.
Daily Republican Banner. (Wed., Sept. 27, 1837)

Porter, Alexander Esq.   Of Nashville.   Died at Dresden.
National Banner & Nashville Daily Advertiser. (Wed., April 24, 1833)

Porter, Archibald.   From Hamilton County.   Died at the Tenn. State
Prison of Cholera.
National Banner & Nashville Whig. (Fri., Aug. 14, 1835)

Porter, Charles T. Esq.   Died in Jefferson County, Tenn.
Nashville Republican & State Gazette. (Tues., May 31, 1831)

Porter, Charles T. Esq.   Late Marshall of East Tenn. and Postmaster
at Chuckybend.   Died at Chucky Bend, Jefferson County on the 28th
March.
National Banner & Nashville Whig. (Mon., May 30, 1831)

Porter, Miss Eliza.   Died in the Parish of St. James, La.
Nashville Republican & State Gazette. (Sat., Oct. 8, 1831)

Porter, Mrs. Elizabeth L.   Died at Indianapolis.
National Banner & Nashville Whig. (Sat., Sept. 1, 1827)

Porter, Mrs. Elizabeth T.   Widow of the late Maj. Joseph B. Porter.
Died in Colubmia.
National Banner & Nashville Daily Advertiser. (Wed., Jan. 9, 1833)

Porter, Mr. Enour J.   Died in Fayette County, Ill.
National Banner & Nashville Whig. (Sat., July 22, 1826)

Porter, His Excellency, Governor. Died at Detroit, Michigan former Governor of that Territory and formerly of Pennsylvania.
National Banner & Nashville Daily Advertiser. (Mon., July 21, 1834)

Porter, Mrs. Jane. Wife of Mr. William Porter. Died in Columbia.
National Banner (May 27, 1836)

Porter, Mr. James. Merchant of this place. Died on Wednesday morning last. He has left an amiable wife, four small children. On Wednesday evening his remains were interred with Masonic honors.
The Nashville Whig. (June 16, 1817)

Porter, Private John B. Of Company C. Died - killed in the Battle of Monterey with the Mexicans.
Nashville Whig. (Sat., Oct. 24, 1846)

Porter, Rev. John C. Rector of the Episcopal Church, at Natchez. Died at Woodville, Miss. on the 20th ult.
National Banner & Nashville Whig. (Mon., Nov. 15, 1830)

Porter, Joseph B. Esq. Died in Maury County on the 20th ult. in the 58th year of age.
National Banner & Nashville Whig. (Sat., Nov. 1, 1828)

Porter, Dr. Joshua. Brother of Gen. Peter B. Porter. Died at Saratoga, N. Y.
National Banner & Nashville Whig. (Fri., Nov. 18, 1831)

Porter, Dr. Joshua. Brother of Gen. Peter B. Porter. Died at Saratoga, N. Y.
National Banner & Nashville Whig. (Fri., Nov. 18, 1831)

Porter, Mrs. Judith. Consort of Benjamin Porter, Esq. Died in Dyer County on Saturday the 20th ult. in the 47th year of her age.
National Banner & Nashville Daily Advertiser. (Wed., Aug. 7, 1833)

Porter, Mrs. Letitia P. Wife of Gen. Peter B. Porter, and daughter of the late John Breakingridge, of Ky.
National Banner & Nashville Whig. (Wed., Aug. 17, 1831)

Porter, Mrs. Letitia P. Wife of Gen. Peter B. Porter and daughter of the late John Breakinridge of Ky. Died at Black Rock, N. Y.
National Banner & Nashville Whig. (Wed., Aug. 17, 1831)

Porter, Mrs. Martha. Wife of Charles B. Porter Esq. Died in Haywood County, Tenn.
National Banner & Nashville Daily Advertiser. (Mon., Aug. 26, 1833)

Porter, Miss Mary Louisa. Eldest daughter of Mr. John Porter. Died on March 11th at the home of her father in Tallahatchee County, Miss.
Nashville Republican. (Thurs., April 13, 1837)

Porter, Mr. Nathaniel S. Died at Lexington, Ky.
National Banner & Nashville Whig. (Sat., Sept. 15, 1827)

Porter, Mrs. Polly G. Wife of the Rev. James B. Porter in the 29th year of her age. Died on the 25th ult. of a pulmonary disease.
The Nashville Whig. & Tenn. Advertiser. (July 4, 1818)

Porter, Robert Sen. Aged 68. Died in Nashville on June 8th. of Cholera.
National Banner & Nashville Daily Advertiser. (Mon., June 10, 1833)

Porter, Mr. Robert. Aged 77. Died near Falmouth, Ky.
National Banner. (March 3, 1826)

Porter, Mr. Samuel. Died in Clarksville.
National Banner & Nashville Whig. (Fri., July 15, 1831)

Porter, Sarah Ann. Wife of Mr. James A. Porter of this City. Died
on the 6th inst. at the residence of Donaldson Coffrey Esq. in St.
Mary's Attakas Law in the 18th year of her age.
Nashville Whig. (May 3, 1824)

Porter, Mrs. Susannah. Wife of the Late Col. William Porter. Died
in Butler County, Ky.
National Banner & Nashville Whig. (Thurs., Aug. 5, 1830)

Porter, William Sen. Esq. Age 66. Died in Henry County.
National Banner & Nashville Advertiser. (Mon., April 30, 1832)

Porter, Young G. Esq. Attorney at law aged 24 years. Died in Giles
County on the 14th inst.
National Banner & Nashville Daily Advertiser. (Thurs., March 21, 1833)

Porterfield, Miss Elizabeth. Died in Washington County, Virginia on
the 6th inst.
Nashville Republican & State Gazette. (Fri., Dec. 14, 1832)

Porterfield, Francis, Esq. Died in Nashville, after an illness of
about 18 hours with the Cholera.
National Banner & Nashville Daily Advertiser. (Mon., June 3, 1833)

Posey, Col. Thornton. Lately second in command to Gen. M'Gregory
at Amelia Island. Died lately at Wilmington, N. C.
The Nashville Whig. & Tenn. Advertiser. (Oct. 13, 1817)

Post, Roswell. Infant son of Dr. R. P. Hayes aged 18 months. Died
in this town of Cholera infamtus.
National Banner. (Sat. Aug. 1, 1829)

Post, Dr. Wright. One of the most eminent physicians of our country.
Died at New York.
National Banner & Nashville Whig. (Fri., July 11, 1828)

Poston, Mrs. Adeline F. Consort of Mr. Alexander H. Poston on Cadiz,
Ky. Died on Friday the 20th inst.
Nashville Whig. (Sat., Oct. 28, 1846)

Poston, John H. Jr. Of Mississippi, formerly of Clarksville, Tenn.
Died at Bon Air Springs.
Nashville Whig. (Mon., Sept. 7, 1840)

Potter, Ebenezer D. D. President of the Theological Seminary. Died
in Andover, Mass.
National Banner & Nashville Daily Advertiser. (Thurs., May 1, 1834)

Potter, Mrs. Eunice. Wife of Mr. Daniel Potter, aged 57. Died at
Ipswich, she was the mother of 14 children.
National Banner & Nashville Daily Advertiser. (Sat., Oct. 19, 1833)

Potter, Mrs. Gillyan. Consort of James O. Potter Esq. of Spring Hill,
Tenn. daughter of Col. John Sneed, near Nashville. Died in Williamson
County in the 23rd year of her age.
National Banner & Nashville Whig. (Mon., Dec. 12, 1836)

Potter, Mrs. Gillyan. Consort of James O. Potter Esq. of Spring Hill,
Tenn. Died in Williamson County on 2d of Dec.
Nashville Republican. (Mon., Dec. 12, 1836)

Potter, Milton. Died 14th at Cincinnati, Ohio of Cholera.
National Banner & Nashville Daily Advertiser. (Tues., Oct. 23, 1832)

Potter, Hon. W. W. Member of Congress from the 14th District in
Pennsylvania. Died recently.
Daily Republican Banner. (Fri., Nov. 22, 1839)

Potts, Mr. John C. Aged 35. Died near Bowling-Green, Ky.
National Banner & Nashville Daily Advertiser. (Sat., Aug. 2, 1834)

Potts, Dr. John W. Late of Tarbarough, N. C. Died in Little Rock,
Ark.
National Banner & Nashville Whig. (Mon., Aug. 3, 1835)

Powell, Alfred H. Esq. Member of the legislature of Virginia. Died
suddenly at Winchester, Va. on the 3d inst.
National Banner & Nashville Whig. (Wed., Aug. 17, 1831)

Powell, Mr. Dempsey. Aged 85 years. Died in Davidson County on the
30th ult.
National Banner & Nashville Daily Advertiser. (Tues., July 3, 1832)

Powell, Mrs. Elizabeth. Wife of Major Seymour Powell. Died in
Davidson County on Friday last.
Daily Republican Banner. (Tues., Oct. 20, 1840)

Powell, Leven Esq. Postmaster and President of the Senate of Alabama.
Died in Tuscaloosa.
National Banner & Nashville Daily Advertiser. (Sat., July 6, 1833)

Powell, Mrs. Mary. Wife of Mr. Dempsey Powell. Died in Carroll
County on the 7th inst.
National Banner & Nashville Daily Advertiser. (Thurs., March 21, 1833)

Powell, Mrs. Mary. Wife of Dr. L. B. Powell of Nashville. Died on
the 25th inst.
The Christian Record. (Sat., Oct. 30, 1847)

Powell, Mr. Nathaniel. A Veteran of the Revolution. Died in Wilson
County on the 19th Feb.
National Banner & Nashville Daily Advertiser. (Wed., March 26, 1834)

Powell, Thomas C. Infant son of William T. Powell. Died in Nashville,
aged 4 years.
National Banner & Nashville Whig. (Wed., June 24, 1835)

Powell, Capt. William. Died in Rutherford County.
National Banner. (March 10, 1826)

Poyntz, Mrs. Sarah E. Consort of Mr. Nathaniel Poyntz. Died in
Maysville, Ky. on Sunday last. (Obituary)
The Christian Record. (Sat., May 20, 1848)

Poyzer, Mr. Benjamin. Died in Nashville. last night.
National Banner & Nashville Daily Advertiser. (Wed., Sept. 12, 1832)

Poyzer, George. Formerly a Merchant of this place. Died lately in
Philadelphia.
The Nashville Whig. & Tenn. Advertiser. (March 14, 1818)

Pratt, Private A. J. Company K. First Regiment Tenn. Volunteers.
Died was killed in the Battle of Monterey with the Mexicans on Sept.
21st. 1846
Nashville Whig. (Sat., Oct. 24, 1846)

Preble, Commodore. Died in Portland on August 25, 6 P.M.
Impartial Review and Cumberland Repository. (Oct. 1, 1807)

Precise, Mrs. Sarah. Died in Logan County, Ky.
National Banner & Nashville Whig. (Sat., May 19, 1827)

Prentiss, George W. Esq. Formerly editor of the N. Y. Statesman.
Died at Keene, N. H.
National Banner & Nashville Whig. (Sat., March 28, 1829)

Preston, Mr. Charles S. In the 23d year of his age. Died at his
residence in Smith County, Tenn. on the 29th Sept.
National Banner & Nashville Whig. (Mon., Oct. 31, 1831)

Preston, Mr. Charles S. Age 23. A member of the (Liberty Blues) in
which rank he occupied a place of honor. Died in Smith County on 29th
Sept.
National Banner & Nashville Whig. (Mon., Oct. 31, 1831)

Preston, Gen. Francis. Of Abingdon, Virginia. Died near Columbia,
S. C.
National Banner & Nashville Whig. (Wed., July 1, 1835)

Preston, Miss Sarah Gillam. Daughter of Mrs. John S. Young. Died
Thursday the 7th inst. in Abingdon, Virginia, aged 18 years and 8 months.
(Obituary)
Nashville Whig. (Sat., May 16, 1846)

Prewett, Mrs. Sarah. Aged 36. Wife of Mr. Moses H. Prewett. Died in
Jackson, Madison County.
National Banner & Nashville Whig. (Thurs., July 29, 1830)

Prewett, Thomas. From Hawkins County. Died at the Tenn. State Prison
of Cholera.
National Banner & Nashville Whig. (Fri., Aug. 14, 1835)

Prewitt, Lavinia. Infant daughter of M. W. Prewitt. Died near
Jefferson, Rutherford County.
National Banner & Nashville Daily Advertiser. (Sat., Sept. 6, 1834)

Prewitt, Capt. Vaulallen. Died in Scott County, Kentucky.
National Banner. (March 31, 1826)

Prewitt, Zachariah. Died in Danville, Ky. of Apoplexy.
National Banner & Nashville Daily Advertiser. (Mon., Aug. 5, 1833)

Price, Mr. Albert C. Died in Philadelphia, Tenn.
National Banner & Nashville Advertiser. (Tues., Dec. 18, 1832)

Price, Mr. Bird. Aged 74. Died in Fayette County, Ky.
National Banner. (Sat., July 18, 1829)

Price, E. With the second Tenn. Regiment. Died - was killed in the
battle of Sierra Gorda with the Mexicans.
The Politicians & Weekly Nashville Whig. (Fri., May 21, 1847)

Price, Mrs. Elizabeth L. A native of Virginia. Died at the mouth of
White River, Ark.
National Banner & Nashville Daily Advertiser. (Sat., May 18, 1833)

Price, Mr. Francis D. Aged 30. Died in Rutherford County.
National Banner & Nashville Whig. (Mon., June 7, 1830)

Price, Mr. Grief. Formerly of Henrico County, Virginia and late of
Louisville, Ky. Died in this town on the 8th inst.
National Banner (Sat., Aug. 15, 1829)

Price, Mr. John. Died in Georgetown, Ky.
National Banner & Nashville Whig. (Sat., Dec. 16, 1826)

Price, Mrs. Letitia. Died in Nashville, very suddenly, on Monday 24th
inst.
National Banner & Nashville Daily Advertiser. (Tues., Sept. 25, 1832)

Price, Mr. Isaac W. Aged 31. Died in Monroe County.
National Banner & Nashville Daily Advertiser. (Mon., Dec. 3, 1832)

Price, Mrs. Nancy. Died in Logan County, Ky.
National Banner & Nashville Whig. (Mon., Sept. 26, 1831)

Price, Major William. Aged 73. Died in Richmond, Va.
National Banner & Nashville Whig. (Mon., July 19, 1830)

Pride, James Henry. Only son of Dr. A. W. Pride, aged 3 years, 7
months, 12 days. Died in Memphis on the 15th Dec. after a short illness.
Nashville Daily Gazette. (Dec. 22, 1857)

Priestley, Mrs. Elizabeth. Widow of the late Rev. Dr. Priestley.
Died in this town on Tuesday last.
National Banner & Nashville Whig. (Sat., Feb. 21, 1829)

Priestly, Capt. James. Aged 35. Died at Jackson.
National Banner & Nashville Whig. (Thurs., Oct. 14, 1830)

Priestley, Doctor James. President of Cumberland College. Died in
Nashville yesterday evening. Whig of the 7th inst.
The Nashville Gazette. (Sat., Feb. 10, 1821)

Prince, Col. Enoch. A member of the Senate of that State. Died at
Princeton, Ky.
National Banner & Nashville Daily Advertiser. (Tues., July29, 1834)

Prince, Mrs. Nancy. Died in Logan County, Ky.
National Banner & Nashville Whig. (Mon., Sept. 26, 1831)

Prince, Robert Esq. Age 24. A native of Tennessee. Died in Warren
County, Miss.
National Banner & Nashville Whig. (Sat., Nov. 3, 1827)

Prince, William. Died in Princeton, Indiana, a member of Congress
from that state.
Nashville Whig. (Oct. 4, 1824)

Prince, Mr. William. An old and well known citizen of Gallatin,
Tenn. Died on the 11th inst. of Consumption.
Nashville Daily Gazette, (Dec. 22, 1857)

Pritchard, Mr. James. Aged 65. Late of Pettersburg, Va. Died in
Pyeatt, Ark.
National Banner & Nashville Whig. (Sat., Sept. 9, 1826)

Pritchard, Richard O. An eminent merchant of New Orleans. Died -
was drowned on the 16th ult. from on board S. Boat Brilliant near
New Orleans.
Nashville Whig. (Fri., Nov. 8, 1839)

Pritchart, Mr. William. Died in Lexington, Ky.
National Banner & Nashville Whig. (Mon., Oct. 4, 1830)

Probart, Robert. Died lately in Springfield.
The Nashville Whig. & Tenn. Advertiser. (March 7, 1818)

Probart, Mr. William Y. Of Nashville. Died on Tuesday morning.
The Nashville Gazette. (Sat., Dec. 18, 1819)

Proctor, Mr. Hezakiah. Died in Russellville, Ky.
National Banner & Nashville Whig. (Mon., Aug. 1, 1831)

Proctor, Mr. Maxwell. Died in Logan County.
National Banner & Nashville Whig. (Sat., Oct. 7, 1826)

Proctor, Miss Nancy. Died in Logan County, Ky.
National Banner & Nashville Whig. (Sat., April 12, 1828)

Prosser, Dr. Albert. Died at Holnesville, Miss.
National Banner & Nashville Whig. (Sat., Dec. 23, 1826)

Prosser, Dr. Albert H. Died inWilkinson County, Mississippi.
National Banner & Nashville Whig. (Sat., Dec. 9, 1826)

Proudfit, John H. Died in Clarksville, Tenn.
Nashville Whig. (Mon., Sept. 7, 1840)

Prout, Mr. Geo. Wade. Died in Florence, Ala.
Nashville Republican & State Gazette. (Sat., May 28, 1831)

Prout, Joshua Esq. Died in Tuscumbia, Ala. on the 13th inst. suddenly
was Post Master at Tuscumbia.
National Banner & Nashville Daily Advertiser. (Mon., Aug. 19, 1833)

Prouty, Mr. Joel Senior. The Firm Daniel Bates & Co. Died near Boston
when the Boat Bunker Hill was upset by the wind.
National Banner & Nashville Daily Advertiser. (Sat., June 30, 1832)

Provost, Mr. William. Aged 28, formerly of London. Died at Cincinnati.
National Banner. (March 10, 1826)

Prunty, Mr. Burwell R. Died in Warren County, Ky.
National Banner & Nashville Whig. (Sat., Aug. 30, 1828)

Pryor, Mr. Asa. Died in Huntsville on the 19th inst. well known as
an assistant in the office of the clerk of the Circuit Court.
National Banner & Nashville Daily Advertiser. (Mon., March 26, 1832)

Pryor, Capt. Beverly B. Aged 20 years and 7 months. Died at Columbus,
Mis. on the 4th inst.
Nashville Republican. (Tues., May 31, 1836)

Pryor, Private Edward. Company G. First Regiment Tenn. Volunteers.
Died was killed in the Battle of Monterey with the Mexicans on Sept.
21st 1846.
Nashville Whig. (Sat., Oct. 24, 1846)

Pryor, Capt. Nathaniel. Very suddenly. Sub-Agent and formerly an
officer of the Army. Died at the Osage Agency.
National Banner & Nashville Whig. (Mon., July 4, 1831)

Pryor, Nicholas B. Esq. Died in Nashville.
National Banner & Nashville Daily Advertiser. (Mon., Jan. 14, 1833)

Pryor, Mrs. Susannah. Age 89. Died in Davidson County on Monday
16th inst.
National Banner & Nashville Advertiser. (Wed., April 25, 1832)

Pryor, Mr. Zachariah B. Aged 55 years. A native of Virginia. Died
in this vicinity on the 17th inst.
Daily Republican Banner. (Wed., Sept. 20, 1837)

Puchen, Mr. J. Bookkeeper in the U. S. Branch Bank. Died in New
Orleans.
National Banner & Nashville Advertiser. (Thurs., Feb. 16, 1832)

Pugh, Mrs. Elizabeth. In the 61st year of her age. Died in Davidson
county on the 26th inst.
National Banner & Nashville Daily Advertiser. (Sat., March 29, 1834)

Pugh, Samuel D. From Marion County. Died in the Tenn. State Prison
of Cholera.
National Banner & Nashville Whig. (Fri., Aug. 14, 1835)

Pugsley, Doctor Charles. Of Nashville. Died in Sumner County, last
night at half past 10 o'clock.
National Banner & Nashville Daily Advertiser. (Thurs., April 19, 1832)

Pullen, Dr. James T. Died - was killed at Pine Bluff, Ark. on Thursday
last by John N. Outlaw.
Daily Republican Banner. (Thurs., June 27, 1839)

Pullum, Benjamin. Died in Madison County, Ky. of pulmonary complaint.
National Banner & Nashville Daily Advertiser. (Sat., Aug. 10, 1823)

Purdy, Col. John. A member of the convention of 34. Died in Henderson County.
Nashville Whig. (Mon., Dec. 31, 1838)

Purdy, Gen. Robert. Died in this place, yesterday morning.
Nashville Republican & State Gazette. (Thurs., March 24, 1831)

Purdy, Gen. Robert. U. S. Marshal for the District of West Tennessee.
Died in Nashville this morning.
National Banner & Nashville Whig. (Wed., March 23, 1831)

Purris, John Esq. Died in Kingston.
National Banner. (Sat., Oct. 3, 1829)

Puryer, Mrs. Nancy. Died in Courtland, Ala.
National Banner & Nashville Daily Advertiser. (Mon., June 18, 1832)

Pulliam, Mrs. Sarah. Wife of Mr. Jas. Pulliam. Died in Lincoln Cty,
Tenn.
National Banner & Nashville Whig. (Mon., Oct. 20, 1834)

Putnam, Ann Eliza. Daughter of Dr. J. R. Putnam. Died in Nashville
on the 23d July, aged about 7 years.
National Banner & Nashville Whig. (Mon., July 25, 1836)

Putnam, Mrs. Cornelia V. Consort of A. W. Putnam Esq. Died in the
vicinity of Nashville on Thursday July 30th.
Nashville Whig. (Sat., Aug. 1, 1846)

Putnam, Col. Daniel. Died in Connecticut.
Nashville Republican & State Gazette. (Thurs., May 26, ___)

Putnam, Mr. Jesse. Aged 60 years. Died in Bedford County, Tenn.
National Banner & Nashville Daily Advertiser. (Mon., Sept. 2, 1833)

Putnam, Mr. Nathan. Died in Lexington, Ky. of Cholera.
National Banner & Nashville Daily Advertiser. (Tues., July 2, 1833)

Putnam, 2 Lieut. S. M. With Company E. Died - was killed in the
Battle of Monterey with the Mexicans on Sept. 21st.
Nasvhille Whig. (Sat., Oct. 24, 1846)

Putney, Miss Eliza. Died in Madison County.
National Banner & Nashville Daily Advertiser. (Fri., July 6, 1832)

Pybass, William. Aged 20 months. Died in Tuscumbia, Ala.
National Banner & Nashville Daily Advertiser. (Mon., Aug. 19, 1833)

Pypas, Mr. William. Died in M'Nairy County.
National Banner & Nashville Whig. (Sat., Feb. 7, 1829)

Pyle, Mr. Benjamin. A native of Chatham County, N. C. Died yesterday
afternoon at the Nashville Inn. Aged about 30 years.
Nashville Whig. (Sat., July 13, 1844)

Pyle, Mr. John. Died in Gallatin.
National Banner & Nashville Daily Advertiser. (Mon., Dec. 3, 1832)

Quarles, Mr. Ambrose. Died in Franklin County, Ky.
National Banner & Nashville Whig. (Mon., Aug. 30, 1830)

Quarles, John A. A citizen of Montgomery County, Tenn. Died
was accidentally shot by his wife last week.
Nashville Whig. (Mon., April 16, 1838)

Quarles, John H. Esq. Attorney at law. Died in Clarksville, Tenn.
on 29th Aug.
National Banner & Nashville Whig. (Fri., Sept. 23, 1836)

Quarles, Mrs. Letitia B. Died in Clarksville.
National Banner & Nashville Whig. (Fri., June 20, 1828)

Quarles, Major Robt. Aged 64. Died in Ferdinand Township, Missouri.
National Banner & Nashville Whig. (Sat., Sept. 15, 1827)

Quarles, Col. Tunstall. Died in Versailles, Ken. on the night of
the18th Feb. last.
The Nashville Whig & Tenn. Advertiser. (March 14, 1818)

Quesenberry, Mr. Henry. Died in Davidson County on the 21st inst.
National Banner & Nashville Whig. (Mon., Dec. 27, 1830)

Ragan, Mr. Levi. Died in Lexington, Ky.
National Banner & Nashville Whig. (Fri., March 13, 1835)

Ragsdale, Mr. Edward. Died in Williamson County.
Nashville Whig. (June 4, 1823)

Ragsdale, Mr. John. Died in Hartsville.
National Banner & Nashville Daily Advertiser. (Wed., Feb. 8, 1832)

Rains, Mrs. Christiana. Wife of Mr. John Rains. Died in this
county.
National Banner (March 24, 1826)

Rains, John. Late a Senator in the Alabama Legislature from Marengo
County. Died in Linden, Alabama.
Nashville Whig. (Fri., Sept. 11, 1840)

Rains, Captain John. Aged upwards of 80 years. Died in this vicinity
on the 26th inst.
National Banner & Nashville Daily Advertiser. (Fri., March 28, 1834)

Ralston, Mr. David. Aged 90. A patriot of the revolution an honest
man and a christian. Died in Davidson County.
National Banner & Nashville Whig. (Mon., Aug. 29, 1831)

Ramage, Christina Stewart. Infant daughter of John & Mary C. Ramage.
Died on Wednesday 14th April.
The Politician & Weekly Nashville Whig. (Fri., May 14, 1847)

Ramsey, Charles R. Esq. Senior editor of the Cincinnati Republican.
Died at Galveston, Texas where he had gone for his health.
Daily Republican Banner. (Mon., April 22, 1839)

Ramsey, Mrs. Eliza H. C. Wife of Col. W. B. A. Ramsey. Editor of
the Knoxville Register. Died in Knoxville on Monday last in the 30th
year of her age.
Nashville Whig. (Wed., Oct. 23, 1839)

Ramsey, Col. Francis A. Aged 56. Died at one o'clock yesterday
morning. From the Knox. Reg.
The Nashville Gazette. (Sat., Mov. 18, 1820)

Ramsay, Col. John. Of Pittsburgh, aged 57. Died at Cincinnati.
National Banner & Nashville Whig. (Fri., Sept. 9, 1831)

Ramsey, Mrs. Susan P. Consort of W. B. A. Ramsey. Died on the
morning of the 18th inst. at the residence of A. V. S. Lindsley Esq.
near Nashville. (Obituary) Jan. 27.
The Christian Record. (Sat., Jan. 20, 1849)

Ramsey, Hon. W. S. Member of Congress from the Carlisle District of
Penn. Died by shooting himself at Barnums Hotel, Baltimore on the
17th inst.
Nashville Whig. (Wed., Oct. 28, 1840)

Ramsay, Hon. William. Member of Congress. Died in Carlisle, Penn.
National Banner & Nashville Whig. (Mon., Oct. 17, 1831)

Ramsey, Mr. William S. Of Carlisle, Penn. Died by shooting himself
in Baltimore. He was a member of Congress.
Daily Republican Banner. (Fri., Nov. 6, 1840)

Randall, Elizabeth. Daughter of David Randall. Died in Nashville
yesterday morning.
Daily Republican Banner. (Fri., April 13, 1838)

Randolph, James M. Second son of the late Thomas Mann Randolph and
grandson of Mr. Jefferson. Died at Edge-Hill, Va.
National Banner & Nashville Daily Advertiser. (Wed., March 5, 1834)

Randolph, Hon. John. Of Roanoke in the 60th year of his age. Died in
Philadelphia on the 25th ult.
National Banner & Nashville Daily Advertiser. (Mon., June 3, 1833)

Randolph, Lewis Jackson. Aged 5 years. Died at the residence of
William Donelson Esq. in Davidson County, on Friday evening.
Nashville Whig. (Mon., June 7, 1841)

Randolph, Mrs. Mary. Died in Rutherford County.
National Banner & Nashville Whig. (Sat., May 19, 1827)

Randolph, Mrs. Mary B. Wife of Dr. P. G. Randolph. Late Chief
Clerk in the War Department. Died at Washington.
National Banner & Nashville Whig. (Fri., Nov. 11, 1831)

Randolph, Mrs. Nancy T. Died in Fayette County, Ky.
National Banner & Nashville Whig. (Wed., Aug. 17, 1831)

Randolph, Hon. Peter. Judge of the U. S. District Court for
Mississippi. Died in Wilkinson County, Miss.
National Banner & Nashville Daily Advertiser. (Thurs., Feb. 16, 1832)

Randolph, Tho. M. Esq. Died at Montecillo, Va. Formerly Governor
of Va.
National Banner & Nashville Whig. (Fri., July 11, 1828)

Rankin, Rev. Adam. Late of Lexington, Ky. Died in Philadelphia.
National Banner & Nashville Whig. (Sat., Dec. 15, 1827)

Rankin, Hon. Christopher. Representative from the state of Mississippi. Died at Washington City.
National Banner. (April 7, 1826)

Rankin, Mr. David. Aged 61. Died in Rutherford County.
National Banner & Nashville Whig. (Fri., Feb. 11, 1831)

Rankin, Rev. James P. Died in Rutherford County.
Nashville Republican & State Gazette. (Sat., Sept. 17, 1831)

Rankin, John W. Died in Rutherford County.
National Banner & Nashville Whig. (Sat., Feb. 10, 1827)

Rankin, Mrs. Margaret. Wife of Mr. John Rankin of Maysville, Ky. Died at Cincinnati.
National Banner. (April 21, 1826)

Rankin, Mr. Thos. C. Died in Bedford County, Tenn. on the 4th inst.
Daily Republican Banner (Fri., Oct. 30, 1840)

Ransom, Richard Esq. Merchant. Died in Williamson County, Ten. in the 32nd year of his age.
National Banner & Nashville Whig. (Fri., March 20, 1835)

Rapier, Capt. Richard. Formerly of the House of Rapier & Simpson. Died in Florence, Ala.
National Banner (Jan. 13, 1826)

Rapp, Frederick. Died in Beaver Co., Pennsylvania. The founder of the settlement at Economy.
National Banner & Nashville Daily Advertiser. (Tues., July 15, 1834)

Raser, Mr. George. Of Mobile, aged 24, died in St. Stephens, Ala.
National Banner & Nashville Whig. (Sept. 2, 1826)

Ratcliff, Mrs. Adah. Aged 32. Died in Amite County, Miss.
National Banner. (March 17, 1826)

Ratcliff, Mr. John. Died at St. Francisville, Lauts.
National Banner & Nashville Whig. (Sat., Dec. 23, 1826)

Ratcliff, R. M. Of Va. Died in New Orleans of Yellow Fever.
Daily Republican Banner. (Wed., Oct. 4, 1837)

Rather, Mrs. Barbara W. Died in Sommerville, Ala.
National Banner & Nashville Whig. (Sat., Nov. 18, 1826)

Rather, Mr. Thomas. Died in Huntsville.
National Banner (Sat., Dec. 19, 1829)

Ratrie, Dr. George T. Died in Lexington, Ky.
National Banner & Nashville Whig. (Sat., Jan. 10, 1829)

Ravenel, Dr. Edward Daniel. Aged 21 years. Died in Pineville, S. C. on the 4th Aug.
National Banner & Nashville Daily Advertiser. (Wed., Aug. 28, 1833)

Rawley, Mrs. Mary Ann. Wife of Dr. M. Rawley. Died in Montgomery County.
National Banner & Nashville Whig. (Sat., June 2, 1827)

Rawling, Dr. Edward G. Died in Nashville on Thursday the 23d of May in the 34th year of his age, formerly a resident of Sumner County.
National Banner & Nashville Daily Advertiser. (Sat., May 25, 1833)

Rawling, Mr. William in the 74th year of his age. Died in Franklin County on the 2d inst. A soldier of the Revolution.
National Banner & Nashville Whig. (Fri., May 20, 1836)

Rawlings, Mrs. Adeline. Wife of Dan R. Rawlings esq. and daughter of Col. John Kelly. Died at Jasper, Marion County.
National Banner & Nashville Whig. (Mon., May 9, 1831)

Rawlings, Eldred Jr. Son of Eldred Rawlings Esq. of Madison County, Ala. Died in Athens, Ala.
National Banner & Nashville Whig. (Wed., Nov. 12, 1834)

Rawlings, Mr. John S. Aged about 27 years. Died in Davidson County at the residence of Mrs. Wingfield on Sunday last.
Daily Republican Banner. (Sat., March 10, 1838)

Rawlings, Mrs. Margaret C. Wife of Dr. Edward C. Rawlings and
daughter of the Hon. Felix Grundy. Died near Pleasant Hill, Jefferson County, Miss. on the 9th inst.
National Banner & Nashville Daily Advertiser. (Wed., Aug. 22, 1832)

Rawlings, Mr. Rufus K. Died in Gallatin.
National Banner & Nashville Daily Advertiser. (Mon., July 29, 1833)

Rawlins, Elizabeth Marion. Eldest daughter of Mr. John T. Rawlins
Died at Richmond, Va.
National Banner & Nashville Whig. (Mon., May 25, 1835)

Rawlins, Thomas James. Son of Eldred Rawlins Esq. of Nashville.
Died on the 3d inst. at the residence of his Uncle Mr. James Bass in
Rutherford County, in his 12th year.
Nashville Whig. (Tues., Feb. 15, 1842)

Raworth, Mrs. Elizabeth. Consort of Mr. George Raworth and daughter
of the late Maulton Dickson Esq. of Dickson County, Tenn. Died on
the 13th ultimo. in the 30th year of her age.
The Christian Record. (Sat., March 6, 1847)

Raworth, Mrs. Priscilla. Died in this place, on Wednesday.
The Nashville Whig. & Tenn. Advertiser. (Jan. 5, 1818)

Ray, Mr. Logan. Died near Danville, Ky.
National Banner & Nashville Whig. (Sat., Jan. 6, 1827)

Rayburn, Mrs. Wife of Samuel S. Rayburn and daughter of John Davis,
esq.
National Banner & Nashville Whig. (Mon., Dec. 5, 1831)

Rayburn, Janet Hobson. Eldest daughter of John K. and Sarah Jane
Rayburn. Died on Saturday 23rd ult. at Pass Christian, aged 18
years.
The Christian Record. (Sat., Oct. 14, 1848)

Rayburn, Mrs. Susan C. Consort of S. S. Rayburn and daughter of John
Davis Esq. Died in Nashville on the 4th inst. in the 21st year of her
age.
National Banner & Nashville Whig. (Fri., Dec. 16, 1831)

Read, Mr. Defrafton. Principal of the female Academy. Died in
Russellville, Ky. on 1st Aug.
Daily Republican Banner. (Mon., Aug. 6, 1838)

Read, Edmond R. In the 27th year of his age. Died at the residence
of his Mother in Rutherford County, on Sunday the 10th inst.
Nashville Whig. (Tues., Sept. 19, 1843)

Read, Mr. Hezeliah. A native of Connecticut. Died on Wednesday night
last of a lingering illness (nervous)
Impartial Review and Cumberland Repository. (Sat., July 26, 1806)

Read, John J. D. Esq. Late co-editor of the Stateman. Died at
Charlotte, Tenn. on the 17th inst. in the 20th year of his age. He
was the only child of Jno. Read, Esq. Attorney of Jackson, Ten.
National Banner & Nashville Daily Advertiser. (Thurs., June 20, 1833)

Read, Mrs. Mary. Wife of Col. John Read. of that Place. Died at
Huntsville, Ala. on the 4th inst.
National Banner & Nashville Whig. (Sat., April 12, 1828)

Read, Samuel D. Esq. of Sumner County, Tenn. Died April 30th 1838.
Nashville Union. (Wed., May 9, 1838)

Read, William Harrison. Son of the late Capt. John N. Read. Died in Rutherford County, near Jefferson in the 21st year of his age.
National Banner & Nashville Whig. (Fri., Oct. 3, 1843)

Reading, Mrs. Mary. Relict of Mr. John Reading, who died in Franklin County, several years ago. Died in Franklin County, Kentucky on the 18th Feb. Aged 82 years.
The Christian Record. (Sat., March 13, 1847)

Ready, Mr. Charles. Died at Cincinnati.
National Banner. (April 7, 1826)

Ready, William F. Son of Charles Ready Sr. of Rutherford County, Ten. Died on the 14th day of Nov. late at Velasco, Texas, aged 32 years 11 months and one day.
Daily Republican Banner. (Mon., Dec. 23, 1829)

Reaves, Mr. Samuel B. Died in Columbia.
Nashville Republican & State Gazette. (Wed., Dec. 5, 1832)

Reavis, Mrs. Elizabeth. Age about 55 years. Died in Henry County, Ten.
National Banner & Nashville Whig. (Mon., Aug. 3, 1835)

Record, Mrs. Elizabeth D. Consort of George M. Record. Died in Maury County, Ten.
National Banner & Nashville Whig. (Mon., March 30, 1835)

Record, daughter of Rev. John Record. Of Williamson County, age 7 was cruelly strangled to death in a branch of water six inches deep by a negro girl.
Impartial Review and Cumberland Repository. (Sat., Aug. 30, 1806)

Rector, Mr. Stephen. Died in St. Louis.
National Banner & Nashville Whig. (Sat., July 29, 1826)

Rector, Gen. Wm. Formerly survey general for Missouri , Illinois and Arkansas. Died in Illinois.
National Banner & Nashville Whig. (July 1, 1826)

Reddick, William R. Attorney at Law. Died at Dover, Tenn. on the 19th inst.
National Banner & Nashville Daily Advertiser. (Thurs., May 24, 1832)

Redman, Mrs. Ann. Aged 70. Died in Bourbon County, Ky.
National Banner & Nashville Whig. (Mon., Dec. 27, 1830)

Reece, Mr. Charles T. Aged 80. A veteran of the Revolution. Died in Lincoln County.
National Banner & Nashville Whig. (Thurs., June 24, 1830)

Reed, Mr. Alexander. Printer, late of this town. Died at New Orleans on the 10th inst.
National Banner & Nashville Whig. (Sat., Nov. 1, 1828)

Reed, Mr. Elijah. Died at Natchitoches.
National Banner. (June 10, 1826)

Reed, Mrs. Grisse. Wife of Mr. J. S. Reed. Died in Green County.
National Banner. (Feb. 24, 1826)

Reed, Jacob. Of the town of St. Louis. Died on the 25th September of yellow fever, after 2 days illness.
The Clarion & Tennessee Gazette. (Nov. 21, 1820)

Reed, Mr. James. Aged 20. Died in Mobile.
National Banner & Nashville Whig. (Sat., Sept. 16, 1826)

Reed, Mrs. Jane. Died in Washington County.
National Banner & Nashville Whig. (Sat., July 15, 1826)

Reed, Mrs. Margaret M. Aged about 60 years. Died in Bourbon County,
Ky. sister of Mrs. Grundy of Nashville and Mrs. McGavock, near Franklin.
National Banner & Nashville Whig. (Mon., Nov. 16, 1835)

Reed, Mr. Samuel. Aged 21 years. Died in Little Rock, Ark.
National Banner & Nashville Daily Advertiser. (Tues., Aug. 5, 1834)

Reed, Hon. Thomas B. Senator in Congress from Mississippi. Died at
Lexington, Ky.
National Banner (Sat., Dec. 5, 1829)

Reed, Maj. Wm. Aged 37. Died near Selma, Ala.
National Banner (Feb. 10, 1826)

Reese, Mrs. Elizabeth. Aged 83. Died in Maury County.
National Banner & Nashville Whig. (Fri., Sept. 16, 1831)

Reese, Mrs. Sarah M. Wife of Wm. B. Reese Esq. Died at Knoxville.
National Banner. (Sat., April 25, 1829)

Reeves, An infant daughter of Mr. Willis Reeves. Died in Bedford
County.
National Banner & Nashville Advertiser. (Fri., July 6, 1832)

Reeves, Mr. Isaiah. 34, died in Mobile.
National Banner & Nashville Whig. (Sept. 2, 1826)

Reeves, Mrs. Susannah. Wife of Reeves, Willis L. Esq. Died at Elkton,
Ky.
National Banner. (Sat., May 9, 1829)

Reid, Mrs. Consort of Mr. Thos. Reid. Died in Memphis, Ten.
National Banner & Nashville Daily Advertiser. (Mon., Sept. 2, 1833)

Reid, Maj. John. Aid to Maj. Gen. Jackson. Died on the 18th of Jan.
near New London, Virginia.
The Nashville Whig. (Feb. 7, 1816)

Reiley, Dr. David. Died at the mouth of Salt River, Ky.
National Banner & Nashville Whig. (Sat., Oct. 7, 1826)

Reinagle, Mr. Hugh. Artist of the American Theatre. Died in New
Orleans.
National Banner & Nashville Daily Advertiser. (Tues., June 24, 1834)

Reinhard, Mr. George. Died at Louisville, Ky.
National Banner. (Sat., July 25, 1829)

Reinhard, Mrs. Susanah. Died at Louisville, Ky.
National Banner & Nashville Whig. (Sat., Oct. 6, 1827)

Renwick, Mr. John. Died at St. Louis.
National Banner & Nashville Daily Advertiser. (Fri., Sept. 7, 1832)

Reno, Mrs. Mary C. Wife of James G. Reno. Esq. Died in Nashville
on the 25th Ult. and on the 8th inst. his infant daughter and only
child.
Nashville Whig. (Sat., May 11, 1844)

Reynolds, Mrs. From Richmond, Va. Died in Nashville, yesterday.
National Banner & Nashville Whig. (Mon., Aug. 23, 1830)

Reynolds, Mrs. Elizabeth G. Died at Cincinnati.
National Banner & Nashville Whig. (Sat., July 22, 1826)

Reynolds, Mr. James. Died in Knox County.
National Banner. (Feb. 3, 1826)

Reynolds, Mrs. Jane B. Consort of Mr. James Reynolds, Merchant of this
Place. Died at Clarksville on the 25th ult.
Impartial Review and Cumberland Repository. (Thurs., Oct. 8, 1807)

Reynolds, Mr. Leroy W. Of Davidson County. Died at Sawannee Old Town
on the 28th.
Nashville Republican. (Mon., Nov. 28, 1836)

Reynolds, Mrs. Mary W. Relict of the late Richard Reynolds. Died
in Williamson County on the 15th inst.
Nashville Whig. (Tuesday, March 24, 1846)

Reynolds, Mr. Obadiah. Died at St. Louis.
National Banner & Nashville Whig. (Sat., Dec. 9, 1826)

Reynolds, Richard Esq. Aged 35- years. Died on Lepers Fork, Williamson County of Cholera.
National Banner & Nashville Whig. (Fri., June 10, 1835)

Reynolds, Mr. Thoma L. In the 21st year of his age. Died in Nashville
on Sunday morning 23d inst.
The Christian Record. (Sat., July 29, 1848)

Reynolds, William. Died in Dickson County, Ten. on Wednesday the
29th of Oct. 1834, in the 71st year of his age.
National Banner & Nashville Whig. (Fri., Oct. 2, 1835)

Rhea, Elizabeth Mrs. Died at her house near Bluntville, in this
Territory, Mrs. Elizabeth Rhea, relict of the late Rev. Joseph Rhea,
of Maryland.
Knoxville Gazette (Thurs., Feb. 13, 1794)

Rhea, Hon. John. For many years a member of Congress from the first
Congressional district in Tennessee. Died on Sunday the 27th of May
at the residence of Mrs. Francis Rhea near Blountsville, Tenn.
National Banner & Nashville Daily Advertiser. (Wed., June 13, 1832)

Rhea, Miss Ruth Jane. Of Tuscumbia. Died at Huntsville, Ala.
National Banner & Nashville Whig. (Sat., July 15, 1826)

Rhea, William. Died on Wednesday, July 15, 1795 Mr. William Rhea of
Knox County, in the 27th year of his age.
Knoxville Gazette (Fri., July 31, 1795)

Rhoades, Private William. Company K. First Regment Tenn. Volunteers.
Died - was killed in the Battle of Monterey with the Mexicans on
Sept. 21st, 1846.
Nashville Whig. (Sat., Oct. 24, 1846)

Rhodes, Mr. Wm. Formerly of North Carolina. Died in Tipton County,
Ten.
National Banner & Nashville Advertiser. (Wed., April 4, 1832)

Rhoton, Mrs. Dr. Died at Versailles, Ky. 14 miles from Lexington,
of Cholera.
National Banner & Nashville Whig. (Fri., Sept. 4, 1835)

Rhoton, Mrs. Juliet. Consort of Dr. Josiah Rhoton. Died in New
Market, Ten.
National Banner & Nashville Whig. (Mon., Oct. 20, 1834)

Rice, Rev. Ebenezer. Age 75 of the Baptist Church. Died in Maury
County.
National Banner & Nashville Whig. (Fri., June 17, 1831)

Rice, Mrs. Elizabeth. Consort of Mr. Joel Rice, of Ala. on 19th inst. Died at the Residence of Maj. J. P. Hickman in Davidson County.
National Banner & Nashville Whig. (Wed., Jan. 26, 1831)

Rice, Mr. Horace. Died in Hawkins County, Tenn. on the 15th ult. in the 34 year of his age.
National Banner & Nashville Daily Advertiser. (Wed., April 4, 1832)

Rice, Mr. John. Of Cincinnati, Ohio. Died in New Orleans.
National Banner & Nashville Daily Advertiser. (Tues., June 24, 1834)

Rice, Rev. John H. D. D. President of the Union Theological Seminary.
Died in Richmond, Va.
National Banner & Nashville Whig. (Fri., Sept. 30, 1831)

Rice, Mrs. Kezia. Age 78. Died in Hawkins County, Ten. on 22d ult.
National Banner & Nashville Advertiser. (Wed., April 4, 1832)

Rice, Col. Nathan. In his 81st year. Died in New Hampshire. A patriot of the Revolution.
National Banner & Nashville Daily Advertiser. (Mon., May 12, 1834)

Rich, Mr. Henry S. Aged 26 years. Died in Monroe County, Ten.
National Banner & Nashville Whig. (Fri., Nov. 21, 1834)

Richards, Mrs. Mary Antonia. Wife of Col. W. C. Richards and daughter of the late C. C. Mayson. Died at Jackson, Miss. on the 19th ulto. in the 21st year of her age.
Nashville Whig. (Sat., Oct. 3, 1846)

Richards, W. P. Died at Cincinnati, Ohio on 13th of Cholera.
National Banner & Nashville Daily Advertiser. (Sat., Oct. 20, 1832)

Richardson, Charles H. Infant son of D. P. and Ellen M. Richardson
Died on the 15th July.
National Banner & Nashville Whig. (Wed., July 26, 1837)

Richardson, David Porter Esq. Died in Houston, Texas on Aug. 12th.
Private Sec'y. to the President.
Daily Republican Banner. (Thurs., Oct. 26, 1837)

Richardson, Dr. J. L. Died at Moulton, Ala.
National Banner. (Sat., Sept. 19, 1829)

Richardson, Mr. Jonas. Of the house of Homer & Richardson. A native of Salem, Mass. Died in Mobile, Ala. of Yellow Fever.
Daily Republican Banner. (Tues., Oct. 1, 1839)

Richardson, Joseph esq. Died in New Lisbon, Ohio.
Nashville Republican & State Gazette. (Tues., July 12, 1831)

Richardson, Mrs. Mary Ann. Died in Fayette County, Ky.
National Banner & Nashville Daily Advertiser. (Mon., Aug. 19, 1833)

Richardson, Mrs. Mary Ann. In the 61st year of her age. Died in Alexandria on Thursday 22d ult. formerly of Nashville, Tenn.
Daily Republican Banner. (Tues., Dec. 11, 1838)

Richardson, Mrs. Mary H. Wife of Samuel Q. Richardson of Frankfort, Ky. Died in Paris, Ky.
National Banner & Nashville Daily Advertiser. (Mon., June 30, 1834)

Richardson, Mr. Moses. In the 26th year of his age. Died in Jackson, Ten.
National Banner & Nashville Whig. (Mon., Aug. 3, 1835)

Richardson, Robert esq. Aged 65 died at Washia, La.
National Banner & Nashville Whig. (Sat., Sept. 15, 1827)

Richardson, Mr. Wm. Died in Maury County.
National Banner. (May 10, 1826)

Richardson, Hon. William M. Chief Justice of the Supreme Court of
New Hamshire. Died -
Daily Republican Banner. (Sat., April 7, 1838)

Richie, Edward Esq. Died on Aug. 20th near Lexington formerly of
Philadelphia.
National Banner & Nashville Daily Advertiser. (Wed., Sept. 3, 1834)

Richie, Mr. Nathaniel D. Died in Jefferson County, Tenn.
National Banner & Nashville Whig. (Sat., Dec. 16, 1826)

Richie, Mrs. Rachel. Formerly of Jefferson County, Ten. Died near
Georgetown, Ill.
National Banner & Nashville Daily Advertiser. (Tues., Aug. 5, 1834)

Richman, Mr. John S. Aged 25. Died in Sumner County, Ten.
National Banner & Nashville Daily Advertiser. (Tues., Aug. 5, 1834)

Richmond, Mrs. Nancy F. Consort of Dr. Andrew Richmond and daughter
of Mr. Richardson Phipps of Davidson County. Died in Wilson County,
Ten. on the 24th Oct. 1831, in the 23d year of her age.
National Banner & Nashville Whig. (Mon., Nov. 7, 1831)

Richmond, Mrs. Nancy F. Wife of Dr. Andrew Richmond. Died in Wilson
County, Tenn.
National Banner & Nashville Whig. (Mon., Nov. 7, 1831)

Rick, Mr. Peter. A native of Germany. Died in New Orleans.
National Banner & Nashville Daily Advertiser. (Tues., June 24, 1834)

Riddit, Mrs. Priscilla A. Wife of Mr. Alfred J. Riddit. Died in
Madison County.
National Banner (Sat., June 27, 1829)

Riddle, James. Died at Versailles, Ky. 14 miles from Lexington of
Cholera.
National Banner & Nashville Whig. (Fri., Sept. 4, 1835)

Riddle, Lewis. Died at Cincinnati, Ohio of Cholera.
National Banner & Nashville Daily Advertiser. (Wed., Oct. 24, 1832)

Riddle, Mrs. Susan. Consort of Mr. E. Riddle. Died in Giles Co.,
Ten.
National Banner & Nashville Daily Advertiser. (Thurs., June 19, 1834)

Rider, John. Of Sumner County. Died at Sea in Oct. on board the
U. S. Steamer American, in Oct.
National Banner & Nashville Whig. (Wed., Nov. 2, 1836)

Ridgely, Charles Esq. Late Governor of that State. Died in Hampton,
Maryland.
National Banner. (Sat., Aug. 8, 1829)

Ridgely, Hon. Nicholas. Chancellor of the State. Died in Delaware.
National Banner & Nashville Whig. (Tuesday April 27, 1830)

Ridgely, Nicholas G. Esq. Died at Baltimore of the house of McDonald
and Ridgely.
National Banner & Nashville Whig. (Fri., Jan. 22, 1830)

Ridley, Capt. George. Aged 98 years. Died a few months ago.
Nashville Republican. (Thurs., April 7, 1836)

Ridley, James Esq. In the 63rd year of his age. Died at his residence in Davidson County, on Monday 30th inst.
The Christian Record. (Sat., Sept. 4, 1847)

Ridley, Mrs. Sarah. We announced only a few months ago, the death of Capt. George Ridley, age 98, one of that hardy race of men who first pierced the wilderness west of the Allegheny Mountains, and who providently lingered almost the last of his brace comrades. He left behind him Mrs. Sarah Ridley. She died of cancer on the ___ day of last month, in the 87th year of her age at the residence of her son Mr. James Ridley in the neighborhood of Nashville.
Nashville Republican. (Thurs., April 7, 1836)

Riggs, Mary Charlotte. Wife of James Riggs Esq. of Philadelphia and only daughter of the late Richard C. Napier. Died in Nashville on Sunday 25th inst.
Nashville Whig. (Wed., July 28, 1841)

Riggs, Overton C. The only son of Gideon Riggs, in Williamson County on the morning of the 30th of December in the 18th year of his age.
Nashville Republican. (Sat., Jan. 9, 1836)

Riggs, Mr. Samuel J. Late of Philadelphia, Pa. and son-in-law of Col. L. P. Cheatham, of Nashville. Died at Tyrees Springs on the 4th inst. aged 36 years.
The Christian Record. (Sat., July 10, 1847)

Rigney, Henry. Died at his residence in this county, on the 30th ult. Age 39. Was a native of Virginia, emigrated to Tennessee and from that State to this. Came to his death by a stab given him on the 5th by one Kennedy, who is in jail and will be tried at the next May term of Court. From the Huntsville Democrat.
National Banner & Nashville Daily Advertiser. (Mon., April 9, 1832)

Riley, Captain James. Died on the 15th of March on board his brig. the William Tell bound to Magadore in the 63d year of his age.
Daily Republican Banner. (Sat., April 18, 1840)

Riley, Mr. Wm. Died in St. Louis, Mo.
National Banner & Nashville Whig. (Sept. 2, 1826)

Ring, Charles Grattan. Oldest son of Dr. L. D. Ring. Died on the morning of the 18th inst.
National Banner & Nashville Whig. (Fri., Sept. 25, 1835)

Ring, Miss Elizabeth. Of Todd County, Ky. Died in Nashville on the 5th inst.
Nashville Union. (Thurs., March 8, 1838)

Ringgold, Alexander. Died 19th at Cincinnati, Ohio of Cholera.
National Banner & Nashville Daily Advertiser. (Fri., Oct. 26, 1832)

Ringland, Mr. C. Formerly of Augusta, Ga. and a Saddler by trade. Died Tuesday the 18th inst. in Robinson County, Ten.
National Banner & Nashville Daily Advertiser. (Wed., Feb. 26, 1834)

Ripley, Dorthea. Died on Friday 23, Dec. at the residence of Wm. Green in Mecklenburg County, Va.
National Banner & Nashville Advertiser. (Wed., Jan. 25, 1831)

Ripley, Gen. Eleazer W. Died at his plantation on the 2nd of March. Clinton Louisianian.
Nashville Union. (Mon., March 18, 1839)

Ripley, Mr. Nathaniel. Died in Cincinnati. Formerly of Plymouth, Mass.
National Banner & Nashville Whig. (Sat., Sept. 2, 1826)

Rising, Mr. Franklin. Died at New Orleans.
National Banner & Nashville Whig. (Sat., Feb. 2, 1828)

Rison, Virginia & Richard. Children of Peter R. Rison. Died in
Franklin, Ten. on the 21st ult.
National Banner & Nashville Daily Advertiser. (Mon., Feb. 11, 1833)

Rison, Virginia and Richard. Children of Peter R. Rison.
The Western Weekly Review. Franklin, Tenn. (Fri., Feb. 8, 1833)

Ritchie, Mrs. Charlotte S. Wife of Dr. James Ritchie. Died at
Lexington, Ky. She was a daughter of John S. Martin, Esq.
National Banner & Nashville Daily Advertiser. (Thurs., May 16, 1833)

Ritner, Lieutenant Joseph. Of the U. S. Army. Died in Pennsylvania.
National Banner & Nashville Daily Advertiser. (Thurs., March 20, 1834)

Rivers, Col. John H. Died in Giles County.
Nashville Republican. (Sat., July 16, 1836)

Rivers, Capt. Thomas. Died in Montgomery County.
National Banner & Nashville Whig. (Sat., Oct. 6, 1827)

Roach, Mary Elizer. Infant daughter of Mr. Benjamin Roach, of Mississippi. Died in Hopkins County, Ky.
National Banner & Nashville Daily Advertiser. (Tues., Aug. 27, 1833)

Roan, Mrs. Ann. Widow of the late Judge Roane. Died in Nashville
at the residence of her son, Dr. James Roane.
National Banner & Nashville Whig. (Fri., April 15, 1831)

Roane, Mrs. Ann. Relict of the late Judge Roane. Died at the residence
of Dr. James Roane.
Nashville Republican & State Gazette. (Thurs., April 14, 1831)

Roane, Mr. David C. Merchant of Big Springs, Ala. Died recently at
the residence of his Mothers in Knox County.
The Nashville Gazette. (Sat., Dec. 23, 1820)

Roane, Dr. James. Died in Nashville of Cholera. Feb. 27th.
National Banner & Nashville Daily Advertiser. (Thurs., Feb. 28, 1833)

Roark, Miss Delilah. Formerly of Surry County, N. C. Died on Sunday
the 28th of Sept. in the 22nd year of her age.
National Banner & Nashville Whig. (Mon., Oct. 20, 1834)

Roane, John Sen. Esq. Of King William County, in the 74th year of
his age. Died in Virginia (from Lynchburg Virginian)
Nashville Union. (Mon., Jan. 7, 1839)

Robb, Mr. James. Died in Memphis. National Banner & Nashville
Daily Advertiser. (Mon., June 17, 1833)

Robb, Mr. Washington S. Died in Jefferson County, Ky.
National Banner (Sat., Sept. 5, 1829)

Robert, Mrs. Ann Eliza T. Consort of Alexis J. Robert, aged 20 years
and 2 months. Died in Nashville on Friday the 6th inst.
Nashville Whig. (Wed., March 11, 1840)

Robert, The Hermit. Aged 70. Died at his Hermitage, near Washington
Bridge.
National Banner & Nashville Advertiser. (Wed., April 18, 1832)

Robert, Julia Isabell. Infant daughter of Alexis J. and Mary A. Robert.
Died in Nashville yesterday the 18th inst.
The Christian Record. (Sat., Dec. 26, 1846)

Roberts, A. J. Son of Samuel Roberts. Died in Knoxville, Tenn.
Daily Republican Banner. (Sat., Oct. 6, 1838)

Roberts, Mr. Alfred. Died in Logan County.
National Banner & Nashville Whig. (Sat., Oct. 7, 1826)

Roberts, Mrs. Ann. Died in Franklin County, Ky.
National Banner & Nashville Whig. (Sat., Feb. 10, 1827)

Roberts, Capt. Charles. Of Henry County, Tenn. Died at New Orleans.
National Banner & Nashville Daily Advertiser. (Wed., March 6, 1833)

Roberts, Dr. Of Manchester, Vermont. Died at Natchez by shooting
himself.
National Banner & Nashville Whig. (Mon., July 25, 1836)

Roberts, Mrs. Elizabeth. Wife of Mr. Samuel Roberts. Died in Knoxville.
National Banner & Nashville Whig. (Sat., Feb. 23, 1828)

Roberts, Elijah Esq. Son of General Roberts of Maury County. Died
on Wednesday evening.
The Nashville Whig. (Feb. 7, 1816)

Roberts, James. From Perry County. Died in Tenn. Penitentiary of
Cholera.
National Banner & Nashville Whig. (Fri., Aug. 14, 1835)

Roberts, Mr. James Madison. Second son of Mr. Samuel Roberts aged
25 years. Died in Knoxville, Ten.
National Banner & Nashville Whig. (Fri., Jan. 23, 1835)

Roberts, Josedeck. Died in Knoxville, Tenn.
Daily Republican Banner. (Sat., Oct. 6, 1838)

Roberts, Josiah Esq. Age 68 years. Died in Sevier County.
National Banner & Nashville Daily Advertiser. (Tues., Sept. 16, 1834)

Roberts, Julia Isabell. Infant daughter of Alexis J. and Mary A.
Roberts. Died in Nashville the 18th inst.
Nashville Whig. (Sat., Dec. 19, 1846)

Roberts, Mrs. Wife of Jezedach Roberts. Died in Knoxville, Tenn.
Daily Republican Banner. (Sat., Sept. 29, 1838)

Roberts, Pamelia. Daughter of the Rev. L. C. Roberts. Died at
Shelbyville, Miss.
National Banner (May 20, 1826)

Roberts, Mrs. Susan. Aged 69, died in Logan County.
National Banner & Nashville Whig. (Sat., Oct. 7, 1826)

Roberts, Miss Susan E. Died in Logan County, Ky.
National Banner & Nashville Whig. (Sat., Oct. 6, 1827)

Roberts, Dr. Thomas H. Died at New Albany, Ind.
National Banner & Nashville Whig. (Sat., April 21, 1827)

Roberts, Mr. William B. Formerly of New York. Died in Mobile, Ala.
of Yellow fever.
Daily Republican Banner.(Tues., Oct. 1st., 1839)

Robertson, Alfred Balch. Died yesterday at the residence of Mr. Snell,
six miles north of Nashville.
Daily Republican Banner. (Fri., May 4, 1838)

Robertson, Doctor Benjamin F. Departed this life at his place of
residence in the county of Maury on 1st of this instant in his 27th
year.
Nashville Whig. (Nov. 22, 1825)

Robertson, Col. C. Died Jan. 28th by drowning in Harpeth River.
Nashville Republican (Thurs., Feb. 18, 1836)

Robertson, Col. C. Drowned in Harpeth River, on 23rd January, Col.
C. Robertson of Dickson County, an enterprising and industrious
citizen, who has left numerous friends and relations - an only son and
a disconsolate wife to lament his untimely death. He was a good
master, an indulgent father, a kind and affectionate husband.
Nashville Republican. (Thurs., Feb. 18, 1836)

Robertson, Mrs. Catherine. Relict of the late Duncan Robinson Esq.
Died in Nashville on the 15th inst.
National Banner & Nashville Daily Advertiser. (Tues., Aug. 19, 1834)

Robertson, Mrs. Charlotte. The aged Mother of Dr. Felix Robertson
and relict of Gen. James Robertson.
Nashville Whig. (Thurs., June 15, 1843)

Robertson, Mr. Duncan. Bookseller. Died in Nashville on Wednesday
May 1st. in the sixty third year of his age.
National Banner & Nashville Daily Advertiser. (Thurs., May 2, 1833)

Robertson, Mrs. Elizabeth. Aged 71 widow of Wm. Robertson, Esq. and
Mother of the late Thomas Bolling Robertson, former governor of
Louisianna. Died at Richmond, Va.
National Banner & Nashville Whig. (Thurs., Sept. 2, 1830)

Robertson, Facomba K. Infant daughter of Mr. Duncan Robertson. Died
in Nashville on Thursday last (Jan. 30, 1806)
Impartial Review and Cumberland Repository. (Sat., Feb. 1, 1806)

Robertson, Mr. George S. Died in New Orleans on 19th March. A printer
of Pittsburgh and late junior editor of the Louisville Focus.
National Banner & Nashville Daily Advertiser. (Mon., April 2, 1832)

Robertson, Henry P. U. S. N. Son of Dr. Peyton Robertson of
Davidson County. Died at Brooklin, N. Y. on the 10th inst. in the
21st year of his age.
Nashville Union. (Wed., Feb. 27, 1839)

Robertson, Jacobina M. Infant daughter of Duncan Robertson of this
place. (Nashville) Died on Thursday last.
Impartial Review & C. R. (Feb. 1, 1806)

Robertson, Dr. James B. Son of Dr. Felix Robertson of Nashville.
Died in Jackson, Miss.
Nashville Republican. (Sat., Sept. 24, 1836)

Robertson, Mr. James H. Died in Hardeman County.
National Banner & Nashville Whig. (Fri., April 29, 1831)

Robertson, Mrs. Joana. In this city on the 29th inst., Mrs. Joana
Robertson in the 38th year of her age consort of Col. A. C.
Robertson formerly of Overton.
Nashville Republican, (Sat., Dec. 31, 1836)

Robertson, Mr. John. Died at Selma, Ala.
National Banner & Nashville Whig. (Sat., Jan. 12, 1828)

Robertson, Mr. Joseph W. Died at the residence of James Woods Esq.
in Nashville on Friday 5th inst.
Nashville Whig. (Tues., Aug. 9, 1842)

Robertson, Mrs. Lydia. Consort of Dr. Felix Robertson. Died in
Nashville on the 13th inst.
National Banner & Nashville Daily Advertiser. (Mon., Nov. 19, 1832)

Robertson, Melissa. Consort of Mr. John Robertson. Died in Bedford
County, Tenn.
National Banner & Nashville Daily Advertiser. (Wed., March 26, 1834)

Robertson, Dr. Peyton. Died in this Davidson County, yesterday.
Daily Republican Banner. (Fri., Sept. 18, 1840)

Robertson, Richard Jonas. Aged 10 years. Son of Capt. H. Robertson.
Died in Lincoln City, Tenn.
National Banner & Nashville Whig. (Mon., Oct. 20, 1834)

Robertson, Robert. Son of Mr. John Robertson. Died in Bedford County
just two days after his Mother died.
National Banner & Nashville Daily Advertiser. (Wed., March 26, 1834)

Robertson, Hon. Thomas Bolling. U. S. District Judge of La. Died at
the Sulpher Springs, Virginia.
National Banner & Nashville Whig. (Sat., Nov. 1, 1828)

Robertson, Private William H. Of Company C. Died was killed in the
Battle of Monterey with the Mexican on the 21st of Sept.
Nashville Whig. (Sat., Oct. 24, 1846)

Robeson, Moses, Sen. Aged 68 years 6 months and 20 days. Died in
Madison County, Ten.
National Banner & Nashville Whig. (Fri., March 13, 1835)

Robeson, Gen. William L. A native of North Caroline. Died in New
Orleans on the 15th June.
National Banner & Nashville Whig. (Mon., June 29, 1835)

Robins, Mrs. Anne. Aged 88 years. Died in Wilkes City, N. C.
National Banner & Nashville Daily Advertiser. (Sat., Aug. 10, 1833)

Robinson, Mrs. Ann. Died in Mason County, Ky.
National Banner. (March 24, 1826)

Robinson, Mrs. Elizabeth. Wife of Hiram D. Robinson, Esq. Died in
Rutherford County, Ten.
National Banner & Nashville Daily Advertiser. (Mon., Nov. 25, 1833)

Robinson, Mr. J. Black. Merchant, formerly of Fayette County, Ky.
Died in Nashville on Saturday last of consumption.
Nashville Whig. (Wed., June 26, 1839)

Robinson, Mr. Joshua. Died at Smithville.
National Banner & Nashville Whig. (Sat., July 22, 1826)

Robinson, Mr. Littleberry. Died in Logan County, Ky.
National Banner & Nashville Whig. (Mon., Jan. 5, 1835)

Robinson, Hon. Peter. A Judge of the Superior Court of Delaware. Died
in Delaware.
The Union. (Sat., June 18, 1836)

Robinson, Hon. Peter. A Judge of the Superior Court of Delaware.
Died in Deleware.
The Union. (Sat., June 18, 1836)

Robinson, Mr. Samuel. Died in Madison County, Ky.
National Banner & Nashville Whig. (Sat., Sept. 9, 1826)

Robinson, Maj. Tully. Died in St. Francisville, La.
Nashville Republican & State Gazette. (Thurs., March 17, 1831)

Robinson, Mr. William. Aged 24. Died in Nashville on Wed. night 8th inst. He was a native of England.
National Banner & Nashville Daily Advertiser. (Fri., May 10, 1833)

Robison, Mary. Wife of Moses Robenson, dec'd. Died in Madison County, Ten. within 12 hours of her husband aged 68 years lacking 3 days.
National Banner & Nashville Whig. (Fri., March 13, 1835)

Rochester, Dr. E. Died in Danville, Ky. of Cholera.
National Banner & Nashville Daily Advertiser. (Mon., Aug. 5, 1833)

Rochester, Margaret Ann. Daughter of W. H. Rochester, aged 5 years, four months and 25 days. Died near Bowling Green, Ky.
National Banner & Nashville Daily Advertiser. (Mon., Aug. 12, 1833)

Rochester, Col. Nathaniel. Died in Rochester, N. Y.
Nashville Republican & State Gazette. (Sat., June 4, 1831)

Rochester, Mr. William. Died near Bowling Green, Ky. Killed by a fall from his horse.
National Banner & Nashville Daily Advertiser. (Sat., Aug. 2, 1834)

Rodes, Mr. Clifton, aged 59. Died in Barren County, Ky.
National Banner & Nashville Whig. (Sat., Feb. 16, 1828)

Rodgers, John Esq. Died at the residence of Randall McGavock Esq. in Williamson County, Aug. 30, aged 90 years. Obituary.
The Union. (Thursday, Sept. 8, 1836)

Roe, Mrs. Mary M. Died at Cincinnati.
National Banner. (May 13, 1826)

Rogers, Mrs. Consort of Major Samul J. Rogers 35. Died in Pulaski, on June 7, of Cholera.
National Banner & Nashville Daily Advertiser. (Wed., June 19, 1833)

Rogers, Mr. Amos M. A member of the medical class in Transylvania University. Died at Lexington, Ky.
National Banner & Nashville Daily Advertiser. (Fri., March 9, 1832)

Rogers, Mr. Edmund. In the 82nd year of his age. Died in Barren County, Kentucky on the 28th ult. He was a Revolutionary soldier.
Nashville Whig. (Thurs., Sept. 14, 1843)

Rogers, Frederick J. Late a door keeper of the House of Representative of this State. Died in Bledsoe County.
National Banner & Nashville Daily Advertiser. (Mon., Feb. 24, 1834)

Rogers, Mr. George. Of Cincinnati. Died on Sat. the 10th inst.
(N. O. Bulletin)
National Banner & Nashville Whig. (Fri., Jan. 6, 1837)

Rogers, Mr. Harden J. Died in Hardeman County.
National Banner & Nashville Whig. (Wed., Oct. 12, 1831)

Rogers, James F. Second son of John A. Rogers Esq. Died suddenly on Wednesday the 10th inst. He was 20 years old. (Rogersville E. Tenn.)
Nashville Whig. (Mon., July 22, 1839)

Rogers, Com. John. Died in Philadelphia Aug. 1st. and was buried on Aug. 3d with military honors.
Nashville Whig. (Mon., Aug. 13, 1838)

Rogers, Dr. Joseph. Son of Col. Joseph Rogers. Died in Rogersville.
National Banner & Nashville Daily Advertiser. (Fri., June 14, 1833)

Rogers, Mr. Joseph. Died in Scott County, Ky.
National Banner & Nashville Whig. (Fri., July 11, 1828)

Rogers, Mrs. Margaret. Wife of Mr. Linton Rogers. Died at Chambers-
burg on Sat., Aug. 9, just a few hours after her marriage, age 16.
Daughter of Mr. William Mackey.
National Banner & Nashville Daily Advertiser. (Sat., Sept. 6, 1834)

Rogers, Mr. Mathew. Of Jackson, County. Died in Smith County.
National Banner & Nashville Advertiser. (Fri., June 22, 1832)

Rogers, Samuel. Inkeeper. Died in Cincinnati, Ohio of the Cholera.
National Banner & Nashville Daily Advertiser. (Thurs., Oct. 18, 1832)

Rogers, Dr. W. An old and respectable physician. Died in New Orleans.
National Banner & Nashville Daily Advertiser. (Sat., Sept. 13, 1834)

Rogers, Capt. William H. Of the Texas Volunteers, a native of Fayetteville, Tenn. Died in Texas.
Nashville Republican (Tues., Jan. 24, 1832)

Roland, Miss Margaret. Eldest daughter of Mr. Hugh Roland in the 16th
year of her age. Died in Nashville on Wednesday last.
National Banner & Nashville Whig. (Fri., July 29, 1831)

Roland, Richard. Infant son of Mr. Hugh Roland. Died in this town.
National Banner & Nashville Whig. (Fri., June 27, 1828)

Rollins, Mr. Andrew. Of Green County, Tenn. Died in Greenville,
S. C.
Nashville Union. (Fri., Dec. 20, 1839)

Roots, Mrs. Died in Knoxville, on Sunday evening.
Daily Republican Banner. (Sat., Oct. 20, 1838)

Roper, Hon. William B. Judge of the Maysivlle Judicial Circuit. Died
in Flemingsburg, Ky.
National Banner & Nashville Daily Advertiser. (Tues., Aug. 27, 1833)

Roscoe, William Esq. Died yesterday at his residence in the 79th
year of his age. (Liverpool Mercery)
National Banner & Nashville Whig. (Wed., Aug. 31, 1831)

Rose, Miss Almedy. Died in Jackson.
Nashville Whig. (Tues., April 21, 1846)

Rose, David J. New Orleans, a Passenger. Died on the Steamer
George Collier about 80 miles below Natches, scalded to death.
Daily Republican Banner. (Tuesday, May 14, 1839)

Rose, Maj. Neil B. In the 58th year of his age. Died on the 28th
a native of N. C. and an early settler of Huntsville, Ala.
Daily Republican Banner. (Tues., March 6, 1838)

Rose, Dr. Robert H. Died in Shelby County, Ten.
National Banner & Nashville Daily Advertiser. (Tues., Aug. 27, 1833)

Ross, Mrs. Amelia. Consort of J. F. Ross, died in Mobile.
National Banner & Nashville Whig. (Sat., Sept. 16, 1826)

Ross, Mr. Christopher C. Died at Indianapolis.
National Banner & Nashville Whig. (Sat., Sept. 1, 1827)

Ross, Mrs. Elizabeth. Consort of Thomas Ross, Esq. Died in Marshall
County, Tenn. aged 30 years.
Nashville Republican. (Tues., April 11, 1837)

Ross, Hon. James F. Died in Charleston, Indiana. Judge of the second Judicial Circuit of that State.
National Banner & Nashville Daily Advertiser. (Thurs., June 19, 1834)

Ross, Mrs. Martha. Consort of Rev. Thomas Ross. Died eight miles north of Dresden, Weakley County, in the 61st year of her life.
National Banner & National Whig. (Mon., Sept. 22, 1834)

Ross, Mrs. Martha Claiborne. Wife of Capt. Daniel Ross, age 23. Died in Davidson County.
Impartial Review and Cumberland Repository. (Sat., April 5, 1806)

Ross, Mrs. Nancy. Aged 65 years. Consort of Rev. Thomas Ross. Died near Dresden, Ten. on Sat., 18th inst.
National Banner & Nashville Whig. (Mon., March 6, 1837)

Ross, Rev. O. B. Of the Methodist Church. Editor of the Gospel Herald Died in Lexington, Ky.
National Banner & Nashville Whig. (Mon., Aug. 15, 1831)

Ross, V. Died at Versailles, Ky. 13 miles from Lexington, Ky. of Cholera.
National Banner & Nashville Whig. (Fri., Sept. 4, 1835)

Roszel, Rev. Stephen George. One of the oldest ministers of the Baltimore Conference of Methodist Conference. Died in Leesburg County, Va. on Friday last.
Nashville Whig. (Fri., May 8, 1841)

Roth, A little girl, age 2 yrs old. Died in Florence, Ala. See paper for notice of accident.
National Banner & Nashville Daily Advertiser. (Mon., March 19, 1832)

Roudet, Mr. Cornelle. A native of France, but far many years a citizen of Mobile. Died in Mobile, Ala. of Yellow fever, aged about 50.
Daily Republican Banner. (Tues., Oct. 1, 1839)

Roulston, Mrs. E. Died in Davidson County.
National Banner & Nashville Advertiser. (Mon., Nov. 19, 1832)

Roulston, George. Died Aug. 10, 1804.

Rountree, Mr. Chesley B. Died in Lauderdale County, Ala.
National Banner & Nashville Daily Advertiser. (Tues., March 19, 1833)

Rowan, Col. Atkinson Hill. Second son of the Hon. John Rowan. Died at Federal Hill near Bardstown, Ky. of Cholera.
National Banner & Nashville Daily Advertiser. (Sat., Aug. 10, 1833)

Rowan, Mrs. Eliza. Consort of Capt. Wm. L. Rowan. Died at Federal Hill near Bardstown, Ky. of Cholera.
National Banner & Nashville Daily Advertiser. (Sat., Aug. 10, 1833)

Rowan, Captain William L. Eldest son of Hon. John Rowan. Died Federal Hill, near Bardstown, Ky. on the 26of July, of Cholera.
National Banner & Nashville Daily Advertiser. (Sat., Aug. 10, 1833)

Rowe, Mrs. M. A. Consort of the Rev. James Rowe. Died on Monday morning at 9 o'clock, 18th inst. she was a native of Lexington, Ky.
National Banner & Nashville Daily Advertiser. (Tues., Dec. 3, 1833)

Rowland, Mr. Robert. Died in Madison County, Ky.
National Banner. (Sat., July 25, 1829)

Rowle, William. A distinguished member of the bar. Died lately at Philadelphia.
The Union. (Tuesday, April 26, 1836)

Royster, Mr. Granderson C. Of Mecklenburg County, Va. Died at Knoxville,
National Banner & Nashville Advertiser. (Mon., January 23, 1832)

Ruby, Mrs. Polly. Wife of Leonard Ruby. Died in the vicinity of Sommersville.
Nashville Whig. (Thurs., March 19, 1846)

Ruckel, Miss Rebecca. Eldest daughter of Mr. John W. Ruckel. Died in Fayette County, Ky.
National Banner & Nashville Whig. (Fri., March 6, 1835)

Rucker, Mr. Barnett. A day watchman . Died in Lexington, Ky. from the Cholera.
National Banner & Nashville Daily Advertiser. (Mon., June 10, 1833)

Rucker, Mrs. Wife of Mr. Benjamin Rucker. Died in Rutherford County, on the 17th inst.
National Banner & Nashville Whig. (Fri., Dec. 9, 1831)

Rucker, Major Elliot. An officer of the Revolutionary Army, aged 77 years. Died in Shelby County, Ky.
National Banner & Nashville Daily Advertiser. (Fri., March 30, 1832)

Rucker, Gideon Esq. Of Rutherford County. Died in Minnville.
National Banner & Nashville Whig. (Sat., Aug. 19, 1826)

Ruckholt, Captain Jacob. Aged 70 a soldier of the Revolution. Died in Amite County, Miss.
National Banner & Nashville Whig. (Sat., Aug. 12, 1826)

Rucks, Rev. Josiah. Died in Smith County on the 5th inst. in the 80th year of his age.
National Banner & Nashville Whig. (Mon., Aug. 15, 1836)

Rucks, Mary W. Infant daughter of James C. Rucks esq. Died in Nashville.
Nashville Republican & State Gazette . (Thurs., June 16, 1831)

Rudd, Mr. Herod. Aged 91. Died in M'Minn County.
National Banner. (Sat , July 11, 1829)

Ruffin, Mrs. Ellen V. Consort of William Ruffin Esq. Died at Clifton, Hardeman County, on the 27th of Aug.
National Banner & Nashville Daily Advertiser. (Sat., Sept. 6, 1834)

Rule, Mr. Press G. Died at Newport, Mo.
National Banner & Nashville Whig. (Thurs., Aug. 19, 1830)

Runkle, Mrs. Nancy. Died in Nashville on Tuesday the 10th inst.
National Banner & Nashville Daily Advertiser. (Fri., Jan. 13, 1832)

Runkle, Mr. Samuel. Died in Memphis.
National Banner & Nashville Daily Advertiser. (Mon., June 24, 1833)

Runnels, Col. Hardin D. Aged 59. Died in Madison County, Miss. one of the first settlers of the county.
Nashville Whig. (Wed., July 10, 1839)

Rush, Julia Roberts. Daughter and only child of Doctor William Rush Died at Pine Grove near Philadelphia.
National Banner & Nashville Daily Advertiser. (Fri., July 25, 1834)

Rush, Mrs. Mary Ursula. Consort of William L. Rush and eldest daughter of Nimrod R. Selser, late of Washington County, Miss. aged 22 years. Died in Lake Providence, La.
National Banner & Nashville Daily Advertiser. (Sat., Aug. 10, 1833)

323

Rush, William. In the 77th year of his age. Died in Philadelphia, on the 17th ult.
National Banner & Nashville Daily Advertiser. (Thurs., Feb. 7, 1833)

Rushbook, Mr. Robert. Died in Madison County, Ky.
National Banner. (Sat., April 25, 1829)

Rushing, Mrs. Jane. In Dickson County, Tenn., 3rd Nov. late consort of D. Rushing.
Nashville Republican. (Tues., Jan. 19, 1836)

Rushing, Richard. A soldier of the revolution. Died in Perry County in the 96th year of his age.
Nashville Whig. (Mon., Nov. 1, 1841)

Russ, Mr. Jonas. Died in Maury County.
National Banner & Nashville Whig. (Mon., Oct. 4, 1830)

Russell, Mr. Manager of the Camp St. Theatre. Died in New Orleans on the 19th inst.
Daily Republican Banner. (Sat., May 26, 1838)

Russell, Mrs. Ann M. Wife of Capt. Thomas A. Russell. Died in Fayette County, Ky.
National Banner & Nashville Whig. (Sat., June 14, 1828)

Russell, Miss Caroline. Age 19. Died in Monroe County.
National Banner & Nashville Advertiser. (Mon., Nov. 12, 1832)

Russell, Mrs. Hannah. Aged 65. Died near Louisville.
National Banner & Nashville Whig. (Sat., Sept. 16, 1826)

Russell, James Garrard. Infant son of Maj. Thos. A. Russell. Died in Fayette County, Ky.
National Banner & Nashville Daily Advertiser. (Mon., Aug. 19, 1833)

Russell, Major John. Died at Knoxville.
The Nashville Whig. and Tenn. Advertiser. (Dec. 15, 1817)

Russell, Maj. John. Aged 65 years. Died at his residence in Henry Cty, Kentucky, on Sunday the 31st. December last.
The Clarion & Tennessee Gazette. (Jan. 23, 1821)
(From the St. Louis Enquirer of Jan. 6)

Russell, Mr. John. Died in Pittsburg, Pa.
Nashville Republican & State Gazette. (Sat., June 4, 1831)

Russell, Mr. John. Aged 25. Died in Lincoln County on the 20th
National Banner & Nashville Whig. (Thurs., May 27, 1830)

Russell, Hon. Jonathan. Age 60. Died at Milton, near Boston.
National Banner & Nashville Advertiser. (Thurs., March 8, 1832)

Russell, Mrs. Mary R. Consort of Rev. George Russell. Died in Knox County on Sunday last, aged 25 years.
Daily Republican Banner. (Sat., Oct. 20, 1838)

Russell, Mr. Samuel. Died in Hopkins County, Ky.
National Banner & Nashville Whig. (Sat., Oct. 28, 1826)

Russell, Rev. Samuel. Minister of the Gospel in the Cumberland Presbyterian Church. Died near Tuscaloosa, Ala. on the 27th Jan.
National Banner & Nashville Daily Advertiser. (Thurs., Feb. 13, 1834)

Russell, Mr. Wm. Died in Lawrence County, Ark.
National Banner & Nashville Whig. (Sat., Jan. 13, 1827)

Rust, David Esq. Died in St. Stephens, Ala. formerly of New York.
National Banner & Nashville Whig. (Sept. 2, 1826)

Ruter, Rev. Dr. Martin. An eminent Divine and well known in the United States. Died in Texas.
Daily Republican Banner. (Thurs., June 19, 1838)

Rutherford, Mr. James. Aged 77. Died in Giles County.
National Banner & Nashville Daily Advertiser. (Wed., Oct. 3, 1832)

Rutherford, Mr. Joseph. Aged 29 years. Died near Little Rock, Ark.
National Banner & Nashville Whig. (Mon., Jan. 5, 1835)

Rutherford, Mrs. Nancy. Of Alabama, aged 59. Died near Milledgeville, Ga.
National Banner & Nashville Whig. (Sat., Sept. 9, 1826)

Rutherford, Mrs. Nancy. Consort of Mr. Benjamin S. Rutherford. Died in Sumner County on the 14th inst.
National Banner & Nashville Daily Advertiser. (Fri., May 24, 1833)

Ruths, David. Child of G. W. Ruths. Died in Shelbyville, Tenn. of Cholera.
National Banner & Nashville Daily Advertiser. (Thurs., July 11, 1833)

Ruths, Mary. Child of G. W. Ruths. Died at Shelbyville, Tenn. of Cholera.
National Banner & Nashville Daily Advertiser. (Thurs., July 11, 1833)

Ruths, Platina. Daughter of G. W. Ruths. Died in Shelbyville, Tenn. of Cholera.
National Banner & Nashville Daily Advertiser. (Thurs., July 11, 1833)

Rutland, Abednego. Aged 85. Died in Wilson County on the 17th ult. at the residence of his son Joseph Rutland was a soldier of the revolution.
Nashville Whig. (Thurs., Dec. 7, 1843)

Rutledge, Major Henry M. The only son of Hon. Edward Rutledge. Died at the residence of his son-in-law Francis B. Fogg, Esq.
Nashville Whig. (Tues., Jan. 23, 1844)

Ryan, Joseph J. Esq. Of Bertee County, N. C. Died at Clarksville, Montgomery County, on Wednesday 13th inst.
National Banner & Nashville Whig. (Fri., Jan. 22, 1836)

Ryburn, Mrs. Eliza. Wife of Matthew Ryburn Esq. Died in Montgomery County on the 11th inst.
National Banner & Nashville Whig. (June 14, 1826)

Sabin, Mr. Charles. A native of New England. Died in the Parish of Lafourche Interior, La.
National Banner & Nashville Daily Advertiser. (Thurs., Aug. 8, 1833)

Saffarans, Mrs. Elizabeth. Wife of David Saffarans. Died in the vicinity of Nashville on the 2nd inst. in the 36th year of her age.
The Christian Record. (Sat., Dec. 9, 1848)

Saffrans, Mrs. Catharine. Aged 70. Died at Hopkinsville.
National Banner & Nashville Whig. (Thurs., Aug. 5, 1830)

Salkeld, Geo. Esq. His Britanie Majesty Consul, aged 66. Died in New Orleans.
National Banner & Nashville Daily Advertiser. (Wed., May 7, 1834)

Saltonstall, Mr. Gilbert. Formerly of New London, Connecticut, aged 42 years. Died in Tuscaloosa, Ala.
National Banner & Nashville Daily Advertiser. (Fri., Feb. 15, 1833)

Saltonstall, Dr. Gurdon. Formerly of N. Y. Died in Tuscaloosa, Ala.
National Banner & Nashville Daily Advertiser. (Mon., Aug. 25, 1834)

Sample, Mr. John. and Col. Thomas T. Maury. Both of Franklin. These gentlemen were afflicted with a pulmonary disease and were on a voyage for the purpose of repairing their health. Died at sea in April last.
The Nashville Whig. (June 16, 1817)

Sample, Mrs. Parthania. Wife of Mr. James Sample. Died in Florence, Ala.
National Banner & Nashville Daily Advertiser. (Mon., Aug. 25, 1834)

Sample, Captain Robert. Aged 76 years. Was a native of Bucks County, Pennsylvania. Died on Friday night last. after a short illness.
Nashville Whig. (June 30, 1823)

Sampson, Charles. With the Second Tenn. Regiment. Died was killed in the Battle of Seirra Gorda, with the Mexicans.
The Politicians and Weekley Nashville Whig. (Fri., May 21, 1847)

Sampson, William. Counsellor at law, aged 73 years. Died at New York on Thursday evening last. He was a native of Ireland.
Nashville Republican. (Tues., Jan. 19, 1837)

Samuel, Miss Eliza G. Daughter of Larkin Samuel. Died in Frankfort, Ky. of Cholera.
National Banner & Nashville Daily Advertiser. (Sat., Aug. 17, 1833)

Samuel, Mr. Ethelbert. Died in Giles County.
National Banner & Nashville Whig. (Sat., Oct. 4, 1828)

Samuel, Reuben. Died - Franklin County, Ky.
National Banner & Nashville Advertiser. (Fri., Jan. 27, 1832)

Samuel, Mr. Ulysses. Died in Giles County.
National Banner & Nashville Whig. (Tues., April 27, 1830)

Sandeford, Joseph A. Of Shelby County, Tennessee. Died on the 20th age 26 years.
Nashville Republican. (Tues., March 8, 1836)

Sanders, Mrs. Ann. Consort of Mr. Charles H. Sanders. Died on March 30th.
National Banner & Nashville Whig. (Fri., April 1, 1836)

Sanders, Mrs. Barbara F. Wife of John W. Sanders. Died in Louisville, Ky.
National Banner & Nashville Whig. (Sat., Jan. 31, 1829)

Sanders, Dr. Bennett P. Died at Rodney, Miss. on the 5th inst.
National Banner & Nashville Daily Advertiser. (Tues., July 17, 1832)

Sanders, Holloway Esq. of McNairy County. Died in Calhoun.
National Banner & Nashville Whig. (Wed., March 9, 1831)

Sanders, Mr. James. Died in Haywood County.
National Banner & Nashville Whig. (Wed., Nov. 2, 1831)

Sanders, James Esq. Aged 72 years. Died in Sumner County.
Nashville Republican (Thurs., Sept. 1, 1836)

Sanders, Maj. Richard. A soldier of the revolution. Died in Wilson County, Ten.
National Banner & Nashville Daily Advertiser. (Mon., March 3, 1834)

Sanders, Mr. Robert H. Died in Nashville.
Ntional Banner & Nashville Whig. (Fri., Jan. 1st. 1830)

Sanders, Mr. Taliaferro. Aged about 45 years. Died in Fayette Co., Ky.
National Banner & Nashville Whig. (Fri., March 6, 1835)

Sanders, Mr. Wm. Sen. Died in Sumner County.
National Banner & Nashville Whig. (Sat., Dec. 20, 1828)

Sanford, Mrs. Cornelia L. Wife of Mr. Thaddeus Sandford, editor of
the Commercial Register. Died in Mobile.
National Banner & Nashville Whig. (Mon., Aug. 15, 1831)

Sandford, Henrietta. Infant daughter of R. W. Sandford Esq. aged
eight months and 28 days. Died in Covington, Ten. on the 28th ult.
National Banner & Nashville Daily Advertiser. (Fri., Oct. 11, 1833)

Sandford, Col. James T. In Maury County.
Nashville Republican and State Gazette. (Thurs., Dec. 23, 1830)

Sandford, Hon. Nathan. For many years a Senator in Congress. Died in
New York.
Daily Republican Banner. (Wed., Oct. 31, 1838)

Sandford, Mr. Richard C. Aged 17 years. Died in Covington.
National Banner & Nashville Whig. (Fri., Feb. 19, 1830)

Sandors, Dr. Lewis. Of Smithville, Ky. Died in Smithville, Ky. On
the 25th ult. was shot dead by a man named Aston.
Nashville Republican (Thurs., Jan. 21, 1836)

Sandridge, Mr. M. C. Formerly of Greenburgh, Ky. Died at Louisville,
Ky.
National Banner & Nashville Advertiser. (Tues., July 3, 1832)

Sands, Col. P. M. One of the principal clerks in the Post Office here.
Died in Nashville on Sunday evening last.
Nashville Whig. (Tues., April 14, 1846)

Sannover, Mr. J. Died at Florence, Ala.
National Banner & Nashville Whig. (Mon., Nov. 7, 1831)

Sansom, Dr. Dorrell N. Died at his residence in Mount Pleasant of
consumption.
National Banner & Nashville Daily Advertiser. (Wed., May 7)

Sappington, Mrs. Susannah. Relict of the late Dr. Roger H. Sappington
of Nashville. Died at Memphis on the 19th inst.
Daily Republican Banner. (Thurs., June 28, 1838)

Sargent, Dr. Thomas F. Minister of the Methodist Church. Died in
Cincinnati, on the 29th Jan.
National Banner & Nashville Daily Advertiser. (Thurs., Feb. 13, 1834)

Satterfield, William P. Esq. Died in Russellville, Ky.
National Banner & Nashville Whig. (Thurs., June 17, 1830)

Saudek, Mrs. Nancy E. Wife of Dr. J. Saudek. Died on Thursday last
the 18th inst. near Sycamore, in Robertson County in the 26th year of
her age.
The Politician & Weekly Nashville Whig. (Fri., Jan. 28, 1848)

Saul, Mrs. Bienaimee. Wife of T. S. Saul Esq. of Opelouses. Died in
New Orleans.
National Banner & Nashville Whig. (Sat., June 2, 1827)

Saunders, Mr. Americus. Son of Mr. Thomas G. Saunders. Died in
Gallatin.
National Banner & Nashville Whig. (Thurs., July 29, 1830)

Saunders, Mrs. Ann. Wife of Mr. Charles L. Saunders. Died in Nashville.
Nashville Republican. (Sat., April 2, 1836)

Saunders, David M. Esq. Son of James Saunders Esq. Died at Gallatin.
National Banner & Nashville Whig. (Fri., May 8, 1835)

Saunders, Mrs. H. Elizabeth. Wife of Mr. D. T. Saunders, of Sumner
County and daughter of Capt. John Canfield of Robertson Co. at the
age of 21 years. Died Friday the 9th of June 1837.
The Union. (Tues., June 27, 1837)

Saunders, Rev. Hubbard. A local preacher in the Methodist Church for
37 years. Died on Tuesday morning 7th inst.
National Banner. (Sat., Sept. 12, 1829)

Saunders, Joseph. Of Hart County, Ky. Died in the loss of the Steam
Boat Brandywine.
National Banner & Nashville Daily Advertiser. (Mon., April 23, 1832)

Saunders, Mr. Junius M. C. Son of Wm. Saunders Esq. Died in this
county on Monday night 11th inst. in the 20th year of his age.
National Banner. (Sat., May 16, 1829)

Saunders, Mrs. Mary. Formerly of Hartford, Con. Died at St. Louis.
National Banner & Nashville Daily Advertiser. (Mon., Sept. 10, 1832)

Saunders, Mrs. Mary. Formerly of Hartford, Conn. Died in St. Louis.
National Banner & Nashville Daily Gazette. (Mon., Sept. 10, 1832)

Saunders, Mrs. Mary K. Wife of Benjamin J. Saunders. Died in
Huntsville, Ala.
National Banner & Nashville Daily Advertiser. (Mon., May 12, 1834)

Saunders, Mrs. Sarah. Consort of William Saunders Esq. Died at the
fountain of Health, Davidson County in the 50th year of her age.
National Banner & Nashville Whig. (Mon., July 27, 1835)

Saunders, Mr. Wm. Died at Athens.
National Banner & Nashville Whig. (Sat., Dec. 30, 1826)

Saunders, William Esq. Age 70. Died at the Fountain of Health in
Davidson County on the 22nd inst.
Nashville Whig. (Thurs., Sept. 24, 1846)

Saunderson, Mrs. Elizabeth. Died in Madison County, Ala. Killed by
the falling of a tree.
National Banner & Nashville Whig. (Sat., May 12, 1827)

Saunderson, Mr. James. Of Alexandria, district of Columbia, aged 53.
Died in Nashville on the 6th inst.
National Banner & Nashville Whig. (Mon., Dec. 27, 1830)

Sawtell, Rev. Eli N. Pastor of the second Presbyterian Church of
Louisville. Died in Louisville, Ky.
National Banner & Nashville Whig. (Wed., Dec. 3, 1834)

Sawyer, Mrs. Cecilia. Died near Chillicothe.
National Banner & Nashville Whig. (Sat., Dec. 16, 1826)

Sawyer, Elizabeth. Daughter of Thomas L. and Henreitta Sawyer.
Died in Gallatin on the 21st inst., aged 1 year five months and ten
days.
The Christian Record. (Sat., Nov. 27, 1847)

Sawyer, Mr. Henderson. Died at Russellville, Ky. Was accidently shot
to death while turkey hunting.
National Banner & Nashville Daily Advertiser. (Sat., Oct. 27, 1832)

Say, Thomas. Of Philadelphia. Died at New Harmony, Indiana on the
10th ultimo. in the 47th year of his age.
National Banner & Nashville Whig. (Fri., Nov. 21, 1834)

Sayre, Foster. An old and respectable inhabitant of Nashville. Died very suddenly on Sunday night, last.
The Nashville Gazette. (Wed., June 7, 1820)

Scales, Mr. Daniel. Aged 60. Died at Harpeths Lick, in Williamson County of Cholera.
National Banner & Nashville Whig. (Fri., June 10, 1835)

Scales, Capt. Henry. Aged 45 years. Died in Tuscumbia, Ala.
National Banner & Nashville Whig. (Fri., Jan. 9, 1835)

Scallion, John Esq. Died in Madison County, Ala.
National Banner & Nashville Whig. (Wed., Aug. 17, 1831)

Schaeffer, Rev. F. C. Pastor of the Evangelical Lutheran Church of St. James in that City. Died in New York.
National Banner & Nashville Whig. (Fri., April 15, 1831)

Schaeffer, Rev. F. C., D. D. Died in New York.
Nashville Republican & State Gazette. (Thurs., April 14, 1831)

Schaeffer, Rev. F. C. Pastor of the Evangelical Luthern Church of St. James in New York City. Died in New York.
National Banner & Nashville Whig. (Fri., April 15, 1831)

Schaff, Mr. Arthur. Died in the State Department at Washington at his office as Librarian on the 9th.
National Banner & Nashville Daily Advertiser. (Wed., Aug. 20, 1834)

Scheide, Charles. One of the workman in the branch Mint. Died in New Orleans on the 17th of Yellow fever.
Daily Republican Banner. (Wed., Sept. 11, 1839)

Schell, Alexander R. In the 19th year of his age. Died at Jalapa Mexico, on the 16th of Dec. 1847. His residence was Gallatin, Tenn.
The Christian Record. (Sat., April 15, 1848)

Schenck, Caroline A. Wife of John B. Schenck. Died in Nashville on Tuesday the 22nd inst. aged 23 years and 10 months.
The Politician & Weekly Nashville Whig. (Fri., June 25, 1847)

Schenck, John B. Aged 8 months. Died on Yesterday morning the 14th inst. son of John and Caroline A. Schenck.
The Politician & Weekly Nashville Whig. (Fri., June 18, 1847)

Schmiyz, Mr. Charles. Died in Maysville, Ky.
National Banner. (Sat., Aug. 8, 1829)

Schrool, John. Died 15th at Cincinnati, Ohio of Cholera.
National Banner & Nashville Daily Advertiser. (Wed., Oct. 24, 1832)

Schultz, Mrs. Ann. Wife of Mr. Charles Schultz. Died in Cincinnati, Ohio.
National Banner & Nashville Daily Advertiser. (Thurs., Aug. 8, 1833)

Schultz, Robert. Of New York. Died in the wreck of the steam boat Lexington.
Daily Republican Banner. (Fri., Jan. 31, 1840)

Scoggin, Mr. John. A citizen of Robinson County, Ten. Died on the 5th inst. aged 62 years.
National Banner & Nashville Whig. (Mon., Aug. 21, 1837)

Scorch, Mrs. Hannah. Aged 32 years. Died at Louisville, Ky.
National Banner & Nashville Daily Advertiser. (Mon., Feb. 18, 1833)

Scott, Mr. Overseer at the Brands factory and 9 negroes. Died at Lexington, Ky of Cholera.
National Banner & Nashville Daily Advertiser. (Tues., July 2, 1833)

Scott, Mrs. Abigail F. Wife of Mr. Chastine Scott. Died in Boone
County, Ky.
National Banner & Nashville Whig. (Fri., Dec. 10, 1830)

Scott, Mr. Charles. A native of Philadelphia. Died in Randolph, Tenn.
on the 20th ulto. in the 26th year of his age.
Nashville Whig. (Tues., Jan. 11, 1842)

Scott, Mrs. Eliza. Formerly of Missouri, aged 40 years. Died in
Arkansas.
National Banner & Nashville Whig. (Fri., April 10, 1835)

Scott, Henry. Infant son of Dr. D. T. Scott. Died at White Creek
Springs.
Nashville Whig. (Mon., Sept. 7, 1840)

Scott, Captain Isaiah. Late of the firm of Young, Green & Co.
Died was drowned from the Steam Boat, General Jackson.
The Nashville Gazette. (Sat., May 20, 1820)

Scott, Col. James W. Died in Knox County.
Daily Republican Banner. (Sat., Oct. 20, 1838)

Scott, Mrs. Jane. Died in Nashville, this morning.
Nashville Whig. (Fri., Feb. 5, 1841)

Scott, Mr. John Sen. Died in Jessamine County, Ky.
National Banner & Nashville Whig. (Sat., Jan. 10, 1829)

Scott, Miss Mary Ann. Died in Huntsville, Ala.
National Banner & Nashville Whig. (Sat., Sept. 6, 1828)

Scott, Mr. Moses G. of the Theatre. Died at New Orleans.
National Banner (May 10, 1826)

Scott, Mr. Nathaniel. Died in Garrard County, Ky.
National Banner. (Jan. 27, 1826)

Scott, Mr. Newton. Died at the residence of Mr. Hugh L. White. A
student at law in Knoxville.
Nashville Gazette. (Sat., June 26, 1819)

Scott, Mrs. Patsey Larew. Died near Knoxville.
National Banner & Nashville Advertiser. (Mon., April 16, 1832)

Scott, Miss Rebecca. Died at Indianapolis
National Banner & Nashville Whig. (Sat., Sept. 1, 1827)

Scott, Mrs. Rebecca T. Consort of M. J. G. Scott. Died in
Huntsville, Ala.
National Banner & Nashville Whig. (Mon., Dec. 6, 1830)

Scott, Robert Jun. Of Bedford County. Departed this life on Friday
last.
The Clarion & Tennessee Gazette. (July 20, 1813)

Scott, Mr. Samuel. Died in St. Louis.
National Banner & Nashville Whig. (Sat., Aug. 30, 1828)

Scott, Mr. Samul. Formerly of Lexington, Ky. and more recently of
Florence, Ala. Died at Shippingpoint, Ky.
National Banner. (Sat., Aug. 22, 1829)

Scott, The lady of Sir Walter. Died at Abbotsford, Eng. daughter of
John Carssantier of Lyons.
National Banner & Nashville Whig. (Sat., July 15, 1826)

Scrape, Fanny W. Infant daughyer of Mr. J. D. Scrape. Died in the vicinity of Murfreesborough.
National Banner & Nashville Daily Advertiser. (Thurs., June 19, 1834)

Scruggs, Mr. Wm. B. Died in Limestone County, Ala.
National Banner. (Sat., Dec. 19, 1829)

Scull, John I. Esq. Formerly editor of the Pittsburgh Gazette. Died at Pittsburgh.
National Banner & Nashville Whig. (Sat., March 10, 1827)

Scull, John Esq. Original propieter of the Pittsburgh Gazette. Died in Westmoreland County, Pa.
National Banner & Nashville Whig. (Sat., March 1, 1828)

Scurry, Capt. Thomas. Died in Tipton County.
National Banner & Nashville Whig. (Sat., Oct. 28, 1826)

Seabolt, Andrew. Died in Knoxville, Tenn.
Daily Republican Banner. (Sat., Sept. 22, 1838)

Seal, Mr. Charles. Age 75. Died in Robertson County, near Springfield on the 26th Sept. at 1 o'clock P. M. Interred on the 27th at 4 P.M.
National Banner & Nashville Daily Advertiser. (Mon., Oct. 1, 1832)

Seal, John Randolph. Infant son of William Seal Esq. Died in Robertson County near Springfield on the 27th of Sept. aged 6 months.
National Banner & Nashville Daily Advertiser. (Mon., Oct. 1, 1832)

Seales, Mary. Aged 87. Died in Rockingham County, N. C. on Monday the 2nd of Jan.
National Banner & Nashville Whig. (Fri., March 4, 1831)

Searcy, Mr. Anderson. In the 59th year of his age. Died in Rutherford County.
National Banner & Nashville Daily Advertiser. (Fri., Jan. 27, 1832)

Searcy, Richard Esq. A native of Tennessee in the 30th year of his age. Died in Batesville, Ark. on the 25th Dec.
National Banner & Nashville Daily Advertiser. (Sat., Feb. 9, 1833)

Searcy, Maj. Robert. Clerk of the Federal Courts for West Tenn. Died in Nashville on the 26th ult. in the 52d year of his age.
The Nashville Gazette. (Sat., Sept. 2, 1820)

Searcy, Maj. Robt. Clerk of the Federal Courts for West Tenn. and for many years. A citizen of this place. Pres. of the Branch Bank at Nashville. Clerk of the U. S. Court, served during Creek War as aid to Gen'l Jackson with honor and ability.
Gazette. (Sept. 2, 1820)

Searcy, Mrs. Sarah M. Wife of Col. William W. Searcy, age 50. Died in Rutherford County, April 29.
National Banner & Nashville Advertiser. (Wed., May 9, 1832)

Searcy, Mrs. Sarah M. Consort of Col. William W. Searcy. Died in Rutherford County on the 29th April. In the 50th year of her age.
National Banner & Nashville Daily Advertiser. (Wed., May 9, 1832)

Searcy, Solon. Son of W. W. Searcy. Died on Saturday the 6th inst. at Onward Furnace, aged four years, 3 months and 17 days.
Daily Republican Banner. (Tues., Sept. 15, 1840)

Searle, Hon. Nathaniel. Age 58. One of the ablest advocate at the Rhode Island Bar. Died at Procience, R. I.
National Banner & Nashville Advertiser. (Thurs., March 8, 1832)

Seaton, Mr. James K. Aged 43. Died in Jefferson County, Ky.
National Banner & Nashville Whig. (Sat., Sept. 16, 1826)

Seawell, Mrs. Susannah. Wife of Col. Benjamin Seawell. Died on
Tuesday, June 27, 1815 in the 56 year of her age, Mrs. Susannah Seawell
consort of Col. Benjamin Seawell, of Nashville. Member of Methodist
Church.
Whig. (July 4, 1815)

Seay, Mrs. Jane. Consort of Mr. Samuel Seay. and daughter of the late
George Wharton Esq. Died on the 16th inst. in her 44th year.
The Christian Record. (Sat., Jan. 23, 1847)

Sedgwick, Hon. Theodore. Died at Stockbridge Mass.
Daily Republican Banner. (Fri., Nov. 22, 1839)

Sedgwick, The Hon. Theodore. Died suddenly on the 17th inst. at
Stockbridge, Mass.
Nashville Union. (Wed., Dec. 4, 1839)

Sedilla, Rev. Antonio de. Died at New Orleans. A venerable Roman
Catholic prelate.
National Banner & Nashville Whig. (Sat., Feb. 7, 1829)

Sedwell, Mrs. Rachel. Died in Bourbon County, Ky.
National Banner & Nashville Whig. (Sat., Sept. 9, 1826)

Seek, Mr. Nicholas. Died at Fort Meigs.
National Banner. (March 17, 1826)

Segur, Mr. Nathan. of Maine. Died in New Orleans, La.
National Banner & Nashville Whig. (Fri., Nov. 14, 1834)

Sellman, Mr. John. Died at Cincinnati.
National Banner & Nashville Whig. (Sat., Feb. 23, 1828)

Sennott, J. F. Of Baltimore. Died in New Orleans of Yellow Fever.
Daily Republican Banner. (Fri., Sept. 29, 1837)

Senter, Elizabeth. Infant daughter of Col. W. S. Senter. Died near
Athens, Ten.
National Banner & Nashville Daily Advertiser. (Fri., July 25, 1834)

Senter, Nelson A. Esq. Died in Grainger County in the 43rd year of
his age.
Nashville Whig. (Tuesday, July 14, 1846)

Severs, Mr. Theoderic L. A native of Virginia. Died in Utica, Ind.
National Banner & Nashville Daily Advertiser. (Thurs., Aug. 8, 1833)

Sevier, Hon. A. H. Of Arkansas. Died at the home of a relative,
Mr. Johnson.
The Christian Record. (Sat., Jan. 13, 1849)

Sevier, Mrs. Catharine H. Died at the residence of her husband, Col.
George W. Sevier of this vicinity.
Nashville Whig. (Wed., Aug. 5, 1840)

Sevier, Mr. Joseph. Died in Overton County.
National Banner & Nashville Whig. (Sat., July 22, 1826)

Sevier, Mr. Richard. Son of General Sevier. Died.
Knoxville Gazette. (Thurs., Jan. 2, 1794)

Sevier, Richard. Died Mr. Richard Sevier, son of General Sevier.
Knoxville Gazette. (Thurs., Jan. 2, 1794)

Sevier, Mrs. Sophia. Wife of Maj. John Sevier. Died in Green County,
Ten. aged 45 years. Natl. Banner & Nashvl Whig. (Wed., Apr. 8, 1835)

Sevier, Mrs. Sophia. Wife of Maj. John Sevier. Died in Green County, Ten. aged 45 years.
National Banner & Nashville Whig. (Wed., April 8, 1835)

Sexton, Benj. Esq. Died in Shawneetown, Ill.
National Banner. (Jan. 6, 1826)

Sexton, Mr. Merit E. Died at Tuscaloosa, Ala.
National Banner. (May 27, 1826)

Seymour, Daniel. Died 16th at Cincinnati, Ohio of Cholera.
National Banner & Nashville Daily Advertiser. (Wed., Oct. 24, 1832)

Shackleford, Mr. David L. Died in Vicksburg, Miss.
National Banner & Nashville Daily Advertiser. (Wed., March 26, 1834)

Shacklefort, Miss. Died at Versailles, Ky. 14 miles from Lexington of Cholera.
National Banner & Nashville Whig. (Fri., Sept. 4, 1835)

Shaffer, Mr. George. Teacher of dancing. Died at Providence.
National Banner & Nashville Whig. (Mon., Aug. 2, 1830)

Shaffer, William H. Infant son of R. W. E. C. Shaffer. Died on Friday the 11th inst.
National Banner & Nashville Whig. (Fri., Aug. 11, 1837)

Shaiffer, James H. In the 28th year of his age. Died at the Western Thrological Seminary in Allegheny city, on Dec. 13th (Obituary).
The Christian Record. (Sat., Jan. 6, 1849)

Sahll, Russell Avery. Infant son of George and Martha Shall. Died in Memphis.
Nashville Whig. (Tuesday, March 31, 1846)

Shall, William H. Avery. Son of Ephraim P. Shall, of New Orleans. Died on the 4th inst. at Bethleham, Pa. aged about 11 years.
The Politician & Weekly Nashville Whig. (Wed., Sept. 1, 1847)

Shank, Mrs. Charles. Died in Shelbyville, Tenn. of Cholera.
National Banner & Nashville Daily Advertiser. (Thurs., July 11, 1833)

Shanks, Charles Sen. Died in Shelbyville, Tenn. of Cholera.
National Banner & Nashville Daily Advertiser. (Thurs., July 11, 1833)

Shanks, Infant child of John T. Shanks. Died at Shelbyville, Tenn. of Cholera.
National Banner & Nashville Daily Advertiser. (Thurs., July 11, 1833)

Shanks, Miss Martha. Daughter of the late Mr. Charles Shanks. Died in Shelbyville, Ten.
National Banner & Nashville Daily Advertiser. (Tues., Aug. 5, 1834)

Shannon, Mr. Charge of d'Affairs for Guatemala and his niece. Died at Ysabal on their way thither.
National Banner & Nashville Daily Advertiser. (Sat., Aug. 25, 1832)

Shannon, Miss Polly. Died in Shelby County, Ky.
National Banner. (June 10, 1826)

Shannon, Mrs. Ioraria. Wife of Thomas Shannon. Died in Madison County.
National Banner & Nashville Whig. (Dec. 2, 1826)

Shannon, Mr. William. Died in the neighborhood of Danville, Ky.
National Banner & Nashville Daily Advertiser. (Mon., Aug. 5, 1833)

Shopard, Joshua. Infant son of Mr. Booker Shoppard of Shelbyville. Died in Rutherford County, Ten.
National Banner & Nashville Daily Advertiser. (Mon., Sept. 2, 1833)

Sharp, Mr. Charles. Died at Lexington, Ky.
National Banner & Nashville Whig. (Sat., Feb. 17, 1827)

Sharp, Mr. J. Jailor. Died in Lexington, Ky.
National Banner & Nashville Whig. (Sat., Dec. 2, 1826)

Sharp, Major John. A soldier of the Revolution, aged 76. Died in
Rutherford County.
Nashville Whig. (Nov. 15, 1824)

Sharp, Mr. R. Died in Lexington, Ky.
National Banner & Nashville Whig. (Dec. 2, 1826)

Sharp, Mr. Walter, Aged 24 years. Died in Lincoln Cty., Ten.
National Banner & Nashville Whig. (Wed., Nov. 19, 1834)

Shaw, Charles Esq. Died in Montgomery, Ala. formerly of Boston.
National Banner & Nashville Whig. (Sat., Dec. 6, 1828)

Shaw, Capt. Christopher. A Revolutionary soldier. Died in Bedford
County on 22 ult.
National Banner & Nashville Advertiser. (Wed., March 7, 1832)

Shaw, Captain John. Aged 54. Died at Louisville, Ky.
National Banner & Nashville Daily Advertiser. (Thurs., Jan. 2, 1834)

Shaw, Mrs. L. C. Daughter of Gen. Nathaniel Green of the Revolutionary
Army.
National Banner & Nashville Whig. (Wed., June 1, 1831)

Shaw, Mrs. L. C. Daughter of Gen. Nathaniel Green of the revolutionary
army. Died on Cumberland Island, near St. Mary's Geo.
National Banner & Nashville Whig. (Wed., June 1, 1831)

Shearon, Laetitia H. Consort of Thomas W. Shearon, Esq. of Davidson
County. Died on the 13th inst.
Nashville Whig. (Thurs., Nov. 16, 1843)

Sheddon, Thomas. Died in Fredericksburg, Va.
Nashville Republican & State Gazette. (Tues., Oct. 25, 1831)

Sheed, Capt. William W. Of Philadelphia. A gallant Naval Officer
during the last War. Died in Europe.
Nashville Republican & State Gazette. (Thurs., April 19, 1831)

Sheffey, Daniel Esq. Died in Augusta County, Va. A man of great
talent. He died suddenly of Apoplexy.
National Banner & Nashville Whig. (Mon., Dec. 27, 1830)

Sheffield, Mr. Patrick H. Died in Tuscumbia, Ala.
National Banner & Nashville Whig. (Fri., Jan. 9, 1835)

Shegog, Mr. Richard M. Died at Courtland, Ala.
National Banner & Nashville Whig. (Tues., March 2, 1830)

Shegog, Mr. Richard W. Died at Duck River Furnance Hickman County in
the 24th year of his age.
National Banner Nashville Whig. (Mon., July 27, 1835)

Shields, Mrs. Mariah. On the 24th of March, 1836, in this city,
Mrs. Mariah, consort of Wm. Shields; after a distressing affliction
of only a few days. Among the many that flee from time every hour,
probably, the loss of but few, are to be more regretted, than Mrs.
S's. But those who sorrow for her, do it not without hope. She
had been a member of the Church of Christ several years, and during
her perigrination, naught could be predicted of her exemplary, pious,
and most religious life. Devoted to her friends, her husband and

her God, she flitted across the arena of existence; in the calm sun-
shine of Gospel grace, her path growing brighter and brighter, till her
change come. Before the flickering lamp of life was extinguished,
she gave ample testimony of her acceptance on high. When asked if she
believed death was her immediate lot, she replied "No doubt" but
continued, "the Lord has been merciful and gracious to me all my life,
and not forsaken me in this trying hour." She desired to hear hymns
of praise, in honor of her risen Savior,, and requested the disciples
of Christ in her expiring moments, to "speak of the goodness of God".
The following passage of scripture, bore her spirit up to the last,
while she would quote it, with an accuracy seldom observed, "For we
know, that if our earthly house of this tabernacle were disolved, we
have a building of God, not made with hands, eternally in the heavens."
Nashville Republican. (Thurs., April 7, 1836)

Shelburn, Mr. James. Died in Franklin, Williamson County from
injury received when thrown from his horse.
Daily Republican Banner. (Fri., Aug. 9, 1839)

Shelby, Mrs. Elizabeth Caroline. Daughter of Gen. James Winchester.
Died in Sumner County on the 25th ult. in the 25th year of her age.
National Banner & Nashville Whig. (Sat., Nov. 17, 1827)

Shelby, Mrs. Elizabeth Caroline. Consort of Orville Shelby, Esq. and
third daughter of Gen. James Winchester, dec'd. Died in Sumner County,
on the morning of the 25th ultimo. in the 25th year of her age. By
the death of this interesting woman, a chasm is refilled, and more
especially in the heart of her bereaved husband; which probably time
with its "gentlest opiates" can never close. Here we are again taught
the solemn lessons how feeble is the tenure, by which life is holden,
even in its utmost bloom and vigor. A short time since I saw her
placid & cheerful, surrounded by everything calculated to make life
endearing; a few short days have passed, "how changed the scene."
Instead of paying a friendly visit, I now take up the pen to pay the
last sad tribute of respect, to one whom I have long known, and as
long respected I would willing offer the least mitigating thought, to
lessen the grief of her friends and relatives but what thought so fit,
and what so great, for this purpose as that rising from witnessing her
"parting breath." When worn down by a long and painful illness, I
am informed she disclosed an entire resignation to her approaching
fate; and no longer trusting to "an arm of flesh" she gave up the world,
by resigning her two infant children to the care and protection of
that God who gave them, and herself to his infinite mercy. Then with
the calmness and serenity of Christian faith, arising from the prospects of a happy immortality, she fearlessly "launched away."
National Banner & Nashville Whig. (November 17, 1827)

Shelby, Col. John. Died at his resident, in Montgomery County on
the ___ inst.
The Nashville Whig & Tenn. Advertiser. (April 25, 1818)

Shelby, Mrs. Martha. Wife of Shelby, Mr. Albert. Died in Sumner Co.
National Banner. (Sat., April 18, 1829)

Shelby, Mrs. Mary. Consort of Gen. James Shelby. Died in Fayette
County, Ky. on the 30th ult. aged 49 years.
National Banner & Nashville Whig. (Fri., Aug. 12, 1836)

Shelby, Mrs. Susan. Relict of the late Gov. Shelby aged 70. Died in
Lincoln County, Ky.
National Banner & Nashville Daily Advertiser. (Mon., Sept. 2, 1833)

Shelby, Mrs. Susan. Widow of the late Gov. Shelby. Died in Lincoln
County, Ky.
National Banner & Nashville Daily Advertiser. (Mon., Aug. 5, 1833)

Sheldon, Mr. John S. Died at Pittsburgh.
National Banner & Nashville Whig. (Sat., Feb. 9, 1828)

Shelley, Mr. William. Aged 24. A native of Canterbury, England. Died in New Orleans, La.
National Banner & Nashville Daily Advertiser. (Sat., Sept. 13, 1834)

Shelton, Robert. Died at Versailles, Ky. 12 miles from Lexington of Cholera.
National Banner & Nashville Whig. (Fri., Sept. 4, 1835)

Shelton, Miss Susan V. Daughter of James Shelton. Died in Smith County on the 19th ult.
National Banner & Nashville Daily Advertiser. (Fri., Jan. 27, 1832)

Shelton, Mr. William B. D. In the 31st year of his age. Died at his residence in Lincoln County, Tenn. on the 14th Feb.
The Christian Record. (Sat., March 13, 1847)

Shelton, Mr. W. H. Aged 24 years. Died in Memphis on the 13th inst. (Memphis Enquirer)
Nashville True Whig. & Weekly Commercial Register. (Fri., Jan. 24, 1851)

Shepard, August H. A native of Mass. Died yesterday at Sycamore Factory in Davidson County.
Daily Republican Banner. (Thurs., Sept. 5, 1839)

Shephard, Mrs. Booker. Died in Shelbyville, Tenn. of Cholera.
National Banner & Nashville Daily Advertiser. (Thurs., July 11, 1833)

Shephard, Francis Adela. Only child of Mr. & Mrs. Thos. Sheppard aged 1 year and 7 months. Died in Nashville on the 28th.
National Banner & Nashville Whig. (Wed., Oct. 29, 1834)

Shepherd, Dr. Of Illinois. Died at the house of Mr. Little near Reynoldsburg, Tenn.
National Banner & Nashville Whig. (Wed., Jan. 14, 1835)

Shepherd, Mrs. Mary A. In the 56th year of her age. Died on Friday night last at the residence of her son-in-law, W. C. Hurt.
Nashville True Whig & Weekly Commercial Register. (Fri., April 17, 1850)

Sheppard, Mr. Austin. Died in Marshall County, Tenn. on the 9th of Aug. 1847.
The Politician & Weekly Nashville Whig. (Wed., Sept. 8, 1847)

Sheppard, Mr. Austin. Died at his residence in Marshall County, Tennessee on the 9th of Aug. 1847.
The Christian Record. (Sat., Sept. 11, 1847)

Sheppard, Harper. Youngest son of Benjamin H. and Phereby R. Sheppard. Died in Nashville on the night of the 24th inst.
The Christian Record. (Sat., May 27, 1848)

Sheppard, Mr. Lewis. Died in Rutherford County.
National Banner & Nashville Daily Advertiser. (Sat., June 22, 1833)

Sheppard, Mary Elizabeth. Eldest daughter of Mr. Benjamin H. and Mrs. Phereby R. Sheppard. Died in Nashville on the 7th inst. in the 9th year of her age.
The Christian Record. (Sat., June 10, 1848)

Sherman, Hon. Charles R. Judge of the Supreme Court of the State. Died at Lebanon, Ohio.
National Banner (Sat., July 11, 1829)

Shew, Elizabeth. Died in Natchez.
National Banner & Nashville Whig. (Sat., Oct. 7, 1826)

Shields, David Esq. Of the firm of D. & M. Shields & Co. paper

manufactures. Died in Grainger County, Tenn.
Daily Republican Banner. (Sat., April 13, 1839)

Shields, Honore Carlin. Infant daughter of Benjamin F. and Susan A.
Shields. Died in Nashville, yesterday.
Nashville Whig. (Thurs., June 27, 1844)

Shields, Mrs. Jane. Mother of the Hon. E. J. Shields. Died in Giles
County on the 11th inst.
Nashville Republican. (May 20, 1837 Sat.)

Shields, Mr. John. Died in Henry County.
National Banner & Nashville Whig. (Mon., Sept. 20, 1830)

Shields, Mr. John. Died in Lexington, Ky.
National Banner & Nashville Advertiser. (Sat., Feb. 4, 1832)

Shields, Mrs. Maria. Consort of Mr. William Shields. Died in Nashville
on March 24th.
Nashville Republican (Tues., April 7, 1836)

Shields, Mrs. Martha. Consort of Mr. William Shields. Died in Nashville, Ten. on 24th March.
National Banner & Nashville Whig. (Fri., March 25, 1836)

Shields, Mr. Patrick. Of Lexington. Died in Logan County, Ky.
National Banner & Nashville Daily Advertiser. (Mon., Jan. 2, 1832)

Shields, Samuel Esq. Died in Giles County on the 9th inst.
National Banner & Nashville Whig. (Sat., May 26, 1827)

Shields, Thomas. Of the U. S. Navy. Died in New Orleans.
National Banner & Nashville Whig. (Sat., June 16, 1827)

Shields, Maj. William. In the 36th year of his age. Died in Giles
County, Ten. on the 23d.
National Banner & Nashville Whig. (Mon., Nov. 2, 1835)

Shinn, Ch. A. Late of the firm of Woodnut & Co. of Cincinnati, Ohio.
Died in Jamacia, West Indies.
National Banner & Nashville Daily Advertiser. (Wed., July 9, 1834)

Shipley, Adam. And three of his children. Died in the vicinity of
Jonesborough, East Tenn.
Daily Republican Banner. (Wed., July 29, 1840)

Shippe, Edward Esq. Cashier of the U. S. Branch Bank in that City.
Died in Louisville, Ky.
National Banner & Nashville Advertiser. (Sat., Dec. 29, 1832)

Shireey, Mr. Paul. A highly respectable merchant of Nashville.
Died at Whites Creek Spring, in Davidson County, on Tuesday the 16th
April.
National Banner & Nashville Daily Advertiser. (Wed., April 16, 1834)

Shirley, Mr. James A. Son of the late Paul Shirley, of Nashville.
Died in Nashville, yesterday afternoon in the 22nd year of his age.
The Christian Record. (Sat., June 26, 1847)

Shirley, Mr. James A. Son of the late Paul Shirley, of Nashville.
Died in Nashville on yesterday in the 22nd year of his age.
The Politician & Weekly Nashville Whig. (Fri., June 25, 1847)

Shoeman, Mr. F. Died in this town on Wednesday.
National Banner & Nashville Whig. (Sat., Sept. 27, 1828)

Shofner, Capt. Christopher. Aged 36. Died in Lincoln County, T.
National Banner & Nashville Whig. (Sat., Sept. 9, 1826)

Shopard, Joshua. Infant son of Mr. Booker Shoppard of Shelbyville.
Died in Rutherford County, Ten.
National Banner & Nashville Daily Advertiser. (Mon., Sept. 2, 1833)

Shopard, Miss Martha Jane. Daughter of William B. Shopard Esq. Died
at Memphis on Saturday last 20th inst.
The Christian Record. (Sat., Jan. 27, 1849)

Shores, Mr. Martin. Aged 27 years. Died in Lincoln County, Tenn.
National Banner & Nashville Whig. (Mon., Oct. 20, 1834)

Short, William. Died 16th at Cincinnati, Ohio of Cholera.
National Banner & Nashville Daily Advertiser. (Wed., Oct. 24, 1832)

Shorter, Judge Eli. Died at his residence in Columbus, Ga. on the 13th
ult.
Nashville Republican. (Sat., Jan. 7, 1837)

Shriver, James Esq. Died at Fort Wayne, Ia.
National Banner & Nashville Whig. (Sat., Sept. 16, 1826)

Shuler, Dr. Lawrence S. Died in Indiana.
National Banner & Nashville Whig. (Sat., Sept. 8, 1827)

Shute, Mr. Thomas. Formerly of Davidson County. Died in Perryville.
National Banner & Nashville Whig. (Thurs., June 10, 1830)

Sills, Isham. Died at his residence in Stewart County, Tenn. on Monday the 23rd. Extensively known throughout this and adjoining states
as The Faith Doctor.
National Banner & Nashville Daily Advertiser. (Fri., April 27, 1832)

Sills, Mr. Isham. Died in Stewart County.
Nashville Republican & State Gazette. (Sat., April 28, 1832)

Simmons, Mr. James Fitz. Of the firm of Gaines & Fitz Simmons, aged
about 30 years. Died in Mobile, Ala. of Yellow fever.
Daily Republican Banner. (Tues., Oct. 1, 1839)

Simmons, Mrs. Nancy. Died in Knox County.
National Banner & Nashville Whig. (Sat., May 19, 1827)

Simmons, Mr. Reuben. Died on Friday last 11th Oct. in the 24th year
of his age. Son of Alexander Simmons Esq. formerly of Virginia.
National Banner & Nashville Daily Advertiser. (Thurs., Oct. 17, 1833)

Simmons, William L. A soldier of the 8th U. S. Infantry. Died -
departed this life in the 23d of his age on Wednesday the 14th inst.
By the ruthless hand of violence. Mr. Simmons was a native of South-
ampton.
The Nashville Whig. (May 19th 1817)

Simms, Douglass R. Printer. Died in Shelbyville formerly of Nashville.
Nashville Whig. (Tues., July 21, 1846)

Simms, John B. Esq. Died at Columbus, Mi. Post Master at that place.
National Banner & Nashville Daily Advertiser. (Tues., July 15, 1834)

Sims, John M. In Davidson County, on the 12th inst. of scarlet fever.
John M. Sims, son of William P. Sims, age 4 years and month.
Nashville Republican. Thurs., Jan. 14, 1836

Sims, Walter Jennings. On Monday night last Walter Jennings, infant
son of Walter Sims, esq. of this County.
Nashville Republican, (Sat., Jan. 9, 1836)

Simns, John G., Esq. Attorney at Law. Died at Gallatin on Saturday
the 21st inst.
Nashville Whig. (Aug. 30, 1824)

Simpson, Mr. A. Age 101. Died at Montreal said to have been the last survivor of Gen. Wolf's Companion in arms.
National Banner & Nashville Advertiser. (Wed., May 16, 1832)

Simpson, James. Died 13th at Cincinnati, Ohio of Cholera.
National Banner & Nashville Daily Advertiser. (Tues., Oct. 23, 1832)

Simpson, Mr. John S. Aged 51 years. Died in Nashville on Sunday last, he commenced the publication of the paper that bears the name of the Nashville Banner.
The Christian Record. (Sat., Aug.12, 1848)

Simpson, Hon. Josiah. One of the Judges of the State of Mississipi. Died lately the Hon. Josiah Simpson.
The Nash. Whig. and Tenn. Advertiser. (Oct. 20, 1817)

Sims, Mrs. Asenath. In the 43d year of her age. Died at the residence of Mrs. Nancy L. Hightower, Williamson County, Tenn. on the 23d inst.
Daily Republican Banner. (Fri., Nov. 29, 1839)

Sims, Henry Clay. Son of Walter Sims, Esq. Died in Davidson County, aged 3 months.
National Banner & Nashville Whig. (Wed., Sept. 30, 1835)

Sims, Mr. Henry W. In his 21st year. Died in Rutherford County, Ten.
National Banner & Nashville Whig. (Fri., Oct. 13, 1834)

Sims, John. Died in Shelbyville, Tenn. of Cholera.
National Banner & Nashville Daily Advertiser. (Thurs., July 11, 1833)

Sims, John M. Son of William P. Sims, in Davidson County on the 12th inst. of scarlet fever, age 4 years and month.
Nashville Republican. (Thurs., Jan. 14, 1836)

Sims, Mr. Parish. Died in Fayette County.
National Banner & Nashville Whig. (Mon., Aug. 16, 1830)

Sims, Capt. Walter. Formerly Merchant of Philadelphia. Died in Davidson County, on the morning of the 8th inst.
The Nashville Gazette (Sat., Jan. 15, 1820)

Sims, Walter Jennings. Infant son of Walter Sims Esq. in this County (Davidson) on Monday night last.
Nashville Republican, (Sat., Jan. 9, 1836)

Sims, Walter Jennings. Son of Walter Sims Esq. Died in Davidson County on the 5th inst. aged 2 years and 5 months.
National Banner & Nashville Whig. (Mon., Jan. 11, 1836)

Sinclair, Com. Arthur. Of the U. S. Navy. Died at Norfolk, Va.
National Banner & Nashville Whig. (Mon., March 7, 1831)

Sinclair, Commodore Arthur. Of the United States Navy and commanding Officer. Died in Norfolk, Va.
Nashville Republican & State Gazette. (Thurs., March 3, 1831)

Sinclair, Com. Arthur. Of the U. S. Navy. Died at Norfolk, Va.
National Banner & Nashville Whig. (Mon., March 7, 1831)

Singleton, Mrs. Rebecca. Wife of Mr. Lewis Singleton. Died in Jessamine County, Ky.
National Banner & Nashville Whig. (Fri., July 11, 1828)

Sisson, Miss Dianna G. Daughter of William and Polly Sisson. Died in Henry County, late of Culpepper County, Va.
National Banner & Nashville Whig. (Fri., Feb. 12, 1836)

Sitler, Col. Isaac. Died at his residence near Nashville.
Daily Republican Banner. (Wed., Sept. 6, 1837)

Sitler, Col James W. Died in this town on Saturday last in consequence of a fall from his horse.
National Banner. (Feb. 10, 1826)

Sittler, Mrs. Juda. The amiable consort of Col. James Sittler of this town. Died on the 2d inst.
The Nasahville Whig. (April 9th, 1818)

Sitler, Mrs. Sarah Winston. Wife of Isaac Sitler Esq. of Nashville. Died on Thursday last.
The Nashville Gazette. (Sat., Sept. 11, 1819)

Skillman, Mr. Henry C. Died in Nashville.
National Banner & Nashville Whig. (Mon., July 13, 1835)

Slack, Mrs. Consort of Mr. Daniel Slack. Died in Wilkinson County, Miss.
National Banner & Nashville Whig. (Sat., Sept. 30, 1826)

Slade, Hon. Mr. A representative in Congress from that state. Died in Knox County, Illinois.
National Banner & Nashville Daily Advertiser. (Mon., July 21, 1834)

Slade, Mrs. Eliza A. Wife of Capt. H. A. Slade. Died in Mobile, Ala.
National Banner & Nashville Whig. (Wed., Nov. 19, 1834)

Slater, Dr. John Thomas. Age 79. Died in Nashville on the 22d inst. suddenly.
National Banner & Nashville Whig. (Fri., Dec. 23, 1831)

Slater, Dr. John Toms. Died in Nashville on the 22nd inst. suddenly, aged 79.
National Banner & Nashville Whig. (Fri., Dec. 23, 1831)

Slater, Mrs. Mary. Aged 36. Died in Fayetteville.
National Banner & Nashville Whig. (Sat., July 8, 1826)

Slaton, Mr. James. Aged 70. Died in Bedford County.
National Banner & Nashville Daily Advertiser. (Sat., May 11, 1833)

Slatter, Mrs. Polly P. Died at her residence in the vicinity of Winchester, Tenn. on the 26th June 1844
Nashville Whig. (Thurs., July 4, 1844)

Slaughter, Col. Gabriel. Formerly Lieut. Governor and nearly 4 years acting Governor of Kentucky. Died in Mercer County, Ky.
National Banner & Nashville Whig. (Mon., Oct. 4, 1830)

Slaughter, Mr. George S. Jun. Died in Madison County, Ky.
National Banner. (Sat., July 4, 1829)

Slaughter, Mrs. Mary P. Wife of John B. Slaughter and only daughter of Presley Edwards. Died at Russellville, Ky.
National Banner & Nashville Daily Advertiser. (Sat., Aug. 4, 1832)

Sloan, Archibald Esq. Died in Smith County on the 9th Oct. in the 64th year of his age.
National Banner & Nashville Whig. (Fri., Nov. 4, 1836)

Sloan, Mrs. Artemisia. Consort of the Rev. J. L. Sloan. Died in Henderson County on the 18th Sept.
National Banner & Nashville Whig. (Wed., Oct. 1, 1834)

Sloan, James. Formerly a member of Congress from N. J. Died.
Nashville Republican & State Gazette. (Thurs., Oct. 6, 1831)

Sloan, Louis Philippe. Eldest son of Martin W. and Eliza W. Sloan.
Died on the 3d inst. aged 6 years and six months.
Nashville True Whig & Weekley Commercial Register. Fri., April 12, 1850

Sloan, Quinton, Mr. Died in Nashville.
National Banner & Nashville Whig. (Fri., Oct. 23, 1835)

Sloss, Joseph Esq. Died in Simpson County, Ky.
National Banner. (Sat., April 18, 1829)

Sluder, Mrs. Elizabeth. Wife of Mr. A. B. Sluder. Died in Nashville
on Sunday evening last.
National Banner & Nashville Whig. (Mon., March 9, 1835)

Sluder, Mrs. Mary. Wife of Mr. A. B. Sluder. Died in Nashville on
Thurs., 14th inst.
Nashville Whig. (Sat., March 16, 1844)

Sluder, William G. E. Infant son of A. B. Sluder of Nashville. Died
in Williamson County on the 14th inst.
National Banner & Nashville Whig. (Wed., Aug. 19, 1835)

Small, Mrs. Elizabeth. Died in Logan County, Ky.
National Banner & Nashville Whig. (Sept. 2, 1826)

Small, Maj. Henry. Died at his residence on Tuesday the 27th ult.
in Tipton County. Formerly of Montgomery county age 61. Left a family
of young children.
National Banner & Nashville Daily Advertiser. (Fri., April 6, 1832)

Small, Mr. Henry. In the 61st year of his age formerly of Montgomery
County, Tenn. Died in Tipton County, Tenn. Tuesday the 27th ult.
National Banner & Nashville Daily Advertiser. (Wed., April 6, 1832)

Smilet, Robert. (Smiley). Died - departed this life on Sunday morning
about 6 o'clock. An elder of the Presbyterian church of Nashville.
Nashville Whig. (Sept. 8, 1823)

Smiley, Elizabeth Boyd. Only daughter of Robert G. and Rachel D.
Smiley. Died on Monday the 23d inst. aged 1 year and 18 days.
Nashville True Whig and Weekly Commercial Register (Wed., Dec. 25, 1850)

Smith, Mrs. Consort of the Rt. Rev. Bishop of this Diocess. Died in
Lexington, Ky.
National Banner & Nashville Daily Advertiser. (Tues., July 2, 1833)

Smith, Alban Weams. Son of Dr. E. B. Smith, aged 4 years 11 months
and 15 days. Died in Davidson County. Aug. 31, 1833.

Smith, Alice M. Daughter of John H. & Caroline Smith. Died on
Sunday evening.
The Politician and Weekley Nashville Whig. (Wed., Oct. 6, 1847)

Smith, Angelina M. Aged 12 years. Died in Nashville of Cholera.
National Banner & Nashville Whig. (Fri., June 19, 1835)

Smith, Augustus C. Died on board the Steamboat Memphis, on their
return from the Seminole War. He was of Capt. Henry's Company,
of Sumner County.
National Banner & Nashville Whig. (Fri., Feb. 3, 1837)

Smith, Col. Benard. Register of the Land Office. Died in Little
Rock, Ark. aged 59 years.
National Banner & Nashville Whig. (Mon., Aug. 3, 1835)

Smith, Mr. Benjamin Jr. Of the firm of Smith & Nye. Died near Boston
from drowning when the Boat Bunker Hill was wrecked by the wind.
National Banner & Nashville Daily Advertiser. (Sat., June 30, 1832)

Smith, General Byrd. Feb. 20, 1815. Died it is with regret that we
learn that our gallant fellow citizen, General Byrd Smith departed
this life on the 20th, Instant, at New Orleans. General Smith was an
early settler in this state, had been a member of the Legislature
and at the day of his death commanded the West Tennessee brigade of
militia, which acted so conspicious a part in the several battles
below N. O.
Whig. (March 14, 1815)

Smith, Calvin M. Esq. Formerly of Columbia. Died in Shelby County.
National Banner & Nashville Whig. (Fri., April 23, 1830)

Smith, Charles William. Infant son of Charles W. and Augusta Smith.
Died in Nashville yesterday afternoon.
Nashville Whig. (Sat., June 27, 1845)

Smith, General Daniel. Died on June 16, 1818. General Daniel Smith,
of Sumner County.
Nashville Whig. (June 27, 1818)

Smith, Daniel. Of N. Y. Died in New Orleans of Yellow Fever.
Daily Republican Banner. (Fri., Sept. 29, 1837)

Smith, Gen. Daniel. Died on the 16th inst. A respectable citizen
of Sumner County.
The Nashville Whig. and Tennessee Advertiser. (June 27, 1818)

Smith, Edith Graves. Daughter of John T. and Elizabeth Smith. Died
in Henry County on the 2nd inst. in her seventeenth year.
The Politician & Weekly Nashville Whig. (Wed., Sept. 8, 1847)

Smith, Edith Graves. Daughter of John T. and Elizabeth Smith. Died
in Henry County, on the 2nd inst. in her seventeenth year.
The Christian Record. (Sat., Sept. 11, 1847)

Smith, Mr. Edward W. Died at Montgomery, Ala.
National Banner & Nashville Whig. (Sat., Nov. 18, 1826)

Smith, Eliza E. Wife of Capt. James D. Smith. Died in Jackson County,
Tenn. on the 19th Feb. Obituary. (From the Knoxville Register)
Nashville Whig. (Wed., March 24, 1841)

Smith, Elizabeth. Eldest daughter of Nicholas Smith Post master of
Three Forks. Died in Wilson County, on Friday the 11th Oct. eight
years old.
National Banner & Nashville Daily Advertiser. (Wed., Oct. 16, 1833)

Smith, Miss Elizabeth W. Daughter of Mr. William C. Smith. Died in
Madison County, Ala.
National Banner. (Sat., Oct. 10, 1829)

Smith, Miss Frances. Daughter of Mr. Daniel Smith. Died in Bowling-
Green, Ky.
National Banner & Nashville Advertiser. (Mon., June 4, 1832)

Smith, Mrs. Francis. Wife of Mr. Charles Smith. Died in Smith
County, Tenn.
National Banner & Nashville Daily Advertiser. (Tues., Aug. 5, 1834)

Smith, George Mr. Died in Wilson County of Cholera on the 3d inst.
National Banner & Nashville Daily Advertiser. (Wed., June 5, 1833)

Smith, George Esq. Merchant of Paris, Tenn. Died at the City Hotel,
New York on the 17th ult, formerly a member of the Tennessee Legis-
lature.
Nashville Whig. (Mon., Dec. 3, 1838)

Smith, Mr. George N. Age 20. Died in Louisville, Ky.
National Banner & Nashville Advertiser. (Mon., Aug. 27, 1832)

Smith, Capt. George Sterling. Died suddnely last evening the father
in law of A. W. Johnson and Nichols Hobson Esqs.
Nashville Whig. (Sat., Jan. 22, 1842)

Smith, Mr. George W. Son of George Sterling Smith Esq. Died on
Wednesday 21st inst. at Tyrees Springs.
National Banner & Nashville Whig. (Thurs., July 29, 1830)

Smith, Mr. Griffin. Aged 21. Died in Antauga County, Ala.
National Banner. (Feb. 24, 1826)

Smith, Mrs. Hannah. Consort of Elisha Smith, on Friday, March 30th.
Died in Lebanon, Tenn.
National Banner & Nashville Advertiser. (Mon., April 9, 1832)

Smith, Henry. Died 15th at Cincinnati, Ohio of Cholera.
National Banner & Nashville Daily Advertiser. (Wed., Oct. 24, 1832)

Smith, Mr. Henry. Of Ala. of the firm of Smith, Gorin & Co. of New
Orleans. Died in Henderson County.
Nashville Whig. (Tues., May 5, 1846)

Smith, Mr. Henry O. Died at St. Louis.
National Banner. (Sat., Aug. 8, 1829)

Smith, J. F. City. Died in New Orleans of Yellow Fever.
Daily Republican Banner. (Wed., Sept. 27, 1837)

Smith, Rev. James. Of Greenville County, N. Carolina. Died in
Knox County, at the residence of H. G. Bennett, Esq.
National Banner & Nashville Daily Advertiser. (Tues., Nov. 19, 1833)

Smith, Mr. James B. In the 33d year of his age. Died in Bolivar.
National Banner & Nashville Whig. (Thurs., May 27, 1830)

Smith, Mrs. Jane. Consort of Joseph Smith, aged 31 years. Died in
Fayette County, Ky.
National Banner & Nashville Daily Advertiser. (Wed., Aug. 14, 1833)

Smith, Mrs. Jane P. Wife of Elisha H. Smith. Died at Mt. Vernon
Hardeman County.
National Banner & Nashville Whig. (Wed., Dec. 14, 1831)

Smith, Mrs. Jeanette. Died in Nashville on the 15th inst.
The Christian Record. (Sat., March 18, 1848)

Smith, Mrs. Jennette. Died in Nashville on the morning of the 15th
inst.
The Politician and Weekly Nashville Whig. (Fri., March 17, 1848)

Smith, Mrs. Jessey. A native of New York. Died in Nashville, recently
from Louisville, Ky.
The Christian Record. (Sat., March 25, 1848)

Smith, Mr. John. Died at Courtland, Ala.
National Banner & Nashville Whig. (Sat., Sept. 8, 1827)

Smith, Mr. John. Died in Knox County.
National Banner & Nashville Whig. (Mon., Sept. 19, 1831)

Smith, Mr. John. Aged 106 years. Died recently in Hardin County, Ky. He has a son living between 80 or 90 years old.
Nashville Whig. (Fri., Sept. 24, 1841)

Smith, Mr. John. Died in Lexington.
National Banner & Nashville Whig. (Sat., Aug. 5, 1826)

Smith, John. Died in Knox County.
National Banner & Nashville Whig. (Mon., Sept. 19, 1831)

Smith, Mr. John C. Died in Williamson County.
National Banner & Nashville Whig. (Sat., Feb. 16, 1828)

Smith, Rev. John C. Died in Carroll County, Tenn. on the 7th inst. Was in the 35th year of his age.
National Banner & Nashville Whig. (Fri., March 5, 1830)

Smith, Mr. John F. Died at Franklin, Williamson County of Cholera.
National Banner & Nashville Whig. (Wed., July 15, 1835)

Smith, Mr. John H. Died in Sumner County at the residence of Col. H. Bate of Consumption.
National Banner & Nashville Daily Advertiser. (Mon., March 31, 1834)

Smith, Jno. H. Late Merchant. Died in Nashville.
National Banner & Nashville Daily Advertiser. (Tues., June 24, 1834)

Smith, Mr. John L. 32. Died in Pulaski on June 7 of Cholera.
National Banner & Nashville Daily Advertiser. (Wed., June 19, 1833)

Smith, John M. In the 34th year of his age. Died at Montgomery Point, Ark. A native of East Tennessee and a son-in-law of the late Genl. Montgomery.
Nashville Whig. (Mon., Nov. 5, 1838)

Smith, Mr. Jonathan S. Died in New Orleans, late bookkeeper in the U. S. Branch Bank in that City.
National Banner & Nashville Daily Advertiser. (Thurs., Feb. 16, 1832)

Smith, Capt. Joseph. Late of the Steamboat Tennessee. Died in Nashville on the 1st of March.
National Banner & Nashville Whig. (Fri., March 3, 1837)

Smith, Captain Joseph. Commander of the steam boat, Tennessee. Died in Nashville, on Tuesday evening last.
Nashville Republican. (Thurs., March 2, 1837)

Smith, Capt. Joseph. of the Steamboat, Tenn. Died suddenly in Nashville after two days illness.
The Union. (Thurs., March 2, 1837)

Smith, Mr. Joseph M. Died at Dover Furnace, on the 26th.
National Banner & Nashville Whig. (Sat., April 5, 1828)

Smithers, Mr. John A. Died in Lexington, Ky.
National Banner. (March 24, 1826)

Smith, Mrs. Louisa. Wife of Mr. John Smith. Died at St. Louis.
National Banner & Nashville Daily Advertiser. (Wed., March 7, 1832)

Smith, Mrs. Louisa. Wife of Mr. John Smith. Died at St. Louis.
National Banner & Nashville Advertiser (Wed., March 7, 1832)

Smith, Mrs. Martha. Nearly 90 years old. Died at Murfreesborough, on the 10th inst.
National Banner (Sat., July 18, 1829)

Smith, Martha Ann. Daughter of Mr. Joel M. Smith. Died in Nashville
on the 20th inst.
The Union. (Thurs., Jan. 21, 1836)

Smith, Mr. Martin. Aged 21. Died in Rutherford County, killed by
the falling of a tree.
National Banner (Feb. 10, 1826)

Smith, Mary. Infant daughter of Thomas F. and Elizabeth S. Smith.
Died on Friday 29th ult. aged 2 years and 11 months.
The Christian Record. (Sat., Oct. 7, 1848)

Smith, Mary Elizabeth. Eldest daughter of Col. Joel R. Smith in the
12th year of her age. Died in Huntingdon on the 17th inst.
National Banner & Nashville Daily Advertiser. (Mon., March 25, 1833)

Smith, Mary Jane. Wife of Pleasant Smith Esq. Merchant and daughter
of William Ewing Esq. of Davidson County. Died.
Nashville Whig. (Thurs., May 19, 1842)

Smith, Mr. Michael. Of Louisville, Ky. Died near Natchez, drowned
by falling from the Steamboat, Robert Emmet.
National Banner & Nashville Whig. (July 1, 1826)

Smith, Dr. Nathan. Professor in the Medical institution of Yale
College. Died at New Haven, Con.
National Banner & Nashville Whig. (Sat., Feb. 21, 1829)

Smith, Nicholas P. Esq. Counsellor at law. Died in Franklin, Williamson County.
National Banner and Nashville Advertiser. (Sat., Oct. 13, 1832)

Smith, Nicholas P. Esq. Died on Wednesday morning at his residence
near Franklin.
Nashville Banner & Nashville Daily Advertiser. (Tues., Oct. 16, 1832)

Smith, Peter. Of New Orleans. A passenger. Died on the Steamer George
Collier, about 80 miles below Natchez. Scalded to death.
Daily Republican Banner. (Tues., May 14, 1839)

Smith, R. B. A student of the University of Nashville. Died at the
residence of Professor Cross, in Nashville.
Nashville Whig. (Wed., July 28, 1841)

Smith, Hon. Robert. In the 8th year of his age. Died in Baltimore
on the 26th. He was in the Revolutionary war.
Nashville Whig. (Thurs., Dec. 8, 1842)

Smith, Mr. Robert. Of Louisville on the evening of the 9th inst.
Died by suicide.
Impartial Review and Cumberland Repository. (Sat., Nov. 1, 1806)

Smith, Gen. Sam G. Died at Elizabethtown, Ky. on the 2nd Sept.
His remains were brought to Nashville and interred with Military honors
on Saturday the 6th inst.
National Banner & Nashville Whig. (Mon., Sept. 8, 1835)

Smith, Mr. Samuel and his wife. Died near Pikeville, Bledsoe County
on the 18th and 20th within two days of each other.
The Nashville Gazette. (Sat., Nov. 11, 1820)

Smith, Mrs. Sarah. Consort of Dr. P. Smith. Died on the 6th inst.
The Politician and Weekly Nashville Whig. (Fri., 10, 1848)

Smith, Mrs. Sarah. Wife of Dr. P. Smith. Died at the residence of
Mrs. Hawlett eight miles from Nashville on the 6th inst.
The Christian Record. (Sat., March 11, 1848)

Smith, Sarah Elizabeth. Daughter of Mr. Francis Smith in the 9th
year of age. Died in Wilson County on Monday 9th inst.
National Banner & Nashville Whig. (Mon., Aug. 16, 1830)

Smith, Capt. Shelton. He was born in Virginia in 1762. Died near
Hartsville, Sumner County, Tenn. on the 9th July in the 77th year of
his age, a soldier of the Revolution.
Daily Republican Banner. (Mon., July 30, 1838)

Smith, Mr. Stanhope P. Died in Madison County, Ala.
National Banner & Nashville Daily Advertiser. (Fri., Sept. 20, 1833)

Smith, Mr. Stanhope P. Aged 22 years. Died in Madison County, Ala.
National Banner & Nashville Daily Advertiser. (Mon., Sept. 9, 1833)

Smith, Mr. Stephen. A citizen of Philadelphia. Died on the 9th inst.
The Nashville Whig. (April 16, 1817)

Smith, Miss Susan P. Youngest daughter of Maj. Meriwether Smith.
Died in Roane County on the 22d ult.
National Banner & Nashville Advertiser. (Mon., March 12, 1832)

Smith, Miss Susan W. Wife of Philip A. Smith. Died in Mobile, Ala.
of Yellow fever, aged 28 years.
Daily Republican Banner. (Tues., Oct. 1, 1839)

Smith, Tennessee. Daughter of O. B. Smith. Died in Henry County.
National Banner & Nashville Daily Advertiser. (Mon., April 30, 1832)

Smith, Waters Esq. Marshal of the district of East Florida. Died
at St. Augustine.
National Banner & Nashville Whig. (Fri., Dec. 2, 1831)

Smith, William Esq. Died on Sunday the 25th in Franklin, in the
56th year of his age.
The Western Weekly Review. (Franklin, Tenn. Friday, Jan. 6, 1832)

Smith, Mr. William. Died in Murfreesborough.
National Banner & Nashville Whig. (Fri., Jan. 22, 1830)

Smith, William Esq. Age 55. Clerk of the circuit court of Williamson
County, for nearly 20 years. Died at Franklin on Sunday 25 ult.
National Banner & Nashville Advertiser. (Mon., Jan. 9, 1832)

Smith, Mr. William Jun. Son of William Smith Esq. Died in Franklin.
National Banner & Nashville Whig. (Mon., May 16, 1831)

Smith, Mr. Wm. Aged 19. Died in New Orleans.
National Banner & Nashville Daily Advertiser. (Tues., June 24, 1834)

Smith, Mr. William. Son of William Smith Esq. Died on the 6th of May
in Franklin.
The Western Weekly Review. Franklin, Tenn. (Fri., May 13, 1831)

Smith, Col. William H. Postmaster. Died at Cotton Grove, Madison
County.
National Banner & Nashville Whig. (Sat., Dec. 27, 1828)

Smith, Mr. William H. Son of Mrs. S. M. Smith and a citizen of Nash-
ville. Died at the residence of his brother, Joseph J. Smith
Pine Bluff, Texas.
Nashville True Whig & Weekly Commercial Register. (Fri., April 26,1850)

Sneed, Mr. William. Aged 58 years. Died in Rutherford County on the
13th of Cholera.
National Banner & Nashville Whig. (Fri., Aug. 14, 1835)

Smiley, Maj. James. Aged 70. Died at Bardstown, Ky.
National Banner. (Sat., Dec. 26, 1829)

Snelling, Col. Josiah. Of the U. S. Army in the 46 year of his
age. Died at Washington City.
National Banner & Nashville Whig. (Sat., Sept. 13, 1828)

Snipes, Mr. Jno. Aged 107 years. Died in Giles County.
Nashville Republican & State Gazette. (Thurs., May 5, 1831)

Snodgrass, Mrs. J. B. Died in Shelbyville, Tenn. of Cholera.
National Banner & Nashville Daily Advertiser. (Thurs., July 11, 1833)

Snow, Hannah. Consort of Mr. David C. Snow in the 43d of her
age. Died - departed this life, this morning at five o'clock.
Nashville Whig. (March 8, 1824)

Snowden, Dr. Isaac C. Died in Bucks County, Penn. Editor of the
Philadelphia Monthly Magazine.
National Banner & Nashville Whig. (Sat., Aug. 16, 1828)

Snowden, Mrs. Susan Bayard. Aged 74 years. Died on the 8th ult. at
Sacketts Harber, New York. Mrs. Snowden was the relict of the late
Rev. Samuel Finley Snowden.
The Christian Record. (Sat., July 29, 1848)

Soaper, Benjamin. Company G. First Tenn. Volunteers. Died - killed
in the battle of Monterey with the Mexicans, on Sept. 21, 1846)
Nashville Whig. (Sat., Oct. 24, 1846)

Soffrans, Peter. A valuable citizen of Florence, Ala. Died at
Florence, Ala.
Nashville Whig. (Wed., Sept. 16, 1840)

Solomon, Jeremiah. Aged 19, son of Mr. Jordon Solomon. Died in
Fayetteville, Tenn.
National Banner & Nashville Whig. (Wed., Oct. 1, 1834)

Solomon. An infant son of Mr. Wm. Solomon. Died in Gallatin.
National Banner & Nashville Daily Advertiser. (Thurs., Feb. 14, 1833)

Somervell, Mr. Jno. Died in Greenville County, N. C.
Nashville Republican & State Gazette. (Sat., March 19, 1831)

Sommersville, Mr. John. One of our oldest and most respected citizens.
Died on Sunday morning last, the 26th inst. age 75 years and 10 months.
Nashville Whig. (Thurs., April 30, 1846)

Sommerville, Capt. John H. Register of the Land Office of the United
States at Montgomery, Ala. Died in Montgomery, Ala. on the 8th.
Daily Republican Banner. (Mon., March 2, 1840)

Sommerville, Capt. John H. Died at Montgomery, Ala. on the 18th.
Register of the Land Office of the United States at Montgomery.
Nashville Whig. (Mon., March 2, 1840)

Sommerville, Mrs. Mary. Aged 75 years. Died in the county of Greenville
N. C. on the 14th of July.
Daily Republican Banner. (Thurs., Aug. 2, 1838)

Sommerville, Pierce Butler. Eldest son of John Sommerville, in the
39th year of his age. Died in Nashville on last evening.
Daily Republican Banner. (Wed., Jan. 3, 1838)

South, Gen. Samuel. Formerly, Treasurer of Kentucky. Died in
Fayette County, Ky.
National Banner & Nashville Advertiser. (Mon., Sept. 17, 1832)

Southerland, Mrs. Sarah. Wife of Mr. William B. Southerland and only
child of Mr. John Mauray. Died at Stenbenville on the 24th inst.
From the Wheeling Times.
National Banner & Nashville Whig. (Fri., Jan. 22, 1836)

Southworth, Mr. Peter. Aged 42, late of Natchez. Died on Lake
Concordia, La.
National Banner & Nashville Whig. (Sat., Sept. 15, 1827)

Spain, Mrs. Eliza Ann. Consort of John N. Spain of Nashville. Died
in Nashville on the 3d ot June.
The Union. (Sat., June 3, 1837)

Spain, Mrs. Eliza Ann. Wife of John Spain. Died in Nashville on the
3d inst.
National Banner & Nashville Whig. (Mon., June 6, 1837)

Spain, Mr. Stephens. Of this town. Died on Monday evening last.
The Nashville Whig. (June 9, 1817)

Spain, Mr. Thomas B. Died on Saturday the 18th at his residence 8
miles from Nashville, age 63.
National Banner & Nashville Daily Advertiser. (Mon., July 21, 1834)

Spain, Wm. G. Aged 13 years and 4 months. Died in Nashville.
National Banner & Nashville Daily Advertiser. (Mon., Sept. 1, 1834)

Spallman, David. Died at Cincinnati, Ohio of the Cholera.
National Banner & Nashville Daily Advertiser. (Thurs., Oct. 18, 1832)

Sparhowe, Edward N. Esq. Editor of the Petersburg Intelligencer.
Died suddenly Saturday afternoon.
(Richmond Whig)
Nashville Whig. (Sat., Jan. 27, 1838)

Sparks, William. Of Vicksburgh. Died in the loss of the Steamboat
Brandywine.
National Banner & Nashville Daily Advertiser. (Mon., April 23, 1832)

Spaulding, T. J. Fireman on the Boat George Collier. Died by being
scaulded to death on the morning of the 6th about 80 miles below
Natchez.
Daily Republican Banner. (Tues., May 14, 1839)

Speece, James Nelson. Died on the 28th inst. after an illness of
several months.
National Banner & Nashville Daily Advertiser. (Tues., July 29, 1834)

Speece, Capt. Lewis. Died in this town.
National Banner. (Sat., May 30, 1829)

Speed, Mr. William Jun. Aged 22. Died in this town.
National Banner & Nashville Whig. (Sat., Sept. 15, 1827)

Sperry, Elizabeth Offutt. Infant daughter of Mr. Lewis Sperry. Died
in Murfreesborough.
National Banner & Nashville Daily Advertiser. (Sat., Sept. 6, 1834)

Spence, Mr. John. Died on Friday last, at his residence. A respectable Merchant of this place, his remains were interred on Saturday
evening with Masonic Honors.
Nashville Whig. (Dec. 20, 1824)

Spence, John Esq. Died in Madison County.
National Banner & Nashville Whig. (Sat., Sept. 16, 1826)

Spence, Mr. Joseph. Died in Columbia.
National Banner. (Sat., Aug. 1, 1829)

Spence, Sarah Louisa. Daughter of Mrs. R. B. C. Spence. Died in
Nashville. She was the daughter of Mrs. R. B. C. Spence.
National Banner & Nashville Daily Advertiser. (Thurs., Dec. 6, 1832)

Spencer, Mrs. Caroline R. H. Wife of Mr. Samuel Spencer. Died in
Huntsville, Ala.
National Banner & Nashville Daily Advertiser. (Wed., Aug. 29, 1832)

Spencer, Mrs. Caroline R. H. Wife of Mr. Samuel Spencer. Died at
Huntsville, Ala.
National Banner & Nashville Advertiser. (Wed., Aug. 29, 1832)

Spencer, Mr. David. In the 63rd year of his age. Died in Logan
County, Ky.
National Banner & Nashville Whig. (Fri., March 27, 1835)

Spillman, Mr. Charles. Aged 80. Died in Garrard County, Ky.
National Banner. (April 7, 1826)

Spence, Capt. Robert T. Of the U. S. Navy. Died at his seat near
Baltimore.
National Banner & Nashville Whig. (Sat., Oct. 7, 1826)

Spinning, Mr. James D. Died at Cincinnati.
National Banner. (March 10, 1826)

Sprague, Mr. Joseph. Aged 28. Died in Hanover, N. H. This gentleman
resided for sometime in Nashville.
National Banner & Nashville Whig. (Fri., Nov. 4, 1831)

Sprain, Mrs. Nancy. Wife of Mr. Solomon D. Sprain. Died in Lauderdale County.
National Banner & Nashville Whig. (Sat., Sept. 9, 1826)

Springer, Mr. John. Died in Fayette County, Ky.
National Banner & Nashville Whig. (Sat., Sept. 9, 1826)

Springman, Mrs. Sarah. Wife of Mr. P. A. Springman. Died at Cincinnati.
National Banner (May 10, 1826)

Sprout, Mrs. Elizabeth. Died - 16th at Cincinnati, Ohio of Cholera.
National Banner & Nashville Daily Advertiser. (Wed., Oct. 24, 1832)

Spurzheim, Dr. Gaspard. Died in this city on Saturday night last.
(Copied from the Boston Daily Advertiser).
National Banner & Nashville Daily Advertiser. (Mon., Nov. 26, 1832)

Spyert, Mr. Thomas. Age 80, on Saturday 22, inst. The deceased was
a native of Virginia and Volunteer soldier of the revolutionary war.
National Banner & Nashville Whig. (Fri., Jan. 28, 1831)

Srite?, Mr. Thomas. Died in Sullivan County.
National Banner (Sat., May 2, 1829)

Stacker, Miss Elizabeth. Daughter of Samuel Stacker Esq. Died at
Cumberland Iron Works aged 14 years.
National Banner & Nashville Whig. (Wed., June 24, 1835)

Stacker, Mrs. Margaret. Wife of Mr. Samuel Stacker. Died in Montgomery County.
National Banner & Nashville Whig. (Wed., June 29, 1831)

Stacker, Mrs. Margaret. Wife of Mr. Samuel Stacker. Died in Montgomery County.
National Banner & Nashville Whig. (Wed., June 29, 1831)

Stacker, Mrs. Margaret. Wife of Mr. Samuel Stacker and daughter of
Mr. Jacob Beltzhoover. Died at the Lafayette Iron Works.
National Banner & Nashville Whig. (Wed., June 29, 1831)

Stacks, Mrs. Margaret Ann. Wife of Mr. Reuben Stacks. Died at Huntsville, Ala.
National Banner & Nashville Whig. (Tues., May 11, 1830)

Stacy, Mrs. Rebecca B. Wife of Mr. Alexander Stacy. Died in Hardeman
County on the 22th inst. and on the 19th Maryetta their infant daughter.
National Banner & Nashville Whig. (Thurs., July 19, 1830)

Staggs, Mr. Felix. Died in Williamson County.
National Banner & Nashville Whig. (Fri., Oct. 20, 1826)

Staggs, Pleasant. Aged 35 years. Died in Nashville on Wednesday
5th inst.
National Banner & Nashville Whig. (Fri., Oct. 7, 1836)

Stanback, F. With the Second Tenn. Regiment. Died was killed in the
Battle of Sierra Gorda, with the Mexicans.
The Politicians and Weekly Nashville Whig. (Fri., May 21, 1847)

Standifer, Col. James. Died on Sunday morning last 20th inst. on his
way to Washington, a member of Congress.
Daily Republican Banner. (Thurs., Aug. 24, 1837)

Standfield, John. Died - 13th at Cincinnati, Ohio of Cholera.
National Banner & Nashville Daily Advertiser. (Tues., Oct. 23, 1832)

Standlee, Mrs. Nancy. Died in Conway County, Ark. Ter.
National Banner. (March 24, 1826)

Stanly, Hon. John. Died in Newbern, S. C. on the 3d inst.
National Banner & Nashville Daily Advertiser. (Tues., Aug. 27, 1833)

Stannard, Franklin Esq. Died at Rodney, Miss.
National Banner & Nashville Daily Advertiser. (Mon., March 10, 1834)

Stark, Rt. Rev. John. Died in Raleigh, N. C. On Friday morning 5th
inst. in the 58th year of his age.
National Banner & Nashville Whig. (Fri., March 26, 1830)

Stark, Mr. John. Died in Nashville yesterday at the residence of
W. Lowe.
Nashville Whig. (Wed., Sept. 25, 1839)

Starling, Jno. L. Esq. Died in Columbus, Ohio.
Nashville Republican & State Gazette. (Sat., June 4, 1831)

Starling, Col. Wm. Age 72. Died in Springfield, Ky.
National Banner & Nashville Whig. (Sat., Feb. 10, 1827)

Starmer, George. Died in Knoxville, Tenn. with Fever.
Daily Republican Banner. (Sat., Oct. 13, 1838)

Starnes, Mr. Shubael. Died in Williamson County.
Nashville Whig. (Tues., May 5, 1846)

Statter, Mr. Abraham. Died in Murfreesborough.
National Banner & Nashville Whig. (Mon., Dec. 27, 1830)

Staughton, Dr. James M. An eminant physician. Died in Cincinnati, O.
National Banner & Nashville Daily Advertiser. (Wed., Aug. 14, 1833)

Staughton, Rev. William D. D. Died in Washington City. Recently
elected President of the College at Georgetown, Ky.
National Banner & Nashville Whig. (Fri., Jan. 1st. 1830)

Stout. The infant child of Mr. J. V. D. Stout. Died in this town on
Monday last.
National Banner & Nashville Whig. (Fri., July 25, 1828)

Steagall, Mrs. Rebecca E. Daughter of William D. and Elizabeth
McClary and consort of J. Steagall. Died at her residence in Marshall
County on the 1st ult. in the 19th year of her age.
The Christian Record. (Sat., June 24, 1848)

Stearns, Mrs. Catharine. Late of Watertown, Mass. Died on Monday
last Aug. 3 at the residence of her son-in-law, W. A. Eichbaum Esq.
of Nashville.
Nashville Whig. (Wed., Aug. 5, 1840)

Stearns, Mrs. Catherine. Late of Watertown, Mass. Died on Monday
Aug. 3, at the residence of her son-in-law W. A. Eichbaum, Esq. of
Nashville.
Daily Republican Banner. (Thurs., Aug. 13, 1840)

Steaurt, Mr. Samuel. Aged 82. Died in Sumner County.
National Banner & Nashville Daily Advertiser. (Tues., April 9, 1833)

Steel, Dr. Hugh. Editor of the Illinois Gazette. Died at Shanee-
town, Ill.
National Banner & Nashville Whig. (Sat., Sept. 27, 1828)

Steel, Miss Mary Jane. Grand-daughter of the Hon. John Rowan.
Died at Federal Hill, near Bardstown, Ky.
National Banner & Nashville Daily Advertiser. (Sat., Aug. 10, 1833)

Steel, Mr. Robert. Age 90. One of the Pioneers of the West. Died in
Sumner County.
National Banner & Nashville Whig. (Mon., May 9, 1831)

Steel, Mr. Robert. Aged 91. Died in Sumner County.
Nashville Republican & State Gazette. (Tues., May 10, 1831)

Steele, Mr. Of Nashville on the 7th inst. Died of a wound received
by an assassin he left a wife and several small children.
Impartial Review and Cumberland Repository. (Sat., June 14, 1806)

Steele, Rev. Elijah. Aged 25 years. Died in New Orleans, on the 10th
Pastor of the Methodist Church in New Orleans.
Nashville Whig. (Fri., Sept. 24, 1841)

Steele, Mr. James. Died in Natchez.
National Banner & Nashville Whig. (Sat., Aug. 5, 1826)

Steele, Capt. James C. Died in Louisville, Ky.
National Banner & Nashville Whig. (Sat., April 21, 1827)

Steele, Mrs. Lucy J. Wife of Edward G. Steele of Nashville. Died on
Tuesday 4th inst.
The Politician & Weekly Nashville Whig. (Fri., May 7, 1847)

Steele, Mrs. Mary. Wife of John Steele Esq. Died at Little Rock,
Ark. Editor of the Political Intellingencer.
National Banner & Nashville Daily Advertiser. (Mon., Aug. 25, 1834)

Steele, Miss Mary P. Aged 20. Died in Sumner County.
National Banner. (Sat., May 2, 1829)

Steele, Miss S. C. To Thomas H. Bradford. Died in Woodford County, Ky.
National Banner & Nashville Whig. (Sat., Dec. 16, 1826)

Steele, Mr. William. Died in Blount County.
National Banner & Nashville Whig. (Mon., Nov. 29, 1830)

Steele, Wm. F. Esq. Died in Mobile.
National Banner & Nashville Whig. (Sat., Oct. 7, 1826)

Steele, Wilson Esq. Aged about 32. Died in Bedford County, Ten.
National Banner & Nashville Daily Advertiser. (Sat., Sept. 6, 1834)

Steen, Mr. James. A native of Ireland. Died in Natchez.
National Banner & Nashville Whig. (Sat., Aug. 12, 1826)

Stemmons, Mr. Jacob. Died in Logan County, Ky.
National Banner. (Jan. 20, 1826)

Stephens, Rev. A. Died on Saturday last.
Nashville Whig. (Mon., March 1, 1841)

Stephens, Mr. Adam. Died at Louisville, Ky.
National Banner. (Feb. 17, 1826)

Stephens, Mr. Roger. Died in Huntsville, Ala.
National Banner & Nashville Whig. (Mon., Nov. 22, 1830)

Stephens, Samuel N. Esq. Principal of the Jackson Male Academy.
Died in Jackson, Tenn. on the 28th ult. Brother of the late Professor
A. Stephens, of Nashville.
Nashville Whig. (Sat., Aug. 12, 1843)

Stephens, Susan F. Aged 4. Died at Cincinnati, Ohio of Cholera.
National Banner & Nashville Daily Advertiser. (Wed., Oct. 24, 1832)

Stephenson, Ebenezer. Died at Cincinnati, Ohio of the Cholera, on the
12th.
National Banner & Nashville Daily Advertiser. (Thurs., Oct. 18, 1832)

Stephenson, Rev. James D. D. Died in Maury County, on the 6th inst.
For many years minister of Zions Church.
National Banner & Nashville Daily Advertiser. (Fri., Jan. 13, 1832)

Stephenson, Mr. John W. In his 63d year. Died at his residence in
Maury County, Tenn. on the 29th Oct. 1847.
The Christian Record. (Sat., Nov. 20, 1847)

Sterns, Mr. Ebeneztr. Mate of the Steamboat Tennessee late of the
City of New York. died on the 16th inst.
National Banner & Nashville Whig. (Fri., Sept. 18, 1835)

Stevens, Henry Esq. Aged near 26 years. Died at the residence of
his Mother in the vicinity of Nashville.
Nashville Whig. (Tues., June 27, 1843)

Stevens, Mr. Miller. Pilot of Cincinnati. Died in Randolph, T.
National Banner & Nashville Daily Advertiser. (Tues., July 15, 1834)

Stevens, P. T. Infant son of Moses Stevens, Esq. Died on Sunday 20,
inst. in Nashville.
National Banner & Nashville Advertiser. (Mon., May 21, 1832)

Stevens, Mrs. Sarah. Wife of Mr. Robert Stevens. Died in Lincoln
County.
National Banner & Nashville Whig. (Fri., Jan. 29, 1830)

Stevens, Sarah B. Daughter of Moses Stevens, Esq. Died in the vicinity
of Nashville the 9th June, she was in the 16th year of her age.
Daily Republican Banner. (Wed., June 12, 1839)

Stevens, Sarah B. Daughter of Moses Stevens Esq. Died last evening
in this vicinity, aged 16 years.
Nashville Whig. (Mon., June 10, 1839)

Stevens, Capt. Thomas L. In the 36th year of his age. Died on the
27th inst. had just been married 2 days. Copyed from the Milton,
N. C. Spectator.
The Western Weekly Review. (Fri., Aug. 17, 1832) Franklin, Tenn.

Stevenson, Dr. D. Died in Versailles, Ky. 12 miles from Lexington
of Cholera.
National Banner & Nashville Whig. (Fri., Sept. 4, 1835)

Stevenson, Mrs. Eleonor S. Aged 55 years. Died near Russellville,
Ky.
National Banner & Nashville Daily Advertiser. (Sat., Feb. 16, 1833)

Stevenson, Elizabeth. Aged 3. Died in Nashville of Cholera. on
Sat., June 8th.
National Banner & Nashvile Daily Advertiser. (Mon., June 10, 1833)

Stevenson, Hugh Esq. Aged about 78 years. Died near Russellville, Ky.
on the 13th inst.
Nashville True Whig & Weekly Commercial Register. (Fri., June 21, 1850)

Stewart, Andrew. Only son of William Stewart Esq. Died at Stewarts
ferry on the 6th inst. aged 33 years.
Daily Republican Banner. (Mon., July 13, 1840)

Stewart, Mr. H. T. President of the Iredale County Temperance Society.
Died in Ireland County, N. C.
National Banner & Nashville Daily Advertiser. (Thurs., Jan. 2, 1834)

Stewart, Col. J. Indian Agent. Died at Detroit on the 21st ult.
National Banner & Nashville Daily Advertiser. (Tues., Sept. 10, 1833)

Stewart, Col. James. An Officer of the Indian Department. Died at
Carey Mission, near Niles, M. T. in the 47th year of his age.
National Banner & Nashville Daily Advertiser. (Fri., Sept. 27, 1833)

Stewart, Mr. Jas. Died in Rutherford County.
National Banner & Nashville Whig. (Sat., Sept. 23, 1826)

Stewart, Mrs. Janette C. Died near Woodville, Miss.
National Banner. (June 10, 1826)

Stewart, Mrs. Margaery. Died at Jonesborough daughter of Wm.
McConnell Esq.
National Banner & Nashville Whig. (Sat., Jan. 20, 1827)

Stewart, Mrs. Sarah. Wife of Capt. William Stewart aged 65. Died at
Stewarts Ferry, Stones River in this County on the 29th inst.
National Banner & Nashville Whig. (Thurs., June 24, 1830)

Stewart, Mrs. Susan E. Wife of Isaac Stewart. Died in Louisville, Ky.
National Banner & Nashville Daily Advertiser. (Wed., July 9, 1834)

Stewart, Mr. Wm. For many years a citizen of this place. Died this
morning in the Market House (Banner).
Nashville Whig. (Mon., Feb. 22, 1841)

Stewart, Mr. William. Died in Madison Co., Ten. A soldier of the
revolution.
National Banner & Nashville Daily Advertiser. (Fri., Dec. 27, 1833)

Stewart, Col. William. Died at Paris, Henry County.
National Banner & Nashville Whig. (Sat., Sept. 20, 1828)

Stickney, Miss Harriet Eliza. Eldest daughter of Mr. John Stickney.
Died at Cincinnati.
National Banner & Nashville Whig. (Fri., Dec. 17, 1830)

Still, Mr. John. Aged 21 years. Died in Williamson County, Ten.
National Banner & Nashville Whig. (Fri., April 10, 1835)

Stinson, E. D. Merchant of Ireland. Died in New Orleans of Yellow
Fever.
Daily Republican Banner. (Wed., Sept. 27, 1837)

Stith, William Dickson. Infant son of Dr. F. Stith. Died on Monday
last.
The Western Weekly Review. (Franklin, Tenn. Fri., Feb. 22, 1833)

Stripe, Mr. D. Died in Bardstown, Ky.
National Banner & Nashville Whig. (Sat., Dec. 23, 1826)

Stockton, Mrs. Wife of Dr. Stockton. Died in Bowling Green, Ky.
National Banner & Nashville Whig. (Thurs., June 17, 1830)

Stockton, Lucius Esq. Died in the City of Trenton an eminent Lawyer
of New Jersey.
National Banner & Nashville Whig. (Wed., July 1, 1835)

Stockton, Richard Esq. Died in New Orleans late Attorney General of
the State of Mississippi.
National Banner & Nashville Whig. (Sat., Feb. 24, 1827)

Stockwell, J. B. Of Ky. Died in New Orleans of Yellow Fever
Daily Republican Banner. (Wed., Sept. 27, 1837)

Stoddart, William Esq. Attorney at Law. Died in Jackson Tenn.
Nashville Whig. (Mon., Jan. 21, 1839)

Stodder, Mrs. Mary P. Wife of Mr. C. Stodder. Aged 51. Died in
Nashville on the 24th ulto.
Nashville Whig. (Wed., Nov. 3, 1841)

Stoddert, William Esq. Died in Jackson.
Daily Republican Banner. (Sat., Jan. 19, 1839)

Stokes, Mr. John. Aged 53. Died at Cincinnati.
National Banner & Nashville Whig. (Mon., June 7, 1830)

Stokes, Mrs. Penelope. Wife of Jordon Stokes Esq. and daughter of
Hon. Nathaniel W. and Sarah J. Williams aged about 20 years. Died
in Carthage, Smith County, Tenn. on the 5th Nov.
Daily Republican Banner. (Sat., Nov. 14, 1840)

Stokes, Mrs. Penelope. Wife of Jordan Stokes, Esq. and daughter of
Nathaniel W. and Sarah J. Williams. Died at Carthage, Smith County,
Tenn. on the 5th of Nov. aged about 20 years.
Nashville Whig. (Fri., Nov. 13, 1840)

Stokes, William. A citizen of Obion County. Died in the vicinity
of Brownsville, Haywood County, on Thursday Aug. 1st inst.
National Banner & Nashville Daily Advertiser. (Wed., Aug. 14, 1833)

Stone, Eli H. Died at Bloomfield, Ky.
National Banner. (May 13, 1826)

Stone, Hendley Esq. Died in Williamson County, Tenn.
National Banner & Nashville Daily Advertiser. (Wed., Aug. 20, 1834)

Stone, Mrs. Mary. Wife of the Hon. George W. Stone and daughter of
George Gillespie, of Williamson County. Died at her home in Talla-
dega, Ala. on the 12th Sept. in the 36th year of her age.
The Christian Record. (Sat., Sept. 30, 1848)

Stone, Philemon, William and Cyrus. The three sons and only
children of Mr. Saphna and Mrs. Lois Stone of Kinsman, Trumbull

County, Ohio. Were drowned by the hand of their Mother. The
eldest was about four years and six months old; the youngest about
eleven months and yet at the breast. These children were uncommonly
bright and promising and a fond father doted upon them with the most
pleasing anticipations. The next day a jury of inquest was called
upon the dead bodies. Their verdict was, that these children came to
an untimely death by the hand of Mrs. Louis Stone, their Mother, who
in a fit of insanity drowned them in a hollow log set in the spring.
The Clarion and Tennessee Gazette. (July 25, 1820)

Stone, Mrs. Polly. Died in Madison County, Ky
National Banner & Nashville Whig. (Sat., Sept. 9, 1826)

Stone, William. A son of Mrs. Stone of the Theatre. Died in Nashville
aged 8 or 10 years old.
National Banner & Nashville Whig. (Mon., June 29, 1835)

Stones, Esther Maria. Infant daughter of Liston and Elizabeth Stones.
Died on the 18th inst.
Daily Republican Banner. (Thurs., Aug. 20, 1840)

Stones, Robena Armstead. Infant daughter of L.& W. E. Stones. Died
on Thursday evening aged 13 months and 2 days.
The Politician &Weekly Nashville Whig. (Fri., July 9, 1847)

Stones, Robena Armstead. Youngest daughter of L. & W. E. Stones
aged 13 months and 2 days. Died on Thursday evening.
The Christian Record. (Sat., July 10, 1847)

Storke, Rev. Charles A. G. Died in Rowan County, N. C.
Nashville Republican & State Gazette. (Thurs., April 19, 1831)

Storrs, Rev. Charles B. Late President of the Westen Reserve College,
Ohio. Died on the 15th ult. at Braintree.
National Banner & Nashville Daily Advertiser. (Sat., Oct. 19, 1833)

Story, Samuel L. M. D. Aged 33 years. Died in Pikeville, Tenn.
27th Sept.
Daily Republican Banner. (Sat., Nov. 9, 1839)

Stouthart, Mr. Robert. Of Nashville. Died in the loss of the boat,
Brandywine.
National Banner & Nashville Daily Advertiser. (Mon., April 23, 1832)

Stout, Banjamin C. M. D. In the 40th year of his age. Died at Athens,
Tenn.
National Banner. (Sept. 12, 1829)

Stout, Miss Elizabeth. Died at Tuscumbia, Ala.
National Banner & Nashville Daily Advertiser. (Tues., Aug. 19, 1834)

Stout, Mr. Ira. Died on the 18th of May last of a pulmonary complaint.
The Nashville Whig. (June 2, 1817)

Stout, Mr. Samuel. Died at Cincinnati, Ohio of Cholera on the 12th.
National Banner & Nashville Daily Advertiser. (Sat., Oct. 20, 1832)

Stowell, Mrs. Maria. Died in Knoxville.
National Banner & Nashville Whig. (Fri., Feb. 12, 1830)

Strause, Capt. Henry. Late of the Steam boat Saratoga. He retired
in usual health and was found dead next morning, cause unknown.
Died in Louisville, Ky.
Nashville Banner & Nashville Whig. (Fri., Sept. 9, 1831)

Stratton, Anthony M. Son of Madison & Mary Stratton. Died on the
2d in Davidson County, aged 6 months and 6 days.
National Banner & Nashville Whig. (Mon., Nov. 9, 1835)

Stratton, Mr. Henry M. Son of James Stratton, Esq. Died in Sumner County on Thursday morning 1st inst.
National Banner & Nashville Whig. (Mon., Sept. 5, 1831)

Stratton, Mrs. Sarah C. Consort of Mr. Edward Stratton. Died in Sumner County, Ten.
National Banner & Nashville Daily Advertiser. (Thurs., June 19, 1834)

Stratton, Miss Sarah F. Daughter of Thomas & Elizabeth Stratton. Died in Davidson County on the 30th Sept.
National Banner & Nashville Whig. (Fri., Oct. 3, 1834)

Street, Mr. Franklin, aged 21. Died in Frankford, Ky.
National Banner & Nashville Whig. (Sat., Sept. 9, 1826)

Street, Mr. Pleasant. Aged 23. Died in Lincoln County, T.
National Banner & Nashville Whig. (Sat., Oct. 7, 1826)

Stribling, Mrs. Maria. Died in Washington, City.
Nashville Republican & State Gazette. (Thurs., March 31, 1831)

Stringfield, Mrs. Sarah. Consort of Rev. Thomas Stringfield. Died at Strawberry Plains Jefferson County, Tenn. on the 5th inst.
Nashville Whig. (Thurs., April 14, 1842)

Striplin, O. With the Second Tenn. Regiment. Died was killed in the Battle of Sierra Gorda with the Mexicans.
The Politicians and Weekly Nashville Whig. (Fri., May 21, 1847)

Stroddard, W. C. Aged 19 years. Died at the residence of his father E. C. Stroddard, in Nashville.
Daily Republican Banner. (Thurs., Nov. 1, 1838)

Strodder, W. C. Son of E. C. Strodder. Died in Nashville on Thursday last.
Nashville Whig. (Mon., Nov. 5, 1838)

Strong, Hon. Caleb. Late Governor of Mass. Died suddenly at Northampton, Mass. on Sunday last.
The Nashville Gazette. (Wed., Dec. 1, 1819)

Strong, Miss Jane. Daughter of Dr. J. C. Strong. Died in Knoxville, Tenn.
Daily Republican Banner. (Sat., Sept. 29, 1838)

Strong, Mrs. Jane. Wife of the late Dr. J. C. Strong. Died at Knoxville on the 3d inst. aged 59.
Nashville Whig. (Tues., Oct. 13, 1846)

Strong, Dr. Robert N. Died at Tuscumbia, Ala.
National Banner (Sat., Nov. 14, 1829)

Strother, Capt. George. Late of the U. S. Army. Died in this place on Sunday evening last.
Nashville Whig. (Tues., Feb. 20, 1816)

Strother, Olivia. Daughter of James W. Strother, Esq. Died in Rutherford County.
National Banner & Nashville Whig. (Sat., Jan. 27, 1827)

Stroud, Miss Sarah. Aged 37. Died in Paris, on the 7th inst.
National Banner & Nashville Daily Advertiser. (Fri., Feb. 15, 1833)

Stuart, Capt. John. Of the U. S. Army. Died in the Cherokee Nation, west.
Nashville Whig. (Mon., Jan. 21, 1839)

Stuart, Gen. Philip. A revolutionary Officer. Died at Washington.
National Banner & Nashville Whig. (Mon., Aug. 30, 1830)

Stuart, Hon. Sophia Margaret. Granddaughter of William Penn. Founder
and proprietor of Pennsylvania. Died on the 29th inst. at the house
of her son-in-law the Earl of Ranfurley.
The Politician & Weekly Nashville Whig. (Fri., June 18, 1847)

Stuart, Mr. Stockton J. Died at Port Gibson, Mi.
National Banner & Nashville Whig. (Wed., April 27, 1831)

Stuart, Hon. Thos. Aged about 70 years. Died in the vicinity of
Franklin, Tenn. on Tuesday evening last.
Daily Republican Banner. (Fri., Oct. 19, 1838)

Stuart, Hon. Thomas. Aged 70 years. Died near Franklin, Williamson
County, Tenn. on Friday last. For twenty six years a Judge of Cir-
cuit Court of Tenn.
Nashville Union. (Fri., Oct. 19, 1838)

Stuart, Hon. Thomas. Aged 70 years. Died near Franklin on Friday
evening last for 26 years, a Judge of the Circuit Court of Tenn.
Nashville Whig. (Fri., Oct. 19, 1838)

Stubbins, Capt. John J. In the 30th year of his age. Died at New
Castle, Ky.
National Banner & Nashville Daily Advertiser. (Sat., Aug. 10, 1833)

Stubblefield, Mrs. Aannah. Aged 57 years. Died in Logan County,
Ky.
National Banner & Nashville Daily Advertiser. (Mon., Sept. 9, 1833)

Stubberfield, Mr. Michael. Aged 70 years, of Jefferson County, Tenn.
Died - was thrown from his horse and killed near Cincinnati.
Nashville Whig. (Wed., Dec. 19, 1838)

Stubbs, Mr. Michael. Died near Bowling Green, Ky.
National Banner & Nashville Daily Advertiser. (Tues., Sept. 10, 1833)

Studley, Mrs. Susan. Wife of Mr. N. Studley. Died in St. Louis.
National Banner & Nashville Whig. (Thurs., Aug. 19, 1830)

Stump, Mary L. Youngest daughter of Col. John Stump. Died in Davidson
County on the 25th ult.
National Banner & Nashville Daily Advertiser. (Mon., March 4, 1833)

Stump, Mrs. Sarah. Consort of Maj. Christopher Stump, of this Place.
Died on Thursday morning last.
Impartial Review and Cumberland Repository. (Sat., June 6, 1807)

Stump, Selinda Parallee. Age 17. Died in Davidson County on 15
inst.
National Banner & Nashville Advertiser. (Mon., Aug. 20, 1832)

Sturdevant, Ashley Page. Son of William Sturdevant and his wife
Elizabeth. Died in Williamson County in the 8th year of his age.
National Banner & Nashville Whig. (Wed., Nov. 26, 1834)

Sublett, Capt. William. Died in Jackson County, Ala.
National Banner & Nashville Daily Advertiser. (Mon., July 23, 1832)

Sublett, George and William Sublett. Both children of Capt. Geo.
A. Sublett. Died in Rutherford County on Satuday last.
National Banner & Nashville Whig. (Sat., Feb. 14, 1829)

Suderd, Miss Nancy. Aged 80. Died in M'Minn County.
National Banner & Nashville Whig. (Wed., Sept. 7, 1831)

Suffringe, Mr. John. Died in Hopkinsville.
National Banner & Nashville Whig. (Sat., Aug. 26, 1826)

Sullivan, Mr. Young. Died at Murfreesborough.
The Nashville Whig. & Tenn. Advertiser. (Dec. 15, 1817)

Sullivan, Dr. Benj. F. Died in Smith County.
National Banner & Nashville Whig. (Sat., Aug. 9, 1828)

Sullivan, Col. John C. Died in St. Louis.
National Banner & Nashville Whig. (Thurs. Aug. 19, 1830)

Sullivan, Mr. J. O. Died at Decatur, Ala.
National Banner & Nashville Whig.' (Sat., Aug. 18, 1827)

Sumner, Mrs. Lavinia. Wife of Isaac W. Sumner in the 24th year of her
age. Died in Davidson County on the 11th inst.
National Banner & Nashville Daily Advertiser. (Sat., June 15, 1833)

Sumner, Mrs. Mary. Age 53. Wife of Duke W. Sumner of Davidson
County and daughter of Mathew Drake, Esq. formerly a merchant in Nash
County, N. C. Died on Friday 22nd leaving 10 children, 3 grand
children.
National Banner & Nashville Daily Advertiser. (Tues., June 26, 1832)

Sumner, Mrs. Mary. Aged 53. Died in Davidson County.
Nashville Republican & State Gazette. (Mon., June 25, 1832)

Sumner, Thomas E. Esq. In the 50th year of his age. Died at his
residence in Williamson County, Tenn. on the 21st inst. He was a
son of General Sumner of North Carolina.
The Nashville Gazette. (Wed., July 28, 1819)

Sumner, Thos. J. Esq. Sen. Editor of the Democrat. Died in Huntsville, Ala.
National Banner & Nashville Advertiser. (Thurs., June 28, 1832)

Sumter, General. Died on the 1st inst. at South Mount age 100.
Nashville Republican & State Gazette. (Wed., June 27, 1832)

Sumter, Gen. Thomas. Died on Friday last in the 97th year of his
age. (Columbia Telescope)
The Western Weekly Review. (Franklin, Tenn. (Fri., June 22, 1832)

Sumpter, General Thomas. Of South Caroline. Died at his residence
at South Mount, on the 1st inst. full of years and full of honors.
A veteran soldier of the Revolution.
National Banner & Nashville Daily Advertiser. (Mon., June 18, 1832)

Sutherland, Mrs. Died at Tuscumbia.
National Banner & Nashville Whig. (Sat., March 10, 1827)

Sutherland, Mr. James. Died in the neighborhood of Danville, Ky. of
Cholera.
National Banner & Nashville Daily Advertiser. (Mon., Aug. 5, 1833)

Sutton, Mr. Of Blount County. Died on board Steamboat Atlantic,
near Memphis.
National Banner & Nashville Daily Advertiser. (Wed., June 12, 1833)

Sutton, Mr. James. Died in Memphis.
National Banner & Nashville Whig. (Sat., Nov. 3, 1837)

Sutton, Col. John. Died in Louisville, Ky.
National Banner & Nashville Whig. (Mon., June 28, 1830)

Sutton, Mr. John. Died in Todd County, Ky.
National Banner. (Feb. 3, 1826)

Sutton, Mrs. Wm. B. Died in Shelbyville, Tenn. of Cholera.
National Banner & Nashville Daily Advertiser. (Thurs., July 11, 1833)

Swan, Col. James. Formerly of Boston, who has been confined in
prison for debt for the last 25 years. Died in Paris, France on the
18th of March.
National Banner & Nashville Whig. (Fri., May 6, 1831)

Swan, Miss Jane. Died in Davidson County, Ten.
National Banner & Nashville Daily Advertiser. (Thurs., Sept. 11, 1834)

Swan, John A. Esq. Died in Knox County.
National Banner & Nashville Daily Gazette. (Mon., Sept. 10, 1832)

Swan, Mrs. Mary L. Died at Knoxville, daughter of Hugh L. White Esq.
National Banner & Nashville Whig. (Sat., May 24, 1828)

Swan, Mr. Samuel H. Formerly of Knoxville. Died in Jackson, Western
District.
National Banner & Nashville Whig. (Mon., Nov. 22, 1830)

Swann, Mrs. Elizabeth B. Died on the 18th inst. in Nashville.
Nashville Whig. (Sat., June 20, 1846)

Swancut, Mr. David. Late of Philadelphia. Died in Mobile, Ala.
of Yellow fever.
Daily Republican Banner. (Tues., Oct. 1, 1839)

Swanson, Mr. Westley. Died in Monroe County, Ten.
Nashville Republican & State Gazette. (Tues., March 15, 1831)

Swassey, Henry S. Of Maine. Died in New Orleans of Yellow Fever.
Daily Republican Banner. (Fri., Sept. 29, 1837)

Swan, Mrs. Ann K. Wife of Capt. John C. Swan. Died at St. Louis.
National Banner & Nashville Daily Advertiser. (Wed., Aug. 22, 1832)

Sykes, Mrs. Sarah W. Consort of Col. James T. Sykes. Died in
Decatur, Ala.
National Banner & Nashville Whig. (Fri., March 6, 1835)

Sylar, Mr. Jacob. Age 62. Died in Roane County.
National Banner. (April 14, 1826)

Syle, Rev. John. In the 43d year of his age. Died in Fayette County,
Ky. on the 23d of Nov. last.
The Christian Record. (Sat., Jan. 9, 1847)

Symmes, Capt. John Cleves. Died in Hamilton, Ohio well known for his
theory of a hollow globe and concentric spheres.
National Banner. (Sat., June 17, 1829)

Sypest?, Thomas Sen. Aged about 80 years. Died in Wilson County.
A soldier of the Revolutionary War.
National Banner & Nashville Whig. (Fri., Jan. 28, 1831)

Taggart, Mr. Patrick. A native of Ireland. Died in Jefferson County,
Ky.
National Banner & Nashville Whig. (Sat., Aug. 26, 1826)

Tailer, Leonard. Died 14th at Cincinnati, Ohio of Cholera.
National Banner & Nashville Daily Advertiser. (Tues., Oct. 23, 1832)

Tait, Hon. Charles. In the 68th year of his age. Died in Wilcox
County, Ala. on the 7th of Oct.
National Banner & Nashville Whig. (Wed., Nov. 4, 1835)

Tait, Mr. William. For thirty years one of the most respectable citizens of this town, on Sunday his remains was intered with masonic honors. Died on Saturday last about 2 o'clock p.m.
The Nashville Whig. (Feb. 7, 1816)

Talbot, Eli, Esq. Clerk of the Chancery Court for this district. Died in Nashville last night.
National Banner & Nashville Advertiser. (Tues., Aug. 14, 1832)

Talbot, John Felix. Infant son of Eli Talbot, Esq. Died in Nashville on Sunday last.
National Banner & Nashville Daily Advertiser. (Tues., Aug. 7, 1832)

Talbot, Mr. Levi. Of the U. S. Navy.
Nashville Republican & State Gazette. (Sat., Aug. 6, 1831)

Talbot, Mrs. Ruth. Consort of Thomas Talbot Esq. Died on Thursday the 7th inst. in the fifty second year of her age.
The Nashville Gazette. (Sat., Oct. 9, 1819)

Talbot, Thomas, Esq. On Friday evening last. Died in Davidson County.
National Banner & Nashville Whig. (Mon., Jan. 31, 1831)

Talbot, Thomas Esq. Died at his residence near Nashville on last evening.
Nashville Republican & State Gazette. (Sat., Jan. 29, 1831)

Talbot, Thomas Esq. Died in Davidson County, on Friday evening last. An old and respectable citizen.
National Banner & Nashville Whig. (Mon., Jan. 31, 1831)

Talbot, Thomas A. Died on the 8th inst. of Cholera.
National Banner & Nashville Whig. (Mon., July 13, 1835)

Talbot, William Charles. Son of Mr. Eli Talbot Esq. Died in Nashville
National Banner & Nashville Whig. (Thurs., Sept. 23, 1830)

Taliaferro, Caroline P. Consort of John A. Taliaferro and daughter of Joshua Harrison. Died at Quincy, Gibson County, on the 7th Jan.
Nashville Republican. (Sat., Feb. 20, 1836)

Taliaferro, Mrs. Wife of Mr. Hay Taleaferro. Died at Winchester, Ky.
National Banner & Nashville Whig. (Sat., Jan. 13, 1826)

Talley, Mr. William Nelson. Died in Sumner County on the 14th inst.
National Banner & Nashville Whig. (Sat , Feb. 21, 1829)

Tandy, Major Gabriel. Died at Harrodsburg, Ky.
National Banner & Nashville Whig. (Mon., July 19, 1830)

Tannehill, Gen. Adamson. Died on Saturday morning the 23d of December, in the seventy-first year of his age.
The Clarion & Tennessee Gazette. (Jan., 23, 1821)

Tannehill, Mrs. Eliza Wife of Wilkins Tannerhill Esq. Died in Nashville on 26th inst. in the 54 year of her age.
Nashville Whig. (Sat., Jan. 28, 1843)

Tannehill, Ephraim Foster. Youngest son of Wilkins Tannehill. Died at Louisville on Sat. the 24th.
Nashville Republican (Tues., June 27, 1837)

Tannehill, Foster. Son of Wilkin Tannehill Esq. Died on Sunday evening last aged 3 years and 3 months old.
Nashville Whig. (Tues., May 30, 1843)

Tannehill, Mr. John. Died in Logan County, Ky.
National Banner (Sat., Sept. 19, 1829)

Tannehill, Mrs. Margaret. In the 73d year of her age. Died in
Nashville on the 21st inst. at the residence of her son Wilkins
Tannehill, relict of the late Capt. Josiah Tannehill.
Nashville Whig. (Wed., Dec. 25, 1839)

Tannehill, Virginia Wilkins. Daughter of Wilkins Tannehill. Died
suddenly on Tuesday night aged 3 years.
Nashville Whig. (Fri., Aug. 27, 1841)

Tannehill, Mr. Wilkins F. Only son of Wilkins Tannehill, Esq. Died
in Memphis on Friday the 15th inst. in the 39th year of his age.
Nashville True Whig & Weekly Commercial Register. (Fri., Nov. 22, 1850)

Tanner, Mrs. Julia. Wife of Tanner, Mr. Wm. Died at Harrodsburg, Ky.
National Banner. (Sat., May 16, 1829)

Tanner, Mrs. Susan F. Consort of Mr. John A. Tanner. Died in Maury
Co. on Thursday the 7th of Aug. in the 24th year of her age.
National Banner & Nashville Daily Advertiser. (Fri., Aug. 22, 1834)

Tantall, Col. Edward. Died in Savannah, Ga. on 21st November.
Nashville Republican & State Gazette. (Wed., Dec. 12, 1832)

Tapp, Mr. John. Aged 76. Died in Scott County, Ky.
National Banner & Nashville Whig. (Mon., Aug. 30, 1830)

Tappan, Mrs. Margaret B. Wife of Col. B. S. Tappan. Died in Williamson County on Tuesday evening 28, ult.
National Banner & Nashville Whig. (Mon., July 4, 1831)

Tappan, Mrs. Margaret B. Consort of Col. B. S. Tappan. Died at her
residence in the vicinity of Franklin on Tuesday last.
The Western Weekly Review. (Fri., July 1, 1831) Franklin, Tenn.

Tarver, Col. Samuel. In the 71st year of his age. Died in Wilson
County on the 20th inst.
National Banner & Nashville Whig. (Thurs., Nov. 4, 1830)

Tate, Miss Eliza Julia. Died in Limestone County, Ala.
National Banner & Nashville Whig. (Wed., Sept. 28, 1831)

Tate, Zedekiah. Died near Belleview, Ala.
National Banner & Nashville Whig. (Wed., Feb. 4, 1835)

Tatum, Major Howell. Officer of the Revolution. Died Monday night,
remains were interred yesterday evening by the Nashville Guard with
military honors.
Nashville Whig. (Sept. 11, 1822)

Taul, Mrs. _aroline P. Aged 21. Wife of Thomas P. Taul, of Huntsville and daughter of Col. Wm. P. Anderson. Died at Winchester, Ten.
on the 30th Aug. 1828.
National Banner & Nashville Whig. (Sat., Sept. 13, 1828)

Taul, Col Micah. Died in Mardisville, Talladega County, Alabama,
on the 27th ultimo. In the 64th year of his age. He was born in
Maryland but was reared in Ky.
Nashville True Whig & Weekly Commercial Register. (Fri., July 19, 1850)

Taws, Mr. Charles Jun. Formerly of Philadelphia. Died at Louisville,
Ky.
National Banner & Nashville Daily Advertiser. (Mon., Oct. 15, 1832)

Taylay, Mrs. Hannah. Died in Fayette County, Ky. on the 16th inst.
aged 78 years.
National Banner & Nashville Daily Advertiser. (Tues., May 29, 1832)

Taylor, Anthony Esq. in the 65th year of his age. Died on the 2d
Dec. 1837 was President of the Farmers Bank of Buck County, Penn.
Daily Republican Banner. (Tues., Jan. 9, 1838)

Taylor, Mr. Bently B. Died in Christian County, Ky.
National Banner. (May 27, 1826)

Taylor, E. H. Died in Louisville, Ky.
National Banner & Nashville Daily Advertiser. (Fri., Oct. 19, 1832)

Taylor, Mrs. Eleanor Hart. Wife of Mr. Nathaniel P. Taylor. Died in
Jefferson County, Ky.
National Banner. (Sat., Sept. 19, 1829)

Taylor, Elizabeth R. B. Died in Lexington, T. daughter of Mr. Jesse
Taylor.
National Banner & Nashville Whig. (Sat., Jan. 20, 1827)

Taylor, Mr. Goodwyn. Died in Lauderdale County, Ala.
National Banner & Nashville Daily Advertiser. (Tues., March 26, 1833)

Taylor, Mrs. Henrietta B. Consort of Mr. A. B. Taylor, age 25. Died
in Robertson County, Ten.
National Banner & Nashville Advertiser. (Fri., June 8, 1832)

Taylor, Hugh P. Esq. Died in Covington, Alleghany County, Va.
Nashville Republican & State Gazette. (Thurs., Jan. 27, 1831)

Taylor, Mr. James. Died in Coffeeville, Ala.
National Banner & Nashville Whig. (Sat., Oct. 7, 1826)

Taylor, James F. Esq. Died at Raleigh, N. C.
National Banner & Nashville Whig. (Fri., July 25, 1828)

Taylor, Col. James P. Attorney General for the first solicitorial
district in the 41st year of his age. Died in Carter County.
National Banner & Nashville Daily Advertiser. (Mon., Feb. 4, 1833)

Taylor, John. The venerable aged 87. Died at Albany, N. Y.
National Banner (Sat., April 18, 1829)

Taylor, Mr. John. Aged 39. A native of Glasgow, Scotland formerly
a resident of Charleston, S. C. Died in New Orleans, La.
National Banner & Nashville Whig. (Fri., Nov. 21, 1834)

Taylor, John of Carolina. A Senator in Congress from the State of
Virginia.
Nashville Whig. (Sept. 13, 1824)

Taylor, Hon. John Lewis. Chief Justice of the Supreme Court of North
Carolina. aged 58. Died near Raleigh, N. C.
National Banner & Nashville Whig. (Sat., March 7, 1829)

Taylor, Miss Louisa O. C. Died on the 27th Jan. at the residence of
her father in Montgomery County.
Nashville Whig. (Wed., Feb. 20, 1839)

Taylor, Mrs. Lucy. Wife of Col. C. H. Taylor, Died in Clarke County,
Ky.
National Banner. (Sat., May 16, 1829)

Taylor, Mrs. Lydia H. Wife of Jesse Taylor, Esq. Died in Madison
County, Ten.
National Banner & Nashville Whig. (Fri., Nov. 25, 1831)

Taylor, Mrs. Mary. Aged 79. Died in Sparta.
National Banner. (Sat., Aug. 8, 1829)

Taylor, Mrs. Mary H. Consort of Mr. Henry Taylor. Died at St. Louis.
National Banner & Nashville Daily Advertiser. (Sat., Aug. 10, 1833)

Taylor, Michael Esq. Died at St. Stephens, Ala.
National Banner. (March 17, 1826)

Taylor, Mrs. Nancy. Wife of Mr. Richard Taylor. Late of Montgomery
County. Died in Haywood County.
National Banner. (Sat., Aug. 22, 1829)

Taylor, Col. Parmenas. Aged 70. Died in Jefferson County.
National Banner & Nashville Whig. (Sat., Feb. 24, 1827)

Taylor, Capt. Richard. Died near Gallatin, on Thursday 29th ult. he
left a wife and four children.
Impartial Review and Cumberland Repository. (Thurs., Sept. 3, 1807)

Taylor, Col. Richard. Aged 83. Died in Jefferson County, Ky.
National Banner & Nashville Whig. (Sat., Feb. 7, 1829)

Taylor, Col. Richard. Aged 69. Died at Frankfort, Ky.
National Banner & Nashville Whig. (Thurs., July 29, 1830)

Taylor, Judge Robert B. Age 60 years. Died at Norfolk, Va. after an
illness of three months.
National Banner & Nashville Daily Advertiser. (Thurs., May 1, 1834)

Taylor, Mrs. Sarah A. Consort of William A. Taylor Esq. Formerly of
Granville, County, N. C. Died in Tipton County, Ten. on the 27th
Dec.
National Banner & Nashville Whig. (Fri., Jan. 23, 1835)

Taylor, Theodosia. Died in Woodford County, Ky.
National Banner & Nash. Whig. (Sat., Dec. 9, 1826)

Taylor, Mr. Thomas. Died in Tipton County on Sunday the 21st inst.
Aged about 42 years.
National Banner & Nashville Whig. (Fri., Jan. 21, 1831)

Taylor, Mr. Thomas W. Died in Franklin County.
National Banner & Nashville Whig. (Sept. 2, 1826)

Taylor, Col. Thomas. A native of Virginia. Died in Columbia, South
Carolina. A soldier of the revolution.
National Banner & Nashville Daily Advertiser. (Thurs., Dec. 5, 1833)

Taylor, Mr. Thomas. Died in Tipton County.
National Banner & Nashville Whig. (Mon., Jan. 31, 1831)

Taylor, Mr. Thomas W. Died in Franklin County.
National Banner & Nashville Whig. (Sat., Sept. 2, 1826)

Taylor, Maj. William. Died Oldham County, Ky.
National Banner & Nashville Whig. (Mon., July 12, 1830)

Taylor, Dr. Willis L. Died in Hardeman County, Ten.
Nashville Republican & State Gazette. (Thurs., March 10, 1831)

Taylor, Dr. Willis L. Died in Hardeman County.
National Banner & Nashville Whig. (Mon., March 14, 1831)

Taylor, Mr. Zackarish S. Died in Mercer County, Ky.
National Banner. (March 10, 1826)

Taylor, President Z. Died at the Presidential Mansion on Tuesday
night the 9th inst.
Nashville True Whig & Weekly Commercial Register. (Fri., July 12, 1850)

Teibout, James W. Died at Cincinnati, Ohio on 13th of Cholera.
National Banner & Nashville Daily Advertiser. (Sat., Oct. 20, 1832)

Telfair, Dr. David A. Died in Washington, N. C.
Nashville Republican & State Gazette. (Thurs., March 17, 1831)

Temple, Rev. Benjamin. Of the M. E. Church. Died near Russellville,
Ky. on the 17th.
Daily Republican Banner. (Mon., March 26, 1838)

Temple, Joseph Selden. Son of Mr. William Temple. Died in Davidson
County on the 26th of Feb. aged 22 years.
National Banner & Nashville Whig. (Fri., March 26, 1830)

Temple, Col. L. E. Died at his residence in this vicinity yesterday
morning.
Nashville True Whig & Weekly Commercial Register. (Fri., Jan. 17, 1851)

Templeton, George. Died at Cincinnati, Ohio on 13th of Cholera.
National Banner & Nashville Daily Advertiser. (Sat., Oct. 20, 1832)

Templin, Mrs. Agnes. Died at Cincinnati.
National Banner. (March 10, 1826)

Templin, Susan. Aged 98. Wife of Mr. William Templin.
Nashville Union. (Fri., Dec. 20, 1839)

Tendall, John D. Died on the 25th near Columbia at the residence of
his father, aged 25 years.
Daily Republican Banner. (Sat., Aug. 1, 1840)

Tenison, Mrs. Sarah Green. Consort of Joseph Tenison of Franklin.
Died on Saturday the 24th ult.
The Western Weekly Review. Franklin, Tenn. (Fri., Jan. 13, 1832)

Tennison, Mrs. Sarah Green. Died in Franklin, Tenn. on the 24th.
Nashville Republican & State Gazette. (Tues., Jan. 17, 1832)

Terrass, Miss Ann T. Daughter of Mr. H. Terrass, aged 25 years, 5
months and 22 days. Died in Nashville the 22d inst.
National Banner & Nashville Whig. (Mon., July 25, 1836)

Terrass, Mrs. Lavinia. Consort of Mr. John W. Terrass and daughter of
Mr. J. T. Hill, all of Nashville. Died on the 15th.
The Christian Record. (Sat., Feb. 20, 1847)

Terrell, Dabney C. Esq. Late of Louisville. Died in New Orleans.
National Banner & Nashville Whig. (Sat., Sept. 15, 1827)

Terrell, Hon. James C. Late a member of Congress from Georgia. Died
at his residence in Carnesville, on the 1st inst.
The Union. (Sat., Dec. 26, 1835)

Terrill, Mr. Pleasant M. In the 21st year of his age. Died in Smyth
County, Va. on the 2nd inst.
Daily Republican Banner. (Tues., Oct. 8, 1839)

Terry, Mr. David. In the 61st year of his age. Died in Maury County,
Tenn.
National Banner & Nashville Whig. (Mon., March 30, 1835)

Terry, Col. Nathaniel. A soldier of the Revolution in his 82nd year.
Died in Todd County, Ky. on Feb. 8th.
National Banner & Nashville Whig. (Fri., March 3, 1837)

Terry, Mrs. Susan. Wife of Mr. Thomas Terry. Died in Bedford County.
National Banner & Nashville Daily Advertiser. (Fri., Nov. 2, 1832)

Tevis, Nester C. Died in Madison County, Ky. of Cholera.
National Banner & Nashville Daily Advertiser. (Sat., Aug. 10, 1833)

Thatcher, Capt. Carey. Died in Knoxville.
National Banner. (Feb. 3, 1826)

Thatcher, Henry. Of N. J. Died in New Orleans of Yellow Fever.
Daily Republican Banner. (Wed., Sept. 27, 1837)

Thaxter, Mr. Benjamin L. Of Abington, Miss. Died in Nashville on
Tuesday morning, 8th inst.
National Banner & Nashville Whig. (Wed., March 9, 1831)

Theill, Catharine. A native of Germany, Died at Harvestraw, N. Y.
26 ult. 108 years old.
National Banner (Sat., June 6, 1829)

Third, Mr. Henry. Died 14th at Cincinnati, Ohio of Cholera.
National Banner & Nashville Daily Advertiser. (Wed., Oct. 24, 1832)

Thom. Mr. Isaac. Died at Louisville, Ky.
National Banner & Nashville Whig. (Sat., Aug. 11, 1827)

Thomas, Mr. Cornelius and his wife. He died in the morning at 10 o'
clock and she died at 6 in the evening. Died in Sumner County on the
29th.
National Banner (Sat., June 6, 1829)

Thomas, Col. David. Attorney General of that Republic. Died at
Galveston Bay, Texas formerly of Wilson County, Tenn.
Nashville Republican. (Sat., June 18, 1836)

Thomas, Col. David. Formerly of Wilson County, Tenn. Died in Texas
at the time of his death was Attorney General of Texas.
The Union. (Sat., June 18, 1836)

Thomas, Miss Elizabeth. Daughter of Mr. Phenas Thomas. Died in
Lauderdale County, Ala.
National Banner & Nashville Daily Advertiser. (Mon., Aug. 27, 1832)

Thomas, Private E. W. With Company E. Died was killed in the Battle
of Monterey with the Mexicans on Sept. 21st.
Nashville Whig. (Sat., Oct. 24, 1846)

Thomas, Mrs. Harriet M. Aged 26 years. Wife of Capt. Wm. Thomas.
Died in Rutherford County.
National Banner (Jan. 27, 1826)

Thomas, Mr. Henry. Died in Bourbon County, Ky.
National Banner & Nashville Whig. (Sat., Sept. 9, 1826)

Thomas, Isabella. Infant daughter of Mr. William Thomas. Died in
Cincinnati, Ohio.
National Banner & Nashville Daily Advertiser. (Wed., Aug. 14, 1833)

Thomas, Isaiah, Esq. President of the American Antiquartan Societ. and
Patriarch of American Printers. Died at Worchester, Mass.
National Banner & Nashville Whig. (Wed., April 27, 1831)

Thomas, Mr. Jacob. Age 82. Died in Nashville.
National Banner & Nashville Whig. (Wed., March 2, 1831)

Thomas, Mrs. Jane. Consort of W. H. Thomas. Died in Nashville on
yesterday.
Daily Republican Banner. (Wed., May 16, 1838)

Thomas, Mr. Jesse W. A respectable citizen of this county.
Nashville Whig. (Tues., Feb. 20, 1816)

Thomas, Mr. John. Died in Iredell County, N. C.
National Banner (Sat., June 17, 1829)

Thomas, Mr. John C. Died in Maury County on the 1st inst.
National Banner & Nashville Daily Advertiser. (Wed., Feb. 6, 1833)

Thomas, Robert. In the 80th year of his age. Died in the vicinity of
Nashville on the 15th day of Aug. A soldier of the Revolutionary War.
Nashville Union. (Fri., Sept. 21, 1838)

Thomas, Tristam Harris. Son of John Thomas Jr. Died in Weakley County
on the 8th inst. in the 18th year of his age.
Nashville Republican (Tues., Feb. 21, 1837)

Thomas, Mr. William Sen. Died in Rutherford County
National Banner & Nashville Daily Advertiser. (Fri., Jan. 27, 1832)

Thomas, Mr. William. Aged 71. Died in Dyer County.
National Banner & Nashville Daily Advertiser. (Wed., April 24, 1833)

Thomas, Mr. William. In the 72nd year of his age. Died in Dyer
County, Ten. on the evening the 1st of April.
National Banner & Nashville Daily Advertiser. (Mon., April 15, 1833)

Thomason, Mr. Paul Piere. Died at Savannah, Ga. on the 13th ult.
French Consul for that Port.
National Banner & Nashville Daily Advertiser. (Tues., Feb. 11, 1834)

Thompson, Mrs. Died in Richmond, Va.
Nashville Republican & State Gazette. (Tues., Dec. 13, 1831)

Thompson, Dr. Asa. Died in Madison County, Ala.
National Banner & Nashville Whig. (Sat., Jan. 12, 1828)

Thompson, Burwell. Aged 75 years. Died in Franklin County, Ten. He
was a revolutionary soldier and fought in the Battle of Kings Mountain.
National Banner & Nashville Daily Advertiser. (Mon., Nov. 25, 1833)

Thomas, Mrs. Charity. Wife of Mr. Rob. Thompson, aged 19. Died in
Jackson.
National Banner & Nashville Whig. (Sat., June 2, 1827)

Thomas, Dr. Geo. G. The funeral sermon will be preached on Sunday,
16th inst. at the house of John M. Goodloe near Nashville.
Impartial Review and Cumberland Repository. (Thurs., Oct. 13, 1808)

Thompson, Charles. 95th year. Died near Philadelphia. Secretary of
Congress during the American Revolution.
Nashville Whig. (Sept. 13, 1820)

Thompson, Dr. Charles B. Late of Nashville. Died in Vickburg, Miss.
National Banner & Nashville Daily Advertiser. (Tues., June 11, 1833)

Thompson, Comm. Charles C. B. Of the U. S. Navy, aged 49. Died at
Hot Springs, on the 1st inst.
Nashville Republican & State Gazette. (Wed., Sept. 26, 1832)

Thompson, Mrs. Charlotte. Wife of Capt. Allen C. Thompson. Died near
Florence, Ala. in Lauderdale County, in the 64th year of her age.
National Banner & Nashville Whig. (Fri., Jan. 23, 1835)

Thompson, Mr. Duncan. Died in Fayetteville, N. C.
National Banner & Nashville Daily Advertiser. (Sat., Aug. 10, 1833)

Thompson, Mrs. Eliza B. Died at St. Louis.
National Banner. (May 10, 1826)

Thompson, Mrs. Elizabeth. Died in Maryville.
National Banner & Nashville Daily Advertiser. (Mon., June 24, 1833)

Thompson, Mrs. Elizabeth. Wife of Mr. John Thompson. Died in
Rutherford County.
National Banner & Nashville Daily Advertiser. (Sat., Feb. 23, 1833)

Thompson, Miss Elizabeth. Died in Blount County.
National Banner & Nashville Daily Advertiser. (Mon., June 17, 1833)

Thompson, Franklin Deaderick, aged eleven years. Died at Columbus,
Crawford County, Arkansas on the 4th. Son of Mr. David Thompson,
formerly of Nashville.
Nashville Republican. (Tues., Nov. 8, 1836)

Thompson, Franklin Deaderick. Aged 11 years. Son of Mr. David
Thompson. Died at Columbus, Crawford County, Arkansas.
National Banner & Nashville Whig. (Mon., Nov. 7, 1836)

Thompson, George Madison. Eldest son of Maj. Geo. C. Thompson. Died
in Mercer County, Ky.
National Banner (Sat., Aug. 22, 1829)

Thompson, Henry. Of D. C. Died in New Orleans of Yellow Fever.
Daily Republican Banner. (Wed., Sept. 27, 1837)

Thompson, Mr. Jason. Died in Davidson County.
National Banner & Nashville Daily Advertiser. (Wed., April 24, 1833)

Thompson, Jason H. Esq. Son of Mr. Jason Thompson of Davidson.
Died on the 20th of Aug. last, at Cambridge, Maryland.
National Banner. (Sat., Oct. 17, 1829)

Thompson, Jason H. Esq. Son of Mr. Jason Thompson of Davidson. Died
on the 20th of Aug. last, at Cambridge, Maryland.
National Banner. (Sat., Oct. 17, 1829)

Thompson, John Col. Aged 72. Died in Rutherford County.
National Banner & Nashville Whig. (Sept. 2, 1826)

Thompson, Mr. John. A soldier of the revolution, aged 81. Died in
McMinnville.
National Banner & Nashville Daily Advertiser. (Wed., May 15, 1833)

Thompson, Capt. John. Of the Steamboat Ploughboy, aged about 32.
Died in Mobile, Ala. of Yellow Fever.
Daily Republican Banner. (Tues., Oct. 1, 1839)

Thompson, Col. John. Aged 72. Died in Rutherford County.
National Banner & Nashville Whig. (Sat., Sept. 2, 1826)

Thompson, John B. Esq. Died in Mercer County, Ky. Member of the
Senate of that state.
National Banner & Nashville Daily Advertiser. (Mon., July 8, 1833)

Thompson, John W. Esq. Died in St. Louis. on Wednesday the first of
October.

Thompson, Mr. Joseph. Died at Maryville.
National Banner. (Sat., Nov. 14, 1829)

Thompson, Mrs. Joseph. Died in Shelbyville, Tenn. of Cholera.
National Banner & Nashville Daily Advertiser. (Thurs., July 11, 1833)

Thompson, Mrs. Lauretta C. Consort of Mr. David Thompson, merchant.
Died at Van Buren, Arkansas on the 24th ult. aged 35 years.
National Banner & Nashville Whig. (Mon., Feb. 20, 1837)

Thompson, Mrs. Lauretta C. Aged 35 years. Consort of Mr. David
Thompson. Died at Van Buren, Arkansas on the 24th ult.
Nashville Republican. (Tues., Feb. 21, 1837)

Thompson, Mrs. Lucy T. Wife of George B. Thompson Esq. Died in Mercer
County, Ky.
National Banner & Nashville Whig. (Sat., March 1, 1828)

Thompson, Mrs. Margaret Ann. Wife of Mr. Charles A. R. Thompson and
daughter of the Rev. Dr. Edgar. Died in Nashville on Friday the 2nd
inst. at the residence of her father.
The Christian Record. (Sat., June 10, 1848)

Thompson, Martha Ann. Aged 12 years. Died in Nashville on Sunday
last, the daughter of Mr. D. L. Thompson.
National Banner & Nashville Daily Advertiser. (Thurs., April 17, 1834)

Thompson, Mrs. Martha. Wife of Mr. John Thompson and daughter of M. C.
Dunn Esq. Died on the 26th ult. in the vicinity of Nashville in the
39th year of her age.
The Christian Record. (Sat., Nov. 4, 1848)

Thompson, Mrs. Mary. Consort of J. W. Thompson. Died in Claiborne
County, Mi.
National Banner & Nashville Daily Advertiser. (Wed., Aug. 20, 1834)

Thompson, Mrs. Mary. Died in this County. Consort of Capt. Wm.
Thompson of Mill Creek.
National Banner & Nashville Whig. (Sat., Aug. 2, 1828)

Thompson, Mrs. Mary E. Died in this County.
National Banner. (April 28, 1826)

Thompson, Mrs. Nancy. Consort of Mr. Thomas Thompson. Died in this
County on the 22nd inst.
National Banner & Nashville Whig. (Sat., Aug. 30, 1828)

Thompson, Capt. Robert. Of Huntsville, aged 77. Died in Limestone
County, Ala.
National Banner. (Sat., July 4, 1829)

Thompson, Mrs. Sally. Consort of Mr. Robert Thompson Esq. Died in
Hardeman County, Ten. age 37 years.
National Banner & Nashville Whig. (Wed., Oct. 22, 1834)

Thompson, Capt. Samuel. In the 69th year of his age. A Revolutionary
soldier. Died on Monday 7th inst. (From the Raleigh, N. C. Star)
National Banner & Nashville Daily Advertiser. (Fri., June 1, 1832)

Thompson, Samuel. Died in Covington, Ten.
Nashville Republican & State Gazette. (Thurs., March 24, 1831)

Thompson, Mr. Samuel. Depty Sheriff of Tipton County. Died in
Covington on the 10th inst.
National Banner & Nashville Whig. (Wed., March 23, 1831)

Thompson, Sarah. Aged 12, daughter of John Thompson Esq. Died in
Bedford County.
National Banner & Nashville Whig. (Sat., Sept. 30, 1826)

Thompson, Mr. Thomas. Died in La Grange, Tenn.
Nashville Whig. (Tues., May 5, 1846)

Thompson, William. Aged 82 years. Died in Washington County, Ten.
National Banner & Nashville Whig. (Wed., April 8, 1835)

Thompson, Mr. Wm. On the 21st of March, at his residence near Winchester, Franklin County, Tenn. of a hemorrhage of the lungs.
Nashville Republican. (Sat., April 2, 1836)

Thompson, Mr. William. Died on the 21st of March near Winchester, Franklin County, Tenn.
Nashville Republican. (Sat., April 2, 1836)

Thompson, Dr. W. L. Died in Murfreesborough, Ten. on the 10th inst.
National Banner & Nashville Daily Advertiser. (Tues., Nov. 19, 1833)

Thompson, William M'Allister. Aged 9 years son of Mr. David Thompson. Died at Columbus, Crawford Co., Arkansas on the 13th ult.
National Banner & Nashville Whig. (Mon., Nov. 7, 1836)

Thompson, William MʼAllister. Aged 9 years. Died at Columbus, Crawford County, Arkansas on the 13th. Son of Mr. David Thompson, formerly of Nashville.
Nashville Republican. (Tues., Nov. 8, 1836)

Thorndike, Hon. Israel. Aged 76 years. Died at Boston. He was for many years a distinguished member of the Senate of Massachusetts.
National Banner & Nashville Daily Advertiser. (Thurs., May 31, 1832)

Thorton, Capt. Arthur W. Of the U. S. Army. Died in Nashville on Wednesday the 2d inst.
Nashville Republican (Fri., Nov. 25, 1836)

Thornton, Mrs. Mary A. Wife of James I. Thornton Esq. Died at Tuscaloosa, Ala.
National Banner & Nashville Whig. (Mon., June 7, 1830)

Thornton, Mrs. Mary S. H. Wife of Dr. John H. Thornton and third daughter of the late Gen. Harrison. Died at North Bend on the 16th inst.
Nashville Whig. (Sat., Dec. 3, 1842)

Thornton, Miss Rachel. Daughter of Nelson and Nancy Thornton. Died in Carriage on the 14th Sept. aged 19 years.
Nashville Whig. (Wed., Sept. 30, 1840)

Thornton, Dr. Reuben L. Aged 62. Died in this county.
National Banner & Nashville Whig. (Sat., July 29, 1826)

Thornton, Robert G. Esq. The first settler of that County. Died in Fayetteville County, Tn.
National Banner & Nashville Whig. (Sat., Sept. 30, 1826)

Thornton, Dr. William. Register of the Patent Office. Died at Washington.
National Banner & Nashville Whig. (Sat., April 19, 1828)

Throp, Mr. Andrew. Died in Mason County, Ky.
National Banner & Nashville Whig. (Sat., Jan. 27, 1827)

Tibbattst, Miss Susan A. Died in Lexington, Ky.
National Banner & Nashville Whig. (Sat., Feb. 3, 1827)

Tibbetts, Mrs. Harriett. Wife of Henry Tibbetts Esq. Died in Louisville, Ky.
National Banner & Nashville Daily Advertiser. (Fri., July 25, 1834)

Tier, Dr. Principal of the female Institute. Died in Princeton, Ky. of Cholera.
National Banner & Nashville Daily Advertiser. (Wed., July 9, 1834)

Tiffin, Dr. Edwards. Age 63, died at Chollicoth, O.
National Banner. (Sat., Aug. 22, 1829)

Tilford, Miss Asabella Olivia. Daughter of Mr. James Tilford. Died in Nashville.
National Banner & Nashville Daily Advertiser. (Mon., Jan. 14, 1833)

Tilford, Mrs. Elizabeth. Aged 82 years. Died in Williamson County, on the 26th.
National Banner & Nashville Whig. (Mon., March 20, 1835)

Tilford, Mr. Hugh. A soldier of the revolution. Died in Wilson County.
National Banner & Nashville Daily Advertiser. (Tues., June 11, 1833)

Tilford, James Jr. In the 32nd year of his age. Died in Wilson County on the 25th ulto.
Nashville Whig. (Sat., Oct. 3, 1846)

Tilford, James McCount. A native of Tennessee. Died in Macon, Ga. on Wednesday the 5th inst. for the last 10 years a resident of Macon, County, Ga.
The Politician & Weekly Nashville Whig. (Fri., Feb. 4, 1848)

Tilford, Margaret Sophia. Daughter of Mr. Samuel Tilford. Died in Nashville, this morning.
National Banner & Nashville Advertiser. (Thurs., Sept. 27, 1832)

Tilford, Child of Mr. Robert Tilford. Died in Danville, Ky. of measles.
National Banner & Nashville Daily Advertiser. (Mon., Aug. 5, 1833)

Tilghman, William. Died in the 71th year of his age.
Chief Justice of Penn.
National Banner & Nashville Whig. (Sat., May 19, 1827)

Timberlake, Miss Eliza. Died at Paris, Ky.
National Banner & Nashville Whig. (July 1, 1826)

Tindall, John D. Aged 25 years. Died on the 15th ulto. at the residence of his father, near Columbia, Tenn.
Nashville Whig. (Mon., Aug. 3, 1840)

Tindle, Mr. George. Aged 22. Died in Knox County.
National Banner. (Feb. 3, 1826)

Tingle, Mr. James S. Died in St. Augustine, Fla.
National Banner & Nashville Whig. (Sat., Sept. 9, 1826)

Tinley, John Senior. Died in Knoxville, Tenn.
Daily Republican Banner. (Sat., Sept. 29, 1838)

Tinsley, Mr. Richard B. Died in Hardeman County.
National Banner & Nashville Whig. (Wed., Sept. 21, 1831)

Tipton, Gen. Late a Senator of the U. S. from the state of Indiana. Died on the 5th inst. He was a native of Tennessee, aged about 55 years.
Nashville Union. (Fri., May 10, 1839)

Tipton, Col. John. A member of the House of Representative, of Tenn. Died in Nashville on Saturday last. Obituary Oct. 10. Nash. Banner.
The Western Weekly Review. Franklin, Tenn. (Fri., Oct. 14, 1831)

Tipton, Col. John. Died in Nashville on Sat. last. A member of the house of Representative from the County of Washington.
National Banner & Nashville Whig. (Mon., Oct. 10, 1831)

Tipton, Hon. John. Late of the U. S. Senate. Died at his residence in Indiana.
Daily Republican Banner. (Fri., April 18, 1839)

Tipton, Joshua. Aged 52 years. Died 13th at Cincinnati, Ohio of Cholera.
National Banner & Nashville Daily Advertiser. (Tues., Oct. 23, 1832)

Tisdale, William H. Esq. Attorney at law. Died at Carrillton, Ill.
National Banner & Nashville Daily Advertiser. (Sat., Aug. 10, 1833)

Titsworth, John G. Aged 27 years. Died in Nashville of Cholera.
National Banner & Nashville Whig. (Wed., July 8, 1835)

Titus, Mrs. Anne. Consort of Mr. George Titus of this County. Died on the 5th inst.
Impartial Review and Cumberland Repository. (Thurs., July 14, 1808)

Titus, Mr. Ebenezer. Of Davidson County. Died on Monday last.
Impartial Review and Cumberland Repository. (Thurs., Sept. 17, 1807)

Todd, Charles Stewart. Aged 4 years. Died in Shelby County, Ky on the 31st May. Son of Col. Charles Todd.
National Banner & Nashville Daily Advertiser. (Mon., June 18, 1832)

Todd, George Mr. Aged 48. Died at Frankfort, Ky.
National Banner & Nashville Whig. (Mon., Aug. 1, 1831)

Todd, Henry Clay. Aged 2 years. Died in Shelby County, Ky. on the 30th May.
National Banner & Nashville Daily Advertiser. (Mon., June 18, 1832)

Todd, Mr. John. Died in Madison County. Wednesday, Dec. 14, 1831
National Banner and Nashville Whig.

Todd, Mr. John. Died suddenly on Tuesday the 29th inst. Also the following day the infant son of Mr. Todd died about 2 years old.
Nashville Whig. (Sat., Nov. 2, 1844)

Todd, Mr. John. Died in Madison County.
National Banner & Nashville Whig. (Wed., Dec. 14, 1831)

Todd, Mrs. Mary. Wife of George Todd Esq. Died in Madison County.
National Banner. (Sat., Oct. 3, 1829)

Todd, Mrs. Mary E. Wife of Mr. George Todd. Died at Frankfort, Ky.
National Banner. (Sat., Aug. 15, 1829)

Todd, Robert R. S. Died near Louisville Ky. Aged 35 years.
National Banner. (Jan. 27, 1826)

Todd, Susan Hart. Aged 10 years. Died in Shelby County, Ky on the 6th June. Daughter of Col. Charles P. Todd.
National Banner & Nashville Daily Advertiser. (Mon., June 18, 1832)

Todd, Hon. Thomas. One of the judges of the supreme court of the United States. Died at Frankfort, Ky. on the 6th inst.
National Banner. (Feb. 17, 1826)

Toland, Mrs. Aged 75 years. Mother of Hon. George W. Toland. Died on the 4th inst. at Germantown, Pennsylvania.
Daily Republican Banner. (Tues., Oct. 17, 1837)

Tolman, Mr. Jesse. 36. Died in Mobile.
National Banner & Nashville Whig.(Sept. 2, 1826)

Tomlinson, Mr. Richard. Died in Madison County.
National Banner & Nashville Whig. (Wed., Sept. 14, 1831)

Thompkins, Mr. John. Died in Glasgow, Ky.
National Banner & Nashville Whig. (Thurs., Oct. 14, 1830)

Toncray, Mr. Daniel C. Formerly of Louisville, Ky. aged 64. Died in Memphis.

Toncray, Mrs. Elizabeth. Died at Louisville, Ky.
National Banner & Nashville Whig. (Sat., Jan. 19, 1827)

Toob, Capt. Mathew. Died in Woodville, Mi.
National Banner & Nashville Whig. (Wed., April 27, 1831)

Toob, Capt. Matthew. Died in Woodville, Miss.
National Banner & Nashville Whig. (Wed., April 27, 1831)

Toole, Thomas. Of N. Y. Died in New Orleans of Yellow Fever.
Daily Republican Banner (Wed., Oct. 4, 1837)

Toombes, Mrs. Rebecca D. Consort of Capt. Thomas Toombes. Died in the vicinity of La Grange, Tenn. in the 40th year of her age.
National Banner & Nashville Whig. (Mon., June 29, 1835)

Topp, Mr. James H. Died at Pulaski, Tenn. Leaving a young widow to whom he had been married to about two months.
National Banner & Nashville Daily Advertiser. (Tues., July 15, 1834)

Torode, Mrs. Mercy. Wife of John Torode. Died in St. Louis, Mo.
National Banner & Nashville Advertiser. (Wed., June 20, 1832)

Torrey, Mr. Charles. In the 27th year of his age. Died in this town on Friday night last.
National Banner & Nashville Whig. (Sat., Feb. 17, 1827)

Totten, Elizabeth S. Consort of Benjamin C. Totten. Died in Huntingdon on the 18th.
National Banner & Nashville Whig. (Fri., Oct. 23, 1835)

Townsend, Mrs. Jane H. Died in Logan County, Ky.
National Banner & Nashville Whig. (Mon., Sept. 26, 1831)

Townsent, Mr. Edwin. Died in Mercer County, Ky.
National Banner & Nashville Whig. (Sat., Sept. 1, 1827)

Townsent, Mr. G. B. Aged 23. Died in Henry County.
National Banner & Nashville Whig. (Mon., Nov. 1, 1830)

Townsent, Mrs. Jane H. Died in Logan County, Ky.
National Banner & Nashville Whig. (Mon., Sept. 26, 1831)

Townsent, Mr. Thomas. Aged 67 years. Died in Cincinnati, O.
National Banner & Nashville Daily Advertiser. (Mon., Sept. 3, 1833)

Trabue, Mary. Wife of Edward Trabue Esq., Merchant. Died in the vicinity of Nashville, yesterday noon.
Nashville Whig. (Mon., Sept. 13, 1841)

Tracy, L. Of Hamilton, Ohio. Died in the loss of the Steamboat, Brandywine.
National Banner & Nashville Daily Advertiser. (Mon., April 23, 1832)

Tracy, Uriah, Esq. Senator from Connecticut, age 54. Died at the City of Washington, on 19th ult. he was intered with honors, due him as a stateman and rank as Maj. General.
Impartial Review and Cumberland Repository. (Thurs., Aug. 20, 1807)

Trask, Thos. S. Died at Memphis.
National Banner & Nashville Whig. (Sat., Aug. 16, 1828)

Trask, Dr. Wm. P. Died in Wilkinson County, Miss.
National Banner & Nashville Whig. (Sat., March 27, 1827)

Travis, James. Died in Shelbyville, Tenn. of Cholera.
National Banner & Nashville Daily Advertiser. (Thurs., July 11, 1833)

Trebuchet, Mr. Francis Ettienne. Native of France and Professor of
the French Language in Georgetown College.
National Banner & Nashville Advertiser. (Mon., April 30, 1832)

Trebuchet, Mr. Francis Ettienne. A native of France recently, Pro-
fessor of the French language, in Georgetown College. Died in
Lexington, Ky.
National Banner & Nashville Daily Advertiser. (Mon., April 30, 1832)

Treeslow, William. Died in Knxoville, Friday night 12th inst.
Daily Republican Banner. (Sat., Oct. 20, 1838)

Treppard, Mr. Francis L. A native of Tennessee. Died in Houston,
Texas, on Sat., Aug. 17.
Nashville Whig. (Mon., Sept. 9, 1839)

Treppard, Mr. Francis. Painter, aged 21 years. Died in Houston,
Texas on Sat., Aug. 17th. He was a native of Nashville, Tenn.
Daily Republican Banner. (Tues., Sept. 10, 1839)

Treppard, Mr. Francis I. Printer, aged 21 years. Died in Houston,
Texas at the residence of Mr. Mark H. Moore, He was a native of
Nashville, Tenn.
Nashville Union. (Mon., Sept. 16, 1839)

Treppard, William Franklin. Aged 11 years son of Mr. William Treppard.
Died in Nashville on Saturday the 21st inst.
National Banner & Nashville Whig. (Mon., March 23, 1835)

Tribble, Mr. Peter. Died in Bedford County.
National Banner & Nashville Whig. (Thurs., Nov. 24, 1831)

Tribble, Mr. Peter. Died in Bedford County.
National Banner & Nashville Whig. (Thurs., Nov. 24, 1831)

Trice, Mrs. Wife of Mr. N. F. Trice. Died in Montgomery County.
National Banner & Nashville Whig. (Fri., July 15, 1831)

Trice, Mrs. Mary H. Wife of N. F. Trice, Esq. of Montgomery County.
Died near Clarksville on the 15th inst.
Nashville Whig. (Mon., June 25, 1838)

Trigg, Mr. William. Died in Denmark, Western District.
National Banner & Nashville Whig. (Wed., Sept. 7, 1831)

Trimble, Mrs. Elizabeth W. Consort of James Trimble, Esq. Died near
Batesville, Independant County, Arkansas on the 13th of April in the
47th year of her age.
National Banner & Nashville Whig. (Mon., May 30, 1836)

Trimble, James Esq. In the 45th year of his age. Died in this town
on the evening of his age.
Nashville Whig. (Aug. 9, 1874?)

Tripps, Susan. Aged 8 years. Died in New York. Weighed several
months since 227 pounds.
Nashville Republican & State Gazette. (Sat., June 4, 1831)

Trott, Mr. Henry B. (Late firm Trott & Whitney). Died near Boston
by drowning when the Steamboat, Bunker Hill was wrecked by the wind.
National Banner & Nashville Daily Advertiser. (Sat., June 30, 1832)

Trotter, Mr. George. Died at Lexington, Ky., aged 16 years.
National Banner & Nashville Daily Advertiser. (Mon., July 30,1832)

Trotter, Col. Jas. Died at Lexington, Ky.
National Banner & Nashville Whig. (Sat., Aug. 18, 1827)

Trotter, Capt. James. Aged 35. Died in Fayette County, Ky.
National Banner & Nashville Whig. (Sat., Aug. 5, 1826)

Trotter, Mrs. Mary Ann. Wife of Mr. George James Trotter, Editor of
the Kentucky Gazette. Died in Lexington, Ky.
National Banner & Nashville Daily Advertiser. (Fri., Nov. 2, 1832)

Trotter, Miss Sarah L. Daughter of the late Samuel Trotter. Died
in Lexington, Ky.
National Banner & Nashville Daily Advertiser. (Mon., Aug. 19, 1833)

Trotter, William J. Son of B. Y and Julia A. Trotter. Died in the
vicinity of Sommersville, aged 4 years.
Nashville Whig. (Thurs., March 19, 1846)

Trousdale, Ophelia Allice. Daughter of Gov. Trousdale. Died in
Gallatin on Tuesday night last, in the 16th year of her age.
Nashville True Whig & Weekly Commercial Register. (Fri., June 21, 1850)

Troy, Mr. Joseph. Died at Detroit.
National Banner. (May 20, 1826)

True, James Esq. Sheriff and for many years, representative for
Fayette County. Died in Fayette County, Ky.
National Banner & Nashville Whig. (Mon., July 11, 1831)

Trumble, Judge John, Esq. Age 81. Died in Detroit, Michigan, on the
10 inst.
National Banner & Nashville Whig. (Fri., May 27, 1831)

Trumbull, Jno. Esq. Died in Detroit, Michigan, Ter. Aged 81.
Nashville Republican & State Gazette. (Sat., May 28, 1831)

Tucker, Charles Esq. Died in Memphis, Tenn.
National Banner & Nashville Whig. (Fri., Oct. 17, 1834)

Tucker, Gen. Starling. For many years a distinguished member of
Congress from S. C. Died in Laurens District, S. C.
National Banner & Nashville Daily Advertiser. (Tues., Feb. 11, 1834)

Tucker, Stephen Dandridge. Son of Hon. Henry St. George Tucker of
Virginia. Died in Philadelphia.
Nashville Whig. (Fri., Sept. 25, 1840)

Tucker, St. George Esq. Died in Nelson County, Va. A distinguished
jurist.
National Banner & Nashville Whig. (Sat., Dec. 15, 1827)

Tucker, Mr. William. Printer, aged about 50. A native of Worcester
County, Mass.
National Banner & Nashville Whig. (Mon., June 7, 1830)

Tufts, Mr. Addison. Printer formerly of Boston aged 27. Died in
Mobile, Ala. of Yellow Fever.
Daily Republican Banner. (Tues., Oct. 1, 1839)

Tunnell, Mr. John. Died in Knox County of Anderson County.
National Banner & Nashville Whig. (Sat., July 29, 1826)

Tunstall, Mrs. Lucy Ann. Died in Todd County, Ky.
National Banner & Nashville Whig. (Fri., Feb. 12, 1830)

Turbeville, Mrs. Sarah. Died in Blount County.
National Banner & Nashville Daily Advertiser. (Mon., June 3, 1833)

Turley, William P. Only son of Hon. William B. Turley. Died in
Jackson.
Nashville Whig. (Tues., July 21, 1846)

Turnbull, Benj. J. Esq. Died in St. Louis, was burned to death on
Sat., Aug. 31st.
Daily Republican Banner. (Mon., Sept. 9, 1839)

Turnbull, Robert J. Esq. Died in Charleston, S. C. on the 15th ult.
National Banner & Nashville Daily Advertiser. (Wed., July 3, 1833)

Turner, Mrs. Anne. Consort of Mr. John Turner. Died in Sumner County.
National Banner & Nashville Daily Advertiser. (Wed., March 19, 1834)

Turner, Charles Lucian. Aged in his 17th- year. Son of Mr. D. B.
Turner of Nashville. Died by the accidental discharge of his gun which
he was carrying.
The Christian Record. (Sat., Feb. 13, 1847)

Turner, Mr. Donaldson. Died in Morgan County, Ala. aged 69 years.
National Banner & Nashville Whig. (Fri., Feb. 6, 1835)

Turner, Mr. Jacob. Died in Sumner County.
National Banner & Nashville Daily Advertiser. (Tues., Nov. 13, 1832)

Turner, Mr. Jacob. Died in Sumner County.
National Banner & Nashville Advertiser. (Tues., Nov. 13, 1832)

Turner, James B. Company I with First Tenn. Volunteers. Died was
killed in the Battle of Monterey with the Mexicans on Sept. 21st.
Nashville Whig. (Sat., Oct. 24, 1846)

Turner, Mr. John E. Died in Robertson County.
National Banner (Jan. 6, 1826)

Turner, Col. John H. Died at Gallatin on the 9th. A prominent
citizen of Sumner County.
National Banner & Nashville Whig. (Mon., Oct. 13, 1834)

Turner, Joseph B. Of this county. Died on Saturday last.
The Nashville Whig & Tenn. Advertiser. (May 9, 1818)

Turner, Laura Shackelford. Infant daughter of James H. Turner Esq.
Died in Columbus, Miss.
Daily Republican Banner. (Wed., July 10, 1838)

Turner, Mr. Lemuel T. Died on Wednesday last (December 6, 1815) after
an illness of 4 or 5 days. Of the firm of Rapier & Turner of this
town. On the next day he was buried with Masonic Honors.
Nashville Whig. (Dec. 13, 1815)

Turner, Mr. Medicus R. Died in this County on the 9th inst.
Nashville Republican & State Gazette. (Thurs., Feb. 10, 1831)

Turner, Medicus R. Died in Davidson County on the 9th inst.
National Banner & Nashville Whig. (Fri., Feb. 11, 1831)

Turner, Gen. Robert B. Former Treasurer of the State.
Died on the morning of the 17th.
The Christian Record. (Sat., June 10, 1848)

Turner, Miss Sarah. Died in Richmond, Ky.
National Banner & Nashville Whig. (Sat., Oct. 28, 1826)

Turner, Thomas. Aged 50. Died in Madison County, Ala.
National Banner & Nashville Whig. (Tues., May 11, 1830)

Turner, Mr. Thomas. Of Madison County, Ala. Student of the University of Nashville. Died on Sunday last in the 19th year of his age.
National Banner. (Sat., Aug. 15, 1829)

Turnery, Dr. Daniel. Died at Columbus, Ohio.
National Banner & Nashville Whig. (Sat., Jan. 20, 1827)

Turpin, Maj. Thomas. Aged 69. Died in Courtland, Ala.
National Banner & Nashville Whig. (Mon., March 21, 1831)

Turpin, Maj. Thomas. Died in Courtland, Ala.
Nashville Republican & State Gazette. (Thurs., March 17, 1831)

Turrentine, Maj. Alexander. Died at his residence in Shelbyville the 11th inst. in the 63d year of his age.
Nashville Whig. (Dec. 20, 1824)

Turrentine, Daniel. Died in Shelbyville, Tenn. of Cholera.
National Banner & Nashville Daily Advertiser. (Thurs., July 11, 1833)

Twiddy, Mrs. Of Snailwell, New Market. Died recently in England at the extraordinary age (within a few months) of 110 years, leaving her youngest child, now 84 years old.
National Banner & Nashville Daily Advertiser. (Mon., April 2, 1832)

Twyman, Mr. James. Aged 73. Died in Scott County, Ky.
National Banner & Nashville Daily Advertiser. (Thurs., March 20, 1834)

Tyler, Isaac H. Esq. Counsellor and Attorney at Law of Louisville, Ky. Died at Baton Rogue, La., Oct. 25th.
National Banner. (Sat., Dec. 5, 1829)

Tyree, Mr. Pleasant. Died in the vicinity of Gallatin.
Nashville Whig. (Tues., May 5, 1846)

Tyson, Henry T. Esq. Formerly of Baltimore, died at Covington, Tenn.
National Banner & Nashville Daily Advertiser. (Wed., March 26, 1834)

Underwood, Mr. Levi S. Died in Rutherford County.
National Banner & Nashville Daily Advertiser. (Fri., June 14, 1833)

Upjohn, Mrs. Sarah. Died at Cincinnati.
National Banner & Nashville Whig. (June 24, 1826)

Upshaw, Mrs. Martha Ann. Died at Pulaski.
National Banner & Nashville Whig. (Sat., May 17, 1828)

Upshaw, Wm. M'Neill. Infant son of Col. A. M. M. Upshaw. Died in Pulaski.
Nashville Republican & State Gazette. (Wed., Aug. 8, 1832)

Upson, Mrs. Lois. Died at Worthington, Ohio.
National Banner. (March 17, 1826)

Urguhart, Mr. David. Of New Orleans. Died suddenly of heart trouble, in Baltimore where he and his daughter was visiting.
Nashville Whig. (Sat., June 25, 1842)

Ury, Lieut. Asbury. Of the first regiment of United State Dragoons. A native of Tennessee. Died at Matanazas Cuba, on the 13th April.
Nashville Whig. (Monday, May 14, 1838)

Ury, Lieut. Asbury. Of the 1st Regiment of U. S. Dragoons. A native of Tennessee. Died in Matanzas, Cuba.
Daily Republican Banner (Sat., May 19, 1838)

Usher, Mr. Luke. Died in Lexington, Ky.
National Banner & Nashville Whig. (Fri., Jan. 1st, 1830)

Ustick, Mr. John S. Printer, formerly of Nashville. Died at Wilmington, Del.
National Banner & Nashville Whig. (Sat., March 22, 1828)

Uxore, Miss Rachel. Died in Mercer County, Ky.
National Banner & Nashville Whig. (Sat., Dec. 23, 1826)

Valois, Mr. Francis X. Died at St. Louis, Misso.
National Banner & Nashville Whig. (Sat., June 16, 1827)

Van, Mrs. Sarah. Relict of the late Mr. James Van. and the Mother of Mr. James Diggons. Died on High Street, Nashville on the 22nd Dec. in the 88th year of her age.
Nashville Whig. (Thurs., Dec. 24, 1846)

Van Buren, Miss Jane. A sister of the President of the U. S. Died recently at the village of Kinderhook, New York in the 59th year of her age.
Nashville Whig. (Mon., July 9, 1838)

Vance, Mr. Andrew. Late of Clarksville and elder partner of the firm of Vance & Dicks. Died on the 12th Nov. at Galveston, Texas.
Daily Republican Banner. (Mon., Dec. 7, 1840)

Vance, Miss Catherine Maria. Daughter of Wm. K. Vance Esq. age 15. Died in Greenville, Tennessee.
National Banner & Nashville Advertiser. (Fri., July 2, 1832)

Vance, Mr. Robert. Died at Clarksville.
National Banner. (Sat., Oct. 3, 1829)

Vance, Dr. Robert. In the 30th year of his age. Died in Buncombe County, N. C. on the 6th inst.
National Banner & Nashville Whig. (Sat., Dec. 1, 1827)

Vance, Mr. William. Died in Bowling Green, Ky.
National Banner & Nashville Whig. (Mon., June 7, 1830)

Van Cortlandt, Gen. Philip. An Officer of the revolution. Died in Westchester County, N. Y. in the 82nd year of his age.
National Banner & Nashville Whig. (Fri., Dec. 2, 1831)

Vandaren, Mrs. Died in Cynthiana, Ky. Killed from a fall from a horse.
National Banner & Nashville Whig. (Sat., July 22, 1826)

Vanderventer, Col. Chrispher?. Formerly of the U. S. Army and afterwards for several years, Chief Clerk of the War Department. Died in Georgetown, D. C. on 22d.
Nashville Whig. (Mon., May 14, 1838)

Vandervoort, Theodore B. Infant son of Mr. William H. Vandervoort. Died in Nashville on Sunday last.
National Banner & Nashville Whig. (Thurs., Sept. 30, 1830)

Vandervoort, Mr. William H. Died at Trenton, Ky. Formerly a Merchant of Nashville.
National Banner & Nashville Whig. (Mon., Nov. 9, 1835)

Vandike, John Jr. Died by fatel accident in Montgomery County, on
last Saturday afternoon.
National Banner & Nashville Daily Advertiser. (Tues., Nov. 6, 1832)

Vandike, Mr. William. Died in Rutherford County.
National Banner & Nashville Whig. (Fri., Nov. 11, 1831)

Van Dyke, Nicholas Esq. Senator in Congress, from Deleware. Died
at Newcastle, Del.
National Banner & Nashville Whig. (June 17, 1826)

Vanhook, Mrs. Died in Memphis on Tuesday morning of Cholera.
National Banner & Nashville Daily Advertiser. (Wed., Nov. 14, 1832)

Vanhook, Mrs. Elizabeth. Consort of John Vanhook Esq. Died in
Henderson County, on the 5th inst. age 54 years.
Daily Republican Banner. (Sat., June 20, 1840)

Vanice, Barney. Died in Danville, Ky. of Cholera.
National Banner & Nashville Daily Advertiser. (Mon., Aug. 5, 1833)

Vanice, John. Died in Danville, Ky. of Cholera.
National Banner & Nashville Daily Advertiser. (Mon., Aug. 5, 1833)

Vanleer, Mr. Bernard. Aged 55. Died in Nashville on Wednesday 16th
inst.
National Banner & Nashville Daily Advertiser. (Thurs., Jan. 17, 1833)

Van Ness, Gen. John. Died in Washington City on the 7th inst. In
the 77th year of his age.
Nashville Whig. (Thurs., March 19, 1846)

Vannoy, Anderson. Died in Shelbyville, Tenn. of Cholera.
National Banner & Nashville Daily Advertiser. (Thurs., July 11, 1833)

Van Pelt, Mrs. Ann H. Late consort of the editor of this paper,
in the 37th year of her age. Died on Thursday last the 28th ult.
Obituary in Weekly Record.
Nashville Union. (Sat., Jan. 6, 1838)

Van Vechten, Abraham. Died in Albany, New York.
Nashville Republican. (Thurs., Jan. 26, 1837)

Van Wart, Capt. Isaac. Aged 71. Died at Mount Pleasant, N. Y.
National Banner & Nashville Whig. (Fri., June 20, 1828)

Vardeman, Mr. Dudley. Son of the Rev. Jeremiah Vardeman. Died in
Fayette County, Ky.
National Banner. (Sat., July 1829)

Varick, Col. Richard. Died in New York.
National Banner & Nashville Whig. (Wed., Aug. 17, 1831)

Vaughan, Mr. Edward W. Died in Wilson County.
National Banner & Nashville Advertiser. (Sat., Dec. 8, 1832)

Vaughn, David. Infant son of Mr. Elisha Vaughan. Died at Murfreesborough.
National Banner & Nashville Advertiser. (Mon., Aug. 27, 1832)

Vaughn, Mr. Edward W. Died in Wilson County.
National Banner & Nashville Daily Advertiser. (Sat., Dec. 8, 1832)

Vaughn, Mr. Elisha B. Died in Murfreesboro, Tenn. on the 25th.
National Banner & Nashville Daily Advertiser. (Mon., March 31, 1834)

Vaughn, Eugene Catherine. Infant daughter of Elisha B. Vaughn. Died in Murfreesborough, Tenn.
National Banner & Nashville Daily Advertiser. (Mon., March 31, 1834)

Vaughn, Mr. John. Aged 34 years. Died in New Orleans, La.
National Banner & Nashville Whig. (Fri., Nov. 14, 1834)

Vaughn, Joshua P. Esq. Died in Montgomery County.
National Banner. (Sat., April 11, 1829)

Vaughn, Mary Elizabeth. In the thirteenth year of her age. Died in Lafayette County, Missouri formerly of Tennessee and grand daughter of Martin Green, dec'd. of this county.
National Banner & Nashville Daily Advertiser. (Fri., Nov. 1, 1833)

Vaughn, Samuel Esq. Died in Jamaica on Feb. 9th.
National Banner & Nashville Whig. (Sat., May 12, 1827)

Vaughn, Mr. William A. Aged 18 years. Died in Rutherford County on the 6th inst.
National Banner & Nashville Daily Advertiser. (Fri., Feb. 15, 1833)

Vaugine, Miss Mary D. Aged 18 years. Died in Little Rock, Ark.
National Banner & Nashville Daily Advertiser. (Tues., Aug. 5, 1834)

Vaugn, Mrs. Nancy. Aged 42. Wife of Mr. Jesse Vaugn. Died in Roane County.
National Banner & Nashville Whig. (Mon., Nov. 29, 1830)

Vaulx, Daniel. Son of Joseph and E. R. N. Vaulx. Died on the 15th inst. aged one year and seven days.
Nashville Whig. (Tues., July 23, 1844)

Vaulx, Mrs. Susan. Wife of Joseph Vaulx, Merchant of Nashville. Died in Nashville on Wednesday the 14th.
National Banner & Nashville Whig. (Mon., Oct. 26, 1835)

Veal, Mrs. Polly. Wife of Jno. C. Veal, aged 45 years. Died in Knoxville, Tenn.
National Banner & Nashville Whig. (Fri., Nov. 21, 1834)

Veech, Miss Elizabeth. Died in Louisville, Ky.
National Banner & Nashville Whig. (Sat., Jan. 31, 1829)

Velman, Enoch. Died 15th at Cincinnati, Ohio of Cholera.
National Banner & Nashville Daily Advertiser. (Wed., Oct. 24, 1832)

Verplanck, Daniel C. Esq. In the 73d year of his age. Died suddenly near Fishkill Landing in the state of New York.
National Banner & Nashville Daily Advertiser. (Wed., April 16, 1834)

Vestal, Mr. Silas. Died in Green County.
Nashville Republican & State Gazette. (Wed., Dec. 5, 1832)

Vick, Col. Willis B. Of Vicksburgh, Mississippi.
National Banner & Nashville Whig. (Mon., Sept. 6, 1830)

Villere, Jaques Esq. Died at New Orleans, formerly Governor of Louisiana.
National Banner & Nashville Whig. (Fri., March 26, 1830)

Vining, Mr. James H. Oldest son of John Vining, Esq. aged 25 years. Died in Madison County, Ala.
National Banner & Nashville Whig. (Wed., Nov. 19, 1834)

Vison, Miss Martha. Died in Sumner Co., Ten.
National Banner & Nashville Daily Advertiser. (Thurs., June 19, 1834)

Virden, Mrs. Caroline. Wife of Mr. Daniel Virden. Died at Lexington, Ky.
National Banner. (Sat., April 18,1829)

Von Tagen, Mr. Henry. Died in Louisville, Ky.
National Banner & Nashville Whig. (Mon., June 28, 1830)

Voorhees, Mr. Peter. Died at New Orleans on the 28th of Yellow Fever.
National Banner & Nashville Daily Advertiser. (Tues., Sept. 10, 1833)

Vorschoyle, Dr. Bishop of Killala, age 85 years. Died in Ireland.
He is the third Protestant Irish Bishop, who has died within the
last twelve months.
National Banner & Nashville Daily Advertiser. (Thurs., June 19, 1834)

Waddle, Mrs. Lucinda J. Wife of Joseph P. Waddle, Esq. Died at
Florence, Ala.
National Banner & Nashville Daily Advertiser. (Mon., Sept. 3, 1832)

Wade, Mrs. Edward. Died in Shelbyville of Cholera.
National Banner & Nashville Daily Advertiser. (Thurs., July 11, 1833)

Wade, Mr. Edward. Aged 28 years. Died in Hardeman County, Ten.
National Banner & Nashville Whig. (Wed., Nov. 19, 1834)

Wade, Mrs. Eliza. Died in Rutherford County.
National Banner & Nashville Whig. (Sat., Feb. 10, 1827)

Wade, Mrs. Elizabeth. Aged 60. Wife of Capt. John Wade Sen. Died
in Rutherford County.
National Banner & Nashville Daily Advertiser. (Fri., Aug. 10, 1832)

Wade, Mrs. Nancy. Wife of Rev. M. Wade. Died in Franklin County,
T.
National Banner & Nashville Whig. (Sat., Sept. 9, 1826)

Wade, Wm. Allen. Aged 25 years. Died at Carthage, Ten. on Thursday
last.
National Banner & Nashville Daily Advertiser. (Sat., March 15, 1834)

Wade, W. W. Esq. Attorney at law, and a member of the late General
Assembly of this State. Died in Smith County, Tenn.
National Banner & Nashville Daily Advertiser. (Tues., March 11, 1834)

Waggoner, Mr. John. Aged 65. Died in Adair County, Ky.
National Banner & Nashville Whig. (Mon., July 19, 1830)

Waggoner, Mr. John. Died in Union County, Ky.
National Banner. (March 10, 1826)

Wagnon, Maj. John P. Died in Sumner County, an old revolutionary
officer.
National Banner & Nashville Whig. (Sat., Sept. 20, 1828)

Wahrendroff, Mr. Charles. Died at St. Louis.
National Banner & Nashville Whig. (Wed., Sept. 7, 1831)

Wair, Mrs. Louisa G. Consort of George G. Wair. Died in Raleigh,
Shelby County, Tenn. on the 20th July, formerly a resident of
Davidson County.
Nashville Whig. (Fri., Aug. 14, 1840)

Waite, Miss J. Died in Shelbyville, Tenn. of Cholera.
National Banner & Nashville Daily Advertiser. (Thurs., July 11, 1833)

Waite, Robert. Died in Shelbyville, Tenn. of Cholera.
National Banner & Nashville Daily Advertiser. (Thurs., July 11, 1833)

Waite, Mr. Robert D. A native of New York in the 19th year of his age. Died in New Orleans.
National Banner & Nashville Whig. (Wed., Feb. 4, 1835)

Walcott, Mr. Alexander. Died at Chicago, Ill.
National Banner & Nashville Whig. (Mon., Jan. 10, 1831)

Wald, Mrs. Terese. Died at Cincinnati, Ohio on 12th of Cholera.
National Banner & Nashville Daily Advertiser. (Sat., Oct. 20, 1832)

Wale, Mr. Patrick Jr. Died in Alexander, La.
National Banner & Nashville Whig. (Sat., Aug. 5, 1826)

Walfenbargen, Mrs. Elizabeth. Died in Knoxville.
National Banner & Nashville Daily Advertiser. (Sat., Sept. 22, 1832)

Walker, Mrs. and Infant. Of Nashville. Died in the destruction of the boat Brandywine.
National Banner & Nashville Daily Advertiser. (Mon., April 23, 1832)

Walker, Alice. Infant daughter of Mr. James Walker. Died in Nashville yesterday.
National Banner & Nashville Daily Advertiser. (Mon., July 8, 1833)

Walker, Mr. H. D. Auctioneer. Died in Nashville on Tuesday morning 14th inst.
Nashville True Whig & Weekly Commercial Register. (Fri., May 17, 1850)

Walker, Jacob W. Esq. President of the Branch of the State Bank of Arkansas. Died at Fayetteville, Arkansas.
Nashville Whig. (Mon., Jan. 21, 1839)

Walker, Capt. John. In the 81st year of his age. Died lately at his resident in this county after a short illness.
The Nashville Whig & Tenn. Advertiser. (March 28, 1818)

Walker, Major John. Died in Madison County. Recently a member of the Senate of the United States from Ala.
Nashville Whig. (April 9, 1823)

Walker, John M. C. Formerly of Nashville. Died at Pine Bluff, Ark. Aug. 21.
Nashville Whig. (Fri., Sept. 4, 1840)

Walker, Mrs. Margaret. In the sixtieth year of her age. Died at the residence of her son-in-law Rev. Mr. Lapsley in Nashville on Monday 19th inst.
Nashville Whig. (Wed., July 21, 1841)

Walker, Mrs. Martha. Died near Columbia, K.
National Banner & Nashville Whig. (Sat., Dec. 16, 1826)

Walker, Miss Nancy L. Daughter of Henry Walker dec'd. aged 16 years. Died on Friday morning the 11th inst. near Franklin, Tenn.
The Western Weekly Review. Franklin, Tenn. (Fri., May 18, 1832)

Walker, Mr. Nichols T. Having been found dead, suspended to a tree. Died in this County yesterday.
National Banner & Nashville Whig. (June 24, 1826)

Walker, Mr. Reuben. In the 54th year of his age. Died in Knox County.
Nashville Whig. (Thurs., April 30, 1846)

Walker, Mr. Robert F. In the 21st year of his age. Died in La Grange, Tenn. on the 11th inst. formerly of Nashville.
National Banner & Nashville Whig. (Fri., July 24, 1835)

Walker, Robert. Merchant, of Houston. Died in Houston, Texas.
Nashville Republican (Thurs., Aug. 3, 1837)

Walker, Capt. Samuel. Aged 82. A soldier of the Revolution. Died
in Roane County.
National Banner & Nashville Whig. (Thurs., July 29, 1830)

Walker, Mr. Zachariah J. Died at Kingston.
National Banner & Nashville Daily Advertiser. (Tues., July 17, 1832)

Wallace, Mr. Barkley M. Of the firm of Jacobs & Wallace. Died in
Knoxville, Ten.
National Banner & Nashville Whig. (Fri., Jan. 23, 1835)

Wallace, Mr. Hugh. Died at St. Louis.
National Banner. (Sat., Aug. 1, 1829)

Wallace, Mr. James H. Died in Nashville on the 17th inst.
National Banner & Nashville Daily Advertiser. (Sat., March 22, 1834)

Wallace, Mr. John. Aged 24 years. Died in South Nashville on Tuesday
24th inst.
Nashville True Whig. & Weekly Commercial Register. (Fri., Jan. 3, 1851)

Wallace, Capt. John. For many years a respectable citizen of Rutherford County. Died on Sunday the 18th of August.
The Nashville Whig. (Sept. 3, 1816)

Wallace, Mrs. Louisa. Wife of Mr. Richard Wallace. Died in Fayette
County, Ky.
National Banner & Nashville Whig. (Sat., April 14, 1827)

Waller, Mr. Richard. Aged 86. Died in Rutherford County.
National Banner & Nashville Whig. (Mon., Oct. 25, 1830)

Wallis, Mr. John. About 20 years of age. Died at Haweis Missionary
Station on Oct. 23d.
Nashville Republican & State Gazette. (Mon., Nov. 26, 1832)

Wallis, Phillip. Formerly of Baltimore. Died in the Explosion of
the Steamboat, Lucy Walker.
Nashville Whig. (Tues., Oct. 29, 1844)

Wallis, Mr. Robert. Died in Columbia, Tennessee on the 22nd Oct. at
the age of 91 years.
The Christian Record. (Sat., Jan. 2, 1847)

Walls, Mr. Noah. Died in Murfreesborough.
National Banner & Nashville Advertiser. (Mon., Aug. 27, 1832)

Walsh, Mr. Bartholomew. In the 93d year of his age. Died in St.
Louis, Mo.
National Banner & Nashville Daily Advertiser. (Mon., Aug. 26, 1833)

Walsh, Mr. Edmond. Died in Knox County.
Nashville Republican & State Gazette. (Thurs., April 19, 1831)

Walsh, Michael. Author of the Mercantile Arithmetic. Died in Ames-
bury, Mass.
Nashville Whig. (Fri., Sept. 4, 1840)

Walton, Mrs. Cynthia Ann. Aged 22 years. Died in New Orleans, La.
National Banner & Nashville Whig. (Fri., Nov. 14, 1834)

Walton, Mrs. Mary. Consort of Edward S. Walton Esq. Died in Montgomery County, Tenn.
National Banner & Nashville Whig. (Fri., March 6, 1835)

Walton, Mr. William. Aged 83. Died at St. Louis.
National Banner (May 13, 1826)

Wappan, Mr. Joseph J. Aged 33, a native of New York. Died in New Orleans.
National Banner & Nashville Daily Advertiser. (Tues., June 24, 1834)

Ward, Albert. Late of this vicinity and son of Col. Edward, deceased. Died in Tipton County.
Nashville Whig. (Fri., Dec. 18, 1840)

Ward, Albert G. Esq. Formerly of this neighborhood. Died on the 8th inst. in Tipton County.
Daily Republican Banner. (Fri., Dec. 18th, 1840)

Ward, Mr. Conrad. Died in Logan County, Ky.
National Banner & Nashville Whig. (Wed., Feb. 25, 1835)

Ward, David L. Esq. Died in Jefferson County, Ky.
National Banner & Nashville Whig. (December 2, 1826)

Ward, Henry Esq. Of the House of Prime Ward and King Brokers of New York. Died on the 27th ult.
Nashville Whig. (Mon., Aug. 6, 1838)

Ward, James. Died in Shelbyville, Tenn. of Cholera.
National Banner & Nashville Daily Advertiser. (Thurs., July 11, 1833)

Ward, Mrs. Mary Jane. Aged 27. Consort of Albert G. Ward, Esq. Died in Davidson County on the 26th ult.
National Banner & Nashville Whig. (Mon., Dec. 1, 1834)

Ward, Mr. Samuel. Died in Franklin.
National Banner & Nashville Whig. (Mon., April 25, 1831)

Ward, Maj. William C. Died in this county.
National Banner & Nashville Whig. (Sat., Aug. 18, 1827)

Wardlaw, Mrs. Hugh. Died in Shelbyville, Tenn. of Cholera.
National Banner & Nashville Daily Advertiser. (Thurs., July 11, 1833)

Wardlow, Mr. W. W. Died in Maury County.
National Banner & Nashville Whig. (Mon., March 16, 1831)

Ware, Captain I. Aged 78 years. Died in Amherst County, Va.
National Banner & Nashville Daily Advertiser. (Thurs., Aug. 14, 1834)

Ware, Hon. Henry. A Senator from the State of Georgia. Died in New York, on the 7th ult.
Nashville Whig. (Oct. 4, 1824)

Ware, John Esq. aged 80. Died at Hingham, Mass.
National Banner & Nashville Daily Advertiser. (Sat., Oct. 19, 1833)

Ware, Priscilla. Died 14th at Cincinnati, Ohio of Cholera.
National Banner & Nashville Daily Advertiser. (Tues., Oct. 23, 1832)

Ware, Robert Esq. Died near Montgomery, Ala.
National Banner & Nashville Whig. (Sat., June 9, 1827)

Wareham, Joseph. Died at Cincinnati, Ohio of Cholera.
National Banner & Nashville Daily Advertiser. (Thurs., Oct. 25, 1832)

Warfield, Mrs. Wife of Dr. George W. Warfield, of Nashville.
Died at the City Hotel, on Tuesday last 25th inst., late of Maryland.
National Banner & Nashville Whig. (Fri., July 28, 1837)

Warfield, Dr. Charles H. Died in Lexington, Ky.
National Banner & Nashville Whig. (Mon., Aug. 30, 1830)

Warfield, Henry Esq. Died in Cynthiana, Ky.
National Banner & Nashville Whig. (Mon., Dec. 27, 1830)

Warfield, Doctor Walter. Died in Lexington, Ky.
National Banner (March 24, 1826)

Warnack, Miss Eliza L. Died in Knox County.
National Banner & Nashville Whig. (Sat., Feb. 7, 1829)

Warner, Mr. Elijah of Lexington. Died in Philadelphia.
National Banner (Sat., Nov. 14, 1829)

Warner, Miss Elizabeth Ann. Daughter of Dr. Wm. M. Warner. Died one
mile north of Moscow, Ten. on the 28th May, aged 12 years and 3 months.
National Banner & Nashville Whig. (Mon., June 8, 1835)

Warner, Gen. John. Died at Columbus, Ohio.
National Banner & Nashville Whig. (Mon., March 7, 1831)

Warren, Mrs. Caroline. Aged 26. Died at Spring Hill, Ala.
National Banner & Nashville Whig. (Sept. 2, 1826)

Warren, Mrs. Catherine. Age 40. Wife of Mr. William, and daughter
of late Col. John Thompson. Died in Rutherford County.
National Banner & Nashville Advertiser. (Fri., Aug. 10, 1832)

Warren, Elizabeth H. Late of Franklin, Tennessee. Died at the
residence of her father in Hinds County, Miss. on the 22nd inst.
aged nine years and 6 months.
National Banner & Nashville Daily Advertiser. (Thurs., April 10, 1834)

Warren, Henry. Aged 71 years. Died in Lincoln County.
Nashville Whig. (Thurs., March 19, 1846)

Warren, Mr. Lawrence R. Aged 35. Died in Huntsville.
National Banner & Nashville Whig. (Fri., Feb. 12, 1830)

Warren, Mr. Washington, age 18. Son of Mr. Samuel D. Warren. Died
in Blount County.
National Banner & Nashville Whig. (Fri., July 18, 1831)

Warwick, Maj. William. President of the Branch Bank of the Bank of
Virginia, at Lynchburg. Died at the Salt Sulphur Springs in Virginia.
National Banner & Nashville Daily Advertiser. (Thurs., Aug. 30, 1832)

Washburn, Mr. John. Died in Logan County, Ky.
National Banner & Nashville Whig. (Sat., Oct. 7, 1826)

Washburn, Mr. Phillip. Died in Logan County, Ky.
National Banner & Nashville Whig. (Sat., Sept. 30, 1826)

Washburn, Mr. Whiting. Died in Logan County.
National Banner & Nashville Whig. (Sat., Oct. 7, 1826)

Washington, Bushrod. Died in Fairfax County, Va.
Nashville Republican & State Gazette. (Sat., May 14, 1831)

Washington, James. Aged 35 years. Died in Nashville on Wednesday
last. A member of the house of James Woods and Co.
Nashville Whig. (Sat., Jan. 27, 1838)

Washington, Dr. G. P. Aged about 28. Died in Rankin, Holmes County,
Miss.
National Banner & Nashville Daily Advertiser. (Tues., Nov. 5, 1833)

Washington, George Esq. Son of Mrs. Lucy Todd, widow of the late
Judge Todd, of Kentucky. Died in Jefferson County, Va. on Oct. 13th.
National Banner & Nashville Whig. (Mon., Oct. 31, 1831)

Washington, Mr. George. Of this town. Died on Monday evening.
The Nashville Whig. (Feb. 7, 1816)

Washington, Mr. Gray. Of Davidson County. Died on Sunday night of
consumption.
Impartial Review and Cumberland Repository. (Thurs., Sept. 1, 1808)

Washington, James G. Esq. Aged 39 years. Of the firm of James
Woods & Co. Died in Nashville on Tuesday night last.
Daily Republican Banner. (Thurs., Jan. 25, 1838)

Washington, Mrs. Margaret. Wife of George A. Washington and daughter
of Maj. William B. Lewis. Died in Robertson County on the 21st inst.
aged 21.
Nashville Whig. (Thurs., Nov. 28, 1844)

Washington, Mary Eliza. Daughter of Thomas Washington, Esq. Died on
Monday 24th inst. aged 7 years.
Nashville Whig. (Thurs., Jan. 27, 1842)

Washington, Mrs. Needham. Aged 64 years. Died in Nashville on
Sunday 29th ult. late of Waterloo, Virginia.
Nashville Whig. (Sat., Sept. 5, 1846)

Washington, Dr. Samuel W. Died in Jefferson County, Va. on Oct. 12th.
National Banner & Nashville Whig. (Mon., Oct. 31, 1831)

Washington, Miss Sarah Jennette. In the 21st year of her age. Died
at the residence of her Mother, Mrs. Elizabeth H. Washington in
Nashville on Wednesday the 17th inst. eldest daughter of the late
Gilbert G. Washington.
The Christian Record. (Sat., March 27, 1847)

Washington, Thomas Esq. Died in New York formerly Governor of Ohio.
National Banner & Nashville Whig. (Sat., July 14, 1827)

Washington, Gen. Thomas. Who was born in Virginia on the first day
of March, 1764. Died on Saturday the 13th inst. at his seat, Rutherford County, Tennessee.
The Nash. Whig & Tenn. Advertiser. (June 20, 1818)

Washington, Mr. Whitting. Died in Logan County, Ky.
National Banner & Nashville Whig. (Sat., Oct. 7, 1826)

Washington, Major William L. Attorney at law of Nashville, Tenn.
Died at Tallahassee, Florida on the 20th Sept. aged 30 years.
Nashville Republican (Tues., Oct. 11, 1836)

Washington, Major William L. Died also, on the 20th Sept. at Tallahassee, Florida Major William L. Washington Atty at law of this city
age 30 years. In this untimely bereavement, Tennessee has lost another
of her brave and generous Sons; his numerous and afflicted, a bright
ornament to their family; the circle of his acquaintances a warm and
cherished friend; and his amiable and affectionate wife, a fond and
devoted husband. Ardent, patriotic and aspiring he left the dear
companion of his love and the friends, the land of his nativity and
home for the toils of the camp and the dangers of battle. Brave,
open and generous. Having enrolled his name in the company of the
Nashville Independent Highlanders he was chosen to command that
band of heroes. He was soon promoted to the rank of Maj. He also

fell a victim to the Billious fever originating in the same causes
that eventuated in the death of the gallant Yerger.
Nashville Republican. (Tues., Oct. 11, 1836)

Waterbury, Mr. Joseph G. Died at Cincinnati.
National Banner & Nashville Daily Advertiser. (Thurs., Sept. 6, 1832)

Waterhouse, Mrs. Ann Eliza. Consort of Eucled Waterhouse of Cleve-
land and second daughter of Thomas J. Campbell, Esq. Died in
Chattanooga at the residence of James W. Smith on the 27th ult.
Daily Republican Banner. (Tues., July 7, 1840)

Waterhouse, Richard. Died Rhea County.
National Banner & Nashville Whig. (Sat., March 31, 1827)

Waters, Mrs. Died by the accidental discharge of a gun. In Madison
County.
National Banner & Nashville Whig. (Wed., Dec. 14, 1831)

Waters, Mrs. Martha. Consort of Mr. P. A. Waters in the 27th year of
her age. Died in Knoxville, Ten.
National Banner & Nashville Whig. (Mon., Oct. 20, 1834)

Waters, Mrs. Martha Ann. Consort of Mr. Lindslay Waters. Died in
in Williamson County.
National Banner & Nashville Whig. (Wed., Feb. 4, 1835)

Waties, Judge. Aged 68. Died near Statesburgh, S. C.
National Banner & Nashville Whig. (Sat., Aug. 9, 1828)

Watkins, Mrs. Cabella. Wife of Mr. James C. Watkins. Died in
Florence, Ala.
National Banner & Nashville Whig. (Mon., Nov. 7, 1831)

Watkins, E. B. Esq. Died in Monroe County.
National Banner & Nashville Whig. (Sat., Feb. 21, 1829)

Watkins, Mrs. Elizabeth. Wife of Mr. Albert Watkins. Died in
Meridianville, Ala.
National Banner & Nashville Whig. (Mon., Aug. 22, 1831)

Watkins, Mr. Henry. And Ten days later Mrs. Elizabeth Watkins, his
widow and Mother of Hon. Henry Clay. Died in Woodford County.
National Banner. (Sat., Dec. 19, 1829)

Watkins, Mr. John K. Died in Henry County.
National Banner & Nashville Whig. (Sat., Dec. 15, 1827)

Watkins, Mrs. Margaret. Aged 24. Died in Sumner County.
National Banner & Nashville Whig. (Sat., Feb. 2, 1828)

Watkins, Mrs. Maria. Consort of A. Watkins Esq. Died in Breckenridge County, Ky.
National Banner & Nashville Daily Advertiser. (Fri., July 25, 1834)

Watkins, Owen T. Esq. In the 51st year of his age. Died on Wednesday
near Franklin.
The Western Weekly Review, Franklin, Tenn. (Fri., Nov. 9, 1832)

Watkins, Mr. Richard. Died in Wilson County on the 30th ult.
National Banner & Nashville Daily Advertiser. (Mon., July 2, 1832)

Watkins, Dr. Thomas G. Died in Jefferson County. on the 2nd inst.
National Banner & Nashville Whig. (Fri., Jan. 22, 1830)

Watkins, Mr. Thomas H. A member of the Legislature. Died in Jefferson
County, Miss.
National Banner & Nashville Daily Advertiser. (Mon., May 26, 1834)

Watkins, William Esq. Aged 68. Died in Breckenridge County, Ky.
National Banner & Nashville Whig. (Sat., Jan. 6, 1827)

Watlington, Harriet McClain. Infant daughter of H. S. & M. B.
Watlington. Died at Gallatin, Tenn.
National Banner & Nashville Daily Advertiser. (Wed., July 9, 1834)

Warmough, Mrs. Ellen. Died in Germantown, Pa.
Nashville Republican & State Gazette. (Thurs., March 3, 1831)

Watson, Anna. Daughter of Samuel Watson. Died at Sycamore, Robertson County, aged about 6 years.
Nashville Whig. (Tues., March 26, 1844)

Watson, Mr. Augustus P. H. Aged about 19 years. Died in Franklin,
Tenn. on 3d inst. of Cholera.
National Banner & Nashville Whig. (Fri., July 10, 1835)

Watson, Midshipman Clarance. Of the U. S. Navy in the 22nd year of
his age. Died in Washington, City.
National Banner & Nashville Daily Advertiser. (Fri., Aug. 1, 1834)

Watson, Mr. George H. Formerly of Warren County, Ky. Died in
Shelby County.
National Banner & Nashville Whig. (Thurs., July 29, 1830)

Watson, Mr. John. Of the House of Fisher, Burk and Watson. Died in
New Orleans.
National Banner (Sat., Sept. 12, 1829)

Watson, John Dexter. Infant son of Matthew and Rebecca Watson. Died
yesterday afternoon at 4 o'clock.
Nashville Whig. (Thurs., Nov. 21, 1844)

Watson, Joseph. Aged 23, formerly of Nashville. Died on Thursday
the 30th ulto. in Jefferson County, Ky. in the vicinity of Louisville,
Ky.
Nashville Whig. (Thurs., April 6, 1843)

Watson, Marquis Morton. Infant son of Samuel and Charlotte Watson.
Died at Sycamore, Robertson County on the 15th inst.
Nashville Whig. (Thurs., Oct. 19, 1843)

Watson, Mary Frances. In the 16th year of her age. Died yesterday
at the residence of Samuel Watson Esq. in Robertson County. Daughter
of Mathew Watson, Esq. of Nashville.
Nashville Whig. (Wed., Aug. 18, 1841)

Watson, Rev. Richard. Of the Wesleyan Methodist Conference. Died in
London Jan. 8th.
The Western Weekly Review. Franklin, Tenn. (Fri., March 29, 1833)

Watson, Mr. Robert B. 35. Died in Mobile.
National Banner & Nashville Whig. (Sept. 2, 1826)

Watson, Mr. Ruel A. Died at Vicksburg, Miss. on the 7th May of
Cholera.
National Banner & Nashville Daily Advertiser. (Mon., May 20, 1833)

Watson, Mrs. Tabitha. Wife of Dr. John M. Watson just beginning
the 22nd year of age. Died on the 13th inst.
National Banner. (Sat., Dec. 26, 1829)

Watson, Dr. Thomas F. Died at his residence at the Empire Iron
Works on the Cumberland River in Trigg County, Ky. on the 16th inst.
Nashville Whig. (Tues., April 21, 1846)

Watterson, Mr. Wesley K. Died in Shelbyville.
National Banner & Nashville Advertiser. (Wed., April 25, 1832)

Watts, Dr. Jno. Jun. M. D. Died in New York. President of Physicians and Surgeons College.
Nashville Republican & State Gazette. (Thurs., Feb. 24, 1831)

Watts, Col. John. A gallant and distinguished Revolutionary Officer.
Died in Bedford County, Virginia at an advanced age.
National Banner & Nashville Whig. (Thurs., July 1, 1830)

Watts, Mr. Thomas G. Died in Madison County, Ala.
National Banner (May 4, 1826)

Weakley, Mrs. Jane. Consort of Col. Robert Weakley. Died in
Davidson County.
Daily Republican Banner. (Thurs., Sept. 20, 1838)

Weakley, Mrs. Jane. Consort of Col. Robert Weakley. Died on yesterday
evening. Funeral at his residence, 2 miles east of Nashville.
Nashville Union. (Wed., Sept. 19, 1838)

Weakley, Samuel. Aged 65. Died in Montgomery County was of this
County.
Nashville Republican & State Gazette. (Wed., Oct. 24, 1832)

Weakley, Samuel Esq. Died in Montgomery County, near Palmyra, aged
nearly 65 years for many years County surveyor for Davidson County.
National Banner & Nashville Daily Advertiser. (Mon., Oct. 22, 1832)

Weathered, Miss Mary C. Daughter of Major Robert Weathered. Died
in Sumner County.
National Banner & Nashville Whig. (Thurs., Oct. 14, 1830)

Weathers, Mr. John. Died in Lincoln County, Ky.
National Banner & Nashville Whig. (Sat., Sept. 1, 1827)

Weatherspoon, Col. John. Aged 79. Died in Wayne County on the 14th
ult. He was a soldier of the Revolution and was in the battle of
Kings Mountain.
Daily Republican Banner. (Sat., Feb. 8, 1840)

Weatherspoon, Nathaniel Green. Son of Col. John Weatherspoon. Died
in Wayne County on the 17th inst. In the 16th year of his age, by
the accidental discharge of a pistol.
National Banner & Nashville Daily Advertiser. (Tues., Jan. 24, 1832)

Weaver, Mr. Eli. Died in Knox County.
National Banner & Nashville Daily Advertiser. (Tues., May 8, 1832)

Weaver, Mr. J. E. Died in Niagra, N. York.
Nashville Republican & State Gazette. (Sat., Sept. 17, 1831)

Weaver, Mrs. Mary D. In the 19th year of her age wife of Dempsey
Weaver and daughter of James Johnson Esq. Died yesterday morning.
Nashville Whig. (Tues., March 1st 1842)

Webb, Amy T. Infant daughter of Col. Ezra Webb. Died in Lauderdale
County, Ala.
National Banner & Nashville Advertiser. (Mon., Aug. 27, 1832)

Webb, Dr. Henry Y. Son of Dr. William S. Webb. Died in Williamson
County on Friday Oct. 9th. at the residence of his father.
National Banner & Nashville Whig. (Mon., Nov. 2, 1835)

Webb, John Esq. Died in Weakly County, Ten.
Nashville Republican & State Gazette. (Tues., March 8, 1831)

Webb, John R. Died at Greenville, Virginia by shooting himself
through the head.
The Union. (Sat., March 12, 1836)

Webb, Nelson. Died 14th at Cincinnati of Cholera.
National Banner & Nashville Daily Advertiser. (Tues., Oct. 23, 1832)

Webb, Dr. Thomas. Druggist. Died in Washington City by suicide.
National Banner. (Jan. 13, 1826)

Webster, Charles R. Esq. A native of Hartford, Conn. Died at Saratoga Springs in the 72nd year of his age.
National Banner & Nashville Daily Advertiser. (Fri., Aug. 1, 1834)

Webster, Charles R. Esq. Died at Saratoga Springs, New York. For
forty years, editor of the Albany (N.Y.) Gazette.
National Banner & Nashville Daily Advertiser. (Sat., Sept. 6, 1834)

Webster, Hon. Ezekiel. Aged 52. Died at Concord, N. H. very
suddenly.
National Banner (Sat., May 2, 1829)

Webster, Mrs. Grace. Wife of Hon. Daniel Webster. Died at New York.
National Banner & Nashville Whig. (Sat., Feb. 9, 1827)

Webster, Col. Jonathan. In the 66th year of his age. Died at his
residence in Coffee County on the 5th ulto.
Nashville Whig. (Thurs., Dec. 8, 1842)

Webster, Mrs. Mary. Consort of Col. Jonathan Webster in the 48th
year of her age. Died in Bedford County, Tenn.
National Banner & Nashville Whig. (Mon., Jan. 5, 1835)

Weigart, Mr. George. Architect, late of Lexington, Ky. Died in
Little Rock, Ark.
National Banner & Nashville Daily Advertiser. (Tues., Aug. 5, 1834)

Weir, Mr. James. Died at Lexington, Ky.
National Banner & Nashville Daily Advertiser. (Mon., March 5, 1832)

Weisiger, Capt. Daniel. Died at Frankfort, Ky. an innkeeper in that
place.
National Banner & Nashville Whig. (Sat., Feb. 14, 1829)

Welch, Denning N. Formerly of Chatham Ct. Died in Plaquemine, La.
National Banner & Nashville Daily Advertiser. (Tues., June 24, 1834)

Welch, Mr. John. Age 83. Died near Nicholasville, Ky. on the 12th
inst.
National Banner & Nashville Advertiser. (Tues., May 29, 1832)

Welch, Mr. Thomas. Died in Nashville of Cholera on the 25th inst.
National Banner & Nashville Daily Advertiser. (Tues., Feb. 26, 1833)

Welcker, Wm. L. Esq. Died at Athens.
National Banner & Nashville Whig. (Wed., March 9, 1831)

Weller, Miss Elizabeth. In the 12th year of her age. Died in
Hopkinsville, Ky. on the 19th Aug. daughter of Mr. B. S. Weller of
Nashville.
National Banner & Nashville Whig. (Wed., Aug. 24, 1836)

Weller, Elizabeth. Of Nashville daughter of Mr. B. S. Weller. Died
at Hopkinsville, Ky. on the 17th inst.
Nashville Republican (Thurs., Aug. 25, 1836)

Weller, Miss Elizabeth Ann. Daughter of Mr. C. G. Weller of Nashville.
Died on Saturday July 4th inst.
Nashville Whig. (Tues., July 7, 1846)

Weller, James E. Son of Rev. C. G. and B. M. Weller. Died in
Nashville on the 14th inst. aged 8 years and 8 months.
The Politician & Weekly Nashville Whig. (Fri., June 25, 1847)

Welles, Gen. Arnold. Died in Boston.
National Banner & Nashville Whig. (Sat., March 31, 1827)

Wells, Mrs. Eliza. Consort of Dr. Thos. Wells of Nashville. Died
on Wednesday morning 1st inst. in the 22nd year of her age.
National Banner & Nashville Whig. (Thurs., Sept. 9, 1830)

Wells, Mr. James. Died in Williamson County.
National Banner & Nashville Whig. (Sat., Feb. 10, 1827)

Wells, Rev. Martin. Died in Arkansas, by drowning. Of the traveling
connection of the Methodist Episcopal Church.
National Banner & Nashville Daily Advertiser. (Tues., Aug. 27, 1833)

Welsh, Mrs. E. and two children of New Orleans. Died on the Steamer
George Collier about 80 miles below Natchez. Scalded to death.
Daily Republican Banner. (Tues., May 14, 1839)

Welsh, Dr. Tho. Aged 79. Died in Boston, Mass.
Nashville Republican & State Gazette. (Thurs., March 24, 1831)

Welsh, Thomas J. Infant son of Mr. Thomas Welsh. Died in this town
on Friday 22nd inst.
National Banner & Nashville Whig. (Sat., Aug. 30, 1828)

Wendel, David. For many years, Post Master of Murfreesboro. Died
in Rutherford County.
Daily Republican Banner. (Wed., Oct. 21, 1840)

Wendel, Mrs. Sarah. Wife of David Wendel Esq. Died in Murfreesboro on the 17th Aug.
Daily Republican Banner. (Thurs., Aug. 23, 1838)

Wendel, Mrs. Sarah H. Wife of David Wendel Esq. of Murfreesboro.
Died in Murfreesboro on Friday the 17th inst. (Obituary)
Nashville Whig. (Fri., Aug. 24, 1838)

West, Mrs. Wife of Mr. Claiborne West. Died in Christian County, Ky.
National Banner & Nashville Daily Advertiser. (Mon., April 29, 1833)

West, Mr. Austin M. Age 25. Died in Lexington, Ky.
National Banner & Nashville Advertiser. (Mon., April 30, 1832)

West, Mr. Austin M. Aged 25 years. Died in Lexington, Ky.
National Banner & Nashville Daily Advertiser. (Mon., April 30, 1832)

West, Mr. Benjamin F. Formerly a resident of Nashville. Died at
New Orleans on the 1st inst.
Nashville Whig. (Thurs., May 16, 1844)

West, Mrs. Cornelia C. Consort of Mr. William G. West. Died on the
4th inst. in Davidson County of Consumption in the 21st year of her
age.
Nashville Whig. (Tues., June 11, 1844)

West, Mr. Edward. An old and respected citizen. Died in Lexington,
Ky.
National Banner & Nashville Whig. (Sat., Sept. 1, 1827)

West, Miss Eliza. Daughter of Mr. Isaac West. Died in Williamson
County.
National Banner & Nashville Daily Advertiser. (Mon., June 17, 1833)

West, Emanuel J. Esq. U. S. Charge d'Affairs at Chili. Died at
Rio Janeiro.
National Banner & Nashville Whig. (Tues., April 27, 1830)

West, Mr. Francis G. Died in Lexington, Ky.
National Banner & Nashville Whig. (Fri., Jan. 1st, 1830)

West, Col. George. Attorney at Law. Died at his residence in Montgomery County on the ___ ult.
Nashville Whig. (May 10, 1824)

West, Mrs. Jane West. Wife of Mr. John B. West. Died in this town
on Friday 18th inst.
National Banner & Nashville Whig. (Sat., April 26, 1828)

West, Mr. John. Died in Dickson County.
National Banner. (April 7, 1826)

West, Mr. Joseph S. Formerly of Sumner County. Died at Equality,
Ill.
National Banner & Nashville Whig. (Fri., Nov. 26, 1830)

West, Mrs. Penelope. Died in Russellville, Jefferson County.
National Banner & Nashville Whig. (Sat., July 22, 1826)

West, Mrs. Sarah. Wife of Mr. James West. Died in Dickson County.
National Banner & Nashville Whig. (Sat., March 7, 1829)

West, Capt. William. Died at Lexington, Ky.
National Banner & Nashville Whig. (Mon., Sept. 26, 1831)

West, Capt. William. Died at Lexington, Ky.
National Banner & Nashville Whig. (Mon., Sept. 26, 1831)

Westbay, Mr. Mathew R. Died on Harrode Creek, Ky.
National Banner & Nashville Whig. (Sat., Sept. 30, 1826)

Western, Miss Sophia. Died in Nashville on the 12th inst.
National Banner & Nashville Whig. (Thurs., May 20, 1830)

Weston, Mr. Daniel F. (Firm Whiting & Weston) Died near Boston by
drowning when the Steamboat, Bunker Hill was wrecked by the wind.
National Banner & Nashville Daily Advertiser. (Sat., June 30, 1832)

Whaley, Mrs. Frances. Died in Lexington, Ky.
National Banner & Nashville Daily Advertiser. (Wed., July 31, 1833)

Wharton, Mrs. Amanda. Eldest sister of Henry C. Walker Esq. of
Nashville. Died at La Grange, Tennessee, at the residence of her
Mother, Mrs. Walker.
Nashville Whig. (Fri., Nov. 8, 1839)

Wharton, Mrs. Elizabeth. Wife of Jesse Wharton, of Davidson County.
Died in Nashville.
National Banner & Nashville Daily Advertiser. (Thurs., May 30, 1833)

Wharton, Ellen Josephine. Infant daughter of Dr. W. H. and Priscilla
Wharton, aged 1 year and 8 days. Died on Tuesday the 2nd inst.
Nashville Whig. (Thurs., April 8, 1844)

Wharton, George Esq. Died at his residence in this County on the
21st inst. in the 58th year of his age.
Nashville Whig. (Aug. 30, 1824)

Wharton, George M. (Dr.) Notice of his death at Hernando, Miss on
Aug. 27, 1853 of Yellow fever.
Republican Banner and Nashville Whig. (No. 214 Thurs., Sept. 1, 1853)

Wharton, Jesse Esq. Formerly a member of Congress from this District. Died in Davidson County.
National Banner & Nashville Daily Advertiser. (Tues., July 23, 1833)

Wharton, Miner. Infant son of Henry & Mary Wharton. Died on the 31st ulto in Nashville.
Nashville Whig. (Sat., June 6, 1846)

Wharton, Mrs. P. Consort of Dr. William H. Wharton. Died on the6th inst. in the vicinity of Nashville.
The Politician & Weekly Nashville Whig. (Wed., Aug. 18, 1847)

Wharton, Mrs. Rhoda. Widow of the late John Wharton Esq. Died at the residence of Jesse Wharton.
National Banner & Nashville Whig. (Sat., April 19, 1828)

Wharton, Mr. Samuel. Died in Nashville on the 20th ult.
National Banner & Nashville Daily Advertiser. (Tues., Jan. 22, 1833)

Wharton, Mr. William. A respectable citizen of this County. Died on Monday morning.
The Nashville Whig. (Feb. 7, 1816)

Wheat, Reginald Heber. Infant son of Rev. John T. Wheat. Died in Nashville this morning.
Nashville Whig. (Fri., June 7, 1839)

Wheatley, Mr. William. Aged 56. Died in Memphis.
National Banner & Nashville Daily Advertiser. (Mon., June 17, 1833)

Wheaton, Mr. John L. Formerly of Williamson County. Died in the Island of Curracoa.
National Banner & Nashville Daily Advertiser. (Tues., July 2, 1833)

Wheeler, Capt. Chester. Died after an illness of 37 hours, near Marthasville, Mo. on Jan. 9.
National Banner & Nashville Advertiser. (Sat., Feb. 11, 1832)

Wheeler, Capt. Chester. Mrs. Johanna Wheeler, his wife. Died on the same day the 9th of Jan. at Marthasville, Mo.
National Banner & Nashville Daily Advertiser. (Sat., Feb. 11, 1832)

Wheeler, George P. Of the house of Charles Lane & Co. Died in Boston on the 18th aged 25 years.
National Banner & Nashville Whig. (Mon., July 31, 1837)

Wheeler, Mr. James D. Of Georgia. Died in Fayett County, Ky.
National Banner & Nashville Whig. (Sat., Jan. 27, 1827)

Wheeler, Mrs. Jane. Wife of Mr. Henry J. Wheeler. Died at Huntsville.
National Banner & Nashville Whig. (Sat., May 26, 1827)

Wheeler, Mrs. Johanna. Consort of Capt. Chester Wheeler. Died on 9, after an illness of 20 hours, near Marthasville, Mo.
National Banner & Nashville Advertiser. (Sat., Feb. 11, 1832)

Wheeler, Mr. William. Died in Bourbon County, Ky.
National Banner (March 17, 1826)

Whelan, Julius Friedlander. Son of Eli W. and Maria A. C. Whelan. Died on the 7th inst. aged about 15 months.
Nashville Whig. (Tues., June 9, 1846)

Wherry, Mr. William. In the 83 year of his age. Died at his residence near Cairo on Saturday April 21.
National Banner & Nashville Whig. (Sat., May 12, 1827)

Whetsell, Mr. Michael. Aged 30. Died at Athens.
National Banner & Nashville Whig. (Fri., May 30, 1831)

Whetsell, Mr. Mitchael?. Age 30. Died in Athens.
National Banner & Nashville Whig. (Fri., May 20, 1831)

Whipple, Mr. James. Died in this town yesterday.
National Banner. (Sat., Aug. 22, 1829)

Whistler, Mrs. Wife of Maj. John Whistler. Died at Contonment,
Belle Fontaine, Mo.
National Banner. (April 28, 1826)

Whitaker, Mrs. Lucinda. Wife of Mr. David Whitaker. Died near
Denmark.
National Banner. (Sat., Nov. 7, 1829)

White, Mrs. Consort of Mr. John A. White. Died in Elizabethtown,
Ky.
National Banner & Nashville Daily Advertiser. (Tues., July 15, 1834)

White, Mrs. Wife of Mr. Davis White. Died in Warren County, Ky.
National Banner. (Sat., May 16, 1829)

White, Mrs. Abigail. Consort of the Hon. John White. Died in
Courtland, Ala.
National Banner & Nashville Daily Advertiser. (Thurs., June 19, 1834)

White, Mrs. Ann Elizabeth. Relict of Hon. Hugh Lawson White. Died
at Flint Hill, her late residence near Knoxville, on the 2nd inst. aged
70 years.
The Politician & Weekly Nashville Whig. (Fri., April 16, 1847)

White, Mr. Benjamin. Died at Franklin.
National Banner & Nashville Whig. (Sat., Oct. 6, 1827)

White, Capt. Beverly W. Formerly of the steamboat Erin and half
brother of Samuel Seay Esq. of Nashville. Died in this vicinity
on Monday night.
Nashville Whig. (Fri., Feb. 8, 1839)

White, C. A. C. Esq. Aged 26. Son of the Hon. Hugh L. White. Died
at Knoxville.
National Banner (Feb. 3, 1826)

White, Rev. Caleb. Aged 64. Died in Jefferson County.
National Banner & Nashville Whig. (Sat., Feb. 24, 1827)

White, Mrs. Catharine L. Consort of Col. William F. White. of
Montgomery County. Died at the residence of Rev. J. W. Ogden in
the vicinity of Nashville on the 26th inst.
Nashville Whig. (Thurs., Jan. 29, 1846)

White, Mr. Chilian. Of Russellville, Ala. formerly of Davidson
County. Died on the 25th. He was murdered near Columbus, Miss.
Daily Republican Banner. (Sat., May 4, 1839)

White, Cynthia. Infant daughter of Hugh A. M. White. Died in
Knoxville, Tennessee.
National Banner & Nashville Daily Advertiser. (Mon., Aug. 26, 1833)

White, Miss Cynthia W. Daughter of Hugh L. White, Esq. aged 16.
National Banner & Nashville Whig. (Sat., Feb. 14, 1829)

White, Hon. David. Judge of the Circuit Court. Died in Franklin
County, Ky.
National Banner & Nashville Whig. (Fri., March 13, 1835)

White, Mrs. Elizabeth. Wife of the Hon. Hugh L. Senator in Congress, from this State. Died in Rockbridge County, Va. on 29 ult.
National Banner & Nashville Whig. (Mon., April 11, 1831)

White, Miss Elizabeth. Daughter of Mr. Robert White. Died in Williamson County, Ten.
National Banner & Nashville Daily Advertiser. (Tues., June 24, 1834)

White, Miss Elizabeth Lawson. Granddaughter of Judge White. Died in Knoxville, Tenn.
Daily Republican Banner. (Sat., Sept. 29, 1838)

White, Elizabeth Lawson. Stepdaughter of Col. R. A. Ramsey. Died in Knoxville on the 20th ult.
Daily Republican Banner. (Wed., March 13, 1839)

White, Miss Emma C. Died in Nashville on the 29th inst. at the residence of William Davis Esq.
The Politician & Weekly Nashville Whig. (Wed., Aug. 4, 1847)

White, Green, From Davidson County. Died at the Tenn. State Prison, of Cholera.
National Banner & Nashville Whig. (Fri., Aug. 14, 1835)

White, Rev. Henry. Died in Monroe County, Ala.
National Banner. (Sat., May 2, 1829)

White, Judge Hugh L. Died - no date given.
Daily Republican Banner. (Fri., April 17, 1840)

White, Dr. Jackson. In Franklin, Tenn. Dr. Jackson White.
Nashville Republican, (Tues., Feb. 9, 1836)

White, Mr. James J. Died in Franklin County, Ky.
National Banner & Nashville Whig. (Sat., June 2, 1827)

White, James. In the 76th year of his age. Died in Maury County A soldier of the revolution.
National Banner & Nashville Daily Advertiser. (Fri., July 6, 1832)

White, James M. M. Esq. Attorney at law at Huntsville and son of Hugh L. White Esq. of Knoxville. Died at Tuscaloosa, Ala.
National Banner & Nashville Whig. (Sat., Dec. 20, 1828)

White, Mrs. Jane. Died in Williamson County. 22nd of Oct. 99 years of age.
National Banner. (Sat., Oct. 31, 1829)

White, Mrs. Jane S. Wife of Maj. William White. Died on 16th inst.
Nashville Whig. (Tues., March 26, 1816)

White, Mr. Jefferson. Died in Madison County, Ky.
National Banner. (Sat., July 4, 1829)

White, Hon. Joseph M. Well known as a distinguished lawyer of Florida. Died - his death announced by St. Louis papers.
Daily Republican Banner. (Mon., Oct. 28, 1839)

White, Rev. Joshua. Departed this life on the morning of the 21st ult. at his resident in this County.
The Nashville Whig & Tenn. Advertiser. (June 6, 1818)

White, Lee Esq. Died at Louisville, Ky.
National Banner & Nashville Daily Advertiser. (Thurs., July 4, 1833)

White, Miss Lucinda B. Daughter of the Hon. Hugh L. White. Died in Knox County.
National Banner & Nashville Whig. (Sat., April 7, 1827)

White, Mrs. Lucy. Aged 65. Died in Franklin County, Ky.
National Banner (June 10, 1826)

White, Miss Lydia. Daughter of Judge White of this place.
Nashville Whig. (June 21, 1824)

White, Melinda. Daughter of the Hon. Hugh L. White. Died at
Knoxville.
National Banner & Nashville Whig. (Tues., April 20, 1830)

White, Mr. Moses. Aged 54. Died in Knox County.
National Banner & Nashville Whig. (Mon., June 7, 1830)

White, Mrs. Nancy. Relict of the late C. A. C. White. Died in
Knoxville.
National Banner & Nashville Whig. (Sat., Feb. 17, 1827)

White, Mrs. Pamela B. H. Wife of Mr. Thomas E. White. She was born
in Mecklenburg County, Va. June 20, 1814. Died in Courtland, Ala.
National Banner & Nashville Whig. (Fri., Aug. 19, 1831)

White, Hon. Robert. Of the General Court of Virginia. A soldier
of Revolution, one of the brightest ornament of the Judiciary of the
state. Died at Winchester, Va.
National Banner & Nashville Whig. (Mon., March 28, 1831)

White, Robert M. Attorney at law, son of Henry White Esq. of Rutherford County. Died on Monday 9th inst. at Woodbury Tennessee.
Nashville Whig. (Mon., Aug. 16, 1841)

White, Miss Sarah. Died in Bowling Green, Ky.
National Banner & Nashville Whig. (Fri., April 10, 1835)

White, Miss Sophia. In the 19th year of her age. Died in the vicinity
of Nashville on the 19th inst.
Nashville Whig. (Sat., March 21, 1846)

White, Mr. Thomas, Sen. Died in Maury County, in the 84th year of
his age.
National Banner & Nashville Whig. (Fri., Aug. 5, 1831)

White, Mr. Thomas A. Died in Bedford County.
Nashville Whig. (Thurs., May 7, 1846)

White, Gen. William. An early settler and a highly respectable
citizen. Died in Davidson County.
National Banner & Nashville Daily Advertiser. (Wed., Aug. 7, 1833)

White, Rt. Reverend William, D. D. Bishop of the Episcopal Diocese
of Pennsylvania. Died - he was more than 88 years old. (From the
U. S. Gazette)
The Union. (Tues., Aug. 23, 1836)

White, Capt. Wilson. Aged 29. Died in Franklin.
National Banner & Nashville Whig. (Sat., Oct. 28, 1826)

White, Woodson P. Formerly Representative from White County in the
Legislature. Died in White County, Ten. on the 4th inst.
Daily Republican Banner. (Thurs., Oct. 10, 1839)

Whitefield, Rev. George. Aged 79 years. Died in London on the 24th
Dec.
The Western Weekly Review. Franklin, Tenn. (Fri., March 29, 1833)

Whiteside, Gen. John D. A distinguished citizen of Illinois having
helt the Office of State Treasurer and many others. Died on the 3d
inst. at his residence in Monroe County, Illinois.
Nashville True Whig & Weekly Commercial Register. (Fri., Sept. 20, 1850)

Whiteside, Mrs. Margaret. Consort of David WHiteside, aged 33 years.
Died in Davidson County on Sunday last 15th inst.
Daily Republican Banner. (Wed., July 19, 1838)

Whitfield, Albert. Of the firm of Carney & Whitfield, Murfreesboro, Tenn. Died at Jones Hotel, Philadelphia, on Friday the 28th
inst.
Nashville Whig. (Tues., Sept. 8, 1846)

Whitfield, Reverend John, D. D. and M. D. President of Washington
College and Pastor of Salem and Leesburg, Churches. He was an
excellent physician; a sincere christian, a useful member of and an
ornament to society. Died on the 15th inst. near Blountsville on
his way to Abbington Presybtery.
The Clarion & Tennessee Gazette. (Oct. 24, 1820)

Whitlock, Mr. Andrew. A native of Virginia and late of St. Louis.
Died at the residence of Henry T. Yeatman, Esq. in Nashville on
4th inst.
Nashville Whig, (Tues., Aug. 9, 1842)

Whitman, Mrs. Amanda. Buford, consort of Mr. Gabriel Buford aged
30 years. Died in Williamson County.
National Banner & Nashville Whig, (Mon., Nov. 10, 1834)

Whitman, Captain Daniel. Died in Bedford County.
National Banner & Nashville Whig. (Wed., Oct. 1, 1834)

Whitney, Andrew G. Esq. U. S. Attorney for Michigan. Died at
Detroit.
National Banner & Nashville Whig. (Sat., Nov. 4, 1826)

Whitney, Mrs. J. G. Died at Shelbyville of Cholera.
National Banner & Nashville Daily Advertiser. (Thurs., July 11, 1833)

Whitney, W. W. Of N. Y. Died in New Orleans of Yellow Fever.
Daily Republican Banner. (Wed., Sept. 27, 1837)

Whitsell, Mrs. E. Died in Bedford County.
National Banner & Nashville Advertiser. (Fri., July 6, 1832)

Whitsitt, Mrs. Jane. Wife of the Rev. James Whitsitt. Died on the
16th inst. of Davidson County.
Daily Republican Banner. (Mon., June 22, 1840)

Whitson, Mrs. Polly. Died in this county, on Thursday last.
Nashville Republican & State Gazette. (Fri., Nov. 16, 1832)

Whitson, Mrs. Priscilla. Died in Bedford County.
National Banner. (March 17, 1826)

Whittington, Southey. Died at Versailles, Ky. 14 miles from Lexington, of Cholera.
National Banner & Nashville Whig. (Fri., Sept. 4, 1835)

Whitworth, Frances Elizabeth. Daughter of Mr. Jacob Whitworth.
Died in Bedford County, Tenn.
National Banner & Nashville Whig. (Fri., Oct. 31, 1834)

Whorton, Mr. George. Aged 85. Died in Jessamine County, Ky.
National Banner. (Sat., May 9, 1829)

Whyte, Hon. Robert. In the 78th year of his age. Died in Nashville
on Tuesday the 12th inst. late one of the Judges of the Supreme
Court of Errors and Appeals of Tenn.
Nashville Whig. (Thurs., Nov. 21, 1844)

Wiatt, Dr. Edwin. Formerly of Knoxville. Died in Paris, T. on the 12th inst.
National Banner & Nashville Whig. (Sat., July 22, 1826)

Wickliffe, B. Howard Esq. Son of Robert Wickliff Sr. of Lexington, Ky. Died in New York, on the 31st May.
Daily Republican Banner. (Tues., June 19, 1838)

Wicks, Mr. William. Died in Lexington, Ky.
National Banner & Nashville Whig. (Sat., Feb. 3, 1827)

Wier, Mr. George. Died in Madison County, T.
National Banner & Nashville Whig, (Sat., Sept. 9, 1826)

Wiggins, James Esq. Died in Madison County, Ala.
National Banner & Nashville Whig. (Mon., Sept. 12, 1831)

Wilcher, Henry. Died in Roane County.
Daily Republican Banner. (Sat., Sept. 22, 1838)

Wilcox, Moses & Aaron. Aged 54. They were twin Brothers. Died in Twinsburgh, Ohio on the 21st of Sept.
National Banner & Nashville Whig. (Sat., Dec. 1, 1827)

Wilcox, Peter. Died 18th at Cincinnati, Ohio of Cholera.
National Banner & Nashville Daily Advertiser. (Fri., Oct. 26, 1832)

Wildman, Hon. Z. A member of the House of Representative in Congress from Connecticut. Died in Washington City. on the 12th.
The Union. (Sat., Dec. 26, 1835)

Wilds, Dr. Samuel J. Late of Jonesborough. Died at Browns Ferry.
National Banner. (Sat., Dec. 19, 1829)

Wiley, Mr. Hezekiah B. Died at Greenville.
National Banner & Nashville Whig. (Sat., Nov. 18, 1826)

Wiley, Mr. Jacob. Died at Natchitoches.
National Banner & Nashville Whig. (Sat., Jan. 19, 1828)

Wiley, Mrs. Sarah. Aged 73. Wife of the late Mr. Robert Wiley. Died in Maury County on Tuesday 10th ultimo.
National Banner & Nashville Whig. (Thurs., Sept. 2, 1830)

Wilgus, Mrs. Elizabeth. Widow of the late Mr. Asa Wilgus. Died in Logan County.
National Banner & Nashville Whig. (Mon., Aug. 22, 1831)

Wilgus, Mrs. Elizabeth. Died in Logan County, Ky. Wife of Mr. Asa Wilgus.
National Banner & Nashville Whig. (Mon., Aug. 22, 1831)

Wilkerson, James H. Esq. Died at Jasper, Marion County.
National Banner & Nashville Daily Advertiser. (Tues., Sept. 16, 1834)

Wilkinson, Charlotte R. Consort of John M. Wilkinson. Died near Hendersonville, Sumner County, Tenn. in the 43d year of her age. Daughter of John Bosley near Nashville.
The Union. (Thurs., Feb. 9, 1837)

Wilkinson, Gen. James. Formerly of the U. S. Army. Died in Mexico.
National Banner. (March 3, 1826)

Wilkinson, Mr. James. Died in Memphis.
National Banner & Nashville Daily Advertiser. (Wed., May 22, 1833)

Wilkinson, Mr. John. Formerly of Florence, Ala. Died in Vicksburg, Miss.
National Banner & Nashville Daily Advertiser. (Wed., May 22, 1833)

Wilkinson, Doctor K. T. Of this County. Died on Thursday last of
a pulmonary complaint.
The Nashville Whig. (April 23, 1817)

Wilkinson, Miss Lucinda. Died in Giles County.
National Banner & Nashville Whig. (Fri., June 17, 1831)

Wilkinson, Miss Lucinda. Died in Giles County.
Nashville Republican & State Gazette. (Thurs., June 16, 1831)

Wilkinson, Theophilus J. Esq. Receiver of public money at the land
office of St. Stephens, Ala.
Nashville Whig. (Fri., Sept. 11, 1840)

Wilkinson, Mr. William. Died in Williamson County.
National Banner & Nashville Whig. (Mon., Nov. 1, 1830)

Wilkinson, Mrs. Lucinda. Wife of Major Peter A. Wilkinson. Died
near Pleasant Shade, Smith County, Tenn. on the 1st inst. in the 27th
year of her age.
Daily Republican Banner. (Thurs., Oct. 8, 1840)

Wilkerson, Mrs. Lucinda. Wife of Mr. James Wilkinson, Died in
Hardeman County.
National Banner & Nashville Whig. (Fri., July 18, 1828)

Wilkes, Mr. Benjamin. Died in Maury County.
National Banner & Nashville Whig. (Sat., Nov. 3, 1827)

Wilkieson, Charlotte R. Consort of John M. Wilkieson. Died near
Hendersonville, Sumner County, Tennessee, in the 43d year of her
age. Daughter of John Bosley near Nashville.
Nashville Republican (Tues., Jan. 31, 1837)

Wilkinson, ___. Son of Maj. Thomas Wilkinson 6 or 7 years old.
Died in Pulaski, Tenn. of Cholera.
National Banner & Nashville Daily Advertiser. (Wed., July 17, 1833)

Williams, Ezra. Died in Danville, Ky. of Cholera.
National Banner & Nashville Daily Advertiser. (Mon., Aug. 5, 1833)

Williams, Henry. Age 11 years. Eldest son of Wm. Williams Esq.
Died in this County.
National Banner & Nashville Whig. (Sat., July 29, 1826)

Williams, Jesse. In the 74th year of his age. Died on the 22d at
his resident in Logan County, Kentucky has left a respectable family.
The Nashville Whig & Tenn. Advertiser. (May 2, 1818)

Williams, Hon. John. Died Suddenly on the 7th inst. An eminent
citizen of Knoxville and formerly Senator in Congress from Tennessee.
National Banner & Nashville Whig. (Fri., Aug. 11, 1837)

Williams, John Milton. Late of North Carolina. Of the House of R.
C. & J. M. Williams aged 24 years. Died in Dresdon, Weakley County,
on the 6th inst.
National Banner & Nashville Whig. (Mon., Aug. 14, 1837)

Williams, John Millon. 24 years old. Died in Dresden, Ten. on the
6th inst. late of North Carolina and a partner of the firm of R. C.
& J. M. Williams, of Dresden, Tenn.
Nashville Republican. (Tues., Aug. 15, 1837)

Williams, John Milton. In the 24th year of his age. Died in Dresden
on Sunday night the 6th inst. late of North Carolina and a partner in
the house of R. C. & J. M. Williams of Dresden, Tenn.
The Union. (Thurs., June 17, 1837)

Williams, Col. Joseph. Aged near 80 years. Died on the 11th ult. at his residence in Surry County, North Carolina.
National Banner & Nashville Whig. (Sat., Sept. 8, 1827)

Williams, Mr. Joseph. Son of William Williams Esq. Died in the vicinity of Nashville on Monday last.
Nashville Whig. (Thurs., April 16, 1846)

Williams, Littleberry. Formerly of Davidson County. Died at Nassau N. P.
The Nashville Whig & Tenn. Advertiser. (Jan. 5, 1818)

Williams, Capt. Luke. In the 67th year of his age. Died in Henderson County, Tenn.
National Banner & Nashville Whig. (Fri., Oct. 17, 1834)

Williams, Mrs. Maria. Wife of Col. John Williams. Died in Mount Sterling, Ky.
National Banner (Sat., Aug. 8, 1829)

Williams, Miss Martha. Eldest daughter of William Williams Esq. Died in Davidson County on Sunday evening last.
National Banner & Nashville Daily Advertiser. (Thurs., Nov. 7, 1833)

Williams, Mrs. Mary. Wife of Mr. Elisha Williams. Died in Rutherford County.
National Banner & Nashville Whig. (Sat., April 26, 1828)

Williams, Mrs. Mary. Wife of Mr. Etheldred Williams. of Knoxville aged about 45 years. Died at Rocky Spring, Grainger County, Ten.
National Banner & Nashville Whig. (Wed., Feb. 4, 1835)

Williams, Mrs. Mary. Died in Rutherford County.
National Banner & Nashville Whig. (Sat., May 17, 1828)

Williams, Mrs. Mary C. Consort of Dr. John P. Williams and daughter of the late Hardy S. Bryan. Died at Port Royal on Sat. the 13th inst.
Daily Republican Banner. (Thurs., July 25, 1839)

Williams, Mrs. Mary L. Wife of Thos. L. Williams Esq. Died at Knoxville on the 16th inst.
National Banner & Nashville Whig. (Fri., June 27, 1828)

Williams, Mrs. Melinda. Widow of the late Col. John Williams. Died near Knoxville on Thursday night last.
Daily Republican Banner. (Tues., March 13, 1838)

Williams, Mrs. Melinda. Relict of the late Col. John Williams of Knoxville. Sister of the Hon. Hugh L. White and Mother to the Hon. Joseph L. Williams. of Tennessee. Died near Knoxville on Thursday night last.
Nashville Whig. (Wed., March 7, 1838)

Williams, Nancy. Daughter of Shadrack Williams. Died in Madison County, Ky. of Cholera.
National Banner & Nashville Daily Advertiser. (Sat., Aug. 10, 1833)

Williams, Mrs. Nancy. Consort of Mr. Joseph Williams. Died in Knoxville, Tenn.
National Banner & Nashville Whig. (Mon., Oct. 20, 1834)

Williams, Mrs. Nancy. Consort of Col. Willoughby Williams. Died on the 18th inst. in the vicinity of Nashville in the 38th year of her age. (Obituary)
Nashville Whig. (Sat., July 27, 1844)

Williams, Hon. Nathaniel W. Died in the vicinity of Knoxville at

at the residence of Col. John Williams, he was one of the judges of the Circuit Court of this State.
National Banner & Nashville Daily Advertiser. (Mon., June 17, 1833)

Williams, Mr. Nathaniel. Died in Maury County.
National Banner & Nashville Whig. (Sat., Aug. 9, 1828)

Williams, Mrs. Paralle. Wife of R. N. Williams Esq. Attorney at law of Nashville. Died on the 13th inst. in the vicinity of Nashville in the 22nd year of her age.
The Politician & Weekly Nashville Whig. (Wed., Sept. 1, 1847)

Williams, R. C. Aged 26. A native of Wilson County, Tennessee. Died at Clinton, Miss. Nashville Whig. (Wed., July 10, 1839)

Williams, Benjamin. Meigs County, Ohio. Died in the loss of the Steamboat, Brandywine.
National Banner & Nashville Daily Advertiser. (Mon., April 23, 1832)

Williams, Mr. Daniel Sen. Aged 78. Died in Lawrence County, Arkansas Territory.
National Banner & Nashville Daily Advertiser. (Thurs., Sept. 11, 1834)

Williams, David L. Son of Mr. Joseph F. Williams, aged 6½ years. Died in this County on the 17th inst.
Sat., Feb. 21, 1829)

Williams, Mrs. Rebecca. Relict of Col. Joseph Williams. Died on the 20th March. in Surry County, N. Carolina.
National Banner & Nashville Daily Advertiser. (Mon., April 16, 1832)

Williams, Rice Esq. Post Master. Died in Troy, Obion County.
National Banner & Nashville Whig. (Thurs., July 29, 1830)

Williams, Robert. Youngest son of the late Capt. John Williams of Nashville. Died in New Orleans, on the 4th inst. aged 20 years.
Nashville Whig. (Tues., Dec. 17, 1844)

Williams, General Robert. Of the state of North Carolina. Died on Sunday evening last at the residence of his brother Hon. John Williams. (Knoxville Intelligencer)
The Nashville Gazette (Sat., June 9, 1821)

Williams, Gen. Samuel H. Aged 67. Died in Maury County, Ten.
National Banner & Nashville Whig. (Wed., May 6, 1835)

Williams, Thomas. Died 14th at Cincinnati, Ohio of Cholera.
National Banner & Nashville Daily Advertiser. (Tues., Oct. 23, 1832)

Williams, Mr. Thos. An industrious and respectable citizen of this town. Died on Thursday last.
The Nashville Whig. (March 26, 1816)

Williams, Col. Thomas H. Formerly Senator in Congress, from Mississippi Died on Saturday in Nashville, of dropsy.
Nashville True Whig & Weekly Commercial Register. (Fri., Dec. 13, 1850)

Williams, Gen. William. Of Warren. Died on the 5th inst. from Raleigh, N. C.
National Banner & Nashville Daily Advertiser. (Sat., March 24, 1832)

Williams, Mr. Wm. Aged 30. Died in Natchez.
National Banner & Nashville Whig. (Sat., Oct. 7, 1826)

Williams, Capt. Duke. In the 67th year of his age. Died in Lexington on the 22 Sept. formerly from Caswell County, North Carolina.
National Banner & Nashville Whig. (Wed., Oct. 20, 1834)

Williams, Elder John. Aged one hundred and one years old. Died at
Columbia, Herkimer Co., N. Y. He was the fourth descendant from
Roger Williams.
Nashville Whig. (Sat., Sept. 23, 1843)

Williams, Mrs. Elizabeth. Consort of the late Capt. John Williams
of Nashville. Died in Memphis on the 26th ult. at the residence of
General Joseph R. Williams.
The Christian Record. (Sat., April 10, 1847)

Williams, Mrs. Elizabeth. Died in Dickson County, on 20 inst.
Nashville Republican & State Gazette. (Sat., April 30, 1831)

Williams, David Shelby. Son of David Williams Esq. of this vicinity
aged 4 years. Died on Sunday morning Jan. 24th.
Nashville Whig. (Mon., Jan. 25, 1841)

Williamson, Mrs. Wife of James Williamson. Died in Davidson County
on the 29th inst.
Daily Republican Banner. (Tues., Jan. 2, 1838)

Williamson, Branch. In the 22nd year of his age. Died in Jackson,
Mississippi late of Amelia County, Virginia.
National Banner & Nashville Daily Advertiser. (Tues., Sept. 16, 1834)

Williamson, Mr. David. Died at Huntsville, Ala.
National Banner & Nashville Whig. (Sat., April 14, 1827)

Williamson, James Esq. Died at Silver Springs, Wilson County.
National Banner & Nashville Whig. (Wed., Sept. 24, 1834)

Williamson, John. Aged 72 years. Died in Davidson County, on the
morning of the 4th inst. He aided during the revolutionary War.
National Banner & Nashville Daily Advertiser. (Wed., Nov. 6, 1833)

Williamson, Mr. John Sen. In the 69th year of his age. Died in
Wilson County on the 6th inst.
National Banner (Sat., Aug. 22, 1829)

Williamson, Mary Malvina G. Aged 6 years. Died on Thursday 13th inst.
in Robinson County.
National Banner & Nashville Whig. (Sat., March 21, 1829)

Williamson, Mrs. Martha. Aged 59. Died in Franklin.
National Banner & Nashville Whig. (Sat., June 14, 1828)

Williamson, Mrs. Nancy. Died on Friday morning 21st inst.
National Banner & Nashville Whig. (Sat., Nov. 29, 1828)

Williamson, Mrs. Mary E. Wife of Thomas Williamson. Died in Robinson
County, on the 2nd of Aug. In the 45th year of her age.
National Banner & Nashville Daily Advertiser. (Thurs., Aug. 14, 1834)

Williamson, Rev. Samuel M. Died in Sommerville.
Nashville Whig. (Tues., July 21, 1846)

Willett, Col. Marinus. Died last Sunday in New York, upwards of 90
years old.
National Banner & Nashville Whig. (Mon., Sept. 6, 1830)

Willie, Mr. John. Late editor of the Commercial Report. Died at New
Orleans on the 13th inst.
National Banner & Nashville Whig. (Tues., Dec. 27, 1831)

Williford, Mr. William H. Aged 19. Died in Maury County.
National Banner & Nashville Whig. (Wed., March 16, 1831)

Williford, Mr. William H. Age 19. Died in Maury County.
National Banner & Nashville Whig. (Wed., March 16, 1831)

Willsford, Mrs. Lucy. Aged 84. Died in Maury County.
National Banner. (Feb. 3, 1826)

Willingham, ___. Infant son of Thomas Willingham. Died in Shelbyville, Tenn. of Cholera.
National Banner & Nashville Daily Advertiser. (Thurs., July 11, 1833)

Willingham, ___. Infant daughter of Thomas Willingham. Died in
Shelbyville, Tenn. of Cholera.
National Banner & Nashville Daily Advertiser. (Thurs., July 11, 1833)

Willis, Mr. John W. Eldest son of Byrd C. Willis Esq. now of Pensacola. Died at Key West, Florida on the 10th ult. in the 26th year
of his age.
National Banner & Nashville Daily Advertiser. (Mon., Aug. 26, 1833)

Willis, Andrew L. Esq. Died on Friday last in Nashville.
National Banner & Nashville Whig. (Mon., July 4, 1831)

Willis, Plumer. Aged 14. Died in Bolivar.
National Banner & Nashville Whig. (Sat., Sept. 30, 1826)

Willis, Mr. Rich. Died in Maury County.
National Banner & Nashville Whig. (Mon., July 12, 1830)

Willis, Mr. Josiah. Died in Claiborne County, Mi.
National Banner & Nashville Daily Advertiser. (Tues., Aug. 5, 1834)

Willis, Mr. Lewis. Late of Virginia, aged 27. Died in Conecuh
County, Ala.
National Banner & Nashville Whig. (Sat., Oct. 7, 1826)

Willis, Dr. Lewis. In the 35th year of his age. Died at Pensacola,
Florida. He was drowned, while crossing the Grand Lagoon.
National Banner & Nashville Whig. (Wed., Nov. 4, 1835)

Willis, Mrs. Mary W. Wife of Byrd C. Willis Esq. Navy Agent. Died
in Pensacola, Florida.
National Banner & Nashville Whig. (Mon., Oct. 27, 1834)

Willis, Mrs. Wife of Mr. Walter Willis. Died in Clarksville.
National Banner. (Sat., June 13, 1829)

Willis, Mrs. Sarah. Wife of Mr. Thomas C. Willis, age 72.
Died in Henry County.
National Banner & Nashville Whig. (Mon., May 9, 1831)

Willis, Miss Sarah P. Daughter of Mr. William Willis. Died in
Nashville on 14th inst. in the 18th year of her age.
Nashville Whig. (Tues., Oct. 18, 1842)

Willis, Mrs. Elizabeth. Widow of Mr. Richard Willis, dec'd. Died in
Maury County.
National Banner & Nashville Advertiser. (Thurs., March 15, 1832)

Wills, Mrs. Sarah. Died in Henry County, consort of Thos. C. Wills
aged 72.
Nashville Republican & State Gazette. (Sat., May 14, 1831)

Willis, Andrew L. Esq. Died in Nashville on Friday last.
National Banner & Nashville Whig. (Mon., July 4, 1831)

Willis, Mr. B. S. Died in Baton Rouge, La.
National Banner & Nashville Daily Advertiser. (Fri., May 16, 1834)

Willis, Mrs. Drucilla I. Relict of the late Major Plummer Willis
and sister of the Hon. Nathaniel Macon. Died in Robertson County
on the 22nd inst.
The Nashville Gazette. (Sat., Jan. 29, 1820)

Willis, David. Of Henry County, formerly of Kentucky. Died in
Montgomery County 25th ult.
Nashville Whig. (Mon., Nov. 5, 1838)

Willis, Mr. George W. Youngest son of Peter Willis in the 24th year
of his age. Died on Dec. 19th at the residence of his father on
Bradly Creek in Franklin County.
National Banner & Nashville Whig. (Mon., Jan. 5, 1835)

Willis, John Mortimer, age 23 years. Died at thee residence of his
Mother, on the 31st.
The Christian Record. (Sat., Jan. 8, 1848)

Willis, Dr. William. Died in Maury County.
National Banner & Nashville Whig. (Mon., Oct. 4, 1830)

Wills, Mr. Barnie B. Aged 28. Died in Athens, Tenn.
National Banner & Nashville Whig. (Sat., Feb. 16, 1828)

Wills, Mr. William. Aged 80 years. Died in Giles County, Ten. on
the 20th Aug.
National Banner & Nashville Daily Advertiser. (Wed., Aug. 28, 1833)

Wilmot, S. S. Died at Lancaster, Ky. of Cholera.
National Banner & Nashville Daily Advertiser. (Wed., July 3, 1833)

Wilson, Mr. William. Aged 80 years. Died at Morganton, N. C. for
many years a citizen of Grainger County, Tenn.
National Banner & Nashville Daily Advertiser. (Mon., July 30, 1832)

Wilson, Mrs. Annie. Consort of Adam Wilson Esq. She was much loved
and respected. Died in Hickman County, on the 10th of June.
The Nashville Whig & Tenn. Advertiser. (Aug. 8, 1818)

Wilson, Mr. William. Died in Russellville, Ky.
National Banner & Nashville Whig. (Mon., Nov. 8, 1830)

Wilson, William M. Died on the 4th ult. in Obion County.
Nashville Republican (Sat., Feb. 18, 1837)

Wilson, Dr. Daniel. Died in Louisville, Ky.
Nashville Republican & State Gazette. (Tues., April 12 ___)

Wilson, Mrs. Elizabeth. Died in Rutherford County.
Nashville Whig. (Sat., April 11, 1846)

Wilson, Elizabeth. Consort of Matthew Wilson formerly of Granville
County, S. C. Died in Gibson County on Sept. 28th in the 53d year
of her age.
Daily Republican Banner. (Tues., Oct. 16, 1838)

Wilson, Mrs. Elizabeth. Died in Shelby County, Ky.
National Banner. (March 17, 1826)

Wilson, Mrs. Elizabeth P. Wife of Mr. Jason H. Wilson and daughter
of Mr. Lemuel Hutchings. Died in Williamson County.
National Banner & Nashville Whig. (Mon., July 19, 1830)

Wilson, Eugenia. Wife of Mr. George Wilson, merchant, and daughter of Capt. Alpha Kingsley. Died on Saturday morning.
Nashville Whig. (Mon., March 15, 1841)

Wilson, George Alexander. Eldest son of Col. George Wilson of Nashville and late of Holly Springs, Miss. Died in the vicinity of Nashville on Monday the 11th inst.
Nashville Whig. (Thurs., May 14, 1846)

Wilson, Private G. W. Company K. First Regiment Tenn. Volunteers. Died was killed in the Battle of Monterey, with the Mexicans on Sept. 21st, 1846.
Nashville Whig. (Sat., Oct. 24, 1846)

Wilson, Hon. Henry M. C. Aged 43. Died in Allentown, Pa.
National Banner & Nashville Whig. (Sept. 2, 1826)

Wilson, Capt. Hugh. Died in Maysville.
National Banner & Nashville Whig. (Sat., Sept. 9, 1826)

Wilson, H. Wright Esq. of New York. Died was killed in a Duel in Norfolk County.
Daily Republican Banner. (Tues., May 7, 1839)

Wilson, Mr. James. Died in Bellefonte, Ala.
National Banner & Nashville Whig. (Thurs., May 27, 1830)

Wilson, James. From Maury County. Died at the Tenn. State Prison of Cholera.
National Banner & Nashville Whig. (Fri., Aug. 14, 1835)

Wilson, Mrs. Consort of James Wilson Esq. age 67. Died in Lincoln County, Ten.
National Banner & Nashville Whig. (Fri., Oct. 17, 1834)

Wilson, Mr. James Esq. Aged about 72 years. Died in Warren County, Ten. on the 8th Nov.
National Banner & Nashville Whig. (Mon., Nov. 24, 1834)

Wilson, John. Aged 91 years. Died on the 25th Nov. last at his residence on Whites Creek Pike.
The Nashville Gazette. (Sat., Dec. 23, 1820)

Wilson, Rev. Jno. M. Died in Caswell City, N. C.
Nashville Republican & State Gazette. (Thurs., Sept. 1, 1831)

Wilson, Mrs. Martha Louisa. Age 34 years and 9 months. Consort of Mr. Sam'l. Wilson. Died in Rutherford County on Wednesday the 18th of June.
National Banner & Nashville Daily Advertiser. (Mon., June 30, 1834)

Wilson, Mary Amanda. Infant daughter of Mr. Thos. W. Wilson. Died in Franklin, Ten. on Sunday 28th June.
National Banner & Nashville Whig. (Fri., July 10, 1835)

Wilson, Mason. Age 13 months, only child of Geo. A. Wilson. Died in Lincoln County, Ten.
National Banner & Nashville Whig. (Mon., Oct. 20, 1834)

Wilson, Mr. Oliver H. Died in Nashville suddenly on Friday, July 26th.
National Banner & Nashville Daily Advertiser. (Sat., July 27, 1833)

Wilson, Capt. Samuel. Aged 72. Died in Rutherford County.
National Banner & Nashville Whig. (Thurs., Sept. 23, 1830)

Wilson, Dr. Samuel. Died in Charleston, S. C. an amiable and
eminent physician.
National Banner & Nashville Whig. (Sat., April 14, 1827)

Wilson, Mrs. Sarah. Died in Henderson County.
National Banner & Nashville Daily Advertiser. (Wed., July 24, 1833)

Wilson, Mrs. Wife of Thos. W. Wilson. Died at the residence of her
Mother, about 3 miles from Franklin, Tenn.
National Banner & Nashville Whig. (Fri., July 10, 1835)

Wilson, Mr. William. Age 80. Died at Morganton, N. C. A citizen
of Grainger County, Tenn.
National Banner & Nashville Advertiser. (Mon., July 30, 1832)

Winbourne, Rev. Alexander. Of the Methodist Episcopal Church. Died
in Davidson County at the residence of his brother, aged 30 years.
Daily Republican Banner. (Mon., July 27, 1840)

Winchester, Alexander Hamilton Esq. Attorney at law in the 22nd
year of his age. Died on the 14th Feb. Cragfont, Sumner County, Ten.
National Banner & Nashville Daily Advertiser. (Mon., March 3, 1834)

Winchester, Gen. James. Died in Sumner County on Thursday night.
National Banner & Nashville Whig. (Sat., July 29, 1826)

Winchester, Mr. Luclius. Of Congestive fever. Died at Cragfont,
Sumner County on the 25th Feb.
National Banner & Nashville Daily Advertiser. (Mon., March 3, 1834)

Winchester, Valerius P. Attorney at law and late of Memphis, Ten.
Died in Nashville on Tuesday last.
Daily Republican Banner. (Thurs., Dec. 7, 1837)

Windel, Mrs. An old lady resident of this county. Died on Friday
night.
Nashville Whig. (Tues., Feb. 20, 1816)

Windel, William. In the 53rd year of his age. Died at Memphis on
the 1st. inst.
Nashville Whig. (Sat., Sept. 9, 1843)

Winder, General William H. A distinguished member of the bar. Died
in Baltimore.
Nashville Whig. (June 21, 1824)

Winder, Elizabeth. Daughter of V. P. Winder Esq. of Louisiana,
aged 8 years. Died at the residence of Mrs. Grundy in Nashville
Nashville Whig. (Thurs., Aug. 4, 1842)

Wingate, Henry. Infant son of Henry Wingate, Esq. Died in Frankfort,
Ky.
National Banner & Nashville Whig. (Fri., March 13, 1835)

Wingate, Judge. A member of the first Congress of the United States.
Died at Strotham, N. H. on the 14th aged 99 years.
Daily Republican Banner. (Fri., March 23, 1838)

Winn, Samuel Esq. Died in Henry County, on the 11th inst.
Nashville Republican & State Gazette. (Mon., Oct. 22, 1832)

Winn, Richard Esq. Formerly of Nashville. Died in Louisiana on the
5th ult.
Daily Republican Banner. (Tues., Nov. 3, 1840)

Winright, Mrs. Elm S. of 3d St. Died 17th at Cincinnati, Ohio of
Cholera.
National Banner & Nashville Daily Advertiser. (Fri., Oct. 26, 1832)

Winslow, R. W. Died at Cincinnati, Ohio on 12 of Cholera.
National Banner & Nashville Daily Advertiser. (Sat., Oct. 20, 1832)

Winston, Mrs. Dorotha. Widow of the celebrated Patrick Henry, her
last husband was the Judge Edmond Winston. Died in Halifax County,
Va. on the 15th ult.
National Banner & Nashville Whig. (Fri., April 1, 1831)

Winston, Mrs. Dorothea. Died in Halifax City, Va. Widow of the
celebrated Patrick Henry.
Nashville Republican & State Gazette. (Tues., March 8, 1831)

Winston, Mrs. Dorothy. Widow of the celebrated Patrick Henry her
last husband was the late Judge Edmond Winston. Died in Halifax
County, Va. on the 15 ultimo.
National Banner & Nashville Whig. (Fri., April 7, 1831)

Winston, Mr. Felix. Late of Nashville and formerly of Hanover County,
Va. Died in New Orleans on the 12th Dec. last in the 31st year of
his age.
National Banner & Nashville Whig. (Wed., June 17, 1835)

Winston, Hon. Fountain. Late Lt. Governor of Mississippi and Senator.
Died in Natches, Miss. on the 1st. Dec. at the time of his death in
the State Legislature from Adams County.
National Banner & Nashville Whig. (Mon., Jan. 5, 1835)

Winston, Mr. George H. Age 18. Died in Hawkins County.
National Banner, (Jan. 20, 1826)

Winston, Hon. Louis. Judge of the 2d District of Mississippi. Died
near Natchez.
Nashville Whig. (Sept. 13, 1824)

Winters, Mr. Daniel. Age 82. Died in Frankford, Ky.
National Banner & Nashville Whig. (Sat., Sept. 20, 1828)

Winters, Mrs. Samuel. Died in Shelbyville, Tenn. of Cholera.
National Banner & Nashville Daily Advertiser. (Thurs., July 11, 1831)

Winterwith, Horatio Esq. Aged 49 years. Died in Elizabethtown, Ky.
National Banner & Nashville Whig. (Fri., March 6, 1835)

Wipple, John. Died at Cincinnati, Ohio on 12th of Cholera.
National Banner & Nashville Daily Advertiser. (Sat., Oct. 20, 1832)

Wirt, Mrs. Caroline. Wife of Mr. John Wirt and daughter of William
Polk, Esq. of Hardeman County.
National Banner (Sat., Dec. 19, 1829)

Wirt, Hon. William. Late Attorney General of the United States.
Died at Washington City, at 8 o'clock on the 19th Feb.
National Banner & Nashville Daily Advertiser. (Mon., March 3, 1834)

Wise, Mrs. Ann. Wife of the Hon. Henry A. Wise and eldest daughter
of the late Rev. Obadiah Jennings, D. D. of Nashville. Died recently
in Accomack County, Virginia.
National Banner & Nashville Whig. (Mon., May 29, 1837)

Wise, Mrs. Ann. Wife of Hon. Henry A. Wise, Mrs. Wise was the daughter of Rev. Dr. Jennings. Died in Accomac County, Virginia on the
14th inst.
Nashville Republican. (Sat., June 3, 1837)

Wise, Mrs. Ann. Wife of the Hon. Henry A. Wise and eldest daughter of
the late Obadiah Jennings, D. D. of Nashville. Died recently in
Accomack County, Virginia.
The Union. (Sat., May 27, 1837)

Wistar, Doct. President of the Philsophical Society, died lately
in Philadelphia.
The Nashville Whig & Tenn. Advertiser. (Feb. 21, 1818)

Withers, Hon. John. Aged 56. Died in Madison County, Ala.
National Banner. (April 28, 1826)

Withers, William Esq. Age 49 years. Died in Courtland, Ala.
Daily Republican Banner. (Mon., March 26, 1838)

Witherspoon, Mrs. Elizabeth. Age 53. Wife of Col. John Witherspoon. Died in Wayne County, Tenn. on Monday 21 ult.
National Banner & Nashville Whig. (Mon., Feb. 7, 1831)

Witherspoon, Mrs. Elizabeth. Aged 53. Consort of Col. John Witherspoon. Died in Wayne County, on Monday the 21st ult.
National Banner & Nashville Whig. (Mon., Feb. 7, 1831)

Witherspoon, Mr. James. Son of Col. John Witherspoon. Died in
Wayne County on the 22d inst.
National Banner & Nashville Whig. (Mon., May 2, 1836)

Wolcott, Dr. Alexander. Died at Chicago, Ill.
National Banner & Nashville Whig. (Mon., Jan. 10, 1831)

Woldridge, Mrs. Consort of Mr. Samuel Woldridge. Died in Clarksville
Tenn. of Cholera.
National Banner & Nashville Whig. (Wed., July 8, 1835)

Wolf, Charles E. Esq. Died in Mayville, Ky. Suddenly of apoplexy.
He was mayor of the city and son of the Gov. of Penn.
National Banner & Nashville Daily. (Sat., Aug. 10, 1833)

Wolf, Mrs. Jane S. Wife of Dr. Michel Wolf. Died at Cincinnati.
National Banner. (March 10, 1826)

Wolf, Mrs. Mary. Consort of Gov. Wolf. Died at Harrisburg, Pa.
National Banner & Nashville Daily Advertiser. (Fri., Dec. 27, 1833)

Womack, Mr. James. Aged 90 years. Died at the residence of his
son at Centre Ridge on the 2nd ult. From the Southern Cahawha,
Ala. Democrat.
Nashville Union. (Thurs., March 29, 1838)

Wood, Mrs. Abby Ann. Wife of William B. Wood and daughter of Elijah
Washington. Died on Friday morning 14th inst. aged 31 years.
Daily Republican Banner. (Fri., Dec. 21, 1838)

Wood, Ann Elizabeth. Only daughter of Larkin F. and Elizabeth Wood,
aged 6 years 2 months. Died in Nashville on the 5th inst.
National Banner & Nashville Whig. (Fri., Nov. 25, 1836)
Nashville Republican. (Thurs., Nov. 24, 1836?)

Wood, Ann Elizabeth. Only daughter of Larkin F. and Elizabeth Wood,
aged six years 2 months and 5 days. Died in Nashville on Sat.,
5th inst.
Nashville Republican (Fri., Nov. 24, 1836)

Wood, Archer S. Aged 61 years. Died at his residence in Wilson
County, Tenn. on the 21st inst. A native of Halifax County, Va.
National Banner & Nashville Daily Advertiser. (Mon., Feb. 24, 1834)

Wood, Archer S. Aged 61 years. Died at his residence in Wilson
County, Tenn. on the 21st inst. A native of Halifax County, Va.
National Banner & Nashville Daily Advertiser. (Mon., Feb. 24, 1834)

Wood, Rev. Bennet. Age 67. Died inLawrence County, Ala.
National Banner & Nashville Whig. (Mon., June 6, 1831)

Wood, Mr. Brewer. Died in Logan County, Ky.
National Banner & Nashville Whig. (Sat., June 16, 1827)

Wood, Isaih B. Age 16 years and 4 months. Son of the late Reuben
Wood. Died at the residence of his brother, in Wilson County, Tenn.
Daily Republican Banner. (Fri., Aug. 14, 1840)

Wood, Mr. James. Died at Cincinnati, Ohio of Cholera on 13th.
National Banner & Nashville Daily Advertiser. (Sat., Oct. 20, 1832)

Wood, Rev. James. Wesleyan Minister. In the 89th year of his age.
Died in Kingswood Hill, England said to be the odlest Methodist
Preacher in the world.
Nashville Whig. (Wed., Sept. 16, 1840)

Wood, Mr. John S. Of Mississippi, a native of Nashville. Died in
Franklin, Tenn. at the residence of Col. B. S. Tappan.
National Banner & Nashville Daily Advertiser. (Tues., July 29, 1834)

Wood, Gen. John. Of Mississippi. Died in this town on Wednesday last.
National Banner & Nashville Whig. (Fri., June 20, 1828)

Wood, Mr. William. Died in Rutherford County.
National Banner & Nashville Daily Advertiser. (Sat., June 22, 1833)

Woodbury, Peter. Father of the Hon. Levi Woodbury, Secretary of the
Treasury. Died at Francistown, N. H.
National Banner & Nashville Whig. (Mon., Oct. 20, 1834)

Woodcock, Mr. John. Died in Nashville.
National Banner & Nashville Advertiser. (Thurs., Dec. 6, 1832)

Woodfin, Henry. Aged 2 years, son of E. B. Bigley. Died in Nashville.
National Banner & Nashville Whig. (Fri., July 24, 1835)

Woodfin, Nicholas. Infant son of Mr. John Woodfin. Died in Henry Co.
National Banner & Nashville Advertiser. (Mon., April 30, 1832)

Woodfin, Mr. Nicholas. Age 73. A soldier of the Revolution. Died in
Bedford County, Dec. 21,
National Banner & Nashville Advertiser. (Mon., Dec. 31, 1832)

Woodfolk, Samuel M. In New Orleans on the 4th inst. Samuel M.
Woodfolk a son of William Woodfork? of Jackson County Tenn.
Nashville Republican. (Sat., Dec. 24, 1836)

Woodford, Lucius Horton. Aged 5 years and 6 months. Died on the 18th
inst. second son of William W. and Ellen D. Woodford.
Nashville True Whig & Weekly Commercial Register. (Fri., July 26, 1850)

Woodfork, Mrs. Martha Williams. Aged 54. Died in Davidson County
on the 12th inst at the residence of Mr. John Wright on Whites
Creek.
National Banner & Nashville Whig. (Wed., Oct. 12, 1831)

Woodlee, Mr. John Senr. Aged about 70 years. Died in Warren County,
Tenn.
National Banner & Nashville Whig. (Mon., April 1st. 1835)

Woodruff, Mr. Ira. Printer of this town. Died on Wednesday last.
The Nashville Whig. (Feb. 7, 1816)

Woodruff, Mrs. Maria. Wife of Mr. Ezra Woodruff. Died at Lexington,
Ky.
National Banner & Nashville Whig. (Sat., May 3, 1828)

Woodruff, Mary Jane. Infant and only daughter of Wm. E. Woodruff
Esq. Editor of the Gazette. Died in Little Rock, Ark.
National Banner & Nashville Daily Advertiser. (Tues., Aug. 5, 1834)

Woods, Major Andrew. Aged 55 years. Died on the 16th June in Jackson
County, Mo.
National Banner & Nashville Daily Advertiser. (Wed., July 11, 1832)

Woods, Mrs. Catherine. Consort of Col. John Woods. Died at Frankford,
Ky. on the 3d inst.
National Banner & Nashville Daily Advertiser. (Sat., Aug. 10, 1833)

Woods, Dr. David. Died in this County on 4th inst.
National Banner & Nashville Whig. (Sat., Oct. 11, 1828)

Woods, Mrs. Elizabeth. Wife of James Woods Esq. in the 41st year of
her age. Died very suddenly yesterday morning.
Nashville Whig. (Sat., March 23, 1844)

Woods, Mrs. Wife of Mr. J. H. Woods. Died at Hopkinsville, Ky.
National Banner & Nashville Whig. (Sat., Jan. 10, 1829)

Woods, Maj. James. A member of the Judicial Bench, of Nelson County.
Died at Lovingston, Va. on the 28th of May.
National Banner & Nashville Daily Advertiser. (Wed., June 20, 1832)

Woods, Mrs. Consort of Mr. James B. Woods. Died in Madison County,
Tenn. daughter of Col. Abel Willis.
National Banner & Nashville Daily Advertiser. (Wed., Aug. 21, 1833)

Woods, Maj. James. Judge in Nelson County. Died at Livingston, Va.
on Monday 28th of May.
National Banner & Nashville Advertiser. (Wed., June 20, 1832)

Woods, Mr. John. Merchant of Nashville. Died on the 4th inst. on
board the Steamboat Eclispe, on his way South for his health.
Nashville Whig. (Sat., Dec. 21, 1844)

Woods, John Esq. Aged 72 years. Died on the 26th of Aug. at his
residence in Henderson County, Tenn.
Nashville Whig. (Sat., Sept. 19, 1846)

Woods, Mr. Patrick, Age 80. Died in Knox County on the 12th of April
last.
Knoxville Gazette. (Fri., June 5, 1795)

Woods, Robert Esq. Aged 56. Member of the Banking House of Yeatman
Woods & Co. Died at West Wood, in the vicinity last evening.
Nashville Whig. (Sat., Jan. 28, 1843)

Woodson, Mrs. C. At the residence of her mother in Gallatin on 6th
inst. Mrs. C. Woodson.
Nashville Republican. (Thurs., March 17, 1836)

Woodson, Peter Sen. In the 77th year of his age. Died in Robertson
County, Tenn. on the 30th June 1846
The Politician & Weekly Nashville Whig. (Fri., July 9, 1847)

Woodson, Samuel H. Esq. Died in Jessamine County, Ky.
National Banner & Nashville Whig. (Sat., Aug. 11, 1827)

Woodson, Mr. T. J. Of the firm of L. S. Green & Co. Died in
Nashville on Monday night last.
National Banner & Nashville Whig. (Wed., Oct. 14, 1835)

Woodstock, Mr. John. Died in Nashville.
National Banner & Nashville Daily Advertiser. (Thurs., Dec. 6, 1832)

Woodward, Baker Esq. Of Memphis. Died in Covington, Tipton County.
National Banner & Nashville Whig. (Tues., Jan. 6, 1829)

Woodward, Mr. Ira. Aged 19. Died in Knoxville.
National Banner & Nashville Whig. (Tues., Feb. 2, 1830)

Woodward, Mr. Jonathan. Died in Gibson County.
Nashville Whig. (Tues., April 21, 1846)

Woodward, Mr. William. Died at Cincinnati. He was founder of the
Woodward High School.
National Banner & Nashville Daily Advertiser. (Thurs., Jan. 31, 1833)

Woolley, Mrs. Elizabeth. Wife of Lt. Col. R. A. Woolley. Died at
Fort Atkinson, Council Bluff.
National Banner. (May 13, 1826)

Woolley, Dr. John. Died in Cincinnati, Ohio for nearly 21 years,
a physician of that place.
National Banner & Nashville Daily Advertiser. (Sat., Aug. 24, 1833)

Woolley, W. Preston. Late editor of the Louisville Journal of
Commerce. Died on the 7th inst. at Buffalo, N. Y. of Cholera.
Nashville True Whig & Weekley Commercial Register. (Fri., Sept. 13,
1850)

Woolfolk, Mr. Richard. Aged 62. Died in Oldham County, Ky.
National Banner & Nashville Whig. (Sat., July 8, 1826)

Woolfolk, Wm. B. Youngest son of Joseph Woolfolk Esq. Died at Port
Royale, on the 27th ult.
National Banner & Nashville Whig. (Sat., March 17, 1827)

Woolsey, Charles. Of Boston. Died in the wreck of the Steam boat
Lexington.
Daily Republican Banner. (Fri., Jan. 31, 1840)

Woolsey, Mrs. Hannah. Daughter of the late Jeremiah Neave. Died at
Cincinnati.
National Banner & Nashville Whig. (Sat., Feb. 9, 1828)

Worchester, Dr. Noah. An eminent physician of Cincinnati. Died in
Cincinnati, on Saturday last.
The Politician & Weekly Nashville Whig. (Fri., April 16, 1847)

Word, Mr. Samuel. Died on the 16th at his residence in Franklin.
Thursday, April 21, 1831
The Western Weekly Review, Franklin, Tenn.

Worly, Mrs. Maria. Wife of Mr. Joseph Worly. Died in Athens.
National Banner & Nashville Whig. (Fri., May 20, 1831)

Worly, Mrs. Maria. Wife of Mr. Joseph Worly. Died at Athens.
National Banner & Nashville Whig. (Fri., May 20, 1831)

Wortham, Mr. William. Died in Maury County, Ten.
National Banner & Nashville Whig. (Fri., April 10, 1835)

Worthington, Mrs. Margaret. Age 23. Daughter of Richard Higgans,
Esq. Died in Lexington, Ky.
National Banner & Nashville Advertiser. (Mon., Dec. 24, 1832)

Wrather, Mrs. Jane W. Died in Rutherford County.
National Banner & Nashville Daily Advertiser. (Sat., June 22, 1833)

Wrather, Mrs. Sarah G. Consort of the Rev. Baker Wrather. Died in
Lebanon of an illness which terminated her useful life in a few days.
On Friday the 31st inst.
The Nashville Whig. (June 4th 1816)

Wray, William Esq. Age 57 years. Died in Livingston, Ten. on the 4th
inst.
Daily Republican Banner. (Wed., Sept. 2, 1840)

Wray, Mr. William. In the 83rd year of his age. Died on Friday
night 8th of Sept. in Neelys Bend where he lived for the past 50
years.
Nashville Whig. (Thurs., Sept. 21, 1843)

Wright, Mrs. Amelia J.   Wife of Hamilton Wright Esq. of New Orleans
and only daughter of Capt. John Williams. Died at the residence of
her father in Nashville on Friday 15th inst.
Nashville Whig. (Mon., Oct. 18, 1841)

Wright, Ansel Howell. Infant son of Jacob O. and Elizabeth Wright.
Died in Nashville on Sunday the 5th inst.
The Christian Record. (Sat., June 10, 1848)

Wright, Captain Byrd. Died at Lebanon in Wilson County on Friday the
15th August in the twenty third year of his age. For some years a
citizen of that place.
The Nashville Whig. (Sept. 3, 1816)

Wright, E. Of Hart County, Kentucky. Died in the loss of the Steamboat, Brandywine.
National Banner & Nashville Daily Advertiser. (Mon., April 23, 1832)

Wright, George. Died in the vicinity of Knoxville, Tenn.
Daily Republican Banner. (Sat., Oct. 6, 1838)

Wright, George R. Esq. Editor of the Alabamian. Died in Haynesville, S. Alabama. A native of Ludlaw, Vermont.
Nashville Whig. (Fri., Oct. 9, 1840)

Wright, Mr. James. Aged 70. Died in this County on the 8th inst.
National Banner (Sat., Aug. 15, 1829)

Wright, Mrs. Mary Ann. In the 22nd year of her age. Died on the 22nd
instant. At the residence of her husband, Mr. Thomas J. Wright.
Nashville Whig. (Thurs., Aug. 24, 1843)

Wright, Mrs. Prudence. Age 55. Died at Russellville, Ky.
National Banner. (Jan. 20, 1826)

Wright, Mr. Robert Esq. Died in Maryland formerly governor of that
State.
National Banner & Nashville Whig. (Sat., Oct. 28, 1826)

Wright, Mr. Robert. Died in Smith County. In the 72d year of his
age. He was a revolutionary soldier.
National Banner & Nashville Whig. (Mon., Sept. 26, 1831)

Wright, Susan. Aged 40 years. Died in Nashville of Measles.
National Banner & Nashville Whig. (Wed., June 24, 1835)

Wright, Mr. Thomas. Aged 45 years. Died in Rutherford County, Ten.
A highly respectable citizen.
National Banner & Nashville Daily Advertiser. (Thurs., June 19, 1834)

Wright, Major Thomas. Died in St. Louis, Mo. He was paymaster of
the United States Army, formerly of Penn.
National Banner & Nashville Whig. (Mon., Jan. 5, 1835)

Wright, Mr. William. Died in Bullitt County, Ky.
National Banner & Nashville Whig. (Sat., April 12, 1828)

Wright, Mr. William P. Died at Russellville, Ky.
National Banner (April 28, 1826)

Wright, Mr. Wm. W. Died at New Madrid, Mo.
National Banner (April 21, 1826)

Wroe, Mrs. Mary D. Consort of H. S. Wroe. Died in Statesville,
Wilson County on the 30th June. In the 34th year of her age.
Daily Republican Banner. (Sat., July 6, 1839)

Wyatt, Mr. Micajah. Died in Fleming County.
National Banner & Nashville Whig. (Sat., Dec. 23, 1826)

Wyche, Dr. W. H. Late of Miss. Died in Meridianville, Ala.
National Banner & Nashville Daily Advertiser. (Sat., Sept. 6, 1834)

Wyche, Mr. William H. Of Miss. formerly of Madison Co., Ala. Died
in Huntsville, Ala.
National Banner & Nashville Daily Advertiser. (Thurs., June 19, 1834)

Wyne, William. In the 32nd year of his age. Died at the residence
of Banjamin S. Weller, Esq. in Nashville on the 9th inst. He was a
native of Caldwell County, Ky.
The Christian Record. (Sat., April 17, 1847)

Wyne, William. In the 32nd year of his age. Died at the residence
of Benjamin S. Weller Esq. in Nashville on the 9th inst. He was a
native of Caldwell County, Ky.
The Politician & Weekly Nashville Whig. (Fri., April 16, 1847)

Yancey, Bartley Esq. Died in Caswell County, N. C.
National Banner & Nashville Whig. (Sat., Sept. 27, 1828)

Yancy, Miss Frances. Died in Shelbyville.
Nashville Whig. (Sat., April 11, 1846)

Yantis, Mary Brown. Daughter of Rev. John L. and Mrs. E. A. Yantis
of the vicinity of Nashville. Died at the residence of Mr. Putnam
Hays, near Salt Pond, Saline Co., Mo. aged 3 years.
The Christian Record. (Sat., Oct. 16, 1847)

Yantis, Mrs. Priscilla A. Relict of the late Col. John Yantis.
Died in Dover at the residence of her son-in-law, Judge J. W. Hall on
1st Sept. aged about 66 years.
The Christian Record. (Sat., Oct. 16, 1847)

Yardly, Mrs. Margaret. Wife of Mr. Thomas Yardly. Died at Murfreesborough.
National Banner. (April 28, 1826)

Yarnell, Mr. Joseph. Aged 62. Died in Knox County, T.
National Banner & Nashville Whig. (Sat., Sept. 16, 1826)

Yates, Mr. David. Died in St. Louis, Mo.
National Banner & Nashville Daily Advertiser. (Mon., Aug. 26, 1833)

Yates, John B. Esq. Died at Chittemango, N. Y.
Nashville Republican. (Tues., Aug. 2, 1836)

Yeates, Mrs. Martha. Wife of Izma Yates, formerly of Davidson County.
Died in Humphreys County near Waverly, in the 63d year of her age.
Daily Republican Banner. (Mon., Sept. 25, 1838)

Yeatman, Mr. Preston. Died in Huntsville, Ala. on Wednesday last.
He left a large circle of relatives and friends in Nashville.
Nashville Whig. (Mon. , March 15, 1841)

Yeatman, Thomas Esq. Of the banking house of Yeatman Woods & Co. of
Nashville. Died on board the Steamboat Mount Vernon of Cholera.
in the 45th year of his age.
National Banner & Nashville Daily Advertiser. (Mon. , June 17, 1833)

Yell, Mrs. Jane. Died in Bedford County.
National Banner & Nashville Daily Advertiser. (Fri. , Jan. 27, 1832)

Yell, Mrs. Nancy J. Consort of Hon. A. Yell one of the Judges of
the Superior Court. Died near Fayetteville, Washington County, Ark.
on the 7th of Oct.
National Banner & Nashville Whig. (Wed. , Nov. 4, 1835)

Yerger, Mrs. Ann Eliza. Consort of John K. Yerger Esq. Died in
Pulaski.
Nashville Republican (Sat. , Aug. 27, 1836)

Yerger, Geo. S. Esq. Died on the 20th inst. , at his plantation on
the Yazoo, of apoplexy, whilst out hunting. Mr. Yerger was formerly
a citizen of Nashville. The deceased was a member of the legal
profession.
Nashville Patriot, Monday, April 23, 1860. Nashville, Tennessee.

Yerger, Harry B. Attorney at law of Nashville, Tenn. Died near
Tallahassee, Florida, age 24 years 7 months and 8 days.
National Banner & Nashville Whig. (Mon. , Oct. 10, 1836)

Yerger, Harry B. Attorney at law, aged 24 years 7 months and 8 days.
Died near Tallahassee, Florida on the 20th Sept. formerly of Nashville,
Tenn.
Nashville Republican. (Tues. , Oct. 11, 1836)

Yerger, Harry B. On the 20th Sept. last, at the residence of Col.
Butler near Tallahassee, Florida, Harry B. Yerger Attorney at law
of Nashville, Tennessee, aged 24 years. He fell victim to the
Billious fever, a most fatal disease of the Southern climate. In
his early and premature death, there is much to lament; the companions
of his youth have lsot a devoted and unwavering friend; society is
deprived of a highly gifted and intelligent member; and the Tenn.
Brigade a noble and chivalrous spirit. While his kind and affectionate relatives mourn their irreparable loss, genius weeps over the
recollection of the untimely grave of one of the noblest and most
entusiactic? of her children. His mind was full of great and noble
elem? Endowed with a rich fancy, which like a fairy threw a nameless
charm over all he did; and an imagination, which lived on excitement
and colored life with the most attractive hues, To what then might
not some dazzling dream of honor and glory lead? As might have been
expected, he promptly responded to his Country's call, and enrolled
himself as a Volunteer for the Creek and Seminole Campaign in the
Nashville Independent Highlanders. Actuated by those would stirring
and thrilling emotions, which find their home in the patriot's bosom,
he longed to strike a blow in defence of bleeding humanity, and his
injured Country; but Alas! too soon he found a tomb: The sound of the
War-Whoop never fell upon his ear; no more will the notes of the bugle
break his repose. Known to his commander to be a brave and choice
spirit, he in company with Maj. Washington was deputed to convey an
express to Gov. Call: Their duty was one of danger and peril; but
they were too bold and patriotic to shrink from the fearless perfor-
mance of their trust. Accordingly they set out together from Camp
Jordan, Ala. for Tallahassee, distant near 300 miles. In obedience
to their order; the trip was performed in four days; but their fatigue
and exposure was great; and the dews of the night were "so heavy
and chill," as to engender their fatal malady. They lingered but a
short time and departed this life on the morning of the same day.
The subject of this obituary was in a state of high and feverish

413

excitement to the hour of his dissolution. Imagining himself about to be engaged in some fierce and coming combat, he cried out in a lofty and swelling (May it prove prophetic) voice "Oseola is surrounded" and then sunk in death.
Nashville Republican. (Tues., Oct. 11, 1836)

oung, Mr. Andrew and his wife. Died in Montgomery County, were both killed by a negro man belonging to Mr. Young.
National Banner & Nashville Daily Advertiser. (Thurs., June 7, 1832)

Young, Mrs. Ann. Aged 43. Died in Owen County, Ind.
National Banner. (May 4, 1826)

Young, Mr. C. Late sheriff of Lauderdale County. Died in Florence, Ala.
Nashville Republican & State Gazette. (Tues., Dec. 13, 1831)

Young, Mrs. Elspy. Died on the same evening of the same day Thurs., October 27, 1814. Mrs. Elspy Young the youthful and affectionate companion of Captain John Young, of this town, Nashville.
Nashville Whig. (Tues., Nov. 1, 1814)

Young, Capt. Emanuel. Late of Memphis. Died on board Steamboat New York, descending from Louisville.
National Banner & Nashville Whig. (Wed., Dec. 14, 1831)

Young, Mrs. Jane. Died in Lauderdale County, Ala.
National Banner & Nashville Daily Advertiser. (Thurs., July 30, 1833)

Young, John Esq. Formerly of Ala. Died in Haywood County.
National Banner & Nashville Whig. (Wed., Sept. 7, 1831)

Young, Jacob. In his 85th year. Died at his residence in Maury County on 23rd, April.
The Politician & Weekly Nashville Whig. (Fri., May 14, 1847)

Young, John Esq. Died in Madison County.
National Banner & Nashville Whig. (Wed., Sept. 14, 1831)

Young, Capt. John C. Died in Knox County. on the 20th ult.
National Banner & Nashville Whig. (Wed., Sept. 7, 1831)

Young, Capt. John C. On 20 ult. Died in Knox County.
National Banner & Nashville Whig. (Wed., Sept. 7, 1831)

Young, Dr. John H. Aged 27. Died in Florence, Ala.
National Banner & Nashville Whig. (Sat., Aug. 12, 1826)

Youngest, Maria M. Daughter of M. Charles Wickliffe. Died in Lexington, Ky.
National Banner & Nashville Whig. (Sat., Sept. 30, 1826)

Young, Mrs. Martha A. Consort of Thomas E. Young. Died in Campbell County, Va. on the 17th inst. In the 79th year of her age.
Nashville True Whig & Weekley Commercial Register. (Fri., Jan. 3, 1851)

Young, Mrs. Rebecca R. Consort of Doctor James Young and daughter of the late Doct. Samuel Hogg. Died in Memphis recently.
The Politician & Weekly Nashville Whig. (Fri., Dec. 10, 1847)

Young, William Esq. Died in Hawkins County.
National Banner & Nashville Whig. (Sat., Jan. 20, 1827)

Young, William Carroll. Aged about 19 years. Died in Robinson County on the 3d inst. at his fathers residence.
National Banner & Nashville Daily Advertiser. (Tues., Nov. 19, 1833)

Young, Dr. William S. Member of Congress elect. Died at Elizabethtown, Ky. National Banner & Nashville Whig. (Sat., Oct. 6, 1827)

Youst, James. Died at Versailles, Ky. 12 miles from Lexington of
Cholera.
National Banner & Nashville Whig. (Fri., Sept. 4, 1835)

Zacharie, Stephen, Esq. Died at New Orleans on the 3d inst. Cashier
of the Louisiana Bank.
Impartial Review and Cumberland Repository. (Thurs., Sept. 24, 1807)

This is a cross index only to names mentioned within the individual
items which are arranged in alphabetical order by surname.

Index Prepared By:
Karon Mac Smith, Rt. 1 Box 190, Nixon, Texas